An Introduction to the Analysis of Variance

Richard S. Bogartz

PRAEGER

Westport, Connecticut
London

Library of Congress Cataloging-in-Publication Data

Bogartz, Richard S.
   An introduction to the analysis of variance / Richard S. Bogartz.
     p.   cm.
   Includes bibliographical references and index.
   ISBN 0-275-94720-3
   1. Analysis of variance.   I. Title.
   QA279.B64   1994
   519.5'38—dc20   93-14135

British Library Cataloguing in Publication Data is available.

Library of Congress Catalog Card Number: 93-14135
ISBN: 0-275-94720-3

First published in 1994

Praeger Publishers, 88 Post Road West, Westport, CT 06881
An imprint of Greenwood Publishing Group, Inc.

Printed in the United States of America

The paper used in this book complies with the
Permanent Paper Standard issued by the National
Information Standards Organization (Z39.48-1984).

10 9 8 7 6 5 4 3 2 1

Copyright Acknowledgments

The author and publisher gratefully acknowledge permission to use the following material:

Excerpts from O. J. Dunn, "Multiple Comparisons among Means," *Journal of the American Statistical Society* 56 (1961): 52-64.

Excerpts from C. W. Dunnett, "New Tables for Multiple Comparisons with a Control," *Biometrics* 20 (1964): 482-91. Reprinted with permission of the Biometric Society.

Excerpts from H. L. Harter, "Critical Values for Duncan's New Multiple Range Test," *Biometrics* 16 (1960): 671-85. Reprinted with permission of the Biometric Society.

Excerpts from E. S. Pearson and H. O. Hartley, "Charts of the Power Function for Analysis of Variance Tests Derived from the Non-Central *F*-Distribution," *Biometrika* 38 (1951): 112-30. Reprinted with permission of the Biometrika Trustees.

Excerpts from E. S. Pearson and H. O. Hartley, *Biometrika Tables for Statisticians*, vol. 1, 3d ed. Cambridge, England: Cambridge University Press, 1970. Reprinted with permission of the Biometrika Trustees.

An Introduction to the
Analysis of Variance

To Norman H. Anderson

Contents

Preface

In teaching the statistics course for first-year psychology graduate students, both in the past at the University of Illinois, Champaign-Urbana, and now at the University of Massachusetts, Amherst, I have encountered each year a group of students diverse in both their backgrounds and their objectives. Students continue to range from those with more than enough mathematical background to understand everything that is going on to those who have avoided things mathematical whenever they could. For some, the course contains information that they know they will need in order to do the work they have chosen. For others, the same course at first glance seems an obstacle to their getting down to the real work for which they came to graduate school. Fortunately, in almost every case the students have been highly motivated self-starters who have risen to the challenges the course offered.

Teaching in the face of this diversity has been my challenge, requiring that the basic statistical ideas be reviewed, the foundational concepts be provided, the tools of the trade be made available to those who will need them, and enough of the depth and the beauty of the formal structures involved be presented to interest and excite those who are capable of going beneath the surface. I have tried to do this in my teaching, and I have tried to do it in this book.

The material covered here, emphasizing the analysis of variance, has been presented in the second semester after a thorough grounding in probability and the logic of inferential statistics has been presented in the first semester. Both the geometric and the algebraic representations of analysis of variance and the general linear model are given because many students get the big ideas from the geometric representations when those ideas seem to be obscured by the algebraic equations. I have stressed the model equation as the basis of all that follows and have shown in detail how degrees of freedom, sums of squares, and expected values of mean squares are interrelated, and all flow from the formulation of the model equation. To do this I have formulated a notation that seems to me to be the simplest and the clearest that I have come across. This notation enables a simple set of rules for obtaining formulas for degrees of freedom, sums of squares, and expected values of mean squares by direct inspection of the model equation. It avoids Greek letters where this is not too unconventional since they tend to perceptually complicate the expressions unnecessarily. On the geometric side, terms in the model equation have been identified with vectors in a vector space, and degrees of freedom are then explained easily and very naturally as the dimensionality of the subspaces that the various vectors lie in. By focusing on general principles and exemplifying them with various models, I have found that students not only come away with the big picture of what is going on but also finish the course fully able to analyze designs they have never seen before and so are prepared to formulate the analyses required for the experimental designs that best suit their own research.

I have also attempted to indicate explicitly the different levels of depth of the material. Material numbered more deeply, such as a section numbered x.y.z as opposed to a section numbered x.y, is intended to be read after material numbered less deeply has been completed. Thus the book is not necessarily to be read in a linear fashion from beginning to end but can be read in multiple passes. I have done my best to build in continuity of the ideas, whether the levels of greater depth are included in a pass through the material or not. Some of the material I view as not at all necessary for all students, but I have included it to satisfy the curiosity of a minority. This material is marked with asterisks. The student and the teacher are encouraged by this layering to engage the big ideas first and to handle the details afterward. The book provides opportunities for getting into the subject deeply, but these are options that are not necessary to getting a great deal out of it.

Another device I have used pertains to matrix algebra. While the appendix presents more than enough of it for the student who chooses, the text introduces matrix algebra gradually, with only those parts that are immediately needed covered in any chapter. These parts are motivated by the context of the particular chapter. I have found that even students for whom this is all new assimilate the matrix algebra quite readily when its use is motivated by the immediate context.

It is my great pleasure to express my gratitude to my teachers and those others who have helped bring this book to fruition in one way or another. In graduate school, John P.Seward, Paul Hoel, and especially Norman H. Anderson helped me to understand and to use statistics in general and the analysis of variance in particular. Over the years I have beenhelped by reading the work of David Grant, Norman Anderson, Henry Scheffé, Jerry Myers, and a vast array of authors who can be found in the reference list of this book. I am especially indebted to Chuck Clifton for his support at a critical time and to Rachel Clifton for her continuing support, encouragement and a well-timed prod. I am grateful to Ladygrith's Friend for her light, her laughter, her support, her insight, her warmth, her caring. Perhaps most of all I am indebted to my students who have shown me what needed to be said, in what order, and in how much depth. Their questions and their remarks in the classroom have led directly to a host of aspects of the structure and content of the book.

An Introduction to the
Analysis of Variance

1

Preliminaries

1.1 Analyzing the variation from score to score. The analysis of variance is a method for considering the variation among a collection of research scores or measurements. The scores differ from each other. The analysis of variance (ANOVA) considers alternative explanations for this score to score variation and provides a method for choosing among these explanations.

In this book we focus on the analysis of variance, although multiple regression and the analysis of covariance will also be treated, but to a lesser extent. These statistical methods are instances of the general linear model (see Chapter 12). The general linear model is a method for analyzing scores into their constituent components. It assumes that a score or measurement is the sum of various values produced as the result of various effects. It allows for the estimation of these various effects and also for testing hypotheses concerning which of a set of possible effects actually do contribute to the score.

1.2 An example experiment. Consider an experiment designed to study the effect of distracting stimuli on attention in children. Twenty 4-year-old and twenty 7-year-old children are shown individually a series of stimulus objects in the center of a computer screen. Their task is to continually watch the objects being shown and to press a button whenever a round object appears. Sometimes when a round object is shown, another stimulus is presented in the lower left-hand corner of the computer screen as a distractor. Half of the children at each age level are given specific verbal instructions not to pay any attention to stimuli that appear in the lower left-hand corner. The other children are not given any instructions concerning the distractor stimuli.

The purpose of the experiment is to determine if older children differ from younger ones in their susceptibility to distraction. A secondary interest is whether the verbal instructions have an effect and, if so, whether this effect is the same for older children as for younger ones.

It seems reasonable that if the distractor stimulus is having an effect, then the probability that the child will notice the round stimulus should be smaller when the distractor stimulus is presented than when it is not. Consequently the observed proportion of times that the child misses the round object should also be smaller with distraction than without it. For each child the proportion of times the child failed to press the button when a round stimulus is shown is calculated for those trials on which a distractor is presented and for those trials on which no distractor is presented. The former proportion minus the latter is taken as the child's susceptibility-to-distraction score in that the more misses caused by distraction, the higher the score should be.

1.3 Conceptual analysis of the variation in the scores. We expect the scores of the 40 children in the experiment to vary. To analyze this variation we conjecture that the score is actually made up of different parts that add together. The parts result from different effects of different events on the different subjects. We assume that the total score may be made either larger or smaller by these different effects. For example, we might expect that being 7 years old, as compared to being 4, has the effect of decreasing susceptibility to distraction. We also might expect that specific verbal instructions to ignore the distractors might also decrease susceptibility.

The effects of age and instructions are the effects of variables that have been intentionally manipulated by the experimenter in an attempt to see if these variables actually do affect susceptibility to distraction. However, there are other reasons scores in the experiment might vary from each other.

1.4 Individual differences. Consider the 10 7-year-old children who were given the instructions concerning ignoring the distractors. So far as manipulation of the two experimental variables, age and instructions, is concerned, these 10 children have all received the same treatment. Yet we do not expect them all to have the same score. We take it for granted, and of course experience has shown, that a group of children will differ in their performance on most tasks even if we do not treat them differently. This is because of individual differences between the children that existed before we selected them.

The fact that children differ from each other complicates our attempt to analyze the scores we obtain. We want to analyze scores into pure constituent components that unambiguously reflect the effects of the events we are interested in. Thus, ideally, we might like to say something like

Susceptibility score = Age effect + instruction effect

or, more commonly,

Susceptibility score = General level + age effect + instruction effect.

In the second form we assume all the subjects would have the same score, which we could call the general level were it not for the age effect that pushes the score up for 4-year-olds and down for 7-year-olds, and the instruction effect that pushes the score down with instructions and up without them. We think of the effects as deflections of the scores from the common general level.

The fact that the children differ even when we treat them alike means that the analysis of our scores will be incomplete if we do not include these individual differences. So, with individual differences in mind, our formulation must be something like

Susceptibility score = General level + age effect + instruction effect + individual subject effect.

1.5 Extraneous or nuisance variables. Laboratory experience has taught us that even this formulation is not adequate. We know that in experiments such as the one described there are all sorts of opportunities for uncontrolled events to affect the scores we obtain. If the experiment is run at a school, there may be uncontrolled noises that affect the scores of some children but not others. Some of the children may be given the task in the morning when they are more alert and less distractible, and others may be given the task in the afternoon when the activities of the day may have tired them. The temperature in the experimental room may vary during the day, producing differences in attentiveness at different times. There may also be effects associated with the particular task. For example, some children may have more experience with being in experiments than others. In general, we find that along with being susceptible to the effects of the experimental variables that we intentionally manipulate, scores are also influenced by what we call extraneous or nuisance variables. There are the subject or individual difference or organismic variables having to do with intrinsic differences that exist among the subjects. There are environmental variables, which are the observable ways in which the experimental environment varies from subject to subject and from measurement to measurement. And there are the task or experimental situation variables, which, if allowed to vary from measurement to measurement, will also influence the scores. This means that our component analysis of the makeup of a score should include a term for each nuisance variable. Unfortunately, we are not always aware of all of the nuisance variables that may be affecting the scores in a given experiment. This will require us to introduce a catchall expression called error which will express in summary fashion the effect of all of the known and unknown nuisance variables that have remained uncontrolled in our experiment. More on this after we consider the control or deliberate noncontrol of nuisance variables.

1.6 Experimental design. An experiment is a planned opportunity for experience that will inform the experimenter about some aspect of the world. If the experiment is well planned, it will use the experimenter's resources efficiently, and it will maximize the information obtained concerning the variables of interest to the experimenter while minimizing the noise introduced by extraneous variables.

Experimental planning employs two important principles: control and randomization. It is rather remarkable that two such opposing ideas can be brought to bear to accomplish the same end.

1.7 Experimental control. Experimental control is an obvious approach to handling the effects of extraneous variables. As an extraneous variable, such as temperature variation in the experimental room, is discovered, experimental control of the variable is exerted, say, by introducing a thermostatically controlled heating or cooling device, in order to hold the range of variation of the extraneous variable within acceptable limits. Effects of time of day are controlled by all the child subjects being run between 9:00 AM and 11:00 AM. Subjects are tested in a sound-shielded research trailer parked in a remote corner of the school parking lot to minimize the effect of noise.

When the values that an extraneous variable takes tend to be associated with the values that an experimental variable takes, we say that the two variables are **confounded**. Literally, the one variable is *found with* the other, and so we cannot tell whether the effects are due to the one variable or to the other. For example, suppose all the 4-year-olds were given the experimental task in the morning and all the 7-year-olds were given the task in the afternoon. Then if the data revealed a difference between the susceptibility scores for 4-year-olds and those for 7-year-olds, we could not know whether the difference was due to the one group's being aged 4 and the other group's being aged 7 or due to the fact that one group performed in the morning and the other group performed in the afternoon, or perhaps partially due to both these circumstances.

In order to avoid this confounding, the experimenter can exert control by requiring that half the 4-year-olds be run in the morning and half be run in the afternoon , and that the same be true for the 7-year-olds. Now, since both the 4-year-olds and the 7-year-olds are to be run during both the morning and the afternoon in equal numbers, if a difference in the scores of the two age groups is found, it cannot be attributed to the time of day at which the subjects were run.

1.8 Randomization. Let us consider another aspect of the experiment we have been discussing. The stimulus objects presented on the computer screen are sometimes to be round and sometimes not. Suppose that one-fifth of them are to be round. How should the round and not-round objects be sequenced for presentation? Obviously it will not do to regularly present four not-round objects followed by a round object. The subjects would quickly learn this sequence rule. Not only would the required level of attention be changed by this learning, but the children could use a counting rule to base their responses on. The effects of distraction would be minimized since a visual distractor would be unlikely to distract the child from the counting process that determined whether it was the point in the sequence where a round object comes up. This, in turn, would make it hard for the experiment to reveal if such effects exist.

A better procedure is to use a randomly generated sequence. For our example sequence of stimulus objects, randomly generated sequences can be constrained or unconstrained. If the sequence is unconstrained, it would be built by allowing each stimulus object to have a probability of one-fifth of being round and a probability of four-fifths of not being round. The practical procedure for doing this would be to use either a table of randomly generated numbers or a computer-generated string of randomly generated numbers. In a table or string of randomly generated numbers, the numbers have been generated so that each position in the table or string has the same chance of containing each of the digits 0 through 9, and the chances for each position are independent of what digit occurs in any other position. Once such a table or string has been created, it can be used to produce random assignments. Returning to the example, the rule might be to proceed through the random number table and assign a round stimulus to the next position in the stimulus sequence if the digit encountered in the table is a 1 or 2 but assign a non-round stimulus if the digit encountered is 3, 4, 5, 6, 7, 8, 9, or 0.

The experimenter may be concerned that too many non-round stimulus objects may occur consecutively before a round one occurs if the assignment of the stimuli to the sequence is left entirely up to the random number table. In this case the experimenter will constrain the sequence. For example, he or she may want at least two round objects in each consecutive string of 10 objects. Then, for each set of 10 objects, he or she could sample random digits until one of each of the 10 digits had been obtained. As each digit is obtained it is assigned to the next position in the stimulus sequence being created for the current string of 10 objects. A round object is assigned to the positions containing a 1 or 2 and a non-round object is assigned to each of the other eight positions. This will ensure that in each consecutive string of 10 stimulus objects there will be 2 round objects and 8 non-round objects located randomly in the string.

Having decided to present the stimulus objects according to a randomly generated sequence, the experimenter is still faced with the question of how many different sequences to use. The minimum is a single sequence that is used with each subject. This is economical so far as effort is concerned. However, if the sequence in which the objects are presented has an effect on performance, the generalizability of results will be weakened by using only one sequence. Also, since every subject receives the same sequence, there will be no way to determine if sequence has an effect or not. The other extreme is to use a different randomly generated stimulus sequence for each subject. This will provide maximum generalizability in that the sequences can all be viewed as random samples from the entire population of possible sequences that might be randomly generated so inference can be properly drawn from the results with the sequences used to results that might have been obtained with any sample of randomly generated sequences. While this procedure provides maximum generalizability, it still does not provide the investigator with any information concerning whether different sequences have an effect. This is because sequences have been completely confounded with subjects.

If the possible effect of sequences is of interest, it would be better to assign at least pairs or more of subjects to the same sequence so that a statistical test of the effect of sequences would be possible by making sequences a factor in the experiment (factors will be explained later).

We considered the desirability of assigning half of the 4-year-olds to being run in the morning and half in the afternoon. Using random numbers, we could do this by deciding randomly for each pair of 4-year-olds whether the first child of the pair would be run in the morning or in the afternoon and assigning the second child to be run at the time not assigned to the first child. The rule for the first child might be to assign to the morning if the next random digit in the table is even (0, 2, 4, 6, or 8) and assign to the afternoon otherwise. Note that this method would result in constrained random assignment in that there would always be the same number of children in each time period. Unconstrained assignment of children to the two time periods could be accomplished by simply following the even or odd rule for each child independently of how other children are assigned.

1.9   If you don't control it, randomize it.   If you do control it, analyze it.   A
rough and ready rule of thumb for dealing with variables that are not of central concern in the
investigation but that may have effects on the response being measured is that if you are not
controlling the variable, you should randomize it over the various experimental conditions
that are of interest. Thus, if time of day at which the subject is run in the experiment is not
of interest, and you do not use time of day as one of the independent variables in the
investigation, then at each time of day that a subject appears, it is best to decide randomly to
which experimental condition the subject will be assigned. In this way experimental
conditions will be associated randomly with time of day.

By randomly assigning subjects to experimental conditions, all sorts of variables are
automatically randomized. Thus, for example, the diet eaten by the subjects might very well
have an influence on the behavior being studied. The problems and expense involved in
controlling the diet are usually so great that randomization is the only course. Random
assignment of subjects to conditions automatically randomizes diet and a host of other
individual difference variables with respect to experimental conditions.

Because we are unable to identify all of the variables that are randomized by random
assignment of subjects to experimental conditions and all of the other variables that remain
uncontrolled and unrandomized in the experiment, we create a composite variable, which we
call error. Error is the sum of the effects of all of the uncontrolled variables that affect the
scores we obtain. The variation in the scores we observe is therefore in part due to the
particular combination of values of the uncontrolled variables that occur.

The extent to which we are able to detect an effect of an experimental variable depends on
the size of the variation in scores that is due to error. **We can think of the variation
due to error as noise and the effects of the experimental variable as a signal
that we are trying to detect against the background of noise created by the
various uncontrolled variables.** The more the scores vary as a result of error, the less
confident we are that differences in the scores from one experimental condition to another are
due to the experimental conditions and not due to error.

**The effect of controlling an extraneous variable is to remove a potential
source of noise.** Controlling the variable reduces the variation due to error because, had
we not controlled this variable, its effects would affect our scores in an uncontrolled fashion
and therefore contribute to error variation. Sometimes we control the extraneous variable by
holding its value to a specific range, as when we control the temperature or the sound level
in the experimental room. Other times we systematically vary the extraneous variable. This
is often the case with individual difference or organismic variables, although it can also
occur with environmental and task variables. When this systematic variation in extraneous
variables is used, we refer to it as **blocking**. We include the blocking variable in our
analysis and thereby use it to remove noise that would otherwise mask the effects of the

TABLE 1.1 SELF-ESTEEM RATINGS BEFORE AND AFTER TREATMENT IN A SIMPLE RANDOMIZED DESIGN

No Boost	Boost	No Boost	Boost
2	2	2	3
2	2	2	3
3	3	3	4
3	3	3	4
4	4	4	5
4	4	4	5
Before		After	

TABLE 1.2 SELF-ESTEEM RATINGS BEFORE AND AFTER TREATMENT IN A RANDOMIZED BLOCKS DESIGN

	No Boost	Boost	No Boost	Boost
Low	2	2	2	3
	2	2	2	3
Medium	3	3	3	4
	3	3	3	4
High	4	4	4	5
	4	4	4	5
	Before		After	

experimental variables of major interest. To clarify this we will take a look in the next section at two experimental designs, one of which uses blocking to control for an extraneous variable and the other of which does not.

1.10 Comparison of a simple randomized design with a randomized blocks design. In each design there are 12 subjects. Six are given a questionnaire designed to boost their self-esteem, and the other six are given a questionnaire that should have no effect on self-esteem. Then all of the subjects are asked to rate their self-esteem. We will make certain simplifying assumptions here so that the point can be made most clearly. We will assume that in both designs there are no sources of error affecting the scores. We will also assume that in each design two of the subjects in each experimental condition have low self-esteem, two have medium self-esteem, and two have high self-esteem.

In the first design, called a simple randomized design, the subjects are simply assigned to one of the two conditions at random, with the constraint that there be six subjects in each condition. Table 1.1 shows what the self-esteem ratings would have been before the delivery of the questionnaires, had we measured them, and what they are after the subjects complete the experiment. We can see that before the questionnaires were given the subjects in the two conditions were the same and we can identify the two subjects at each level of self-esteem. We also see that after the questionnaires, the effect of the No Boost questionnaire was to leave the self-esteem ratings the same and the effect of the Boost questionnaires was to raise each rating by one point.

For reasons that we will discuss later, the statistical test of whether the two different questionnaires have different effects on the scores uses two quantities. The first quantity is the difference between the mean self-esteem rating after the Boost questionnaire and the mean self-esteem rating after the No Boost questionnaire. This difference is 4 - 3 = 1. This is the signal of an effect. Noise is represented by the second quantity, which measures the extent to which the several self-esteem ratings in each different experimental condition differ from each other. To the extent that the scores in a single experimental condition are different from each other, we have unpredictability since we have no explicit explanation of why identically treated subjects should differ. The more such unpredictability there is, the less confidence we have in any difference between the mean from one experimental condition and the mean from another.

In the second design, called a randomized blocks design, we will assume the experimenter knows the initial self-esteem values of the subjects. This will permit blocking the subjects according to these initial self-esteem levels. The design in this case would be as shown in Table 1.2. In this second design the signal value is still the same since the difference between the mean for Boost and the mean for No Boost is still 4 - 3 = 1. But now the measure of noise is zero, because in each cell the scores are identical. The fact that in each cell the scores are identical indicates that there is no unexplained or error variation. If we know which condition and which initial level of self-esteem a subject is at, then we know everything that is needed to determine that subject's score. The situation is exactly analogous to prediction being perfect when there is no scatter around the regression line in simple linear regression (see Chapter 12). We see that at each level of initial self-esteem, each pair of scores for the Boost condition is higher by one score than the corresponding pair of scores for the No Boost condition.

To see in a different way how the second design has reduced the noise, consider presenting the data for the two designs as frequency distributions. We will think of overlap of the two distributions as noise in the sense that the less the distributions overlap, the more clear it is that their means differ. In the case of the simple randomized design, we have the frequency distribution for the No Boost condition and that for the Boost condition. We can

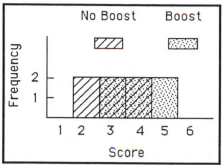

Figure 1.1. Two overlapping frequency distributions for the No Boost and Boost conditions.

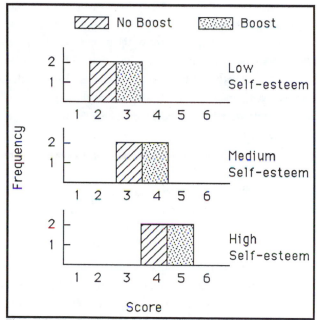

Figure 1.2. The frequency distributions for No Boost and Boost conditions in the randomized blocks design.

observe in Figure 1.1 that two-thirds of the scores in the two distributions overlap in that 3, 3, 4, and 4 occur in both distributions. However, in the case of the randomized blocks design, we have two frequency distributions at each level of the blocking variable, that is, at each level of initial self-esteem. These three pairs of distributions are shown in Figure 1.2. At low self-esteem, we have the No Boost scores of 2, 2 and the Boost scores of 3, 3. We see no overlap of the two distributions. Similarly at the medium level of self-esteem we have 3, 3 and 4, 4, and at the high level we have 4, 4 and 5, 5. In each case there is no overlap. By using the blocking variable the overlap of the two distributions has been completely eliminated so that the picture of an effect due to the Boost questionnaire is very clear at each level of the blocking variable.

What we have seen with this example is how experimental control may be exerted to remove variation that would otherwise be interpreted as error and would consequently tend to obscure the effects of the variables of interest.

1.11   Random sampling and handy sampling.   Usually sampling in behavioral research occurs in the selection of the subjects to be studied and the materials to be presented to those subjects. With random sampling a well-defined collection or population of persons or materials exists, and a part of that collection is sampled according to the condition that each object in the collection has the same chance of being in the sample. When a random sampling process is used to obtain a sample, then the sample will be atypical of the population only as a result of chance. For example, if half of the people in the population are men and half are women, then a random sample of the population will vary from this 50:50 split only as a result of chance. There will be no systematic bias toward including men, say, in the sample because each person in the population had the same chance of appearing in the sample. If the sample were biased, there would be a problem in drawing inferences to the population because the sample would be systematically nonrepresentative.

A sample's being random does not prevent mistakes in inference. For example, suppose in the population half of the people score 10, and half of them score 15 on some test. If we take a random sample of 20 people from this population, the probability is greater than .80 that the mean score in our sample will be different from the mean score in the population. If we use that sample mean to estimate the population mean, more than 80 percent of the time our estimate will not be exactly correct. What we can be sure of is that if we use random sampling, the misrepresentativeness of our sample will not be systematically tilted in any one direction. Only chance will produce misrepresentation of the population by the sample, and we can build procedures into our methods of inference, such as confidence intervals, for example, that take into account the effects of chance.

Almost always, in experimental research, the samples of subjects used are not random samples from some well-defined population. When college students serve as subjects, it is usually because they volunteer or are paid for it. The ones who wind up in the experiment are certainly not random samples from the general population or random samples even from their college class. When young children serve as subjects, it is usually because their mothers answer ads or their preschool is cooperative with research programs. When older children serve as subjects, it is usually the children from the more cooperative school systems who are included. When animals are the subjects, it is usually because they are available in the local animal colony or are easily purchased. In short, the samples that are used are handy samples rather than random samples.

When a handy sample is used, the generalization from the sample to some larger body of persons such as "children of age 4" or "college students" or "people" cannot be made statistically. The absence of random sampling removes the basis for drawing statistically valid inferences from the sample to the population from which it was sampled. Of course, inferences can still be drawn. It is just that in the absence of random sampling, the departures of the sample results from what would be true of the results for the entire population cannot be regarded as merely due to the effects of chance. Still, inferences of an extrastatistical nature can be drawn. Thus, the investigator can claim that even though the sampling of college students is not random, there is no obvious reason why the sampled college students should differ from college students in general on the particular variables being studied. Or the investigator can suggest that these results for the sample apply to the general population, "other things being equal." Such extrastatistical lines of inferences are generally taken by behavioral researchers and tend to be maintained until someone comes along and fails to replicate research results when using a different population of subjects. Then the issue of why the differences exist becomes a subject for inquiry.

1.12 A partial, brief review of introductory statistics. This book is intended for highly motivated students who have taken at least one introductory statistics course. In the remainder of this chapter we will briefly review the typical content of such an introductory course. We touch on only those matters that relate to the subject of this book, the analysis of variance. Typically, such a course ends with how to use data from experiments to test hypotheses about the effects of experimental treatments. Perhaps it stopped at the t-test, perhaps it got to a one-factor experimental design, or maybe even to a two-factor design, but that was probably as far as it went. You were told that methods for analyzing more complicated experiments would have to wait for a more advanced course in statistics. This book is intended to serve as either a textbook in such an advanced course or else as a companion to whatever textbook is used. It starts at the simplest analysis of variance and carries through to some of the most complex. By the time you are finished with it, you will know quite a bit about the analysis of variance and feel very good about how much you have learned. Now the book will jog your memory concerning introductory statistics.

1.13 Three meanings of the word "statistics." **Statistics, the science,** is the theory and practice of accurately and economically describing data and drawing valid, wise, useful inferences from these data. **Statistics, the functions of data,** such as the mean or the standard deviation, serve as descriptive tools for summarizing information in data sets and as inferential tools for drawing inferences from samples of data that are in hand to populations from which those samples have been drawn, (and therefore to samples of data that may later be in hand). **Statistics, the sets of numbers**, are collections of numbers that carry specific information such as vital statistics, test results, or crop harvest values. In this book we will be studying statistics, the science, and in particular, we will be learning about certain statistics, the functions of data, that are used in drawing inferences concerning results of experimental manipulations.

1.14 Differences in the scores give rise to all of the methods of descriptive statistics. All of the problems that statistics the science has been devised to cope with arise because the scores or values making up the data usually do not all have the same value. If they did, we could describe every sample of scores by using at most two values: one telling the common value shared by all the pieces of data and the other telling the number of values in the sample. All of the tools of descriptive statistics such as the mean, the median, the mode, the range, and the standard deviation become unnecessary when all of the values in the sample are the same. So we see that it is this property of samples, that the values in general differ from one another, that gives rise to all of the questions and methods of descriptive statistics.

1.15 The fundamental concept of descriptive statistics is the frequency distribution. The concept of a frequency distribution has been created as an economical device for organizing the differences and samenesses of values in a sample. The differences are enumerated as the possible values that the items in the sample can take. These are enumerated either as individual values or as groups of values, as in the grouped frequency distribution. The samenesses are enumerated by an indication, for each of these possible values, of how many of the items in the sample take that value. Thus the frequency distribution makes a complete statement of the differences between the scores and the frequency with which scores take the same value or fall in the same interval of values.

1.16 Frequency distributions with many values overload perception and memory, giving rise to summary statistics. Because a sample may be very large, containing many values, and because these values may differ greatly from one another, a frequency distribution may carry so overwhelming an amount of information that neither memory nor perception can adequately cope. Principles of economy are then brought to bear, and attempts are made to summarize the information in a sample by using a relatively small number of values. These are called **summary statistics** or **descriptive statistics.** These summary statistics usually answer two questions: What is a value that typifies the entire collection in the sample? and What is a value that indicates how typical this value really is? The question of the typical value is usually answered by some measure of

central tendency, usually the mean, but occasionally the median. The question of how typical is this measure of central tendency is usually answered by some measure of dispersion, spread, or **variability**, usually the standard deviation or its square, the variance, but occasionally some other measure. Usually the measure of dispersion summarizes how discrepant the scores in the sample are from the value chosen as typical.

1.17 Sampling error gives rise to all of the methods of inferential statistics. If we take our samples from some population in such a way as to give each value in the population the same chance of being included in our sample, we say we have taken a **random sample**. It is obvious that if we repeatedly sample from a population in which the values differ, we can expect that the makeup of our samples will differ from sample to sample. Our sample frequency distribution will not be the same each time we draw a random sample from a population in which the values differ from one another. This raises all of the problems of inferential statistics.

The business of inferential statistics is to draw inferences about populations by using the information contained in samples. But if the samples differ from random sample to random sample, a measure of uncertainty is introduced into the inferential process. We refer to these differences from sample to sample as **sampling error**. Because of sampling error we are uncertain how typical the information in our sample is of the information contained in the entire population we are sampling. The point of sampling is to draw an inference from a part of the population to the whole of it. As long as the part is a stable representative of the whole, we feel comfortable and assured. When the possibility of the part's varying from occasion to occasion is introduced, the credibility of the part comes into question, and we become concerned as to how we may draw valid inferences from a varying part to what we assume is a stable whole. The theory and methods of inferential statistics are designed for coping with the uncertainty produced by variation from sample to sample, that is, by sampling error.

1.18 The fundamental concept of inferential statistics is the sampling distribution of a statistic. When we combine (1) the need for economical representation of a sample by some statistic with (2) the variation of the makeup of samples as we go from sample to sample, we encounter the situation in which our summary statistic will vary from sample to sample. Our approach to the problems of inferential statistics is based upon this variation of our summary statistic from sample to sample. We solve the problems by developing a theory of how the summary statistic will vary, that is, how it will behave from sample to sample. **All of this theory rests upon the fundamental concept of inferential statistics: the sampling distribution of a statistic.**

The concept of the sampling distribution of a statistic enables us to bring to bear the well-developed machinery of probability theory upon the problem of understanding the behavior of a statistic from sample to sample and therefore how we can rationally use such a summary of the sample information in drawing inferences from samples to populations.

1.19   The bases of inferential statistics.   Using sample data that result from experiments in order to draw inferences to populations and therefore to data that might result from other experiments rests on a three-part foundation. The first part is the concept of **the statistic and its sampling distribution**. The second part is **probability theory**, which provides a precise understanding of the sampling distribution and therefore of the behavior of the statistic from sample to sample, and the third part involves a **logic of inference** by which we use statistics (the functions of data) together with our knowledge of sampling distributions in order to draw inferences.

1.20 You were first introduced to some basic concepts.   A good deal of introductory statistics was designed to lead you to this. First, you drew a distinction between a **population**, the entire collection of numbers of interest, and a **sample** which was the part of that population you actually observed. Then you learned about a descriptive statistic, the **sample arithmetic mean** (we'll just call it the sample mean from now on), which was defined as the sum of the scores in a sample, divided by the number of scores in that sample. If Y_i stands for the ith score in the sample and N stands for the number of scores in the sample, then $M = \Sigma_i Y_i / N$ is the sample mean. $(\Sigma_i Y_i = Y_1 + Y_2 + ... + Y_{N-1} + Y_N.)$

You also learned about the **variance,** and its square root, the **standard deviation.** These both measured dispersion or the degree to which the sample scores differed from their mean. The variance was defined as a kind of average also. The sample variance averaged the squares of the deviations of the scores from the sample mean, giving $S^2 = \Sigma_i(Y_i - M)^2/N$ as the **sample variance**. Then the **sample standard deviation** was defined as the square root of the variance, $\sqrt{S^2}$. (Some textbooks call $\Sigma_i(Y_i - M)^2/(N-1)$ the sample variance and its square root the sample standard deviation, but in this book $\Sigma_i(Y_i - M)^2/(N-1)$ is called the unbiased estimate of the population variance and its square root is called the estimated standard deviation.)

Similarly, the **population mean** and **population variance** were also defined, the population mean being the average of all of the scores in the population and the population variance being the average squared deviation of the scores in the population from the population mean. Perhaps you also learned to refer to the mean and variance of the sample as **statistics** and the mean and variance of the population as **parameters.**

1.21 Then to the z-distribution. Then you learned about some of the different shapes that population distributions take. You learned about the **normal or Gaussian distribution** (see Statistical Table 1 in Appendix 3) and its properties, including how to use the standard normal distribution, the one with a mean of zero and a standard deviation of one, to find what proportion of scores in some other normal distribution were below some given score, or above some given score, or between that given score and the mean of the distribution, or between two given scores, and so forth. Remember how this went. You converted the given score to a z-score by subtracting the mean of the distribution and then dividing this difference by the standard deviation of the distribution. Then you were either told or shown that this constituted a linear transformation of the given score and that the same linear transformation applied to all the scores in a distribution would preserve the rank order of all these scores. So if a score was in the bottom 30 percent of the old distribution, the z-score it was converted to would be in the bottom 30 percent of the z-distribution (read the same for top 50 percent, middle 20 percent, etc.). Therefore, by knowing the relative position of the z-score in the z-distribution, also known as the **standard normal distribution**, you could know the relative position of the given score in its normal distribution.

With this tool in hand you were able to interpret these proportions as probabilities in the following sense. If, say, the proportion of scores between 100 and 115 in some normal distribution is .34, you could appreciate that the chances of getting a score in that interval of 100 to 115 when you randomly sampled one score from the entire normal distribution would be 34 in 100 or odds of 34 to 66 in favor of it. You then could intuit that the probability of such a score's occurring would be .34. And whenever you wanted to know what the proportion of scores is between two given scores in a given normal distribution, you could use the z-score technique.

1.22 Now you were able to do a z-test. At this point, with the standard normal distribution in hand, and some feeling for probabilities of a score in a certain interval occurring when the score is sampled from a normal distribution, you were guided through your first bit of inference. It went something like this. First you were shown, using the table of a standard normal distribution, that a z-score greater than 1.96 or less than -1.96 occurred only about once in 20 times. Its probability of occurrence is .05. Perhaps this was expressed something like this:

$$\Pr(|\,z\,| \geq 1.96) = .05. \qquad\qquad [1.1]$$

Among other things, this means that if you sample a score at random from a normal distribution, convert that score into a z-score by subtracting the mean and dividing by the standard deviation, then only 1 in 20 times should the absolute value (the value regardless of its + or - sign) of that z-score be so big as 1.96 or bigger. We could say

$$\Pr(\,|Y_i - \mu\,|/\sigma \geq 1.96) = .05. \qquad\qquad\qquad\qquad\qquad [1.2]$$

where μ and σ are the mean and standard deviation of the distribution. And by multiplying the inequality in the parentheses through by σ we could write

$$\Pr(\,|Y_i - \mu\,| \geq 1.96\sigma\,) = .05,$$

which in words says that the probability of a score's being as much as 1.96 standard deviations or more from the mean of its distribution is .05 if the distribution is a normal distribution.

Now at last you could almost test a hypothesis about an unknown mean and standard deviation of a normal distribution. You had the required knowledge of the distribution and the required probability information. The only thing needed was a reasoning pattern, a logic of inference. It went something like this. (And don't worry if this is a brief treatment because we'll go right through the same reasoning pattern again in section 1.21.) We decide to act as if rare events do not occur at all, even though we know that actually they do occur, albeit only rarely. We will use a score's deviating from a conjectured or hypothesized mean by more than 1.96 standard deviations as evidence that the conjecture or hypothesis is false. We do this even though we know that if the hypothesis were true, once in 20 times such a deviation would occur. We guardedly refuse to believe that it has actually happened this time—guardedly, in that we are aware that indeed it may have.

At this point you were able to test a hypothesis about a normal distribution. You said, "I will sample a score randomly from a normal distribution about which I hypothesize that the mean is 50 and the standard deviation is 5. I will convert the score to a z-score, and if the z-score is, in absolute value, as big as 1.96 or bigger, I will reject the hypothesis. I will do this because if the hypothesis were true, I would have to conclude that a rare event, one that would occur only once in 20 times, had actually occurred, and of course I have decided to act as if such rare events do not occur." You came to know and love this first inferential procedure for testing hypotheses as **the z-test**.

1.23 Then the z-test was extended to samples of N scores. As soon as the z-test was mastered you were informed that it could be used with a sample of more than one score. This was an important lesson because it showed you that **changing some of the elements of the procedure was not crucial so long as the distribution theory, the probabilities, and the logic of inference remained unchanged.** You found out that if N scores are sampled randomly and independently of one another from a normal distribution, the sample mean is calculated, and this same process is repeated a very large number of times, the distribution of sample means that is generated will itself be approximately a normal distribution. And if this process is allowed to continue indefinitely, the distribution that is generated will approach more and more closely to a limiting normal distribution with a mean equal to the mean of the population being sampled and a standard deviation, known as the **standard error of the mean**, equal to the standard deviation of the sampled population divided by the square root of the sample size. This limiting normal distribution you knew as the **sampling distribution of the sample mean**. Its standard deviation you knew as the **standard error of the mean**. With this sampling distribution of the sample mean you were able to calculate the probability of sample means departing from a hypothesized population mean by specified amounts, and in particular you were able to say that the probability that a sample mean would differ from the population mean by an absolute difference of 1.96 standard errors of the mean or more is .05. That is,

$$Pr(|M - \mu| \geq 1.96\sigma /\sqrt{N}) = .05$$

This followed as a simple extension of the z-test logic to means, because a sample mean could itself be viewed as a sample of a single score from a population distribution of normally distributed means, that distribution being the sampling distribution of the mean.

You may not have realized at the time that the step from using a single score to using a sample of N scores was a very important transition. When one sample score is used to draw an inference about the population, the inference rests upon the nature of the hypothesized distribution. To repeat the reasoning, in a normal distribution with a mean μ and a variance σ^2 the proportion of scores in this population that are between $\mu - 1.96\sigma$ and $\mu + 1.96\sigma$ is .95 and the proportion of scores outside this interval is .05. The values $\mu - 1.96\sigma$ and $\mu + 1.96\sigma$ cut the number line into three segments. The middle segment consists of points corresponding to numbers that would usually occur as the sample score when μ is the population mean and σ^2 is its variance. The line segment at or below $\mu - 1.96\sigma$ and the line segment at or above $\mu + 1.96\sigma$ consist of points corresponding to numbers that would rarely happen, only about 1 in 20 times. If the sample score is one of these rare values, we decide to reject the hypothesis that the population mean is μ and the population variance is σ^2.

However, when the sample consists of more than one score it can become awkward and inefficient to try to reach a decision about the hypothesis by referring to this hypothesized population distribution. Suppose, for example, the hypothesized population was a normal distribution with a mean of 100 and a variance of 100. Suppose also that we are willing to believe that $\sigma^2 = 100$, but we want to test the hypothesis that $\mu = 100$. Then, only 1 in 20 times would we expect a single score to be at or above 119.6 or at or below 80.4. That is, μ $\pm 1.96\sigma = 100 \pm 1.96(10)$. Suppose that in a sample of nine scores we found the values 119, 112, 95, 87, 124, 98, 105, 117, and 107. Only one score, 124, is the sort that would occur only rarely. The other eight scores are between 80.4 and 119.6. Should we accept or reject the hypothesis that these scores were sampled from a population with a mean of 100, assuming a variance of 100? Certainly different people would reach different conclusions were a standard procedure not available. By using the sample mean, it is possible to extract all of the information in the sample that bears on the question of the location of the population mean (see discussions of <u>sufficient statistics</u> in advanced statistics textbooks for more on this assertion). And by using the sampling distribution of the sample mean, it is possible to know which values of the sample mean are common and which would occur only rarely if our hypothesis about the population mean is true.

We know that repeatedly drawing a sample of nine scores from a normal distribution with a mean of 100 and a variance of 100 would produce a normal distribution of sample means. This normal distribution would have a mean of 100 and a variance of 100/9. Hence the standard deviation of the sampling distribution of the sample mean, that is, the standard error of the mean, would equal $(\sqrt{100/9}) = 10/3$. Therefore only 1 in 20 times would we expect to observe a sample mean greater than or equal to $100 + 1.96(10/3) = 106.53$ or less than or equal to $100 - 1.96(10/3) = 93.47$. With this knowledge we can use the same logic to test the hypothesis as we did with a single score. In fact we can think of our sample mean as a sample of a single mean from that imaginary population of sample means that would be created by repeatedly randomly sampling nine scores from the hypothesized original population of scores. Since the sample mean of our particular sample is actually 107 and is outside the range of common sample means, 93.47 to 106.53, we would reject the hypothesis that $\mu = 100$ since such a sample mean would occur only rarely if the hypothesis were true.

This device of converting a sample of scores into a statistic for which the sampling distribution is known lies at the foundation of hypothesis testing. The sampling distribution informs us which values of the statistic rarely occur and which occur commonly when the tested hypothesis is true. The strategy we adopt is to reject hypotheses when values occur that the hypotheses predict should occur only rarely. In the first part of the book we will attend to the task of showing how we know the sampling distribution of the statistics we will be using to test hypotheses.

1.23.1   A little concrete familiarization with a sampling distribution of a sample mean. We have just asserted that the sampling distribution of the mean of random samples of independent scores from a normal distribution is itself a normal distribution with a mean equal to the population mean and a variance equal to σ^2/N, the population variance

TABLE 1.3 THE 27 POSSIBLE SAMPLES OF THREE SCORES FROM THE POPULATION CONSISTING OF 1, 2, AND 3, AND THE CORRESPONDING SAMPLE MEANS FOR EACH OF THOSE SAMPLES.

Samples

Third Score

	1			2			3		

		Second Score			Second Score			Second Score		
		1	2	3	1	2	3	1	2	3
First	1	1,1,1	1,2,1	1,3,1	1,1,2	1,2,2	1,3,2	1,1,3	1,2,3	1,3,3
Score	2	2,1,1	2,2,1	2,3,1	2,1,2	2,2,2	2,3,2	2,1,3	2,2,3	2,3,3
	3	3,1,1	3,2,1	3,3,1	3,1,2	3,2,2	3,3,2	3,1,3	3,2,3	3,3,3

Corresponding Sample Means

3/3	4/3	5/3	4/3	5/3	6/3	5/3	6/3	7/3
4/3	5/3	6/3	5/3	6/3	7/3	6/3	7/3	8/3
5/3	6/3	7/3	6/3	7/3	8/3	7/3	8/3	9/3

Note: see figure 1.4 for a graph of the sampling distribution of these means.

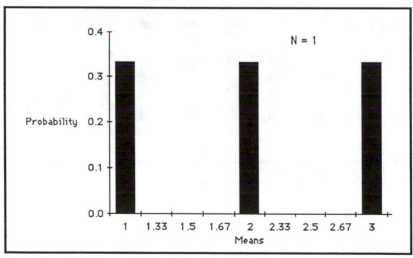

Figure 1.3. The sampling distribution of the sample mean for a sample of one score from the population consisting of the scores 1, 2, and 3.

divided by the sample size. We won't prove the normality of the sampling distribution. Such a proof would take us into moment generating functions and calculus, which we are

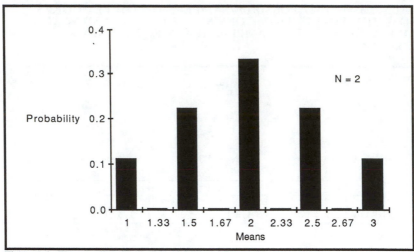

Figure 1.4. The sampling distribution of the sample mean for a sample of two scores from the population consisting of the scores 1, 2, and 3.

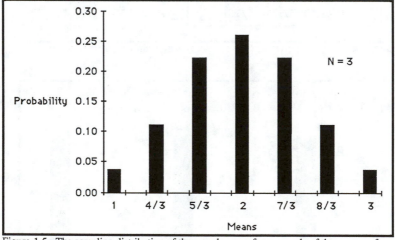

Figure 1.5. The sampling distribution of the sample mean for a sample of three scores from the population consisting of the scores 1, 2, and 3.

Such a proof would take us into moment generating functions and calculus, which we are trying to avoid. Later in the book when we learn about expected values, it will be easy to show that the mean of the sampling distribution of the mean is the mean of the population and the variance of the sampling distribution of the mean is equal to the variance of the population divided by the number of scores in the sample. For now we just want to give an intuitive feeling for these two facts. To do this we will consider samples from a small discrete population and observe the mean and variance of the distribution of all possible sample means.

Let us consider samples of size N from the population consisting of the numbers 1, 2, and 3. This is a population with a mean of 2 and a variance equal to $[(1-2)^2 + (2-2)^2 + (3-2)^2]/3 = 2/3 = \sigma^2$. We will observe the distribution of the sample mean after all possible samples of size N have been drawn by sampling with replacement. Random sampling assures us that each possible sample has the same probability of occurrence. Therefore a simple average of the various sample means will give us the mean of the sampling distribution and the variance of these sample means will be the variance of the sampling distribution of the mean. For N = 1, the three possible samples of one score are 1, 2, and 3. The means of each of these three one-score samples are, of course 1, 2, and 3. The mean of these sample means is 2 which is the mean of the population, and the variance of these sample means is the variance of the population, $[(1-2)^2 + (2-2)^2 + (3-2)^2]/3 = 2/3 = \sigma^2$ since N = 1.

For N = 2 the nine possible samples of two scores are 1,1; 1,2; 1,3; 2,1; 2,2; 2,3; 3,1; 3,2; and 3,3. The means of these samples of two scores are 1, 1.5, 2, 1.5, 2, 2.5, 2, 2.5, and 3. The mean of these sample means is 2, and the variance of these sample means is the average squared deviation of these sample means from their own mean, 2, which gives $[(1 - 2)^2 + 2(1.5 - 2)^2 + 2(2-2)^2 + 2(2.5 - 2)^2 + (3-2)^2]/9 = 1/3 = \sigma^2/N$ since $\sigma^2 = 2/3$ and N = 2.

For N = 3 Table 1.3 shows the 27 possible samples of three scores and the corresponding sample means. Table 1.4 gives each possible sample mean and the frequency with which it occurred. The mean of the distribution of sample means is again the population mean, 6/3 = 2, and the variance of this distribution is $[(3/3 - 2)^2 + 3(4/3 - 2)^2 + 6(5/3 - 2)^2 + 7(6/3 - 2)^2 + 6(7/3 - 2)^2 + 3(8/3 - 2)^2 + (9/3 - 2)^2]/27 = (54/9)/27 = 2/9 = (2/3)/3 = \sigma^2/N$.

TABLE 1.4 FREQUENCY DISTRIBUTION FOR SAMPLE MEANS: N = 3

MEAN	FREQUENCY
3/3	1
4/3	3
5/3	6
6/3	7
7/3	6
8/3	3
9/3	1

It is also instructive to examine Figures 1.3, 1.4, and 1.5 where the sampling distributions for N = 1, 2, and 3 are separately graphed. In Figure 1.3 we see that for N =1 the total probability is equally distributed over the three possible values of the sample mean. But in Figures 1.4 and 1.5 we see that more of the probability is assigned to values of the sample mean that are close to the population mean than to values that are far from it. Examining the three graphs we see that for N = 1 only one-third of the sample means are less than one unit from the population mean, whereas for N = 2, seven-ninths of the sample means are no more than half a unit from the population mean. And for N = 3,nineteen-twenty sevenths of the possible sample means are within one-third of a unit from the population mean. Of course, this is what the decreasing variance of the sampling distribution of the mean is telling us: the average squared distance of a sample mean from the population mean decreases from two-thirds to one-third to two-ninths as N goes from 1 to 2 to 3. Note also for so small a sample size as N = 3 that the sampling distribution of the mean of three scores drawn from a population with a flat distribution (all scores equally probable) has started to look quite a bit like the normal distribution. This is a graphic portrayal of the successively closer approximation of the sampling distribution of the sample mean to the normal distribution that occurs as N gets bigger. Perhaps in your introductory course you encountered this, referred to as the **central limit theorem.**

1.24 An aside regarding the word "distribution." In an effort to help you avoid unnecessary confusion, sometime around now perhaps your attention was brought to the fact that the word "distribution" had been used in at least three important senses which must be distinguished one from another. The **population distribution** is the distribution of scores from which samples are drawn and to which inferences are drawn; the **sample distribution** is the distribution of scores in the sample that has been drawn; and the **sampling distribution** of some statistic (so far only the mean) is the probability distribution of that statistic. (A probability distribution is a function that assigns to each value of a discrete variable or to each interval of a continuous variable the probability that the variable will take that discrete value or occur in that interval.)

1.25 Using t instead of z. No sooner did you learn to use the z-test with a sample of N scores to test a hypothesis about the mean of a normal distribution than you received your first big surprise. You were told that researchers almost never use the z-test. Why? Because to do so the researcher must either know the population standard deviation or have some hypothesis as to its specific value. Most of the time this is not the case. Instead, the researcher uses information from the sample concerning what the population standard deviation is. We will call the population standard deviation σ. The sample information about σ is contained in the sample estimate of σ,

$$\sigma_{est.} = S\sqrt{[N/(N-1)]} = \sqrt{[\Sigma_i(Y_i - M)^2/(N-1)]}.$$

But because $\sigma_{est.}$ was used instead of σ, it was no longer possible to use the standard normal distribution, the z distribution. The statistic $(Y_i - \mu)/\sigma_{est.}$ did not have the z distribution, nor did the statistic $(M - \mu)/(\sigma_{est.}/\sqrt{N})$. Instead a different distribution had to be used. This was called the **t-distribution.** You learned to do a **t-test** of the hypothesis that μ was the population mean by finding

$$t = (M - \mu)/(\sigma_{est.}/\sqrt{N})$$

and determining whether this value of t was in a critical or rejection region which depended on the quantity N-1, the degrees of freedom for t.

Hopefully you were told that of the three aspects of testing the hypothesis, the distribution of the statistic was the only one that changed. Probability theory was used in the same way as with z; the logic of inference was exactly the same as with z—only the statistic being used, t, had a different distribution than did the z statistic, so the value 1.96 was replaced by another value, which depended on the quantity N - 1. If we call the value of t that replaces 1.96 "$t_{critical}$", then we can state that

$$Pr(|t| \geq t_{critical}) = .05$$

so

$$Pr[\ |M - \mu|/(\sigma_{est}/\sqrt{N}) \geq t_{critical}\ ] = .05$$

and therefore

$$Pr[\ |M - \mu| \geq t_{critical}(\sigma_{est}/\sqrt{N})\ ] = .05$$

which is of the same form as

$$Pr[\ |M - \mu| \geq 1.96(\sigma/\sqrt{N})\ ] = .05,$$

the only difference being that because we use σ_{est} instead of σ, we therefore use $t_{critical}$ instead of 1.96.

1.25.1 Why we divide by N - 1. If you never understood why σ^2_{est} was $\Sigma_i(Y_i -$ M$)^2$/(N - 1) instead of the variance of the sample of scores, which would have been $\Sigma_i(Y_i -$ M$)^2$/N, it may help to consider a concrete example of why we divide by N - 1. Consider again the nine possible samples of two scores from the population 1, 2, 3: 1,1; 1,2; 1,3; 2,1; 2,2; 2,3; 3,1; 3,2; 3,3. Each possible sample would be expected to occur about one-ninth of the time so by averaging the sample variance, $\Sigma_i(Y_i - M)^2$/N, for each of these samples we can find out what our estimate of σ^2 would be on the average if we used the sample variance as our estimator of the population variance. Then we can compare that average estimator with the actual variance and see if on the average the estimator equals the variance we are trying to estimate. (This is a nice property of an estimator. An estimator having this property is called an **unbiased estimator**.) The sample variances for the nine possible samples are $[(1 - 1)^2 + (1 - 1)^2]/2$, $[(1 - 1.5)^2 + (2 - 1.5)^2]/2$, $[(1 - 2)^2 + (3 - 2)^2]/2$, $[(2 - 1.5)^2 + (1 - 1.5)^2]/2$, $[(2 - 2)^2 + (2 - 2)^2]/2$, $[(2 - 2.5)^2 + (3 - 2.5)^2]/2$, $[(3 - 2)^2 + (1 - 2)^2]/2$, $[(3 - 2.5)^2 + (2 - 2.5)^2]/2$, and $[(3 - 3)^2 + (3 - 3)^2]/2$, which equal 0, .25, 1, .25, 0, .25, 1, .25, and 0, and average to 1/3. But the variance of the population is $[(1 - 2)^2 + (2 - 2)^2 + (3 - 2)^2]/3 = 2/3$. We see that on the average, the sample variance underestimates the population variance. If we multiply the average sample variance by N/(N - 1) which is 2/(2 - 1) $= 2$ in this case, we obtain a value equal to the population variance. It can be shown, using the expected value operator (see Appendix A1), that it is always true that N/(N - 1) times the average sample variance is equal to the population variance. This means that if instead of using the sample variance, $\Sigma_i(Y_i - M)^2$/N, as our estimator, we use [N/(N - 1)] times the sample variance, then the long-run average of this quantity will actually be the population variance and therefore this quantity, which is

$$[N/(N - 1)] \; \Sigma_i(Y_i - M)^2/N \; = \; \Sigma_i(Y_i - M)^2/(N - 1)$$

is an unbiased estimator of the population variance. This is why we use $\Sigma_i(Y_i - M)^2$/(N - 1) to estimate σ^2: because the long-run average value of $\Sigma_i(Y_i - M)^2$/(N - 1) is σ^2.

1.26   Really getting down to the business of testing hypotheses: The t-test for two independent samples. When the next surprise came it was a little easier to take. You found out that the t-test of a hypothesis about the mean of a single normal distribution, while occasionally being used in research, actually occurred rather rarely. It was not usual for a researcher to have a hypothesis about the mean of a single distribution. Far more often the research question involved a comparison of the means of two distributions. This arose because two sets of scores, one from an experimental condition and another from either a control condition or a different experimental condition, were regarded as samples from two different distributions. The question of whether the effect of an experimental treatment differed from that of a control treatment or that of a second experimental treatment was translated into a question about the effects of those treatments on the scores in the two distributions and therefore on the means of those scores. Thus it became the statistical question of whether the two sets of scores could be regarded as samples from distributions having the same mean and standard deviation or from distributions having different means but the same standard deviation. The unknown common standard deviation was estimated from the data, and a t-test for testing the hypothesis that the two distributions had the same mean was conducted using the t-statistic

$$t = \frac{(M_1 - M_2) - (\mu_1 - \mu_2)}{\sqrt{\{[\Sigma_j(Y_{1j} - M_1)^2 + \Sigma_j(Y_{2j} - M_2)^2](1/N_1 + 1/N_2)/(N_1 + N_2 - 2)\}}}$$

where $(\mu_1 - \mu_2)$ is the hypothesized difference between the two populations means, in this case it being zero, and the denominator of the t being the estimate of the standard deviation of the sampling distribution of the statistic $(M_1 - M_2)$, the difference between the two sample means.

It might be useful to spell out the story of this t-statistic just a little further. This t is actually a substitute for a z just as

$$t = (M - \mu)/\sqrt{\{[\Sigma_i(Y_i - M)^2/(N-1)](1/N)\}}$$

was a substitute for

$$z = (M - \mu)/\sqrt{(\sigma/\sqrt{N})}.$$

Suppose that we were to engage repeatedly in a two step process. The first step of the process is sampling N_1 scores from a normal distribution with a mean μ_1 and a variance σ^2 and then sampling N_2 scores from a normal distribution with the same variance σ^2 but with a mean of μ_2. The second step is to subtract M_2, the sample mean of the N_2 scores from M_1, the sample mean of the N_1 scores, and to record the difference. If we were to do this repeatedly a large number of times, we would create a distribution of such $(M_1 - M_2)$-values. It is possible to show that these $(M_1 - M_2)$-values would be normally distributed with a mean equal to $(\mu_1 - \mu_2)$ and a variance equal to $(\sigma^2/N_1 + \sigma^2/N_2) = \sigma^2(1/N_1 + 1/N_2)$. Therefore, if we were to subtract $(\mu_1 - \mu_2)$ from each $(M_1 - M_2)$ and divide each such $(M_1 - M_2) - (\mu_1 - \mu_2)$ by $\sqrt{[\sigma^2(1/N_1 + 1/N_2)]}$ we would obtain the standard normal distribution. That is,

$$z = [(M_1 - M_2) - (\mu_1 - \mu_2)] / \sqrt{[\sigma^2(1/N_1 + 1/N_2)]}$$

because $(\mu_1 - \mu_2)$ is the mean of the distribution of $(M_1 - M_2)$-values and $\sqrt{[\sigma^2(1/N_1 + 1/N_2)]}$ is its standard deviation.

Since $Pr(\ |z| \geq 1.96) = .05$, it follows that

$$Pr(\ |(M_1 - M_2) - (\mu_1 - \mu_2)| / \sqrt{[\sigma^2(1/N_1 + 1/N_2)]} \geq 1.96) = .05$$

so

$$Pr(|\ (M_1 - M_2) - (\mu_1 - \mu_2)\ | \geq 1.96\sqrt{[\sigma^2(1/N_1 + 1/N_2)]}) = .05.$$

Thus, if we knew σ^2 we could test the hypothesis that $(\mu_1 - \mu_2)$ is the true difference between the means of the two normally distributed populations we were sampling from by comparing $(M_1 - M_2)$ to $(\mu_1 - \mu_2)$. If the absolute difference between $(M_1 - M_2)$ and $(\mu_1 - \mu_2)$ exceeded $1.96\sqrt{[\sigma^2(1/N_1 + 1/N_2)]}$ we would have the standard grounds for rejecting the hypothesis: namely, a rare z has been obtained.

But we do not know σ^2, the variance common to the two populations that were sampled. To remedy this problem we use an unbiased estimate of σ^2 that uses the information about σ^2 contained in both of the two samples of scores we have drawn. This value is

$$\sigma^2_{est} = [\Sigma_j(Y_{1j} - M_1)^2 + \Sigma_j(Y_{2j} - M_2)^2]/(N_1 + N_2 - 2).$$

But when we substitute σ^2_{est} for σ^2 in the formula

$$z = [(M_1 - M_2) - (\mu_1 - \mu_2)] / \sqrt{[\sigma^2(1/N_1 + 1/N_2)]}$$

we no longer have a statistic that has the z distribution. Instead, the statistic is

$$t = [(M_1 - M_2) - (\mu_1 - \mu_2)] / \sqrt{[\sigma^2_{est}(1/N_1 + 1/N_2)]}$$

and is distributed according to the t distribution with $N_1 + N_2 - 2$ degrees of freedom. At this point we can follow the same steps as for a sample from a single population and make the following three equivalent statements:

$$Pr(|t| \geq t_{critical}) = .05;$$

$$Pr(|\ [(M_1 - M_2) - (\mu_1 - \mu_2)\ ] / \sqrt{[\sigma^2_{est}(1/N_1 + 1/N_2)]}\ | \geq t_{critical}) = .05;$$

$Pr(| [(M_1 - M_2) - (\mu_1 - \mu_2)] | \geq t_{critical}\sqrt{[\sigma^2_{est}(1/N_1 + 1/N_2)]}) = .05$.

We reject the hypothesis that the difference between the means of the two populations is $(\mu_1 - \mu_2)$ if the difference between the two obtained sample means, $M_1 - M_2$, differs from $(\mu_1 - \mu_2)$ by more than $t_{critical}\sqrt{[\sigma^2_{est}(1/N_1 + 1/N_2)]}$. Our argument is that we know that a difference this big or bigger would occur only 1 time in 20 and we follow the guarded strategy of refusing to believe that such a rare event has occurred.

For many of you, the course went no further than this so far as the analysis of scores from experiments. You probably had some introduction to the analysis of frequencies, as in the chi-square test for independence, and you probably had a minimal introduction to correlation and simple linear regression. If you did do a little more it was probably to draw the distinction between t-tests for independent samples and t-tests for dependent measures.

1.27 The t-test for two dependent measures. One way to do an experiment on the effects of two different experimental treatments is to apply one treatment to one set of subjects, plants, machines, or something else, and the other to a different set. The two sets are independent of each other, and therefore so are the scores. The t-test in section 1.15 is appropriate to such data. A second way is to give the two treatments to, say, the same group of subjects. Each subject gets first one treatment and then the other, which treatment comes first being decided randomly for each subject. In this case, because the scores for the two different treatments come from the same subjects, we would assume that they are not independent of one another. An experiment of this sort is called a dependent measurements experiment or a repeated measurements experiment because we repeatedly measure the same subjects. You probably learned that for the case of just two measurements per subject, a simple device could be used to test the hypothesis that the two treatments differ in their effects by the amount $(\mu_1 - \mu_2)$, (zero in this case), where μ_1 is the mean of the distribution of scores under the first treatment and μ_2 is the mean of the distribution of scores under the second treatment. The device was to use difference scores $D_j = Y_{1j} - Y_{2j}$, where Y_{ij} is the score for individual j under treatment i. Then a t-test of the hypothesis that the mean of the D_j is equal to $\mu_D = (\mu_1 - \mu_2)$ could be performed using the t-test for a single group of scores, the scores being the D_j. Thus, letting $M_D = \Sigma_j D_j/N$,

$t = [M_D - \mu_D]/\sqrt{[\Sigma_j(D_i - M_D)^2/(N-1)]}$.

What we are saying here is that if the difference between the two means, $(\mu_1 - \mu_2)$, equals the hypothesized value, say zero, then the mean of the differences or difference scores will be μ_D, and equal zero in this case.

1.28 The t-test for independent samples and the t-test for dependent measures as the seeds for many of the analyses to be studied in this book. As we go through the book we will observe that most of it is devoted to generalizing the two t-tests we have just recalled. The one-factor experimental design with independent groups will permit us to ask about differences between the means of more than two distributions, using independent samples. The one-factor repeated measurements design will allow us to do the same when dependent samples are used with more than two treatments. Two and more factor designs allow us to generalize these tests to more than one class of experimental treatments. And mixed designs allow us even to consider the case where some of the samples are independent of the others and some are dependent. It will be helpful to know that while things get a little bit more complicated, the same basic ideas will continue to be used and expanded. In the remainder of this chapter we will briefly review the big ideas of hypothesis testing. Then in Chapter 2 we will start to study how we use the analysis of variance for testing hypotheses about the effects of manipulating experimental variables.

1.29 The purpose of the book. We are going to examine the analysis of variance from various perspectives in order to provide the student with a deep understanding of what is going on. We will try to indicate some of the big ideas and display some of the important little details. We will also provide a geometric perspective on the subject to supplement the standard algebraic treatment. In addition we will display various rules that enable us to express the problems of interest in the form of competing equations. We will learn how to use such equations to obtain the entire computational machinery that we need. In fact, we could say that a reasonable summary of our purpose is just this: **we are going to be refining our understanding of how we find and compute test statistics after we have expressed two or more rival hypotheses as model equations and how we estimate parameters of the model equations.**

1.30 The biggest idea. The drawing of inferences from data samples to populations from which those data were sampled either by testing hypotheses or by estimating parameters is the biggest idea of the analysis of variance. Let us review the general logic of hypothesis testing and of estimation so that we can use it to structure our thinking about the analysis of variance. To do this we use the common coin flip example, which you have no doubt already encountered in your introductory statistics course.

1.31 Testing the hypothesis that a coin is fair. We wish to test the hypothesis that a coin is fair. If the coin is fair, the probability of heads coming up on any toss is one-half. We say: if the coin is fair, $Pr(H) = 1/2$. To test the hypothesis we perform an experiment in

TABLE 1.5 THE SAMPLING DISTRIBUTION OF THE STATISTIC X, THE NUMBER OF HEADS IN 10 INDEPENDENT FLIPS OF A FAIR COIN

x	Pr(X=x)
0	.0010
1	.0098
2	.0439
3	.1172
4	.2051
5	.2461
6	.2051
7	.1172
8	.0439
9	.0098
10	.0010

According to the binomial probability distribution:

$$Pr(X=x) = \frac{10!}{x!(10-x)!} (1/2)^x (1/2)^{10-x}$$

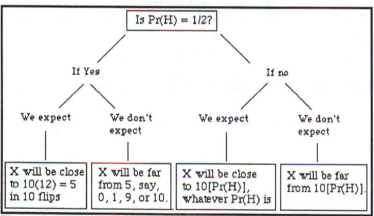

Figure 1.6. Our reasoning concerning the number of heads (X) in 10 flips if Pr(H) does or does not equal 1/2.

which we flip the coin independently on 10 trials. We decide also to use as our test statistic the number of times the coin comes up heads in these 10 flips. We call this number X.

1.32 The logic of our inference. We reason according to the diagram in Figure 1.6. If the coin is fair, the number of heads in 10 flips should be in the vicinity of about 5 heads and only rarely should we see as few as 0 or 1 or as many as 9 or 10. In fact, because we learned about the binomial probability distribution in introductory statistics, we can use the binomial formula to find the probability of each value of X from X = 0 to X = 10. These are given in Table 1.5. The probability that X is between 3 and 7, inclusive, is .8907 and the probability that X is so small as 0 or 1 or so large as 9 or 10 is only .0216.

1.33 The way we decide. We have concluded that if the coin is fair, we do not expect to see 0, 1, 9, or 10 heads since they happen only rarely when Pr(H) = 1/2. So, if we do see any of these values, we must decide either that Pr(H) is not one-half or that it is one-half and a rare event has occurred. Rather than deciding that a rare event has occurred, we prefer to conclude that Pr(H) is not one-half. We reject (decide against) that hypothesis. If the number of heads in 10 flips is not 0, 1, 9, or 10 we do not reject the hypothesis that Pr(H) = 1/2. Does this mean that we conclude that Pr(H) = 1/2? Not exactly. This is because we realize that Pr(H) could be any one of many values that are inferentially compatible with the fact that we did not get 0, 1, 9, or 10 heads. The same evidence that is insufficient to persuade us that Pr(H) ≠ 1/2 is also insufficient to persuade us that Pr(H) ≠ .55. We can say that the hypothesis that Pr(H) = 1/2 is acceptable in the light of the evidence supplied by the data. We can even say that we accept that hypothesis instead of rejecting it so long as we understand that it is in the above sense of accepting it along with a range of other inferentially plausible values. It is just not the only value that is acceptable. To find the entire range of possible values that would be acceptable in the light of the data,we would find a confidence interval (see section 1.29) around the sample proportion of heads. We'll have more to say about confidence intervals throughout the book.

1.34 The sampling distribution as the basis for deciding which events are rare. Recall that the sampling distribution of a statistic is the probability distribution of that statistic. In the case of a statistic such as X that takes discrete values, the sampling distribution is an assignment of a piece of probability to each possible value of X. What we have just done is to use the sampling distribution of our test statistic, X, to determine a collection or region of values of X that are improbable when the tested hypothesis is true. Then we decided that if, when we collect our data and compute X, it turns out to equal one of those rare values, we will choose to believe that the hypothesis we are testing is false rather than believe that (1) it is true and (2) a rare event occurred. The collection or region of rare values that we use to reject the tested hypothesis is called the **critical region** or the **rejection region**.

1.35 The importance of the sampling distribution of our test statistic. W e should note well that it was by knowing the sampling distribution of our test statistic that we were able to decide which values are rare and which values are common if the tested hypothesis is true. We should also note that we chose rare values that were as far from the expected value of X as we could find. This was not simply because these values had small probabilities. It also concerned the power of our test against alternative hypotheses, but we won't be talking about power in detail until Chapter 13.

1.36 The abstract steps in hypothesis testing. Now that we have gone through this concrete example, let us abstract the general ideas so that we can be prepared for using the same general strategy in the analysis of variance. The abstract steps with their concrete examples are given in Table 1.6. The student should refer to Table 1.6 now and carefully compare each abstract step with its concrete example before reading further.

1.37 The big idea of hypothesis testing. The big idea of hypothesis testing is
1. **Formulate a hypothesis;**
2. **choose a test statistic for which the sampling distribution is known when the tested hypothesis is true;**
3. **select a rejection region; and**
4. **reject the tested hypothesis if the value of the test statistic computed from the sample of data equals a value in the rejection region.**

TABLE 1.6 THE STEPS IN TESTING A HYPOTHESIS.

Abstract Step	Concrete Example of Step
1. Formulate a hypothesis	1. Pr(H) = 1/2.
2. Choose a test statistic for which the sampling distribution (probability distribution) can be obtained when the chosen hypothesis is true.	2. Choose X, the number of heads in 10 flips of the coin, for which the sampling distribution is the binomial distribution with N = 10 and p = 1/2.
3. Determine those rare values which depart most from the value expected if the tested hypothesis is true and use them as a critical or rejection region.	3. Choose X = 0,1,9, and 10 as the rejection region or critical region.
4. Collect the sample, calculate the value of the test statistic, and reject the tested hypothesis if the test statistic equals a value in the rejection region.	4. Flip the coin 10 times, count the number of heads, and reject the hypothesis that Pr(H) = 1/2 if the number of heads is 0, 1, 9, or 10.

1.38. Some little details we are skipping. There are many little details we have not pursued here because we want to press on with the big ideas. For example, we have not considered what criteria are used in deciding which test statistic we should choose, if more than one choice is possible. How does the test statistic relate to the hypothesis? Could we ever use, say, a sample mean to test a hypothesis about a population variance? What properties of the test statistic's sampling distribution might lead us to prefer it to some other candidate for a test statistic? If there is more than one way to test a hypothesis, is one way better than another? In what sense? If so, is there a way to identify the best of several tests? Does selection of the rejection region depend on what alternatives to the tested hypothesis one is concerned with? If so, how? These are all interesting questions, but they would take us too far afield from our primary concerns, so we will just mention them and hope that the student will be interested enough to pursue them later. Now we return to the big ideas.

1.39 Point estimation. We will cover point estimation in more detail later. For now we will just say that we will use the method of least squares to estimate population parameters such as population means or differences between the means of two populations. This method permits us to choose as our estimates of the population parameters those values that minimize the squares of the differences between the data we have observed and the values that our model predicts for those data.

1.40 Confidence intervals. Often, but not always, (see Chapter 11), the particular analysis of variance procedure adopted by the investigator permits the determining of a confidence interval for a population mean, μ, or for the difference between two population means, $\mu_1 - \mu_2$, say, or for comparable but more general expressions (called contrasts) that involve more than just two population means. A **confidence interval** is an estimate of a population parameter that takes the form of a range of values that may or may not contain the estimated parameter. This range of values is determined by a process that has a known probability, usually high such as .95 or .99, of producing a range that contains the true value of the parameter. Different areas of investigation place greater or less emphasis on confidence intervals relative to hypothesis testing. Despite much encouragement by statisticians and others, psychologists currently do not make much use of confidence intervals, giving much greater emphasis to hypothesis testing in the form of significance tests. This is unfortunate since confidence intervals are often more useful than significance tests (Box, Hunter & Hunter, 1978, p. 115). Here we will just take a brief look at the logic of confidence intervals and give an example of how we might use one.

We know (see section 1.25) that the probability that a sample mean will differ from the population mean by as much as $t_{critical}(\sigma_{est}/\sqrt{N})$ or more is .05. That is,

$$\Pr[\ |M - \mu| \geq t_{critical}(\sigma_{est}/\sqrt{N})\ ] = .05.$$

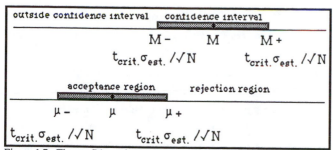

Figure 1.7. The confidence interval not overlapping the hypothesized value of μ is exactly equivalent to the sample mean M not being found in the acceptance region for the hypothesis that μ is the population mean.

Therefore the probability that the sample mean differs from the population mean by less than $t_{critical}(\sigma_{est}/\sqrt{N})$ must be $1 - .05 = .95$. That is, $Pr[\ |M - \mu| < t_{critical}(\sigma_{est}/\sqrt{N})\ ] = .95$. Another way of putting this is that the probability is .95 that μ will be found within a distance $t_{critical}(\sigma_{est}/\sqrt{N})$ of the sample mean. That is,

$$Pr[\ M - t_{critical}(\sigma_{est}/\sqrt{N}) \ < \ \mu \ < \ M + t_{critical}(\sigma_{est}/\sqrt{N})\ ] = .95.$$

The interval from $M - t_{critical}(\sigma_{est}/\sqrt{N})$ to $M + t_{critical}(\sigma_{est}/\sqrt{N})$ is said to be a 95 percent confidence interval for μ. This means that if over and over again we perform the process of taking a sample, finding $t_{critical}(\sigma_{est}/\sqrt{N})$, and creating the interval of values $M - t_{critical}(\sigma_{est}/\sqrt{N})$ to $M + t_{critical}(\sigma_{est}/\sqrt{N})$, then in the long run the population mean will occur somewhere in that interval on 95 percent of the times we do this. It is from this knowledge that we will be correct 95 percent of the time in our asserting that μ is in the confidence interval that we gain our confidence.

It is important to understand that the probability statement we make refers to the process we engage in and not to a given confidence interval after we have drawn our sample and determined that interval. That given interval is no longer a random variable. It is a fixed value. Probability statements no longer apply to it. That given interval now either contains μ or it does not, and we do not know which is true. We could say that the probability that μ is in the interval is now 1 or 0 but that is not very interesting.

Suppose that we have drawn a sample of 20 scores from a normal distribution and created a 95 percent confidence interval for the μ, which turns out to be the interval from 10 to 20. We see that M must be 15 and $t_{critical}(\sigma_{est}/\sqrt{N})$ must be 5. The first thing we can note is that these data would have resulted in the rejection, at the .05 level, of any hypothesis that asserted that the mean was outside this interval. This is because the width of the confidence interval is exactly equal to the width of the acceptance region around a given hypothesized mean. Suppose, for example, we were testing the null hypothesis that μ = 0. Then the critical region would be all values of the sample mean outside the interval 0 -

$t_{critical}(\sigma_{est}/\sqrt{N})$ to $0 + t_{critical}(\sigma_{est}/\sqrt{N})$, which in this case would be all values outside the interval -5 to +5. Since the sample mean was 15, we would reject the hypothesis that the population mean is zero. We see that we will reject the null hypothesis every time the confidence interval fails to overlap the value hypothesized by the null hypothesis because the confidence interval failing to overlap the hypothesized mean is equivalent to the sample mean being outside the region of acceptance and therefore within the rejection region for the hypothesis. We can see this graphically in Figure 1.7. The same number scale is on each line. We see that M on the top line being within the rejection region on the bottom line is exactly equivalent to the hypothesized μ on the bottom line being outside the confidence interval on the top line. **This means that the confidence interval can function as a tool for hypothesis testing as well as for estimation.** But the confidence interval goes beyond the test of a given hypothesis in that it immediately reveals the entire set of hypotheses that would have been rejected and the remaining hypotheses that would have been accepted.

1.41 The analysis of variance is a vehicle for hypothesis testing and estimation. The analysis of variance is a piece of statistical machinery that enables going through the four steps of hypothesis testing and the steps of estimating population parameters either by point or interval estimation. This machinery allows us to execute these processes in a multitude of different situations. In the next chapter we begin to study this by beginning to describe what we do in an analysis of variance. Now that we are familiar with the term "analysis of variance" and growing a little tired of having to repeat such a long phrase, we will frequently abbreviate it as **ANOVA.**

Exercises

1. Would you say that experimental control strengthens the signal or weakens the noise level in an experiment?
2. How does blocking reduce the noise level in an experiment?
3. What are the risks that are incurred when an extraneous variable is not controlled and also not randomized over conditions.
4. What are the components of the error term in the equation for a score (all of the systematic and random uncontrolled effects in the experiment)?
5. What are the consequences of leaving an extraneous variable confounded with an experimental variable?
6. Why would it be difficult to draw conclusions about the effect of stimulus sequences if each subject in the experiment received a different sequence?
7. How do behavioral researchers justify using handy samples rather than random samples?

8. Consider sampling two scores independently and at random with replacement from a population containing 1, 3, and 5.

(a) Find the average value over all possible samples of the sample variance and compare it to the population variance.

(b) Find the average value of $\Sigma_i(Y_i - M)^2/(N - 1)$ over all possible samples and compare it to the population variance.

(c) Find the average value of $[\Sigma_i(Y_i - M)^2/(N - 1)]^{.5}$ over all possible samples and compare it to the population standard deviation. Would you say that the square root of the unbiased estimator of the population variance is or is not an unbiased estimator of the population standard deviation?

9. When the sample size, N, is very large, do you think the long-run average value of the sample variance will be close to the population variance? Why?

10. To test the null hypothesis that a normal distribution had a mean of 25 and a standard deviation of 5 against the alternative that the mean was not 25 but the standard deviation was 5, a single score was sampled. The score turned out to be 31. What was the result of the test if a .05 significance level was used?

11. Suppose that in exercise 10 four scores had been sampled and were 31, 30, 28, and 34. What would the result of the test of the same hypotheses be?

12. Let Y_{1j} be the jth score in population 1 which has a mean of μ_1, and let Y_{2j} be the jth score in population 2 which has a mean of μ_2. Define $D_j = Y_{1j} - Y_{2j}$. Prove that the population mean of the D_j is $\mu_D = (\mu_1 - \mu_2)$. Show that if $\mu_1 = \mu_2$ then $\mu_D = 0$.

13. Explain in your own words why the probability distributions of sample means in section 1.23.1 look more and more like the normal distribution as the sample size increases.

14. What are the three senses of the word "distribution"?

15. A population consists of the scores 1, 1, and 2. Random samples of size 3 are drawn. Each score is replaced before the next is drawn. Find the sampling distribution of the sample mean of samples of size 3. What is the mean of this sampling distribution? What is the variance of this sampling distribution. In this problem, the population distribution is _____; an example of a sample distribution is _____; and the sampling distribution of the mean assigns probabilities to the values _____.

16. When is t used instead of z? Why?

17. State in your own words how the sampling distribution of a statistic is used to test a hypothesis.

18. What are the four points in the big idea of hypothesis testing?

19. How does probability theory enter into testing hypotheses?

20. Make up a table similar to Table 1.5. Use the left-hand side of Table 1.5, but in place of the right-hand side, substitute the steps used in a z-test using a sample of one score from a

normal distribution. Now, repeat the problem but for a t-test based on a sample of N scores from a normal distribution.

21. Suppose a sample of N_1 scores is to be drawn from population 1 and N_2 scores are to be drawn from population 2. Assume that both populations are normal and that sampling is independent and random. Write the formula for a 95 percent confidence interval for the difference between the the mean of population 1 and the mean of population 2, that is, for $\mu_1 - \mu_2$.

22. State how you could use the formula in exercise 5 to test the hypothesis that $\mu_1 = \mu_2$.

23. Suppose that you are sampling two scores independently and at random with replacement from a distribution containing a 1, two 2's, and a 3.

(a) Find the sampling distribution of the sample mean.

(b) Find the variance of the sample mean.

(c) Repeat parts (a) and (b) assuming a sample of size 3. Compare the results with those for a sample of size 2.

(d) How would the results for parts (a) and (b) differ if the population had contained one 4, two 5's, and a 6?

24. Define X_{max} to be the largest score in the sample. Suppose a population consisting of the scores 1, 2, and 3, each occurring once. Assume independent random sampling with replacement. Assume a sample size of N = 2.

(a) Find the sampling distribution of X_{max}.

(b) Find the average value of X_{max}.

(c) Find the variance of X_{max}.

25. Let X_{min} be the smallest score in the sample. Suppose a population consisting of the scores 1 and 0, each occurring once. Assume independent random sampling with replacement. Assume a sample size of N = 3.

(a) Find the sampling distribution of X_{min}. (If you stop and think about this you can get the answer very quickly.)

(b) Find the average value of X_{min}.

(c) Find the variance of X_{min}.

26. For the population defined in exercise 2 and the same sampling process except that the sample size is 2 instead of 3, define the **sample variance** to be

$$S^2 = \Sigma_i(X_i - M)^2/N = \Sigma_i X_i^2/N - M^2$$

where M is the sample mean and N is the sample size.

(a) Find the sampling distribution of the sample variance.

(b) Find the average value of the sample variance.

27. Define $X_{max} - X_{min}$ to be the sample range. Suppose a population consisting of the scores 1, 2, and 4, each occurring once. Assume independent random sampling with replacement. Assume a sample size of N = 2.

(a) Find the sampling distribution of the sample range.

(b) Find the average value of the sample range.

(c) Find the variance of the sample range.

28. Assume that the following scores were independently randomly sampled from a normal distribution: 1, 3, 5, 2, 4, 0, 1, 2, -1, 3. Find a 95 percent confidence interval for μ, the mean of that normal distribution, and use the interval to test the hypothesis that $\mu = 0$.

29. Assume that the following two groups of scores were sampled from two distributions known to be normal. Find a 95 percent confidence interval for $\mu_1 - \mu_2$, the difference between the two population means, and use the interval to test the hypothesis that $\mu_1 - \mu_2 = 10$.

Group 1: 5, 4, 3, 2, 6, 4, 5, 2, 2;

Group 2: 8, 9, 7, 10, 7, 10, 8, 8.

2

What We Do in an ANOVA

2.1 A concrete example. Consider an imaginary research project designed to discover whether people's attitudes about toxic waste disposal can be changed by showing them a movie on the prevalence of dumping poisonous chemicals, the dangers this entails, and some of the unfortunate consequences that already have been observed. The design of the study involves assessing people's attitudes with a preliminary survey, showing them the film, and then assessing their attitudes again with a second survey. Each survey provides a numerical score, which summarizes a person's attitude toward toxic waste disposal issues.

2.2 A small sample. Let us assume five persons were studied to see if their data justified a larger investigation. Call the preliminary survey scores for the five subjects P_1, P_2, P_3, P_4, P_5, and the second survey scores for the five subjects S_1, S_2, S_3, S_4, S_5. If the film had an effect, we expect a difference between a person's S score and her P score. So, the data will be a set of five difference scores: Y_1, Y_2, ..., Y_5, where $Y_i = S_i - P_i$ for i = 1, 2, ..., 5. (We ignore the need for a control group that is measured twice without an intervening film).

2.3 The null and the alternative hypotheses. Assume that the Y scores are sampled from a normal distribution. The null hypothesis of no effect due to the film is that the population mean of the Y_i, μ, is zero. This is because if there is no difference between the mean of the S scores and the mean of the P scores, the mean of the differences must be zero. (This in turn can be seen by noting that the mean of the Y_i will be the mean of the S_i - P_i, and in the population, as in a sample, $\Sigma_i(S_i - P_i)/N = \Sigma_i S_i/N - \Sigma_i P_i/N$.) The alternative hypothesis will be that the mean of the Y scores is not zero, that is, $\mu \neq 0$. We can express a score in the population as $Y_i = \mu + e_i$. Under the null hypothesis ("under the null hypothesis" means "assuming the null hypothesis is true") $\mu = 0$ so $Y_i = e_i$. Note that the null hypothesis is just a special case of the general equation $Y_i = \mu + e_i$. The general equation is "larger" than the null hypothesis equation in that it admits all real numbers as possible values of μ. The null hypothesis is "smaller" in that the set of possible values of μ is limited to contain only zero. Note also that the e_i represent the effects of error discussed in Chapter 1. All of the effects of uncontrolled variation are summarized by this single effect.

**TABLE 2.1 FICTIONAL DATA FROM
A STUDY OF ATTITUDE CHANGE**

$Y_{1,1}$	=	2	$Y_{2,1}$	=	3
$Y_{1,2}$	=	3	$Y_{2,2}$	=	7
$Y_{1,3}$	=	5	$Y_{2,3}$	=	8
$Y_{1,4}$	=	4	$Y_{2,4}$	=	7
$Y_{1,5}$	=	7	$Y_{2,5}$	=	9
$Y_{1,6}$	=	7	$Y_{2,6}$	=	9
$Y_{1,7}$	=	4	$Y_{2,7}$	=	8
$Y_{1,8}$	=	5	$Y_{2,8}$	=	10
$Y_{1,9}$	=	4	$Y_{2,9}$	=	9
$Y_{1,10}$	=	6	$Y_{2,10}$	=	11

2.4 A second experiment. Suppose the Y scores turned out to be 2, 3, 5, 7, 4.   It looks as if a statistical test would reject the null hypothesis that the mean of the population of Y scores is zero, and we would conclude that the film has an effect. Suppose this leads to a larger study in which more persons participate. Here two different films are used, one that stresses negative outcomes of toxic waste dumping and the other that stresses positive actions that people can take toward bringing about positive changes in the practices. Suppose that in this second study we find that with Film 1, the film that stresses negative outcomes, the attitude change scores are 2, 3, 5, 4, 7, 7, 4, 5, 4, 6 and with Film 2 the change scores are 3, 7, 8, 7, 9, 9, 8, 10, 9, 11. Call the scores for Group 1 (Film 1 subjects) the $Y_{1,j}$'s, namely, $Y_{1,1}$, $Y_{1,2}$, ..., $Y_{1,10}$ and the scores for Group 2 (Film 2) the $Y_{2,j}$'s, $Y_{2,1}$, $Y_{2,2}$, ..., $Y_{2,10}$. The first subscript, i, on Y stands for the group, the film, the experimental condition, while the second subscript, j, stands for which person received treatment i. Thus $Y_{2,3}$ is the score for the third person to see Film 2.

2.5 The data for the second experiment. The data are shown in Table 2.1.

2.6 The two hypotheses that can be tested in a two-group experiment. The design of the second experiment allows testing of two null hypotheses: (1) that the population mean of all the change scores is zero and (2) that the population mean of Group 1 equals the population mean of Group 2.

2.7 The experimental treatment effect and error effects. The difference between the S score and the P score is attributed to two possible reasons. If the film had an effect, then this will produce a difference between S and P. And, whether or not the film had an effect, chance variation attributable to all sorts of possible variations in the person between the first survey and the second could produce a difference. For example, the person was sick the first time but not the second, or hadn't had enough sleep the night before one of the survey days but not the other. As we have said, all these experimentally uncontrolled effects are referred to as **error**. Assume that all such chance errors combine to produce one normally distributed **error effect**. For the first experiment, we can represent these two assumptions about the effects on the Y scores by an algebraic equation or **model equation** as it is called. We say $Y_i = \mu + e_i$, where e_i is normally distributed with a mean of zero and some unknown variance. (More about the details of this later). For now it is enough to think of μ as representing the (possibly zero) effect of the experimental treatment, the film, and e_i as representing the combination of all the uncontrolled, known and unknown error effects that affect Y_i. The null hypothesis is that $\mu = 0$, meaning that the film had no effect.

2.8 A model equation for the second experiment. For the second experiment the effects of the two films are conceived as possibly differing so the model equation can be written as $Y_{ij} = \mu_i + e_{ij}$, where Y_{ij} is the score for the jth person who saw film i, μ_i is the mean of the population of scores for those persons who have seen or might have seen film i and e_{ij} is the normally distributed error effect for the jth person who saw film i. It will be useful to conceptualize the film i mean, μ_i, as consisting of two parts, a part μ common to both films and a part α_i specific to film i. Analyzing the film effect in this way enables testing the hypothesis that the common film effect μ is some specific value, say μ_0, and separately testing the hypothesis that the specific film effects α_1 and α_2 are zero versus the alternative that they are not zero. Testing these two hypotheses separately allows for identifying four possible situations and inferentially determining which we should believe is the actual situation.

2.9 The various hypotheses and their model equation forms. The four situations are represented by the following four sets of equations:

Case 1: $\mu = \mu_0$, $\alpha_1 = \alpha_2 = 0$
e.g., $Y_{i,j} = 0 + e_{i,j}$ (assuming $\mu_0 = 0$ in this case and the remaining three cases)
Case 2: $\mu = \mu_0$, $\alpha_1 \neq \alpha_2$
e.g. $\alpha_1 = 8$, $\alpha_2 = -8$, so $Y_{1,j} = 8 + e_{i,j}$ and $Y_{2,j} = -8 + e_{i,j}$
Case 3: $\mu \neq \mu_0$, $\alpha_1 = \alpha_2 = 0$
e.g., $\mu = 10$, $\alpha_1 = \alpha_2 = 0$, so $Y_{i,j} = 10 + e_{i,j}$
Case 4: $\mu \neq \mu_0$, $\alpha_1 \neq \alpha_2$
e.g., $\mu = 10$, $\alpha_1 = 8$, $\alpha_2 = -8$, so $Y_{1,j} = 10 + 8 + e_{i,j}$ and $Y_{2,j} = 10 - 8 + e_{i,j}$.

Notice that all four equations are instances of $Y_{ij} = \mu + \alpha_i + e_{ij}$ but when $\mu = \mu_0$ and or the α_i's are zero, the various special cases corresponding to various null hypotheses result. Although there are exceptions, which we will note later, generally a null hypothesis corresponds to the assumption that some effect is zero.

2.10 F-tests are used like z-tests and t-tests. To test a null hypothesis we use an F-test. An F-test makes use of the fact that when the null hypothesis is true, an appropriate test statistic, called an F-ratio, has the F distribution (analogous to z having the standard normal distribution or t having the t distribution). Then, if an improbably large value of the F-ratio occurs, we reject the null hypothesis just as we reject a null hypothesis if z is greater in absolute value than 1.96 (.05 significance level, two-tailed test) or if t is greater in absolute value than the tabled critical value for the chosen significance level. The F-test procedure follows exactly the same logic. Only the test statistic and its sampling distribution will differ from that used in doing t-tests. We change from t to F because F will apply to more elaborate experiments and will answer more general questions. But t and similar procedures will be used later to pick those elaborate experiments apart to answer more specific and often more interesting questions.

2.11 Families of distributions. We now describe, in an abstract way, how to arrive at a test statistic that has the F distribution. This occurs in two parts. We show first that the chosen statistic is distributed as F, and then we show that it is a reasonable statistic to use to test the null hypothesis.

When we say that a statistic "has the F distribution" or "is distributed as F", or as we will say in a moment, that a variable "is a chi-square variable" or "has the chi-square distribution" or "is chi-square distributed" it is easy for the student to pass this by as some sort of mystery. It is appropriate at this point for this to be partly a mystery, but we should clear up the big idea so that only the details remain perhaps mysterious. When we use the word "distribution" in reference to a statistic, we are talking about the sampling distribution of that statistic. Because the sampling distribution of a statistic provides the probability that the statistic will take the various possible values that it can take if a certain hypothesis is true, we are able to make probabilistic statements, we are able to know which values of that statistic would hardly ever happen if that hypothesis were true, and we can support these inferences with those probabilistic arguments.

To say that a statistic has the F distribution means that the sampling distribution of that statistic is a member of a family of sampling distributions, all the members of which share something in common. That shared something is the **form of the sampling distribution** or the form of the equation of the sampling distribution. It is like a family resemblance. This idea is already familiar in the case of the normal distribution and the t distribution. There are many normal distributions, they all share the same form, and have the same equation, but they can differ from one another in their mean and in their variance. All these normal distributions have the same equation. But there are two parameters, the mean and the variance, the specific values of which determine which particular member of the family a given normal distribution is. With the t distribution there is only one parameter, the "degrees of freedom." This one parameter determines which member of a family of t distributions is associated with a particular statistic.

"Parameter" is a familiar concept with an unfamiliar name. Think about all the possible geometric squares. They are all members of the "square family." They all have the same shape. But they differ in side length and in area. We can take the length of one side of a square as the square's parameter. Changing this value produces all the different possible squares. Thus a parameter is a variable that can take different values, and the value that it takes determines which particular member of a family of similar shapes is obtained. Parameters determine the particular instance of a distribution in just the same way.

Consider the t statistic used to test the hypothesis that a sample of scores has been drawn from a normal distribution with a mean of μ:

$$t \;=\; (M - \mu)/\sqrt{[(\Sigma Y^2 - NM^2)/(N-1)N]}$$

with $N - 1$ degrees of freedom. Now consider the t statistic used to test the hypothesis that two samples of scores, the $Y_{1,i}$ and the $Y_{2,i}$, have been drawn from two normal distributions having the same variance but having a difference between their means equal to $\mu_1 - \mu_2$:

$$t = [(M_1 - M_2) - (\mu_1 - \mu_2)] / \sqrt{[(\Sigma Y_1^2 - N_1 M_1^2 + \Sigma Y_2^2 - NM_2^2)(1/N_1}$$

$$+ 1/N_2)/(N_1 + N_2 - 2)]$$

with $N_1 + N_2 - 2$ degrees of freedom. These two formulas certainly look quite different. And one is based on a single sample from a single population while the other is based on two samples from two populations. Still, mathematical statisticians have shown that the sampling distributions of the two statistics have exactly the same form or equation, except for a difference in the value of a single parameter in the equation, called the degrees of freedom. And, in fact, if the value of $N - 1$ for the first t-statistic happens to equal the value of $N_1 + N_2 - 2$ for the second t statistic, then the two t-statistics will have the identical t distribution. Also, of course, there are many other t-statistics that share in this family resemblance of sampling distributions.

Knowing that many statistics have the same distribution, differing only in a parameter value, produces a great savings in effort. This is already clear insofar as the same table of critical values of t can be used to test a variety of different hypotheses generated in a variety of different situations. An even more useful collection of statistics exists, all of which have F distributions that differ from one another only in the value of two parameters. By means of this family of F sampling distributions, an enormously varied selection of hypotheses can be tested, and confidence intervals can be determined for the parameters of a vast array of models.

2.12 The F family. An F-ratio is a fraction in which the numerator and the denominator are each also fractions. The numerator fraction is a chi-square variable (more later) divided by its degrees of freedom. The denominator is another chi-square variable divided by its degrees of freedom. And the numerator and denominator of the F are independent of each other. We will show what we have to do with the sample of Y scores in order to convert them into an F-ratio. We will use the data to generate a piece that goes in the numerator of the F-ratio and a piece that goes in the denominator. We'll do this by working on the squares of the Y scores and on other squares. These squared values will provide us with variables that have the chi-square distribution, and then we'll divide these variables by values called their degrees of freedom to get the numerator and denominator for the F-ratio. **The way we will show that the statistic we have chosen is the right statistic to test the null hypothesis will be to show that if the null hypothesis is true, then the expected value of the F-ratio numerator is the same as the expected value of the F-ratio denominator, so we would expect values of the F-ratio to be around one, more or less. We will show that if the null hypothesis is not true, then the expected value of the F-ratio numerator is larger than the expected value of the F-ratio denominator so we would expect values larger than one when the null hypothesis is false. Large F-ratios will support the falsity of the null hypothesis, and small F-ratios will support its truth along with the truth of hypotheses close to the null hypothesis. This will tell us to put the critical region or rejection region of F values in the upper or right-hand tail of the F distribution so that improbably large F-ratios will be used to reject the null hypothesis.** (The typical shape of an F distribution is somewhat like a normal distribution in that it is unimodal, continuous, and smooth, but it has no height over values less than zero and it tends to have a long tail stretching out to the right. Thus it is a positively skewed, unimodal asymmetric probability function.)

2.13 Using F where we used to use t. The ANOVA approach to testing hypotheses will be exemplified by approaching two familiar problems in a new way. Recall from introductory statistics the use of a t-test to test a null hypothesis, H_0, that a sample of scores had come from a normal distribution with a mean equal to zero and a standard deviation equal to σ, against an alternative hypothesis, H_1, that the mean was not zero but some other value $\mu \neq 0$. Recall also another t-test for testing the null hypothesis that two samples drawn independently of each other were sampled from the same normal distribution against the alternative that the two samples were drawn from two normal distributions having the same variance but different means. Here the null hypothesis would be that $\mu_1 = \mu_2$ and the alternative would be that $\mu_1 \neq \mu_2$. We will perform an analysis of variance using an F-ratio to test each of these hypotheses. First, however, we will make some general remarks about ANOVA, which the student should return to after we have gone through the two examples.

2.14 Systematic effects and error effects. An ANOVA tests one or more hypotheses about the systematic effects that may be influencing scores.

The basic notions are that in general the scores we obtain in the data collection procedure (experiment, survey, observational method, etc., but for simplicity we will refer only to experiments) are subject to **systematic and error effects.**

The error effects are referred to as **error** or the **effects of error** or the **effects due to error**. Error effects are attributed to nonsystematic, unknown causes assumed to average out to no effect or zero effect in the long run. If an effect due to some source did not average out to zero, it would be a systematic rather than an error effect.

2.14.1 Truth and error. The term "error" comes to us from the dawn of statistics. It was found by various scientists that when a measurement was repeated several times, the same value was not obtained. Thus, astronomers measuring the positions of stars found that if more than one person obtained a measurement, their values differed. What grew up was a conception of a true value of the measured object that was coupled with an error of measurement that produced the differing values when the measurement was taken more than once. It was no doubt a salute to the Platonic notions of the apparent and the real, the true value being the Platonic form and the measured value being its approximation here in the world. In any case, the idea stuck, and statistics devoted much of its development to determining suitable methods for answering questions about the true value when only the measurements, subject to error, are in hand. The whole study of inferential statistics, then, is often viewed as an inquiry into answering questions about true values by applying methods of estimation and hypothesis testing to values combining truth and error.

2.15 Systematic effects. Systematic effects are of two sorts: (1) those due to sources identified in the experimental design and (2) those due to other sources. Those due to other sources may be (a) independent of experimental variables, affecting all of the scores equally, or (b) they may be **confounded** with experimental variables. In case (a) we are generally not concerned since an effect that adds a constant to all scores rarely misleads us concerning an experimental variable. It could happen if we were using difference or gain scores, however, and it will certainly mislead us when the focus is on parameter estimation rather than on hypothesis testing. But usually, in hypothesis testing, we take it as simply setting the general level or mean of the scores. In case (b) confounded effects can distort the results of hypothesis testing as well as those of parameter estimation. This might lead to false inference concerning the presence or absence of systematic effects due to experimental variables or lead us to misestimate the magnitude of the effects due to experimental variables. The experimental design and ANOVA will not reveal anything about the presence, absence, or magnitude of systematic effects due to sources other than those we have included in the experimental design. Perspicacity and good fortune in the selection of variables can protect us against such concealed effects. A course in the design of experiments is helpful. This would teach us, among other things, about holding irrelevant variables constant or assigning their different values at random to the different experimental conditions. For example, if we were not going to keep the number of men and women the same in each of the two film groups, we would want to assign men and women to the two groups randomly. That way any gender effects would affect the results in a chance fashion and the significance level would protect us against such a chance result. The significance level protects us in that it determines the probability that we will obtain a significant result if only chance is at work. (Speaking of the dawn of statistics, when I was an undergraduate, in the first independent class experiment I ever performed, I learned about randomization the hard way. I ran all the subjects in my experimental group and then all the subjects in my control group. When I gave my class report on the work, a fellow student, no less, immediately pointed out that I had confounded the time in the semester at which the subject was run with my experimental conditions, and that I should have created a random sequence in which the experimental and control subjects would be run. Such all-too-public education can be painful. I never forget the lesson of randomization.)

2.16 We use F as we used to use t. In the ANOVA we test hypotheses about the systematic effects that may be influencing scores, and we estimate population parameters using either the method of least squares to arrive at point estimates or the F distribution to arrive at confidence intervals. We test hypotheses by locating a test statistic, the F-ratio, that has a known sampling distribution, the F distribution (named so by George Snedecor in honor of Sir Ronald A. Fisher, the creator of ANOVA), when the systematic effects we are concerned with are not present. We then use the occurrence of a significant F-ratio as inferential evidence against the absence of those effects and therefore as indicating their presence. (A significant F-ratio is a value of the F-ratio that falls within the rejection region of the F distribution for some selected significance level.)

This is completely analogous to what we did with the t distribution. In hypothesis testing we hypothesized some value, say zero, as the mean of a normal distribution of scores. We knew that if we were sampling from a normal distribution with a mean of zero, then the sampling distribution of the ratio of the sample mean to an estimate of the standard error of the mean would have the t distribution with N - 1 degrees of freedom. If we found that the t statistic was one of those rare t values that would hardly ever happen if the mean were zero, we inferred that there was a nonzero value of the population mean. In interval estimation we use the F distribution in essentially the same fashion that we used the t distribution.

2.17 The simplest ANOVA. We now take the simplest possible case of an ANOVA as an example of how we will be proceeding. The tested hypothesis is that we have independently randomly sampled N scores, Y_1, Y_2, ..., Y_N, from a normal distribution of Y scores which has zero as its mean and σ^2 as its variance. An arbitrary score Y_i can be represented then by the equation

$$Y_i = e_i \quad \text{where } e_i \text{ is } N(0, \sigma^2) \tag{2.1}$$

("N(0, σ^2)" means "normally distributed with a mean of zero and a variance of σ^2") and is a statement of the tested null hypothesis. According to this null hypothesis there are no systematic effects and Y_i is composed only of a normally distributed error. The true mean of the variable Y is zero because the mean of the errors is always assumed to be zero. Compare [2.1] to the alternative hypothesis, which says that

$$Y_i = \mu + e_i \quad \text{where } e_i \text{ is } N(0, \sigma^2) \text{ and } \mu \neq 0, \tag{2.2}$$

so that each Y_i is composed of a systematic effect μ and an error effect e_i. Equations [2.1] and [2.2] are known as **model equations**. This is because they provide us with a model or representation of the structure of the obtained scores. One model equation says that the scores are just chance errors, but the other says that the scores are made of two pieces, one a nonzero constant effect which is the same for each score, and another that is a random effect that varies from score to score. (Until we get to what are known as *random effects* models and *mixed models*, we will be assuming that all systematic effects have fixed, constant values. These are known as *fixed effects* and the models that use only fixed effects for systematic effects are known as *fixed-effects models*.) The two hypotheses can be displayed graphically. Figure 2.1 shows (a) a normal distribution of Y scores with a mean of zero and (b) a normal distribution with a mean of μ somewhere on the number line away from zero. Note that the tested hypothesis $Y_i = e_i$ is just a special case of the more general hypothesis $Y_i = \mu + e_i$ where μ happens to be zero and so is not written in.)

2.18 The analysis of $\Sigma_i Y_i^2$. To test hypothesis [2.1] we consider the quantity $\Sigma_i Y_i^2$, which is the sum of the squares of the scores in the sample. We can analyze this sum into two parts since we can use the identity $Y_i = Y_i - M + M$ to write

$$\Sigma_i Y_i^2 = \Sigma_i (Y_i - M + M)^2 \qquad \text{(where } M = \Sigma_i Y_i / N).$$

Using the fact that $(A + B)^2 = A^2 + 2AB + B^2$, this can be rewritten, if we take A to be $(Y_i - M)$ and B to be M, as

$$\Sigma_i Y_i^2 = \Sigma_i [(Y_i - M)^2 + 2(Y_i - M)M + M^2]$$
$$= \Sigma_i (Y_i - M)^2 + 2M\Sigma_i (Y_i - M) + \Sigma_i M^2 = \Sigma_i (Y_i - M)^2 + NM^2 \qquad [2.3]$$

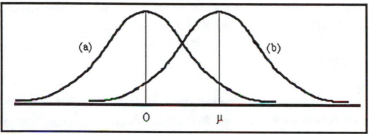

Figure 2.1. (a) A normal distribution with a mean of 0 and (b) a normal distribution with a mean μ not equal to zero.

since $\Sigma_i (Y_i - M) = \Sigma_i Y_i - NM = 0$ because $\Sigma_i Y_i = NM$.

2.19 Abbreviating the pieces of $\Sigma_i Y_i^2$ by Q's. If we divide [2.3] by σ^2 on both sides of the equal sign we have

$$\Sigma Y_i^2 / \sigma^2 = \Sigma_i (Y - M)^2 / \sigma^2 + NM^2 / \sigma^2 \qquad [2.4]$$

which we will abbreviate by $Q/\sigma^2 = Q_1/\sigma^2 + Q_2/\sigma^2$.

2.20 The proper attitude toward big ideas and little details. Before proceeding we will state a few little details about the chi-square probability distribution. These details are presented without proof but proofs are easy to locate in mathematical statistics textbooks. These details should be skipped the first time or two through this chapter. (It is important for the student to realize that big ideas and little details are antagonistic to one another in that they are both in a struggle for the student's attention. Always the student should side first with the big ideas and only later abandon them in order to fill in the complete picture by getting the little details as well. Skipping little details at first is a perfectly respectable procedure and will greatly facilitate your learning. Compulsively trying to assimilate the details before the big ideas are in place will tend to wear you out.)

The big idea behind considering the chi-square distribution is that the statistics we use to test hypotheses are going to have the F distribution when the null hypothesis is true. We want to be able to know if a variable has the F distribution. We will find later that if two variables each have the chi-square distribution and if they are independent of each other, then we can use them to create a statistic that has the F distribution—hence the interest in the chi-square distribution and in knowing whether a variable has that distribution.

2.20.1 The chi-square distribution. A continuous random variable X (see Appendix A1 for a discussion of random variables) with probability density function

$$f(x) = \ x^{r/2-1} \ e^{-x/2} \, / \, \Gamma(r/2) \ (2^{r/2})$$

for $x > 0$ and $f(x) = 0$ elsewhere has the **chi-square distribution** with r degrees of freedom. (It is not necessary for you to know this density function. It is here in case you want to.) We will abbreviate this by saying **X is $\chi^2(r)$.** We are familiar with what a **probability density function** is, but we may not have known it by that name. Recall that the probability that a score, randomly sampled from a normal distribution, is in some numerical interval is given by the piece of area that lies over that numerical interval and under the normal probability curve. You may not have known that for a given normal probability curve, the height of the curve above any value x along the number line was given by the value $f(x) = Ae^{-B}$, where $A = [1/\sqrt{(2\pi\sigma^2)}]$ and $B = (x - \mu)^2/2\sigma^2$. This function that gives the height of a continuous probability curve for any value x is called a probability density function. So just as the areas under the normal curve give probabilities for a normally distributed variable, areas under the curve with the height

$$f(x) = \ x^{r/2-1} \ e^{-x/2} \, / \, \Gamma(r/2)(2^{r/2})$$

above x give the probabilities for a chi-square distributed variable. Some examples of the chi-square probability density function are shown in Figure 2.2.

*2.20.1.1 The gamma function. Notice the quantity $\Gamma(r/2)$ in the chi-square density function. For any value a, the value of $\Gamma(a)$ is given by the **gamma function** with parameter a and is

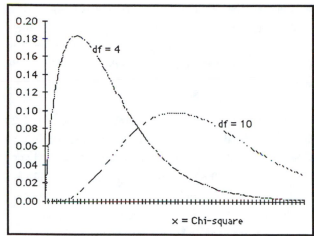

Figure 2.2. The chi-square probability density functions for 4 and 10 degrees of freedom.

$\Gamma(a) = \int y^{a-1} e^{-y} \, dy$ for $a > 0$.

If a is an integer, $\Gamma(a) = (a - 1)!$. (Recall that $N! = 1 \times 2 \times 3 \times ... \times N$, so for example, $3! = 6$.) In any case, if $a > 0$ then $\Gamma(a+1) = a\Gamma(a)$ and of course $\Gamma(a) = \Gamma(a+1)/a$. With these two relations it is only necessary to have a table of $\Gamma(a)$ ranging from 1.00 to 1.99 in order to be able to obtain $\Gamma(a)$ for any positive a. Thus if you wanted $\Gamma(3.5)$, you could find it as $(2.5)\Gamma(2.5) = (2.5)(1.5)\Gamma(1.5)$, and use the table to obtain $\Gamma(1.5)$. The gamma function is extensively tabled in various handbooks and books of statistical tables.

2.20.2 z^2 is $\chi^2(1)$. If X is $N(\mu, \sigma^2)$, that is, if X is normally distributed with mean μ and variance σ^2, then

$(X - \mu)^2/\sigma^2$ is $\chi^2(1)$.

In words this says that the variable created by taking a standard normally distributed variable, that is, a normally distributed z-score, $z = (X - \mu)/\sigma$ and squaring that variable to get $z^2 = (X - \mu)^2/\sigma^2$, has a probability distribution that is a member of the chi-square family, in particular that member having one degree of freedom.

2.20.3 The additivity of independent chi-square variables. If X is $\chi^2(a)$ and Y is $\chi^2(b)$ and if X and Y are independent, then $(X + Y)$ is $\chi^2(a+b)$. This says that we can add independent chi-square variables and the sum will itself be a chi-square variable, with its degrees of freedom equal to the sum of the degrees of freedom of the two added variables.

This additivity property is by far the exception rather than the rule. Independent chi-square variables add to give chi-square variables, and independent normally distributed variables add to give normally distributed variables, but such additivity does not hold for t variables, F variables, binomially distributed variables, and so forth. Assume that such additivity does not hold unless it is otherwise indicated.

2.20.4 A third way to tell that a variable is a chi-square variable. In 2.20.2 and 2.20.3 two different ways of knowing that a variable has the chi-square distribution were given. In 2.20.2 a variable is $\chi^2(1)$ if that variable is the square of a standard normal variable, a squared normal z-score. In 2.20.3, if two variables have the chi-square distribution and they are independent, then their sum is also chi-square distributed with the degrees of freedom equaling the sum of the degrees of freedom of the two separate variables. Here is a third way to know that a variable has the chi-square distribution.

This third way states three conditions that, if satisfied, will establish that a variable is distributed as chi-square. The first condition supposes that you partition the sum of squares of N mutually independent random variables, which are normally distributed with possibly different means but the same variance σ^2, into K pieces. The second condition specifies that we divide the whole sum of squares, call it Q, and K-1 of the K pieces by that same variance σ^2. The third condition specifies that if Q and those K-1 pieces, $Q_1, Q_2, ..., Q_{K-1}$, when divided by that variance σ^2 each has a chi-square distribution, then the last piece, Q_K, if it is greater than or equal to zero, also when divided by that variance has a chi-square distribution and all of the pieces of Q are mutually independent. Furthermore, if the degrees of freedom associated with the chi-squares made with Q, $Q_1, Q_2, ..., Q_{K-1}$ are, respectively, $r, r_1, r_2, ..., r_{K-1}$, then the degrees of freedom for the piece involving Q_K is $r - (r_1 + r_2 + ... + r_{K-1})$. Symbolically, we say let $Q = \Sigma_i Q_i$ be the sum of squares of N mutually independent random variables which are normally distributed with means $\mu_1, \mu_2, ... \mu_N$ and the same variance σ^2. Let $Q/\sigma^2, Q_1/\sigma^2, ..., Q_{K-1}/\sigma^2$ have chi-square distributions with degrees of freedom $r, r_1, ..., r_{K-1}$, respectively. Let $Q_K \geq 0$. Then: $Q_1, ..., Q_K$ are mutually independent and Q_K/σ^2 is $\chi^2[r - (r_1 + ... + r_{K-1}) = r_K]$. The proof of this theorem can be found in advanced mathematical statistics texts.

2.21 Showing that $\Sigma_i(Y_i - M)^2/\sigma^2$ and NM^2/σ^2 are chi-square variables. Using the details in section 2.20.1 to 2.20.4 we can show that Q_1/σ^2 and Q_2/σ^2 in section 2.19 are independent chi-square variables. This takes three steps. First, because the Y_i are independent and each of them is $N(0, \sigma^2)$, it follows from 2.20.2 that $(Y_i - 0)^2/\sigma^2 = Y_i^2/\sigma^2$ is $\chi^2(1)$ and therefore, from 2.20.3, that $Q/\sigma^2 = \Sigma_i Y_i^2/\sigma^2$ is $\chi^2(N)$. In words, since each of the Y_i is normally distributed with a mean of zero, if we subtract that zero mean from each and divide each by its standard deviation and then square that fraction, each will now be the square of a z-score and therefore a variable that has a chi-square distribution with one degree of freedom. If we add all of these N chi-square variables up, we have another chi-square variable, which has N degrees of freedom. We are entitled to add them because they are independent because the Y_i's are independent. The second step is that since all of the Y_i are $N(0, \sigma^2)$, M is $N(0, \sigma^2/N)$. Therefore, by 2.20.2, $(M-0)^2/(\sigma^2/N) = NM^2/\sigma^2$ is $\chi^2(1)$. In words, since all of the Y_i are normally distributed with a mean of zero and variance σ^2, the sample mean of the Y_i must be normally distributed with a mean of zero but with a variance equal to σ^2 divided by the sample size, N. Therefore, subtracting $\mu = 0$ from the sample mean of the Y_i, squaring this difference and dividing by the variance of the Y_i sample mean gives us a squared normal z-score and therefore a variable that is distributed as chi-square with one degree of freedom. Finally, since $Q/\sigma^2 = \Sigma_i Y_i^2/\sigma^2$ is $\chi^2(N)$ and $Q_2/\sigma^2 = NM^2/\sigma^2$ is $\chi^2(1)$, it follows from section 2.20.4 that Q_1 and Q_2 are independent and that $Q_1 = \Sigma_i(Y_i - M)^2/\sigma^2 = \Sigma_i Y_i^2/\sigma^2 - NM^2/\sigma^2$ is $\chi^2(N-1)$. This is just a simple case of section 2.20.4 where $K = 2$. The overall sum of squares, $Q = \Sigma_i Y_i^2$, has been partitioned into two pieces, $Q_1 = \Sigma_i(Y_i - M)^2$ and $Q_2 = NM^2$. The quantity Q and one of the pieces, Q_2, when divided by the variance, are each distributed as chi-square, and therefore by the rule in section 2.20.4, the other piece, Q_1, when divided by the variance, is independent of Q_2, is also distributed as chi-square, and its degrees of freedom are the difference between N, the degrees of freedom for Q, and 1, the degrees of freedom for Q_2.

2.22 An F-ratio. Having shown that $Q_1/\sigma^2 = \Sigma(Y_i - M)^2/\sigma^2$ and $Q_2/\sigma^2 = NM^2/\sigma^2$ are independent chi-square variables, we can use the ratio

$$F = (Q_2/\sigma^2)/1/(Q_1/\sigma^2)/(N-1) = NM^2/\sigma^2/[\Sigma(Y_i - M)^2/\sigma^2]/(N-1)$$

$$= NM^2/\Sigma(Y_i - M)^2/(N-1) \qquad [2.5]$$

as the test statistic. This is because the ratio of two independent chi-square variables, each divided by its degrees of freedom, has the F distribution.

2.22.1 The F distribution. Let U and W be independent chi-square variables with r and s degrees of freedom, respectively. Then the F-ratio

$$F = (U/r)/(W/s)$$

has the F distribution with r and s degrees of freedom such that

$$\Pr(F \leq f') = \int_0^{f'} \Gamma[(r + s)/2]\,(r/s)^{r/2}\,f^{(r/2 - 1)} / [\Gamma(r/2)\Gamma(s/2)(1 + rf/s)^{(r + s)/2}]\,df.$$

Let's face it. This expression looks as if it might chew us up and spit us out if we look at it the wrong way. Still, as soon as we choose values for r and s, it settles down quite a bit, especially when r and s are both divisible by 2. Let $r = 2$ and $s = 10$. Then we have as the quantity inside the integral sign

$$\Gamma[12/2](2/10)^{2/2} f^{(2/2-1)} / [\Gamma(2/2)\Gamma(10/2) (1+2f/10)^{(12)/2}]$$

$$= (6-1)!(1/5)f^0 / (1-1)!(5-1)!(1 + f/5)^6$$

$$= 5!/5 / 0!4! (1 + f/5)^6 = 1/(1 + f/5)^6 = (1 + f/5)^{-6} = [5/(5+f)]^6.$$

Now $[5/(5+f)]^6$ is not only something we can take home to milk and cookies (not to mention graph if we want to see what a member of the F distribution family looks like), but the integral in question turns out to be

$$Pr(F \le f') = 1 - [5/(5+f')]^5,$$

which we can live with quite readily. It says that the probability of getting a value of F that is less than or equal to some selected number f' is equal to $1 - [5/(5+f')]^5$. With this function we can determine which values of F are likely and which values are unlikely. In fact, if we set f' equal to 4.1 we find that $Pr(F \le 4.1) = .9499$. You can use this to confirm the tabled critical value of 4.1 at the .05 significance level in the F table for 2 and 10 degrees of freedom.

2.23 Critical regions for F-ratios. We still need to consider which values of F should be used to reject the hypothesis that $\mu = 0$ and why it makes sense to use those values. We will argue that if the tested hypothesis is true, the F-ratio should be in the neighborhood of one, but the more that μ deviates from zero, the larger do we expect the F-ratio to be.

2.23.1 The expected value of a chi-square variable is its degrees of freedom. If U is $\chi^2(r)$, then $E(U) = r$. In words, if U is a variable that has the chi-square distribution with r degrees of freedom, then the expected value of U is just its degrees of freedom, r. (See Appendix A1 for discussion of the expected value of a random variable.) We should note that because the expected value of a chi-square variable is its degrees of freedom, if we divide a chi-square variable by its degrees of freedom, we create a new variable that has an expected value of one. That is, if U is $\chi^2(r)$, and therefore $E(U) = r$, then $E(U/r) = (1/r)E(U) = (1/r)r = 1$. (Appendix A1 provides a summary of the properties of the expected value operator.) This is of interest to us because under the null hypothesis, the numerator and the denominator of an F ratio are each chi-square variables divided by their degrees of freedom.

2.23.2 The expected values of the numerator and denominator in [2.5]. Therefore

$$E(NM^2/\sigma^2) = 1 \quad \text{and} \quad E(\Sigma_i(Y_i - M)^2/\sigma^2) = N - 1.$$

Thus the numerator and the denominator of the F-ratio in [2.5] each has 1 as its expected value.

2.23.3 What we expect of the ratio in [2.5]. Therefore we expect, if the tested hypothesis is true, that the F-ratio in [2.5] will take values near one since the numerator should tend to be near one and so should the denominator.

2.23.3.1 If X and Y are independent, $E(X/Y) \neq E(X)/E(Y)$. We should note, however, that if X and Y are independent, $E(X/Y) = E(X)E(1/Y)$, but $E(X/Y) \neq E(X)/E(Y)$. For example, consider the following display of joint probabilities where X and Y are independent, and X and Y each take the values 1 or 2 with equal probability.

		Y	
		1	2
X	1	.25	.25
	2	.25	.25

Clearly, $E(X)/E(Y) = 1$ but $E(X/Y) = .25(1 + .5 + 2 + 1) = 1.125$. Thus we cannot conclude that the expected value of the F-ratio is one just because its numerator and denominator each have an expected value of one. As it happens, when s, the degrees of freedom of the denominator chi-square variable in the F-ratio, is greater than 2, the expected value of the F-ratio is $s/(s-2)$. Therefore, the F-ratio in [2.5] has $(N-1)/(N-3)$ as its expected value for N greater than 3, and this value approaches one as N gets larger.

2.23.4 But if the null hypothesis is false ... If the tested hypothesis is false and $Y_i = \mu + e_i$, where $\mu \neq 0$, then $E(NM^2/\sigma^2) = 1 + N\mu^2/\sigma^2$. Note also that the more μ departs from zero, the more does the expected value of NM^2/σ^2 depart from 1.

2.23.4.1 The proof. The equality $E(NM^2/\sigma^2) = 1 + N\mu^2/\sigma^2$ follows because $E(NM^2/\sigma^2) = (N/\sigma^2)E(M^2)$. Since the variance of a random variable is also defined as the expected value of the square of that variable minus the square of the expected value of that variable, the variance of M is $E(M^2) - E^2(M)$, so we have

$$VAR(M) = \sigma^2/N = E(M^2) - E^2(M) = E(M^2) - \mu^2,$$

giving

$$E(M^2) = \sigma^2/N + \mu^2$$

so we can say

$$E(NM^2/\sigma^2) = (N/\sigma^2)E(M^2) = (N/\sigma^2)[\sigma^2/N + \mu^2] = 1 + N\mu^2/\sigma^2,$$

which is what is given in section 2.23.4

2.23.5 Critical values for F-ratios are located in the upper tail of the F distribution. The F-ratio values that are greater than one favor the alternative hypothesis that $\mu \neq 0$. This indicates where to locate the critical region in the F distribution; namely in the upper tail. Values of F greater than the critical value of F will inferentially imply that some systematic nonzero effect μ is affecting all of the scores in the sampled population.

2.24 The F-ratio as a comparison of a numerator to a denominator. Consider again the statistics $\Sigma_i(Y_i - M)^2/(N-1)$ and NM^2. The statistic $\Sigma_i(Y_i - M)^2/(N-1)$ is s^2, an unbiased estimator of the population variance. So, its expected value is σ^2. And, as shown in 2.23.4.1, $E(NM^2) = N[E(M^2)] = N(\sigma^2/N + \mu^2) = \sigma^2 + N\mu^2$. When $\mu = 0$, each of these two quantities has σ^2 as its expected value. Therefore we expect the numerator and the denominator to be equal but for the effects of error. But when μ is not zero, then the numerator of the F-ratio, NM^2, has a larger expected value, larger by the amount $N\mu^2$. When we use the ratio NM^2 divided by $\Sigma_i(Y_i - M)^2/(N-1)$ as the test statistic, we are assuming that large values of this ratio tend to occur more frequently when $\mu \neq 0$ because the numerator has a larger expected value than does the denominator. We therefore use large values to reject the tested hypothesis. We can regard this as comparing the numerator to the denominator to see whether the numerator is large relative to the denominator. Later we will consider this comparison from a geometric perspective, which will cast more light on the approach.

2.25 Review of the abstract steps. The abstract steps we have gone through were:

1. **Expression of a hypothesis to be tested and an alternative to which we contrasted it.**
2. **Partitioning of the sum of the squares of all the scores.**
3. **Determining a test statistic and its distribution.**
4. **Locating the appropriate rejection region in the sampling distribution of the test statistic.**

2.25.1 We contrasted hypotheses by contrasting model equations. We expressed the tested hypothesis in the form of a model equation and we contrasted it with an alternative also expressed as a model equation. These were $Y_i = e_i$ versus $Y_i = \mu + e_i$, where in both cases e_i is normally distributed with a mean of zero.

2.25.2 An important correspondence exists between model equation terms, sums of squares, and computational formulas. We considered the sum of the squares of the scores, and partitioned it into two pieces—a piece for the mean, NM^2, and a piece for error. We haven't said yet how we knew how to partition the sum of squares and why it turned out that there was a piece for the mean and a piece for error. The partitioning is based on the largest model equation. We note that in this case the model equation has a term for the mean, μ, and a term for error, e_i, and the partitioning of the total sum of squares yielded a piece for the mean and a piece for error. This correspondence is not accidental. It will always be the case that the partitioning of the total sum of squares will yield a sum of squares that corresponds to each term in the model equation that represents the largest model under consideration. Later, when we deal with the subject of computational formulas in a very general way, we will find that the model equation has a structure corresponding to all of the computations that we need to perform. The equation expresses itself as sources and as degrees of freedom. The sources tell us which sums of squares need to be computed, and the degrees of freedom tell us exactly how to compute them.

2.25.3 The distribution of the F-ratio and its parts. We determined, using the details in the subsections of section 2.9, that if the scores are independently sampled from a normal distribution, then:

1. **Each piece of sum of squares, when divided by the variance, is distributed as chi-square.**
2. **The pieces are independent.**
3. **We call the ratio of the two pieces, each divided by the variance and by its degrees of freedom, the F-ratio.**
4. **If the tested hypothesis is true, the F-ratio has the F distribution.**

2.25.4 Choice of the rejection region. We also determined that if the alternative hypothesis is true, we expect F-ratios larger than we do if the tested hypothesis is true, so **we choose as the rejection region for the tested hypothesis the upper tail of the F distribution, where the larger values of F occur.**

2.26 Exemplifying the F-test with two groups of scores. To solidify understanding of these steps, let us now repeat them but with a slightly more complex situation. Assume that we have sampled not one but two collections of scores: N_1 of the $Y_{1,j}$'s and N_2 of the $Y_{2,j}$'s. That is, the two samples are $Y_{1,1}$, $Y_{1,2}$, ..., $Y_{1,N1}$ and $Y_{2,1}$, $Y_{2,2}$, ..., $Y_{2,N2}$. It is usual to refer to these as two **groups** of scores. We can think of these two groups of scores as the two groups of difference scores (S - P scores) obtained from the two groups of people who were shown the two different films on toxic waste disposal problems mentioned at the beginning of this chapter.

2.27 The null hypothesis. As the tested or null hypothesis we state that the only reason the scores deviate from zero is due to normally distributed chance errors that have a mean of zero. The null hypothesis is so called because usually it asserts that one or more effects are null or nonexistent (mathematically, they equal zero). The alternative hypothesis asserts the existence of those effects denied by the null hypothesis. It is also standard to refer to the null hypothesis as "H_0" and the alternative as "H_A.") So, the model equation for H_0, the null hypothesis, is

$Y_{ij} = e_{ij}$ where e_{ij} is $N(0, \sigma^2)$.

2.28 The alternative hypothesis. The alternative hypothesis, H_A, to be considered here asserts that H_0 may be false in one or both of two ways. It says that there is a systematic general effect μ that is a part of all the Y scores, both the $Y_{1,j}$'s and the $Y_{2,j}$'s. It also says there is a systematic effect specific to the particular group (film) indicated by α_i, i = 1, 2. The alternative hypothesis is written in model equation form as

$Y_{ij} = \mu + \alpha_i + e_{ij}$ where e_{ij} is $N(0, \sigma^2)$ and $\Sigma_i N_i \alpha_i = 0$.

Thus the $Y_{1,j}$'s are $N(\mu + \alpha_1, \sigma^2)$ and the Y_{2j}'s are $N(\mu + \alpha_2, \sigma^2)$. If $\mu \neq 0$ or $N_1\alpha_1 = -N_2\alpha_2 \neq 0$ or if both $\mu \neq 0$ and $N_1\alpha_1 = -N_2\alpha_2 \neq 0$, then H_0 would be false. (Note that $N_1\alpha_1 = -N_2\alpha_2$ is always true since $N_1\alpha_1 + N_2\alpha_2 = 0$ is always true. It is just that they each equal zero if the α_i are both zero.) Graphically, we can display these alternatives as shown in Figure 2.3.

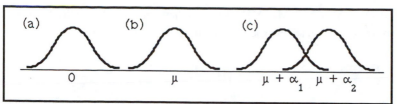

Figure 2.3. (a) The null hypothesis: both distributions centered at zero; (b) both distributions centered at m ≠ 0; (c) the means of the two distributions at two different values, m + a$_1$ and m + a$_2$ where m may or may not equal zero.

2.28.1 Estimating the α_i separately from μ. The requirement that $\Sigma_i N_i \alpha_i = 0$ is necessary if we want to be able to estimate the α_i separately from the overall mean effect, μ. The information about μ, α_1, and α_2 comes from the two group means, μ_1 and μ_2. If we estimate $\mu + \alpha_i$ by M_i, $i = 1, 2$, we have the two equations

$$\mu + \alpha_1 = M_1$$

$$\mu + \alpha_2 = M_2$$

in the three unknowns, μ, α_1, and α_2. A third equation is required for a unique solution. By taking $\Sigma_i N_i \alpha_i = 0$ we introduce a third equation in the three unknowns. Then we obtain

$$N_1(\mu + \alpha_1) = N_1 M_1$$

$$N_2(\mu + \alpha_2) = N_2 M_2.$$

Adding these equations we have $(N_1 + N_2)\mu = N_1 M_1 + N_2 M_2$, so
$$\mu_{est} = (N_1 M_1 + N_2 M_2)/(N_1 + N_2)$$

which is just a weighted average of the two group means, and

$$\alpha_{i,est} = M_i - \mu_{est}$$

as the estimators of the unknown parameters. We will see in Chapter 3 that $\Sigma_i N_i \alpha_i = 0$ requires the α_i to be independent of μ.

2.29. Partitioning the sum of squares. Now, according to the steps we mentioned in 2.25, we next must partition the sum of the squares of all of the scores. We can write

$\Sigma_i\Sigma_j Y_{ij}{}^2 = \Sigma_i\Sigma_j(Y_{ij} - M_i + M_i - M + M)^2$ since we have preserved equality by merely adding and subtracting M_i and adding and subtracting M to Y_{ij}. This gives

$$\Sigma_i\Sigma_j Y_{ij}{}^2 = NM^2 + \Sigma N_i(M_i - M)^2 + \Sigma_i\Sigma_j(Y_{ij} - M_i)^2$$

where $N = N_1 + N_2$, $M_i = \Sigma_j Y_{ij}/N_i$, and $M = \Sigma_i\Sigma_j Y_{ij}/N$. (See section 2.29.1 for the proof.) We do this partitioning in keeping with the goal of finding chi-square distributed statistics that will enable us to establish F-ratios that will serve as the test statistics.

2.29.1 Two useful facts and a proof. Two useful facts that will help the student to follow these manipulations with summation signs are:

1. The sum of the deviations of the scores in a group from their own group mean is zero. That is, $\Sigma_j(Y_{ij} - M_i) = 0$. The student should prove this and remember it. Similarly, the weighted sum of the deviations of the group means from the general mean is also zero. That is, $\Sigma_i N_i(M_i - M) = 0$. Again the student should prove this. (Teachers say students should prove things because they know that when the student proves something, it becomes a part of the student in a way that is very different from just being told it by the teacher or author.) One way to prove a statement such as $\Sigma_i A(B - C) = 0$ is to go through the steps

$\Sigma_i(AB - AC) = 0,$

$\Sigma_i AB - \Sigma_i AC = 0,$

$\Sigma_i AB = \Sigma_i AC,$
and see if that is true.

2. The sum of the scores in a group is always equal to the number of scores in the group times the group mean. This just follows immediately from the definition of the mean as the sum of the scores divided by the number of scores. Similarly, the weighted sum of the group means equals the sum of all the scores and also equals the grand mean of all the scores, multiplied by the grand number of all the scores. That is, $\Sigma_j Y_{ij} = N_i M_i$ and $\Sigma_i N_i M_i = \Sigma_i\Sigma_j Y_{ij} = NM$.

With these facts in hand we can prove the partitioning in section 2.29. We write

$$\Sigma_i\Sigma_j Y_{ij}{}^2 = \Sigma_i\Sigma_j(Y_{ij} - M_i + M_i - M + M)^2$$

and think of it as

$\Sigma_i\Sigma_j[(Y_{ij} - M_i) + (M_i - M) + M]^2$.

Thus the quantity being squared is of the form $[A + B + C]^2$ which we recall can be written as $A^2 + B^2 + C^2 + 2AB + 2AC + 2BC$, so we can continue

$= \Sigma_i\Sigma_j[(Y_{ij} - M_i)^2 + (M_i - M)^2 + M^2 + 2(Y_{ij} - M_i)(M_i - M) + 2(Y_{ij} - M_i)M$

$+ 2(M_i - M)M]$

$= \Sigma_i\Sigma_j (Y_{ij} - M_i)^2 + \Sigma_i N_i(M_i - M)^2 + NM^2$

since

$\Sigma_i\Sigma_j(Y_{ij} - M_i)(M_i - M) = \Sigma_i\Sigma_j(Y_{ij}M_i - M_i^2 - Y_{ij} M + M_iM)$

$= \Sigma_i(N_iM_i^2 - N_iM_i^2 - N_iM_iM + N_iM_iM) = 0,$

$\Sigma_i\Sigma_j(Y_{ij} - M_i)M = M\Sigma_i\Sigma_j(Y_{ij} - M_i) = 0,$

and

$\Sigma_i\Sigma_j(M_i - M)M = M\Sigma_i\Sigma_j(M_i - M) = 0.$

2.30 The pieces of the sum of squares: in words. How can we say in words what these three pieces of the sum of squares of all the scores are? The first piece, NM^2, is the square of the overall mean of all the scores, M^2, multiplied by the number of scores in the entire sample. The second piece adds two quantities, $N_1(M_1 - M)^2$ and $N_2(M_2 - M)^2$. These two pieces take the squared difference between the group mean and the general mean and multiply that squared difference by the number of scores in the respective group. Each piece is a weighted squared deviation of the group mean from the general mean, with the weight equal to the group sample size. The third piece takes the difference of each score from its own group mean, squares it, and adds up all such squared deviations. It looks like this: $(Y_{1,1} - M_1)^2 + (Y_{1,2} - M_1)^2 + ... + (Y_{1,N1} - M_1)^2 + (Y_{2,1} - M_2)^2 + (Y_{2,2} - M_2)^2 + ... + (Y_{2,N2} - M_2)^2$.

2.31 The pieces are called sums of squares. Each of these three pieces is a sum of squared numbers and we call each a **sum of squares**, which we abbreviate by SS (mathematical statisticians call such pieces *quadratic forms*). The first piece is the **sum of**

squares for the mean, $SS_M = NM^2$. The second is the **sum of squares for Groups,** $SS_G = \Sigma_i N_i (M_i - M)^2$. And the third is the **sum of squares for error,** $SS_E = \Sigma_i \Sigma_j (Y_{ij} - M_i)^2$. Later, the geometric representation will make more sense of this partitioning of the sum of squares. Let's take a break from the algebra for a moment and use a tiny set of data to exemplify these three sums of squares. Suppose the three scores in Group 1 are 1, 3, and 5 and the two scores in Group 2 are 4 and 6. Then $N_1 = 3$, $N_2 = 2$, and $N = 5$. Also, $M_1 = 3$, $M_2 = 5$, and $M = 3.8$. Hence:

$$SS_M = NM^2 = 5(3.8)^2 = 72.2;$$

$$SS_G = \Sigma_i N_i (M_i - M)^2 = 3(3 - 3.8)^2 + 2(5 - 3.8)^2 = 4.8$$

$$SS_E = \Sigma_i \Sigma_j (Y_{ij} - M_i)^2 = (1-3)^2 + (3-3)^2 + (5-3)^2 + (4-5)^2 + (6-5)^2 = 10.0.$$

According to the partitioning these three sums of squares should add up to the sum of the squares of each of the scores. And a little addition confirms that $\Sigma_i \Sigma_j Y_{ij}^2 = 1^2 + 3^2 + 5^2 + 4^2 + 6^2 = 87$ and $SS_M + SS_G + SS_E = 72.2 + 4.8 + 10.0 = 87$.

2.32 SS_M. The SS_M serves as a basis for inferring whether $\mu = 0$. When $\mu = 0$ we expect M to be close to zero and therefore NM^2 to be small.

2.32.1 E(M). We expect M to be close to zero when $\mu = 0$ because the expected value of M is the general mean, μ. That is, $E(M) = E_i E_j (\Sigma_i \Sigma_j Y_{ij}/N) = \Sigma_i E_i \Sigma_j E_j (Y_{ij})/N = \Sigma_i E_i \Sigma_j (\mu + \alpha_i)/N = \Sigma_i E_i (N_i \mu + N_i \alpha_i)/N = \Sigma_i (N_i \mu + N_i \alpha_i)/N = \mu + (N_1 \alpha_1 + N_2 \alpha_2)/N = \mu$. (The two subscripted expected values signs indicated that we are first taking the expectation over scores within each group and then taking the expectation over groups.)

2.33 SS_G. Similarly, SS_G measures the extent to which α_1 and α_2 depart from zero. When α_1 and α_2 equal zero, the two group means (in the population, not necessarily in the samples, of course) will equal the general mean, μ, and therefore the departures of M_1 and M_2 from M should be small. If they are large they inferentially indicate that α_1 and α_2 are not zero. So, when $\alpha_1 = \alpha_2 = 0$, we expect SS_G to be small.

2.34 SS_E provides a gauge for measuring SS_M and SS_G. When we say we expect SS_M or SS_G to be small, we need a gauge. The value of SS_E provides us with a gauge of how small is small. The reason for this is that SS_E is measuring the variability of the errors. The quantity SS_E is proportional to an unbiased estimator of the variance of the errors, σ^2. Clearly, if that variance were zero, then the errors would all equal their mean, which is zero. Thus there would be no errors, the sample general mean would exactly equal the population mean, and the Group sample means would exactly equal the Group population means. Hence any slightest deviation of the sample means from the hypothesized values would indicate that the population means deviated from the hypothesized values and the hypotheses could be rejected. But if the variance of the errors is not zero, but instead is rather large, then, from sample to sample, the sample means might deviate rather greatly from the population values. We say that because the sampling error is large, the sampling error of the sample means is large, and large deviations of the sample mean from the population mean are to be expected. This being the case, a large deviation of the sample mean from the null hypothesized value is not grounds for rejecting the null hypothesis. The size of the SS_E, then, gives us a handle on the size of the error variance, and therefore gives us a gauge to use to decide whether the size of the deviation of the sample mean from the hypothesized mean is or is not grounds for rejecting the hypothesis. This argument is intuitive but correct. We will gradually proceed to make it more precise.

2.34.1 Some chi-square variables. To see how SS_E provides such a gauge we'll need some chi-square variables. If the hypothesis that $\mu = 0$ is true, then SS_M/σ^2 will be $\chi^2(1)$. The argument for this is exactly as in 2.21. Also, if $\alpha_1 = \alpha_2 = 0$, then SS_G/σ^2 will be $\chi^2(1)$ also. The argument for this takes a few steps. We know that under the null hypothesis $\Sigma_i\Sigma_j Y_{ij}^2/\sigma^2$ is $\chi^2(N)$ using an argument the same as in 2.21. Also, if we regard each group separately, $\Sigma_j(Y_{ij} - M_i)^2/\sigma^2$ is distributed as $\chi^2(N_i - 1)$ following the argument in 2.21. Therefore, using 2.20.3, $\Sigma_i\Sigma_j(Y_{ij} - M_i)^2/\sigma^2$ is distributed as $\chi^2(N_1 - 1 + N_2 - 1)$ $= \chi^2(N-2)$. Finally, using 2.20.4, $\Sigma_i N_i(M_i - M)^2/\sigma^2$ must be distributed as $\chi^2[N - (N-2) - 1] = \chi^2(1)$ and all of the sums of squares are independent.

2.35 Two F-ratios. Using the results in 2.34.1, if $\mu = 0$,

$$F = \{[(SS_M/\sigma^2)]/1\} / \{[(SS_E/\sigma^2]/(N-2)\} = SS_M/[SS_E/(N-2)]$$

is the ratio of two independent chi-square variables each divided by its degrees of freedom and this same description also applies to

$$F = \{[(SS_G/\sigma^2)]/1\} / \{[(SS_E/\sigma^2]/(N-2)\} = SS_G/[SS_E/(N-2)]$$

when $\alpha_1 = \alpha_2 = 0$. Each of these statistics is an F-ratio and has the F distribution with 1 and N-2 degrees of freedom.

2.36 The magnitude of the F-ratio determines whether SS_M or SS_G is small.
We can say that SS_M or SS_G is small if the appropriate F-ratio we obtain is not so large as to equal one of the improbable values in the rejection region of the F distribution. This is because, as before, improbably large values of the F-ratio, due to large values of the numerator, provide evidence against the null hypothesis either that $\mu = 0$ or that $\alpha_1 = \alpha_2 = 0$.

2.36.1 A useful fact for finding expected values of sums of squares: $E(Y^2)$ = $Var(Y) + E^2(Y)$. (Before proceeding the reader may wish to reread Appendix A1.) To see once again why large values of F provide evidence against the null hypotheses of interest, let's look at the expected value of SS_G/σ^2 and the expected value of SS_E/σ^2. But before we do this we will first recall the definition of the expected value of a random variable and then take note of another fact. If Y is a discrete variable that takes the value Y_i with probability P_i, we call Y a random variable and define the **expected value** of Y to be $E(Y)$ = $\Sigma_i P_i Y_i$. (This is what has been meant when you have heard the expression "the long-run average value of Y." See Appendix A1 for a more complete discussion of random variables and their expectations.) For example, if we define a variable Y that takes the value 1 whenever a fair coin comes up heads and takes the value 0 when it comes up tails, then $E(Y)$ = $.5(1) + .5(0) = .5$.

The definition of the variance of a random variable Y is $Var(Y) = E(Y^2) - E^2(Y)$, where $E^2(Y)$ is the square of the expected value of Y. Thus, for the coin example, $Var(Y) =$ $[(.5)(1^2) + .5(0^2)] - (.5)^2 = .5 - .25 = .25$. This variance formula gives a formula for the expected value of the square of a random variable: **the expected value of the square of a random variable is the variance of the random variable plus the square of the expected value of that random variable.** That is,

$$E(Y^2) = Var(Y) + E^2(Y).$$

If the random variable of interest happens to be a mean, say M, based on N scores ("based on N scores" means we added up N scores to get a sum and then divided by N to get that mean), then using this formula it follows that

$$E(M^2) = Var(M) + E^2(M) \quad = [Var(Y)]/N + \mu^2 \qquad\qquad [2.6]$$

where $\mu = E(M) = E(Y)$. This formula [2.6] is useful over and over again because in finding the expected value of various sums of squares we repeatedly encounter the squares of means and can find their expectations with ease by simply applying [2.6]. We will see this now as we obtain SS_G, SS_E, $E(SS_G)$, and $E(SS_E)$.

Since

$$SS_G = \Sigma_i N_i (M_i - M)^2 = N_1(M_1 - M)^2 + N_2(M_2 - M)^2$$

$$= N_1(M_1^2 - 2M_1 M + M^2) + N_2(M_2^2 - 2M_2 M + M^2)$$

$$= N_1 M_1^2 + N_2 M_2^2 - 2M(N_1 M_1 + N_2 M_2) + NM^2$$

$$= N_1 M_1^2 + N_2 M_2^2 - 2MNM + NM^2 = N_1 M_1^2 + N_2 M_2^2 - NM^2,$$

we can find

$$E(SS_G) = E(N_1 M_1^2 + N_2 M_2^2 - NM^2)$$

$$= E(N_1 M_1^2) + E(N_2 M_2^2) - E(NM^2) = N_1 E(M_1^2) + N_2 E(M_2^2) - NE(M^2)$$

by three applications of [2.6]:

$$E(M_1^2) = \sigma^2/N_1 + E^2(M_1) = \sigma^2/N_1 + (\mu + \alpha_1)^2;$$

$$E(M_2^2) = \sigma^2/N_2 + E^2(M_2) = \sigma^2/N_2 + (\mu + \alpha_2)^2; \text{ and}$$

$$E(M^2) = \sigma^2/N + E^2(M) = \sigma^2/N + \mu^2.$$

Thus

$$E(SS_G) = N_1 E(M_1^2) + N_2 E(M_2^2) - NE(M^2)$$

$$= N_1[\sigma^2/N_1 + (\mu + \alpha_1)^2] + N_2[\sigma^2/N_2 + (\mu + \alpha_2)^2] - N(\sigma^2/N + \mu^2)$$

$$= \sigma^2 + N_1(\mu^2 + 2\mu \alpha_1 + \alpha_1^2) + \sigma^2 + N_2(\mu^2 + 2\mu\alpha_2 + \alpha_2^2) - \sigma^2 - N\mu^2$$

$$= \sigma^2 + (N_1 + N_2 - N)\mu^2 + 2(N_1\alpha_1 + N_2 \alpha_2)\mu + N_1\alpha_1^2 + N_2 \alpha_2^2$$

$$= \sigma^2 + \Sigma_i N_i \alpha_i^2,$$

since $N_1 + N_2 = N$ and $N_1\alpha_1 + N_2\alpha_2 = 0$.

To find $E(SS_E)$ we take

$$SS_E = \Sigma_i\Sigma_j(Y_{ij} - M_i)^2 = \Sigma_i\Sigma_j(Y_{ij}^2 - 2Y_{ij}M_i + M_i^2) = \Sigma_i\Sigma_j Y_{ij}^2 - \Sigma_i N_i M_i^2$$

and apply [2.6] to it. In doing so we have to be careful to make explicit the expectations that are being taken. When we take the expectation within the ith group, this will be expectation over the scores in that group and be denoted by E_j. When we take expectation over groups we will denote it by E_i. This gives

$$E_i E_j(Y_{ij}^2) = E_i[\sigma^2 + (\mu + \alpha_i)^2] \text{ and } E_i E_j(M_i^2) = E_i[\sigma^2/N_i + (\mu + \alpha_i)^2]$$

since $VAR(Y_{ij}) = \sigma^2$, $E_j(Y_{ij}) = \mu + \alpha_i$, $VAR(M_i) = \sigma^2/N_i$, and $E_j(M_i) = \mu + \alpha_i$.

So,

$$E_i E_j(SS_E) = E_i E_j(\Sigma_i\Sigma_j Y_{ij}^2) - E_i E_j(\Sigma_i N_i \mu_i^2) = E_i[\Sigma_i\Sigma_j E_j(Y_{ij}^2) - \Sigma_i N_i E_j(\mu^2)]$$
$$= E_i\{N \sigma^2 + \Sigma_i N_i(\mu + \alpha_i)^2 - \Sigma_i N_i[\sigma^2/N_i + (\mu + \alpha_i)^2]\}$$

$$= E_i\{N\sigma^2 + \Sigma_i N_i(\mu + \alpha_i)^2 - \Sigma_i\sigma^2 - \Sigma_i N_i(\mu + \alpha_i)^2]\} = E_i[(N - 2)\sigma^2]$$

$$= (N - 2)\sigma^2 .$$

2.36.2 What large F-ratios indicate. This little exercise of finding $E(SS_G)$ and $E(SS_E)$, aside from familiarizing us with finding expected values of sums of squares, shows why a large value of the F-ratio

$$(SS_G/1)/[SS_E/(N-2)]$$

provides inferential evidence against the hypothesis that $\alpha_1 = \alpha_2 = 0$. (We divide by 1 and N-2 because these are the degrees of freedom for the two chi-square distributed variables, SS_G/σ^2 and SS_E/σ^2.) We can get a rough idea of how the F ratio behaves by replacing SS_G and SS_E by their expected values in the F-ratio. We obtain

$$[\sigma^2 + \Sigma_i N_i \alpha_i^2]/[\{(N-2)\sigma^2\}/(N-2)] = [\sigma^2 + \Sigma_i N_i \alpha_i^2]/\sigma^2$$

$$= 1 + (\Sigma_i N_i \alpha_i^2)/\sigma^2.$$

We see that if $\alpha_1 = \alpha_2 = 0$, this ratio of expected values would be equal to one and that as α_1 and α_2 depart from zero, the numerator grows bigger and the ratio of the two expected values exceeds one by more and more. Thus large values of the F-ratio appear more

TABLE 2.2 WORKSHEET FOR THE DATA IN TABLE 2.1

Y_1	Y_1^2	$Y_1 - M_1$	$(Y_1 - M_1)^2$	Y_2	Y_2^2	$Y_2 - M_2$	$(Y_2 - M_2)^2$
2	4	-2.7	7.29	3	9	-5.1	26.01
3	9	-1.7	2.89	7	49	-1.1	1.21
5	25	0.3	0.09	8	64	-0.1	0.01
4	16	-0.7	0.49	7	49	-1.1	1.21
7	49	2.3	5.29	9	81	0.9	0.81
7	49	2.3	5.29	9	81	0.9	0.81
4	16	-0.7	0.49	8	64	-0.1	0.01
5	25	0.3	0.09	10	100	1.9	3.61
4	16	-0.7	0.49	9	81	0.9	0.81
6	36	1.3	1.69	11	121	2.9	8.41
Total 47	245	0	24.1	81	699	0	42.9
Mean 4.7				8.1			

$N_1 = 10$, $N_2 = 10$, $N = 20$,   Grand Total = 128,   Grand Mean = 6.4

$SS_M = 819.2$, $SS_G = 57.8$, $SS_E = 67$

compatible with the hypothesis that α_1 and α_2 do not equal zero while values near one appear more compatible with the null hypothesis that $\alpha_1 = \alpha_2 = 0$. Following this reasoning we again would choose the rejection region to lie in the upper tail of the F distribution.

2.37 Analyzing a set of data. We don't want to do too much analyzing of data until we get to Chapter 5, which will tell us some simple ways to perform the computations. But we are able to do an analysis of variance at this point so we should flex our muscles a little. Let's analyze the data in Table 2.1. These were scores for two groups. Table 2.2 shows the scores, their squares, the squared deviations of the scores in each group from their own group mean, and the quantities required to perform the analysis. To test the null hypothesis that the overall mean of all of the scores in both populations is zero, we calculate the F-ratio $(SS_M/df_M)/(SS_E/df_E) = (819.2/1)/(67/18) = 220.08 = F_{1,18}$ and compare it to the tabled critical value of F for 1 and 18 degrees of freedom using a .05 significance level. The tabled critical value shown in Statistical Table 4 is 4.41 so we reject the null hypothesis. To test the null hypothesis that there is no effect due to groups, we calculate the F-ratio $(SS_G/df_G)/(SS_E/df_E) = (57.8/1)/(67/18) = 15.53 = F_{1,18}$ and compare it to the same tabled critical value of F. This F-ratio is also significant at the .05 level and we reject the null hypothesis.

2.38   A confidence interval for $\mu_1 - \mu_2$. We already know that for the case of the experiment with two groups, one having N_1 scores and the other having N_2 scores, the quantity SS_E/σ^2 is $\chi^2(N_1 + N_2 - 2)$. Also, since M_1 and M_2 are independent normally distributed sample means, their difference is normally distributed also. That is, $M_1 - M_2$ is $N[\mu_1 - \mu_2 , \sigma^2(1/N_1 + 1/N_2)]$. Therefore

$$[(M_1 - M_2) - (\mu_1 - \mu_2)] / \sqrt{[\sigma^2(1/N_1 + 1/N_2)]}$$

is a normally distributed z-score and

$$[(M_1 - M_2) - (\mu_1 - \mu_2)]^2 / [\sigma^2(1/N_1 + 1/N_2)],$$

which is the square of a normally distributed z score, must be $\chi^2(1)$. Therefore, taking the ratio of two independent chi-square variables, each divided by their degrees of freedom, we have, letting mean square for error, $MS_e = SS_E/(N_1 + N_2 - 2)$,

$$\{[(M_1 - M_2) - (\mu_1 - \mu_2)]^2 / [\sigma^2(1/N_1 + 1/N_2)]\}/ [(MS_e/\sigma^2)]$$

which has the F distribution with 1 and $N_1 + N_2 - 2$ degrees of freedom. Let $F_{critical}$ be that value in this F distribution for which $Pr(F \geq F_{critical}) = .05$. Cancelling out the σ^2's, it follows that

$$Pr(\{[(M_1 - M_2) - (\mu_1 - \mu_2)]^2 / [(1/N_1 + 1/N_2)]\}/ MS_e \geq F_{critical}) = .05.$$

From this it follows that

$$Pr(\{[(M_1 - M_2) - (\mu_1 - \mu_2)]^2 / [(1/N_1 + 1/N_2)]\}/ MS_e < F_{critical}) = .95,$$

and therefore that

$$Pr([(M_1 - M_2) - (\mu_1 - \mu_2)]^2 < F_{critical} [(1/N_1 + 1/N_2)] MS_e) = .95.$$

This says that the probability that the distance between $(M_1 - M_2)$ and $(\mu_1 - \mu_2)$ is less than $\sqrt{\{ F_{critical} [(1/N_1 + 1/N_2)]MS_e\}}$ is .95. Writing this in the following form

Pr { $(M_1 - M_2) - \sqrt{ F_{critical} [(1/N_1 + 1/N_2)]MS_e} \leq (\mu_1 - \mu_2) \leq (M_1 - M_2) +$

$\sqrt{ F_{critical} [(1/N_1 + 1/N_2)]MS_e} } = .95$

we see that

$(M_1 - M_2) - \sqrt{ F_{critical} [(1/N_1 + 1/N_2)]MS_e} \leq (\mu_1 - \mu_2) \leq (M_1 - M_2) +$

$\sqrt{ F_{critical} [(1/N_1 + 1/N_2)]MS_e}$

is a 95 percent confidence interval for the difference between the two population means, $\mu_1 - \mu_2$.

2.39 What Chapters 3 and 4 will be about. In this chapter we have seen, using two relatively simple examples, how we test hypotheses concerning fixed-effects models by using F-ratios. In Chapter 4 we are going to begin to extend the application of the big ideas of this chapter to increasingly complex experimental designs. But first, while things are still simple, in Chapter 3 we are going to look at ANOVA from a geometric perspective. We will find that this gives us new insight and increased understanding of the beauty of the method and of many aspects that remain relatively mysterious when we look only from the algebraic point of view.

Exercises

1. Instead of two groups with sample sizes N_1 and N_2, assume there are I groups with sample sizes $N_1, N_2, ..., N_i, ..., N_I$. Now $SS_G = \Sigma_i N_i(M_i - M)^2$. Find $E(SS_G)$.

2. Write the model equation for an experiment with three groups. Write, using model equation terms, (a) the null hypothesis concerning the overall mean of all three populations, and (b) the null hypothesis concerning differences between the group population means. Draw a picture similar to that in Figure 2.3 showing these two null hypotheses and their alternatives.

3. Let X be a variable that is normally distributed with a mean of 15 and a variance of 10. Write an expression in terms of X that has the chi-square distribution.

*4. Write an expression that gives the probability that F is less than 4 if F has the F distribution with 2 and 4 degrees of freedom. Do the same for 2 and 6 degrees of freedom and 2 and 10 degrees of freedom. Calculate the value of each expression. What inference do you draw about the relationship of the probability that F is less than some value to the size of the denominator degrees of freedom?

*5. Perform a similar numerical experiment to that in exercise 4, but now vary the numerator degrees of freedom. What inference do you draw?

6. Explain in your own words why the critical region of the F distribution is located in the right hand or upper tail.

7. Find the numerical value of the F-ratio for testing the null hypothesis that the following sample of 10 scores was independently randomly sampled from a normal distribution with a mean of zero. The sample is: 2, 4, 5, 1, 2, -3, 2, 4, 5, 3.

8. Find the expected value of SS_E/σ^2. What rule can you use to check your answer? Hint: what is the distribution of SS_E/σ^2 ?

9. Summarize in your own words the big idea of how we go about testing hypotheses. Include remarks about a fraction, its numerator, its denominator, the distribution of parts of the numerator and the denominator, the distribution of the fraction, the expected values of the numerator and denominator, and what kind of gauge we use.

10. Perform an analysis of variance on the data in Table 2.3 to test the hypothesis that the independent variable Drug Dosage had no effect on the dependent variable Reaction Time. Each score comes from a different subject assigned at random to one of the four Drug Dosages. Drug Dosage is measured in micrograms and Reaction Time is measured in milliseconds.

(a) Write the model equation.

(b) State the null hypothesis with respect to Drug Dosage in terms of the model equation.

(c) Compute the F statistic, compare it to the tabled critical value of F, using a .05 significance level, and accept or reject the null hypothesis. (The tabled critical value is for 3 df in the numerator and 16 df in the denominator.)

11. Let us refer to the population means in exercise 10 as $\mu_{10}, \mu_{20}, \mu_{30},$ and μ_{40}. Suppose you are interested in whether the difference between the means for the first two groups equals the difference between the means for the second two groups. Observe that $(M_{10} - M_{20}) - (M_{30} - M_{40})$ is normally distributed with a mean of $(\mu_{10} - \mu_{20}) - (\mu_{30} - \mu_{40})$ and a variance of $\sigma^2(1/5 + 1/5 + 1/5 + 1/5)$ and extend the reasoning in section 2.38 to find a 95 percent confidence interval for $(\mu_{10} - \mu_{20}) - (\mu_{30} - \mu_{40})$.

12. How could you use the fact that $\Sigma_i(Y_i - M)^2/\sigma^2$ is $\chi^2(N-1)$ to test the hypothesis that σ^2 is some specific value, say 10?

13. What is the justification for using the upper tail of the F distribution as the rejection region?

14. State what each of the following quantities measures:

(a) $SS_M = NM^2$;

(b) $SS_G = \Sigma_i N_i(M_i - M)^2$;

(c) $SS_e = \Sigma_i\Sigma_j(Y_{ij} - M_i)^2$.

15. Speaking loosely, how do we tell if SS_M or SS_G is large?

TABLE 2.3 FICTIONAL REACTION TIME SCORES FOR EXERCISE 10

Drug Dosage			
10	20	30	40
420	430	560	540
400	450	530	550
430	460	520	550
460	480	500	560
430	470	510	560

16. What two statistics do we use to answer exercise 15 more rigorously?

17. If $F = N(M - \mu)^2 / [\Sigma_i(Y_i - M)^2/(N - 1)]$, and $Pr[F \geq F_{critical,1,N-1}] = .05$, then find a 95 percent confidence interval for μ.

18. Suppose you were to add 5 to each of the scores for the second group in Table 2.1. Predict what effect would this have on

(a) NM^2.

(b) SS_G.

(c) SS_E.

(d) The F ratio $(SS_G/ df_G)/(SS_E/ df_E)$ which was found to equal 15.3 in section 2.37.

19. Confirm your answers by performing the addition of 5 to each of the Y_2 scores in section 2.37 and performing the calculations to obtain the quantities for (a)–(d) in exercise 18.

20. How can we tell that a variable is distributed as F?

21. Write the model equations for the following hypotheses:

(a) A single set of Y scores is a sample from a normal distribution with a mean of zero.

(b) Same as in (a) but the mean is μ.

22. What needs to be done to NM^2 so that the result will be distributed as chi-square if $\mu = 0$?

23. Let M be the sample mean of a sample of 10 scores from a normal distribution with a mean of 5 and a variance of 30. What would the expected value of M^2 be?

24. Explain why SS_G measures the extent to which the effects α_1 and α_2 depart from zero in the case of the alternative hypothesis described in section 2.28.

25. Find a 95 percent confidence interval for $\mu_1 - \mu_2$ using the data and analysis results in section 2.37.

26. Using Y_1 scores of 3, 4, 5, 4, 5, 4, 6 and Y_2 scores of 5, 6, 5, 7, 5, 7, 8, 6, perform the same analysis as done in section 2.37. Note that the number of scores in the two groups are different.

27. If α_1 is less than α_2 then (a) α_1 must be _____ ? (b) the distribution with mean μ must lie _____ the distribution with mean $\mu + \alpha_1$ and the distribution with mean $\mu + \alpha_2$.

28. Suppose that you wish to test the null hypothesis that $\mu_1 - \mu_2 = 0$. You find a 95 percent confidence interval for $\mu_1 - \mu_2$ and the interval does not overlap zero. What can you conclude? You may wish to refer back to the section on confidence intervals in Chapter 1.

29. Explain why, in a test of the null hypothesis that the mean is zero, you would expect that exerting experimental control over extraneous variables would tend to produce larger values of F when the null hypothesis is actually false.

30. Let X be a variable that takes the value 10 if a penny comes up heads and 5 if the penny comes up tails. Let Y be a variable that takes the value 3 if a dime comes up heads and 1 if the dime comes up tails. Assume that the penny and the dime are fair coins. Show that $E(X/Y)$ is not equal to $E(X)/E(Y)$.

3

Some Geometry of the ANOVA

3.1 The geometry will clarify the algebra. This chapter will clarify and enrich the algebraic aspects of the analysis of variance for fixed-effects models by showing geometric representations of those algebraic aspects. We will find as a result of introducing this geometric perspective that our understanding takes on a new clarity. Also, many of the details so far taken on faith without understanding their basis will suddenly snap into a new cognitive place and seem not only no longer baseless and disconnected, but obvious, necessary, and seemingly the only natural way to approach the whole business.

3.1.1 Some mysteries. For example, most of us in an undergraduate introductory statistics course memorized the fact that the sum of the squared deviations of a set of scores from their own mean is less than the sum of the squared deviations of those scores from any other number. But very few of us were told why we ought to know such a thing and what relevance it had to anything else. Some of us ran into degrees of freedom, which we dutifully memorized and even followed some mumbo-jumbo about numbers being free to vary. But we still never really understood degrees of freedom, where they came from, what they had to do with the sums of squares they went with, or much of anything else about them except that you needed them to look up critical values for F-tests (or t-tests, or chi-square tests). Some of us ran into the method of least squares, but we didn't understand the meaning of minimizing those squares. Besides, least squares was encountered in the study of regression rather than ANOVA and we were never aware that least-squares procedures were occurring all over the place in the ANOVA. Some of us memorized that a sum of squares in the ANOVA could never be negative and if it was, we had made an error. But we never had any reasonable notion of why it could never be negative.

3.1.2 The mysteries will get solved here. By getting the geometric ideas in the ANOVA well in place, we will reveal in a new light the meaning of the sum of squared deviations of the scores from the mean and why it is smallest, and why that matters. We will discover what degrees of freedom are and how they relate to sums of squares, what least squares is all about and how it occurs in the ANOVA, why sums of squares are never negative, and we will even develop a geometric understanding of the F-ratio and see that the comparison of the numerator and the denominator of the F-ratio has a very sensible geometric meaning. Those of us who lean toward thinking geometrically rather than algebraically will find that the algebra takes on a new simplicity because we now can relate the abstract algebraic pieces to meaningful concrete geometric entities.

3.2 Geometry will represent algebra in many simple ways. In order to establish a correspondence between geometric entities and the algebraic entities that occur in ANOVA we will make use of the mathematical idea known as the **vector.** This will exactly suit our purposes because a vector has both an algebraic and a geometric representation. Consequently we will be able to display simple, intuitively appealing pictures, the parts of which will correspond to algebraic formulas. Also, least-squares procedures that would have required differential calculus if we performed them algebraically can instead be described in terms of the simple geometric idea of determining a line perpendicular to another line.

3.3 Algebraic vectors. Algebraically, a vector is a collection of numbers arranged in an order and enclosed by brackets—for example, [5, 2], or [3], or [7, 2, 3, 7]. Each number can be thought of as a coordinate in a coordinate system. For our purposes we will always be using the Cartesian coordinate system in a space of 1, 2, ..., or N dimensions. The axes will always be orthogonal (at right angles) to one another. A vector containing N elements (numbers) can be thought of as an ordered list of the coordinates or values on each of the N dimensions.

3.4 Geometric vectors. Geometrically, a vector corresponding to a given algebraic vector will be an arrow pointing from the origin of the coordinate system (0, 0, ..., 0) to that point in space (a space of N dimensions for a vector with N coordinates) having the coordinates given in the algebraic vector. Note that we use parentheses ( ) to enclose the coordinates of a point in space but brackets to denote the coordinates of a vector. Also, we will use boldface to distinguish algebraic vectors from algebraic terms.

3.5 Some examples of algebraic vectors and their geometric representations. Some examples would be the algebraic vector $\mathbf{X} = [3]$ corresponding to the one-dimensional geometric vector shown in Figure 3.1, and the algebraic vector $[X_1, X_2] = [1, 3]$ corresponding to the geometric vector shown in Figure 3.2.

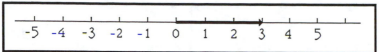

Figure 3.1. The geometric vector corresponding to the algebraic vector [3] and extending from the origin (0) to the point (3) in a one-dimensional straight line space of points.

3.6 Just the essentials of vectors. We will consider properties of vectors as we need them. It will not be necessary for us to acquire an exhaustive knowledge of vector algebra and vector spaces. As a new property of vector algebra is motivated by the discussion in hand it will be introduced. The student will find that this is a painless, easily assimilated approach to learning quite a bit about vectors and their algebra. At this point we only need to know about addition and subtraction of vectors, the length of a vector, and the angle between two vectors.

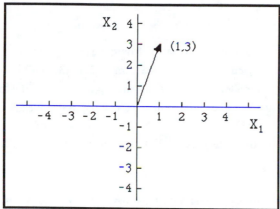

Figure 3.2. The geometric vector, corresponding to the algebraic vector [1, 3], extending from the origin (0, 0) to the point (1, 3).

3.7 The addition of vectors. We add two vectors algebraically by adding corresponding elements (coordinates on the same dimension). That is, if $X = [X_1, X_2, ..., X_N]$ and $Y = [Y_1, Y_2, ..., Y_N]$, then $X+Y = [X_1+Y_1, X_2+Y_2, ..., X_N+Y_N]$, For example, $[2, 2] + [1, 2] = [2 + 1, 2 + 2] = [3, 4]$. Geometrically, one vector is added to another by keeping its direction constant while sliding it so that its tail touches the tip of the arrow head of the vector it is being added to. Consider Figure 3.3. If the vector Y is slid along the vector X, keeping the tip of Y's tail touching X but keeping the whole vector Y pointed in the same direction, then clearly the dotted line from (2, 2) to (3, 4) in Figure 3.3 is where Y will be when the tip of its tail reaches the arrow head of X. The new location of the arrow

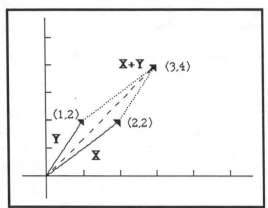

Figure 3.3. The dashed arrow locates the arrow head for **X** + **Y**
due to sliding the **Y** tail to the head of **X**, keeping the direction
of **Y** constant. The same location at (3, 4) would result from
sliding **X** so that its tail was at the arrow head of **Y**, keeping
the direction of **X** constant.

head of **Y** will now locate the arrow head of the vector **X+Y**. The same result would occur
if X was slid along **Y** so that it corresponded to the dotted line from (1, 2) to (3, 4).

Figure 3.4 shows an example of vector addition in three dimensions. Again we think of
the vector **X** as sliding along the vector **Y**, while maintaining its direction, so that it ends up
on the dashed line from (Y_1, Y_2, Y_3) to $(X_1+Y_1, X_2+Y_2, X_3+Y_3)$. The vector from the
origin (0, 0, 0) to the new location of the arrowhead of **X** will be the vector $[X_1+Y_1, X_2
+Y_2, X_3+Y_3] = $ **X** + **Y**.

3.7.1 Some properties of vector addition. The sum of two vectors V_1 and V_2 is a
uniquely determined vector $V_1 + V_2$. Vector addition is commutative in that $V_1 + V_2 =
V_2 + V_1$; is associative in that $(V_1 + V_2) + V_3 = V_1 + (V_2 + V_3)$; has an additive identity
element the zero vector **0** such that **V** + **0** = **V** for all vectors **V**. The vector **0** is a vector
with every coordinate equal to zero. Also, for every vector **V** there is an additive inverse
vector -**V** such that **V** + (-**V**) = **0**. Also $V_1 - V_2 = V_1 + (-V_2)$. The additive inverse of the
vector **X** is that vector -**X** such that if X_i is the ith element of **X**, then $-X_i$ is the ith element
of -**X**. For example, if **X** = [2, 3], then -**X** = [-2, -3]. Then **X** + (-**X**) = [2, 3] + [-2, -3] =
[0, 0].

3.7.2 Scalar multiplication. For any vector **V** = $[V_1, V_2,...,V_N]$ and any real number
k, the scalar product k**V** = $[kV_1, kV_2, ... kV_N]$ is a uniquely defined vector. (Don't get all
upset over the new word "scalar." It just means "regular number," like we grew up with,

rather than vector, the new kind that we are getting used to. It's just that we can multiply vectors by regular numbers, scalars, to get new vectors.) The result of this multiplication of

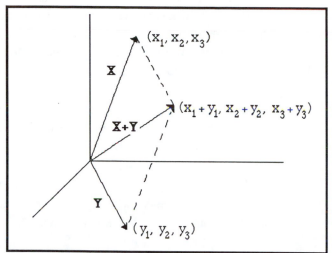

Figure 3.4. The addition of two three-dimensional vectors, **X** and **Y**, giving the vector **X+Y**.

a vector by a scalar is a change in the length of the vector. If the scalar is positive, the direction of the vector remains the same. If the scalar is negative, the direction of the vector is reversed.

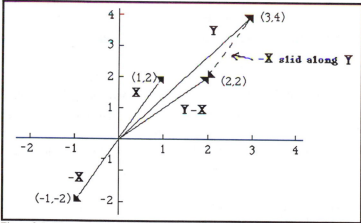

Figure 3.5. The vector **X** = [1, 2] is subtracted from the vector **Y** = [3, 4] by taking -**X** = [-1, -2], the negative of **X**, a vector equal in length pointing in the opposite direction, and adding it by sliding it so its tail coincides with the arrow head of [3,4].

For every vector $\mathbf{V}$, $0\mathbf{V} = \mathbf{0}$, $1\mathbf{V} = \mathbf{V}$, $(-1)\mathbf{V} = -\mathbf{V}$. Also, $k_1(k_2\mathbf{V})=(k_1k_2)\mathbf{V}$ for all scalars k_1 and k_2 and all vectors $\mathbf{V}$ (this just says that the order in which we change the length of a vector twice makes no difference concerning the final length of the vector); and $k(\mathbf{V_1}+\mathbf{V_2}) = k\mathbf{V_1} + k\mathbf{V_2}$ (changing the length of the pieces of a vector by multiplying the pieces by a scalar is equivalent to changing the length of the whole vector by such a multiplication) and $(k_1+k_2)\mathbf{V} = k_1\mathbf{V} + k_2\mathbf{V}$ (a vector $\mathbf{V}$ can be made (k_1+k_2) times as long by adding a vector k_1 times $\mathbf{V}$ to a vector k_2 times $\mathbf{V}$) for all scalars k, k_1, and k_2, and all vectors $\mathbf{V}$, $\mathbf{V_1}$, and $\mathbf{V_2}$.

3.8 The subtraction of vectors. We subtract one vector from another algebraically by subtraction of corresponding elements. Thus, $\mathbf{X} - \mathbf{Y} = [X_1, X_2, ..., X_N] - [Y_1, Y_2, ..., Y_N] = [X_1-Y_1, X_2-Y_2, ..., X_N-Y_N]$. So, $[3, 4] - [1, 2] = [3 - 1, 4 - 2] = [2, 2]$. Geometrically, subtraction of one vector $\mathbf{X}$ from another vector $\mathbf{Y}$ is accomplished by first replacing $\mathbf{X}$ by $-\mathbf{X}$, which is a vector of the same length as $\mathbf{X}$ but oriented in the opposite direction, and then following the procedure for adding. So, $\mathbf{Y} - \mathbf{X} = \mathbf{Y} + (-\mathbf{X})$. This is shown in Figure 3.5.

3.8.1 The length of a vector. The **length** of a vector $\mathbf{X} = [X_1, X_2, ..., X_N]$ is $\sqrt{(\Sigma_i X_i^2)}$. Thus the squared length of a vector $\mathbf{X}$ is $\Sigma_i X_i^2$. Perhaps you have come across a formula for the distance between two points in a Cartesian coordinate system. This formula says that if there are two points $(X_1, X_2, ..., X_N)$ and $(Y_1, Y_2, ..., Y_N)$, then the distance between the two points is defined to be $\sqrt{[\Sigma_i(X_i - Y_i)^2]}$. The length of a vector $\mathbf{X} = [X_1, X_2, ..., X_N]$ is the distance between the point $(X_1, X_2, ..., X_N)$ and the origin, $(0, 0, ..., 0)$. By substituting 0 for each value of Y_i in the general distance formula, the stated formula for the length of a vector results. Soon we will put the squared lengths of vectors to much good use.

3.8.2 What we mean by the "opposite direction." We will rarely be concerned with the direction of a vector. So far as "a vector of the same length pointing in the opposite direction" is concerned, we mean the vector $-\mathbf{X}$ such that if $\mathbf{X} = [X_1, X_2, ..., X_N]$, then $-\mathbf{X} = [X_1, X_2, ..., X_N]$. These two vectors are obviously of the same length, and reversal of direction is produced by the negating of the component coordinates.

3.9 The angle between two vectors. To define the angle between two vectors we first define the **inner product**, $\mathbf{X} \cdot \mathbf{Y}$, of two vectors $\mathbf{X}$ and $\mathbf{Y}$ to equal $\Sigma_i X_i Y_i = X_1 Y_1 + X_2 Y_2 + ... + X_N Y_N$. Then the squared length of $\mathbf{X}$ is $\mathbf{X} \cdot \mathbf{X}$, the squared length of $\mathbf{Y}$ is $\mathbf{Y} \cdot \mathbf{Y}$, and the **cosine** of the angle between $\mathbf{X}$ and $\mathbf{Y}$ is $\mathbf{X} \cdot \mathbf{Y}/(\sqrt{\mathbf{X} \cdot \mathbf{X}})(\sqrt{\mathbf{Y} \cdot \mathbf{Y}})$. For example, if $\mathbf{X} =$

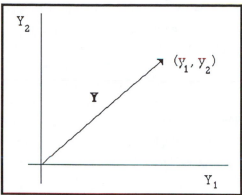

Figure 3.6. The data vector **Y** for a sample of two scores with values y_1 and y_2.

[1,2] and $\mathbf{Y} = [3,4]$, then the cosine of the angle between $\mathbf{X}$ and $\mathbf{Y}$ is $(1\cdot3 + 2\cdot4)/[\sqrt{(1\cdot1 + 2\cdot2)}(\sqrt{(3\cdot3 + 4\cdot4)}] = 11/(5\sqrt{5})$.

3.9.1 If two vectors X and Y form a right angle, then their inner product X·Y must equal zero. Since the cosine of a right angle is zero, it follows that for two vectors to lie at right angles to each other (we say they are **orthogonal** to each other), $\mathbf{X}\cdot\mathbf{Y}$ must equal zero since the cosine of the angle between them can be zero only if $\mathbf{X}\cdot\mathbf{Y}$ is zero. In terms of the coordinates of the two vectors, the sum of the products of the coordinates, $\Sigma_i X_i Y_i$ must equal zero for the two vectors to be orthogonal.

3.10 The sample mean estimates the population mean. We can now begin to think about some statistical notions algebraically and geometrically at the same time. Let's begin by taking a sample of two scores from a population and estimating the mean of that population. The model will be that $Y_i = \mu + e_i$, and we will assume as before that the e_i are error effects that have a mean of zero. Algebraically, if the sample is Y_1 and Y_2, we know that we just average the sample scores to get $M = (Y_1 + Y_2)/2$ as the sample mean, which we use to estimate the population mean, μ. We are familiar from introductory statistics with many of the reasons for using the sample mean to estimate the population mean. For example, if we sampled the entire population, the sample mean would be the population mean and would give exactly the right value for an estimate of the population mean. Now, however, we are going to look at a geometric rationale for using the sample mean as an estimate of the population mean.

3.11 The mean line. A simple way to present the geometric point of view is to consider taking a sample of just two scores, Y_1 and Y_2. The particular values we get will be called y_1

and y_2. and we will represent the sample as a vector $\mathbf{Y} = [y_1, y_2]$. Notice that we have used uppercase "Y" to denote the variable in each case and lowercase "y" to denote the particular value that Y takes. Figure 3.6 shows the sample as a vector. To estimate μ, the mean of the population, we recall the model $Y_i = \mu + e_i$. This says that but for the addition of e_i, the observed Y_i would be μ. Suppose the errors had not occurred. That is, suppose Y_1 and Y_2 were equal to μ. Where would the data vector lie? Well, the vector would be $\mathbf{Y} = [\mu, \mu]$, so it would have to lie on the line $Y_1 = Y_2$. It would lie on the line passing through (0, 0), (1, 1), (2, 2), and so on, and would have to be a scalar multiple of the vector [1, 1]; namely, it would be $\mu[1, 1]$. Let us refer to the line passing through the origin, (1, 1), (2, 2), and of course (μ, μ) as the mean line. Figure 3.7 shows the data vector and the mean line.

3.12 The situation. The problem in estimation is that we do not know the value of μ We know that $[\mu, \mu]$ lies on the mean line somewhere. We also know where the data vector is and that the two values in the data vector depart from μ by errors.

3.13 The natural, commonsensical solution. It seems natural to choose a point on the mean line so that its coordinates estimate $[\mu, \mu]$. It also seems unnatural to choose a point that is far from the data vector, since the data vector, but for error, indicates the location of $[\mu, \mu]$. In fact, it seems reasonable to choose the point on the mean line that is closest to the data vector since this makes the best use of the fact that the data vector is indicative of the location of the μ-vector, $[\mu, \mu]$.

3.14 Estimating μ is finding the point on the mean line closest to the data. So, the task of estimating μ geometrically reduces to finding that point on the mean line closest to the point (y_1, y_2).

3.14.1 Pythagoras provides a perpendicular to pick the proper point. Figure 3.8 shows the data vector, the mean line, a line segment r, that is perpendicular to the mean line and extending from (y_1, y_2) to the point (m, m) on the mean line, and a line segment t extending from (y_1, y_2) to some point (c, c) on the mean line, where $c \neq m$ and therefore t is not perpendicular to the mean line. Call the line segment from (m, m) to (c, c) by the name s. Then the triangle formed by the line segments r, s, and t is a right triangle and we know that r < t. This is so because of the Pythagorean theorem, which assures us that $r^2 + s^2 = t^2$, and so $r = \sqrt{(t^2 - s^2)} < \sqrt{t^2} = t$.

3.15 Estimation is as simple as diving: we just take the "right" angle and drop. We find the point on the mean line closest to the data vector by dropping a perpendicular from the data vector to the mean line.

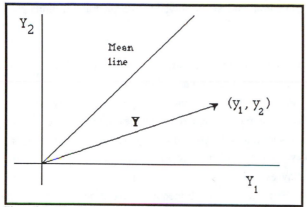

Figure 3.7. The data vector **Y** and the mean-line, the line $Y_1 = Y_2$ passing through the origin (0, 0) and the points (1, 1), (2, 2), and so forth.

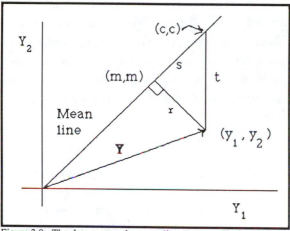

Figure 3.8. The data vector, the mean line, a perpendicular, r, dropped from the data vector to the point (m,m) on the mean line, and the line t from the data vector to some point (c,c) on the mean line such that c does not equal m.

3.16 The sample mean locates the geometrically natural estimate of the population mean. This point on the mean line has as its coordinates the sample mean, $(y_1 + y_2)/2$.

3.16.1 The orthogonality of M and D provides a quadratic formula for the estimator of μ. Clearly, by the rule for the addition of vectors, $[m, m] + [y_1 - m, y_2 - m] = [y_1, y_2]$. And also, following section 3.9.1, since $\mathbf{M} = [m, m]$ and $\mathbf{D} = [y_1 - m, y_2 - m]$ are orthogonal to each other, $\mathbf{M} \cdot \mathbf{D} = m(y_1 - m) + m(y_2 - m) = 0$, which implies that $2m^2$ -

$(y_1 + y_2)m = 0$, which is a quadratic in m that can be solved by the quadratic formula giving $m = (y_1 + y_2)/2$, the sample mean.

3.17 Ah ha! Having done just this little exercise in estimating the population mean from a sample of two scores, several statistical ideas take on new clarity for us. Do you recall (and you cannot be blamed if you don't since it probably was just a meaningless fact) being told that the sum of the squares of the deviations of a set of scores from their own arithmetic mean is less than the sum of the squares of the deviations from any other number? You may even have seen an expression like $\Sigma_i(Y_i - M)^2 \leq \Sigma_i(Y_i - C)^2$, and in some textbooks you may even have seen an algebraic proof accomplished by substitution of $M + f$ for C on the right side of the inequality and doing some algebraic manipulation. But if we just recall the rule for the length of a line segment between two points (x_1,x_2) and (y_1,y_2) as being $\sqrt{[(x_1-y_1)^2 + (x_2-y_2)^2]}$, we can see immediately that since $M = m$ in Figure 3.8, $\Sigma_i(Y_i - M)^2$ is just the squared length of the line segment r while $\Sigma_i(Y_i - C)^2$ is the squared length of t, and we have already satisfied ourselves that $r < t$. The longwinded, seemingly pointless statement that the sum of the squared deviations from the mean is less than that from any other point simply arises from the fact that the point on the mean line closest to the data vector has the sample mean as its coordinates. Also, we see here a simple case of **least-squares estimation.** Choosing a point on the mean line, call it (M, M), that is closest to (y_1, y_2) amounts to finding that M which minimizes $\Sigma_i(Y_i - M)^2$, which is the squared distance between those two points.

3.17.1 Least-squares estimation. Least-squares estimation is always a procedure that, geometrically, finds a point closest to some other point and is always accomplished by dropping a perpendicular from some higher-dimensional space (here, a two-dimensional plane) in which a data vector lies to a lower-dimensional subspace of that higher-dimensional space (here, the one-dimensional mean line lying in the two-dimensional data plane).

3.18 The error estimates. We have seen that the data vector can be expressed as the sum of two vectors: $[Y_1, Y_2] = [M, M] + [Y_1 - M, Y_2 - M]$, which we can write as $\mathbf{Y} = \mathbf{M} + \mathbf{D}$ ("D" for deviations of the scores from their mean). We know that the elements of $\mathbf{M}$ estimate μ. What do the elements of $\mathbf{D}$ estimate? The elements of $\mathbf{D}$, $Y_1 - M$ and $Y_2 - M$, estimate the errors, e_1 and e_2.

3.18.1 The mean vector and the error-estimates vector are orthogonal. These two error estimates, $Y_1 - (Y_1 + Y_2)/2 = (Y_1 - Y_2)/2$ and $Y_2 - (Y_1 + Y_2)/2 = (Y_2 - Y_1)/2$, are of the form b and -b, so $\mathbf{D}$ will be some scalar multiple of the vector [1, -1] (since [b, -b] = b[1, -1]), and will always lie on a line passing through the origin (0,0) and the point (1, -1).

This **error-estimate line** intersects the mean line at a right angle, and we say that the error-estimate line and the mean line are <u>orthogonal</u> (i.e., at right angles) to each other.

3.19 The spatial relationships of Y, M, and D. Figure 3.9(a) shows the data vector **Y**, the mean vector **M**, and the vector of error estimates, **D**. The vectors **M** and **D** are shown as orthogonal to each other. We can also see that **M** is found by dropping a perpendicular from **Y** to the mean line and **D** is found by dropping a perpendicular from **Y** to the error-estimate line.

3.19.1 The proof that M and D are orthogonal. We can show that **M** and **D** are orthogonal, using the detail in section 3.9.3. The inner product $\mathbf{M \cdot D} = [(Y_1 + Y_2)/2][(Y_1 - Y_2)/2] + [(Y_1 + Y_2)/2][(Y_2 - Y_1)/2] = 0$.

3.20 The geometry illuminates the partitioning of the sum of squares in equation [2.3]. Figure 3.9(b) shows that since **M** and **D** are orthogonal and **Y** = **M** + **D**, a right triangle is formed by **Y**, **M**, and **D** with **Y** as the hypotenuse and **M** and **D** as the sides. Since they form a right triangle, the Pythagorean theorem assures us that

$$\mathbf{Y \cdot Y} = \mathbf{M \cdot M} + \mathbf{D \cdot D},$$

that is, that the squares of the lengths of the two sides add to the square of the length of the hypotenuse. Algebraically, this results in

$$Y_1{}^2 + Y_2{}^2 = (Y_1 - M)^2 + (Y_2 - M)^2 + M^2 + M^2$$

which we find, to our great delight, is nothing other than the equation [2.3]

$$\Sigma_i Y_i{}^2 = \Sigma_i (Y_i - M)^2 + NM^2, \quad \text{where } N = 2.$$

Here, then, is the geometric basis of the partitioning of the total sum of squares into two pieces. The two pieces of sums of squares represent the squared lengths of two vectors, the mean vector and the error-estimates vector, which lie at right angles to one another and add to give the squared length of the data vector, simply because the three vectors form a right triangle. Furthermore, the two vectors forming the sides of the triangle are the shortest possible vectors satisfying certain requirements. The vector **D** is the shortest it can be if the

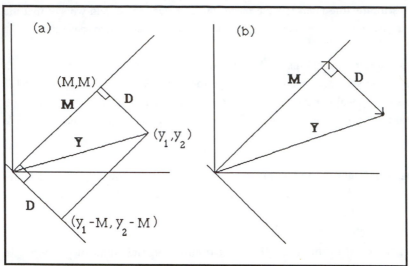

Figure 3.9. (a) The data vector, **Y**; the mean vector, **M**; and the vector of error estimates, **D**; with **M** and **D** orthogonal to each other, each found by dropping a perpendicular from **Y** to the mean line or the line orthogonal to the mean line, the error-estimate line. (b) The vector **M** and **D** are orthogonal and add to **Y**, so **Y**, **M**, and **D** form a right triangle, so that $\mathbf{Y \cdot Y = M \cdot M + D \cdot D}$, which is equivalent to equation [2.3].

other side vector is to lie on the mean line, and the vector **M** is the shortest vector it can be if the other side is to lie on the error-estimate line.

3.21 "A thing of beauty is a joy forever."   Figure 3.9(b) is a thing of beauty. It concisely summarizes so much of what we have expressed.

(a)   **It clarifies the partitioning of the sums of squares.**

(b)   **It makes obvious the method of least squares.**

(c)   **It makes sense of why the sum of squared deviations from the mean is smaller than the sum of squared deviations from any other value.**

(d)   **And now that we know that a sum of squares is the squared length of a vector, we would never dream of supposing that a sum of squares could ever be a negative number because the square of a length is always positive.**

Can we hope that it will also offer some insight into the F-ratio and those pesky little degrees of freedom? Indeed, yes. First, let's consider the degrees of freedom.

3.22 Degrees of freedom are the dimensionalities of subspaces.   Please don't get rattled by the word "subspace." A subspace is just a piece of a space. If you are comfortable with sets, think of a subspace as just a subset of the points in a space. The wall is a two-dimensional subspace of my office. The floor is another. The line where the floor meets the wall is a one-dimensional subspace of my office and is also a one-dimensional subspace of each of those two-dimensional subspaces, the wall and the floor. In fact, it is the intersection of the two. Speaking of intersections, the intersection of two streets is another example of a subspace, it being that portion of the space that the two streets both occupy.

The total number of scores in the sample was two, so we required a two-dimensional plane to locate the data vector. We also located two orthogonal one-dimensional subspaces of that two-dimensional plane. These were the mean line and the error-estimate line. The degrees of freedom for the total sum of squares is <u>two</u>, the degrees of freedom for NM^2 is one, and the degrees of freedom for $\Sigma_i(Y_i - M)^2$ is also one when $N = 2$.

Partitioning the total sum of squares corresponds to dividing the space in which the data vector lies. The degrees of freedom for the total sum of squares is equal to the dimensionality of the space in which the data vector lies. The degrees of freedom for SS_M equals the dimensionality of the subspace in which the mean vector lies, namely, <u>one</u>. And the degrees of freedom for SS_E equals the dimensionality of the subspace in which the vector **D** is constrained to lie, namely, also <u>one</u> in this case. **It is no coincidence that the dimensionality for the data vector space and the two subspaces are 2, 1, and 1 and the degrees of freedom for the total sum of squares, SS_M, and SS_E are 2, 1, and 1. Rather, this correspondence always occurs. A sum of squares, which is the squared length of some vector, always has as its degrees of freedom a number equal to the dimensionality of the space or subspace in which that vector lies.**

Table 3.1 summarizes the situation. We see in Table 3.1 a variety of correspondences. The partitioning of $\Sigma_i Y_i^2$, the sum of squares that we started with in Chapter 2, is not only identical to the Pythagorean relationship between the squared lengths of the sides of a right triangle, **M·M** and **D·D**, and the squared length of the hypotenuse, **Y·Y**, namely, **Y·Y** = **M·M** + **D·D**, but also two corresponding partitions match this partition. The data vector undergoes a partition expressed by **Y** = **M** + **D** and the total degrees of freedom, 2, is partitioned into 1 for the mean and one for error, giving a corresponding expression, 2 = 1 + 1. In what follows we will see that similar correspondences apply regardless of how many scores are in the sample. First we will consider a sample of three scores in order to ease into generalizing, and then we will go on to a sample of N scores.

3.23 The geometry for a sample of three scores. A sample of three scores can be represented by a vector **Y** = [Y_1, Y_2, Y_3] in a three-dimensional space. Figure 3.10 shows

TABLE 3.1 THE PARTITIONING OF THE DATA VECTOR, TOTAL SUM OF SQUARES, AND   DIMENSIONALITY OF THE DATA SPACES INTO A COMPONENT FOR THE MEAN AND A COMPONENT FOR ERROR, AND THE CORRESPONDING ADDITIVITIES THAT EXIST FOR THIS PARTITIONING

	Vector	Sum of squares = Squared length	Degrees of freedom = Dimensionality
Total	$\mathbf{Y} = [Y_1, Y_2]$	$\Sigma_i Y_i^2 = \mathbf{Y \cdot Y}$	2
Mean	$\mathbf{M} = [M, M]$	$2M^2 = \mathbf{M \cdot M}$	1
Error	$\mathbf{D} = [Y_1-M, Y_2-M]$	$\Sigma_i(Y_i - M)^2 = \mathbf{D \cdot D}$	1
Additivity	$\mathbf{Y = M + D}$	$\mathbf{Y \cdot Y = M \cdot M + D \cdot D}$	$2 = 1 + 1$

this vector $\mathbf{Y}$ and the three axes of the coordinate system. Figure 3.11 shows the data vector $\mathbf{Y}$, the mean line passing through the origin $(0,0,0)$ and the point $(1,1,1)$, and the vector $\mathbf{D}$. The mean line is the locus (locus and location have the same root) of all points (Y_1, Y_2, Y_3) in three space such that $Y_1 = Y_2 = Y_3$, therefore the point (μ, μ, μ) will lie on it. We choose that point on the mean line closest to (Y_1, Y_2, Y_3) as the estimate of (μ, μ, μ). That point is (M, M, M). We find that point by dropping a perpendicular from (Y_1, Y_2, Y_3) to the mean line. This perpendicular is the vector $\mathbf{D} = (Y_1 - m, Y_2 - m, Y_3 - m)$, where (m, m, m) is the point on the mean line intercepted by the perpendicular from (Y_1, Y_2, Y_3). Therefore, $\mathbf{D}$ is orthogonal to $\mathbf{m} = [m, m, m]$ and so $\mathbf{D \cdot m} = 0$. Thus, $\Sigma_i[(Y_i - m)m] = 0$ and $\Sigma_i Y_i m - \Sigma_i m^2 = 0$ and so $m(\Sigma_i Y_i) = 3m^2$, therefore $m = 0$ or $m = \Sigma_i Y_i/3 = M$, the sample mean. Obviously m equals zero only when the perpendicular dropped from the data vector intercepts the mean line at the origin. In order for this to happen, the data vector must lie in the plane orthogonal to the mean line, passing through the origin. The equation of this plane is given by the equation $\Sigma_i Y_i = 0$, so even in this case, $m = 0 = (\Sigma_i Y_i/3) = M$.

3.24 D lies in the plane orthogonal to M. Since $\mathbf{D}$ is orthogonal to $\mathbf{M} = [M, M, M]$, $\mathbf{D}$ must lie in that two-dimensional plane that is orthogonal to $\mathbf{M}$. This is because the two-dimensional plane orthogonal to $\mathbf{M}$ contains all the vectors orthogonal to $\mathbf{M}$.

*3.24.1 How do we know that all the vectors orthogonal to M lie in the same plane? It is certainly reasonable to ask how we know that all the vectors orthogonal

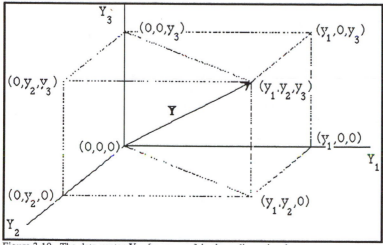

Figure 3.10. The data vector $\mathbf{Y} = [y_1, y_2, y_3]$ in three-dimensional space.

to $\mathbf{M}$ lie in the same plane. Might there not be one vector orthogonal to $\mathbf{M}$ that lies outside that plane? The answer is no. All vectors orthogonal to $\mathbf{M}$ lie in the same plane and we can show this, but it takes
going into a few little details. These are given in Appendix 3.24.1.1-3.24.1.3.

*3.24.2 The independence of vectors. In Appendices 3.24.1.1-3.24.1.3 it is shown that any vector in three space that is orthogonal to a given vector must
lie in a certain plane that contains all the vectors orthogonal to that given vector. There could be no vector orthogonal to that given vector that did not lie in that certain plane. It is also shown that any such vector lying in that plane can be expressed as a linear combination of any two noncollinear vectors also in that plane. Notice that the plane is two dimensional, and in general it requires a linear combination of two vectors to equal a vector in that plane. We can generalize this fact to an N-dimensional space. Then we would say that any vector lying in that N-dimensional space can be written as a linear combination of N vectors in that space provided that the N vectors in the space stand in a relationship to each other that is analogous to two vectors not lying in the same line. This relationship is called **linear independence** or just **independence**, and N vectors are independent if no one of them can be expressed as a linear combination of the other N - 1. (By a linear combination of N vectors $\mathbf{V_1}, \mathbf{V_2}, ..., \mathbf{V_N}$, we mean $a_1 \mathbf{V_1} + a_2 \mathbf{V_2} + ... + a_N \mathbf{V_N}$ where the a_i's are all arbitrary scalars.)

*3.24.3 A geometric example of independent vectors. Let $\mathbf{V_1}, \mathbf{V_2}, ..., \mathbf{V_N}$ be a set of N vectors in N-dimensional space (we'll say "N-space" from now on). They are all

linearly independent of each other if no one of them can be expressed as a linear combination of the others. Otherwise, they are **dependent**. Consider, for example, the vectors $E_1 = [1, 0, 0]$, $E_2 = [0, 1, 0]$, and $E_3 = [0, 0, 1]$. Clearly no linear combination of any two of these could give the third. Thus, $aE_1 + bE_2$ cannot equal E_3 because the third element in E_3, 1, would have to equal $a(0) + b(0) = 0$. Geometrically this fact is shown

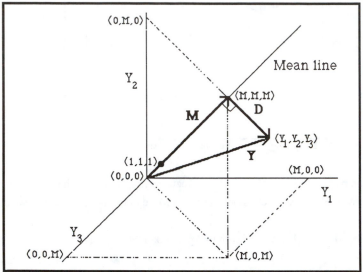

Figure 3.11. The vectors **Y**, **M**, and **D**; **D** is orthogonal to the mean line so **M** is the closest vector to **Y**, with all its coordinates equal. The coordinate is M and estimates μ.

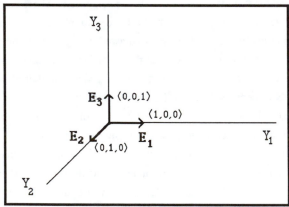

Figure 3.12. Any vector in the Y_1 - Y_2 plane can be written as a linear combination of E_1 and E_2, but no linear combination of E_1 and E_2 can equal E_3 since a linear combination of E_1 and E_2 cannot rise out of the Y_1 - Y_2 plane.

in Figure 3.12. It is clear that no addition of a multiple of E_1 and a multiple of E_2 can ever rise up out of the plane they define so that it could equal E_3.

*3.24.4 A basis for an N-dimensional vector space is any set of N linearly independent vectors in that space. If V_1, V_2, ..., V_N are a set of N independent vectors, then any other vector in N-space can be written as a linear combination of V_1, V_2, ..., V_N. We say that the vectors V_1, V_2, ..., V_N constitute a **basis** for N-space and that they **span** N-space. The **vector space spanned by a basis** is just the set of all vectors that can be written as a linear combination of the vectors in the basis. Thus, for example, we can write the vector $V = [V_1, V_2, V_3]$ as $V_1E_1 + V_2E_2 + V_3E_3 = [V_1, 0, 0] + [0, V_2, 0] + [0, 0, V_3] = V$. While it is now obvious that any vector in 3-space can be written as a linear combination of the vectors E_1, E_2, and E_3, it may not be obvious that any vector in 3-space (N-space) can be written as a linear combination of any three linearly independent vectors (N linearly independent vectors). Suppose $T = [t_1, t_2, t_3]$, $U = [u_1, u_2, u_3]$, and $V = [v_1, v_2, v_3]$ are

linearly independent, and let $S = [s_1, s_2, s_3]$ be any other vector. Then the claim is that there exist real numbers a, b, and c such that $S = aT + bU + cV$. This means that there is a solution for a, b, and c in the system of equations

$s_1 = at_1 + bu_1 + cv_1$
$s_2 = at_2 + bu_2 + cv_2$
$s_3 = at_3 + bu_3 + cv_3$.

(If it is a puzzle why this system of equations follows, just think of the vectors S, T, U, and V as columns of their elements, that is, column vectors, and note that the equation $S = aT + bU + cV$ says that the first element of S is given by the first equation in the system, the second element by the second equation, etc.)

Now this system of three equations in the three unknowns a, b, and c will have a solution provided that the determinant

$$\begin{vmatrix} t_1 & u_1 & v_1 \\ t_2 & u_2 & v_2 \\ t_3 & u_3 & v_3 \end{vmatrix}$$

is not zero. A method for determining the value of a determinant is given in Appendices 3.24.4.1-3.24.4.2. One condition that ensures that a determinant is not zero is if no column (row) of the determinant, thought of as a vector, can be written as a linear combination of the other columns (rows). We are assured that this is the case for this determinant because we have assumed that **T**, **U**, and **V** are linearly independent.

3.25 The general case: A sample of N scores. We can now generalize to a sample of N scores. The data vector will be $Y = [Y_1, Y_2, ..., Y_N]$, the mean vector is $M = [M, M, ..., M]$, and $D = [Y_1 - M, Y_1 - M, ..., Y_N - M]$. Obviously, **M** is orthogonal to **D**. The squared length of **Y** is $\Sigma_i Y_i^2$, the squared length of **M** is NM^2, and the squared length of **D** is $\Sigma_i (Y_i - M)^2$. There are N scores, and therefore the data vector lies in an N-dimensional space. The mean vector must lie on the one-dimensional mean line passing through (0, 0, ..., 0) and (1, 1, ..., 1), and the vector **D** must lie in the (N-1) dimensional hyperplane which contains all those vectors that are orthogonal to the mean line and have coordinates that add to zero. Correspondingly, there is one degree of freedom for the mean, N - 1 degrees of freedom for error, and N degrees of freedom for the total sum of squares.

*3.25.1 Constraining vectors to certain subspaces by fixing a coordinate. How can we understand the idea of a vector being constrained to lie in a subspace of the data space? Suppose we have an arbitrary vector in three-space. We can write it as $V = [V_1, V_2, V_3]$ where all the coordinates are completely free to take any value. The vector can be anywhere in three-space. Now, suppose we consider another vector that is lying in the Y_1, Y_2-plane. We know that its third coordinate must be zero if the vector is in that plane. The vector must be of the form $[V_1, V_2, 0]$. We can say that in three-space, if a vector lies in the Y_1, Y_2-plane, then $V_3 = 0$. Or, reversing the argument, we can also say that if $V_3 = 0$, then the vector must lie in the Y_1, Y_2-plane. This equation $V_3 = 0$ constrains the coordinates of the vector and constrains the vector to lie in a plane. By similar reasoning we could determine that saying $V_2 = 0$ is equivalent to saying that the vector must lie in the Y_1, Y_3-plane, and saying $V_1 = 0$ is equivalent to the vector lying in the Y_2, Y_3-plane.

Now consider the plane that is parallel to the Y_1, Y_2-plane but passes through the point [0, 0, 1]. That is, the plane "floats" one unit up "in the air" above the Y_1, Y_2-plane. Any vector in that plane must have 1 as its third coordinate. All such vectors will be of the form $[V_1, V_2, 1]$. Or, reversing the argument, saying $V_3 = 1$ constrains the vector to lying in that plane. We see that, in general, determining the value of any coordinate to be some constant constrains the vector to lie in some plane.

*3.25.2 Other ways to constrain a vector to a subspace. Is there some other way to constrain the vector to lie in a plane? We expect so since there are many other planes that can lie in three-space besides the ones determined by two axes and the ones parallel to the planes determined by two axes. There are all the planes that go slanting through three-space at various angles. One way to think about some of those possible planes is to think about all the vectors emanating from the origin in three-space and realize that for each such vector there is a plane passing through the origin, perpendicular to that vector.

Let's take some particular vector, say $V_1 = [1, 2, 1]$, and consider the plane passing through the origin orthogonal to V_1. Call that plane P_1. Now P_1 will contain all the vectors orthogonal to V_1. Let $U = [U_1, U_2, U_3]$ be an arbitrary one of those vectors in P_1 orthogonal to V_1. Then, using the fact that the inner product of two orthogonal vectors is zero, we have that $V_1 \cdot U = 0$, so $1(U_1) + 2(U_2) + 1(U_3) = 0$. We see that asserting that the plane P_1 is orthogonal to the vector V_1 says that any vector U in P_1 must satisfy the equation $U_1 + 2U_2 + U_3 = 0$. And we can also tell, by looking at this equation and reversing the argument, that any vector $[U_1, U_2, U_3]$ whose coordinates satisfy this equation must be a vector that is orthogonal to the vector $[1, 2, 1]$ and therefore must lie in the plane P_1.

Ah ha! If we now generalize from the vector $V_1 = [1, 2, 1]$ to an arbitrary vector $[a, b, c]$, we can repeat the whole argument and arrive at the general conclusion that any vector $[U_1, U_2, U_3]$ satisfying the equation $aU_1 + bU_2 + cU_3 = 0$ must lie in the plane orthogonal to the vector $[a, b, c]$. Therefore, an equation such as this constrains the vectors to lie in a plane. Because every plane in three-space must be orthogonal to some vector we see that this equation gives the general form of the equation for any plane in three-space.

What have we shown so far? We have shown that stating that a vector satisfies an equation such as $aU_1 + bU_2 + cU_3 = 0$ restricts that vector to lying in a particular subspace of three-space, namely, a plane.

*3.25.2.1 Linear homogeneous equations. What kind of an equation is this? We call it a **linear homogeneous equation** in U_1, U_2, and U_3. It is <u>linear</u> because the left-hand side is a linear combination of the U's and it is <u>homogeneous</u> because the right hand side of the equation is zero.

*3.25.3 One equation costs one dimension. Writing one equation (we will just say equation from now on but we will mean one linear homogeneous equation) involving the coordinates of an arbitrary vector in three-space results in constraining that vector to lie in a plane. It can be <u>any</u> vector in that plane, so it still retains some of its initial arbitrariness or generality, but some is lost. It now has to reside in a plane that has one dimension less than the three-dimensional space the vector was formerly free to be in. If writing one such equation results in constraining the vector to a space of one less dimension, should we suppose that writing two such equations will result in constraint to a space having two less dimensions than the space the vector began with?

*3.25.4 Two independent equations constrain a vector in 3-space to lie in a one-dimensional subspace of 3-space, that is, on a line. Suppose we start with an arbitrary vector $\mathbf{V} = [V_1, V_2, V_3]$ and require as the first constraint that $V_1 + 2V_2 + V_3 = 0$ and as the second constraint that $2V_1 + V_2 + V_3 = 0$. On the basis of the previous discussion we realize that we have required that $\mathbf{V}$ lie in two planes: the plane orthogonal to [1, 2, 1] and the plane orthogonal to [2, 1, 1]. The vector $\mathbf{V}$ must therefore lie in the intersection of these two planes (geometrically and also set-theoretically, considering the intersection of the two planes as the set of all vectors in both planes). Now we know that two planes intersect in a line if they intersect at all. What is the line that these two planes intersect in? We can find it by finding what the two constraining equations say when considered simultaneously, that is, taken together. By solving for V_3 in the second equation and substituting this solution for V_3 in the first equation we obtain $-V_1 + V_2 = 0$, which means that $V_1 = V_2$. Knowing this it is also now clear from both equations that $V_3 = -3V_1$. Therefore, these two equations taken together require that the vector $\mathbf{V}$ be of the form $[V_1, V_1, -3V_1]$ which is a scalar multiple of the vector [1, 1, -3]. We see then that all such vectors must lie on the line passing through the origin and the point (1, 1, -3). By writing two equations we reduced the dimensionality of the space in which the vector $\mathbf{V}$ could lie from three dimensions to one dimension.

There is a catch, however. Suppose we had written as the two equations $V_1 + 2V_2 + V_3 = 0$ and $2V_1 + 4V_2 + 2V_3 = 0$. Since a 2 can be divided out of the second equation, we see that these two equations state the same fact, and so place only one equation's worth of constraint on $\mathbf{V}$. When two equations state the same fact, we say they are **dependent**. When they state two different facts, we say they are **independent**. In general, when we have N equations but they do not state N different facts, we say the equations are dependent. Otherwise they are independent.

*3.25.4.1 Determining the independence or dependence of equations. How can we tell if N equations are dependent? Let us look at two examples. First consider the two equations $V_1 + 2V_2 + V_3 = 0$ and $2V_1 + 4V_2 + 2V_3 = 0$. The first equation says $\mathbf{V}$ is orthogonal to [1, 2, 1] and the second says $\mathbf{V}$ is orthogonal to [2, 4, 2], which is just a scalar multiple of [1, 2, 1]. If $\mathbf{V}$ is orthogonal to [1, 2, 1] it must be orthogonal to all scalar multiples of it, and therefore the second equation provides no additional information beyond that provided by the first equation. Now consider another case. Suppose a set of equations tells us that a vector $\mathbf{V}$ is orthogonal to a collection of vectors $\mathbf{A} = [a_1, a_2, a_3]$, $\mathbf{B} = [b_1, b_2, b_3]$, and $\mathbf{C} = [c_1, c_2, c_3]$. This set of equations would be

$$a_1V_1 + a_2V_2 + a_3V_3 = 0$$
$$b_1V_1 + b_2V_2 + b_3V_3 = 0$$

$$c_1V_1 + c_2V_2 + c_3V_3 = 0 \ .$$

If **C** were a linear combination of **A** and **B**, then if **A** and **B** are orthogonal to **V**, **V** would have to be orthogonal to **C** since **C** would lie in the plane containing all and only those vectors orthogonal to **V**. Thus the third equation would provide no information beyond that provided by the first two equations. We begin to see that the independence of the equations rests on the independence of the vectors of coefficients of the coordinates of **V** in the equations. The three equations are independent if the vectors **A**, **B**, and **C** are independent. And they are independent, we recall, if no one of them can be expressed as a linear combination of the others.

*3.25.5 Each of a set of independent linear homogeneous equations reduces by one dimension the dimensionality of the space that a vector is free to lie in. So, what is the upshot of all this? What we have seen, for three-space, is that independent linear homogeneous equations in the coordinates of an arbitrary vector constrain that vector to lie in a space that is reduced in dimensionality by the number of equations. One equation constrains the vector to a plane. Two constrain it to a line. And three independent equations in the three unknown coordinates of the vector can be solved for the coordinates, narrowing the space in which the vector must lie to a specific point (having zero dimensions) and therefore specifying all three coordinates of the vector exactly.

*3.25.6 The generalization to N-space. These results generalize to N-space. An arbitrary N-dimensional vector $V = [V_1, V_2, ..., V_N]$ will be constrained to an $(N - 1)$-dimensional **hyperplane** by one independent equation, constrained to an $(N - 2)$-dimensional hyperplane by two independent equations, ..., constrained to a plane by $N - 2$ independent equations, and constrained to a line by $N - 1$ independent equations. A set of N independent equations completely determines the vector, therefore locating it at a particular point, and so reducing the space it is free to lie in to a 0-dimensional point. (Don't let the word "hyperplane" cause your mind to go into a hypertailspin. We have the word "line" to refer to a one-dimensional space, and we have the word "plane" to refer to a two-dimensional space. But when we get to spaces of arbitrary numbers of dimensions, large than two, we need a generic term. We use the words "hyperplane" or "hyperspace" in such situations.)

*3.25.7 The N - 1 equations constraining the mean vector. We recall that the mean vector $M = [M, M, ..., M]$ is constrained to lie on the mean line, a one-dimensional subspace of the N-dimensional data space. We can now anticipate that there must be $N - 1$ linear homogeneous equations in the coordinates of the mean vector that produce this constraint. We can also recall that the mean line was characterized as the locus of all points in N-space such that all the coordinates are equal. That is, let $V = [V_1, V_2, ..., V_N]$ be a vector in N-space. Then if V is to lie on the mean line, it must be that $V_1 = V_2 = ... = V_N$. This is actually quite a few equations lumped into one expression. When we spell out these equations one at a time as linear homogeneous equations, we find that they say that $V_1 - V_2 = 0$, $V_2 - V_3 = 0$, ..., $V_{N-1} - V_N = 0$. There are N - 1 equations. These equations are independent linear homogeneous equations in the V_i's and are the equations that constrain the vector to lie on the mean line, a one-dimensional subspace of the N-dimensional data space.

*3.25.8 The one equation constraining the error-estimates vector. We also recall that the vector D containing the error estimates $Y_1 - M$, $Y_2 - M$, ..., $Y_N - M$ was constrained to lie in an (N - 1)-dimensional subspace of the data space. Why was this? We can now say that it was because we required D to be orthogonal to M (because D was the perpendicular we dropped so its length would be minimal), and requiring D to be orthogonal to M was equivalent to requiring that D be a vector $[d_1, d_2, ..., d_N]$ such that $D \cdot M = 0$, which in turn meant that $d_1 M + d_2 M + ... + d_N M = 0$, which is one linear homogeneous equation in the d_i's and therefore constrains D to an (N - 1)-dimensional subspace.

*3.25.9 The N - 2 equations constraining the vector of group effects in the two groups design. Let's look at one more example. Recall in Chapter 2 we had the model equation $Y_{ij} = \mu + \alpha_i + e_{ij}$ for the experiment with two groups. With N_1 scores in the first group and N_2 scores in the second group, we have a data vector with $N = N_1 + N_2$ scores as the elements. In vector notation the model equation may be written as $Y = \mu + \alpha + e$ A picture of the geometric relations of the vectors is shown in Figure 3.13. Now consider the vector of estimated group effects $[A_1, A_1, ..., A_1, A_2, A_2, ..., A_2]$ for the test involving these samples from two populations. If we consider the constraints imposed on an arbitrary vector $[V_1, V_2, ..., V_N]$ in order for it to be of the form $[A_1, A_1, ..., A_1, A_2, A_2, ..., A_2]$ we find that this vector is constrained to lie on a line. Why? Because the equality of the first N_1 A_1's takes $N_1 - 1$ equations of the form $V_1 - V_2 = 0$, $V_2 - V_3 = 0$, and so forth. The equality of the last N_2 A_2's similarly takes $N_2 - 1$ equations. That makes $N_1 - 1 + N_2 - 1 = N - 2$ equations. And there is also the equation $\Sigma_i N_i A_i = 0$, which when written $A_1 + A_1 + ... + A_1 + A_2 + ... A_2 = 0$ can be seen to be a linear homogeneous equation in the A_i's. That makes $(N - 2) + 1 = N - 1$ equations, leaving only one dimension, a line, for the vector of group effects to lie in. Later we will see that for a design with I groups the vector of group effects always lies in an (I - 1)-dimensional space.

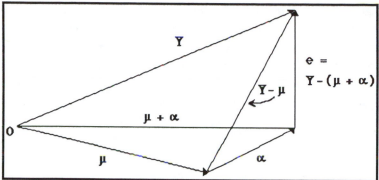

Figure 3.13. The geometric relations of the vectors $Y = [Y_{1,1}, Y_{1,2}, ..., Y_{1,N1}, Y_{2,1}, Y_{2,2}, ..., Y_{2,N2}]$, $\mu = [\mu, \mu, ..., \mu]$, $a = [\alpha_1, \alpha_1, ..., \alpha_1, \alpha_2, \alpha_2, ..., \alpha_2]$, and $e = Y - \mu - \alpha$.

*3.25.10 Summary. What we have seen is that vectors are constrained, by various sets of equations, to lie in certain subspaces of the whole space. The dimensionality of such a subspace equals the dimensionality of the whole space minus the number of independent equations that have been stated.

3.25.11 Degrees of freedom are the dimensionalities of subspaces. This applies to the geometric representation of the analysis of variance in the following way. The vectors of parameters and the error vector are constrained to lie in certain subspaces determined by the model equation. The assumptions embedded in the model equation can be expressed as independent linear homogenous equations. **The dimensionality of the subspace that a parameter vector or error vector must lie in is nothing other than the degrees of freedom that go with the sum of squares that is the squared length of that parameter vector or error vector.**

If, in your introductory statistics course, you got to the analysis of variance of a one-factor design, you may have been told that you started with one degree of freedom for each score. Each score was initially free to be any value. Then one degree of freedom was "lost" when the general mean was calculated, leaving N - 1 degrees of freedom. That is, if you knew N - 1 of the scores and you knew the general mean, then the Nth score was determined. Then you were told that I - 1 additional degrees of freedom were "lost" when the Group means were calculated. Only I - 1 even though there were I Groups because, knowing the general mean meant that you didn't have to calculate the last mean since it was determined by knowledge of the first I - 1 means together with the general mean. Then in a step of blind faith, you were asked to associate these different degrees of freedom with quantities called sums of squares. **We now know that the association of a degrees of freedom value with a sum of squares is mediated by their common association with a**

vector. The degrees of freedom give the dimensionality of the space that the vector can lie in and the sum of squares gives that vector's squared length.

As we shall see later, this very close correspondence between the model equation, the parameter and error vectors, the degrees of freedom and the sums of squares will turn out to be remarkably useful to us. We will find that with the use of a very small number of simple rules, we will be able to use the model equation to generate not only the sources for the analysis of variance, but the degrees of freedom and the computational formulas for the sums of squares.

3.26 An F-ratio can be interpreted geometrically as the ratio of two average squared vector lengths. In Section 3.21 we indicated that figure 3.9(b) which shows the right triangle formed by **Y**, **M**, and **D**, would also shed some light on the F-test. The F-ratio of interest to us is that given in equation [2.5], $F = (NM^2/1)/[\Sigma_i(Y_i - M)^2/(N - 1)]$, which we can now rewrite as

$$F = (\mathbf{M \cdot M}/1)/[\mathbf{D \cdot D}/(N - 1)] .$$

The F-ratio, as a ratio of mean squares, can be thought of as the ratio of two average squared vector lengths that have the same expected value when the null hypothesis is true and that contraindicate the null hypothesis when the two average squared lengths appear too different from each other.

Because the squared length of the data vector divided by the variance is a chi-square variable with N degrees of freedom, its expected value is its degrees of freedom, N, as we indicated in Section 2.12.1. That is,

$$E(\Sigma_i Y_i^2/\sigma^2) = N. \tag{3.1}$$

But this is equivalent to saying that the expected value of the average squared Y score is the variance, since we can rewrite [3.1] in the equivalent form

$$E(\Sigma_i Y_i^2/N) = \sigma^2 \tag{3.2}$$

just by algebraic manipulation. This is true only when $\mu = 0$, of course. As we know from [2.6], the expected value of the square of a random variable is the variance of that variable plus the square of the variable's mean. Since the variable's mean is zero in this case, the expected value of the square of the variable Y is just its variance, which is in agreement with [3.2]. We can also manipulate [3.1] one more time to obtain

$$E(\Sigma_i Y_i^2) = N\sigma^2. \qquad\qquad [3.3]$$

We see from [3.3] that the expected squared length of the data vector is N times the variance and that each of the Y_i-squared has σ^2 as its expected value. It is perfectly appropriate to think of the expected squared length of the data vector as being composed of N pieces, each of which is σ^2.

The data vector then is a vector lying in an N-dimensional space, composed of N coordinates, each of which contributes a piece, σ^2, to the expected squared length of the data vector. We can say that the expected squared length of the data vector per dimension is σ^2.

Now we also know that $Y = M + D$. And we know that M is constrained to lie in a one-dimensional subspace of the N-dimensional data space, the mean line, and D is constrained to lie in the (N - 1)-dimensional subspace orthogonal to the mean line. Furthermore we know that the expected value of the squared length of the mean vector is σ^2, and we know that the expected value of the squared length of the deviations vector, D, is $(N - 1)\sigma^2$. Therefore, we can think of the numerator of the F-ratio, $NM^2/1$, as a measure of the squared length of the mean vector per dimension of the space it must lie in, and the denominator of the F-ratio, $D \cdot D/(N - 1)$, as a measure of the squared length of the deviations vector per dimension of the space it must lie in.

The F-ratio therefore can be thought of as comparing the squared length of the mean vector per dimension of the subspace it must lie in with the squared length of the deviations vector per dimension of the subspace it must lie in.

The squared length of a vector per dimension of the subspace it must lie in can be thought of as a kind of average. It is an average squared length, and we will refer to it as a mean squared length or, following customary usage, as a **mean square**. So, we will say that the mean square for the mean is $NM^2/1$, and the mean square for error is $D \cdot D/(N-1)$.

We see then that the F-ratio can be thought of as a comparison of the mean-squared length of the mean vector per dimension with the mean-squared length of the deviations vector per dimension. Both these mean-squared lengths have σ^2 as their expected values under the null hypothesis. When the numerator mean square exceeds the denominator mean square greatly, we argue that the discrepancy is too unlikely if the null hypothesis were true, and so we infer the null hypothesis is false.

Geometrically, what we are doing is comparing the squared lengths of two vectors after having divided those squared lengths by the dimensionality of the subspaces to which the vectors are respectively constrained to lie in. Thus **the F-ratio, as a ratio of mean squares, is the ratio of two average squared vector lengths that have the same expected value when the null hypothesis is true.** They contraindicate the null hypothesis when the two average squared lengths appear too different from each other and tend to confirm the null hypothesis when their average squared lengths are about the same.

*3.24.1.1 Any two noncollinear vectors define a plane.   Any two noncollinear vectors (vectors that do not lie in the same line; vectors that are not a scalar multiple of one another) define a plane just as any two noncollinear lines do. Consider Figure 3.14 in which two vectors **T** and **U** are shown and the triangle whose vertices are $(0, 0, 0)$, (t_1, t_2, t_3), and (u_1, u_2, u_3) lies in and displays a portion of that plane defined by the two vectors **T** and **U**.

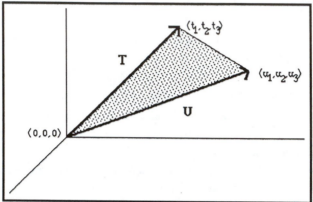

Figure 3.14. The triangle formed by the points $(0, 0, 0)$, (t_1, t_2, t_3), and (u_1, u_2, u_3) lies in and displays a part of the plane defined by the noncollinear vectors **T** and **U**.

*3.24.1.2 Any linear combination of two vectors lies in the plane defined by those two vectors.   A linear combination of the two vectors **T** and **U** is any vector **B** $= a\mathbf{T} + b\mathbf{U}$. Clearly, any linear combination of **T** and **U** will lie in the plane defined by **T** and **U**. This is seen in Figure 3.15, which shows **T**, **U**, $a\mathbf{T}$, $b\mathbf{U}$, and $a\mathbf{T} + b\mathbf{U}$. The vector $a\mathbf{T}$ is a vector in the same direction as **T** only perhaps longer (if $a > 1$) or shorter (if $a < 1$). The same is true for $b\mathbf{U}$ with respect to **U**. The sum of $a\mathbf{T}$ and $b\mathbf{U}$ is obtained by sliding $b\mathbf{U}$ until it is tail to head with $a\mathbf{T}$ while keeping $b\mathbf{U}$ oriented in the same direction. Since $b\mathbf{U}$ has the same direction as **U**, as we slide $b\mathbf{U}$ along $a\mathbf{T}$, it will remain in the plane defined by **U** and **T**. Thus we have that any linear combination of two vectors lies in the same plane as those two vectors.

*3.24.1.3 The proof that all vectors orthogonal to M lie in the same plane.   Now consider two vectors orthogonal to the vector $\mathbf{M} = [M, M, M]$. Call them $\mathbf{T} = [t_1, t_2, t_3]$ and $\mathbf{U} = [u_1, u_2, u_3]$. Then, by the definition of orthogonality, $\mathbf{T} \cdot \mathbf{M} = 0$ and

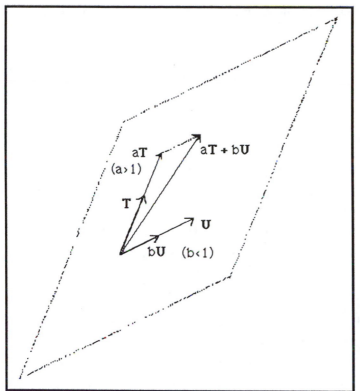

Figure 3.15. The vector aT + bU, which is any linear combination of the vectors **T** and **U**, lies in the same plane as the vectors **T** and **U** do.

U·M = 0, and therefore $\Sigma_i t_i M = 0$ so $\Sigma_i t_i = 0$ and $\Sigma_i u_i M = 0$ so $\Sigma_i u_i = 0$. (We don't have to consider the case of M = 0 since if M = 0, every vector is orthogonal to **M**.) If $\Sigma_i t_i = 0$, we can write **T** = $[t_1, t_2, -(t_1+t_2)]$ and similarly we can write **U** = $[u_1, u_2, -(u_1+u_2)]$. Now consider another vector **V**, also orthogonal to **M**. We want to show that **V** must lie in the plane defined by **T** and **U**. We can write **V** = $[v_1, v_2, -(v_1+v_2)]$ by the same argument as for **T** and **U**. Now we know that **V** is in the plane of **T** and **U** if **V** = a**T** + b**U**. This requires that we solve the systems of equations

$$at_1 + bu_1 = v_1$$
$$at_2 + bu_2 = v_2$$
$$-a(t_1 + t_2) -b(u_1 + u_2) = -(v_1 + v_2)$$

for a and b. Since two of these three equations are independent, we know that we can solve for a and b and therefore that **V** is a linear combination of **T** and **U** and so is in their plane.

3.24.4.1 The value of a 2 x 2 determinant. A 2 x 2 (two rows and two columns) determinant

$$\begin{vmatrix} t_1 & u_1 \\ t_2 & u_2 \end{vmatrix}$$

has the value $t_1 u_2 - t_2 u_1$.

3.24.4.2 The value of N x N determinants. A determinant is always a single numerical value that is characteristic of a given matrix. The value of a 3 x 3 (N x N) determinant can be found as a linear combination of 2 x 2 [(N - 1) x (N - 1)] determinants.

To spell this out in detail we need to speak in terms of the following mathematical concepts:

1.   a **matrix**
2.   a **square matrix**
3.   a **submatrix**
4.   a **minor**, and
5.   a **cofactor** of an element in a matrix.

A **matrix** is a rectangular array of numbers of the form

$$A = \begin{matrix} a_{11} & a_{12} & \cdots & a_{1n} \\ a_{21} & a_{22} & \cdots & a_{2n} \\ \cdots & \cdots & \cdots & \cdots \\ a_{m1} & a_{m2} & \cdots & a_{mn} \end{matrix}$$

with m rows and n columns.

We say that **A** is an m x n matrix ("m by n matrix") and sometimes denote this by writing A_{mxn}.

The rows of **A** are sometimes referred to as the **row vectors of A** and the columns as the **column vectors of A**.

A **square matrix** is a matrix in which the number of rows equals the number of columns, that is, m = n.

A **submatrix** of **A** is obtained by deleting one or more rows and/or columns from **A**. The submatrix obtained by deleting the ith row and jth column of the matrix **A** will be denoted by A_{ij}.

The **minor** of the element a_{ij} in **A** is the determinant $|A_{ij}|$, and the **cofactor** of the element a_{ij} is the signed minor $(-1)^{(i+j)}|A_{ij}|$.

The **determinant** of the matrix **A** is then

$|A| = \Sigma_i(-1)^{(i+j)}a_{ij}|A_{ij}|$ for any particular j   or

$\Sigma_j(-1)^{(i+j)}a_{ij}|A_{ij}|$ for any particular i.

For example, if $A_{3\times3} =$

$$\begin{vmatrix} 1 & 2 & 3 \\ 2 & 1 & 0 \\ 3 & 1 & 1 \end{vmatrix}$$

then, letting i = 1, $|A| = \Sigma_j(-1)^{(i+j)}a_{1j}|A_{1j}|$ =

$$1\begin{vmatrix} 1 & 0 \\ 1 & 1 \end{vmatrix} - 2\begin{vmatrix} 2 & 0 \\ 3 & 1 \end{vmatrix} + 3\begin{vmatrix} 2 & 1 \\ 3 & 1 \end{vmatrix}$$

= 1(1) - 2(2) + 3(2-3) = -6, or letting j = 2, say, $|A| = \Sigma_i(-1)^{(i+j)}a_{i2}|A_{i2}|$ =

$$-2\begin{vmatrix} 2 & 0 \\ 3 & 1 \end{vmatrix} + 1\begin{vmatrix} 1 & 3 \\ 3 & 1 \end{vmatrix} - 1\begin{vmatrix} 1 & 3 \\ 2 & 0 \end{vmatrix}$$

= -2(2) +1(1-9) - 1(-6) = -6.

Exercises

1. Add the two vectors **X** = [1, 3, 5] and **Y** = [2, 2, 1].
2. Add the two vectors **X** = [1, 3, 5, 7, 9] and **Y** = [2, 2, 1, 1, 1].
3. Explain why addition of vectors is commutative and associative in the light of the fact that ordinary addition of numbers is commutative and associative.
4. Write the additive inverse of **X** = [1, 3, 5]. Show that the additive inverse of the additive inverse of **X** is itself **X**.
5. Write the additive inverse of **X** = [2, 4, -5, 6, -1]. Show that the additive inverse of the additive inverse of **X** is itself **X**.
6. If **Y** is the additive inverse of **X**, what does **X+Y** equal?
7. Let **X** = [1, 4, 2], **Y** = [2, 3, 5], k_1 = 2, and k_2 = 3. Find:
       (a) $k_1\mathbf{X} + k_2\mathbf{Y}$ (c) $(-k_1k_2)\mathbf{X} + k_2\mathbf{Y}$

     (b) $k_1X - k_2Y$ (d) $k_1(X + Y)$ and $k_1X + k_1Y$

8. Let $X = [2, -3, 5, 1, -4]$, $Y = [0, 1, 5, -4, -1]$, $k_1 = 2$, and $k_2 = 3$. Find:

     (a) $k_1X + k_2Y$ (c) $(-k_1 k_2)X + k_2Y$

     (b) $k_1X - k_2Y$ (d) $k_1(X + Y)$ and $k_1X + k_1Y$

9. Find the squared length of the vector $Y = [1, 3, 5]$.

10. Find the squared length of the vector $M = [3, 3, 3]$.

11. Find the squared length of the vector $Y - M$.

12. Note that the squared length of M plus the squared length of $Y - M$ is equal to the squared length of Y. Do you think this will be true for any values of the coordinates of M?

13. Find the squared length of the vector $Y = [2, 3, 7, 4, -1]$.

14. Find the squared length of the vector $M = [3, 3, 3, 3, 3]$.

15. Find the squared length of the vector $Y - M$.

16. Compare the results of exercises 13, 14, and 15 to your answer to the second part of exercises 12. Now try $M = [2, 2, 2, 2, 2]$.

17. Let $Y = [1, 3, 5]$ and $M = [3, 3, 3]$. Find the cosine of the angle between M and $Y - M$.

18. Let $Y = [2, 1, 9, 4]$ and $M = [4, 4, 4, 4]$. Find the cosine of the angle between M and $Y - M$.

19. What vector in three-dimensional space is orthogonal to every other vector in that space?

20. What vector in N-space is orthogonal to every vector in N-space?

21. Write a vector in three-dimensional space that is orthogonal to the vector $[1, 1, 1]$.

22. Explain in your own words why, from a geometric perspective, the sample mean is commonsensibly the best estimate of the population mean.

23. What does the fact that the sum of the squared deviations of a set of scores from their mean is less than the sum of the squared deviations of a set of scores from any other number have to do with using the sample mean as the estimate of the population mean?

24. A sample of two scores consisted of the values 4 and 6. Find M and D, and show that they are orthogonal.

25. Show that in exercise 24 the vector D lies on the line passing through $(0, 0)$ and $(1, -1)$.

26. Explain in your own words why the degrees of freedom for total, mean, and error are 2, 1, and 1 with a sample consisting of two scores.

27. What would have to be true about the elements of the vector $D = [d_1, d_2, ..., d_N]$ so that it would necessarily be true that $D \cdot M = 0$?

28. State in your own words the relationship between the fact that the sum of the deviations of a set of scores from their own mean equals zero and the right triangle formed by Y, M, and D.

29. Let $Y_i = \mu + e_i$. Assume the e_i are independent and each is $N(0, \sigma^2)$. Show that:

     (a) $Var(Y_i) = \sigma^2$;

(b) $E(NM^2) = \sigma^2 + N\mu^2$;

(c) $E[\Sigma(Y_i - M)^2] = \sigma^2(N-1)$.

30. Let $Y_{ij} = \mu + \alpha_i + e_{ij}$. Assume the e_{ij} are independently $N(0, \sigma^2)$ and that $\Sigma_i N_i \alpha_1 = 0$. Show that $VAR(Y_{ij}) = E[Y_{ij} - E(Y_{ij})]^2 = \sigma^2 + \Sigma_i N_i \alpha_i^2 / N$.

31. Show that $E[\Sigma_i \Sigma_j (M_i - M)^2] = (I - 1)\sigma^2 + \Sigma_i N_i \alpha_i^2$.

32. Show that $E[\Sigma_i \Sigma_j (Y_{ij} - M_i)^2 / (N-2)] = \sigma^2$.

33. Show that $VAR(\alpha_i) = \Sigma_i (N_i \alpha_i^2) / N$.

34. Let $Y_{ij} = \mu + \alpha_i + e_{ij}$ and let N_1 and N_2 be the two sample sizes with $N_1 + N_2 = N$.

(a) How many equations constrain the location of the vector $\mu = [\mu, \mu, ..., \mu]$? Write those equations.

(b) How many equations constrain the location of the vector $\alpha = [\alpha_1, \alpha_1, ..., \alpha_1, \alpha_2, \alpha_2, ..., \alpha_2]$? Write them.

(c) How many equations constrain the location of the vector $D = [Y_{11} - \mu - \alpha_1, Y_{12} - \mu - \alpha_1, ..., Y_{1N1} - \mu - \alpha_1, Y_{21} - \mu - \alpha_1, Y_{22} - \mu - \alpha_1, ..., Y_{2N2} - \mu - \alpha_1]$? Write them.

35. Using the vectors μ, α, and e in exercise 6, and the rules of vector addition, show that $Y =$

$[Y_{11}, Y_{12}, ..., Y_{1N1}, Y_{21}, Y_{22}, ..., Y_{2N2}]$ is equal to $\mu + \alpha + e$.

36. Show that $Y \cdot Y = \mu \cdot \mu + \alpha \cdot \alpha + e \cdot e$.

37. Draw the vectors Y, μ, α, and e associated with the model in exercise 34 and indicate the dimensionalities of the subspaces to which each of these vectors is constrained.

38. Show that α is orthogonal to μ and that e is orthogonal to $\mu + \alpha$.

39. If $e \cdot e = 0$, what must be true about all the scores in Group 1 and all the scores in Group 2?

40. With a sample of N scores, what is the dimensionality of the space containing each of the following vectors:

(a) Y; (b) M; (c) D; (d) $Y - M$; (e) $M + D$?

41. Let A be a matrix the rows of which are $A_1 = [1, 2, 2, 1]$, $A_2 = [2, 0, -2, 1]$, $A_3 = [1, 3, 5, 1]$, and $A_4 = [4, 3, 2, 1]$. Find the determinant of A, and determine whether the four vectors A_1, A_2, A_3, and A_4 are linearly independent.

42. Write an expression showing the form of any vector in the plane defined by $A_1 = [1, 2, 2, 1]$ and $A_2 = [2, 0, -2, 1]$.

43. State in your own words a geometric interpretation of a sum of squares divided by its degrees of freedom.

44. State in your own words a geometric interpretation of an F-ratio.

45. In the case of a sample of three scores, if two vectors span the space in which D lies, how do we know that they are linearly independent?

46. In the case of a sample of N scores, if N - 1 vectors span the space in which **D** lies, how do we know that they are linearly independent? Suppose a vector in which each element is equal to 1 were added to this collection of N - 1 linearly independent vectors. Would the new collection of N vectors so formed consist of N linearly independent vectors? How do you know?

47. Draw the vectors **Y**, **M**, and **D** for a sample of more than 3 scores. Just omit the axes, and draw the vectors in their appropriate relations to each other, indicating which vectors form a right angle. The result should look like Figure 3.9 or 3.11 without the axes.

48. Write an equation constraining a vector to lie in the plane orthgonal to the vector whose N elements are each the mean of a sample of N scores.

Supplementary Reading

Box, G. E. P., Hunter, W. G., & Hunter, J. S. (1978) *Statistics for experimenters.*
        New York: John Wiley. Chapters 6 and 7.
Saville, D. J. & Wood, G. R. (1986) A method for teaching statistics using
        N-dimensional geometry. *The American Statistician*, 40, 205-214.

4

Two-Factor Designs
and Three-Factor Designs

4.1. Purpose. The purpose of this chapter is to introduce the additional features of the analysis of variance that arise when more than one qualitative independent variable is manipulated. To do this we will consider an experiment with two independent variables. That will introduce us to the concept of **interaction effects**. Then we consider an experiment with three variables. That will introduce **higher-order interaction effects**. Once we see how a two-variable model and a three-variable model work, it will be easy to generalize the whole situation to an arbitrary number of independent variables.

4.2 Factors and their levels. In the analysis of variance the term **factor** denotes an independent variable, two or more values of which are used as treatments of the experimental subjects or materials, or methods of selection of the subjects, and so on. The different values of a factor are called the **levels** of that factor. Thus, for example, if three groups of subjects,

3-year-olds, 5-year-olds and 7-year-olds, served as subjects in an experimental study of moral development, the *factor* would be Age and the three *levels* of that factor would be 3 years, 5 years, and 7 years. Similarly, in our experiment on attitude change due to film presentations on waste disposal, the factor was Film, and the two levels were Film 1 and Film 2.

It is common to represent experimental designs by diagrams showing the factors and their levels. Table 4.1 shows the form of a one-factor design with the three levels of age for the study of moral development. The model equation for the jth score in Level i of the design would be $Y_{ij} = \mu + \alpha_i + e_{ij}$. Our analysis of variance for this single-factor design is apparent from what we have seen in Chapters 2 and 3. We would compare MS_{Groups} to MS_{error}, where if there are I levels and J scores per level, $MS_{Groups} = \Sigma_i \Sigma_j (M_i - M)^2/(I - 1)$ and $MS_{error} = \Sigma_i \Sigma_j (Y_{ij} - M_i)^2/(IJ - I)$. The comparison would, of course, be by calculating the F-ratio MS_{Groups}/MS_{error}. More will be said later about the details of this. For now we

TABLE 4.1 A ONE-FACTOR DESIGN WITH THE LEVELS BEING THREE AGES

3 yr. 5 yr. 7 yr.

TABLE 4.2   A DISPLAY REPRESENTING A TWO-FACTOR EXPERIMENTAL DESIGN, THE ROW FACTOR (COLLEGE CLASS) HAVING TWO LEVELS AND THE COLUMN FACTOR (ADJECTIVE SEQUENCE) HAVING SIX LEVELS

College Class	Adjective Sequence					
	1	2	3	4	5	6
Freshmen						
Seniors						

want to consider more complex designs.

It is easy to imagine wanting to manipulate more than one variable in an experimental design. In an experiment designed to study the effect of order of stimulus presentation, we might present the three adjectives "sincere," "intelligent," and "mature" to different subjects, in the six possible orders of presentation. Each subject would receive only one of the six orders of presentations, the order for each subject being decided randomly. We then might ask each subject to judge some attribute of a person characterized by the three adjectives, say the "likeableness" of such a person. The factor is then Order of Presentation and its six levels are the six possible orders of the three adjectives: (1) serious-intelligent-mature; (2) serious-mature-intelligent; (3) intelligent-serious-mature; (4) intelligent-mature-serious; (5) mature-serious-intelligent; and (6) mature-intelligent- serious. If we decide to study freshmen and seniors as separate groups of subjects, each of whom receives one of the six possible orders of presentation, then College Class would also be a factor in our experiment, with the two levels Freshmen and Seniors. Our experiment would now be said to be a two-factor design, one factor having two levels and the other having six levels. Such a design is referred to as a "2-by-6 factorial design" or "2 x 6 factorial design."

We represent our experimental design by the display in Table 4.2 We describe such a display as consisting of rows of cells and columns of cells. Each of the two rows has 6 cells and each of the six columns has 2 cells. The entire display has 12 cells. Each of the scores that will be presented in a given cell in this design will represent a rating obtained from one student who is in the College Class represented by the row in which the cell occurs and who received the particular Order of Presentation represented by the column in which that cell occurs. Here we see that each of the six levels of the Order of Presentation occurs with each level of College Class. When each level of one factor combines with each level of the other factor in a two-factor design, we say the two factors are **completely crossed**. In Chapter 5 we explore experimental designs in which the factors are not always competely crossed.

4.3 A model equation for a two-factor design. The model equation for our two-factor design will depend on our hypotheses. The most common approach to modeling a two-factor design is to test three major hypotheses. The first is the null hypothesis that there is no Order of Presentation effect. The second is that there is no effect due to College Class. And the third is that there is no effect due to the particular combination of level of College Class with level of Order of Presentation. "No Order of Presentation effect" means that except for the effects of error, the mean value of the likeableness score will be the same for every different order in which the three adjectives are presented. Similarly, "no effect due to College Class" means that except for error, the Freshmen will give the same likeableness ratings as the Seniors, on the average. The third hypothesis, no effect due to the particular combination of levels of the two factors, means that but for error, the average likeableness score in a particular cell in Table 4.1, that is, for a particular Order-Class combination, will be due only to the effect of the Order level and the effect of the Class level as they combine in an additive way.

The model equation for the design under discussion will be

$$Y_{ijk} = \mu + C_i + O_j + CO_{ij} + e_{ijk} \qquad [4.1]$$

where μ, C_i, O_j, and CO_{ij} are the parameters of the model. (We will usually use the more descriptive English letter model terms rather than Greek letters in stating models with more than one factor so that it will be obvious which term goes with which factor.) This equation says that the likeableness score, Y_{ijk}, the score for the kth person to receive Class level i in combination with Order level j, is the sum of a general mean, μ, an effect due to Class, C_i, an effect due to Order, O_j, an effect due to the specific Class-Order combination, CO_{ij}, and an error effect, e_{ijk}, which is a normally distributed error effect with a mean of zero and a variance σ^2. (Note that CO_{ij} is not a product of C and O but is a single term giving the interaction effect for cell$_{ij}$ of the design.)

4.3.1 Effects are deviations. The complete statement of the model equation in [4.1] requires that we include the **"side conditions"** that

$$\Sigma_i C_i = \Sigma_j O_j = 0, \qquad [4.2]$$

$$\Sigma_j CO_{ij} = 0 \text{ for each i}, \qquad [4.3]$$

and

$\Sigma_i CO_{ij} = 0$ for each j. [4.4]

These side conditions parallel our requiring that $\Sigma_i N_i \alpha_i = 0$ in the one-factor design. The N's do not occur in [4.2-4.4] because we are assuming here and throughout this chapter and the next that the same number of scores occurs in each cell of the design and therefore the N_i's, N_j's, and N_{ij}'s are constants and cancel out of the side condition equations.

If the difference $(\mu_{i..} - \mu)$ is zero, we say there is no Row i effect.

Now the general mean must by definition be the average of all of the scores in all of the rows. Therefore the general mean must be the average of all of the row means. From this it follows that the average of all of the Row effects must be zero since it is the average of the deviations of a set of values, the $\mu_{i..}$'s, from their own mean, μ. Since the average of the row effects is zero, the sum of the row effects must be zero. Thus, by defining the Row effects as the deviations of the Row means from the general mean, we have created a model in which the Row effects must sum to zero. This same requirement applies to the Column effects in a completely parallel way.

The interaction effects can also be expressed as differences or deviations. To say that there is an interaction effect characterizing the scores in the cell lying in Row i and in Column j is to say that the true cell mean, $\mu_{ij.}$, is different from the sum of three quantities: the general mean, the effect of Row i, and the effect of Column j. That is, $\mu_{ij.}$ differs from $\mu + (\mu_{i..} - \mu) + (\mu_{.j.} - \mu)$. Putting it as a difference or deviation, the interaction effect is

$\mu_{ij.} - [\mu + (\mu_{i..} - \mu) + (\mu_{.j.} - \mu)]$

which, of course, equals

$\mu_{ij.} - \mu_{i..} - \mu_{.j.} + \mu.$

We say that the interaction effect RC_{ij} for the cell in Row i and in Column j, as for example the effect CO_{ij} in [4.1], is

$$RC_{ij} = \mu_{ij.} - \mu_{i..} - \mu_{.j.} + \mu.$$ [4.5]

Having expressed RC_{ij} as in [4.5] we can see why for any value of j, $\Sigma_i RC_{ij} = 0$ and for any value of i, $\Sigma_j RC_{ij} = 0$. Fixing the value of j,

$$\Sigma_i RC_{ij} = \Sigma_i[\mu_{ij.} - \mu_{i..} - \mu_{.j.} + \mu] = \Sigma_i(\mu_{ij.} - \mu_{.j.}) + \Sigma_i(\mu_{i..} - \mu) = 0$$

**TABLE 4.3 THE LIKEABLENESS SCORES FOR
THE EXPERIMENTAL DESIGN IN TABLE 4.1**

	Order of Presentation					
Class	1	2	3	4	5	6
Freshmen	Y_{111} Y_{112} ... Y_{11n}	Y_{121} Y_{122} ... Y_{12n}	Y_{131} Y_{132} ... Y_{13n}	Y_{141} Y_{142} ... Y_{14n}	Y_{151} Y_{152} ... Y_{15n}	Y_{161} Y_{162} ... Y_{16n}
Seniors ...	Y_{211} Y_{212} ... Y_{21n}	Y_{221} Y_{222} ... Y_{22n}	Y_{231} Y_{232} ... Y_{23n}	Y_{241} Y_{242} ... Y_{24n}	Y_{251} Y_{252} ... Y_{25n}	Y_{261} Y_{262} ... Y_{26n}

since $\Sigma_i(\mu_{ij.} - \mu_{.j.})$ is the sum of the deviations of the cell means in the jth column from the overall mean of the jth column and is therefore zero ($\Sigma_i\mu_{ij.} = I\mu_{.j.}$ and $\Sigma_i\mu_{.j.} = I\mu_{.j.}$). Similarly, $\Sigma_i(\mu_{i..} - \mu)$ is the sum of the deviations of the row means from the general mean and is therefore zero ($\Sigma_i\mu_{i..} = I\mu$ and $\Sigma_i\mu = I\mu$).

A similar analysis applies to all of the effects in a fixed-effects model. The side conditions indicating that the sum of effects is zero are always indicating that the sum of certain deviations from a mean equals zero.

4.4 Where we'll be going now. Now we will consider what the scores look like for this design. Then, just for old times sake we'll take a look at the vector space representation of the scores in their model form and in their data form. After that we will consider a three-factor design. Then in Chapter 5 we will take up how to test the null hypotheses by using F-tests.

4.5 The assumption of equal number of scores in each cell. Until we indicate otherwise, from now on we will be assuming that there are the same number of scores in each cell of the experimental design. Often, when this condition is not satisfied, procedures that we will not take up until Chapter 15 are required to perform the analysis of variance.

4.6 Scores for a two-factor design. Assume that 12n subjects served in the experiment, n in each of the 12 cells in the design in Table 4.3. Then the scores we would collect from these 12n subjects would be as shown in Table 4.3. The model says that $Y_{ijk} = \mu + C_i + O_j + CO_{ij} + e_{ijk}$, so, for example, Y_{122} = the sum of the general mean, μ, the effect for Class 1, C_1, the effect for Order 2, O_2, the effect for the combination of Class 1

TABLE 4.4 EXAMPLE NUMERICAL VALUES SHOWING THE ROW, COLUMN, INTERACTION, AND ERROR EFFECTS COMBINING TO GIVE A SET OF TWO SCORES PER CELL IN THE 2 x 6 FACTORIAL DESIGN

Type of effect		Numerical value Order 1	2	3	4	5	6		Cumulative effects Order 1	2	3	4	5	6
The general mean, having the same effect on all scores.	F	3	3	3	3	3	3	F	3	3	3	3	3	3
		3	3	3	3	3	3		3	3	3	3	3	3
	S	3	3	3	3	3	3	S	3	3	3	3	3	3
		3	3	3	3	3	3		3	3	3	3	3	3
The Class effects, adding -3 to all Freshman scores and 3 to all Senior scores.	F	-3	-3	-3	-3	-3	-3	F	0	0	0	0	0	0
		-3	-3	-3	-3	-3	-3		0	0	0	0	0	0
	S	3	3	3	3	3	3	S	6	6	6	6	6	6
		3	3	3	3	3	3		6	6	6	6	6	6
The Order effects add the same value to each score in the same Order condition.	F	-1	-2	-1	2	1	1	F	-1	-2	-1	2	1	1
		-1	-2	-1	2	1	1		-1	-2	-1	2	1	1
	S	-1	-2	-1	2	1	1	S	5	4	5	8	7	7
		-1	-2	-1	2	1	1		5	4	5	8	7	7
The Interaction effects add a different constant to each score in the same cell.	F	1	-2	-3	1	1	2	F	0	-4	-4	3	2	3
		1	-2	-3	1	1	2		0	-4	-4	3	2	3
	S	-1	2	3	-1	-1	-2	S	4	6	8	7	6	5
		-1	2	3	-1	-1	-2		4	6	8	7	6	5
The Error effects add a different error to each score.	F	1	2	-1	-3	2	-1	F	1	-2	-5	0	4	2
		-1	-2	1	3	-2	1		-1	-5	-3	6	0	4
	S	-1	-3	2	2	1	-1	S	3	3	10	9	7	4
		1	3	-2	-2	-1	1		5	9	6	5	5	6

with Order 2, CO_{12}, and the error associated with the second person to be tested under the conditions of Class 1 and Order 2, e_{122}.

Table 4.4 shows a numerical example of a case where n, the number of scores per cell, is two. This table should be examined carefully to see the role of each type of effect. The sample of scores is shown as the 24 numbers in the lower right-hand corner of the table. These are the results of the cumulative effects of the general mean, which is 3, and are shown as the 24 numbers in the upper left-hand corner, and the other effects, which are shown successively in the succeeding sets of 24 numbers that progress down the column on the left, labeled Numerical Value. As the effects areadded, one after another, their cumulative effect is shown in the successive sets of 24 numbers in the right-hand column, labeled Cumulative effects. Notice that the row effects, -3 for Freshmen and +3 for Seniors, affect every Freshman score and every Senior score, respectively. The next set of effects, that for Order of Presentation of the adjectives, adds the same value to each score receiving the same level of Order. Thus, for example, all the scores corresponding to Order 2 received an Order effect of -2, while all of the scores corresponding to Order 6 received an Order effect of +1. (The student should realize that these numerical values are completely arbitrary and have been composed by pulling numbers out of the air. The particular values used are not intended to relate any true psychological facts but only to show how the numerical combination of the various effects occurs. Other completely different numbers would have served this purpose as well. Of course, the numbers have been constrained to satisfy the side conditions of the model.)

The next set of effects is referred to as **interaction effects**. We will discuss the meaning of this term "interaction" in the next section. For now they are the effects we have referred to above as resulting from the particular combination of some row level with some column level; some Class with some Order. Thus, the table shows an effect of -2 for the particular combination of a Freshman student receiving Order 2. Notice that both freshmen who received Order 2 have this same interaction effect since it is peculiar to the particular cell in which both these scores occur. This is in contrast to the next set of effects, which are error effects. Here notice that while the two freshmen who received Order 2 are in the same cell, their error effects differ, one freshman receiving an error effect of 2 and the other of -2. The error effects have been chosen to add to zero in each cell but in actuality this would not necessarily occur.

4.7 Interaction effects. To discuss interaction effects it will be helpful to ignore the error effects and consider the cumulative effects before and after the interaction effects have been added. This corresponds to considering two models, one in which the interaction effects are all zero and the other in which not all of them are zero. Doing this shows what kind of a difference the interaction effects make.

Since we are ignoring the error effects, we need only look at one score per cell since all scores in the same cell are the same but for the error effects. The scores of interest, then, are the cumulative effects before the interaction effects are added, which are -1, -2, -1, 2, 1, 1 for the Freshmen under the six Orders, and 5, 4, 5, 8, 7, 7 for the Seniors under the same Orders. We can consider these values as the true cell means under the hypothesis that the interaction effects are all zero.

Now the first thing to notice is that at each level of the Order factor, the cell mean for the Seniors is 6 greater than the cell mean for the Freshmen. Another way to say this is that the difference between Freshmen scores and Senior scores is constant from level to level of the Order factor, the constant difference being 6. Still another way to say it is that the Senior means can be obtained by addition of a constant, 6, to the Freshmen means. This relation between the Senior means and the Freshmen means gives rise to referring to zero interaction effects as a relation of **additivity**. Aside from the general mean, the cell means are determined by addition of a row effect and a column effect, so any two rows will differ by a constant, the difference between the two row effects. (Recall that the Row effects were -3 and +3. The difference between them is 6, which is the difference between the row means.) Also, any two columns will differ by a constant, the difference between the two column effects. Hence the additivity can also be seen by looking at the cell means from column to column. For Order 1 the cell means are -1 and 5; for Order 2 they are -2 and 4; Order 3, -1 and 5; Order 4, 2 and 8; Order 5, 1 and 7; and Order 6, 1 and 7. Here we see the additive relation by noting that each pair of means can be obtained from any other pair of means by addition of an appropriate constant. For example, the Order 2 means can be obtained by adding -1 to each of the Order 1 means. Inspection of the six pairs of cell means reveals that each pair can be obtained from each other pair by addition of a positive or negative constant.

Now compare this situation of additivity with that existing after the interaction effects have been added. To do this, look at the cell means in Table 4.4 in the cumulative effects column opposite the Type of Effect row labeled Interaction effects. The cell means are 0, -4, -4, 3, 2, 3 for the Freshmen and 4, 6, 8, 7, 6, 5 for the Seniors. With these it is immediately apparent that the additivity that existed before addition of the interaction effects has been removed. There is now no single constant that we can add to the Freshman means that will give the Senior means. In Order 1 the difference between Freshmen and Seniors is 4, while in Order 2 that same difference is 10.

It is also informative to consider interaction geometrically. Figure 4.1(a) shows a graph , of the means before the addition of the interaction effects and Figure 4.1(b) shows the means after addition of the interaction effects. We see that without interaction, the two curves are parallel, but that addition of the interaction effects destroys the parallelism. (We are used to speaking of straight lines being parallel. Here we extend the notion of parallelism to the curves produced by connecting means at the same level of a factor. For that matter, we are used to using the word "curve" to refer to figures that are smooth, continuous, and arcing, whereas in graphing the results of data collection or the theoretical results pertaining to factorial designs, we refer to the lines connecting points representing means as "curves.")

What we have seen, then, is that

1. **additivity means zero interaction,**
2. **interaction means nonadditivity,**
3. **additivity graphs as parallelism, and**
4. **nonparallelism is equivalent to nonzero interaction effects.**

We will find that this idea of interaction versus additivity arises in more complex experimental designs involving more than two factors. (More about this later.) Now we

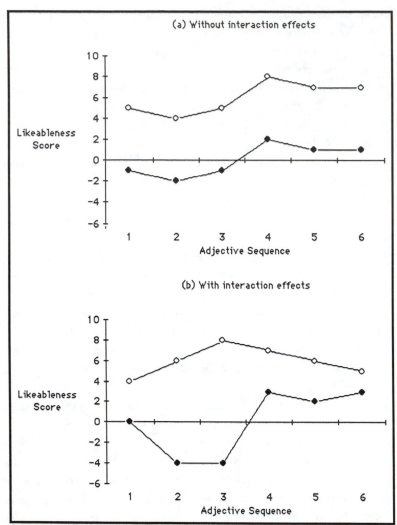

Figure 4.1. The true mean scores, before error effects, under the hypothesis of (a) zero interaction effects and (b) nonzero interaction effects. The numerical values of the effects are given in Table 4.2.

will look briefly at the vector space representation of our data and model equation, so that we can see how the geometry of the analysis of variance generalizes along with the model equations.

4.8 A vector space representation of the two-factor design. Figure 4.2 shows the data vector **Y**, the vector of error effects, e, various

TABLE 4.5 CORRESPONDENCE OF MODEL EQUATION, DEGREES OF FREEDOM, SAMPLE VALUES, AND SUMS OF SQUARES IN THE TWO-FACTOR DESIGN

Source	μ-dot term	M-dot term	df	Sum of Squares
Mean	μ	M	1	$\Sigma_i\Sigma_j\Sigma_k M^2$
Row	$\mu_{i..} - \mu$	$M_{i..} - M$	$I - 1$	$\Sigma_i\Sigma_j\Sigma_k(M_{i..} - M)^2$
Column	$\mu_{.j.} - \mu$	$M_{.j.} - M$	$J - 1$	$\Sigma_i\Sigma_j\Sigma_k M_{.j.} - M)^2$
R x C	$\mu_{ij.} - \mu_{i..}$	$M_{ij.} - M_{i..}$	$IJ - I$	$\Sigma_i\Sigma_j\Sigma_k(M_{ij.} - M_{i..}$
	$- \mu_{.j.} + \mu$	$- M_{.j.} + M$	$- J + 1$	$- M_{.j.} + M)^2$
Error	$Y_{ijk} - \mu_{ij.}$	$Y_{ijk} - M_{ij.}$	$IJK - IJ$	$\Sigma_i\Sigma_j\Sigma_k(Y_{ijk} - M_{ij.})^2$
Total	Y_{ijk}	Y_{ijk}	IJK	$\Sigma_i\Sigma_j\Sigma_k Y_{ijk}^2$

vectors of means, and the vectors of the effects, which are the subject of our null hypotheses for this experimental design. Because our data vector contains 24 scores, each of these vectors has 24 coordinates. The coordinates of these vectors are given in Table 4.4 The column labeled Numerical value in that table shows in order the coordinates of: the mean vector (all 3's); the Class-effects vector (12 -3's and 12 +3's); the Order-effects vector; the interaction-effects vector; and the error-effects vector. The coordinates of the data vector are given by the 24 values in the lower right-hand corner. The coordinates of the μ_i vector are given by the sum of the meanvector, μ, and the Class-effects vector, C_i. These are the 12 0's followed by 12 6's in the second group in the column labeled Cumulative effects in Table 4.4. The vector $\mu_i + \mu_j - \mu$ is the result of adding the Order effects to the vector μ_i, and its coordinates are given in the cumulative column in the third group of 24 from the top. The vector μ_{ij} is the vector of cell means after the interaction effects have been added, and its coordinates are in the next to the bottom group of 24 in the cumulative-effects column.

It is clear from Figure 4.2 that the following vector equations hold:

$$C_i = \mu_i - \mu$$

$$O_j = \mu_j - \mu \qquad\qquad [4.6]$$
$$CO_{ij} = \mu_{ij} - \mu_i - \mu_j + \mu$$

Also, exactly parallel to our model equation we have the vector equation

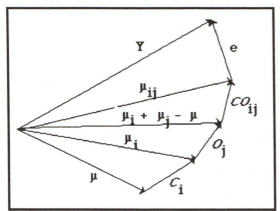

Figure 4.2. Vector representations of the data vector, the error vector, the vectors of means and effects for the two-factor design.

$$Y = \mu + C_i + O_j + CO_{ij} + e. \tag{4.7}$$

The student should also verify that except for e, the vectors on the right side of equation [4.7] are all orthogonal to each other.

4.8.1 The model equation with effects written as deviations. Following the vector equation [4.7] we can write

$$Y_{ijk} = \mu + (\mu_{i..} - \mu) + (\mu_{.j.} - \mu) +$$

$$(\mu_{ij.} - \mu_{i..} - \mu_{.j.} + \mu) + e_{ijk}$$

which gives the model equation by expressing the various effects as deviations. We will find in Chapter 5 that this method of writing the model equation is extraordinarily useful. For now we will just show Table 4.5.

The student should notice in Table 4.5 the correspondence between the indices on the model terms expressed as μ-dot terms, the same indices used in the sum of squares formulas, and the uppercase values of those indices used in the degrees of freedom formulas. Notice that wherever μ occurs in the μ-dot term, 1 occurs in the degrees of freedom formula; wherever i occurs in the μ-dot term, I occurs in the degrees of freedom formula; and so on. We are going to find these correspondences very useful to us in the coming chapters.

There is one more important equation that must be added in Chapter 5, but this must wait until after we have introduced the T-dot notation. Then, that added equation will give the computational formulas for the sums of squares in the analysis of variance.

TABLE 4.6 EXAMPLE OF SCORES IN A THREE-FACTOR DESIGN

	Block 1			Block 2			Block 3		
	Col. 1	Col. 2	Col. 3	Col. 1	Col. 2	Col. 3	Col. 1	Col. 2	Col. 3
Row 1	Y_{1111} Y_{1112}	Y_{1211} Y_{1212}	Y_{1311} Y_{1312}	Y_{1121} Y_{1122}	Y_{1221} Y_{1222}	Y_{1321} Y_{1322}	Y_{1131} Y_{1132}	Y_{1231} Y_{1232}	Y_{1331} Y_{1332}
Row 2	Y_{2111} Y_{2112}	Y_{2211} Y_{2212}	Y_{2311} Y_{2312}	Y_{2121} Y_{2122}	Y_{2221} Y_{2222}	Y_{2321} Y_{2322}	Y_{2131} Y_{2132}	Y_{2231} Y_{2232}	Y_{2331} Y_{2332}
Row 3	Y_{3111} Y_{3112}	Y_{3211} Y_{3212}	Y_{3311} Y_{3312}	Y_{3121} Y_{3122}	Y_{3221} Y_{3222}	Y_{3321} Y_{3322}	Y_{3131} Y_{3132}	Y_{3231} Y_{3232}	Y_{3331} Y_{3332}

4.9 A three-factor design. We now consider a three-factor design. In a three-factor design the score Y_{ijkm} is the mth score in Cell ijk. Cell ijk lies in Row i, Column j, and Block k of the design. Table 4.6 provides an example with three factors, each having three levels. For example, the score Y_{3212} is the second score in Row 3, Column 2 of the first Block.

The model equation for this three factor design is

$$Y_{ijkm} = \mu + R_i + C_j + B_k + RC_{ij} + RB_{ik} + CB_{jk} + RCB_{ijk} + e_{ijkm} \qquad [4.8]$$

TABLE 4.7 AN EXAMPLE TABLE OF TRUE MEANS SHOWING HOW THE μ-DOT NOTATION INDICATES AVERAGING BY DOTTING THE INDEX AVERAGED OVER

	Block 1				Block 2				Block 3			
	Col_1	Col_2	Col_3		Col_1	Col_2	Col_3		Col_1	Col_2	Col_3	
Row 1	μ_{111}	μ_{121}	μ_{131}	$\mu_{1.1}$	μ_{112}	μ_{122}	μ_{132}	$\mu_{1.2}$	μ_{113}	μ_{123}	μ_{133}	$\mu_{1.3}$
Row 2	μ_{211}	μ_{221}	μ_{231}	$\mu_{2.1}$	μ_{212}	μ_{222}	μ_{232}	$\mu_{2.2}$	μ_{213}	μ_{223}	μ_{233}	$\mu_{2.3}$
Row 3	μ_{311}	μ_{321}	μ_{331}	$\mu_{3.1}$	μ_{312}	μ_{322}	μ_{332}	$\mu_{3.2}$	μ_{313}	μ_{323}	μ_{333}	$\mu_{3.3}$
	$\mu_{.11}$	$\mu_{.21}$	$\mu_{.31}$	$\mu_{..1}$	$\mu_{.12}$	$\mu_{.22}$	$\mu_{.32}$	$\mu_{..2}$	$\mu_{.13}$	$\mu_{.23}$	$\mu_{.33}$	$\mu_{..3}$

TABLE 4.7a   CELL, ROW, AND COLUMN MEANS   AVERAGED OVER BLOCKS IN TABLE 4.4

	Col 1	Col 2	Col 3	Row means
Row 1	$\mu_{11.}$	$\mu_{12.}$	$\mu_{13.}$	$\mu_{1..}$
Row 2	$\mu_{21.}$	$\mu_{22.}$	$\mu_{23.}$	$\mu_{2..}$
Row 3	$\mu_{31.}$	$\mu_{32.}$	$\mu_{33.}$	$\mu_{3..}$
Column means	$\mu_{.1.}$	$\mu_{.2.}$	$\mu_{.3.}$	μ

TABLE 4.8 FAKE SPELLING ERROR SCORES FOR BOYS AND GIRLS IN THE FOURTH, FIFTH, AND SIXTH GRADES IN THREE SCHOOLS TO ILLUSTRATE THE Y-DOT MEANS

	Hark School			Lark School			Dark School		
	4th	5th	6th	4th	5th	6th	4th	5th	6th
Girl	5	3	1	10	7	4	2	1	1
	6	5	3	12	8	6	1	2	1
Boys	6	4	2	14	9	7	1	0	0
	5	6	2	18	11	8	1	0	1

with the side conditions that $\Sigma_i R_i = \Sigma_j C_j = \Sigma_k B_k = 0$, $\Sigma_i RC_{ij} = 0$ for each j, $\Sigma_j RC_{ij} = 0$ for each i, similar conditions for RB_{ik} and CB_{jk}, and the sum of the RCB_{ijk} over any index for fixed values of the other two indices equals zero. The mth score in Cell ijk is composed of a general mean, a Row effect, a Column effect, a Block effect, three two-factor interaction effects, a three-factor interaction effect, and an error effect. A two-factor interaction effect such as RC_{ij} is the effect of the particular combination of a level of one factor with a level of another, for example, level i of the Row factor and level j of the Column factor. A three-factor interaction effect is the effect of the combination of the particular levels of three factors, say Row i, Column j, and Block k. In deviation form, using the μ-dot notation, the model equation is

$$Y_{ijkm} = \mu + (\mu_{i...} - \mu) + (\mu_{.j..} - \mu) + (\mu_{..k.} - \mu) + (\mu_{ij..} - \mu_{i...} - \mu_{.j..} + \mu) +$$

$$(\mu_{i.k.} - \mu_{i...} - \mu_{..k.} + \mu) + (\mu_{.jk.} - \mu_{.j..} - \mu_{..k.} + \mu) +$$

TABLE 4.9 AVERAGING WITHIN TABLE 4.5 TO GET CELL MEANS AND MARGINAL MEANS

$M_{ij1.}$			$M_{i.1.}$	$M_{ij2.}$			$M_{i.2.}$	$M_{ij3.}$			$M_{i.3.}$
5.50	4.00	2.00	3.83	11.00	7.50	5.00	7.83	1.50	1.50	1.00	1.33
5.50	5.00	2.00	4.17	16.00	10.00	7.50	11.17	1.00	0.00	.5	.50
5.50	4.50	2.00	4.00	13.5	8.75	6.25	9.50	1.25	.75	.75	.92

$$(\mu_{ijk.} - \mu_{ij..} - \mu_{i.k.} - \mu_{.jk.} + \mu_{i...} + \mu_{.j..} + \mu_{..k.} - \mu) + e_{ijkm} \qquad [4.9]$$

wherein μ is an abbreviation for $\mu_{....}$.

4.9.1 Clarifying the μ-dot notation. To understand the various μ-dot terms in this expression it will be helpful to consider Table 4.7 in which we ignore the error effects and consider only parameter values for the three-factor design. We will consider a few examples. Locate μ_{231}. This is the true or population mean for the cell in Row 2, Column 3, of Block 1. That is, it is the mean of the population of scores having the combination of the Row 2, Column 3, and Block 1 experimental conditions, from which the scores in Cell 2,3,1 are considered to be a sample. Now consider the other means in that same column (columns go up and down like columns of marble; rows go across like rows in a theater). These are μ_{131} and μ_{331}.

The average of these three cell means is $\mu_{.31}$, the mean for the third column in Block 1, and is given in the third column of Block 1 at its bottom margin. Notice that to get $\mu_{.31}$ we average μ_{131}, μ_{231}, and μ_{331}. This averaging over the three different <u>rows</u> is denoted by the dot in the position of the <u>row</u> index, i. Similarly, the average of $\mu_{.11}$, $\mu_{.21}$, and $\mu_{.31}$ is $\mu_{..1}$, which is the true average value of a score in the overall population from which scores in Block 1 were sampled. (I hope that the student appreciates that these "population means" are nothing other than <u>expected values</u> traveling around in disguises that appeal to the intuition.) Also notice that $\mu_{..1}$ is the average of $\mu_{1.1}$, $\mu_{2.1}$, and $\mu_{3.1}$. The value $\mu_{..1}$ is obtained by averaging over the rows and the columns of Block 1 so both the row index i and the column index j are dotted, while the block index is 1, indicating which block $\mu_{..1}$ is the mean of.

There are averages that occur in the model equation but are not shown in Table 4.7. We can obtain these by averaging over Blocks. This gives the means shown in Table 4.7a. The reason these means are missing in Table 4.5 is because we averaged over Rows and over Columns but not over Blocks.

TABLE 4.10 THE GENDER x CLASS (ROW x COLUMN) MEANS, $M_{ij..} = \Sigma_k\Sigma_m Y_{ijkm}/KM$.

	4th	5th	6th	Row Means
Girls	6.00	4.33	2.67	4.33
Boys	7.50	5.00	3.33	5.28
Col. means	6.75	4.66	3.00	4.80

4.10 Estimation of the effects. To estimate one of these effects on the right side of equation [4.8] we take the corresponding quantity expressed in μ-dot notation in equation [4.9] and substitute for each μ-dot term its sample estimator, which is the corresponding sample mean. The generic score in a three-factor design is Y_{ijkm}. To obtain a sample mean that corresponds to a μ-dot term we simply average over the index m which indexes the different scores in the same cell and also average over the indices, which are dotted in the μ-dot term. We can call these estimators the M-dot terms. Of course they are nothing other than the cell sample means or the marginal sample means. Any M-dot term is a simple average, so it is obtained by summing over all of the dotted indices and dividing by the number of scores summed. If we use the uppercase value of each index to denote how many values this index ranges over, then the number of scores we sum will always just equal the product of the uppercase values of all of the indices over which we have summed, so it will be this product that we will divide the sum by. (This is another of those simple ideas that is painfully tedious to say in words but very easy to understand from a few examples.) Thus, $M_{i...} = \Sigma_j\Sigma_k\Sigma_m Y_{ijkm}/JKM$, where the summation over j is from 1 to J, that over k is from 1 to K, and over m is from 1 to M, so we divide by JKM. Similarly, $M_{.12.} = \Sigma_m Y_{i12m}/IM$. (Be careful to distinguish between an M that denotes a sample mean and the M that denotes the uppercase value of m, which is the number of levels of a factor. The former will have subscripts except when it denotes the overall mean, and the latter will never have a subscript.)

4.10.1 Obtaining M-dot values: A numerical example. As a numerical example of obtaining M-dot values, consider the data in Table 4.8, which pretend to be spelling error scores from Girls and Boys in three Grades at three Schools. The values of the $M_{ijk.}$ are obtained by averaging the two scores in each cell (M = 2; this is M, the number of scores per cell, not M, the abbreviation of $M_{....}$. Such an ambiguity occasionally arises in the notation, but the context will keep things clear). This gives the cell means in Table 4.9. These cell

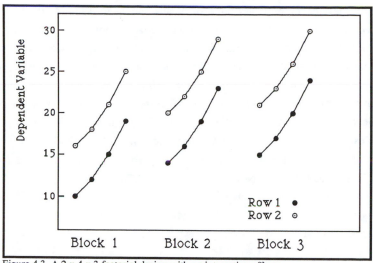

Figure 4.3. A 2 x 4 x 3 factorial design with no interaction effects.

TABLE 4.11 THE GENDER x SCHOOLS INTERACTION TABLE OF MEANS, THE $M_{i.j.}$

	Hark	Lark	Dark	Row Means
Girls	3.83	7.83	1.33	4.33
Boys	4.17	11.17	.50	5.28
Col. Means	4.00	9.50	.92	4.80

TABLE 4.12 THE GRADES x SCHOOLS INTERACTION TABLE OF MEANS, THE $M_{.jk.}$

	Hark	Lark	Dark	Row Means
Fourth	5.5	13.5	1.25	6.75
Fifth	4.5	8.75	.75	4.66
Sixth	2.0	6.25	.75	3.00
Means	4.00	9.50	.92	4.80

means can be averaged across Gender and Grade for each School separately, giving the marginal means also shown in Table 4.9 Averaging the cell means in Table 4.9 over schools, we obtain the Gender by Class table of means shown in Table 4.10 (this is averaging over "Blocks"). Table 4.9 is referred to as a three-factor table of means or as the Gender x Grade x Schools interaction table of means. This is because if we wanted to represent graphically the presence or absence of the three-factor interaction effects, we would graph the means in Table 4.9. Similarly, Table 4.10 is referred to as the Gender x Grade interaction table of means. If we wanted to represent graphically the presence or absence of the Gender x Grade interaction effects we would show a graph of the means in Table 4.10. Tables 4.11 and 4.12 display the Gender x Schools and the Grade x Schools interaction tables of means. Notice that the values in these two tables have been collected from the marginal means in Table 4.9. Now, following Table 4.7, we can estimate all of the various effects. For example, the estimate of R_1 is $M_{1..} - M_{...} = 4.33 - 4.80 = -.47$, the estimate of RC_{12} is $M_{12.} - M_{1..} - M_{.2.} + M_{...} = 4.33 - 4.33 - 4.66 + 4.80 = .14$, and that of RCB_{212} is $M_{212.} - M_{21..} - M_{2.2.} - M_{.12.} + M_{2...} + M_{.1..} + M_{..2.} - M_{....} = 16 - 7.5 = 11.17 - 13.5 + 5.28 + 6.75 + 9.5 - 4.80 = .56$.

4.11 What the F-test for interaction will tell us. The F-test for the Row x Column x Block interaction, which we will take up in Chapter 5, will test whether the departure from zero of the estimates of the three-factor interaction effects such as RCB_{212} is consistent with what we would expect to result from sampling error. A significant F-ratio will inferentially indicate that these estimates such as .56 depart from zero more than we would expect in the light of our estimate of the variance of the errors. A nonsignificant F would indicate that these departures could be due to error variance alone rather than indicating that the true three-factor interaction effects are not zero.

4.12 Data without errors occurs only as a teaching device, not in research. Before we go on to Chapter 5 and the analysis of variance for two-or-more factor designs, we want to

look at some graphical representations of data from a three-factor design in which we either build in or leave out the two- or three-factor interaction effects. This is so that we can gain some understanding of what data look like when they display these kinds of nonadditivities. We will start with a design in which pure additivity occurs and then add some of the other effects to show how the picture changes. For this purpose, it is best to omit the error effects so the clearest picture emerges. We will do this, but the student should realize that this construction and graphical representation of error-free data is a teaching device. In research we never obtain error-free data. Presenting artificial data without errors is taking a God's-eye view of the situation. We pretend that we can know the parameter values themselves, all the time realizing that this is an idealized version that is never encountered outside the teaching context.

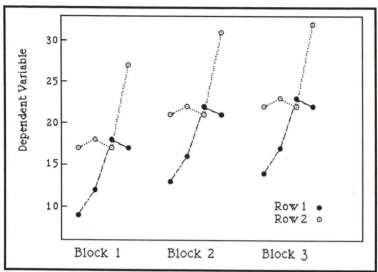

Figure 4.4. A three-factor design with a Row x Column interaction. At each block, the curves for the two rows are not parallel. But the entire pattern for any block is equal to the entire pattern for any other block, plus or minus some constant.

An additional aspect of this idealization is separating the score into its component effects. In research we have only the score. The separate effects are part of the idealization that is the model equation. We can use estimation procedures to estimate the effects, but we can never know their true values. Dropping off the errors and partitioning the score into component pieces is therefore for the purpose of clarifying the roles that the various pieces play in the model that we are using, and the student should avoid slipping into the pattern of thought that takes these values as obtainable or knowable as opposed to estimable.

4.13 The additive case. All of these graphical representations will be equally applicable to designs with repeated measurements (Chapter 8), but we will assume for simplicity that there are no repeated-measurement factors. The first model we will consider is the model for a three-factor design with no interaction effects. The general model equation for a three-factor design would be, excluding the error term,

$$Y_{ijkm} = \mu + R_i + C_j + B_k + RC_{ij} + RB_{ik} + CB_{jk} + RCB_{ijk} \qquad [4.10]$$

By eliminating all of the interaction effects we obtain the model equation

$$Y_{ijkm} = \mu + R_i + C_j + B_k \qquad [4.11]$$

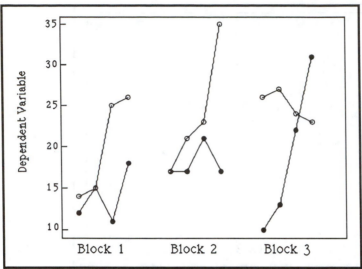

Figure 4.5. A three-factor design with Row, Column, and Block main effects and a three-factor interaction. The differences between Row 1 and Row 2 vary from column to column, and the pattern of this variation is not the same for all three blocks.

Suppose that we have two rows, four columns, and three blocks. Also suppose that $\mu = 20$, the Row effects are -3 and +3, the Column effects are -4, -2, 1, and 5, and the Block effects are -3, 1, and 2. The student should verify that the graph in Figure 4.3 is a display of the cell means that would result from this completely additive combination of effects.

4.14 The three-factor design with Row, Column, and Block effects and a Row x Column interaction. Suppose now that a row by column interaction is added to give the model equation

$$Y_{ijkm} = \mu + R_i + C_j + B_k + RC_{ij} \qquad\qquad [4.12]$$

and that along with the values given in Section 4.13 the RC_{1j} are -1, 0, 3, and -2, and the RC_{2j} are 1, 0, -3, and 2. Then the cell means would be as shown in Figure 4.4. We can see that in Figure 4.4 there no longer exists the separation of Row 1 from Row 2 by a constant as there was in Figure 4.3. But corresponding points in Block 1 and Block 2 differ by a constant. In fact, for any selection of two blocks, corresponding points in the two blocks differ by a constant. This additivity between blocks indicates that there are no interactions involving the Blocks factor.

Suppose in the case of a Row x Column interaction we did not think of the Row effects and the Interaction effects separately but instead combined them and thought of them as Row effects that differed from column to column. For the first column they would be -3 -1 = -4

TABLE 4.13   FICTIONAL DATA FOR A TWO-FACTOR DESIGN

	B_1	B_2	B_3
A_1	2	3	6
	4	5	7
A_2	8	9	4
	8	5	5
A_3	6	7	8
	5	5	6
A_4	6	9	10
	8	10	10

for Row 1 and +3 +1 = +4 for Row 2; for the second column they would be -3 + 0 = -3 and +3 + 0 = 3; for the third, -3 +3 = 0 and +3 - 3 = 0; and for the fourth, -3 - 2 = -5 and +3 + 2 = +5. These values would give the very same curves of course. Viewing the effects in this way provides us with still another way of thinking about interaction. **We can think of the Row x Column interaction as the Row effects differing from column to column. A similar combination of the interaction effects with the column effects could have been performed, in which case we could have regarded the interaction as the differing of the column effects from row to row. From this perspective we can regard a two-factor interaction as the differing of the effects of one factor from level to level of another factor. In similar fashion we could generalize the perspective to see a three- (or more) factor interaction as the differing of the effects of a two- (or more) factor interaction from level to level of the third (or higher) factor.**

4.15   The three-factor design with Row, Column, and Block effects and a Row x Column x Block interaction. Now we will remove the Row by Column interaction effects and replace them with three-factor interaction effects. This gives the model equation

$$Y_{ijkm} = \mu + R_i + C_j + B_k + RCB_{ijk} . \qquad [4.13]$$

We will take as the interaction effects the values 2, 3, -4, -1 as the RCB_{1j1}'s,
and the side conditions therefore require that the RCB_{2j1}'s be -2, -3, 4, 1. Next we will take
as the RCB_{1j2}'s the values 3, 1, 2, -6, so the side conditions require that the RCB_{2j2}'s be
-3, -1, -2, 6. By now the side conditions completely determine the rest of the values. The
RCB_{1j3}'s must be -5,-4, 2, 7, and the RCB_{2j3}'s must be 5, 4, -2, -7. Adding these
interaction effects to the value of G and the appropriate main effects used before, we obtain
the values graphed in Figure 4.5.

Exercises

1. Using a design with two rows, three columns, and four blocks, choose numerical values
for the parameters in the following models so that the appropriate side conditions are
satisfied. Then graph the values similarly to the graphing in Table 4.6 (here too ignoring
error effects):
(a) $Y_{ijkm} = \mu + B_k$
(b) $Y_{ijkm} = \mu + R_i + CB_{jk}$
(c) $Y_{ijkm} = RC_{ij}$
(d) $Y_{ijkm} = \mu + RC_{ij} + RB_{ik}$
(e) $Y_{ijkm} = \mu + R_i + C_j + B_k + RC_{ij} + RB_{ik} + CB_{jk} + RCB_{ijk}$
2. For the data in Table 4.13 the model equation is $Y_{ijk} = \mu + A_i + B_j + AB_{ij} + e_{ijk}$. Use
the M-dot values to estimate the values of:
(a) $\mu_{i.}$ for i = 1 to 4
(b) the $\mu_{.j}$ for j = 1 to 3
(c) the μ_{ij} for i = 1 to 4 and j = 1 to 3
(d) all the A_i
(e) all the B_j
(f) all the AB_{ij}
3. Estimate e_{231} and e_{232} for the data in exercise 2.
4. Why does additivity result in parallelism?
5. What are the side conditions on the various effects in a two-factor design? In a three-
factor design?
6. Suppose a four-factor design with model equation $Y_{ijklm} = \mu + A_i + B_j + C_k + D_l +$
$AB_{ij} + AC_{ik} + AD_{il} + BC_{jk} + BD_{jl} + CD_{kl} + ABC_{ijk} + ABD_{ijl} + ACD_{ikl} + BCD_{jkl} +$
$ABCD_{ijkl} + e_{ijklm}$. Define the following quantities:
(a) $\mu_{i...}, \mu_{.jk.}, \mu_{..12}, \mu_{.21.}, \mu_{1212}, \mu_{.312}$
(b) $M_{i...}, M_{.jk.}, M_{..12}, M_{.21.}, M_{1212}, M_{.312}$
(c) $\mu_{i...} - \mu$, $\mu_{i.k.} - \mu_{i...} - \mu_{..k.} + \mu$
(d) Write the estimators of the quantities in exercise 6c.

TABLE 4.14 GENDER x SCHOOL
TABLE OF MEANS

	Hark	Lark	Dark	Row Means
Girls	3.83	7.83	1.33	4.33
Boys	4.17	11.17	.50	5.28
Col. Means	4.00	9.50	.92	4.80

TABLE 4.15 THE CELL
MEANS IN TABLE 4.14
MINUS THEIR RESPECTIVE
ROW MEANS

	Hark	Lark	Dark
Girls	-.50	3.50	-3.00
Boys	-1.11	5.89	-4.78

(e) Write BCD_{jkl} in μ-dot notation.

7. If all of the scores in the population in exercise 6 were averaged over the levels of Factor D, how would you denote these various means?

8. (a) Is it possible to have a three-factor interaction without having a two-factor interaction?

(b) Is it possible to have a two-factor interaction even if the effects of the factors involved are all zero?

9. What do you think the degrees of freedom would be for a source that had as its μ-dot term the quantity $\mu_{ijk} - \mu_{ij.} - \mu_{i.k} - \mu_{.jk} + \mu_{i..} + \mu_{.j.} + \mu_{..k} - \mu$?

10. Describe what the graph of a two-factor interaction would look like. Do the same for a three-factor interaction.

11. If we can think of a three-factor interaction as a two-factor interaction varying from level to level of the third factor, how is it possible for us to have a three-factor interaction without having any two-factor interactions?

12. Write the model equation for a three-factor design in which one factor has no main effect, is involved in no two-factor interactions, but is involved in a three-factor interaction.

13. Using the information in Tables 4.8-4.12, estimate the following effects:

(a) RB_{22}

(b) RCB_{222}

(c) RC_{21}

14. Change the data in Table 4.5 so that the estimates of R_1 and R_2 are equal.

15. Now change the table that you constructed in exercise 2 so that the estimates of C_1, C_2, and C_3 are also equal.

16. Because $\mu_{ij} - \mu_{i.} - \mu_{.j} + \mu$ is the two-factor interaction and therefore $m_{ij} - m_{i.} - m_{.j} + m$ is the estimate of that interaction, we can see that an interaction effect for a given cell in a row x column design is estimated by starting with the cell mean, subtracting the row mean and the column mean, and adding the general mean. This can be done for a whole table essentially all at once. Thus for Table 4.11 we start with the table of cell means shown again in Table 4.14, subtract the row means from each cell to get Table 4.15, subtract the column means from each cell to get Table 4.16, and add the general mean to get Table 4.17 which are the estimates of the Gender x School interaction effects. (Note that summed over each row and each column these estimates sum to zero.) Use the same process with Table 4.12 to obtain the table of Grade x School interaction effects.

17. How could you use the estimated interaction effects to obtain the sum of squares for interaction? (Hint: see Table 4.5).

18. Describe what you would do, using Table 4.9, to obtain a table of estimates of the Gender x Grade x School interaction effects.

19. How would your procedure in exercise 18 differ from the one you described if you had available to you the three tables of estimates of the two-factor interaction effects?

TABLE 4.16 SUBTRACTING THE COLUMN MEANS FROM THE VALUES IN TABLE 4.15

	Hark	Lark	Dark
Girls	-4.50	-6.00	-3.915
Boys	-5.11	-3.61	-5.695

TABLE 4.17 ADDING THE GENERAL MEAN TO TABLE 4.13: THE ESTIMATES OF THE INTERACTION EFFECTS

	Hark	Lark	Dark
Girls	.305	-1.195	.890
Boys	-.305	1.195	-.890

20. In Table 4.18, containing fictional scores obtained from first- and third-grade boys and girls under three methods of teaching, Rote, Abstract, and both combined, estimate the following quantities:

(a) The population mean score for Boys

(b) The effect of being a Boy

(c) The interaction effect of being a Girl and learning by the Abstract method

(d) The interaction effect of being a third-grade girl and learning by the Abstract method

TABLE 4.18 SCORES FROM GIRLS AND BOYS IN TWO DIFFEREN GRADES WITH THREE TEACHING METHODS

	Rote		Abstract		Both	
	Grade		Grade		Grade	
	1	3	1	3	1	3
Boys	2	5	4	7	9	12
	4	6	3	6	8	15
	3	5	4	8	9	13
Girls	3	6	5	8	10	15
	4	7	5	7	10	15
	4	7	5	9	12	16

21. Let $Y_{ijk} = \mu + A_i + B_j + AB_{ij} + e_{ijk}$. (a) Ignore the errors and assume that $I = 2$, $J = 3$. Assume that $\mu = 10$, $A_1 = 5$, $A_2 = -5$, $B_1 = 3$, $B_2 = 4$, $B_3 = -7$, the AB_{1j} are 2, 3, and -5, and the AB_{2j} are -2, -3, and 5. Graph the six cell means as you progressively add to μ the A effects (Graph 1), the A and B effects (Graph 2), and the A, B, and AB effects (Graph 3).

(b) Compare the first and second graphs, and describe how their comparison reveals the effect of the B variable.

22. State in your own words the meaning of the expression "effects are deviations."

23. In a one-factor design, if all of the effects are zero and we ignore error, what do we expect concerning the means at each level?

24. Why does additivity mean zero interaction?

25. Draw the vector representation of the data vector, the error vector, and the vectors of means and effects for the three-factor design.

26. Write a table corresponding to Table 4.5 but for the three-factor design. Show a source, μ-dot term, M-dot term, df, and sum of squares column. (If you can do this, you understand in quite a bit of detail much of this chapter. If you can't do it, get someone to show you how—even the professor.)

27. (a) How would the cell means in a two-factor design plot if there are no interaction effects?

(b) How would they plot in a three-factor design if there are no interaction effects?

28. What part of Table 4.4 helps you to deduce which is the Freshman curve and which is the Senior curve in Figure 4.2?

29. Which part of Table 4.4 produces the nonparallelism in Figure 4.1(b)?

30. Consider a design with two rows, three columns, and two blocks. The model equation is $Y_{ijkm} = \mu + A_i + B_j + C_k + AB_{ij} + AC_{ik} + BC_{jk} + ABC_{ijk} + e_{ijkm}$. Let there be two scores per cell. Create a table analogous to Table 4.4 that shows each of the separate effect values for each combination of levels (each cell) of the design as a number you select. Give these values on the left side and the cumulative numerical effects on the right side. You will need a section for each term in the model equation. Make sure all of the side conditions are satisfied.

31. Graph each of the sections on the right side, and comment on how the addition of each model term alters the graph.

32. Verify that the μ-dot expression for the three-factor interaction effect is the discrepancy between the cell mean, $m_{ijk.}$, and the value predicted for the cell by the sum of the general mean, the Row, Column, and Block effects and the three two-factor interaction effects—that is, that it equals $\mu_{ijk.} - [\mu + (\mu_{i...} - \mu) + (\mu_{.j..} - \mu) + (\mu_{..k.} - \mu) + (\mu_{ij..} - \mu_{i...} - \mu_{.j..} + \mu) + (\mu_{i.k.} - \mu_{i...} - \mu_{..k.} + \mu) + (\mu_{.jk.} - \mu_{.j..} - \mu_{..k.} + \mu)]$.

5

Computations and Display

5.1 The correspondences between the μ-dot, M-dot, degrees of freedom, and sums of squares terms. In Chapter 4 we summarized the correspondences that exist between the symbolic representations of the model equation, the degrees of freedom, the μ-dot notation for the parameters, and the M-dot estimators of the μ-dots. We saw, for example, that in a two-factor design with crossed factors,

$$Y_{ijk} = \mu + (\mu_{i..} - \mu_{...}) + (\mu_{.j.} - \mu_{...}) + (\mu_{ij.} - \mu_{i..} - \mu_{.j.} + \mu_{...}) + e_{ijk} \qquad [5.1]$$

corresponds to

$$Y_{ijk} = M + (M_{i..} - M_{...}) + (M_{.j.} - M_{...}) + (M_{ij.} - M_{i..} - M_{.j.} + M_{...}) + e_{ijk} \qquad [5.2]$$

and to

$$IJK = 1 + (I - 1) + (J - 1) + (IJ - I - J + 1) + (IJK - IJ) \qquad [5.3]$$

We also saw in Table 4.3 that the sums of squares also follow the exact same correspondence.

5.2 Using means to compute sums of squares is not economical. The formulas for the sums of squares given in Table 4.5 are excellent for showing the sums of squares conceptually. They show what estimated effects are squared and summed. For example, the sum of squares for the row effects, the $(\mu_{i..} - \mu_{...})$, is the sum of the squared values of the estimates of the row effects, the $(M_{i..} - M_{...})$, giving $\Sigma_i\Sigma_j\Sigma_k(M_{i..} - M_{...})^2$, which we recognize from the geometric discussions as just the squared length of the vector of estimated row effects. But the sums of squares formulas in Table 4.5 are unnecessarily complicated so far as computations are concerned. There is no need to compute all those means mentioned in the formulas. It is simpler to work with **sums**. To facilitate working with sums instead of means, we will introduce the **T-dot notation**.

5.3 A know-at-a-glance notation for sums. To begin the introduction, let us suppose a collection of scores in a two-factor design with I rows, J columns, and K scores per cell. As usual, we let Y_{ijk} be the arbitrary kth score in the cell in row i and column j of the design. So far, if we wanted to represent a sum of such scores, we did so by using the summation sign notation as with $\Sigma_j\Sigma_k Y_{ijk}$, which would be the sum of all the scores in the ith row. This notation is not revealing, however. When we glance at it, it does not immediately show what it is the sum of. We must go through some reasoning process. And even after we become proficient at such reasoning, the notation still slows us down. An alternative notation for this same sum is $T_{i..}$. The 'T' tells us it is a <u>total</u> or sum of scores, the "i" in the index tells us it is the total for the ith level of the factor the index of which is i (in this case Rows) so it is the total for the ith row, and the two dots in the index tell us that we summed over the two indices that are dotted, j and k. So, $T_{i..} = \Sigma_j\Sigma_k Y_{ijk}$. Similarly, $T_{.3.}$ tells us at a glance that we have the total of the scores in the third column, having summed over i (rows) and k (scores in cells). Thus, $T_{.3.} = \Sigma_i\Sigma_k Y_{i3k}$ is the sum of all the scores having 3 as their column index. Again, for another example, we take $T_{12.}$ which we can read at a glance to be the total of all the scores in the cell in Row 1, Column 2 and is therefore $\Sigma_k Y_{12k}$.

In Figure 5.1(a) we show a set of data for a two-factor design with three rows, four columns, and three scores per cell. The scores that are added to obtain $T_{2..}$ are shown in the dotted area of the design diagram. In Figure 5.1(b) the scores added to get $T_{.3.}$ are in one dotted area, and those added to get $T_{31.}$ are in another.

5.4 Knowing at a glance how many scores have been summed to obtain a particular total. We can also tell at a glance how many scores are

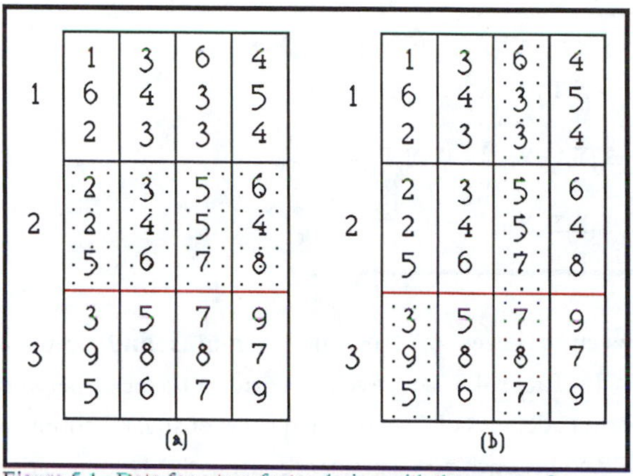

Figure 5.1. Data for a two-factor design with three rows, four columns, and three scores per cell are shown in panels (a) and (b). The stippled region in panel (a) shows the scores added to get $T_{2..}$, the sum of the scores in the second row; the stippled regions in panel (b) show the scores added to get $T_{.3.}$, the total of the scores in the third column, and the scores added to get $T_{31.}$, the total of the scores in the cell in row 3, column 1.

added to get a given T-dot quantity. Consider $T_{i..}$. We know that the dots replace the indices that are summed over. Therefore, since j and k have been replaced, we must have summed over j and k. This means that for each of the J levels of j, we summed K numbers. Thus JK numbers are summed in all to get $T_{i..}$. By similar reasoning, K numbers are summed to get $T_{12.}$, and IK numbers are summed to get $T_{.j.}$. The rule is simply that **to determine the number of scores that are summed to get a T-dot term, we take the product of the uppercase values of the indices that have been replaced by dots.** We will see shortly why we need this rule. As a final example, if the basic score is Y_{ijkmp}, then we see immediately that $T_{12...}$ is the sum of KMP scores and $T_{.3..}$ is the sum of IJMP scores.

TABLE 5.1 SOURCES, DEGREES OF FREEDOM, AND SUMS OF SQUARES COMPUTING FORMULAS FOR THE TWO-FACTOR DESIGN

Source	df	Sums of Squares
Mean	1	$T_{...}^2/IJK$
Rows	$I - 1$	$\Sigma_i T_{i..}^2/JK - T_{...}^2/IJK$
Columns	$J - 1$	$\Sigma_j T_{.j.}^2/IK - T_{...}^2/IJK$
Interaction	$IJ - I - J + 1$	$\Sigma_i\Sigma_j T_{ij.}^2/K - \Sigma_i T_{i..}^2/JK$ $- \Sigma_j T_{.j.}^2/IK + T_{...}^2/IJK$
Error	$IJK - IJ$	$\Sigma_i\Sigma_j\Sigma_k Y_{ijk}^2 - \Sigma_i\Sigma_j T_{ij.}^2/K$
Total	IJK	$\Sigma_i\Sigma_j\Sigma_k Y_{ijk}^2$

5.5 The correspondence between degrees of freedom formulas and sums of squares computing formulas. In Table 4.5 we saw the correspondences between model equation terms in M-dot notation, degrees of freedom, and sums of squares formulas. In this section we will develop still another such correspondence, using the T-dot notation. This correspondence will simplify obtaining the computational formulas and doing the computing of the sums of squares. The simplification will be such that the student will be able to write each sum of squares computing formula simply by inspecting one model equation term or even more conveniently, by inspecting the degrees of freedom term that corresponds to that sum of squares. The easiest way to explain this simple correspondence is to display an example, comment on it, and state the general rules. We follow the form of Table 4.5 in Table 5.1 which shows the sources, degrees of freedom, and computational formulas for sums of squares for the two-factor design we have been discussing.

Let us now consider Table 5.1, one row at a time. In the first row of the body of the table, we see that the Mean has one degree of freedom and the sum of squares for the Mean is the squared total of all the scores, divided by the total number of scores. **We should note that we are dividing this squared total by the number of scores we added to get the total.** We also note that that divisor is, as we have said, the product of the uppercase values of the dotted subscripts in the T-dot term. The subscripts replaced by dots in $T_{...}$ are i, j, and k, so the number of scores is IJK since $T_{...} = \Sigma_i\Sigma_j\Sigma_k Y_{ijk}$, where i ranges from 1 to I, j from 1 to J, and k from 1 to K. **The general rule for sums of squares will follow this example exactly in that every squared total will be divided** by the number of scores added to get that total, and this number will always be the product of the uppercases of the dotted subscripts.

Now let's move to the second row. Here we find I - 1 degrees of freedom for the Row source. First we note that there are two parts for the degrees of freedom term. The part I is added, and the part 1 is subtracted. Looking at the sums of squares term for rows, we see there are two parts there also. One is added, and the other is subtracted. The sum of squares part, which is subtracted, $T_{...}^2/IJK$, corresponds to the 1 degree of freedom in the formula and is subtracted in correspondence to the subtraction of 1 in the degrees of freedom. Now look back at the row for the Mean. Here we also see 1 degree of freedom going with $T_{...}^2/IJK$, but in this case the 1 degree of freedom has a positive sign, and so does the sum of squares part, $T_{...}^2/IJK$. These two rows illustrate two very important rules for determining sums of squares. The first rule is that **a degrees of freedom term always corresponds to the <u>same</u> sum of squares term.** The second rule is that **the arithmetic sign, plus or minus, on the sum of squares term is <u>always the same</u> as the arithmetic sign on the degrees of freedom term that it corresponds to.** These two rules imply that wherever we see a one or a minus one in some row of the degrees of freedom column, we will see in that same row, in the sum of squares column, the quantity $T_{...}^2/IJK$ and the sign on the one in the degrees of freedom term will be the same as the sign on the quantity $T_{...}^2/IJK$. Inspecting the first four rows of Table 5.1 confirms that this is indeed the case.

Returning to the degrees of freedom for Rows, we consider the other term, I, and the sum of squares that corresponds to it, $\Sigma_i T_{i..}^2/JK$. At this point we can infer that in whatever row of the degrees of freedom column I occurs, in that same row we will find $\Sigma_i T_{i..}^2/JK$ in the sum of squares column. *Note that by " occurs" we mean I by itself and not as part of a product ,such as IJ or IJK.* Thus we see I in the degrees of freedom for Rows and the degrees of freedom for Interaction. In the Rows term, I is positive, and so is the sum of squares terms it corresponds to, $\Sigma_i T_{i..}^2/JK$. In the Interaction term, I is subtracted in the degrees of freedom, and so is the term it corresponds to in the sum of squares. The first two rules determined all this.

Now we want to prepare for the third rule. This third rule will tell us how to write the sum of squares term in T-dot notation by using the degrees of freedom term. To exemplify this third rule before we state it, let us examine three sums of squares terms: those corresponding to the degrees of freedom terms I, J, and IJ. The correspondences are:

$$I \longleftrightarrow \Sigma_i T_{i..}^2/JK; \quad J \longleftrightarrow \Sigma_j T_{.j.}^2/IK; \quad \text{and} \quad IJ \longleftrightarrow \Sigma_i \Sigma_j T_{ij.}^2/K.$$

How are the sums of squares terms alike and how do they differ? Each sum of squares term is a sum of squared totals (squared T-dots) divided by a number. By knowing:

(1)   over which variable the summation occurs,

(2)   which squared T-dot we are summing, and

(3)   what number it is divided by,

we specify the entire quantity. As it happens, each of these specifications concerning the sum of squares term is completely determined by the degrees of freedom term. Let's look at how the degrees of freedom term determines the summation specification:

$$I \longleftrightarrow \Sigma_i; \quad J \longleftrightarrow \Sigma_j; \quad \text{and} \quad IJ \longleftrightarrow \Sigma_i\Sigma_j .$$

We see that **we always sum over the lowercase values of the uppercase letters in the degrees of freedom term.** Next, the correspondence of the degrees of freedom term to which squared T-dots we are summing:

$$I \longleftrightarrow T_{i..}^2; \quad J \longleftrightarrow T_{.j.}^2; \quad \text{and} \quad IJ \longleftrightarrow T_{ij.}^2.$$

The squared T-dot always has as its index the lowercase value of each letter in the degrees of freedom term and always has all other letters in its index replaced by dots. Finally, the correspondence between the degrees of freedom terms and the numbers dividing the squared T-dots is:

$$I \longleftrightarrow JK \quad ; \quad J \longleftrightarrow IK; \quad \text{and} \quad IJ \longleftrightarrow K.$$

The dividing number is always the product of all the uppercase letters not contained in the degrees of freedom term. Or, alternatively, the dividing number is the product of the uppercase values of all the letters that are dotted in the index of the T-dot term. This dividing number, by the way, is just the number of scores that were added to obtain the T-dot term. For example, the number dividing $T_{i..}$ is JK and $T_{i..} = \Sigma_j\Sigma_k Y_{ijk}$, which is the sum of JK scores, K scores in each of the J columns.

To generate some examples, consider the following model equation for a four-factor design:

$$Y_{ijkmn} = \mu + A_i + B_j + C_k + D_m + AB_{ij} + AC_{ik} + AD_{im} + BC_{jk} + BD_{km} + CD_{km}$$

$$+ ABC_{ijk} + ABD_{ijm} + ACD_{ikm} + BCD_{jkm} + ABCD_{ijkm} + e_{ijkmn}.$$

Some of the sources, degrees of freedom, and sums of squares are

A, I - 1, $\Sigma_i T_{i...}^2/JKMN - T^2/IJKMN$;

D, M - 1, $\Sigma_m T_{...m.}^2/IJKN - T^2/IJKMN$;

BD, JM - J - M + 1, $\Sigma_j\Sigma_m T_{.j.m.}^2/IKN - \Sigma_j T_{.j..}^2/IKMN - \Sigma_m T_{...m.}^2/IJKN +$

$T^2/IJKMN$;

ABD, IJM - IJ - IM - JM + I + J + M - 1, $\Sigma_i\Sigma_j\Sigma_m T_{ij.m.}^2/KN -$

$\Sigma_i\Sigma_j T_{ij...}^2/KMN - \Sigma_i\Sigma_m T_{i..m.}^2/JKN - \Sigma_j\Sigma_m T_{.j.m.}^2/IKN + \Sigma_i T_{i...}^2/JKMN +$

$\Sigma_j T_{.j..}^2/IKMN + \Sigma_m T_{...m.}^2/IJKN + T^2/IJKMN$.

To see that the T-dot sum of squares formula gives the same value as the M-dot sum of squares formula, we can consider an example. For the sum of squares corresponding to $\mu_{.j.}$ - $\mu_{...}$ we have $\Sigma_i\Sigma_j\Sigma_k(M_{.j.} - M)^2$ for the M-dot notation and $\Sigma_j T_{.j.}^2/IK - T^2/IJK$ for the T-dot notation. Therefore these two quantities should be equal. Now

$\Sigma_i\Sigma_j\Sigma_k(M_{.j.} - M)^2 = IK\Sigma_j(M_{.j.} - M)^2 = IK\Sigma_j(M_{.j.}^2 - 2M_{.j.}M + M^2)$

$= IK(\Sigma_j M_{.j.}^2 - 2M\Sigma_j M_{.j.} + \Sigma_j M^2) = IK\Sigma_j M_{.j.}^2 - 2IKM\Sigma_j M_{.j.} + IJKM^2$.

Consider the next to the last term on the right side of the equation, $-2IKM\Sigma_j M_{.j.}$. By definition, $M_{.j.} = T_{.j.}/IK$. Therefore

$\Sigma_j M_{.j.} = T_{.1.}/IK + T_{.2.}/IK + ... + T_{.J.}/IK = T/IK = JM$

since the sum of the column totals is the grand total and $M = T/IJK$. So the next to the last term on the right turns out to be $-2IKM\Sigma_j M_{.j.} = -2IKMJM = -2IJKM^2$. Combining this with the last term on the right gives $-2IJKM^2 + IJKM^2 = -IJKM^2 = -IJK(T/IJK)^2 = T^2/IJK$. The remaining quantity on the right, $IK \Sigma_j M_{.j.}^2 =$
$IK[(T_{.1.}/IK)^2 + (T_{.2.}/IK)^2 + ... + (T_{.J.}/IK)^2] = \Sigma_j T_{.j.}^2/IK$. Hence, $\Sigma_i\Sigma_j\Sigma_k(M_{.j.} - M)^2 = \Sigma_j T_{.j.}^2/IK - T^2/IJK$.

5.6 An important caution. It is important to note that this correspondence between the degrees of freedom formulas and the sum of squares formulas *does not hold* if the degrees of freedom are not multiplied out to remove all parentheses. For example, the degrees of freedom for AB_{ij} can also be written as $(I - 1)(J - 1)$, but such an expression must not be used in that form to obtain the sums of squares formulas. For example, to do so might lead one to assert mistakenly that since the degrees of freedom for Interaction is $(I - 1)(J - 1)$, the sum of squares for Interaction is the product of the sum of squares that corresponds to $(I - 1)$ and the sum of squares that corresponds to $(J - 1)$, namely, $(\Sigma_i T_{i.}^2/JK -$ $T_{...}^2/IJK)(\Sigma_j T_{.j}^2/IK - T_{...}^2/IJK)$. This is *not true* and can be avoided by multiplying out $(I - 1)(J - 1)$ so that the parentheses are removed, giving $IJ - I - J + 1$ to which the correct quantities will correspond.

To summarize, given that we know the model equation, we can immediately write for each source (model term) the degrees of freedom, and using the degrees of freedom we can immediately write for that source the sum of squares.

5.7 Some shortcuts. The great power and ease of using this method can be even further enhanced by noting certain short cuts. For example, note that for the Interaction, the degrees of freedom can be written as $IJ - I - (J - 1)$. Since we have already computed the sum of squares that goes with $J - 1$, we need not do it again. We can just write that the sum of squares for Interaction is $\Sigma_i\Sigma_j T_{ij}^2/K - \Sigma_i T_{i.}^2/JK - SS_{Cols.}$, where $SS_{Cols.}$ stands for the sum of squares for Columns, which is the sum of squares that corresponds to $J - 1$ degrees of freedom.

The savings is not so great in this example, but consider a three-factor design with factors A, B, and C in which the degrees of freedom for the three-factor Interaction is, say, $(I - 1)(J - 1)(K - 1) = IJK - IJ - IK - JK + I + J + K - 1$. It is helpful to recast this as $IJK - IJ - JK - I - (JK - J - K + 1)$ since the terms in parentheses are all that are required for the BC interaction. Then we can write that the sum of squares for the A x B x C Interaction is $\Sigma_i\Sigma_j\Sigma_k T_{ijk}^2/M - \Sigma_i\Sigma_j T_{ij.}^2/KM - \Sigma_i\Sigma_k T_{i.k}^2/JM + \Sigma_i T_{i..}^2/JKM - SS_{BC interaction}$.

Please note also that by writing $(JK - J - K + 1)$ we have not violated the dictum to clear the parentheses. *We need only be concerned about clearing the parentheses when the terms inside the parentheses are* multiplied *by a degrees of freedom term outside them.*

5.8 The form of an analysis of variance summary table. We recall from Chapter 3 that **a mean square is always a sum of squares divided by its degrees of freedom and an F-ratio is always the ratio of two mean squares.** The results of an analysis of variance are usually presented in a standard format, which shows each source or model term together with the degrees of freedom, sum of squares, mean square, and F-ratio associated with that model term. (Sometimes, where space is at a premium, either the sum of squares column or the mean square column is omitted since they are redundant. In scientific journals, when the design is clear, often only the F-ratios are presented in the text rather than in a table. This is okay if the means are presented since the combination of knowing the design, the means, and the F-ratios permits recovery of the entire table. When the means are omitted and only the F-ratios are presented, the reader has no way of recovering the table or of doing any further tests not performed by the writer. This extreme skimpiness of presentation is a trend in the current literature that should be reversed.) The F-ratio for a model term is used to test the null hypothesis that the effects represented by that model term are all zero. Usually we present the name or abbreviation of the factor or interaction of factors in a column labeled Source rather than presenting the model term itself. In the following sections we will analyze some fictitious data for a one-factor, a two-factor, and a three-factor design, present the computational formulas in the appropriate format for the summary table, and then present the actual results of the analysis in that appropriate format.

5.9 The analysis of a one-factor design. Consider first an experiment in which 20 infants were randomly assigned to experimental conditions with the restraint that there be 5

TABLE 5.2 FICTITIOUS LOOKING TIMES FOR DIFFERENT STIMULI

STIMULUS			
UNSCRAMBLED		SCRAMBLED	
PICTURE	DIAGRAM	PICTURE	DIAGRAM
26	11	4	6
22	13	6	6
19	12	5	5
21	15	7	8
24	15	9	4
$T_{1.} = 112$	$T_{2.} = 66$	$T_{3.} = 31$	$T_{4.} = 29$

infants in each of four stimulus conditions. Each infant was shown one of four different stimuli: a picture of a face, a schematic diagram of a face, a scrambled picture of a face made by cutting the first picture into pieces and rearranging the pieces, or a scrambled schematic diagram of a face made by cutting the diagram into pieces and rearranging them. Each subject saw only one stimulus. The four different stimuli constitute the levels of the Stimulus factor. The dependent variable is the amount of time in seconds that the infant spent looking at the stimulus before looking away for the first time. The model equation for this experiment is $Y_{ij} = \mu + A_i + e_{ij} = \mu + (\mu_{i.} - \mu) + (Y_{ij} - \mu_{i.})$. The null hypothesis to be tested is that the different stimuli do not produce different effects on the looking time. That

TABLE 5.3 SUMMARY TABLE OF THE ANALYSIS OF VARIANCE FOR THE ONE-FACTOR DESIGN

Model Term	Source	df	SS	MS	F
μ	The Mean	1	T^2/IJ	$SS_M/1$	MS_M/MS_e
$\mu_{i.}- \mu$	A	I-1	$(\Sigma_i T_{i.}^2/J) - T^2/IJ$	$SS_A/(I-1)$	MS_A/MS_e
$Y_{ij}- \mu_{i.}$	Error	IJ-I	$\Sigma_i\Sigma_j Y_{ij}^2 - (\Sigma_i T_{i.}^2/J)$	$SS_e/(IJ-I)$	

TABLE 5.4 SUMMARY TABLE OF THE ANALYSIS OF VARIANCE FOR THE ONE-FACTOR DESIGN

Model Term	Source	df	SS	MS	F
μ	The Mean	1	$238^2/20$	$2832.2/1$	$(2832.2/1)/4.1$ = 690.78
$\mu_{i.}- \mu$	Stimuli	3	$112^2/5 + 66^2/5 + 31^2/5$ $+ 29^2/5 - 238^2/20$ $= 3740.4 - 2832.2 = 908.2$	$908.2/3$ = 302.73	$302.73/4.1$ = 73.84
$Y_{ij} - \mu_{i.}$	Error	16	$3806 - 3740.4 = 65.6$	$65.6/16 = 4.1$	

is, the A_i are all zero. A fictitious set of data for such an experiment is given in Table 5.2. The abstract form of the ANOVA summary table for a one-factor design is given in Table 5.3. In conventional presentations the column labeled Model Term is not included. It is included here so that the correspondence between the subscripts on the model terms and the formulas for degrees of freedom and sums of squares will be apparent. Also, often the row for The Mean is omitted. Table 5.4 shows the summary table for the data in Table 5.2. (Of course in a scientific report the computations in Table 5.4 would not be shown, only the final values.) If we have adopted the .05 significance level, we test the null hypothesis that $\mu = 0$ by comparing the obtained F-ratio of 690.78 with the tabled critical value of F for 1 and 16 degrees of freedom in the table giving the upper 5 percent points of the F distribution. (see Statistical Table 4). Note that every F-ratio has a numerator mean square and a denominator mean square. Each mean square has an associated degrees of freedom, which we refer to as the numerator degrees of freedom and the denominator degrees of freedom. For the Mean the numerator df is 1 and the denominator df is 16. We use these

TABLE 5.5 FICTITIOUS LOOKING TIMES FOR DIFFERENT STIMULI

	STIMULUS			
	UNSCRAMBLED		SCRAMBLED	
	PICTURE	DIAGRAM	PICTURE	DIAGRAM
3 MON THS	26	11	4	6
	22	13	6	6
	19	12	5	5
	21	15	7	8
	24	15	9	4
6 MON THS	15	18	10	11
	12	21	9	10
	14	23	9	12
	12	21	8	10
	14	20	9	9

two df values to locate the tabled critical value. The numerator df locates the correct column in the table, and the denominator df locates the correct row. The tabled value in that column and row is the critical value for that combination of degrees of freedom. For 1 and 16

TABLE 5.6 LOOKING TIME TOTALS

Age	Picture	Diagram	Scrambled Picture	Scrambled Diagram	
3 Months	$T_{11.} = 112$	$T_{12.} = 66$	$T_{13.} = 31$	$T_{14.} = 29$	$T_{1..} = 238$
6 Months	$T_{21.} = 67$	$T_{22.} = 103$	$T_{23.} = 45$	$T_{24.} = 52$	$T_{2..} = 267$
	$T_{.1.} = 179$	$T_{.2.} = 169$	$T_{.3.} = 76$	$T_{.4.} = 81$	$T = 505$

TABLE 5.7 SUMMARY TABLE FOR THE ANOVA OF THE TWO-FACTOR DESIGN

Model Term	Source	df	SS	MS	F
μ	The Mean	1	T^2/IJK	$SS_M/1$	MS_M/MS_e
$\mu_{i..}-\mu$	A	$I-1$	$(\Sigma_i T_{i..}^2/JK) - T^2/IJK$	$SS_A/(I-1)$	MS_A/MS_e
$\mu_{.j.}-\mu$	B	$J-1$	$(\Sigma_j T_{.j.}^2/IK) - T^2/IJK$	$SS_B/(J-1)$	MS_B/MS_e
$\mu_{ij.}-\mu_{i..}$ $\mu_{.j.}+\mu$	AB	$IJ-I-J+1$	$(\Sigma_i\Sigma_j T_{ij.}^2/K) -(\Sigma_i T_{i..}^2/JK)$ $-(\Sigma_j T_{.j.}^2/IK)+T^2/IJK$	$SS_{AB}/(IJ-I-J+1)$	MS_{AB}/MS_e
$Y_{ijk}-\mu_{ij.}$	Error	$IJK - IJ$	$\Sigma_i\Sigma_j\Sigma_k Y_{ijk}^2 - (\Sigma_i\Sigma_j T_{ij.}^2/K)$	$SS_e/(IJK - IJ)$	

degrees of freedom, that tabled critical value is 4.49. (Check this right now in Statistical Table 4.) If μ actually equals zero, the probability is only .05 that an F-ratio of 4.49 or larger would be obtained in replications of the present experiment. Since 690.78 exceeds 4.49, we reject the null hypothesis. (Some researchers have adopted the practice of reporting the smallest significance level at which the null hypothesis would have been rejected. Such a researcher might look in a table that shows that the critical value of F at the .001 level for 1 and 16 degrees of freedom is 16.12 and report this by stating that "the null hypothesis is rejected, $p < .001$." I do not understand the logic of this practice. I object to the practice because in setting a .05 level in advance, I have decided that I will use as a basis for rejecting the null hypothesis at the .05 level all of those values of the F-ratio that exceed 4.49. Having found one of those that greatly exceeds 4.49 does not justify my now adopting a new significance level. Furthermore, there is a rationale to discussing the probability of an event's occurring or not occurring prior to conducting the experiment in which it may occur or not occur, but that rationale disappears after the experiment is run. There no longer is a probability associated with the outcome once the outcome has occurred. The outcome, for example, an F-ratio of 690.78, has simply occurred. I prefer to set a significance level in advance and accept or reject the null hypothesis at the preset significance level. If other researchers habitually use a different significance level, they can always test my results using their significance level.)

To test at the .05 significance level the null hypothesis that the A_i are all zero, we compare the obtained F-ratio of 73.84 with the tabled critical of F for 3 and 16 degrees of freedom, which is 3.24. Again the null hypothesis is rejected.

5.10 An analysis of a two-factor design. To exemplify the analysis of the two-factor design, we will enlarge the experiment on infant looking times to consider two groups of infants, one group at 3 months of age and the other at 6 months. The fictitious data for this enlarged experiment are shown in Table 5.5. (The scores for the 3-month-old children are the same as those in Table 5.2 for computational convenience for the author. If the experiment comparing the two age groups were actually performed, all of the subjects would be run in random order rather than collecting all the data from one age group before collecting that from the other.) Because all of the sums of squares terms are computed using the sum of the squares of all of the scores, $\Sigma_i\Sigma_j\Sigma_kY_{ijk}^2$, and various squared totals, it is a convenience in computing if we begin by obtaining a table of totals. Table 5.6 shows the table of totals for the design in Table 5.5. The value of $\Sigma_i\Sigma_j\Sigma_kY_{ijk}^2$ is 7799. It is useful to note that the row totals 238 and 267 sum to the grand total of 505, as do the column totals, 179, 169, 76, and 81. If the computations are being done by hand, this provides an easy check for errors. Table 5.7 shows the formulas for the two-factor design,

TABLE 5.8 TWO-FACTOR DESIGN ANOVA SUMMARY

Model Term	Source	df	SS	MS	F
μ	The Mean	1	6375.625	6375.625	2189.06
$\mu_{i..}-\mu$	Age	1	21.025	21.025	7.22
$\mu_{.j.}-\mu$	Stimulus	3	918.275	306.0917	105.10
$\mu_{ij.}-\mu_{i..}-\mu_{.j.}+\mu$	AB	3	390.875	130.2917	44.74
$Y_{ijk}-\mu_{ij.}$	Error	32	93.2	2.9125	

and Table 5.8 shows the application of these formulas to the two-factor looking time experiment with Age and Stimulus as the two factors. Table 5.8 presents the summary of the analysis of variance of the data in the two-factor design shown in Table 5.5. When the formulas in Table 5.7 are applied to the data in Table 5.5: $I = 2$, $J = 4$, $IJ = 8$, and $IJK = 40$; the value of T^2/IJK is $505^2/40 = 6375.625$; the value of $\Sigma_iT_{i..}^2/JK$ is $238^2/20 + 267^2/20$; the value of $\Sigma_jT_{.j.}^2/IK$ is $179^2/10 + 169^2/10 + 76^2/10 + 81^2/10 = 7293.9$; the value of $\Sigma_i\Sigma_jT_{ij.}^2/K$ is $112^2/5 + 66^2/5 + 31^2/5 + 29^2/5 + 67^2/5 + 103^2/5 + 45^2/5 + 52^2/5 = 38529/5 = 7705.8$; and $\Sigma_i\Sigma_j\Sigma_kY_{ijk}^2 = 7799$. Using the model equation we can immediately arrive at the degrees of freedom and sums of squares formulas given in Table 5.10.

5.11 An analysis of a three-factor design. The next example we will consider is a three-factor design in which the investigators are not only interested in the effects of Age and Stimulus but also wish to consider the possibility that infant boys and infant girls may differ in their looking times. Gender is introduced into the design as a third factor. Suppose that when 80 3- and 6-month-old boy and girl infants were shown one of the four stimuli

An Introduction to the Analysis of Variance

TABLE 5.9 FICTITIOUS LOOKING TIMES FROM 3- AND 6-MONTH-OLD BOY AND GIRL INFANTS

		STIMULUS			
		UNSCRAMBLED		SCRAMBLED	
		PICTURE	DIAGRAM	PICTURE	DIAGRAM
GIRLS	3 MO.	26	11	4	6
		22	13	6	6
		19	12	5	5
		21	15	7	8
		24	15	9	4
	6 MO.	15	18	10	11
		12	21	9	10
		14	23	9	12
		12	21	8	10
		14	20	9	9
BOYS	3 MO.	23	10	4	4
		22	9	5	6
		24	12	3	6
		24	8	3	3
		21	9	4	4
	6 MO.	14	19	8	7
		13	21	8	6
		15	24	7	8
		12	21	9	8
		13	18	6	6

described above and the same looking time measure was taken, the data in Table 5.9 were collected. The model equation for the experimental design in Table 5.9 is

$$Y_{ijkm} = \mu + G_i + A_j + S_k + GA_{ij} + GS_{ik} + AS_{jk} + GAS_{ijk} + e_{ijkm}$$

$$= \mu + (\mu_{i...} - \mu) + (\mu_{.j..} - \mu) + (\mu_{..k.} - \mu) + (\mu_{ij..} - \mu_{i...} - \mu_{.j..} + \mu)$$

$$+ (\mu_{i.k.} - \mu_{i...} - \mu_{..k.} + \mu) + (\mu_{.jk.} - \mu_{.j..} - \mu_{..k.} + \mu) + (\mu_{ijk.} - \mu_{ij..} - \mu_{i.k.} - \mu_{.jk.}$$

$$+ \mu_{i...} + \mu_{.j..} + \mu_{..k.} - \mu) + e_{ijkm}.$$

TABLE 5.10 THREE-FACTOR DESIGN ANOVA SUMMARY

Source	df	SS
Mean	1	$T^2/IJKM$
G	I-1	$\Sigma_i T_{i...}^2/JKM - T^2/IJKM$
A	J-1	$\Sigma_j T_{.j.}^2/IKM - T^2/IJKM$
S	K-1	$\Sigma_k T_{..k.}^2/IJM - T^2/IJKM$
GA	(I-1)(J-1)	$\Sigma_i \Sigma_j T_{ij..}^2/KM - \Sigma_i T_{i...}^2/JKM - \Sigma_j T_{.j.}^2/IKM + T^2/IJKM$
GS	(I-1)(K-1)	$\Sigma_i \Sigma_k T_{i.k.}^2/JM - \Sigma_i T_{i...}^2/JKM - \Sigma_k T_{..k.}^2/IJM + T^2/IJKM$
AS	(J-1)(K-1)	$\Sigma_j \Sigma_k T_{.jk.}^2/IM - \Sigma_j T_{.j.}^2/IKM - \Sigma_k T_{..k.}^2/IJM + T^2/IJKM$
GAS	(I-1)(J-1)(K-1)	$\Sigma_i \Sigma_j \Sigma_k T_{ijk.}^2/M - \Sigma_i \Sigma_j T_{ij..}^2/KM - \Sigma_i \Sigma_k T_{i.k.}^2/JM -$ $\Sigma_j \Sigma_k T_{.jk.}^2/IM + \Sigma_i T_{i...}^2/JKM + \Sigma_j T_{.j.}^2/IKM$ $+\Sigma_k T_{..k.}^2/IJM - T^2/IJKM$
Error	IJKM - IJK	$\Sigma_i \Sigma_j \Sigma_k \Sigma_m Y_{ijkm}^2 - \Sigma_i \Sigma_j \Sigma_k T_{ijk.}^2/M$

Applying the values in Table 5.10 to the data in Table 5.9 gives the results in Table 5.11. It will be useful to examine the worksheet for obtaining these results shown in Table 5.12.

TABLE 5.11 SUMMARY TABLE FOR ANALYSIS OF THE THREE-FACTOR DESIGN

Source	df	SS	MS	F
Mean	1	11,328.80	11,328.80	4,681.32
G	1	42.05	42.05	17.39
A	1	57.80	57.80	23.90
S	3	2,121.70	707.23	292.40
GA	1	1.25	1.25	.52
GS	3	18.85	6.28	2.60
AS	3	904.30	301.43	124.62
GAS	3	22.45	7.48	3.09
Error	64	154.80	2.42	

The worksheet shows the cell totals for the 16 cells in the 2 x 2 x 4 design. These are the $T_{ijk.}$'s. Letting Gender be Factor G, Age be Factor A, and Stimulus Condition be Factor S, we also see in the various margins: the G x S totals 179, 169, 76, 81, 181, 151, 57, and 58, which are the $T_{i.k.}$'s; the G x A totals 238, 267, 204, and 243, which are the $T_{ij..}$'s; and the

A x S totals in the table at the bottom of the worksheet, which are 226, 114, 50, 52, 134, 206, 83, aand 87, the $T_{jk.}$'s. The margins also show the various totals for the main effects: for Factor G the $T_{i...}$'s are 505 and 447; for Factor A the $T_{.j..}$'s are 442 and 510; and for Factor S the $T_{..k.}$'s are 360, 320, 133, and 139. Finally the grand total $T_{....}$ or just T is found to be 952. The student should locate all of these totals in the worksheet and note how each of the values for the two-factor totals may be found by summing in the table of $T_{ijk.}$'s, each of the one-factor totals may be found by summing the values in the two-factor tables, and the grand total is obtained by summing any set of one-factor totals. This provides checks on the various computations if the analysis is done by hand. The only other value needed to perform the computations is the sum of the squares of all of the scores in the design, which turns out to be 14,652.

Since the basic computations are performed using sums of squared totals, it is useful to extend the worksheet in Table 5.12 by squaring all the entries. This gives the worksheet in Table 5.13. Summing the appropriate entries in Table 5.13 and dividing gives the values $\Sigma_i\Sigma_j\Sigma_k T_{ijk.}^2/M = 14497.20$; $\Sigma_i\Sigma_j T_{ij..}^2/KM = 11,429.90$; $\Sigma_i\Sigma_k T_{i.k.}^2/JM = 13,511.40$; $\Sigma_j\Sigma_k T_{.jk.}^2/IM = 14,412.60$; $\Sigma_i T_{i...}^2/JKM = 11,370.85$; $\Sigma_j T_{.j..}^2/IKM = 11,386.60$; $\Sigma_k T_{..k.}^2/IJM = 13,450.50$; and $T^2/IJKM = 11,328.80$. Inserting these in the formulas of Table 5.10 completes the work for the analysis shown in Table 5.11.

TABLE 5.12 A WORKSHEET FOR OBTAINING THE VARIOUS CELL TOTALS AND MARGINAL TOTALS FOR THE THREE-FACTOR ANALYSIS OF VARIANCE IN TABLE 5.14

		P	D	SP	SD	
Girls	Three	112	66	31	29	238
	Six	67	103	45	52	267
		179	169	76	81	505
Boys	Three	114	48	19	23	204
	Six	67	103	38	35	243
		181	151	57	58	447
		360	320	133	139	952

	P	D	SP	SD	
Three	226	114	50	52	442
Six	134	206	83	87	510

5.12 The alternation rule. There is a simple rule for writing out the various formulas for any source in a factorial design regardless of how many factors there are. This rule

TABLE 5.13 THE SQUARES OF ALL OF THE VARIOUS CELL AND MARGINAL TOTALS IN THE WORKSHEET OF FIGURE

		P	D	SP	SD	
Girls	Three	12544	4356	961	841	56644
	Six	4489	10609	2025	2704	71289
		32041	28561	5776	6561	255025
Boys	Three	12996	2304	361	529	41616
	Six	4489	10609	1444	1225	59049
		32761	22801	3249	3364	199809
		129600	102400	17689	19321	906304
	Three	51076	12996	2500	2704	195364
	Six	17956	42436	6889	7569	260100

applies to μ-dot, degrees of freedom, and sums of squares formulas. We will call it the **alternation rule**. We will express the rule in terms of the degrees of freedom since they involve the simplest notation. Consider the degrees of freedom for the sources in a three-factor design. There is the degree of freedom for the mean, 1. Then, for the main effects there are I - 1, J - 1, and K - 1. Note that for the mean, there is only one term, and it is positive. For each of the main effects, the first term is positive and the second term is negative. Now consider the degrees of freedom for the three two-factor interactions. They are

IJ - I - J + 1,

IK - I - K + 1, and

JK - J - K + 1.

Notice that the terms at the two-factor level, IJ, IK, and JK, are each positive. Then all of the terms at the next level down are negative. Then the sign switches back to the positive at the level of the mean, 1. We always start with one N-letter term as positive. Then at the next level, we have all of the (N - 1)-letter terms included in the beginning N-letter term, and they are all negative. Then we switch back to positive for the $(N - 2)$-letter terms, and so forth until we get down to the 1 for the mean. Thus, for the three-factor interaction we have

IJK - IJ - IK - JK + I + J + K - 1.

For a four-factor interaction the rule gives

IJKM - IJK - IJM - IKM - JKM + IJ + IK + IM + JK + JM + KM - I - J - K -

M + 1.

Because of the complete correspondence between degrees of freedom and the μ-dot notation, and also between degrees of freedom and the sum of squares notation, this same alternation rule gives

μ, $\mu_{i..} - \mu, \mu_{.j.} - \mu, \mu_{..k} - \mu$,   and $\mu_{ij.} - \mu_{i..} - \mu_{.j.} + \mu$

as the μ-dot formulas and

T^2/IJK, $\Sigma_i T_{i..}^2/JK - T^2/IJK$, $\Sigma_j T_{.j.}^2/IK - T^2/IJK$, $\Sigma_k T_{..k}^2/IJ - T^2/IJK$,

and

$\Sigma_i \Sigma_j T_{ij.}^2/K - \Sigma_i T_{i..}^2/JK - \Sigma_j T_{.j.}^2/IK + T^2/IJK$

as the corresponding sums of squares formulas. The alternation rule applies only to factorial designs and not to the types of designs to be considered in the next chapter.

5.13 On to nested factors. With this chapter we have almost exhausted the many quantities that can be obtained directly from the model equation. The last to be considered will be the expected values of mean squares. These also can be gotten immediately by an orderly inspection of the model equation according to a few simple rules. But before taking that up, we will get a chance to see in the next chapter how the rules for getting degrees of freedom and sums of squares apply to designs with nested factors. Then we'll take up random effects models and see how they require expected values of mean squares.

Exercises

*1. Explain from a vector perspective why:

(a) a degrees of freedom term always corresponds to the same sum of squares term.

(b) the arithmetic sign, plus or minus, on the sum of squares term is always the same as the arithmetic sign on the degrees of freedom term that it corresponds to.

2. The student should show algebraically that the conceptual formula for a sum of squares as given in Table 4.5 and the T-dot formula for the same sum of squares are equivalent. Specifically, show the equality of $\Sigma_i\Sigma_j\Sigma_k(M_{i..} - M_{...})^2$ and $\Sigma_i T_{i..}^2/JK - T_{...}^2/IJK$ by performing the indicated operations in the former term and converting M-dot terms to T-dots divided by uppercase products.

3. Perform the analysis of variance on the data in Table 5.9. Check your final results against the analysis of variance in Table 5.11. If there is a discrepancy, try to locate the error by backtracking using the worksheets in the text.

4. Assume that the scrambled diagram condition had not been used in the experiment for which the data are shown in Table 5.5. Thus only three levels of the stimulus factor are used. This leaves a 2 x 3 factorial design. Using the data in Table 5.5

(a) Write the model equation for this design

(b) Write out a summary table showing the Sources, the df, and the sums of squares for this design. (Hint: a lot of the work is already done in Table 5.6.)

(c) Write the model term for each source, using μ-dot notation

5. Use the data in Table 5.9. Again assume that the scrambled diagram condition was not used in the experiment, leaving a 2 x 2 x 3 design.

(a) Write the model equation

(b) write a summary table showing the sources, the df, and the sums of squares. Much of the work has been done for you in Tables 5.12 and 5.13

(c) Write the model term for each source, using μ-dot notation.

6. Perform a separate two-factor analysis of variance for just the Girls data in Table 5.9, and then do the same for just the Boys data.

(a) Compare the results of these two analyses with the results of the three-factor analysis in Table 5.11. Are the same F values obtained for the Stimulus and Age factors? Why did this happen?

(b) What is missing from the two separate analyses that is obtained with the overall analysis of the three-factor design?

7. (a) Write out the formula for the sum of squares for a source with

$(I - 1)(J - 1)(K - 1)(L - 1)$ degrees of freedom, using the T-dot notation. Assume a four-factor design.

(b) Suppose a two-factor design could exist in which some source has $I(J - 1)$ degrees of freedom. What would the sum of squares be for that source, written in T-dot notation?

8. What shortcut could you use in answering exercise 7a?

**TABLE 5.14 FICTIONAL DATA
FOR A MEMORY EXPERIMENT**

	List Length		
	Short	Medium	Long
Abstract Words	7	8	14
	8	9	13
	8	12	9
	9	13	12
	7	11	10
Concrete Words	12	13	19
	14	14	20
	13	14	16
	10	13	15
	12	16	14

**TABLE 5.15 DATA FOR AN INFANT
PERCEPTION TASK**

	STIMULUS			
	UNSCRAMBLED		SCRAMBLED	
	PICTURE	DIAGRAM	PICTURE	DIAGRAM
3 MO.	14	9	4	6
	17	8	6	6
	15	11	5	5
	22	10	7	8
	21	9	9	4
6 MO.	6	16	10	11
	8	15	9	10
	7	14	9	12
	9	18	8	10
	10	12	9	9

9. Assume the data in Table 5.14, and give the number of remembered items in a memory experiment in which words belonging in different categories were shown to subjects in lists of various lengths. Perform the analysis of the data, and write out the summary table, including all of the columns in Table 5.4.

10. Graph the cell means for the data in exercise 9, and describe how the results of the analysis of variance are refelcted in the graph.

11. Perform an analysis of variance on the data in Table 5.15, and present the results in a summary table.

12. Write the degrees of freedom and T-dot sums of squares formulas associated with the following m-dot expressions:

(a) $\mu_{ij.}$

(b) $\mu_{i..}$

(c) μ

(d) $\mu_{ijk..}$

(e) $\mu_{i.k.}$

13. Assume that Table 5.16 gives the cell **totals** in a 2 x 4 x 3 factorial design and that there are four scores per cell. Find the sums of squares for A, C, AB, AC and ABC.

TABLE 5.16 FICTIONAL DATA FOR A 2 x 4 x 3 FACTORIAL DESIGN

	C_1					C_2					C_3		
	B_1	B_2	B_3	B_4		B_1	B_2	B_3	B_4		B_1	B_2	B_3	B_4
A_1	8	11	12	15	A_1	14	13	15	17	A_1	8	10	14	16
A_2	6	8	11	12	A_2	10	11	12	16	A_2	7	12	13	15

14. Given the information provided in exercise 13, what additional information is needed in order to calculate the sum of squares for error?

15. Assuming that for the data summarized in exercise 13, the model equation is

$$Y_{ijkm} = \mu + A_i + B_j + C_k + AB_{ij} + AC_{ik} + BC_{jk} + ABC_{ijk} + e_{ijkm},$$

find $T_{1...}$, $T_{.3..}$, $T_{23..}$, and $T_{223.}$.

16. Assume a five-factor design with score Y_{ijkmno}. Use the alternation rule to write the degrees of freedom for:

(a) each of the four-factor interactions

(b) the five-factor interaction

17. Using the alternation rule, write the sum of squares formula in T-dot notation for the four-factor interaction for a four-factor design with score Y_{ijkmn}.

18. Inspect Table 5.10 to see that the sum of squares formulas follow the alternation rule in every case.

Supplementary Reading

Lackritz, J. R. (1984) Exact p values for F and t tests. *The American Statistician, 38,* 312-314. Gives a hand calculator method for calculating p values.

6

Nested Factors

6.1 Crossed and nested factors. When a level of one factor occurs in the experimental design with more than one level of another factor, we say the two factors are **crossed**. If every level of each of the two factors occurs with every level of the other factor, the two factors are **completely crossed**. Otherwise the crossed factors are said to be partially crossed. So far, we have looked only at designs in which if there was more than one factor, the factors were completely crossed. Now, **if every level of factor B occurs with <u>one and only one</u> level of factor A, we say B is nested within A.**

Think of nests full of young birds. There may be several birds in each of several nests, but no bird occurs in a nest other than its own (too young to fly, etc.).

Let's consider an example. In a large city, four fourth-grade classrooms are selected in each of three grammar schools. Twenty students in each class are selected at random and given a mathematics achievement test in order to assess the homogeneity of mathematics achievement throughout the city school system. We denote Grammar Schools as Factor A and Classrooms as Factor B. Classrooms are nested in Grammar Schools since a given classroom cannot occur in more than one grammar school. We can also note that children are nested in classrooms in that a given child occurs in one and only one classroom. We can call children Factor C. We will treat the effects of individual children as error, however.

6.2 Model equation notation for nested factors. There are four classrooms in each of three schools; therefore there are 12 levels of Factor B. It will be useful, however, to denote each classroom by indicating which classroom it is in which school it is nested. Thus, in each school, calling the classrooms 1, 2, 3, and 4, we would denote the effect of the jth classroom in the ith school by the factor name B with the index j(i), giving the effect $B_{j(i)}$, the index denoting the jth classroom nested in the ith level of Factor A. **The index for the nested-factor effect is written so that the nested factor's level occurs first, and the nesting factor's level is appended to it in parentheses.** First we indicate the bird; then, in parentheses, which nest it lives in—first, the classroom; then, which school.

6.3 The data in model equation form for a design with a nested factor. Let us look at a fixed-effects model for this experimental design. The model equation would be

$$Y_{ijk} = \mu + A_i + B_{j(i)} + e_{ijk} \qquad [6.1]$$

with the side conditions that $\Sigma_i A_i = 0$ and at each value of i (i.e., level of factor A), $\Sigma_j B_{j(i)} = 0$. A representation of the scores in their model equation form for this design is shown in Table 6.1.

6.4 There is never an interaction effect for two factors when one is nested within the other. One of the first things we notice about the model equation [6.1] is that we have a two-factor design but there is no interaction effect in the model equation. Let us first state the rule that bears on this situation and then justify it. **There is never an interaction effect for two factors when one is nested within the other.** Or, putting it positively, interaction effects occur only for crossed factors. Now, why is this?

TABLE 6.1 MODEL EQUATION VALUES FOR FOUR LEVELS OF B NESTED IN EACH OF THREE LEVELS OF A WITH 20 SUBJECTS PER CELL

A_1	A_2	A_3
$\mu + A_1 + B_{1(1)} + e_{1,1,1}$	$\mu + A_2 + B_{1(2)} + e_{2,1,1}$	$\mu + A_3 + B_{1(3)} + e_{3,1,1}$
...	...	...
$\mu + A_1 + B_{1(1)} + e_{1,1,20}$	$\mu + A_2 + B_{1(2)} + e_{2,1,20}$	$\mu + A_3 + B_{1(3)} + e_{3,1,20}$
$\mu + A_1 + B_{2(1)} + e_{1,2,1}$	$\mu + A_2 + B_{2(2)} + e_{2,2,1}$	$\mu + A_3 + B_{2(3)} + e_{3,2,1}$
...	...	...
$\mu + A_1 + B_{2(1)} + e_{1,2,20}$	$\mu + A_2 + B_{2(2)} + e_{2,2,20}$	$\mu + A_3 + B_{2(3)} + e_{3,2,20}$
$\mu + A_1 + B_{3(1)} + e_{1,3,1}$	$\mu + A_2 + B_{3(2)} + e_{2,3,1}$	$\mu + A_3 + B_{3(3)} + e_{3,3,1}$
...	...	...
$\mu + A_1 + B_{3(1)} + e_{1,3,20}$	$\mu + A_2 + B_{3(2)} + e_{2,3,20}$	$\mu + A_3 + B_{3(3)} + e_{3,3,20}$
$\mu + A_1 + B_{4(1)} + e_{1,4,1}$	$\mu + A_2 + B_{4(2)} + e_{2,4,1}$	$\mu + A_3 + B_{4(3)} + e_{3,4,1}$
...	...	...
$\mu + A_1 + B_{4(1)} + e_{1,4,20}$	$\mu + A_2 + B_{4(2)} + e_{2,4,20}$	$\mu + A_3 + B_{4(3)} + e_{3,4,20}$

The simplest way to see why no interaction effect is included is to realize that an interaction effect is built into a model equation in order to account for a departure from additivity in the data. For example, consider the case of two crossed factors, A and B. The model equation is $Y_{ijk} = \mu + A_i + B_j + AB_{ij} + e_{ijk}$. Now consider the true means for $Cell_{1,1}$, $Cell_{1,2}$, $Cell_{2,1}$, and $Cell_{2,2}$. These would be μ_{11}, μ_{12}, μ_{21}, and μ_{22}. If there are no interaction effects, $\mu_{11} - \mu_{12} = \mu_{21} - \mu_{22}$ since

$$\mu_{11} - \mu_{12} = (\mu + A_1 + B_1) - (\mu + A_1 + B_2) = B_1 - B_2$$

and

$$\mu_{21} - \mu_{22} = (\mu + A_2 + B_1) - (\mu + A_2 + B_2) = B_1 - B_2.$$

Interaction effects are included to account for any difference between $(\mu_{11} - \mu_{12})$ and $(\mu_{21} - \mu_{22})$. Thus, with interaction effects included,

$$\mu_{11} - \mu_{12} = (\mu + A_1 + B_1 + AB_{11}) - (\mu + A_1 + B_2 + AB_{12}) = (B_1 - B_2) + (AB_{11} - AB_{12})$$

and

$$\mu_{21} - \mu_{22} = (\mu + A_2 + B_1 + AB_{21}) - (\mu + A_2 + B_2 + AB_{22}) = (B_1 - B_2) + (AB_{21} - AB_{22}).$$

Therefore the model with interaction effects accounts for the difference between the two cell means in column 1 not equaling the difference between the two corresponding cell means in column 2. It accounts for the difference by the difference between $(AB_{11} - AB_{12})$ and $(AB_{21} - AB_{22})$.

But now consider the nested factors model:

$$\mu_{11} = \mu + A_1 + B_{1(1)}; \quad \mu_{12} = \mu + A_1 + B_{2(1)}; \quad \mu_{21} = \mu + A_2 + B_{1(2)};$$

$$\mu_{22} = \mu + A_2 + B_{2(2)}.$$

Therefore $\mu_{11} - \mu_{12} = B_{1(1)} - B_{2(1)}$ and $\mu_{21} - \mu_{22} = B_{1(2)} - B_{2(2)}$. Thus there is already included in the model an explanation for why $\mu_{11} - \mu_{12}$ does not equal $\mu_{21} - \mu_{22}$. These differences are expected to differ from each other since there is no reason why $B_{1(1)} - B_{2(1)}$ should equal $B_{1(2)} - B_{2(2)}$. In terms of the example with classrooms in schools, there is no expectation that the difference between the scores of two classrooms in School 1 should equal the difference between the scores of two other classrooms in School 2. These four classrooms are unrelated except that each pair shares the same school. That common effect of sharing the same school is represented by the fact that two have A_1 and the other two have A_2 as their School effects.

We say that the B factor is **completely confounded** with any AB interaction effect. This means that if there were some effect specific to the particular combination of a level of A with a level of B, we would be unable to estimate this effect separately from the effect of the level of B itself. Therefore there is no point to including it in the model equation.

6.5 The effects of nested factors and their estimates in M-dot form. The μ-dot form of the model equation [6.1] is

$$Y_{ijk} = \mu_{...} + (\mu_{i..} - \mu_{...}) + (\mu_{ij.} - \mu_{i..}) + e_{ijk} \qquad [6.2]$$

where $\mu_{...}$ is the general mean, $\mu_{i..}$ is the mean for the ith level of A, and $\mu_{ij.}$ is the mean for the jth level of B at the ith level of A. **The effect of the level of a nested factor is defined** not as the deviation of that level from the general mean but instead **as the deviation of that level of B from the mean of the level of A in which it is nested.** As usual the estimates of the various effects are obtained by substituting the sample means for the corresponding population means. Thus

TABLE 6.2 THE SOURCES, df, AND SUMS OF SQUARES FOR THE DESIGN DESCRIBED BY EQUATION [6.2]

Source	df	SS
Mean	1	$T_{...}^2/IJK$
A	I-1	$\Sigma_i T_{i..}^2/JK - T_{...}^2/IJK$
B nested in A	IJ - I	$\Sigma_i\Sigma_j T_{ij.}^2/K - \Sigma_i T_{i..}^2/K$
Error	IJK - IJ	$\Sigma_i\Sigma_j\Sigma_k Y_{ijk}^2 - \Sigma_i\Sigma_j T_{ij.}^2/K$

the estimates of $\mu_{...}$, $\mu_{i..}$, and $\mu_{ij.}$ are $M_{...} = \Sigma_i\Sigma_j\Sigma_k Y_{ijk}/IJK$, $M_{i..} = \Sigma_j\Sigma_k Y_{ijk}/JK$, and $M_{ij.} = \Sigma_k Y_{ijk}/K$, and the estimates of μ, A_i, and $B_{j(i)}$ are $M_{...}$, $M_{i..} - M_{...}$, and $M_{ij.} - M_{i..}$.

6.6 The ANOVA for the model equation in [6.2]. The analysis of variance for the model equation in [6.2],

$$Y_{ijk} = \mu_{...} + (\mu_{i..} - \mu_{...}) + (\mu_{ij.} - \mu_{i..}) + e_{ijk},$$

follows the procedures completed in Chapter 5. The sources come from the effects equation, and the degrees of freedom and sums of squares are obtained using the model equation [6.2]. The essentials for the analysis are given in Table 6.2.

TABLE 6.3 FICTIONAL SCORES: FOUR CLASSROOMS IN THREE SCHOOLS

SCHOOL 1				SCHOOL 2				SCHOOL 3			
CLASSROOM				CLASSROOM				CLASSROOM			
1	2	3	4	1	2	3	4	1	2	3	4
1	2	2	4	3	5	3	4	3	1	3	1
3	4	1	4	4	5	4	3	4	2	3	1
2	3	3	3	3	3	6	3	5	3	1	2
2	5	3	4	4	4	4	3	5	3	2	2
1	5	2	5	4	5	5	4	3	2	2	2

To exemplify this analysis in simplified form, we assume that the scores from five children obtained in four classrooms at the three schools are given in Table 6.3. We find that $\Sigma_i\Sigma_j\Sigma_k Y_{ijk}^2 = 686$, $T_{...}^2/60 = 589$, $\Sigma_i T_{i..}^2/20 = 611$, and $\Sigma_i\Sigma_j T_{ij.}^2/5 = 650$, giving the analysis of variance shown in Table 6.4.

TABLE 6.4   ANOVA OF TABLE 6.3 SCORES

Source	df	SS	MS	F
Mean	1	589	589.00	785.00
Schools	2	22	11.00	14.70
Classrooms	9	39	4.33	5.78
Error	48	36	.75	

TABLE 6.5   THE DESIGN DIAGRAM FOR A FOUR-FACTOR DESIGN IN WHICH D IS NESTED IN B x C AND A IS CROSSED WITH B, C, AND D

	B_1						B_2					
	C_1			C_2			C_1			C_2		
	$D_{1(1,1)}$	$D_{2(1,1)}$	$D_{3(1,2)}$	$D_{1(1,2)}$	$D_{2(1,2)}$	$D_{3(1,2)}$	$D_{1(2,1)}$	$D_{2(2,1)}$	$D_{3(2,1)}$	$D_{1(2,2)}$	$D_{2(2,2)}$	$D_{3(2,2)}$
A_1	2	3	4	6	7	6	4	3	4	8	7	9
	3	3	1	2	4	3	7	6	5	4	8	8
A_2	4	5	4	5	6	6	7	6	5	6	7	8
	4	5	5	4	5	6	7	7	8	7	8	9
A_3	4	5	6	5	6	7	4	4	5	6	7	7
	4	4	5	4	6	7	5	5	5	3	8	8

6.7 The ANOVA for a more complex design. In this section we consider a more complex design in which there are four factors, A, B, C, and D, and in which B and C are crossed, D is nested in B cross C, and A is crossed with B, with C, and with D. The design diagram together with two scores per cell is shown in Table 6.5. When we say that A is crossed with B, C, and D, we mean that each level of A occurs with each level of B, with each level of C, and with each level of D. We can see in the diagram in Table 6.5 that this is so. Factors B and C are obviously also crossed since each level of B occurs with each level of C and vice versa. Factor D, however, is nested in C and nested in B since each level of Factor D occurs with one and only one level of B and one and only one level of C.

Remember here that all of the levels of Factor D are unique even though the first subscript repeats at each different combination of B with C. The fact that there are 12 different subscripts denotes this fact that all 12 levels of Factor D are different from one another.

The model equation for the experimental design displayed in Table 6.5 is

$$Y_{ijkmp} = \mu + A_i + B_j + C_k + D_{m(j,k)} + AB_{ij} + AC_{ik} + AD_{im(j,k)} + BC_{jk} +$$

$$ABC_{ijk} + e_{ijkmp} \qquad\qquad [6.3]$$

Let's inspect the right side of equation [6.3] in detail. In addition to μ, the general mean, we first find the main-effects terms A_i, B_j, C_k, and $D_{m(j,k)}$. The indices on $D_{m(j,k)}$ denote that the D factor is nested in the factors for which j and k are the indices, namely, B and C. Next we have the two-factor interaction terms. The terms AB_{ij} and AC_{ik} show A crossed with B and with C. The factors B and C are also crossed, so we find the term BC_{jk}. Also, since A, B, and C are crossed we have the three-factor interaction term, ABC_{ijk}. Then, along with error, we find $AD_{im(j,k)}$, showing A crossed with D, the index being the combination of the i for A and the m(j,k) for D. We also note that since D is nested in B and C, there are no interaction terms containing B and D or C and D. In μ-dot form, equation [6.3] becomes

$$Y_{ijkmp} = \mu + (\mu_{i...} - \mu_{.....}) + (\mu_{.j..} - \mu_{.....}) + (\mu_{..k..} - \mu_{.....}) + (\mu_{.jkm.} - \mu_{.jk..})$$

$$+ (\mu_{ij...} - \mu_{i...} - \mu_{.j...} + \mu_{.....}) + (\mu_{i.k..} - \mu_{i...} - \mu_{..k..} + \mu_{.....}) + (\mu_{ijkm.} - \mu_{ijk..} -$$

$$\mu_{.jkm.} + \mu_{.jk..}) + (\mu_{.jk..} - \mu_{.j...} - \mu_{..k..} + \mu_{.....}) + (\mu_{ijk..} - \mu_{ij...} - \mu_{i.k..} - \mu_{.jk..} +$$

$$\mu_{i...} + \mu_{.j...} + \mu_{..k..} - \mu_{.....}) + e_{ijkmp}. \qquad\qquad [6.4]$$

We obtain the formulas for the degrees of freedom and the sums of squares by following the simple rules developed in Chapters 4 and 5 and shown in Table 6.6. We note in Table 6.6 that the degrees of freedom and sums of squares formulas for the nested factors reflect, as we would expect, that the effect for a nested factor is viewed as the deviation of the mean for the nested-factor level from the mean of the level of the factor in which it is nested, thus conforming to the M-dot expression of the model equation as usual. Numerical values are included in Table 6.6 for checking computations using the data in Table 6.5.

6.8 On the definition of nested-factor effects. A question that often arises for the student is why we define the effect of the level of a nested factor as

TABLE 6.6 THE DEGREES OF FREEDOM AND SUMS OF SQUARES FORMULAS FOR THE MODEL EQUATION [6.4]

Source	df	Sums of Squares
Mean	1	$T_{....}^2/IJKMP = 2123.35$
A	$I-1 = 2$	$\Sigma_i T_{i....}^2/JKMP - T_{....}^2/IJKMP = 15.19$
B	$J-1 = 1$	$\Sigma_j T_{.j...}^2/IKMP - T_{....}^2/IJKMP = 48.35$
C	$K-1 = 1$	$\Sigma_k T_{..k..}^2/IJMP - T_{....}^2/IJKMP = 42.01$
D	$JKM-JK = 8$	$\Sigma_j\Sigma_k\Sigma_m T_{.jkm.}^2/IP - \Sigma_j\Sigma_k T_{.jk..}^2/IMP = 30.78$
AxB	$IJ-I-J+1 = 2$	$\Sigma_i\Sigma_j T_{ij...}^2/KMP - \Sigma_i T_{i....}^2/JKMP - \Sigma_j T_{.j...}^2/IKMP +$ $T_{....}^2/IJKMP = 15.53$
AxC	$IK-I-K+1 = 2$	$\Sigma_i\Sigma_k T_{i.k..}^2/JMP - \Sigma_i T_{i....}^2/JKMP - \Sigma_k T_{..k..}^2/IJMP$ $+T_{....}^2/IJKMP = 6.03$
AxD	$IJKM-IJK-$ $JKM+JK = 16$	$\Sigma_i\Sigma_j\Sigma_k\Sigma_m T_{ijkm.}^2/P - \Sigma_i\Sigma_j\Sigma_k T_{ijk.}^2/MP -$ $\Sigma_j\Sigma_k\Sigma_m T_{.jkm.}^2/IP + \Sigma_i\Sigma_j T_{ij...}^2/KMP = 8.22$
BxC	$JK-J-K+1 = 1$	$\Sigma_j\Sigma_k T_{.jk..}^2/IMP - \Sigma_j T_{.j...}^2/IKMP - \Sigma_k T_{..k..}^2/IJMP +$ $T_{....}^2/IJKMP = 0.68$
AxBxC	$IJK-IJ-IK-$ $JK+I+J+K-1 = 2$	$\Sigma_i\Sigma_j\Sigma_k T_{ijk.}/MP - SSAxB - \Sigma_i\Sigma_k T_{i.k..}/JMP -$ $\Sigma_j\Sigma_k T_{.jk..}^2/IMP - \Sigma_k T_{..k..}^2/IJMP = 0.36$
Error	$IJKMP-IJKM = 36$	$\Sigma_i\Sigma_j\Sigma_k\Sigma_m\Sigma_p Y_{ijkmp}^2 - \Sigma_i\Sigma_j\Sigma_k\Sigma_m T_{ijkm.}^2/P = 56.50$

Note: the numerical values are for the data in Table 6.5

the deviation of the mean for that nested level from the mean for the level of the factor it is nested in. That is, if $Y_{ijk} = \mu + A_i + B_{j(i)} + e_{ijk}$, why is $B_{j(i)}$ defined as $\mu_{ij.} - \mu_{i..}$? This is a reasonable question because prior to discussing nested factors we have always defined the effect of a level of some factor as the difference between the mean of the effect for that level and the general mean. Thus in the model for a two-factor design with crossed factors, $Y_{ijk} = \mu + A_i + B_j + AB_{ij} + e_{ijk}$, we have defined A_i as $\mu_{i..} - \mu_{...}$ and B_j as $\mu_{.j.} - \mu_{...}$. Now, in a two-factor design with B nested in A, we define A_i, as before, as $\mu_{i..} - \mu_{...}$, but we define $B_{j(i)}$ as $\mu_{ij.} - \mu_{i..}$. Often students find this irregular and desire an explanation.

Let's take an example. Suppose we want to compare the performances of students, having various majors, on the common final exam in the Introductory Statistics course. The exam is used by all three sections of the course, although the sections have different teachers and use different statistics textbooks. Furthermore, due to scheduling constraints, Section 1 of the Statistics course has enrolled in it only Psychology, Nursing, and Journalism majors; Section 2, only Business, Communication Disorders, and Engineering majors; and Section

3, only Economics, Anthropology, and Sociology majors. Thus, the factor Majors is nested in the factor Sections, since a given major occurs in one and only one section.

Before we get to the point, one little digression about confounded variables. We do not use Teachers and Textbooks as separate factors because they are completely confounded in this design. No way exists for estimating a Teacher effect separate from the effect of the textbook. We lump such effects together, along with any other effects specific to a section such as time of day taught or classroom used, and consider these all as summarized by the Sections effect. This is not to say that we believe time of day, classroom, textbook, and teacher do not have separate effects. They well may. It merely recognizes the limitations of this particular experimental design. Separate effects may exist, but this experiment cannot reveal them. The simple fact is that we never expect a single experiment to answer all the questions we might have, nor do we try to manipulate every variable we can think of that might have an effect. We manipulate the variables of central concern to us and try to hold the others constant or randomize their values over the experimental conditions. When we cannot do either of these, we at least try to be aware of such confounding of variables that exists.

When we are aware that two or more variables are confounded, we may choose to leave them that way if we don't care to separate them, or we may postpone separating them to another experiment.

Now back to the point. If we now were to try to estimate the effect of a particular Major, say Sociology, by subtracting the sample mean for Sociology Majors from the general mean, we would be ignoring the fact that all of the Sociology Majors were in Section 3 and that therefore their scores are affected not only by their being Sociology Majors but also by any Section 3 effect that exists. We can say that except for error, the mean Sociology Major's score consists of the general effect, μ, the effect of being a Sociology Major, call it $B_{Soc(3)}$ and the effect of being in Section 3, call it $A_{Sect. 3}$. We can write

$$\mu_{Soc} = \mu + B_{Soc(3)} + A_{Sect. 3} \, .$$

Then the effect $B_{Soc(3)}$ is $\mu_{Soc} - \mu - A_{Sect. 3}$ and $A_{Sect. 3}$ is defined as $\mu_{Sect. 3} - \mu$, so we have that

$$B_{Soc(3)} = \mu_{Soc} - \mu - (\mu_{Sect. 3} - \mu) = \mu_{Soc} - \mu_{Sect. 3} \, .$$

In μ-dot notation, except for error,

$$\mu_{Soc} = \mu + (\mu_{Soc} - \mu_{Sect. 3}) + (\mu_{Sect. 3} - \mu)$$

TABLE 6.7 FACTOR B NESTED IN FACTOR A AND CROSSED WITH FACTORS C AND D

		C_1			C_2			C_3			C_4		
		D_1	D_2	D_3	D_1	D_2	D_3	D_1	D_2	D_3	D_1	D_2	D_3
A1	B1(1) B2(1) B3(1)												
A2	B1(2) B2(2) B3(2)												
A3	B1(3) B2(3) B3(3)												

so that $A_{\text{Sect. }3} = (\mu_{\text{Sect. }3} - \mu)$ but $B_{\text{Soc}} = (\mu_{\text{Soc}} - \mu_{\text{Sect. }3})$.

In general, for the design with model equation $Y_{ijk} = \mu + A_i + B_{j(i)} + e_{ijk}$ we see that except for error $\mu_{ij.} = \mu + A_i + B_{j(i)}$ and $\mu_{ij.} - \mu_{...}$ would estimate $A_i + B_{j(i)}$, whereas if we want an estimate of $B_{j(i)}$ itself we must estimate $\mu_{ij} - \mu - A_i$ using $M_{ij.} - M_{...} - (M_{i..} - M_{...}) = M_{ij.} - M_{i..}$.

6.9 Diagramming designs with nested factors. Another question that often arises concerns diagramming designs with nested factors. Crossed-factor designs seem to raise no particular problem. But when some factors are crossed and others are nested, there seems to be some difficulty in deciding how to lay out the diagram. In general, experience has indicated that the easiest way to diagram a design with a nested factor is first to draw the levels of the factor nesting the nested factor. This can be across the left-hand side of the diagram. Then, draw the levels of the nested factor contained within each of the levels of the nesting factor. Then, draw all of the factors that are crossed with the nested factor along the top of the diagram. For example, suppose B is nested in A, and C and D are crossed with each other and with A and B. First lay out A and the levels of B nested in A along the side, giving

A_1 $B_{1(1)}$
$\quad\quad B_{2(1)}$
$\quad\quad B_{3(1)}$

$B_{1(2)}$

A_2 $B_{2(2)}$

$B_{3(2)}$

$B_{1(3)}$

A_3 $B_{2(3)}$

$B_{3(3)}$

Then create the cross of C with D across the top. This will produce not only the cross of C with D but also all the other crosses needed. Thus the diagram would be finished off as in Table 6.7. If the nested variable were nested in the cross of two variables, say C nested in A x B and C is also crossed with D and E, it seems to draw easily if we first draw the cross of A and B, then nest the levels of C in that cross, and if we have done this on the side of the diagram, then draw the cross of D and E across the top. The student will find that just a little practice and you become an expert at drawing even quite complex diagrams. A couple of more hints might be that if you wind up with two nested factors and neither is nested in the other, locate one along the top of the diagram along with its nesting factors, and locate the other on the side with its nesting factors. Of course, if one is nested in the other, they must both be located either at the top or at the side but not separately. Finally, one can imagine, but almost never run into, a design that requires more than one subdiagram to complete the whole diagram. For these, play a little with two diagrams at once or seek help from a diagram master. Diagrams are most useful when computations are to be done by hand since they facilitate finding the various T-dot quantities. Super complex designs will almost always be analyzed by computer so it is nice that the need for diagramming fades out just as diagramming becomes difficult.

6.10 A nested factor nested within another nested factor. In the last section we mentioned a design with two nested factors, one nested in the other. What might this look like, and how would we write its model equation? We can imagine an experiment in which we study children from several different classrooms in several different schools in several different school districts. Classes are nested in Schools, and the Schools are nested in Districts. The model equation would be

$$Y_{ijk} = \mu + A_i + B_{j(i)} + C_{k(i,j)} + e_{ijk}$$

where A_i is the Districts effect, $B_{j(i)}$ is the Schools effect, and $C_{k(i,j)}$ is the Classrooms effect. All previous considerations continue to apply to this model equation so far as degrees of freedom, sums of squares, and so on. If three tests were given to each child so that Classrooms, Schools, and Districts were crossed with Tests, the equation might be

$$Y_{ijkm} = \mu + A_i + B_{j(i)} + C_{k(i,j)} + D_m + AD_{im} + BD_{j(i)m} + CD_{k(i,j)m} + e_{ijkm}$$

and the diagram for this design might look something like Table 6.8. This design is a repeated-measurements design, and we do not know how to perform its analysis of variance yet (see Chapter 8).

TABLE 6.8   C NESTED IN B NESTED IN A;
A, B, AND C CROSSED WITH D

			D_1	D_2	D_3
		$C_{1(1,1)}$			
	$B_{1(1)}$	$C_{2(1,1)}$			
		$C_{3(1,1)}$			
A_1					
		$C_{1(1,2)}$			
	$B_{2(1)}$	$C_{2(1,2)}$			
		$C_{3(1,2)}$			
		$C_{1(2,1)}$			
	$B_{1(2)}$	$C_{2(2,1)}$			
		$C_{3(2,1)}$			
A_2					
		$C_{1(2,2)}$			
	$B_{2(2)}$	$C_{2(2,2)}$			
		$C_{3(2,2)}$			

6.11 A shortcut to obtaining degrees of freedom from a model equation.
Consider the model equation $Y_{ijkm} = \mu + A_i + B_{j(i)} + C_{k(i,j)} + D_m +$
$AD_{im} + BD_{j(i)m} + CD_{k(i,j)m} + e_{ijkm}$. We know from Chapters 4 and 5 that if we write this equation in μ-dot notation we can use the subscripts of the μ's to obtain the degrees of freedom. Thus, $A_i = \mu_{i...} - \mu_{....}$, so the degrees of freedom for A_i are $I - 1$, and $C_{k(i,j)} = \mu_{ijk.} - \mu_{ij..}$ so the degrees of freedom are $IJK - IJ$.

An alternative procedure that will permit you to write the degrees of freedom with only a glance at the model equation is to take each letter in the subscript for any model term and write the product of the uppercase values of each of those letters that are in parentheses, and then multiply that by the product of the uppercase-value-minus-one for each letter in the subscript

**TABLE 6.9 SOURCES AND df FOR
DESIGN WITH C NESTED IN B
NESTED IN A; E NESTED IN D; A, B,
AND C CROSSED WITH D AND E**

Source	df
Mean	1
A	$I - 1$
B	$I(J - 1)$
C	$IJ(K - 1)$
D	$M - 1$
E	$M(N - 1)$
AD	$(I - 1)(M - 1)$
AE	$M(I - 1)(N - 1)$
BD	$I(J - 1)(M - 1)$
BE	$IM(J - 1)(N - 1)$
CD	$IJ(K - 1)(M - 1)$
CE	$IJM(K - 1)(N - 1)$
Error	$IJKMN(n - 1)$

TABLE 6.10 FICTIONAL DATA: EXERCISE 3

	Professor							
	A			B			C	
Teaching Assistant			Teaching Assistant			Teaching Assistant		
a_A	b_A	c_A	a_B	b_B	c_B	a_C	b_C	c_C
47	49	38	37	42	29	41	37	39
41	45	6	19	49	35	39	33	36
39	50	33	29	38	32	45	36	29
46	42	36	30	39	28	46	35	31
48	45	40	18	37	29	42	42	40

that is not in parentheses. **Then multiply out to get rid of the parentheses in
this expression.** Thus, following this rule, $C_{k(i,j)}$ gives $IJ(K - 1) = IJK - IJ$, which

agrees with the previous result. Similarly, $CD_{k(i,j)m}$ gives $IJ(K - 1)(M - 1) = IJKM - IJK - IJM + IJ$ and $B_{j(i)}$ gives $I(J - 1) = IJ - I$. This rule works for all of the balanced design ANOVA model equations we will consider in this book.

6.12   A device for ensuring that you get all of the terms in the model equation and therefore all of the sources in the ANOVA.   When the design involves many factors, some crossed and some nested, it can be tedious getting all of the interaction terms that belong and none of the ones that do not belong.   A simple, straightforward procedure for doing this is to write out all of the possible sources and then to exclude those that cannot occur because they involve interaction of a nested factor with a factor it is nested in. Let us consider some examples.

Suppose a design in which B is nested in A, C is crossed with B and therefore with A, and A, B, and C are crossed with the cross of D and E. We have five factors. If there were no nested factor, the possible sources would be

μ (1)

A, B, C, D, E (5)

AB, AC, AD, AE, BC, BD, BE, CD, CE, DE (10)

ABC, ABD, ABE, ACD, ACE, ADE, BCD, BCE, BDE, CDE (10)

ABCD, ABCE, ABDE, ACDE, BCDE (5)

ABCDE (1).

(The numbers in parentheses to the right of each list give the number of possible terms at each level of sources, providing a handy check on the completeness of the list. If there are N factors, then these numbers are given by the values $N!/[i!(N - i)!]$ for $i = 0, 1, ..., N$. They are the numbers of combinations of N things taken i at a time.) The next step is to exclude from the list all those terms that involve both a nested factor and a factor it is nested in. Since B is nested in A, any term with an A and a B is excluded. The reduced list would be

μ

A, B, C, D, E

AC, AD, AE, BC, BD, BE, CD, CE, DE

ACD, ACE, ADE, BCD, BCE, BDE, CDE

ACDE, BCDE.

For the next example, suppose that C is nested in B, B is nested in A, E is nested in D, and A, B, and C are each crossed with D and with E. The same list of possible terms would be generated as for the first example since again there are five factors. Then any term involving A and B or B and C or A and C or D and E would be deleted. The remaining terms would be

μ

A, B, C, D, E

AD, AE, BD, BE, CD, CE.

The model equation would be $Y_{ijkmno} = \mu + A_i + B_{j(i)} + C_{k(i,j)} + D_m + E_{n(m)} + AD_{im} + AE_{in(m)} + BD_{j(i)m} + BE_{j(i)n(m)} + CD_{k(i,j)m} + CE_{k(i,j)n(m)} + e_{ijkmno}$ and the sources and degrees of freedom, assuming n scores per cell, are shown in Table 6.9.

Exercises

1. (a) Write the model equation for a design in which Age is crossed with Sex, Age is nested in Teaching Method, and Teaching Method is also crossed with Sex.

(b) Now write out the analysis of variance table showing degrees of freedom and sums of squares.

(c) Write the df directly from the model equation using the new short-cut methods.

(d) Then check your results using the M-dot system of generating df and sums of squares.

2. For the design in exercise 1, let there be three ages nested in each of two teaching methods, with Boys and Girls used as subjects. Draw the design.

3. Suppose the Undergraduate Affairs Committee in a Psychology Department desired to assess the progress of students in the Introductory Statistics course by administering a standard test to all students taking the course. As it happens there are three different sections of the course taught by

TABLE 6.11   STIMULUS WORDS FOR EXPERIMENT ON EFFECTS OF CATEGORY MEMBERSHIP ON SHORT-TERM MEMORY

			Column		
	1	2	3	4	5
Row					
1	Cod	Salmon	Swordfish	Tuna	Trout
2	Cow	Pig	Horse	Dog	Goat
3	Rose	Carnation	Tulip	Poppy	Marigold
4	Red	Blue	Green	Yellow	Brown
5	Car	Truck	Wagon	Bicycle	Motorcycle

three different professors whose anonymity we will protect by calling them professors A, B, and C. Also, each section being large, there are three teaching assistants in each section. The three in Professor A's section will be called a_A, b_A, and c_A; the three in Professor B's section will be called a_B, b_B, and c_B; and the three in Professor C's section will be called a$_C$, b$_C$, and c$_C$. The Undergraduate Affairs Committee realized that the progress of the students might well depend not only on the section they were in but also on which teaching assistant they had. Sections and teaching assistant were incorporated in the design in Table 6.10 and the data shown in that design were analyzed. Perform the analysis of variance on the portion of those data shown in Table 6.10.

4. Why is there never an interaction effect for two factors when one is nested within the other?

5. Does the answer to exercise 4 mean that there is no possibility of interaction of Professor with Teaching Assistant in the design in exercise 3, or does it mean that with the design in #3 there is no possibility of assessing such an interaction? How does the term "completely confounded" apply here?

6. Write the degrees of freedom for each term in the model equation

$$Y_{ijkm} = \mu + A_i + B_{j(i)} + C_{k(i,j)} + D_m + AD_{im} + BD_{j(i)m} + CD_{k(i,j)m} + e_{ijkm}.$$

7. Write the model equation for a design in which factors A, B, and C are crossed, D is nested in A x B x C, and E is nested in D. Find the degrees of freedom for each term in the equation.

8. Write the model equation for a design in which factors A and B are crossed, C is nested in A x B, D is crossed with A, B, and C, and E is nested in D. Find the degrees of freedom for each term in the equation.

9. Diagram the design in exercise 8.

10. Using μ-dot notation, rewrite the model equation in exercise 6.

11. Describe the design represented by the following model equations. Indicate which factors are crossed, which are nested, and which are nesting the nested factors:

(a) $Y_{ijkmno} = \mu + A_i + B_j + C_k + D_{m(k)} + E_{n(m,k)} + AB_{ij} + AC_{ik} + AD_{im(k)} + AE_{in(m,k)} + BC_{jk} + BD_{jm(k)} + BE_{jn(m,k)} + e_{ijkmno}$

(b) $Y_{ijkmn} = \mu + A_i + B_{j(i)} + C_{k(i,j)} + D_{m(i,j,k)} + e_{ijkmn}$

(c) $Y_{ijkmno} = \mu + A_i + B_{j(i)} + AC_{ik} + BC_{j(i)k} + e_{ijkm}$

(d) $Y_{ijkmno} = \mu + A_i + B_{j(i)} + C_k + D_{m(k)} + AC_{ik} + AD_{im(k)} + BC_{j(i)k} + BD_{j(i)m(k)} + e_{ijkmn}$

12. Draw a diagram for each of the model equations in exercise 11. Assume two levels for each factor.

13. In an experiment to study the effects of category membership on short-term memory for briefly presented stimuli, the stimulus words shown in Table 6.11 were used.

The stimuli were presented in a tachistoscope for a very brief interval of time. They were presented as a group of five words, one above another. In the Single Category condition the five words presented were all the words in one of the five rows. Thus, all five words belonged to a single category. In the Multiple Category condition, the five words were those

TABLE 6.12 DESIGN FOR EXERCISE 14

		C_1			C_2		
		D_1	D_2	D_3	D_4	D_5	D_6
A_1	B_1						
	B_2						
A_2	B_3						
	B_4						
A_3	B_5						
	B_6						

in one of the five columns. Thus, factor A is Type of Category (single or multiple) and factor B is particular list. Lists are nested in Type of Category.

(a) Write the model equation for this design.

(b) Write the sources and degrees of freedom for the analysis of variance.

14. For the design in Table 6.12:

(a) Write the model equation.

(b) Assuming four scores per cell, write the sources and degrees of freedom for the ANOVA table.

15. If Factor D is crossed with Factor C and Factor C is nested in Factor E, is Factor D crossed with or nested in Factor E?

16. Draw a diagram for the following model equation:

$$Y_{ijkmno} = \mu + A_i + B_{j(i)} + C_{k(n)} + D_m + E_n + AC_{ik(n)} + AD_{im} + AE_{in} + BC_{j(i)k(n)}$$

$$+ BD_{j(i)m} + BE_{j(i)n} + CD_{k(n)m} + DE_{mn} + ACD_{ik(n)m} + ADE_{imn} + BCD_{j(i)k(n)m}$$

$$+ BDE_{j(i)mn} + ACDE_{ik(n)mn} + BCDE_{j(i)k(n)mn} + e_{ijkmno}$$

17. Which factors are crossed and which are nested in exercise 16?

18. Write the sources and degrees of freedom for the model equation in exercise 16.

7

Random-Effects Models

7.1 Sampling levels from a population of levels for a given factor.

Thus far we have considered only fixed-effects models. Now we introduce another class of models. Consider a psychology experiment on memorization in which the experimental subjects are given a prose passage to study for five minutes and then are tested for recall of the passage's content. Suppose that after the study period, but before the recall test, the subjects are given one of 10 different photographs to examine. The expectation is that these photographs may differentially interfere with memory for the prose passages. We could consider that we have 10 groups of subjects, one group for each different photograph, and treat the experiment as a one-factor design with Photographs as the factor and each different photograph as a level of the Photographs factor. This would, as before, be a fixed-effects design. The standard assumption would be that the sum of the effects for the 10 photographs is zero and the analysis of variance would test the null hypothesis that each of the 10 effects is zero against the alternative that while their average is zero, not all of them are zero. (In a fixed-effects model the average is always zero because the sum of the effects is always zero.)

But suppose that interest is in the effects of a large population of photographs. Also, suppose we have only 100 subjects available to us. We might still be interested in drawing an inference concerning the entire population of effects associated with the many different levels of the Photographs factor even though there are more photographs than we have subjects. We could adopt an alternative approach that would use only 10 photographs as in a fixed-effects design but would permit us to draw inferences to the entire population of photographs and their effects. Suppose that we randomly sampled 10 photographs from the large population of photographs. We give one photograph to one group of 10 subjects, a second to another group of 10, and so on, so that each group of 10 people sees one of the 10 photographs. Naturally the subjects are assigned to photographs at random, with the restriction that there be 10 assigned to each photograph.

7.2 The sum of the effects in our sample is no longer zero. As a consequence of sampling only some of the levels in the population of levels that we are concerned with, we do not assume that the sum of the Photograph effects is zero in the experiment. We assume this is true in the population of effects from which we have sampled the 10 since we can define the effect of a photograph as the difference between the mean response to that photograph and the overall mean response, but it does not have to be the case with the 10 photographs in the sample. Of course, it will be so if the null hypothesis is true and therefore all the Photograph effects in the population are zero. However, it will not in general be the case if the null hypothesis is not true. In order to test the hypothesis that all of the effects in the population of effects are zero, we adopt a different approach. We argue as follows: if all of the Photograph effects in the population of effects are zero, then these effects are all the same value, zero, and so the population of effects has a variance equal to zero. (For numbers that are all the same, all the numbers equal the mean number, and therefore the variance, being the average squared deviation of the numbers from their mean, is zero because every such deviation is zero.) This means that we can test the null hypothesis about the effects in the population all being zero by using an estimate of the variance of these population effects.

7.3 Balanced designs. In what follows we will make considerable use of Scheffé's presentation (Scheffé, 1959, chs. 7-8). The procedures that we will present will apply to balanced experimental designs. A one-factor design is **balanced** if the number of observations at each level are the same, as we have been assuming with the fixed-effects models. Designs with more than one factor are balanced if the numbers of scores in each cell are equal. If there are nested factors, the design is balanced provided that the number of levels of the nested factor is the same at each combination of levels of the factors that it is nested within, and the factors that are crossed are completely crossed. Again, this is just as we have been doing with the fixed-effects models.

7.4 Random-effects models. We begin by formulating a model for the experiment. Models for experiments in which the levels of the factors are sampled at random from a population of such levels are called **random-effects models**. The model says that

$$Y_{ij} = \mu + a_i + e_{ij} \, .$$

That is, the jth score in the ith level is a fixed constant effect μ, plus a random effect a_i particular to the ith level in the experiment, plus an error particular to the jth observation at the ith level. Something new has been added to the notation, which will be important when we consider expected mean squares. **Notice that the model term for the random effect is written as a lowercase letter, contrary to previous usage in which we have written model effects as uppercase letters.** We will use the distinction between uppercase and lowercase letters to distinguish between fixed effects and random effects. From now on, **fixed-effects terms will be denoted by uppercase and random effects will be denoted by lowercase letters.**

We will assume, as before, that the e_{ij} are normally distributed with a mean of zero and variance of σ^2_e. We will also assume that the population of a_i from which we have drawn a sample of a_i is a normal distribution with a mean of zero and variance σ^2_A. Furthermore, we will assume that all of the e_{ij} and all of the a_i are completely independent. Then the variance of the Y_{ij} is

$$\sigma^2_y = \sigma^2_A + \sigma^2_e,$$

since the variance of the sum of independent variables is the sum of the variances of those variables and of course, μ, being a fixed constant, has a variance of zero. That is,

$$\text{Var}(Y_{ij}) = \text{Var}(\mu + a_i + e_{ij}) = \text{Var}(\mu) + \text{Var}(a_i) + \text{Var}(e_{ij}) = 0 + \sigma^2_A + \sigma^2_e.$$

7.5 The null hypothesis in a random-effects model. The null hypothesis that we wish to test is that the effects in the population from which we have sampled the a_i are all equal and therefore all equal to zero since their mean is equal to zero whether or not the null hypothesis is true. This means that under the null hypothesis, $\sigma^2_A = 0$. It may seem that in the fixed-effects case the null hypothesis is about the population means, and in the random-effects model it seems to be about a variance. In fact, the random-effects model is often presented in that way but it tends to be a little confusing to start off thinking about it that way. Perhaps it will be a little clearer if we consider two one-factor designs, each with two levels. For one design we will formulate a fixed effects model; for the other, a random effects model. For Design 1, $Y_{ij} = \mu + A_i + e_{ij}$ and the null hypothesis is that $A_1 = A_2 = 0$. For Design 2, $Y_{ij} = \mu + a_i + e_{ij}$ and the null hypothesis is that $a_1 = a_2 = a_3 = ... = a_I = 0$, where I, the number of levels in the population of levels, may be infinite. In the case of Design 1, we sample scores from two populations, one with a mean $\mu + A_1$ and the other with a mean $\mu + A_2$. In the case of Design 2, the sampling goes in two stages. First we randomly sample two of the populations to sample the scores from; then we sample scores from them. Those two populations have means $\mu + a_i$ and $\mu + a_{i'}$. We denote i by 1 and i' by 2 in the design since they are the first and second level of the factor, but they are the ith and the i'^{th} level in the population of levels from which we have sampled the two.

We have already seen for fixed-effects models how the F test permits us to draw an inference concerning whether $A_1 = A_2$. Now we would like to see how by looking at just two of the I levels from which we sample in the random-effects case, we may draw an inference concerning the equality or lack of equality of all of the a_i.

7.6 The F-test for a one-factor design with random effects. The F statistic to test the null hypothesis for the random-effects design will be the same as for the fixed-effects design. This is true for a one-factor design but not for designs with more than one factor. Thus for the design in question,

$$F = MS_A/MS_e = [SS_A/(I - 1)]/[SS_e/(IJ - I)] = [(IJ - I)/(I - 1)]SS_A/SS_e,$$

where for the example $I = 2$, but we may as well treat I as being of arbitrary value so we don't have to go through the same argument again to make it general.

The distribution of MS_A/MS_e is that of a constant times a variable that has the F distribution with $I - 1$ and $IJ - I$ degrees of freedom. The constant is $(1 + J \sigma^2_A/ \sigma^2_e)$. We can say that

$$F = MS_A/MS_e = (1 + J \sigma^2_A/ \sigma^2_e)F_{I-1,IJ-I}.$$

Recall that we used the subscripts of the model terms to generate degrees of freedom formulas and sums of squares formulas. For example, in the model equation $Y_{ij} = \mu + A_i + e_{ij}$ we used the subscript "i" to obtain the formula "I - 1" as the degrees of freedom for the factor A, and this expression was used to obtain a formula for the sum of squares for that factor. Notice that in the random-effects model $Y_{ij} = \mu + a_i + e_{ij}$ the subscripts of the model terms have not been changed. Only the symbol "A" has been changed to "a." We can use this stability of the subscripts to indicate to ourselves that **since the subscripts are not changed when a model term changes from a fixed effect to a random effect, the computations of degrees of freedom and sums of squares do not change either.** We will see that **what does change is not the computations of sums of squares and mean squares, but rather it will be which ratios of mean squares we use as F statistics.** This change will not happen, however, until we get to a two-factor design.

7.6.1 The distribution of SS_A and SS_e. Recall that $SS_A = J\Sigma_i(M_{i.} - M_{..})^2$, and $SS_e = \Sigma_i\Sigma_j(Y_{ij} - M_{i.})^2$. Under the random-effects model, $M_{i.} = \mu + a_i + e_{i.}$, and $M_{..} = \mu + a_. +$

$e_{..}$, where $e_{i.} = \Sigma_j e_{ij}/J$ and $e_{..} = \Sigma_i \Sigma_j e_{ij}/IJ$, $a_{.} = \Sigma_i a_i/I$, $M_{i.} = \Sigma_j Y_{ij}/J$, and $M_{..} = \Sigma_i \Sigma_j Y_{ij}/IJ$. (Notice here that the $a_{.}$ do not sum to zero as would be the case in the fixed-effects model.) Then

$$SS_A = J\Sigma_i(\mu + a_i + e_{i.} - \mu - a_{.} - e_{..})^2 = J\Sigma_i(a_i + e_{i.} - a_{.} - e_{..})^2 \quad \text{and}$$

$$SS_e = \Sigma_i\Sigma_j(Y_{ij} - M_{i.})^2 = \Sigma_i\Sigma_j[(\mu + a_i + e_{ij}) - (\mu + a_i + e_{i.})]^2 = \Sigma_i\Sigma_j(e_{ij} - e_{i.})^2.$$

Now if we write $b_i = a_i + e_{i.}$, then $b_{.} = a_{.} + e_{..}$ and

$$SS_A = J\Sigma_i(b_i - b_{.})^2. \qquad\qquad [7.1]$$

Because we have assumed that the a_i and the e_{ij} are independently normally distributed, the a_i being $N(0, \sigma^2_A)$ and the e_{ij} being $N(0, \sigma^2_e)$, it follows that b_i is $N(0, \sigma^2_b)$ where the variance of b_i is the variance of $a_i + e_{i.}$. Since a_i and $e_{i.}$ are independent, the variance of this sum is the sum of their separate variances. The variance of a_i is as we have said σ^2_A and the variance of $e_{i.}$ is the variance of the mean of J independent variables, each of which has the variance σ^2_e; therefore it is σ^2_e/J. So $\sigma^2_b = \sigma^2_A + \sigma^2_e/J$. Since the b_i are normally distributed with a mean of zero and variance σ^2_b, we have that $(b_i - b_{.})/\sqrt{\sigma^2_b}$ is a standard normal variable, and therefore we know that $\Sigma_i(b_i - b_{.})^2/\sigma^2_b$ is a chi-square variable with I - 1 degrees of freedom, which we will denote by $\chi^2_{(I-1)}$. Using this fact and equation [7.1] we have that

$$SS_A = J\Sigma_i(b_i - b_{.})^2 = J \sigma^2_b [\Sigma_i(b_i - b_{.})^2/\sigma^2_b]$$

$$= J \sigma^2_b \chi^2_{(I-1)} = J(\sigma^2_A + \sigma^2_e/J) \chi^2_{(I-1)} = (J \sigma^2_A + \sigma^2_e) \chi^2_{(I-1)}. \qquad [7.2]$$

In words, the sum of squares for the A factor is the product of a chi-square variable with I - 1 degrees of freedom and a quantity equal to the variance of the A effects times the number of observations at each level of A, plus the error variance.

To find the distribution of SS_e we observe that

$$SS_e = \Sigma_i\Sigma_j(Y_{ij} - Y_{i.})^2 = \Sigma_i\Sigma_j(\mu + a_i + e_{ij} - \mu - a_i - e_{i.})^2 = \Sigma_i\Sigma_j(e_{ij} - e_{i.})^2.$$

Again we can note that the e_{ij} are $N(0, \sigma^2_e)$, and so at each value of i, the quantity $(e_{ij} - e_{i.})/\sqrt{\sigma^2_e}$ is a standard normal variable, so $\Sigma_j(e_{ij} - e_{i.})^2/ \sigma^2_e$ is a chi-square variable on J - 1 degrees of freedom, and since all of the e_{ij} are independent, if we sum over I we will have the sum of I independent chi-square variables, each having J - 1 degrees of freedom. We recall that the sum of independent chi-square variables is also a chi-square variable with its degrees of freedom equal to the sum of the degrees of freedom for the chi-square variables being summed, so the sum of these I chi-square variables will be a chi-square variable having $I(J - 1) = IJ - I$ degrees of freedom. Since $\Sigma_i\Sigma_j(e_{ij} - e_{i.})^2/\sigma^2_e = SS_e/\sigma^2_e = \chi^2_{(IJ-I)}$, it follows that $SS_e = \sigma^2_e\chi^2_{(IJ-I)}$.

7.6.2 The distribution of MS_A/MS_e.

Since SS_A is $(J \sigma^2_A + \sigma^2_e)\chi^2_{(I-1)}$,

$$MS_A = SS_A/(I - 1) = (J \sigma^2_A + \sigma^2_e)\chi^2_{I-1}/(I - 1),$$

which is a constant times a chi-square variable divided by its degrees of freedom. Similarly,

$$MS_e = SS_e/(IJ - I) = \sigma^2_e\chi^2_{(IJ-I)}/(IJ - I),$$

which is also a constant times a chi-square variable divided by its degrees of freedom. Therefore,

$$MS_A/MS_e = [(J \sigma^2_A + \sigma^2_e)/\sigma^2_e][\chi^2_{(I-1)}/(I - 1)]/[\chi^2_{(IJ-I)}/(IJ - I)]$$

which we see is a constant times the ratio of two chi-square variables each divided by its degrees of freedom. We can rewrite the constant $[(J \sigma^2_A + \sigma^2_e)/\sigma^2_e] = 1 + J \sigma^2_A/\sigma^2_e$. It can be shown that SS_A and SS_e are statistically independent and therefore that the two chi-square variables are independent. The ratio of two independent chi-square variables each divided by its degrees of freedom has the F distribution and therefore

$$MS_A/MS_e = (1 + J \sigma^2_A/\sigma^2_e)F_{I-1,IJ-I}.$$

7.7 The statistic for testing the null hypothesis that $\sigma^2_A = 0$.

The statistic $MS_A/MS_e = (1 + J \sigma^2_A/\sigma^2_e)F_{I-1,IJ-I}$ is appropriate for testing the hypothesis that $\sigma^2_A = 0$. When $\sigma^2_A = 0$, the statistic is just $F_{I-1,IJ-I}$, so it has a known distribution under the null hypothesis. When σ^2_A is not zero, the test statistic will tend to be larger than $F_{I-1,IJ-I}$ so the choice of the rejection region is clear. As with the fixed-effects models we will use large values of $F = MS_A/MS_e$ to reject the null hypothesis, where by large values we will mean values exceeding the tabled critical value of $F_{I-1,IJ-I}$ for the chosen significance level.

7.8 The expected values of MS_A and MS_e and an important relationship between them.

We are now going to find the expected values of MS_A and MS_e and point out a relationship between them. The form of this relationship will be central to the procedure throughout the rest of this chapter in developing the usual procedure for hypothesis testing in random-effects models and mixed models. First,

$$E(MS_A) = E[SS_A/(I - 1)] = E(SS_A)/(I - 1) = E[(J \sigma^2_A + \sigma^2_e)\chi^2_{(I-1)}/(I - 1)].$$

We recall that the expected value of a constant times a variable is equal to the constant times the expected value of the variable, so we can write $E(MS_A) =$
$[(J \sigma^2_A + \sigma^2_e)/(I - 1)]E(\chi^2_{(I-1)})$. We also recall that the expected value of a chi-square variable is its degrees of freedom. Therefore, $E(MS_A) = [(J \sigma^2_A + \sigma^2_e)/(I - 1)] E(\chi^2_{(I-1)}) =$
$[(J \sigma^2_A + \sigma^2_e)/(I - 1)](I - 1) = J \sigma^2_A + \sigma^2_e$. Following parallel steps, we find that $E(MS_e) =$
$E[SS_e/(IJ - I)] = E(SS_e)/(IJ - I) = E(\sigma^2_e \chi^2_{(IJ-I)})/(IJ - I) = \sigma^2_e E(\chi^2_{(IJ-I)})/(IJ - I) = \sigma^2_e(IJ -$
$I)/(IJ - I) = \sigma^2_e$. When we compare $E(MS_A) = J \sigma^2_A + \sigma^2_e$ to $E(MS_e) = \sigma^2_e$ we see that $E(MS_A)$ is equal to $E(MS_e)$ plus one more term, $J \sigma^2_A$, and when the null hypothesis that σ^2_A is zero is true, $E(MS_A) = E(MS_e)$. Otherwise $E(MS_A)$ is greater than $E(MS_e)$. We see that **the test statistic, MS_A/MS_e, has a mean square in the numerator, which has as its expected value a quantity that contains all of the terms in the expected value of the denominator mean square plus one additional term. This additional term is zero when the null hypothesis that we are testing is true and positive when it is false.** We will use this relationship between the expected values of the numerator and denominator mean squares as the general criterion for determining test statistics in the more complex experimental designs involving random effects. In the next section we begin the discussion of these more complex models by considering a two-factor design in which both factors involve random effects.

7.9 A two-factor design with random effects. Suppose that a team of university educators becomes concerned with the ability of first-year college students to apply their quantitative skills to some practical problems. The team's primary concern is getting some quick, preliminary information, which they will then follow up with a more extensive, systematic procedure. They decide to sample at random five departments in the university and to test 25 students from each sampled department on a "quick and dirty" test produced by sampling 20 test items from a 200-item test that was available but would take too long to administer. We can regard the effect of each of the items as a random effect because we think of these effects as sampled from the population of 200 effects associated with the 200 test items that might have been used. The inferences about test item effects will be from the 20 sampled item effects to the population of 200 item effects. (We might even regard the sampled population as consisting of item effects associated with the 200 items on the test and the countless other similar, equivalent items that might be written.) Similarly, we can regard the effects of the five sampled departments as random effects, and the inferences will be to the population of departments in the university from which these departments were sampled. We will make the probably unreasonable assumption that the errors associated with the responses of each person to each of the 20 items are statistically independent just so that we can avoid, for the moment, the more complicated treatment that is required when we have to take this dependence into account. Later we will take up such dependence in Chapter 8.

7.10 The model equation for a two-factor design with random effects. Let the Department effects be the a_i and the Test Item effects be the b_j. We can write as the model equation

$$Y_{ijk} = \mu + a_i + b_j + ab_{ij} + e_{ijk}.$$

7.10.1 On the notation. We should note here that in this equation the double subscript "ij" is on the entire symbol "ab" in the fourth term on the right side of the equation. The symbol "ab" is not a product of a and b but instead denotes an interaction effect. Using both letters to denote a single effect is convenient because the notation then indicates which two factors are involved. The subscript "ij" denotes the row and column combination that determines the cell to which the ab_{ij} interaction effect applies.

7.10.2 The ab_{ij} are random effects. The ab_{ij} effects are random effects because they are selected at random by virtue of the random selection of the levels associated with a_i and b_j. The inferences based on the estimates of the variance of the ab_{ij} effects will be to the population of such interaction effects from which these are considered to have been sampled.

7.10.3 The effects sum to zero in the population but not in the sample. The sum of the a_i is not zero in the sample, although it is so in the population of a_i from which the sampled effects have been drawn. Parallel remarks apply to the b_j. We recall that if this were a two-factor design with fixed effects, the interaction effects would sum to zero in various ways. For each value of i, $\Sigma_j AB_{ij} = 0$, and for each value of j, $\Sigma_i AB_{ij} = 0$. These same relationships hold in the population of interaction effects from which those in the experiment have been sampled, but they do not in general hold for the effects in the experiment. This is because the sample has not exhausted the population. Thus, we are likely to have drawn a sample of effects that do not have the population mean as their sample mean and so do not necessarily sum to zero.

TABLE 7.1 ROW, COLUMN, AND CELL MEANS FOR A RANDOM-EFFECTS MODEL

$\mu+a_1+b_1+ab_{11}+e_{11.}$	$\mu+a_1+b_2+ab_{12}+e_{12.}$	$\cdots$ $\mu+a_1+b_J+ab_{1J}+e_{1J.}$	$\mu+a_1+b_.+ab_{1.}+e_{1..}$
$\mu+a_2+b_1+ab_{21}+e_{21.}$	$\mu+a_2+b_2+ab_{22}+e_{22.}$	$\cdots$ $\mu+a_2+b_J+ab_{2J}+e_{1J.}$	$\mu+a_2+b_.+ab_{2.}+e_{2..}$
$\cdots$	$\cdots$	$\cdots$ $\cdots$	$\cdots$
$\mu+a_I+b_1+ab_{I1}+e_{I1.}$	$\mu+a_I+b_2+ab_{I2}+e_{I2.}$	$\cdots$ $\mu+a_I+b_J+ab_{IJ}+e_{IJ.}$	$\mu+a_I+b_.+ab_{I.}+e_{I..}$
$\mu+a_.+b_1+ab_{.1}+e_{.1.}$	$\mu+a_.+b_2+ab_{.2}+e_{.2.}$	$\cdots$ $\mu+a_.+b_J+ab_{.J}+e_{.J.}$	$\mu+a_.+b_.+ab_{..}+e_{...}$

7.11 Distribution assumptions for the random-effects model. The assumptions concerning this model will be that the population distributions of the a_i, the b_j, and the ab_{ij} are, along with the e_{ijk}, all independently normally distributed with means equal to zero and variances σ^2_A, σ^2_B, σ^2_{AB}, and σ^2_e, respectively.

7.11.1 On the notation. We note that the subscripts on the several variances are written as upper case letters even though they refer to random-effects factors and their interaction. This is because the only place we need to draw the distinction between random effects and fixed effects is in the model equation. As long as the distinction is drawn there, we will not go astray since we use the model equation to obtain the expected mean squares and these expected mean squares will be the guides in formulating the appropriate F-tests. Similarly, it will not be necessary for us to distinguish between fixed effects and random effects in the subscripts for sums of squares or for mean squares, so we will use the conventional uppercase values.

7.12 The expected values for MS_A, MS_B, MS_{AB}, and MS_e. In this section we will find the expected values for the various mean squares associated with the different terms of interest in the model equation. The degrees of freedom and the sums of squares are computed for random-effects models according to the same formulas as for fixed-effects models so we can determine these quantities directly by inspection of the model equation. Thus, $df_A = I - 1$, and

$$SS_A = JK\Sigma_i(M_{i..} - M_{...})^2 = JK\Sigma_i(\mu + a_i + b_. + ab_{i.} + e_{i..} - \mu - a_. - b_. - ab_{..} - e_{...})^2$$

$$= JK\Sigma_i(a_i - a_. + ab_{i.} - ab_{..} + e_{i..} - e_{...})^2.$$

The dots on the subscripts of the model terms indicate averaging over the dotted subscript. It may be helpful to inspect Table 7.1 to see how the marginal means and the grand mean, in model terms, result from averaging over rows, over columns, and over the column or row averages. The entries in the cells are averaged over the scores in the cells so the k subscript is dotted. We recall that the kth score in the cell in row i, column j is Y_{ijk}. We see that $M_{i..}$ $= \mu + a_i + b_. + ab_{i.} + e_{i..}$, and that $M_{...} = \mu + a_. + b_. + ab_{..} + e_{...}$. Therefore $(M_{i..} - M_{...}) =$ $a_i - a_. + ab_{i.} - ab_{..} + e_{i..} - e_{...}$ and $SS_A = JK\Sigma_i(M_{i..} - M_{..})^2 = JK\Sigma_i(a_i - a_. + ab_{i.} - ab_{..} + e_{i..} - e_{...})^2$. If we set $c_i = a_i + ab_{i.} + e_{i..}$, then c_i is normally distributed with a mean of zero and a variance $\sigma^2_c = \sigma^2_A + \sigma^2_{AB}/J + \sigma^2_e/JK$, and $SS_A = JK\Sigma_i(M_{i..} - M_{..})^2 = JK\Sigma_i(c_i - c_.)^2$. Now we know that $\Sigma_i(c_i - c_.)^2/ \sigma^2_c$ is distributed as $\chi^2_{(I-1)}$ so

$$SS_A = JK\, \sigma^2_C\, \chi^2_{(I-1)} = JK(\, \sigma^2_e/JK + \sigma^2_A + \sigma^2_{AB}/J\,)\, \chi^2_{(I-1)}.$$

Then, since $MS_A = SS_A/(I - 1)$, substituting for SS_A, it follows that $MS_A = JK(\, \sigma^2_e/JK + \sigma^2_A + \sigma^2_{AB}/J\,)\, \chi^2_{(I-1)}/(I - 1)$. Therefore

$$E(MS_A) = E[SS_A/(I - 1)] = E(SS_A)/(I - 1) = JK(\sigma^2_e/JK + \sigma^2_A + \sigma^2_{AB}/J)E(\chi^2_{(I-1)})/(I - 1)$$

$$= E[JK(\sigma^2_e/JK + \sigma^2_A + \sigma^2_{AB}/J\,)\, \chi^2_{(I-1)}\, /(I - 1)]$$

$$= JK(\, \sigma^2_e/JK + \sigma^2_A + \sigma^2_{AB}/J\,)(I - 1)/(I - 1) = \sigma^2_e + JK\, \sigma^2_A + K\, \sigma^2_{AB}.$$

(We recall again that the expected value of a chi-square variable is its degrees of freedom.) We can see now that SS_A is just $SS_A = E(MS_A)\, \chi^2_{(I-1)}$ The student should now follow the parallel steps to show that $E(MS_B) = \sigma^2_e + IK\, \sigma^2_B + K\, \sigma^2_{AB}$, and that $SS_B = E(MS_B)\, \chi^2_{(J-1)}$. Instead of pursuing details further, we will just state that $E(MS_{AB}) = \sigma^2_e + K\, \sigma^2_{AB}$, $E(MS_e) = \sigma^2_e$, $SS_{AB} = E(MS_{AB})\chi^2_{[(I-1)(J-1)]}$, $SS_e = E(MS_e)\chi^2_{(IJK-IJ)}$, and that the four sums of squares SS_A, SS_B, SS_{AB}, and SS_e are independent. The details may be found in Scheffé (1959, Ch. 7).

7.13 Testing the main effects in a two-factor random-effects model against MS_e is incorrect because MS_A/MS_e and MS_B/MS_e are positively biased toward Type I errors. In 7.12 we saw that each of the sums of squares was equal to an expected mean square times a chi-square variable. We can write this in the general form

$$SS = E(MS)\, \chi^2.$$

Therefore, if we divide the SS by its degrees of freedom, we will have

$SS/df = MS = E(MS) \chi^2/df$.

For the four sources in the design, $MS_A = E(MS_A) \chi^2_{(I-1)}/(I - 1)$, $MS_B = E(MS_B) \chi^2_{(J-1)}/(J - 1)$, $MS_{AB} = E(MS_{AB}) \chi^2_{[(I-1)(J-1)]}/[(I - 1)(J - 1)]$, and $MS_e = E(MS_e) \chi^2_{(IJK-IJ)}/(IJK - IJ)$. When we were working with a two-factor design with fixed effects, we used the MS_e as the denominator for each of the three F-ratios for testing the null hypotheses concerning the two main effects and their interaction. Let's see what would happen if we were to try to follow the same procedure with the random-effects model. The first ratio would be

$$MS_A/MS_e = [(\sigma^2_e + JK\ \sigma^2_A + K\ \sigma^2_{AB})\chi^2_{(I-1)}/(I - 1)] / \sigma^2_e\ \chi^2_{(IJK-IJ)}/(IJK - IJ)$$

$$= [(\ \sigma^2_e + JK\ \sigma^2_A + K\ \sigma^2_{AB})/\ \sigma^2_e][\ \chi^2_{(I-1)}\ /(I - 1)]/[\ \chi^2_{(IJK-IJ)}\ /(IJK - IJ)]$$

$$= [(\ \sigma^2_e + JK\ \sigma^2_A + K\ \sigma^2_{AB})/\ \sigma^2_e]F_{I-1,IJK-IJ},$$

since the ratio of two independent chi-square variables each divided by its degrees of freedom is distributed as F. But this statistic is not suitable as the test statistic because it does not have the F distribution when the null hypothesis that $\sigma^2_A = 0$ is true. Setting σ^2_A equal to 0 we get

$$MS_A/MS_e = [(\ \sigma^2_e + K\ \sigma^2_{AB})/\ \sigma^2_e]F_{I-1,IJK-IJ} = (1 + K\ \sigma^2_{AB}/\ \sigma^2_e)F_{I-1,IJK-IJ}$$

which would not be distributed as F unless $\sigma^2_{AB} = 0$ also. Otherwise, the statistic MS_A/MS_e would be biased toward rejection of the null hypothesis $\sigma^2_A = 0$ even when that hypothesis is true. If the ratio $K\ \sigma^2_{AB}/\ \sigma^2_e$ were sufficiently large, we could expect to reject the null hypothesis almost all of the time even though it was true. Thus while we might select as the significance level the value of .05, the actual significance level could be much greater than .05, leading us to make Type I errors much more frequently than the chosen significance level would suggest. Similarly,

$$MS_B/MS_e = [(\ \sigma^2_e + IK\ \sigma^2_B + K\ \sigma^2_{AB})\chi^2_{(J-1)}/(J - 1)] / \sigma^2_e\ \chi^2_{(IJK-IJ)}/(IJK - IJ)$$

$$= [(\ \sigma^2_e + IK\ \sigma^2_B + K\ \sigma^2_{AB})/\ \sigma^2_e][\chi^2_{(J-1)}/(J - 1)]/[\chi^2_{(IJK-IJ)}/(IJK - IJ)]$$

$$= [(\ \sigma^2_e + IK\ \sigma^2_B + K\ \sigma^2_{AB})/\sigma^2_e]F_{J-1,IJK-IJ},$$

which, when the null hypothesis that $\sigma^2_B = 0$ is true, is equal to $[(\ \sigma^2_e + K\ \sigma^2_{AB})/\ \sigma^2_e]F_{J-1,IJK-IJ}$, which displays the same positive bias as in the case of MS_A/MS_e. Values larger than the critical value of F will tend to occur with a probability greater than the chosen significance level when the null hypothesis is true. Clearly neither MS_A/MS_e nor MS_B/MS_e is suitable as a test statistic. Neither one satisfies the requirement that the test statistic have a *known* distribution when the null hypothesis is true, because when the null hypothesis is true, the distribution of each of these statistics will still depend on the value of an unknown parameter σ^2_{AB}.

7.14 But testing the interaction effects against MS_e is correct. Let us now inquire into the third ratio,

$$MS_{AB}/MS_e = \{(\sigma^2_e + K \sigma^2_{AB})\chi^2_{[(I-1)(J-1)]}/[(I-1)(J-1)]\} / \sigma^2_e \chi^2_{(IJK-IJ)}/(IJK$$

$$- IJ) = [(\sigma^2_e + K \sigma^2_{AB})/ \sigma^2_e]F_{(I-1)(J-1), IJK-IJ} .$$

We see that in this case, when the null hypothesis that $\sigma^2_{AB} = 0$ is true, the statistic MS_{AB}/MS_e is distributed as $F_{(I-1)(J-1), IJK-IJ}$. Therefore, for the test of the hypothesis that $\sigma^2_{AB} = 0$ we can use the ratio of MS_{AB} to MS_e. Also, when the null hypothesis is false, the obtained values of this test statistic will tend to be greater than when it is true, so it will be natural to use values of the test statistic that are greater than the tabled critical value as evidence against the null hypothesis and in favor of the alternative that $\sigma^2_{AB} > 0$.

7.15 How we find the correct F-ratios with random-effects models. What we have seen in the two preceding sections is that the ratio of the mean squares for the sources of interest to us to the mean square for error may or may not be distributed as F when the null hypothesis is true. Each of the mean squares was of the form $E(MS)\chi^2_{df}/df$. When we took the ratio of two of these mean squares, call them MS_1 and MS_2, we obtained a ratio $E(MS_1)\chi^2_{df1}/df_1/ E(MS_2)\chi^2_{df2}/df_2$, which, because the chi-square variables are independent, could be written as

$$MS_1/MS_2 = [E(MS_1)/E(MS_2)]F_{df1, df2}.$$

From this form we can see that whether the ratio is distributed as $F_{df1, df2}$ will depend on whether $E(MS_1)/E(MS_2) = 1$. Thus, to obtain an appropriate test statistic for testing a given null hypothesis, we will want **the ratio of two mean squares that will have the same expected value when the null hypothesis we are testing is true.** Let us now reconsider the four mean squares of interest and their expected values shown in Table 7.2. Inspecting Table 7.2, we can see now why MS_{AB}/MS_e was successful as a test statistic but MS_A/MS_e and MS_B/MS_e were not. In the case of MS_{AB}/MS_e, when $\sigma^2_{AB} = 0$, the numerator and denominator mean square each have the same expected value, σ^2_e, and so the ratio of the two expected mean squares is 1, in which case the ratio of the mean squares is just the ratio of the chi-square variables divided by their degrees of freedom and so is distributed as F. But for MS_A and MS_B, the expected mean squares do not equal the expected mean square for MS_e when the null hypothesis is true, so an F statistic does not result in either case. This analysis, together with inspection of Table 7.2, does suggest to us the appropriate test statistics for testing the null hypotheses concerning σ^2_A and σ^2_B. We can see that $E(MS_A) = E(MS_{AB})$ when $\sigma^2_A = 0$ and $E(MS_B) = E(MS_{AB})$ when $\sigma^2_B = 0$. Therefore MS_A/MS_{AB} will be distributed as $F_{I-1,(I-1)(J-1)}$ when $\sigma^2_A = 0$ and MS_B/MS_{AB} will be distributed as $F_{J-1,(I-1)(J-1)}$ when $\sigma^2_B = 0$ since

$$MS_A/MS_e = [(\sigma^2_e + JK\,\sigma^2_A + K\,\sigma^2_{AB})/(\sigma^2_e + K\,\sigma^2_{AB})]\,F_{I-1,(I-1)(J-1)}$$

which equals

$$[(\sigma^2_e + K\,\sigma^2_{AB})/(\sigma^2_e + K\,\sigma^2_{AB})]\,F_{I-1,(I-1)(J-1)} = F_{I-1,(I-1)(J-1)}$$

when $\sigma^2_A = 0$

and

$$MS_B/MS_e = [(\sigma^2_e + IK\,\sigma^2_B + K\,\sigma^2_{AB})/(\sigma^2_e + K\,\sigma^2_{AB})]\,F_{J-1,(I-1)(J-1)}$$

which equals

$$[(\sigma^2_e + K\,\sigma^2_{AB})/(\sigma^2_e + K\,\sigma^2_{AB})]\,F_{J-1,(I-1)(J-1)} = F_{J-1,(I-1)(J-1)}$$

when $\sigma^2_B = 0$.

7.16 The general approach to finding F-ratios with random-effects models. In general, for a random-effects model, finding the appropriate ratio of mean squares boils down to **finding two mean squares having equal expected values when the null hypothesis is true and using as the numerator of the F-ratio the mean square that has the larger expected mean square when the null hypothesis is false.** The difference between these two expected mean squares is the inclusion in the larger one of *one* term containing the variance that is zero under the null hypothesis. For this reason it

TABLE 7.2   EXPECTED MEAN SQUARES FOR THE TWO FACTOR DESIGN WITH RANDOM EFFECTS

Mean square	Expected mean square
MS_A	$\sigma^2_e + JK\,\sigma^2_A + K\,\sigma^2_{AB}$
MS_B	$\sigma^2_e + IK\,\sigma^2_B + K\,\sigma^2_{AB}$
MS_{AB}	$\sigma^2_e + K\,\sigma^2_{AB}$
MS_e	σ^2_e

will be useful to have a handy device for determining expected mean squares. Since the model equation has served us in such good stead thus far, giving us degrees of freedom formulas and sums of squares formulas, we might expect that it will provide us with expected mean square formulas as well, and we will not be disappointed.

7.17 A rule for finding expected mean squares in designs without nested factors. We will first give a simple rule for random-effects models without nested factors. Then we will elaborate the rule to apply to designs with nested factors and to designs involving mixed models in which random and fixed effects both occur. We will exemplify the use of each rule with the two-factor random-effects model equation

$$Y_{ijk} = \mu + a_i + b_j + ab_{ij} + e_{ijk}.$$

E(MS) Rule 1:   For a given source, e.g. factor A, locate the term in the model equation that expresses the effect of that source, e.g., a_i, determine the subscript(s) of that term, in this case i, and locate just those terms in the model equation that contain those subscripts in their subscript. For the term a_i, these would be the terms containing i in their subscript. They are shown in boldface in the model equation

$$Y_{ijk} = \mu + \mathbf{a_i} + b_j + \mathbf{ab_{ij}} + \mathbf{e_{ijk}}.$$

The term μ is not included since it has no subscripts, so it cannot include the subscript i in its subscript, and the term b_j is not included since i, the subscript of a_i, does not occur in its subscript. However, ab_{ij} does have i in its subscript so it is included. So does e_{ijk}.

For each such model equation term that is located, create a variance term, σ^2, that has as its subscript the label of the source for that model term, giving σ^2_A, σ^2_{AB}, and σ^2_e for the example, **and multiply each such σ^2 term by the**

uppercase value of the subscripts of Y that do not occur in the subscript of that model term. This gives JK σ^2_A, since Y_{ijk} includes i, j, and k in its subscript but a_i does not include j and k; it gives K σ^2_{AB} since k is in the subscript of Y_{ijk} but not in that of ab_{ij}, and it gives σ^2_e since all of the subscripts of e_{ijk} are subscripts of Y_{ijk}. **The sum of these quantities is the desired E(MS).** Thus,

$$E(MS_A) = \sigma^2_e + JK\,\sigma^2_A + K\,\sigma^2_{AB}.$$

Following these rules to find $E(MS_B)$ we obtain the terms

$$Y_{ijk} = \mu + a_i + \mathbf{b_j} + \mathbf{ab_{ij}} + e_{ijk},$$

the boldfaced terms being all those that include j (the subscript of b_j) in their subscript. Creating the σ^2 terms we get σ^2_e, σ^2_B, and σ^2_{AB}, and multiplying by the subscripts that are in Y_{ijk} but not in the term in use, we get σ^2_e, IK σ^2_B, and K σ^2_{AB}. Summing these we get

$$E(MS_B) = \sigma^2_e + IK\,\sigma^2_B + K\,\sigma^2_{AB}.$$

For $E(MS_{AB})$, the model term for the effect of the AB interaction is ab_{ij}, its subscript is ij, and the only terms in the model equation containing all of the letters in that subscript are

$$Y_{ijk} = \mu + a_i + b_j + \mathbf{ab_{ij}} + e_{ijk}.$$

Following the rule, we get σ^2_{AB} and σ^2_e, with σ^2_{AB} multiplied by K, so

$$E(MS_{AB}) = \sigma^2_e + K\,\sigma^2_{AB}.$$

Applying the rule to obtain $E(MS_e)$ we find that the only term to contain all of the subscripts in e_{ijk} is e_{ijk} itself, so $E(MS_e) = \sigma^2_e$. We should note that **it is a consequence of E(MS) Rule 1 that σ^2_e is included in every E(MS) and that $E(MS_e)$ is always just σ^2_e.**

7.18 Applying the rule to a three-factor design with random effects. Now we will apply the rule for obtaining expected mean squares to a three-factor design with random effects. The model equation is

$$Y_{ijkm} = \mu + a_i + b_j + c_k + ab_{ij} + ac_{ik} + bc_{jk} + abc_{ijk} + e_{ijkm}.$$

To find $E(MS_A)$ we go through the following steps: first we locate the model terms containing i in their subscript, since i is the subscript of a_i. This gives us

$$Y_{ijkm} = \mu + a_i + b_j + c_k + ab_{ij} + ac_{ik} + bc_{jk} + abc_{ijk} + e_{ijkm}.$$

Then we create the variance terms σ^2_A, σ^2_{AB}, σ^2_{AC}, σ^2_{ABC}, and σ^2_e, and multiplying them by the appropriate quantities and adding we get

$$E(MS_A) = \sigma^2_e + JKM\, \sigma^2_A + KM\, \sigma^2_{AB} + JM\, \sigma^2_{AC} + M\, \sigma^2_{ABC}.$$

The student should apply the E(MS) Rule to show that:

$$E(MS_B) = \sigma^2_e + IKM\, \sigma^2_B + KM\, \sigma^2_{AB} + IM\, \sigma^2_{BC} + M\, \sigma^2_{ABC}$$

$$E(MS_C) = \sigma^2_e + IJM\, \sigma^2_C + JM\, \sigma^2_{AC} + IM\, \sigma^2_{BC} + M\, \sigma^2_{ABC}$$

$$E(MS_{AB}) = \sigma^2_e + KM\, \sigma^2_{AB} + M\, \sigma^2_{ABC}$$

$$E(MS_{AC}) = \sigma^2_e + JM\, \sigma^2_{AC} + M\, \sigma^2_{ABC}$$

$$E(MS_{BC}) = \sigma^2_e + IM\, \sigma^2_{BC} + M\, \sigma^2_{ABC}$$

$$E(MS_{ABC}) = \sigma^2_e + M\, \sigma^2_{ABC}$$

$$E(MS_e) = \sigma^2_e.$$

Inspection of these expected mean squares shows that the appropriate ratio for testing the null hypothesis that $\sigma^2_{ABC} = 0$ is MS_{ABC}/MS_e and that each of the tests for the two-factor interaction null hypotheses should use the ratio of the mean square for the two-factor interaction to the mean square for the three-factor interaction. But when we consider the expected mean squares for the main effects, we see that there is no appropriate denominator mean square. That is, there is no mean square that has as its expected value a quantity that is the same as the $E(MS_A)$ when the null hypothesis that $\sigma^2_A = 0$ is true.

If we could assume that σ^2_{AB} or σ^2_{AC} were zero, then we could find an appropriate denominator mean square. But even if the F-test for one of these two-factor interactions led to accepting the null hypothesis, we could not be sure that this was the case, inference being what it is. We would therefore run the risk of introducing a bias into the test that would result in the test statistic's being too small and therefore failing to reject the null hypothesis as often as we should when it was in fact false. Some people are willing to accept this risk and regard it as safe since it is conservative against Type I error. However, there is usually as little justification for spurious diminishing of power as there is for spurious inflation of the significance level. In the next section we will consider an alternative in which an approximate F-test can be used when an appropriate denominator mean square cannot be found.

7.19 Approximate F-ratios. The strategy for determining mean square ratios that provide us with test statistics that are distributed as F when the null hypothesis is true has been to use in the numerator of that ratio the mean square for the source we are testing and to use in the denominator of that ratio a mean square that contains all of the terms that the numerator mean square contains except for that one additional term that contains the parameter that is zero under the null hypothesis. But as we saw in 7.18, for the three-factor design with random effects for each factor,

$$E(MS_A) = \sigma^2_e + JKM\,\sigma^2_A + KM\,\sigma^2_{AB} + JM\,\sigma^2_{AC} + M\,\sigma^2_{ABC}.$$

Since MS_A is the numerator mean square for the test that $\sigma^2_A = 0$, we would need to find a mean square with an expected value equal to $\sigma^2_e + KM\,\sigma^2_{AB} + JM\,\sigma^2_{AC} + M\,\sigma^2_{ABC}$. But there is no source in the design for which the expected mean square has this value. **The procedure for obtaining an approximate F-test when there is no mean square with the appropriate expected value to use as the denominator of the F statistic will be to find a linear combination of mean squares that has the appropriate expected value.** We will treat this linear combination of mean squares as if it is itself a mean square and use it as the denominator of the test statistic.

We can write that $E(MS_A) = U + JKM\,\sigma^2_A$, where $U = \sigma^2_e + KM\,\sigma^2_{AB} + JM\,\sigma^2_{AC} + M\,\sigma^2_{ABC}$. Then we can further note that $U = E(MS_{AB}) + E(MS_{AC}) - E(MS_{ABC})$.

When the expression $U = E(MS_{AB}) + E(MS_{AC}) - E(MS_{ABC})$ is first presented in class, students usually go through a preliminary quandary followed by a secondary quandary. The first is that they don't see why the equality holds. That quandary is immediately dispensed with when they refer back to the values of the three expected mean squares on the right side, perform the addition and subtraction, and compare the answer to the value given in the definition of U. The second quandary is where did this expression come from? The teacher usually appears to pull it out of midair, and the student is mystified. Well, there is no mystery, and it isn't pulled out of midair. The entire collection of expected mean squares is searched for a linear combination of some of them that results in a value equal to U. In other words, you play around with the expected mean squares until you find a combination of them that gives the desired result. This is, of course, not just random play. You start with

An Introduction to the Analysis of Variance

the expression $U = \sigma^2_e + KM\,\sigma^2_{AB} + JM\,\sigma^2_{AC} + M\,\sigma^2_{ABC}$. You can see that an E(MS) term with $KM\,\sigma^2_{AB}$ is needed, so you can add in $E(MS_{AB})$ and you can try $E(MS_{AC})$ to get the $JM\,\sigma^2_{AC}$ term. Doing this you would have

$$\sigma^2_e + KM\,\sigma^2_{AB} + M\,\sigma^2_{ABC} + \sigma^2_e + JM\,\sigma^2_{AC} + M\,\sigma^2_{ABC}.$$

Comparing this to the value of U, you would see that it would be just right except that there is one σ^2_e and one $M\,\sigma^2_{ABC}$ too many. That is your signal to find an E(MS) term that has both of these in it and subtract it from the terms already gathered. Fortunately, $E(MS_{ABC}) = \sigma^2_e + M\,\sigma^2_{ABC}$, so you arrive at the desired result, $U = E(MS_{AB}) + E(MS_{AC}) - E(MS_{ABC})$.

Since U is the expected value of $MS_{AB} + MS_{AC} - MS_{ABC}$, we will use $MS_{AB} + MS_{AC} - MS_{ABC}$ as the denominator of the approximate F statistic which we will write as

$$F_{I-1,\ df_{denominator}} = MS_A/(MS_{AB} + MS_{AC} - MS_{ABC}).$$

To determine the degrees of freedom for the denominator "mean square" we will take the square of $MS_{AB} + MS_{AC} - MS_{ABC}$ and divide it by a sum. This sum will be obtained by taking each mean square in the linear combination, squaring it, dividing it by the df for that mean square, and then adding up all these squared-MS's-divided-by-their-df. For the example we would have

$$df_{denominator} = (MS_{AB} + MS_{AC} - MS_{ABC})^2 / [MS_{AB}^2/(I-1)(J-1)$$

$$+ MS_{AC}^2/(I-1)(J-1) + MS_{ABC}^2/(I-1)(J-1)(K-1)]$$

This procedure can be used generally. **Find a linear combination of mean squares for which the expected value equals that of the mean square for the source about which the hypothesis is to be tested, use that linear combination of mean squares as the denominator of the approximate F statistic, and use as the degrees of freedom for that denominator, the square of that linear combination divided by the sum of the squares of each term in the linear combination, each such square being divided by the degrees of freedom for the mean square in that term.**

7.19.1 How $df_{denominator}$ is obtained. To see how the estimation of the degrees of freedom is arrived at, we have to consider a few little details. First, when we treat $MS_{AB} + MS_{AC} - MS_{ABC}$ as if it is a mean square, we are saying that we will treat it as if it is the variable $U\chi^2_{df}/df$, so that when we take the ratio

$MS_A/(MS_{AB} + MS_{AC} - MS_{ABC})$

it will be as if we have taken the ratio

$[E(MS_A)\chi^2_{(I-1)}/(I-1)]/[U\chi^2_{df}/df]$

so that since $E(MS_A) = U$ under the null hypothesis that $\sigma^2_A = 0$, we would have

$MS_A/(MS_{AB} + MS_{AC} - MS_{ABC}) = [\chi^2_{(I-1)}/(I-1)]/[\chi^2_{df}/df] = F_{I-1,df}.$

Now, as we try to solve for the unknown, df, the approximation gets introduced in two ways. The first approximation is that we approximate the variable $MS_{AB} + MS_{AC} - MS_{ABC}$ by the variable $U\chi^2_{df}/df$.

7.19.1.1 Approximating the distribution of one variable by that of another is not new to us. Approximating the distribution of one variable by that of another is not completely foreign to us. Recall in Introductory Statistics when we wanted to use the normal distribution as an approximation to some binomial distribution in order to compute binomial probabilities that would be too tedious to compute if we had to use the binomial formula, as, for example, if we wanted to compute the probability of a fair coin coming up heads between 500 and 550 times in 1000 independent tosses of the coin. The procedure, because we were told that the normal distribution well approximated the binomial distribution under certain conditions that this example satisfies, was to assign to the normal distribution the same mean and the same variance as the binomial distribution that we wanted to approximate. So we used a normal distribution with a mean of $Np = 1,000(.5)$ and a variance of $Np(1 - p) = 1,000(.5)(.5)$ since the binomial distribution, as we recall, has a mean of Np and a variance of $Np(1 - p)$. Then we computed normal distribution probabilities for score intervals in the normal distribution corresponding to the intervals of scores of interest in the binomial distribution. The point here is that we are familiar with a procedure whereby we approximate the distribution of one variable with the distribution of another by setting the mean and variance of the approximating variable equal to the mean and variance of the approximated variable.

7.19.2 Approximating $MS_{AB} + MS_{AC} - MS_{ABC}$ by $U\chi^2_{df}/df$. To approximate $MS_{AB} + MS_{AC} - MS_{ABC}$ by $U\chi^2_{df}/df$ we set the mean and variance of the latter equal to that of the former. Now since both have the same expected value, their means are already equal. That is $E(MS_{AB} + MS_{AC} - MS_{ABC}) = U$ and $E(U\chi^2_{df}/df) = (U/df)E(\chi^2_{df}) = (U/df)df = U.$ To equate their variances we make use of the fact that if $MS = E(MS)\chi^2_{df}/df$, then $Var(MS)$

$= 2[E(MS)]^2/df$. That is, if some mean square is equal to its expected value times a chi-square variable divided by its degrees of freedom, then the variance of that mean square is two times the square of that expected value of the mean square, then divided by the degrees of freedom for that mean square. So, acting as if the linear combination $MS_{AB} + MS_{AC} - MS_{ABC}$ is a mean square, we can write

$$Var(MS_{AB} + MS_{AC} - MS_{ABC}) = Var(U\chi^2_{df}/df) = 2U^2/df.$$

But since the mean squares in the linear combination are independent of one another, the variance of the linear combination is just the sum of the variances of the separate terms, and so we also have

$$Var(MS_{AB} + MS_{AC} - MS_{ABC}) = 2[E(MS_{AB})]^2/[(I - 1)(J - 1)] +$$

$$2[E(MS_{AC})]^2/[(I - 1)(K - 1)] + 2[E(MS_{ABC})]^2/[(I - 1)(J - 1)(K - 1)].$$

Setting these two values equal to each other we can solve for the unknown df. Thus,

$$2U^2/df = 2[E(MS_{AB})]^2/[(I - 1)(J - 1)] + 2[E(MS_{AC})]^2/[(I - 1)(K - 1)]$$

$$+ 2[E(MS_{ABC})]^2/[(I - 1)(J - 1)(K - 1)]$$

so, since $U^2 = [E(MS_{AB} + MS_{AC} - MS_{ABC})]^2$,

$$df = [E(MS_{AB} + MS_{AC} - MS_{ABC})]^2 /\{[E(MS_{AB})]^2/(I - 1)(J - 1)$$

$$+ [E(MS_{AC})]^2 /(I - 1)(K - 1) + [E(MS_{ABC})]^2 /(I - 1)(J - 1)(K - 1)\}$$

This expression is in terms of the unknown expected values, which are defined in terms of the unknown variances. The second level of approximation is introduced by estimating each expected mean square by using the corresponding mean square obtained from the data. This gives the quantity to be used as the degrees of freedom for the denominator,

$$df_{denominator} = [(MS_{AB} + MS_{AC} - MS_{ABC})]^2 /\{[(MS_{AB})]^2/(I - 1)(J - 1)$$

$$+ [(MS_{AC})]^2 /(I - 1)(K - 1) + [(MS_{ABC})]^2 /(I - 1)(J - 1)(K - 1)\}$$

7.20 Extending the method of finding expected mean squares to model equations involving nested factors. We now want to extend the method of deriving expected mean squares to models containing nested as well as crossed factors and to models involving fixed as well as random factors. This will require just a slight elaboration of the rule. We begin by formulating a model equation for a design in which nested and crossed factors occur and in which some effects are fixed and some are random. Models involving both fixed and random effects are called **mixed models**. Suppose we have a design with a fixed-effects factor A, a random-effects factor B, and another random-effects factor C that is nested in B. The model equation for this design would be

$$Y_{ijkm} = \mu + A_i + b_j + c_{k(j)} + Ab_{ij} + Ac_{ik(j)} + e_{ijkm}.$$

(Let us note in passing that **the interaction of a fixed effect with a random effect is a random effect** for the simple reason that the particular combination of interaction effects is a result of random sampling rather than of a predetermination by the experimenter. So far as notation is concerned, any string of letters that names a particular interaction effect will denote a random effect if any one or more of those letters is in lowercase, meaning at least one of the interacting factors has a random effect and therefore the interaction effect results from random sampling.)

Now we want to reconsider E(MS) **Rule 1.** We will write the rule in parts to make it easier to single out the part to be changed.

(1)   **For a given source, locate the term in the model equation that expresses the effect of that source,**

(2)   **determine the subscript(s) of that term, and**

(3)   **locate just those terms in the model equation that contain those subscripts in their subscript.**

(4)   **For each such model equation term that is located, create a variance term, σ^2, that has as its subscript the label of the source for that model term, and**

(5)   **multiply each such σ^2 term by the uppercase value of the subscripts of Y that do not occur in the subscript of that model term.**

(6)   **The sum of these quantities is the desired E(MS).**

It is part (3) that we want to change. **When we are locating those terms in the model equation that include in their subscripts all the letters in the subscript of the term of the source of interest, we will** <u>delete any such term, except the error term, that has in its subscript the subscript for a fixed effect that</u>

does not occur in the subscript of the term of interest unless that subscript for a fixed effect is in parentheses. Let's say this again in another way. As we are collecting the sources that contribute to the expected mean square for some source of interest, we take the model term for the source of interest and find all the other model terms that have in their subscript the same letters as has the model term for the source of interest. Then, of those we have found in this way, some must be deleted. The ones that are deleted are, with two exceptions, those that have in their subscript the letter or letters subscripting a fixed effect source that does not occur in the source of interest. The two exceptions are (1) the error term, which is never deleted, and (2) any model term in which the subscript for the fixed effect that does not occur in the model term for the source of interest occurs in parentheses. This is one of those rules that is so awkward to say but so easy to exemplify and to learn and use. We may as well stop trying to say it now and just show it. So, for example, to find the $E(MS_A)$, we locate

$$Y_{ijkm} = \mu + A_i + b_j + c_{k(j)} + Ab_{ij} + Ac_{ik(j)} + e_{ijkm},$$

since these all contain the subscript i which is the subscript for source A, the source of interest, and we proceed as usual to write

$$E(MS_A) = JKM\, \sigma^2_A + KM\, \sigma^2_{AB} + M\, \sigma^2_{AC} + \sigma^2_e.$$

When we come to locating the terms for $E(MS_B)$, we start with

$$Y_{ijkm} = \mu + A_i + b_j + c_{k(j)} + Ab_{ij} + Ac_{ik(j)} + e_{ijkm},$$

but in accordance with the new rule change we must delete Ab_{ij} and $Ac_{ik(j)}$ since they each contain the subscript i, which is the subscript of a fixed-effect factor that is not contained in the subscript of the source of interest, b_j. We do not exclude e_{ijkm} even though it contains i because σ^2_e is a part of every expected mean square. Thus we arrive at

$$E(MS_B) = IKM\, \sigma^2_B + IM\, \sigma^2_C + \sigma^2_e.$$

7.21 Some more examples. It will be helpful to the student to go through the procedure for finding expected mean squares a few more times to be sure the rules are clear. Notice as we do this how we can arrive at the various expected mean square formulas essentially by just inspecting the model equation in a systematic manner. Let's take a really juicy model equation, say, that for a design having four factors: A and B fixed, C and D random, D nested in B x C, A crossed with B, with C, and with D, and, of course, B crossed with C. This equation would be $Y_{ijkmn} = \mu + A_i + B_j + c_k + d_{m(j,k)} + AB_{ij} + Ac_{ik} + Ad_{im(j,k)} + Bc_{jk} + ABc_{ijk} + e_{ijkmn}$. To find $E(MS_A)$ we locate the terms having i in their subscript, giving A_i, AB_{ij}, Ac_{ik}, $Ad_{im(j,k)}$, ABc_{ijk} and e_{ijkmn}. Since j is the subscript of a fixed-effect factor and j does not occur in the subscript of A_i, we delete AB_{ij} and ABc_{ijk}. Notice that we did not delete $Ad_{im(j,k)}$ even though it has j in its subscript. This is because j occurs in parentheses. We are left with the terms A_i, Ac_{ik}, $Ad_{im(j,k)}$, and e_{ijkmn}, giving

$$E(MS_A) = \sigma^2_e + JKMN\ \sigma^2_A + JMN\ \sigma^2_{AC} + N\ \sigma^2_{AD}.$$

Let's do two more: $E(MS_C)$ and $E(MS_D)$. For $E(MS_C)$ we locate all the terms having k in their subscript, giving

$$c_k, d_{m(j,k)}, Ac_{ik}, Ad_{im(j,k)}, Bc_{jk}, ABc_{ijk} \text{ and } e_{ijkmn},$$

we eliminate Ac_{ik}, $Ad_{im(j,k)}$, Bc_{jk}, and ABc_{ijk} since i and j are fixed-effects subscripts that do not occur in the subscript of c_k and do not occur in parentheses in the subscripts of these terms, and then write

$$E(MS_C) = \sigma^2_e + IJMN\ \sigma^2_C + IN\ \sigma^2_D.$$

To find $E(MS_D)$ we locate the terms having m, j, and k in their subscripts: $d_{m(j,k)}$, $Ad_{im(j,k)}$ and e_{ijkmn}; eliminate the term $Ad_{im(j,k)}$ due to the i; and get

$$E(MS_D) = \sigma^2_e + IN\ \sigma^2_D.$$

7.22 The new rule. The rule for finding expected mean squares will in its new form read:

(1)   For a given source, locate the term in the model equation that expresses the effect of that source,

(2)   determine the subscript(s) of that term, and

(3)   locate just those terms in the model equation that contain those subscripts in their subscript. <u>Delete any such term, except the error term, that has in its subscript the subscript for a fixed effect that does not occur in the subscript of the term of interest unless that subscript for a fixed effect occurs within parentheses.</u>

(4)   For each such model equation term that remains, create a variance term, σ^2, that has as its subscript the label of the source for

that model term, and

(5)   **multiply each such σ^2 term by the upper case value of the subscripts of Y that do not occur in the subscript of that model term.**

(6)   **The sum of these quantities is the desired E(MS).**

In this form the rule is appropriate for fixed, random, or mixed designs. Applying the rule to each source in the example model equation

$$Y_{ijkm} = \mu + A_i + b_j + c_{k(j)} + Ab_{ij} + Ac_{ik(j)} + e_{ijkm},$$

we obtain the expected mean squares given in Table 7.3.

TABLE 7.3   ANALYSIS OF VARIANCE TABLE

Source	df	MS	E(MS)	F
A	I-1	MS_A	$\sigma^2_e + JKM\,\sigma^2_A + KM\,\sigma^2_{AB} + M\,\sigma^2_{AC}$	MS_A/MS_{AB}
B	J-1	MS_B	$\sigma^2_e + IKM\,\sigma^2_B + IM\,\sigma^2_C$	MS_B/MS_C
C	K-1	MS_C	$\sigma^2_e + IM\,\sigma^2_C$	MS_C/MS_e
AB	(I-1)(J-1)	MS_{AB}	$\sigma^2_e + KM\,\sigma^2_{AB} + M\,\sigma^2_{AC}$	MS_{AB}/MS_{AC}
AC	J(I-1)(K-1)	MS_{AC}	$\sigma^2_e + M\,\sigma^2_{AC}$	MS_{AC}/MS_e
Error	IJKM-IJK	MS_e	σ^2_e	

Two things should be noted about the entries in Table 7.3. In general, the ratios given in the F column are not necessarily distributed as F even though the appropriate relationships hold between the expected values of the numerator and denominator mean squares. However, standard usage is to use these ratios as approximately F distributed. An exact test using Hotelling's T^2-statistic is discussed by Scheffé (1959, p. 271) for mixed models. Also, the σ^2 terms in Table 7.3 are not all variances. For example, σ^2_A is actually $\Sigma_i A_i^2/(I - 1)$. For the purpose of determining which ratios are distributed as F or approximately as F, we will not need to distinguish between those σ^2 terms which are actual variances and those which are other quantities.

Exercises

1. Explain in your own words why we assume that σ^2_e is a part of the expected value of every mean square.

2. Find all of the E(MS) terms for the model

$$Y_{ijkmn} = \mu + A_i + B_j + c_k + d_{m(j,k)} + AB_{ij} + Ac_{ik} + Ad_{im(j,k)} + Bc_{jk} + ABc_{ijk} + e_{ijkmn}.$$

3. Find the various E(MS) terms for the model

$$Y_{ijkm} = \mu + A_i + b_j + c_k + Ab_{ij} + Ac_{ik} + bc_{jk} + Abc_{ijk} + e_{ijkm}.$$

TABLE 7.4 FICTIONAL LOOKING TIMES FROM 3- AND 6-MONTH-OLD BOY AND GIRL INFANTS

		STIMULUS			
		UNSCRAMBLED		SCRAMBLED	
		PICTURE	DIAGRAM	PICTURE	DIAGRAM
GIRLS	3 MO.	26	11	4	6
		22	13	6	6
		19	12	5	5
		21	15	7	8
		24	15	9	4
	6 MO.	15	18	10	11
		12	21	9	10
		14	23	9	12
		12	21	8	10
		14	20	9	9
BOYS	3 MO.	23	10	4	4
		22	9	5	6
		24	12	3	6
		24	8	3	3
		21	9	4	4
	6 MO.	14	19	8	7
		13	21	8	6
		15	24	7	8
		12	21	9	8
		13	18	6	6

4. Do exercise 3 again, except assume that A is a random effect and B and C are both fixed effects.

5. An experiment is designed in which a random sample of three Drug Levels is nested within each of four specified Learning Tasks. A different set of 10 randomly sampled subjects is nested within each of the Drug Levels. (Note that Subjects and Error are completely confounded. Take this into account in writing the model equation.)

(a) How many subjects served in this experiment?

(b) What is the model equation for the experiment?

(c) Write out all of the expected mean squares.

(d) What would you use as the denominator mean square to test the null hypothesis that all four learning tasks have the same mean?

(e) What would be the denominator for the test of the drug level effects?

6. What would you use as the denominator for the test of the null hypothesis that the population variance of the B effects in exercise 3 is zero?

7. Find the appropriate F-ratios for testing all of the hypotheses for the model

$$Y_{ijkmn} = \mu + a_i + b_j + c_k + d_{m(j,k)} + ab_{ij} + ac_{ik} + ad_{im(j,k)} + bc_{jk} + abc_{ijk} + e_{ijkmn}.$$

TABLE 7.5   FICTIONAL DATA FROM A NESTED-FACTOR DESIGN

	B_1						B_2					
	C_1			C_2			C_1			C_2		
	$D_{1(1,1)}$	$D_{2(1,1)}$	$D_{3(1,2)}$	$D_{1(1,2)}$	$D_{2(1,2)}$	$D_{3(1,2)}$	$D_{1(2,1)}$	$D_{2(2,1)}$	$D_{3(2,1)}$	$D_{1(2,2)}$	$D_{2(2,2)}$	$D_{3(2,2)}$
A_1	2	3	4	6	7	6	4	3	4	8	7	9
	3	3	1	2	4	3	7	6	5	4	8	8
A_2	4	5	4	5	6	6	7	6	5	6	7	8
	4	5	5	4	5	6	7	7	8	7	8	9
A_3	4	5	6	5	6	7	4	4	5	6	7	7
	4	4	5	4	6	7	5	5	5	3	8	8

8. Table 5.9 is shown here again as Table 7.4. Assume that the levels of the stimulus factor were sampled at random from a population of methods of presenting such stimuli. Regard Gender and Age as fixed effects.

(a) Perform the analysis of variance of these data.

(b) Write out the summary table, including in it the expected mean squares for each of the sources.

9. The data in Table 7.5 are from Table 6.5. Assume that the levels of D, the nested factor, were sampled at random from a population of D levels. Assume the other factors consist of fixed effects.

(a) Perform the appropriate analysis of variance.

(b) Show the expected mean squares for each source.

10. An investigation of children's reading skills in grades 7 through 9 is conducted in a major metropolitan school district. Five schools are sampled at random, and within each school, three classrooms are selected at random from the seventh-grade classes, three from the eighth-grade classes, and three from the ninth-grade classes. A random sample of 10 children is chosen from each class, and their reading skills are assessed.

(a) Which of these effects are fixed and which are random?

(b) Which of these factors are nested and which are crossed?

(c) Write the model equation for this design.

TABLE 7.6 FICTIONAL REACTION TIME DATA

					Stimulus Type							
	Simple				Complex				Compound			
	Sequence				Sequence				Sequence			
1(1)	2(1)	3(1)	4(1)	1(2)	2(2)	3(2)	4(2)	1(3)	2(3)	3(3)	4(3)	
211	209	201	220	241	229	227	235	243	234	229	222	
210	205	208	217	238	217	223	248	245	234	225	227	
199	219	207	212	226	225	248	229	225	229	225	223	
204	203	202	215	223	232	234	221	239	235	231	237	
201	204	223	215	239	219	218	240	240	239	223	224	

d) Draw the design diagram.

11. Assume that in an investigation of reaction time to visual stimuli, three types of stimuli were used: Simple, Complex, and Compound. The investigator was concerned that if the 20 stimuli of each type were presented in a specific sequence, then the finding of a difference in reaction time to different types of stimuli would be specific to the sequence used. For this reason, four different randomly determined sequences were used with each type of stimuli. Thus, each subject received a single sequence of a single type of stimuli, and the subject's score was the mean reaction time in milliseconds to the stimuli in the sequence. This would permit a test of the sequence effect, and a finding of no differences due to sequences would

permit generalization of the differences in reaction time between types of stimuli to the entire three populations of possible stimulus sequences from which these randomly determined sequences could be regarded as random samples. Assume the data in Table 7.6 came from such an investigation, and perform the appropriate F-tests to test for effects due to Type of Stimuli and Sequence.

12. Assume that the data in exercise 11 were the result of 12 different sequences of the same stimulus type. That is, ignore the Stimulus Type factor. Analyze the data as a one-factor random-effects design with the single factor being sequences. How does the test for the effect of sequences differ in this design from that in the design used in exercise 11? Why is the mean square for Sequences different in this design than it was in the design in exercise 11?

13. Do parts (a) and (b) of exercise 9 assuming that B and D are random effects and that A and B are fixed effects.

14. Do parts (a) and (b) of exercise 9 assuming that all of the factors have random effects.

15. Find the appropriate F-ratios for testing all of the hypotheses for the model
$$Y_{ijkmn} = \mu + A_i + b_j + c_k + d_{m(j,k)} + Ab_{ij} + Ac_{ik} + Ad_{im(j,k)} + bc_{jk} + Abc_{ijk} + e_{ijkmn}.$$

16. Find the expected mean squares for all of the sources for the model
$$Y_{ijkmn} = \mu + A_i + b_j + C_k + d_{m(j,k)} + Ab_{ij} + AC_{ik} + Ad_{im(j,k)} + bC_{jk} + AbC_{ijk} + e_{ijkmn}.$$

8

Repeated Measurement Designs

8.1 Two shortcomings of assigning different subjects to different experimental conditions. Consider a one-factor design with I levels of the factor.

TABLE 8.1 TREATMENTS BY SUBJECTS OR REPEATED MEASURES DESIGN: J SUBJECTS CROSSED WITH EACH OF I TREATMENTS

	Treatment 1	Treatment 2	...	Treatment I
Subject 1	$Y_{1,1}$	$Y_{2,1}$	...	$Y_{I,1}$
Subject 2	$Y_{1,2}$	$Y_{2,2}$	...	$Y_{I,2}$
...	...	...	...	...
Subject j	$Y_{1,j}$	$Y_{2,j}$	...	$Y_{I,j}$
...	...	...	...	...
Subject J	$Y_{1,J}$	$Y_{2,J}$	...	$Y_{I,J}$

Suppose these I levels represent I different treatments that are administered to subjects, say, for example, I training procedures, I propaganda films, I amounts of some drug, or I delay durations between a first treatment and a second treatment. Suppose 10 subjects are at each level. This design is a common, acceptable design often encountered in the research literature. It has two aspects that sometimes may be shortcomings. We cannot tell how the same person would react to the I different treatments since we give only one treatment per person. Also, the differences among the subjects in each group of 10 subjects receiving a given treatment manifest themselves as error and contribute to the estimate of error variance. Hence, insofar as there are large between-subject differences within a given treatment level, it is difficult for us to reject the null hypothesis even when it is false. Sometimes for the one reason, sometimes for the other, often for both, an alternative design has been used in which each subject receives each treatment. Graphically, such a design might be represented by Table 8.1.

8.2 In a repeated measurement design Subjects are crossed with at least one other factor. We can see that the design in Table 8.1 is simply a case of a design with two crossed factors. **What is new is that Subjects is one of the crossed factors.** In all of the previous designs, subjects have been a nested factor. It is important to understand how repeated measurement designs differ from the designs we have grown used to and how they do not. There is one very important way they differ, having to do with the underlying assumption of independence of the scores, and one rather superficial but

TABLE 8.2 EXPECTED MEAN SQUARES FOR A TREATMENTS x SUBJECTS DESIGN

Source	df	E(MS)	F
A	I-1	$\sigma^2_e + J\sigma^2_A + \sigma^2_{AS}$	MS_A/MS_{AS}
Subjects	J-1	$\sigma^2_e + I\sigma^2_S$	
A X S	(I-1)(J-1)	$\sigma^2_e + \sigma^2_{AS}$	
Error	0	σ^2_e	

traditional way in which the summary table of the analysis of variance is presented. We will touch on these two differences later. For now we want to emphasize that formally a design in which Subjects are crossed with some other factor is no different from any other crossed design. We can write a model equation for this design in the form $Y_{ij} = \mu + A_i + s_j + As_{ij} + e_{ij}$. Except in the rare case where interest lies in the specific set of subjects used, Subjects is considered a random factor. In the model equation the treatment factor, A, is shown as a fixed-effects factor, but this is not necessary. The analysis of variance for the design in Table 8.1 is given in Table 8.2. **Caution: If I > 2, do not use this analysis as is without reading the considerations of independence given in Section 8.6.** Because each subject is measured only once under each treatment condition, there is only one score per cell in the factorial design. Since the number of scores equals the number of cells, there are zero degrees of freedom for error. This means there is no F-test for Subjects (unless we make the usually unjustified assumption that $\sigma^2_{AS} = 0$, in which case the Subjects effect can be tested using MS_S/MS_{AS}), nor is there one for the Treatments x Subjects interaction. This is not a required condition, however. It is possible to measure the subject more than once under the same condition. If the subject were measured

TABLE 8.3 EXPECTED MEAN SQUARES FOR A TREATMENTS x SUBJECTS DESIGN WITH K OBSERVATIONS PER TREATMENT-SUBJECT COMBINATION

Source	df	E(MS)	F
A	I-1	$\sigma^2_e + J\sigma^2_A + \sigma^2_{AS}$	MS_A/MS_{AS}
Subjects	J-1	$\sigma^2_e + I\sigma^2_S$	MS_S/MS_e
A x S	(I-1)(J-1)	$\sigma^2_e + \sigma^2_{AS}$	MS_{AS}/MS_e
Error	IJK - IJ	σ^2_e	

TABLE 8.4　TREATMENTS x SUBJECTS　DESIGN

		Treatments				
		1	2	3	4	Totals
Subject	1	2	4	5	9	20
	2	3	6	7	10	26
	3	4	5	6	8	23
	4	4	6	7	10	27
	5	5	5	7	9	26
Totals		18	26	32	46	122

TABLE 8.5　ANOVA OF THE DATA IN FIGURE 8.2

Source	df	SS	MS	F
A	4-1	$(18^2+26^2+32^2+46^2)/5 - 122^2/20 = 83.80$	27.93	58.81
Subjects	5-1	$(20^2+26^2+23^2+27^2+26^2)/4 - 122^2/20 = 8.30$	2.075	
A X S	(4-1)(5-1)	$2^2+4^2+...7^2+9^2 - (18^2+26^2+32^2+46^2)/5$		
		$- (20^2+26^2+23^2+27^2+26^2)/4 + 122^2/20 = 5.95$	.496	

K times, the model equation would be $Y_{ijk} = \mu + A_i + s_j + As_{ij} + e_{ijk}$, and the ANOVA would be as shown in Table 8.3. For a short numerical example, consider the data from five subjects given each of four treatments once, shown in Table 8.4. Table 8.5 shows the results of the ANOVA of these data.

Caution is required with the design in Table 8.3. Since the measurements of the same person under the same condition are assumed to differ only due to error variance, and since these errors are assumed to be independently distributed, factors such as fatigue, boredom, or carryover of any sort from one response to another can produce violation of this independence assumption. This will generally result in underestimation of error variance and inflation of the significance level.

8.3 Between-subject sources and within-subject sources. When Subjects are crossed with two factors the design is usually called a Treatments x Treatments x Subjects design or an A x B x S design. Formally, this design can be treated in the usual way so far as degrees of freedom and sums of squares are concerned. The expected mean squares and

TABLE 8.6 SOURCES AND df FOR A DESIGN WITH ONE BETWEEN-SUBJECTS AND ONE WITHIN-SUBJECTS FACTOR

Source	df
Between Subjects	JK - 1 (# of subjects - 1)
B	J - 1
S	J(K - 1)
Within Subjects	JK(I - 1) (# of scores - # of subjects)
A	I - 1
AB	(I - 1)(J - 1)
AS	(I - 1)J(K - 1)

the F-ratios have to be handled somewhat differently and we will come to that shortly. Also, when Subjects are nested within some factors and crossed with others, the degrees of freedom and sums of squares are computed as before, but for historical reasons the various sources customarily are displayed in the analysis of variance table in two categories: **Between-Subjects sources and Within-Subjects sources.**

Between-Subject sources refer to sources of variation that occur between the different subjects. Within-Subject sources are those due to the fact that in general the scores from the same subject vary one from another, and this variation of scores within a given subject is due to these sources of Within-Subject variation. For example, when the same subject is given five memorization trials and the five scores are recorded, the fact that these five scores are not the same does not reflect anything about the differences between the several subjects in the experiment, but instead reflects the fact that the given subject's scores differ under the five treatments. All these differences occur within the same subject's set of scores and are referred to as within-subject variation.

The Between-Subjects sources comprise Subjects and the factors that Subjects are nested in; the Within-Subjects sources are the rest: the factors that Subjects are crossed with, the interactions of Subjects with the factors Subjects are crossed with, and the interactions of the factors Subjects are crossed with with the factors Subjects are nested in. Let's look at two examples. The first will involve Subjects nested in one factor, B, and crossed with another, A. The factor B might be Classrooms and the factor A might be Memorization Trials. The model equation would be

An Introduction to the Analysis of Variance

TABLE 8.7 FICTIONAL DATA FOR A MIXED DESIGN

	Group 1 Treatments						Group 2 Treatments						Group 3 Treatments				
	1	2	3	4			1	2	3	4			1	2	3	4	
1	2	4	5	9	20	6	4	7	8	11	30	11	3	6	7	10	26
2	3	6	7	10	26	7	5	6	8	12	31	12	4	6	8	11	29
3	4	5	6	8	23	8	6	8	6	14	34	13	5	6	6	11	28
4	4	6	7	10	27	9	4	8	9	12	33	14	4	7	8	11	30
5	5	5	7	9	26	10	6	9	10	14	39	15	5	7	9	12	33
	18	26	32	46	122		25	38	41	63	167		21	32	38	55	146

TABLE 8.8 ANOVA OF THE MIXED DESIGN DATA IN FIGURE 8.3

Source	df	SS	MS	F
Between	14			
B	2	50.70	25.35	11.14
S	12	27.30	2.28	
Within	45			
A	3	348.18	116.06	180.87
AB	6	5.97	.99	1.55
AS	36	23.10	.64	

$$Y_{ijk} = \mu + B_j + s_{k(j)} + A_i + AB_{ij} + As_{ik(j)} + e_{ijk},$$

and the Summary Table would be as shown in Table 8.3. In the second example we'll let Subjects be nested in the cross of two factors, B and C. This will give the model equation

$$Y_{ijk} = \mu + B_j + C_k + BC_{jk} + s_{m(j,k)} + A_i + AB_{ij} + AC_{ik} + ABC_{ijk} + As_{im(j,k)}$$

$$+ e_{ijk}.$$

The analysis of variance will be as shown in Table 8.6. As a numerical example for the design in Table 8.6 we can consider Table 8.7 showing five subjects nested in each of three different experimental groups, each subject receiving a different random order of the four

**TABLE 8.9 ANOVA: TWO BETWEEN-VARIABLES
AND ONE WITHIN**

Source	df
Between	JKM - 1
B	J - 1
C	K - 1
BC	(J - 1)(K - 1)
S	JK(M - 1)
Within	IJKM - JKM
A	I - 1
AB	(I - 1)(J - 1)
AC	(I - 1)(K - 1)
ABC	(I - 1)(J - 1)(K - 1)
AS	(I - 1)JK(M - 1)

treatments. The ANOVA for this design is shown in Table 8.8. The computations follow the usual scheme. The sum of squares for Groups is $(122^2 + 167^2 + 146^2)/20 - 435^2/60$. The sum of squares for subjects nested in Groups is $(20^2 + 26^2 + ... + 30^2 + 33^2)/4 - (122^2 + 167^2 + 146^2)/20$. The sum of squares for Treatments (A) is found using the totals for the treatments, added over Groups. That is, $(18 + 25 + 21)^2/15 + (26 + 38 + 32)^2/15 + ... + (46 + 63 + 55)^2/15 - 435^2/60$. The AB interaction sum of squares is found using the Treatment totals for each Group, and so forth, to obtain $(18^2 + 26^2 + ... + 38^2 + 55^2)/5 - (122^2 + 167^2 + 146^2)/20 - [(18 + 25 + 21)^2/15 + (26 + 38 + 32)^2/15 + ... + (46 + 63 + 55)^2/15] + 435^2/60$. The Treatment x Subjects interaction can be obtained by calculating the Treatment x Subjects interaction at each level of the Groups factor and adding them, or more simply by multiplying the degrees of freedom out to obtain IJK - IJ - JK + J and then following the df-to-SS correspondence, taking the sum of the squares of all of the scores, subtracting $(18^2 + 26^2 + ... + 38^2 + 55^2)/5$ and $(20^2 + 26^2 + ... + 30^2 + 33^2)/4$, and adding $122^2/20 + 167^2/20 + 146^2/20$.

Note that in these **"mixed" designs** (having a mixture of "between" and "within" sources) **the sum of all the degrees of freedom for the Between-Subjects sources is always the number of subjects minus one and the sum of all of the degrees of freedom for the Within-Subjects sources is always the number of scores minus the number of subjects.** All of the degrees of freedom for the specific sources are computed from the model equation in the usual way, and the sums of squares

**TABLE 8.10 MIXED DESIGN WITH TWO
BETWEEN-SUBJECT AND ONE WITHIN-SUBJECTS FACTORS**

	Instruction Set 1						Instruction Set 2					
	Condition 1			Condition 2			Condition 1			Condition 2		
	Treatments			Treatments			Treatments			Treatments		
	1	2	3		1	2	3		1	2	3		1	2	3
1	2	4	5	6	4	7	8	11	3	6	7	16	5	7	9
2	3	6	7	7	5	6	8	12	4	6	8	17	6	7	9
3	4	5	6	8	6	8	6	13	5	6	6	18	6	7	8
4	4	6	7	9	4	8	9	14	4	7	8	19	5	9	10
5	5	5	7	10	6	9	10	15	5	7	9	20	8	11	11

**TABLE 8.11 ANOVA OF
THE DATA IN FIGURE 8.4**

Source	df	SS	MS	F
Between Subjects				
Instruction Set	1	14.02	14.02	5.53
Condition	1	50.42	50.42	19.90
Instruct. x Cond.	1	.02	.02	.01
Subjs. in B x C	16	40.53	2.53	
Within Subjects				
Treatments	2	106.43	53.22	77.88
Treats. x Instruct.	2	.43	.22	.32
Treats. x Conds.	2	.63	.32	.46
Tr. x Instr. x Cond.	2	.63	.32	.46
Tr. x Subjs. in B x C	32	21.87	.68	

and mean squares are obtained from the degrees of freedom according to the standard procedures (see Sections 5.5 and 6.11).

Table 8.10 shows a numerical example for the design in Table 8.9. Subjects in one of two experimental conditions were given one of two sets of instructions and then measured under three treatments. Treatments are repeated measures. The subjects are nested in the cross of Instruction Set with Condition. Thus, Instruction Set, Conditions, and their interaction are between-subjects sources, and the rest are within-subjects sources. The ANOVA is shown in Table 8.11.

Frequently Subjects are crossed with more than one factor. For example, Subjects might be crossed with the cross of two factors, A x B. This design is called a Treatments x Treatments x Subjects design or a design with two within-subjects sources or factors. Certainly, Subjects could be nested within one factor and crossed with two others or nested in the cross of two factors and crossed with three others, and so forth. Thus, for example, we could have the following models:

Subjects crossed with A x B

$$Y_{ijk} = \mu + s_k + A_i + As_{ik} + B_j + Bs_{jk} + AB_{ij} + ABs_{ijk} + e_{ijk}. \qquad [8.1]$$

Subjects nested in D and crossed with A x B

$$Y_{ijkm} = \mu + D_m + s_{k(m)} + A_i + AD_{im} + As_{ik(m)} + B_j + BD_{jm} + Bs_{k(m)}$$

$$+ AB_{ij} + ABD_{ijm} + ABs_{ijk(m)} + e_{ijkm}; \qquad [8.2]$$

Subjects nested in D x E and crossed with A x B x C

$$Y_{ijkmnp} = \mu + D_m + E_n + DE_{mn} + s_{p(m,n)} + A_i + AD_{im} + AE_{in} + ADE_{imn}$$

$$+ As_{ip(m,n)} + B_j + BD_{jm} + BE_{jn} + BDE_{jmn} + Bs_{jp(m,n)} + C_k + CD_{km} + CE_{kn}$$

$$+ CDE_{kmn} + Cs_{kp(m,n)} + AB_{ij} + ABD_{ijm} + ABE_{ijn} + ABDE_{ijmn} + ABs_{ijp(m,n)}$$

$$+ AC_{ik} + ACD_{ikm} + ACE_{ikn} + ACDE_{ikmn} + ACs_{ikp(m,n)} + BC_{jk} + BCD_{jkm}$$

$$+ BCE_{jkn} + BCDE_{jkmn} + BCs_{jkp(m,n)} + ABC_{ijk} + ABCD_{ijkm} + ABCE_{ijkn}$$

$$+ ABCDE_{ijkmn} + ABCs_{ijkp(m,n)} + e_{ijkmnp}.$$

8.4 Displaying the sources in a summary table for a mixed design. Note in Table 8.9 that all of the Between sources are presented in one package at the top of the table and the Within sources are presented in a package at the bottom. This is the traditional form

An Introduction to the Analysis of Variance

TABLE 8.12 SOURCE, DF, AND E(MS) FOR THE MODEL IN EQUATION [8.2]

Source	df	E(MS)
Between	KM - 1	
D	M - 1	$\sigma^2_e + IJK\sigma^2_M + IJ\sigma^2_S$
S	M(K - 1)	$\sigma^2_e + IJ\sigma^2_S$
Within	IJKM - KM	
A	I - 1	$\sigma^2_e + JKM\sigma^2_A + J\sigma^2_{AS}$
AD	(I - 1)(M - 1)	$\sigma^2_e + JK\sigma^2_{AD} + J\sigma^2_{AS}$
AS	(I - 1)M(K - 1)	$\sigma^2_e + J\sigma^2_{AS}$
B	J - 1	$\sigma^2_e + IKM\sigma^2_B + I\sigma^2_{BS}$
BD	(J - 1)(M - 1)	$\sigma^2_e + IK\sigma^2_{BD} + I\sigma^2_{BS}$
BS	(J - 1)M(K - 1)	$\sigma^2_e + I\,\sigma^2_{BS}$
AB	(I - 1)(J - 1)	$\sigma^2_e + KM\,\sigma^2_{AB} + \sigma^2_{ABS}$
ABD	(I - 1)(J - 1)(M - 1)	$\sigma^2_e + K\,\sigma^2_{ABD} + \sigma^2_{ABS}$
ABDS	(I - 1)(J - 1)M(K - 1)	$\sigma^2_e + \sigma^2_{ABS}$

TABLE 8.13 DATA ANALYZED IN TABLE 8.14

		Condition 1 Treatments			Condition 2 Treatments		
Subjects		1	2	3	1	2	3
Instruction Set 1	1	2	4	5	4	7	8
	2	3	6	7	5	6	8
	3	4	5	6	6	8	6
	4	4	6	7	4	8	9
	5	5	5	7	6	9	10

		Condition 1 Treatments			Condition 2 Treatments		
		1	2	3	1	2	3
Instruction Set 2	6	3	6	7	5	7	9
	7	4	6	8	6	7	9
	8	5	6	6	6	7	8
	9	4	7	8	5	9	10
	10	5	7	9	8	11	11

of presenting sources in the summary table for a mixed design. It is also traditional that all of the sources using the same mean square as the denominator of the F-test are packaged

TABLE 8.14   SUMMARY OF A MIXED DESIGN

Source	df	SS	MS	F
Between Subjects				
Instructions	1	14.02	14.02	3.28
Subjects in Instructs.	8	34.13	4.27	
Within Subjects				
Conditions	1	50.42	50.42	63.02
Instructions x Conds.	1	.02	.02	.02
Conditions x Subjects	8	6.40	.80	
Treatments	2	106.43	53.22	63.23
Instructions x Treats.	2	.43	.22	.26
Treatments x Subjs.	16	13.47	.84	
Conds. x Treats.	2	.63	.32	.60
Instrs. x Conds. x Treats.	2	.63	.32	.60
Conds. x Treats x Subjs.	16	8.40	.52	

together with the source for that mean square. We can illustrate this with a summary table, Table 8.12, for the model in equation [8.2]. Notice that for the Between sources, all of the mean squares use MS_S as the denominator mean square. Now notice that for the Within sources, (1) each of the factors that is crossed with Subjects (e.g., A) uses the mean square for the interaction of that factor with Subjects (e.g., MS_{AS}) as its denominator for the F-test; (2) each factor that Subjects is nested in (there is only one in this design, D) and the interaction of such a factor with a factor that Subjects is crossed with (e.g., AD) use the same denominator mean square as is used for the factor (A) that Subjects is crossed with (i.e., MS_{AS}). Table 8.14 shows the analysis in Table 8.12 applied to the data in Table 8.13 where Instructions is the between-subjects factor and Conditions and Treatments are the crossed within-subjects factors.

8.4.1 An aside. You might be interested in taking stock at this point. You now know how to write

(a)   model equations,

(b)   degrees of freedom formulas,

(c)   sums of squares formulas,

(d)   expected mean square values,

(e)   and ANOVA summary tables,

and also how to determine which ratios of mean squares to use as F statistics for balanced designs with

(a)   an arbitrary number of crossed or nested factors,

(b)   using fixed or random effects,

(c)   with or without repeated measurements.

   Furthermore, if you remember the small number of simple rules, you should be able to do these analyses without opening a book. If you own a personal computer it will be a simple matter to program it to do your analyses of variance. I find that I can set up a rather complex ANOVA on a spreadsheet such as Multiplan in very short order. But if you don't have easy access to a computer, using what you have learned should make it straightforward and reasonably manageable to do an analysis with a hand calculator except for designs with a staggeringly large amount of data. Even then, the biggest obstacle will be obtaining the sum of the squares of all of the scores. The rest will be working from tables of totals, which can be tedious but not overwhelming.

8.5 We must now reconsider the underlying assumption of independence of the scores. What we have done so far is to go through the same formal motions of writing model equations and calculating degrees of freedom and sums of squares. For the first design, the Treatments x Subjects design with I treatment conditions, we even obtained expected mean squares, and used them to obtain F-ratios as we did in the designs we have examined in previous chapters. We must, however, reconsider the underlying assumptions upon which these formal procedures were based. When we considered the two-or-more factor designs with random or mixed factors, we were always assuming that the various scores were independent of one another. The question of independence must be reconsidered for these repeated measurement designs. We will find that the assumption of independence is no longer completely tenable and that this leads us into alternative procedures.

8.6 The nonindependence of several measures from the same person requires different treatment of the degrees of freedom. When we obtain more than one measurement from the same person, we can expect that these measurements will in general not be independent. This lack of independence in general results in mean square ratios that are not distributed in quite the same way as those we have looked at so far. Consider the repeated measurement design in which J subjects are crossed with I treatments. The design is a Treatments x Subjects design with two factors, Subjects and Treatments. The model equation is

$Y_{ij} = \mu + A_i + s_j + As_{ij} + e_{ij}.$

The statistic MS_A/MS_{AS} will have the F distribution but the degrees of freedom are not necessarily $I - 1$ and $(I - 1)(J - 1)$ as we would expect. In fact, Box (1954) has shown that MS_A/MS_{AS} has the F distribution on $\varepsilon(I - 1)$ and $\varepsilon(I - 1)(J - 1)$ df. We will now consider what affects this quantity ε ("epsilon"), what we can do about it, and some simple general ways to proceed. More or less we will parallel Myers's (1979) treatment of the topic, although in much less detail, and in a different notation. The student may wish to study Myers's treatment (Chapter 7); it is thoughtfully and extensively done and well worth the effort of converting from my notation to his.

8.7 If the Treatment x Subject interaction effects are all zero, F = MS_A/MS_{AS} on $I - 1$ and $(I - 1)(J - 1)$ df. The simplest situation would be if all of the As_{ij} were equal to zero. In this case, ε would equal 1, and MS_A/MS_{AS} would be distributed as F on $I - 1$ and $(I - 1)(J - 1)$ df. It is not so simple to be convinced by the data that these interaction effects are all equal to zero, however. Tukey's (1949) test of additivity can be used in which the statistic

$$F = \{B[(I - 1)(J - 1) - 1]\}/\{[\Sigma_i(M_{.i} - M_{..})^2 \Sigma_j(M_{j.} - M_{..})^2]SS_{AS} - B\}$$

has the F distribution on 1 and $(I - 1)(J - 1) - 1$ df, and in which the quantity

$$B = [\Sigma_i \Sigma_j Y_{ij}(M_{.i} - M_{..})(M_{j.} - M_{..})]^2.$$

A significant F indicates the presence of nonzero interaction effects. But this test will not detect all nonzero interaction effects, and failing to detect interaction effects with Tukey's test may not be enough for us to accept completely the null hypothesis of zero interaction.

8.8 Homogeneity of the variance of the difference scores. To continue the discussion of the df for MS_A/MS_{AS} we will need to define **the variance of the difference scores** for two levels of the treatment factor A. Let these two levels be A_i and $A_{i'}$. Then for the jth subject in the population, the difference score $d_{jii'} = Y_{ij} - Y_{i'j}$. Define the variance of all these difference scores in the population from which the subjects are sampled to be $\sigma^2_{dii'}$. Then we will say that **the variances of the difference scores are homogeneous** if for any pair of levels i and i' of factor A, $\sigma^2_{dii'}$, the variance of the difference scores, equals the variance of the difference scores for any other choice of a pair of levels. Huynh and Feldt (1970) have shown that with homogeneous variances of the difference scores the degrees of freedom for MS_A/MS_{AS} are $I - 1$ and $(I - 1)(J - 1)$. That is, the quantity ε in the expressions $\varepsilon(I - 1)$ and $\varepsilon(I - 1)(J - 1)$ is equal to 1. Furthermore, the more heterogenous the variances of the difference scores are, the closer does ε approach the quantity $1/(I - 1)$. This means that even with the most extreme heterogeneity, the df will still be at least 1 and $J - 1$. **Note that for the case of only two treatments, there is only one set of difference scores. Thus no heterogeneity can exist and no problem arises.**

8.9 Some ways to proceed. Given these results, how should we proceed? Suppose we ignore the issue, as still occurs in the research literature, and act as if the correct df are $I - 1$ and $(I - 1)(J - 1)$. The test statistic will generally be positively biased, meaning that when the null hypothesis of no treatment effects is true, we will reject it with a greater frequency than the chosen significance level indicates, and we will not know how much greater that frequency is. The test will be biased toward Type I errors. We can get a rough idea of the bias by inspecting the table of critical F-values for various amounts of degrees of freedom. For example, suppose we had a Treatments x Subjects design with 5 treatments and 11 subjects. Ignoring the issue we would assume the mean square ratio MS_A/MS_{AS} has 4 and 40 df. If we were conducting the F-test with a .05 significance level, the tabled critical value would be 2.61. But suppose extreme heterogeneity of variance of the difference scores exists. Then the actual df would be more like 1 and 10. Inspection of the table of critical values of F indicates that with 1 and 10 df, a value of F greater than 2.61 will occur between 10 and 20 percent of the time when the null hypothesis is true. Therefore by ignoring the issue, we would more than double the actual significance level.

A second option that is almost as easy as ignoring the issue but is much more favorable is to conduct the F-test twice, first with $I - 1$ and $(I - 1)(J - 1)$ df and the second time with 1 and $J - 1$ df. If the null hypothesis is not rejected on the first test, it would not be rejected if heterogeneity of variance of the difference scores exists and we could determine the correct df. Also, if we reject the null hypothesis on the second test with only 1 and $J - 1$ df, we can feel confident in the conclusion again since if heterogeneity of variance of the difference scores exists and we could determine the correct df, they would be greater than the ones we used and we would certainly reject the null hypothesis with those correct df.

The difficulty exists in reaching a decision if we reject the null hypothesis on the first test, with $I - 1$ and $(I - 1)(J - 1)$ df but do not reject it with 1 and $J - 1$ df. Since the correct df may be in between the values used for the two tests, the first test may be positively biased and the second may be negatively biased. That is, the first test will give more significant statistics than the chosen significance level indicates, and the second test will give fewer significant statistics than should occur for a given amount of falsity of the null hypothesis. The heart of the problem lies in not knowing what the value of ε is. As we know, the statistical approach to not knowing the value of a parameter is estimation of that parameter and it is to estimation of ε that we turn for help when we reject with the first test but accept with the second. We will do this in section 8.10, but first we must introduce the notion of the covariance of two variables and the estimate of a covariance.

8.9.1 The covariance of two variables. We want to introduce the concept of **covariance** now since it will be needed to estimate d. Consider the variance of a variable Y. It is the average of the squared deviations of each of the Y values from the mean of the Y's. That is,

$$\sigma^2_Y = \Sigma_i(Y_i - \mu_Y)^2/N.$$

We can rewrite this as

$$\sigma^2_Y = \Sigma_i(Y_i - \mu_Y)(Y_i - \mu_Y)/N$$

and describe the variance as the average of the products obtained by multiplying each deviation by itself. When we have two variables, say Y_1 and Y_2, which take the values Y_{1i} and Y_{2i}, then we can not only define their variances as $\sigma^2_{Y1} = \Sigma_i(Y_{1i} - \mu_{Y1})(Y_{1i} - \mu_{Y1})/N$ and $\sigma^2_{Y2} = \Sigma_i(Y_{2i} - \mu_{Y2})(Y_{2i} - \mu_{Y2})/N$, but we can define a third quantity, which we obtain by averaging the products of the deviations of the Y_{1i} from their mean and the deviations of the Y_{2i} from their mean. That is, the **covariance** of Y_1 and Y_2 is

$$Cov_{Y1Y2} = \Sigma_i(Y_{1i} - \mu_{Y1})(Y_{2i} - \mu_{Y2})/N.$$

A quantity $\Sigma_i(Y_{ji} - \mu_{Yj})(Y_{j'i} - \mu_{Yj'})/N$ is either a variance or a covariance, depending on whether $j = j'$.

We now want to introduce the estimate of the variances and covariances which we will call the $S_{jj'}$.
This will be

$$S_{jj'} = \Sigma_i(Y_{ji} - M_j)(Y_{j'i} - M_{j'})/(N - 1)$$

which is the variance estimate $S_{jj} = \Sigma_i(Y_{ji} - M_j)^2/(N - 1)$ when $j = j'$ and is the covariance estimate when $j \neq j'$.

8.10 Using an estimate of ε. If there are I levels of the Treatment factor, then a given level i will have a variance and I - 1 covariances with the other I - 1 Treatment levels. Let S_i be the average of the estimates of these I quantities That is,

TABLE 8.15   VARIANCE-COVARIANCE ESTIMATES FOR THE DATA IN TABLE 8.3

			i'				
$S_{ii'}$	i	1	2	3	4	$S_{i.}$	$S_{i.}^2$
	1	1.3	.35	.70	-.15	.5500	.3025
	2	.35	.7	.65	.45	.5375	.2889
	3	.70	.65	.8	.40	.6375	.4064
	4	-.15	.45	.40	.70	.3500	.1225

TABLE 8.16 $S_{ii'}^2$ VALUES FOR THE DATA IN TABLE 8.3

i	1	2	3	4
1	1.69	.1225	.49	.0225
2	.1225	.49	.4225	.2025
3	.49	.4225	.64	.16
4	.0225	.2025	.16	.49

$S_{i.} = \Sigma_{i'}S_{ii'}/I = (S_{i1} + S_{i2} + ... + S_{iI})/I$.

Also, let $S_{..}$ be the average of all I of the $S_{i.}$, so $S_{..} = \Sigma_i S_{i.}/I$. Then, Collier, Baker, Mandeville, and Hayes (1967) have provided an estimate of ε which is

$$\varepsilon_{est} = [I^2(\Sigma_i S_{ii}/I - S_{..})^2]/[(I - 1)(\Sigma_i\Sigma_{i'}S_{ii'}^2 - 2I\Sigma_i S_{i.}^2 + I^2 S_{..}^2)].$$

Note that the term $\Sigma_i S_{ii}/I$ is the average of the I variance estimates. Collier, Baker, Mandeville, and Hayes (1967) and Stoloff (1966) have shown by computer simulation that the actual significance level is very close to the chosen significance level when the estimate ε_{est} is used to determine the df for the F test.

The procedure which Myers (1979, p. 482; see also Greenhouse & Geisser, 1959) has recommended and which seems to be the best we have now for testing the overall effect for Treatments in the Treatments by Subjects design is to do the first test with I - 1 and (I - 1)(J - 1) df, the second test with 1 and J - 1 df, and if the two tests yield inconsistent results, find ε_{est}, the estimate of ε, and do the test with $\varepsilon_{est}(I - 1)$ and $\varepsilon_{est}(I - 1)(J - 1)$ df.

Huynh and Feldt (1976) have provided an improvement on the use of ε_{est}, which is seriously biased when ε is not a low value, say, less than .75 or so. In a Treatments x Subjects design with I treatments and S subjects they suggest using $\varepsilon_{est'} = [S(I - 1)\varepsilon_{est} - 2]/\{(I - 1)[S - 1 - (I - 1)\varepsilon_{est}]\}$. See their article for details and extensions of the result and considerations of power and control of the Type I error rate. For a numerical example we calculate the value of ε_{est} for the data in Table 8.5. Table 8.15 shows the variance-covariance estimates for the data in Table 8.5. The value 1.3 in the upper left-hand corner is just the variance estimate of the set of scores under Treatment 1: 2, 3, 4, 4, 5. That is, [(2^2 + 3^2 + 4^2 + 4^2 + 5^2) - $18^2/5$]/4. The next value, .35, is the estimate of the covariance of the Treatment 1 scores with the Treatment 2 scores. That is, [(2x4 + 3x6 + 4x5 + 4x6 + 5x5) - 18x26 /5]/4. And so on. The first column in the margin contains the $S_{i.}$ values and their average, .5188, is the value of $S_{..}$. The second column in the margin contains the $S_{i.}^2$ values, which sum to 1.1203. The formula also requires the $S_{ii'}^2$ values, which are shown in Table 8.16. The sum of these is 6.15. The final value needed is the average of the variance estimates, (1.3 + .7 + .8 + .7)/4 = .875. Inserting the various values into the formula

$$\varepsilon_{est} = [I^2(\Sigma_i S_{ii}/I - S_{..})^2]/[(I - 1)(\Sigma_i \Sigma_{i'} S_{ii'}^2 - 2I\Sigma_i S_{i.}^2 + I^2 S_{..}^2)]$$

gives

$$\varepsilon_{est} = [4^2(3.5/4 - .5188)^2]/[(4 - 1)(6.15 - 2(4)1.1203 + (4^2).2691)] = .1472.$$

The above remarks about dealing with the problem of possible heterogeneity of the variances of the difference scores in repeated measurement designs all refer to the question of testing the overall null hypothesis that all of the Treatment effects are zero. In the next chapter we shall see that this overall null hypothesis is usually of much less interest than are more specific questions that can be asked about the effects of the particular levels of the Treatment factor. In fact, often it is possible to ignore the overall null hypothesis altogether and focus directly on these more specific questions. We shall find that when this is the case, we can completely sidestep the problem of heterogeneity of difference score variances in repeated measurement designs.

There is a multivariate analysis of variance (MANOVA) procedure that can be adapted to analyzing repeated measures designs. Consideration of MANOVA is beyond the scope of this book but the reader is referred to O'Brien and Kaiser (1985), which will serve as a good primer for this approach.

*8.11 The necessary and sufficient conditions for within-subject F-ratios to be distributed as F. Huynh and Mandeville (1979) (see also Huynh, 1978; Huynh &

Feldt, 1970; Mendoza, Toothaker & Crain, 1976; Rouanet & Lépine, 1970) have provided the necessary and sufficient conditions for mean square ratios (F-ratios) to be distributed as F for tests of within-subjects factors. To state these conditions we must introduce a few more matrix ideas.

Orthonormal vectors and orthonormal transformations. A set of **orthonormal vectors** is a set of vectors that satisfy two requirements: (1) they are mutually orthogonal (that's the "ortho" part), and (2) they are of length one (that's the "normal" part). If we have a set of mutually orthogonal vectors, then we can change them to orthonormal vectors by dividing each element in each vector by the square root of the sum of the squares of values of the elements in that vector. Thus we could start with the vectors [1, -1, 0, 0], [1, 1, -2, 0] and [1, 1, 1, -3], which are obviously mutually orthogonal, and convert them to the set of orthonormal vectors $[1/2^{.5}, -1/2^{.5}, 0, 0]$, $[1/6^{.5}, 1/6^{.5}, -2/6^{.5}, 0]$ and $[1/12^{.5}, 1/12^{.5}, 1/12^{.5}, -3/12^{.5}]$.

Let X_1 be a 1 x S row vector of the S scores obtained by S subjects on the first level of a within-subjects factor, and let X_2, X_3, ..., X_I be the row vectors of S scores for those S subjects on the remaining levels of that factor. Let X be the I x S matrix the rows of which are X_1, X_2, ..., and X_I. Let M be an (I - 1) by I matrix of I - 1 orthonormal vectors. Then $Y = MX$ is an **orthonormal transformation** of the data that results in an (I - 1) by S matrix of scores, which, following Huynh and Mandeville, we will refer to as the **orthonormal variables**. If Σ_X is the covariance matrix of X, then $M\Sigma_X M^T$ is the covariance matrix of the orthonormal variables, Y.

We chose (I - 1) orthonormal vectors because that many are required to provide an orthonormal basis for the space in which the vector of within-subject variable effects lies. In a more complex design involving more than one within-subject source, we will need a different set of orthonormal vectors for each source or cluster of sources that uses a different error term. (For example, in a design with one between-subjects with J - 1 df and one within-subjects factor with I - 1 df, the within-subjects source and the interaction of the between with the within sources are tested against the same error term. Therefore only I - 1 orthonormal vectors would be needed.) These sets of orthonormal vectors will be mutually orthogonal, and there will be as many vectors in a set as there are degrees of freedom for the source it applies to.

Sphericity is the independence and equal variability of the orthonormal variables. Recall from your study of simple correlation the case of two variables that are independent and therefore have zero correlation. If you converted them to z-scores (so one variable would not spread out more than the other) and graphed the scatterplot, the points would fall in a circular pattern around the origin, but with nonindependence, the pattern would be elliptical. With three independent variables converted to z scores the scatterplot would be in three dimensions and the points would fall in a spherical pattern around the origin. Sphericity is the generalization of this circular or spherical pattern to an arbitrary number of dimensions We can also define sphericity in terms of the covariance matrix for the orthonormal variables, $M\Sigma_X M^T$. The sphericity pattern holds if $M\Sigma_X M^T = \lambda I_{I-1}$, where λ is a constant and I_{I-1} is an identity matrix of order $I - 1$ (a square matrix with 1's down the main diagonal and zeroes everywhere else). Thus each orthonormal variable has variance λ, and all the variables are uncorrelated.

For a one-factor design with repeated measures, the F-ratio for the repeated measure source will be distributed as F if and only if the covariance matrix for the orthonormal variables is characterized by sphericity. For a two-factor design with one between-subjects or independent factor and one repeated measures or within-subjects factor, the F-ratios for the within-subjects sources will be distributed as F if and only if two conditions hold: (1) at each level of the between-subjects factor, sphericity must apply to the orthonormal variables for that level, and (2) the covariance matrices for the different levels of the between-subjects factor must be identical.

In a design with two repeated measures factors, call them factors B and C, there are different error terms for B, C, and the B x C interaction. A different set of orthonormal variables is obtained for each. If B, C, and B x C have $(I - 1)$, $(J - 1)$ and $(I - 1)(J - 1)$ df, then the M matrices of orthonormal vectors corresponding to B, C, and B x C will have $(I - 1)$, $(J - 1)$, and $(I - 1)(J - 1)$ rows respectively. There will be a covariance matrix for each set of orthonormal variables, and the F-ratio for each source will be distributed as F provided that the corresponding covariance matrix displays sphericity. The variances in the three different covariance matrices need not be equal from matrix to matrix.

In a design with one independent factor, A, and two repeated measures factors, B and C, B and A x B are tested against one error term, C and A x C against a second, and B x C and A x B x C against a third. For each such cluster, a set of orthonormal variables is obtained, following the case for two repeated measures without an independent factor. For any one of these clusters, in order for the F-ratios to be distributed as F, the covariance matrix of orthonormal variables must be the same at each level of the A factor, and this common covariance matrix must display sphericity. These results generalize to designs with more independent and repeated measures factors.

*8.12 Testing for sphericity. Huynh and Mandeville (1979) also indicate statistical tests for sphericity and for equality of covariance matrices. These tests will be given here but the reader should refer to their article for more details, examples, and considerations of the effect of the violations of the assumption of normality. The sphericity null hypothesis for a given covariance matrix Σ for p orthonormal variables is that $\Sigma = \lambda I_p$, where I_p is the p x p identity matrix. The alternative hypothesis is that $\Sigma \neq \lambda \mathbf{I_p}$. Let S be the sample covariance estimate that estimates Σ. Then

W = | **S** |/| trace **S**/p |p   (trace of a square matrix is the sum of the elements on the main diagonal)

is the likelihood ratio test of the null hypothesis (Mauchly, 1940). See Consul (1967, 1969), Pillai and Nagarsenker (1971) Mathai and Rathie (1970), and Nagarsenker and Pillai (1972, includes tables of critical values of W) for the exact sampling distribution of W.

*8.13   Testing for equality of covariance matrices. Let Σ_i be the covariance matrix of the p orthonormal variables for the ith of I levels of the independent (between-subjects) factor. Let S_i be the unbiased estimate of Σ_i based on n_i degrees of freedom. The null hypothesis $\Sigma_1 = \Sigma_2 = ... = \Sigma_I$ is tested using the Box criterion (Morrison, 1976; Timm, 1975)

$M = \Sigma n_i \ln|\mathbf{S}| - \Sigma_i n_i \ln|\mathbf{S_i}|$,

where **S** is a pooled estimate of the common covariance matrix obtained by taking the weighted average of the S_i, $\Sigma_i n_i S_i / \Sigma_i n_i$. Under the null hypothesis,

$\{1 - [(2p^2 + 3p - 1)/(6(p + 1)(k - 1)][\Sigma_i(1/n_i) - 1/\Sigma_i n_i]\}M$

is approximately distributed as chi-square on $(k - 1)p(p + 1)/2$ degrees of freedom. Huynh and Mandeville refer to tables of critical values of M at the .05 level in Korin (1969) and Pearson & Hartley (1972).]

Huynh and Mandeville suggest a two-step procedure when independent factors are present, first testing for equality of the covariance matrices using the Box criterion, and then, if equality is tenable, testing for sphericity in the common covariance matrix. They suggest that if an α Type I error rate is desired for the overall test, the two steps each use an $\alpha/2$ level of significance.

Keselman, Rogan, Mendoza, and Breen (1980) indicate that these tests for sphericity are "sensitive to all but the most minute departures from their respective hypotheses," and for this reason they consider their use as a preliminary test superfluous. They recommend adopting the above described three-step procedure due to Greenhouse and Geiser rather than automatically computing ε. However, their rationale is based on the possibility of avoiding extra computations. This will perhaps apply if the computations are done by hand, but many computer programs compute ε_{est} so their argument has lost force with the tendency of most researchers to use mainframe or other computer-based analyses.

Exercises

1. Decide for each term in each of the model equations [8.1], [8.2], and[8.3] whether it corresponds to a between-subjects source or a within-subjects source.

2. Write the model equation for a design with Subjects nested in D x E and crossed with A x B. Which are the Between and which are the Within sources?

3. Using the data in Table 8.6 for the experiment with Treatments, Instruction Sets, and Conditions, perform the analysis of variance. Check your results with those in Table 8.4a. (Save your calculations for this exercise. You'll be reusing many of the numbers in an exercise coming up soon.)

4. Find the E(MS) for the sources corresponding to each term in equation [8.3]. Determine which denominator mean square should be used for each source. Do this separately for each of the rows of terms in which the equation is arranged. What do you notice about the terms in each of these rows of terms so far as their expected mean square and the appropriate denominator mean square is concerned? Save this information. You will need it for exercise 6.

5. Write out the summary table, appropriately packaged, for the model given by equation [8.3].

6. In Table 8.8 the data are the same numbers as in the previous design except now Conditions and Treatments are both repeated measures variables and only Instruction Set is a between-subjects variable, so the design is of the form in Table 8.8. Perform the analysis, and check that the results correspond to those in Table 8.9.

7. Bernstein, Treneer, Goehler, and Murowchick (1985) wanted to determine whether frequent changes in diet would attenuate the decline in food intake and body weight that accompanies tumor growth in rats. In their experiment 4, 20 rats in all were assigned to two groups. One group of rats, the Varied Diet group, was fed a variety of diets, three days each, presented in ascending order of diet preference, in the sequence Puppy Chow, Friskies, Soymeal Diet, Blue Mountain, AIN, and C-21. The other group, the Constant Diet group, was fed a single diet through the whole test period of the experiment, that single diet being the most palatable of the assortment of six diets, C-21 for 18 days. Assume that five animals in each group were implanted with LTW(m) tumors and the other five received control incisions (in Bernstein et al., it was six animals with tumors and 4 with control incisions). Diet exposure began 10 days after the surgery. Suppose that Table 8.17 shows the data found by Bernstein et al.

TABLE 8.17 FICTIONAL DATA FOR THE BERNSTEIN ET AL. EXPERIMENT

Mean Daily Food Intake in Grams

		Blocks of 3 Days				
	1	2	3	4	5	6
Varied Diet						
	18	11	12	11	12	12
	17	11	13	14	12	12
Tumor	10	12	13	13	12	11
	18	13	12	14	11	10
	19	12	14	13	13	9
	20	19	17	21	17	17
	21	17	19	22	10	19
Control	22	20	19	22	19	18
	20	21	18	21	18	19
	17	19	21	23	19	20
C-21						
	19	10	6	6	6	6
	18	9	4	5	7	7
Tumor	19	8	5	6	7	7
	17	8	5	4	7	7
	21	6	6	5	6	8
	22	20	19	18	14	14
	23	21	18	19	13	13
Control	23	21	20	18	15	14
	24	23	20	20	17	15
	23	21	22	16	16	14

TABLE 8.18 DATA FOR A TREATMENTS x SUBJECTS DESIGN

A_1	A_2	A_3
8	5	10
9	6	11
5	4	12
7	7	10
7	4	9

(a) Write the model equation for this design.

(b) Which are the between subjects sources and which are the within-subjects sources?

(c) What statistical test will reveal whether the Varied Diet produced the effect that the experimenter's were interested in? What is the value of F for this test? Does this test the effect of a between subject's source or a within subject's source?

(d) How would you test whether food intake declined over Blocks of three days?

(e) How would you test whether the decline over Blocks occurred at the same rate in the four different experimental groups?

(f) What is the problem in trying to determine whether Food Intake of Soymeal Diet was equal to Food Intake of Friskies? Does this same problem exist for the test of changes over Blocks in part (d)? How can you take this problem into account and still test for changes over Blocks?

8. Assume that the data in table 8.18 were gathered using a Treatments x Subjects design with three treatments and five subjects.

(a) Calculate the values of the $S_{jj'}$;

(b) Find the estimate of ε.

(c) What degrees of freedom (give numerical values) would you use for the two preliminary tests?

(d) What degrees of freedom (numerical values) would you use if the two preliminary tests gave inconsistent results?

9. Write the sources, df, and E(MS) for the model in exercise 8.

10. Spencer, Pontecorvo, and Heise (1985) tested the ability of rats to remember the brightness of a visual display. The rats were trained to press a bar if the new display of a light did not match in brightness the previous light display. If the rat pressed the bar when no change had occurred, this response was labeled a false alarm. When the rat pressed the bar following a change, this was called a hit. For reasons that may be found in Grier (1971), a measure of the rats' sensitivity to the change in brightness can be computed by obtaining an estimate of x, the probability of a false alarm, and y, the probability of a hit, and calculating the value of

$$A' = .5 + (y - x)(1 + y - x)/[4y(1 - x)]$$

These sensitivity measures formed the basic measures for the test of how the different drug dosages affected memory of light brightness.

The interval between offset of the previous light display and onset of the new one varied randomly among the three values 2.5, 5, and 10 seconds. Appropriate measures were taken to prevent carry over effects from one drug dosage to another. For example, the order of drug dosages and retention intervals was randomized, and caution was taken not to repeat the same drug or dosage in consecutive or near-consecutive sessions.

TABLE 8.19 FICTIONAL DATA: SPENCER ET AL. EXPERIMENT

Mean Daily Food Intake in Grams

			Blocks of 3 Days			
Varied Diet	1	2	3	4	5	6
Tumor	18	11	12	11	12	12
	17	11	13	14	12	12
	18	12	13	13	12	11
	18	13	12	14	11	10
	19	12	14	13	13	9
Control	20	19	17	21	17	17
	21	17	19	22	18	19
	22	20	19	22	19	18
	20	21	18	21	18	19
	17	19	21	23	19	20
C-21						
Tumor	19	10	6	6	6	6
	18	9	4	5	7	7
	19	8	5	6	7	7
	17	8	5	4	7	7
	21	6	6	5	6	8
Control	22	20	19	18	14	14
	23	21	18	19	13	13
	23	21	20	18	15	14
	24	23	20	20	17	15
	23	21	22	16	16	14

Sixteen rats were given two injections each of four Drug Dosage conditions. The four conditions were either Saline, or Scopolamine hydrobromide in dosages of .125 mg/kg, .25 mg/kg, or .50 mg/kg. For each rat, the data were pooled over injections and light display presentations to obtain a sensitivity measure for each Drug Dosage at each Retention Interval. With four Dosages and three intervals, there were 12 measures for each rat, and thus 16 x 12 scores in the

TABLE 8.20 SUMMARY OF BOWEY'S DATA

	Easy List	Words Story	Hard List	Words Story
Fourth Grade				
Less Skilled	10.76	4.28	24.65	21.18
Skilled	1.74	1.74	7.29	8.33
Fifth Grade				
Less Skilled	6.25	2.78	14.24	15.28
Skilled	1.04	2.08	4.17	4.17

design. Table 8.19 shows data that might have been gathered from just five of those rats.

(a) Write the model equation for this design.

(b) Perform the appropriate ANOVA in order to test the hypothesis that there is no effect of retention interval and no effect of Drug Dosage.

11. This exercise poses a problem which computers are usually not programmed to solve and so illustrates why the researcher should be familiar with computational formulas even in the day of computer analyses. Suppose a study is reported in the literature and, as is common, the entire summary table of the ANOVA is not presented. Only the group means and some of the F-ratios are given. If you would like to perform some comparisons that were not performed by the author, how do you recover the appropriate error mean squares? We will cast this exercise within the context of a study by Bowey (1985). The compensatory interactive hypothesis of information processing in reading says that processes at different levels of cognitive functioning interact to result in word identification. Bowey reasoned that children lower in decoding skills would make more use of the effect of word context, since when decoding of the word itself ran into a problem, the interaction of this process with processes involving word context would result in compensatory facilitation of identification by using contextual information, and she expected this to happen more frequently with such children than with children with higher decoding skills, since for the latter identification would more frequently result from use of the word itself, therefore requiring less compensatory help from interaction with context processing. Putting it more concisely, Bowey expected that reading words embedded in a story would be more helpful to children who are less skilled at decoding words than to children who are more skilled. The subjects were 48 fourth- and fifth-grade children assigned to skilled and less skilled decoding ability groups on the basis of median split performance on a word reading test.

(Median split means the children with performance scores in the top 50 percent of the group go into one group and the rest of the children go into the other group.) The children were

TABLE 8.21 FICTITIOUS LOOKING TIMES FROM 3- AND 6-MONTH-OLD BOY AND GIRL INFANTS

| | | STIMULUS | | | |
| | | UNSCRAMBLED | | SCRAMBLED | |
	Subj.	PICTURE	DIAGRAM	PICTURE	DIAGRAM
Girls	1	26	11	4	6
	2	22	13	6	6
3 Mo.	3	19	12	5	5
	4	21	15	7	8
	5	24	15	9	4
	6	15	18	10	11
	7	12	21	9	10
6 Mo.	8	14	23	9	12
	9	12	21	8	10
	10	14	20	9	9
Boys	11	23	10	4	4
	12	22	9	5	6
3 Mo.	13	24	12	3	6
	14	24	8	3	3
	15	21	9	4	4
	16	14	19	8	7
	17	13	21	8	6
6 Mo.	18	15	24	7	8
	19	12	21	9	8
	20	13	18	6	6

required to read 24 easy and 24 hard words. Half the words at each difficulty level were read in a list and the other half in a passage from a story. Thus the design has two between-subjects variables, School Grade (fourth or fifth) and Group (Less Skilled or More Skilled), and two within-subjects variables, Difficulty (Hard Words or Easy Words) and Context

(List or Story Passage). Percentage of errors in reading the words was the basic score for each child in each condition. Table 8.20 summarizes the mean percentage of reading errors in the two context conditions as a function of grade level, decoding ability, and word difficulty. Bowey reported the following F-ratios for the indicated source: Grade, F = 6.55; Group, F = 34.28; Difficulty, F = 72.79; Difficulty x Group, F = 16.93; Difficulty x Grade, 4.14; Context, F = 2.27; Context x Group, 4.11; and Difficulty x Context x Group = 1.68.
(a) Write the model equation for this design.
(b) Write out the summary table for the ANOVA and fill in the various F-ratios that Bowey reported.
(c) How many scores did Bowey collect?
(d) Fill in the degrees of freedom for each source. Check that these add up to one less than the total number of scores Bowey used (unless, of course, you included the mean as a source in your ANOVA table)
(e) Calculate the sums of squares and the mean squares for all of the sources except the four error terms (denominator mean squares), using your knowledge of the cell means and the numbers of scores collected in order to get the marginal and cell totals needed for these computations.
(f) Use your knowledge of how the F-ratios given by Bowey were computed in order to find the mean squares for the four error terms, and from those obtain the sums of squares for each source of error. You now have the complete summary table, and you also have all of the information needed to perform contrasts of your own.

12. We now redesign the experiment in exercise 8 of Chapter 7 by assuming that there were only 20 infants in the experiment: 5 girls and 5 boys at age 3 months and 5 girls and 5 boys at age 6 months. Each infant saw all four stimuli in a different random sequence. We also assume Stimulus is a fixed effect. The data are shown in Table 8.21.
(a) Which factors are crossed, and which are nested?
(b) Which factors are between-subjects, and which are within-subjects?
(c) Perform the analysis of variance for these data.
(d) What potential advantage does this design have over that in Chapter 7?

13. We now redesign the situation in exercise 11 of chapter 7 by assuming that there were only 15 subjects in the experiment—5 in each Stimulus Type condition. Each subject received each of four different random sequences of the stimuli. The order in which the sequences were presented to a given subject was decided by generating a random sequence of the numbers 1 to 4. The new design is shown in Table 8.22.
(a) Are Subjects crossed with or nested in Stimulus Types?
(b) Are sequences crossed with or nested in Stimulus Types?
(c) Are Subjects crossed with or nested in Sequences?

TABLE 8.22 EXPERIMENT 11, CHAPTER 7, REDESIGNED

	Subj.	Sequence 1	2	3	4
	1	211	209	201	220
	2	210	205	208	217
Simple	3	199	219	207	212
	4	204	203	202	215
	5	201	204	223	215
	6	241	229	227	235
	7	238	217	223	248
Complex	8	226	225	248	229
	9	223	232	234	221
	10	239	219	218	240
	11	243	234	229	222
	12	245	234	225	227
Compound	13	225	229	225	223
	14	239	235	231	237
	15	240	239	223	224

(d) Identify the between-subjects and the within-subjects factors.

(e) Write the model equation for this design.

(f) Perform the appropriate analysis of variance.

14. We now reinterpret the design shown in exercise 9 of Chapter 7. Let D be Subjects nested in the cross of B with C and let A be a within-subjects variable. Assume two measurements are obtained from each subject at each level of A. Thus, the second subject at B_1C_2 scored 6 the first time she was tested on A_2 and 5 the second time. Assume A, B, and C are fixed and D is random.

(a) Write the model equation for this design.

(b) Perform the analysis of variance.

15. Suppose that the experiment in exercise 3 had been performed at two different levels of motivation of the subjects involved. Thus, Motivation would be a between-subjects factor and Instruction Sets would be crossed with Motivation Level. Write out:

(a) the model equation

TABLE 8.23 FICTIONAL RETENTION DATA

	Abstract Words			Concrete Words		
	List Length			List Length		
Subj.	Short	Medium	Long	Short	Medium	Long
1	7	8	14	12	13	19
2	8	9	13	14	14	20
3	8	12	9	13	14	16
4	9	13	12	10	13	15
5	7	11	10	12	16	14

(b) the sources and the degrees of freedom

(c) the expected mean squares

(d) the appropriate F-ratios

16. Suppose that the subjects in exercise 14 had been run through the entire experiment not once, but twice. Call the first time through Trial 1 and the second time through Trial 2. Thus, Trials is another repeated measurement fixed-effect factor.

(a) Write out the model equation.

(b) Write out the sources and degrees of freedom.

17. Assume that the data in Table 8.23 were obtained from five subjects who were tested on retention of six word lists. Half the lists contained abstract words, and the other half contained concrete words. There were two short, two medium, and two long lists. A different random order of presentation of the six lists was used with each subject.

(a) Write the model equation.

(b) Perform the analysis of variance.

18. Write the model equation for the design with Subjects nested in the cross of B with C and Subjects crossed with the cross of A with D. The factors B and C are crossed with A and D. Assume all factors except Subjects are fixed-effects.

Supplementary Readings

Kenny, D. A., & Judd, C. M. (1986) Consequences of violating the independence assumption in analysis of variance. *Psychological Bulletin*, 99, 422-431.

Maxwell, S. E., & Bray, J. H. (1986) Robustness of the quasi F statistic to violations of sphericity. *Psychological Bulletin*, 99, 416-421.

O'Brien, R. G., & Kaiser, M. K. (1985) MANOVA method for analyzing repeated measures designs: An extensive primer. *Psychological Bulletin, 97*, 316-333.

9

Contrasting Effects

9.1 We are usually interested in a detailed understanding of how the overall null hypothesis is false. So far, in considering the effects of a factor in an experimental design, we have focused on how to test the hypothesis that the effects are all equal to zero. This is a simple question and would most often apply when the experimenter has almost no knowledge about the effects. The experimenter wants to show that manipulation of the independent variable represented by the factor has *some* effect on the dependent variable. But the effects for the several levels can differ from zero in many ways, and usually the experimenter is not working at the level of ignorance that asks if the variable has any effect at all. Often, the experimenter already knows or is confident that there is some effect but wants to ask more precise questions about the effects of the specific levels included in the design. Logically following the question, "Does the factor have some effect?" is the question, "What kind of effect does it have?" "What kind of effect does it have?" means, What are the relative effects of the different levels? How do the different levels differ in their effects. This calls for a comparison of some levels with others.

Consider, for example, an experiment in which the question concerns the effect of the medium of communication on the effectiveness of the communicated message. An experimenter decides to compare the persuasiveness of an article arguing for free enterprise and against a controlled economy when it is presented in five different media: a newspaper editorial, a magazine article, a televised reading of the article, an audiotape of the televised reading, and the same article printed in a book. The article is prepared for presentation to the subjects in the various media. The wording of the article in each medium is the same, and various other possibly confounding variables are controlled. Assume that the experimenter knows, on the basis of previously gathered information, that the experiment will be sufficiently powerful if 150 subjects are assigned at random to the five Medium conditions with the restriction that there be 30 subjects in each condition. (We continue to assume throughout this chapter that the designs we study are balanced.)

We will conjecture that on the basis of previous work, the experimenter is convinced that different media differ in their effectiveness. The questions to be asked in this experiment are more specific than do they differ. One question that might be asked is whether the printed communications are more or less effective than are electronically presented communications. The experimenter might couch this question in the form of the null hypothesis that the average score for the newspaper, magazine, and book conditions equals the average score for the televised and audiotaped readings. Suppose we set up the model equation for this experiment as

$$Y_{ij} = \mu + A_i + e_{ij} \, ,$$

where Y_{ij} is the score for the jth subject in Medium condition i. We will define the A_i to be A_n, A_m, A_t, A_a, and A_b as the effects, respectively, of the newspaper, magazine, televised, audiotaped, and book media. Then the null hypothesis that the average score for the newspaper, magazine, and book condition equals the average score for the televised and audiotaped reading can be written in terms of the effects as $(A_n + A_m + A_b)/3 = (A_t + A_a)/2$, or alternatively, $(A_n + A_m + A_b)/3 - (A_t + A_a)/2 = 0$. We might also note, at this point, that statements of this sort about the effects of levels are equivalent to statements about the means of the levels since $A_i = \mu_i - \mu$, so that $(A_n + A_m + A_b)/3 = (A_t + A_a)/2$, implies that $(\mu_n - \mu + \mu_m - \mu + \mu_b - \mu)/3 = (\mu_t - \mu + \mu_a - \mu)/2$ in which the μ terms all cancel out and we are left with $(\mu_n + \mu_m + \mu_b)/3 = (\mu_t + \mu_a)/2$. We can therefore anticipate that we will be using the sample means for the various levels to test null hypotheses such as these.

Another hypothesis that the experimenter might wish to test is that the visual component in the televised presentation makes a difference compared to the audiotaped presentation, which has the same sound component but no visual component. The null hypothesis, in several different forms, would be that: $\mu_t - \mu_a = 0$; $A_t - A_a = 0$; $\mu_t = \mu_a$; or $A_t = A_a$. The question might arise as to whether current sources of printed communications such as newspapers and magazines are more or less effective than are books, which may lack the indication of being based on the most current information available but on the other hand may have a greater sense of time-testedness or reliability about them. The null hypothesis here would be $(\mu_n + \mu_m)/2 = \mu_b$ or $(\mu_n + \mu_m)/2 - \mu_b = 0$.

9.2 Contrasts. We will adopt just one way of the several equivalent ways of stating the null hypotheses shown above. The adopted way will use the means and state a numerical relation among the means such that some linear combination of the means for selected levels is equal to zero. So, we will state the null hypotheses as $(\mu_n + \mu_m + \mu_b)/3 - (\mu_t + \mu_a)/2 = 0$, or $\mu_t - \mu_a = 0$, or $(\mu_n + \mu_m)/2 - \mu_b = 0$. The linear combination of means on the left side of the equality is of the form $\Sigma_i c_i \mu_i$. That is, it is the sum of the μ's, each multiplied by a coefficient, c. So, for example, in the case of $(\mu_n + \mu_m)/2 - \mu_b = 0$, which can be rewritten $(1/2)\mu_n + (1/2)\mu_m + (-1)\mu_b = 0$, the values of c for μ_n, μ_m, and μ_b are 1/2, 1/2, and -1.

When the sum of the coefficients for the means, the c_i, in such a linear combination is equal to zero, that is, when $\Sigma_i c_i = 0$, we call the linear combination a **contrast of the means** and usually refer to it simply as a **contrast**. Since the summation is over all the levels of the factor, in some of the contrasts some of the c_i will be zero. Thus in the contrast $(\mu_n + \mu_m + \mu_b)/3 - (\mu_t + \mu_a)/2$ where we think of μ_n, μ_m, μ_t, μ_a, and μ_b as μ_1, μ_2, μ_3, μ_4, and μ_5, we have $c_1 = c_2 = c_5 = 1/3$ and $c_3 = c_4 = -1/2$, but in the contrast $(\mu_1 + \mu_2)/2 - \mu_5$, we have $c_1 = c_2 = 1/2$, $c_3 = c_4 = 0$, and $c_5 = -1$.

9.2.1 Contrasts are comparisons that are independent of the general mean.

A linear combination $\Sigma_i c_i \mu_i$ in which the $\Sigma_i c_i$ is not necessarily zero is called a **comparison of the means** or just a **comparison**. To see why most of the time we focus on contrasts we need to define the **independence of two comparisons**. Let $C_1 = \Sigma_i c_{1i} \mu_i$ and $C_2 = \Sigma_i c_{2i} \mu_i$ be two different comparisons. They differ because they have different values for the coefficients—that is, for at least one value of i, $c_{1i} \neq c_{2i}$. Then we say that C_1 and C_2 are independent if $\Sigma_i c_{1i} c_{2i} = 0$. (Can you think of a vector space interpretation of this independence in terms of orthogonality? See section 3.9.1.) For example, suppose we have the two comparisons of three means $C_1 = \mu_1 + \mu_2 - 2\mu_3$ and $C_2 = \mu_1 - \mu_2$. We can make up a table of the coefficients and the products of those coefficients and determine whether the sum of the products of those coefficients is zero, thereby determining if the comparisons are independent. Doing this for C_1 and C_2 we obtain

	μ_1	μ_2	μ_3
c_{1i}	1	1	-2
c_{2i}	1	-1	0
$c_{1i}c_{2i}$	1	-1	0

and we see that the sum of the elements in the third row, $\Sigma_i c_{1i} c_{2i} = 1 + (-1) + 0$ is zero. The two comparisons are independent.

Now let us consider the comparison in which each of the c_i equals $1/I$. We have

$$\Sigma_i c_{1i} \mu_i = \Sigma_i (1/I)\mu_i = \Sigma_i \mu_i/I = \Sigma_i(\mu + A_i)/I = I(\mu/I) + \Sigma_i A_i/I = \mu.$$

Thus the general mean is a comparison of the group means with the coefficients all equal and equal to the reciprocal of the number of groups (so long as the number of subjects is the same in each group). It follows then that **every contrast is a comparison that is independent of the general mean** since if $\Sigma_i c_{1i} \mu_i$ is a contrast, then $\Sigma_i c_{1i} = 0$ and therefore $\Sigma_i (1/I)c_{1i} = (1/I)\Sigma_i c_{1i} = 0$, satisfying the condition for two comparisons to be independent. Note that if $\Sigma_i c_i = 0$, then $\Sigma_i c_i \mu_i = \Sigma_i c_i \mu + \Sigma_i c_i A_i = \Sigma_i c_i A_i$ so the contrast only reflects on the A_i's, but if $\Sigma_i c_i \neq 0$, then $\Sigma_i c_i \mu_i = \Sigma_i c_i \mu + \Sigma_i c_i A_i$ and reflects both the value of μ and the values of the A_i. (A similar result holds for unequal numbers of scores in each group. Can you explain why in this case $\Sigma_i n_i c_i = 0$?) **The motivation behind using contrasts, then, is to make sure that the tests of hypotheses concerning differences between group or level effects are not influenced by the value of the general mean.** With contrasts, we know that the value of the contrast is independent of the general mean, so that the conclusions rest solely on the relative values of the scores at the various levels of interest, rather than on the general tendency of all of the scores to be either high or low.

9.3 An F-test for testing the significance of a contrast. Now that we can express detailed null hypotheses concerning possible relations between the effects of the various levels of a factor, we want to know how to test these hypotheses. We follow the general approach of creating a mean square ratio that is distributed as F when the null hypothesis is true. Then we can compare the obtained mean square ratio with the tabled critical value of F, just as we do when we test the overall null hypothesis concerning whether any of the effects differs from zero. In fact, the numerator of the mean square ratio will involve a sum of squares that is a piece of the sum of squares used in the overall test.

Let $\Sigma_i c_i \mu_i = 0$ be some null hypothesis of interest. Let M_i be the sample mean of all the scores obtained at the ith level of the experimental factor, and let n_i be the number of scores at that level. Then $\Sigma_i c_i M_i$ is an estimator of $\Sigma_i c_i \mu_i$, and the sum of squares for this contrast,

$$SS_{\Sigma_i c_i \mu_i} = (\Sigma_i c_i M_i)^2 / (\Sigma_i c_i^2 / n_i)$$

is that portion of the sum of squares for the factor in question that is associated with the contrast $\Sigma_i c_i \mu_i$. There will always be one degree of freedom for each such sum of squares. Thus the mean square for the contrast will equal the sum of squares for the contrast. If there are I levels of the factor, there will be I - 1 df for that factor. If I - 1 orthogonal contrasts are created, then their sums of squares will be a partitioning of the total sum of squares for the factor into I - 1 independent pieces such that the sum of those pieces equals the total sum of squares for the factor and in the usual corresponding fashion, the sum of the single df for each of the I - 1 contrasts will equal the I - 1 df for the factor.

The denominator of the mean square ratio will, except in the case of repeated measurement designs dealt with later, be the same error mean square that we would use to test the overall effect of the factor.

9.3.1 The expected value of the mean square for a contrast. To see that this is the correct choice of an error term we can find the expected value of the mean square for a contrast. We may as well do it for the generic contrast $C = \Sigma_i c_i \mu_i$. Since each contrast has one df,

$$MS_C = SS_C = (\Sigma_i c_i M_i)^2 / (\Sigma_i c_i^2 / n_i).$$

So we want to find

$$E(MS_C) = E[(\Sigma_i c_i M_i)^2 / (\Sigma_i c_i^2 / n_i)].$$

As usual, we pull the constant out of the expectation, giving

$$[1/(\Sigma_i c_i^2 / n_i)] \; E(\Sigma_i c_i M_i)^2.$$

Now we can work on the expectation in the usual way, recalling that the $E(X^2) = VAR(X) + E^2(X)$, we can write

$$E(\Sigma_i c_i M_i)^2 = VAR[(\Sigma_i c_i M_i)] + E^2(\Sigma_i c_i M_i) = \Sigma_i c_i^2(\sigma^2_i / n_i) + (\Sigma_i c_i \mu_i)^2.$$

By the usual homogeneity of variance assumption, $\sigma^2_i = \sigma^2_e$, so we have

$$E(\Sigma_i c_i M_i)^2 = \Sigma_i c_i^2(\sigma^2_e / n_i) + (\Sigma_i c_i \mu_i)^2 = \sigma^2_e(\Sigma_i c_i^2 / n_i) + (\Sigma_i c_i \mu_i)^2$$

and therefore

$$E(MS_C) = [1/(\Sigma_i c_i^2 / n_i)] [\sigma^2_e(\Sigma_i c_i^2 / n_i) + (\Sigma_i c_i \mu_i)^2] = \sigma^2_e + (\Sigma_i c_i \mu_i)^2 / (\Sigma_i c_i^2 / n_i)$$

which equals the $E(MS_e)$, σ^2_e, when the null hypothesis $\Sigma_i c_i \mu_i = 0$ is true. When the null hypothesis is not true, then the more false it is, the larger do we expect $(\Sigma_i c_i \mu_i)^2 / (\Sigma_i c_i^2 / n_i)$ to be. Thus, the upper tail of the F distribution is again the appropriate location for the critical region of the F-test.

*9.3.2 Orthogonal partition of the vector of group means. (You may need to refer to appendix 2 on vector and matrix algebra in going through this section.) The sum of squares for a contrast is the squared length of one of I - 1 orthogonal vectors, which when added to the mean vector give the vector of group means. To exemplify this, consider the one factor design

A_1	A_2	A_3
Y_{11}	Y_{21}	Y_{31}
Y_{12}	Y_{22}	Y_{32}

with two scores in each of three groups. Let M_1, M_2, and M_3 be the means for the three groups. Let $C_2 = M_1 - M_2$ and $C_3 = M_1 + M_2 - 2M_3$ be two orthogonal contrasts exhausting the two degrees of freedom for Groups. Also let C_1, C_2, and C_3 be the column vectors of a matrix C such that

$$
\begin{array}{ccc}
\mathbf{M} & \mathbf{C} & \mathbf{b}
\end{array}
$$

$$
\begin{bmatrix} M_1 \\ M_1 \\ M_2 \\ M_2 \\ M_3 \\ M_3 \end{bmatrix}
=
\begin{bmatrix}
1 & 1 & 1 \\
1 & 1 & 1 \\
1 & -1 & 1 \\
1 & -1 & 1 \\
1 & 0 & -2 \\
1 & 0 & -2
\end{bmatrix}
\begin{bmatrix} b_1 \\ b_2 \\ b_3 \end{bmatrix}
$$

It follows, with a little matrix algebra, that

$$
\mathbf{b} = \mathbf{AC^tM} =
$$

$$
\begin{bmatrix}
1/N & 0 & 0 \\
0 & 1/\Sigma_i^T C_{2j}^2 & 0 \\
0 & 0 & 1/\Sigma_i^T C_{3j}^2
\end{bmatrix}
\begin{bmatrix}
1 & 1 & 1 & 1 & 1 & 1 \\
1 & 1 & -1 & -1 & 0 & 0 \\
1 & 1 & 1 & 1 & -2 & -2
\end{bmatrix}
\begin{bmatrix} M_1 \\ M_1 \\ M_2 \\ M_2 \\ M_3 \\ M_3 \end{bmatrix}
=
\begin{bmatrix}
M \\
C_2/\Sigma_i^T C_{2j}^2 \\
C_3/\Sigma_i^T C_{3j}^2
\end{bmatrix}
$$

since $\mathbf{AC^tC}$ is obviously an identity matrix (if this isn't obvious, multiply $\mathbf{AC^tC}$ out) so premultiplying both sides of the equation $\mathbf{M} = \mathbf{Cb}$ by $\mathbf{AC^t}$ gives $\mathbf{AC^tM} = \mathbf{AC^tCb} = \mathbf{Ib} = \mathbf{b}$.

Let b_1, b_2, and b_3 be the three elements of $\mathbf{b}$. Then

$$
SS_{Mean} = b_1^2\, \mathbf{C_1^t\, C_1} = NM^2
$$

$$
SS_{C2} = b_2^2\, \mathbf{C_2^t\, C_2} = n(M_1 - M_2)^2/(\Sigma_i C_{2i}^2)
$$

$SS_{C3} = b_3{}^2 \, \mathbf{C_3}^t \, \mathbf{C_3} = n(M_1 + M_2 - 2M_3)^2/(\Sigma_i C_{3i}{}^2)$

where n is the number of scores per cell and the C_{2i} and C_{3i} are the elements of $\mathbf{C_{2i}}$ and $\mathbf{C_{3i}}$ respectively.

The orthogonal decomposition of the squared length of the vector of group means is accomplished by finding the projections of the group mean vector on the three orthogonal basis vectors in the matrix $\mathbf{C}$. (The projection of a vector $\mathbf{A}$ on a vector $\mathbf{B}$ is the vector from the origin to the point where a perpendicular dropped from $\mathbf{A}$ to $\mathbf{B}$ intersects $\mathbf{B}$. Thus it has the same direction as $\mathbf{B}$ but is of length $\mathbf{A \cdot B}$.) The squared lengths of these projections form the partition of the sum of squares into NM^2, the sum of squares for the general mean, plus the sums of squares for the several orthogonal contrasts. The vector equation is

$$\mathbf{M} = [(\mathbf{M \cdot C_1})/(\mathbf{C_1 \cdot C_1})]\mathbf{C_1} + [(\mathbf{M \cdot C_2})/(\mathbf{C_2 \cdot C_2})]\mathbf{C_2}$$

$$+ [(\mathbf{M \cdot C_3})/(\mathbf{C_3 \cdot C_3})]\mathbf{C_3}$$

where each term in the sum on the right is the projection of $\mathbf{M}$ on one of the basis vectors. The squared length of $\mathbf{M}$ may be gotten by taking the inner product of $\mathbf{M}$ with itself, giving

$$\mathbf{M \cdot M} = [(\mathbf{M \cdot C_1})/(\mathbf{C_1 \cdot C_1})]\mathbf{C_1 \cdot M} + [(\mathbf{M \cdot C_2})/(\mathbf{C_2 \cdot C_2})]\mathbf{C_2 \cdot M}$$

$$+ [(\mathbf{M \cdot C_3})/(\mathbf{C_3 \cdot C_3})]\mathbf{C_3 \cdot M}$$

$$= (\mathbf{M \cdot C_1})^2/\mathbf{C_1 \cdot C_1} + (\mathbf{M \cdot C_2})^2/\mathbf{C_2 \cdot C_2} + (\mathbf{M \cdot C_3})^2/\mathbf{C_3 \cdot C_3}$$

$$= SS_{Mean} + SS_{C2} + SS_{C3}.$$

What we have just seen is that the vector of group means is the sum of the three vectors that are the projections of the vector of group means on the three orthogonal basis vectors, and the squared length of the vector of group means is the sum of the squared lengths of those projections.

9.4 A numerical example of F-tests for two contrasts. A numerical example probably wouldn't hurt at this point. Consider the example data in Table 9.1 with three scores per level of Factor A. Suppose the two contrasts of interest are $C_1 = (\mu_1 + \mu_2)/2 - \mu_3 = 0$ and $C_2 = \mu_1 - \mu_2 = 0$. Satisfy yourself that these two are orthogonal and therefore independent. Now we will compute the df and sums of squares. Factor A has three levels so two df. Each contrast has one df. The two contrasts being independent and their df

TABLE 9.1 FICTIONAL DATA

	A_1	A_2	A_3
	2	5	3
	3	7	5
	4	6	4
Totals	9	18	12
Means	3	6	4

summing to the df for the factor indicates that the sum of squares for the two contrasts should sum to the sum of squares for Factor A. The sum of squares for Factor A is

$$SS_A = (9^2 + 18^2 + 12^2)/3 - 39^2/9 = 14,$$

and the sums of squares for the two comparisons are

$$SS_{C1} = [(3 + 6)/2 - 4]^2 / [.5^2 + .5^2 + (-1)^2]/3 = .25/(1.5/3) = .5,$$

and

$$SS_{C2} = (3 - 6)^2/[1^2 + (-1)^2]/3 = 9/(2/3) = 13.5.$$

TABLE 9.2 SUMMARY OF THE ANOVA

Source	df	SS	MS	F
The Mean	1	169	169	169
A	2	14	7	7
C1	1	0.5	0.5	.5
C2	1	13.5	13.5	13.5
Error	6	6	1	

Ordinarily these results would be assembled in an ANOVA summary table as in Table 9.2. It is surprising that one of the F's is significant, given the small sample sizes for each group. The mean squares for the two contrasts reflect what is evident from the sample means—namely, that the difference between the mean for level 3 and the average for levels 1 and 2, tested by the first contrast is small, while the difference between the mean for level 1 and the mean for level 2, tested by the second contrast, is relatively large.

*As an advanced exercise the student should confirm, using these example data, that

$$(\mathbf{M} \cdot \mathbf{C_1})^2/\mathbf{C_1} \cdot \mathbf{C_1}, \ (\mathbf{M} \cdot \mathbf{C_2})^2/\mathbf{C_2} \cdot \mathbf{C_2}, \ \text{and} \ (\mathbf{M} \cdot \mathbf{C_3})^2 /\mathbf{C_3} \ \mathbf{C_3}$$

are the sums of squares for the mean and the two contrasts. The vector $\mathbf{M}$ is a 9 x 1 vector with the elements 3,3,3,6,6,6,4,4,4. The three columns of the $\mathbf{C}$ matrix are 1, 1, 1, 1, 1, 1, 1, 1, 1; 1/2, 1/2, 1/2, 1/2, 1/2, 1/2, -1, -1, -1, and 1, 1, 1, -1, -1, -1, 0, 0, 0.

9.5 A preliminary word on orthogonal contrasts. Let's suppose that the sample size and error variance was such that we did find a significant difference between the effects for level A_1 with a mean of 3 and level A_2 with a mean of 6. Noticing that level A_3 has a mean of 4, we might then have wondered whether its effect differs significantly from one or both of the other two. We might have considered the contrasts $\mu_1 - \mu_3$ and $\mu_2 - \mu_3$. Now we know in general that we cannot have more independent contrasts than we have df for the source. (We cannot have more mutually orthogonal vectors than we have dimensions to put them in.) If we perform the contrasts $\mu_1 - \mu_2$, $\mu_1 - \mu_3$ and $\mu_2 - \mu_3$ we cannot have three independent contrasts. To verify this, we can make up a table of contrast coefficients and examine the sums of products of the coefficients. This would give

Contrast	μ_1	μ_2	μ_3
$\mu_1 - \mu_2$	1	-1	0
$\mu_1 - \mu_3$	1	0	-1
$\mu_2 - \mu_3$	0	1	-1

and we can see that no two of these three contrasts are independent since in each case $\Sigma_j c_{ij} c_{kj} = 1$ or -1, where j ranges over the three levels and i and k denote the two contrasts being considered. The question of independence or orthogonality of contrasts arises in the context of considering error rates or significance levels when more than one contrast is performed with the same data. We shall take this subject up shortly, but first we will say a few words about contrasts in repeated measurement designs.

9.6 Contrasts and homogeneity of the variances of the difference scores. We saw in Chapter 8 that with repeated measurement designs, if homogeneity of variance and homogeneity of the variances of the difference scores exists, we can proceed in the usual fashion, but that if homogeneity of the variances of the difference scores does not exist, special steps are needed. When we test hypotheses expressed in terms of contrasts, we must also consider this matter. When homogeneity of the variances of the difference scores exists, we can proceed with contrasts in the usual fashion also. We use as the denominator mean square the same mean square that would be used to test the factor, and we use the same df for that denominator. In the Treatments x Subjects design, this denominator mean square would, of course, be the A x S interaction mean square on $(I - 1)(J - 1)$ df. When homogeneity of the variance of the difference scores does not occur, we can either use $\varepsilon_{est}(I - 1)(J - 1)$ as the approximate df for the A x S interaction mean square as the denominator, or we can use a procedure that will always be exactly correct but will cost us some error df. In this second procedure what we do is equivalent to computing an exactly correct denominator mean square with exactly correct df, resulting in exactly correct error terms. The way we will recommend going about these computations is different from most other textbooks but has great simplicity and familiarity going for it.

9.7 Contrast scores used with repeated measures. We will begin with a Treatments x Subjects design with I subjects and three treatments. The score for Subject j under Treatment i is Y_{ij}. Let the two null hypotheses of interest concerning the Treatment means be H_{01}: $\mu_1 - \mu_2 = 0$ and H_{02}: $\mu_1 + \mu_2 - 2\mu_3 = 0$. ($H_{02}$ is equivalent to the null hypothesis that the average of the first two means equals the third. This can be seen by dividing the equation by 2.) In performing each of the contrasts we will find for each subject a new kind of score called a **contrast score**. For the first contrast we define a first-contrast score for subject j, $C_{1j} = Y_{1j} - Y_{2j}$. The "1" in the index of the "C" denotes that this contrast score is for the first contrast of interest and the "j" denotes that it is the first-contrast score for subject j. For the second contrast we define a second-contrast score for subject j, $C_{2j} = Y_{1j} + Y_{2j} - 2Y_{3j}$. We see that the contrast score for each subject uses the same algebraic relation for the subject's three treatment scores as the relation among the treatment population means in the null hypothesis statement of the contrast to be tested. That is, $C_{1j} = Y_{1j} - Y_{2j}$ corresponds to $\mu_1 - \mu_2$ and $C_{2j} = Y_{1j} + Y_{2j} - 2Y_{3j}$ corresponds to $\mu_1 + \mu_2 - 2\mu_3$.

Now if $\mu_1 - \mu_2 = 0$, then the population mean of the C_{1j} will be zero. This follows because $E_j(C_{1j}) = E(Y_{1j} - Y_{2j}) = E(Y_{1j}) - E(Y_{2j}) = \mu_1 - \mu_2$. Therefore, to test the hypothesis that $\mu_1 - \mu_2 = 0$ it will suffice to test the hypothesis that the mean of the C_{1j}, over the whole population of subjects from which these are a sample, is zero.

To test the hypothesis that the population mean of the C_{1j} is zero, we can perform the simple test we developed in Chapter 2 for using a single sample of scores to test the hypothesis that the mean of a population is zero. We recall that in that test, we had a sample of Y scores, the Y_i, and we found that if the population mean of the Y_i is zero, then F =

TABLE 9.3 TREATMENTS x SUBJECTS DESIGN DATA

	Treatments			
Subjects	1	2	3	4
1	5	1	8	2
2	4	2	7	2
3	5	3	8	3
4	3	3	6	1
5	6	2	5	2
6	5	4	4	1

TABLE 9.4 THREE SETS OF CONTRAST SCORES—THEIR SQUARES AND THE SUMS

C_{1j}	C_{1j}^2	C_{2j}	C_{2j}^2	C_{3j}	C_{3j}^2
-3	9	-1	1	5	25
-3	9	0	0	3.5	12.25
-3	9	0	0	3.5	12.25
-3	9	2	4	2.5	6.25
1	1	0	0	3.5	12.25
1	1	3	9	2	4
-10	38	4	14	20	72

$(T^2/N)/(\Sigma Y_i^2 - T^2/N)/(I - 1)$ is distributed as F with 1 and $I - 1$ degrees of freedom. (Recall that $T = \Sigma_i Y_i$.) We can now apply that same test using the C_{1i} to obtain the F statistic

$$F = (\Sigma_j C_{1j})^2/J \;/\; \{[\Sigma_j C_{1j}^2 - (\Sigma_j C_{1j})^2/J]/(J - 1)\}, \qquad [9.1]$$

which we could also write as $F = (T_{C1j}^2/J)/(\Sigma_j C_{1j}^2 - T_{C1j}^2/J)/(J - 1)$ where T_{C1j} is the sum of the C_{1j} in the sample. This F-ratio is distributed as F on 1 and $J - 1$ degrees of freedom when the null hypothesis that $\mu_1 - \mu_2 = 0$ is true. Substituting the C_{2j} for the C_{1j} in formula [9.1] gives the appropriate F-test for the second contrast.

A little numerical example should be helpful here. Suppose we have a Treatments x Subjects design with six subjects and four treatments. The data are as given in Table 9.3.

As usual, let Y_{ij} be the ith score for Subject j. We will consider three contrasts of the Treatment means to test three null hypotheses: that the first and third Treatment means are equal; that the second and fourth Treatment means are equal; and that the average of the first and third Treatment means equals the average of the second and fourth Treatment means. Or, algebraically: $\mu_1 - \mu_3 = 0$, $\mu_2 - \mu_4 = 0$, and $(\mu_1 + \mu_3)/2 - (\mu_2 + \mu_4)/2 = 0$. Following the correspondence of the algebraic form of the contrast score with the algebraic form of the contrast we have: $C_{1j} = Y_{1j} - Y_{3j}$; $C_{2j} = Y_{2j} - Y_{4j}$; and $C_{3j} = (Y_{1j} - Y_{3j})/2 - (Y_{2j} - Y_{4j})/2$. It is convenient to table the contrast scores, their squares, and the sums of each. Table 9.4 shows these values for the three contrasts. Then, using formula [9.1] three times we obtain an F-statistic for testing each of the contrasts:

$$F_1 = [(-10)^2/6]/[(38 - (-10)^2/6]/5 = 3.91;$$

$$F_2 = (4^2/6)/(14 - 4^2/6)/5 = 1.18; \text{ and}$$

$$F_3 = (20^2/6)/(72 - 20^2/6)/5 = 62.5,$$

where each F-ratio has the F distribution with 1 and 5 df when the tested contrast equals zero in the population of subjects.

**TABLE 9.5 TREATMENTS
x SUBJECTS DESIGN**

Subjects	Treatments		
	1	2	3
1	1	2	4
2	2	3	5
3	3	2	6
4	2	1	5
5	2	3	6
6	1	0	5

*9.8 Why do the contrast scores work? Now that we have defined the contrast scores and seen how to use them to test some contrasts in a Treatment x Subjects design, we should attend a little to why they work. Then we can expand their use to higher-order experimental designs. First, intuitively, analyzing the contrast scores seems appropriate. If $\mu_1 - \mu_2$ is equal to zero, then we would expect $Y_{1j} - Y_{2j}$ to be more or less in the neighborhood of zero also since on the average Y_{1j} equals μ_1, and on the average Y_{2j} equals

μ_2, and we know that $\mu_1 = \mu_2$. So, on the average, $Y_{1j} = Y_{2j}$ and the contrast scores for this contrast should not depart too much from zero in the sample, too much or not too much being measured by the F-ratio. But we can also examine the contrasts from a geometric perspective. Let's consider a Treatment x Subjects design with six subjects and three treatments. Suppose the data are those shown in Table 9.5. We can consider the three scores for each subject as the coordinates of a vector in three-dimensional space. Formerly, we analyzed such a vector, call it V, into two vectors, the mean vector $M = M[1,1,1]$ and the vector $D = V - M = [V_1 - M, V_2 - M, V_3 - M]$. We recall that M lies on the one-dimensional mean line passing through $(0, 0, 0)$ and $(1,1,1)$ and D lies in the two-dimensional plane orthogonal to the mean line. Now, suppose we choose two vectors, C_1 and C_2, orthogonal to the mean line and orthogonal to each other. For example, $C_1 = [1, -1, 0]$ and $C_2 = [1, 1, -2]$. We know that these three mutually orthogonal vectors must span the three-dimensional space, so each subject's vector must be a linear combination of the three vectors $1 = [1, 1, 1]$, C_1 and C_2. Thus $V = M1 + b_1C_1 + b_2C_2$. We can rewrite this vector equation as $V = bP$, where P is a 3 x 3 matrix with 1, C_1 and C_2 as its three rows, and b is a 3 x 1 column vector the elements of which are M, b_1, and b_2. To find M (which of course we already know as the sample mean), b_1 and b_2 we note that $VP^{-1} = bPP^{-1} = b$. So, to find M, b_1 and b_2 we need to find the inverse of P and postmultiply V by it. (The inverse of the square matrix P is a square matrix P^{-1} such that the product of P and P^{-1} is the identity matrix I, a matrix with 1's down the main diagonal and 0's everywhere else. I has the property that for any matrix A, $IA = AI = A$. See appendix 2 on vectors and matrix algebra for more on matrix inverses.) Let P_1, P_2, and P_3 be the three row vectors of P, and let P_1^t, P_2^t, and P_3^t be the three column vectors of P^t, the transpose of P. Then

$$PP^t = \begin{bmatrix} P_1 \\ P_2 \\ P_3 \end{bmatrix} [P_1^t P_2^t P_3^t] = \begin{bmatrix} P_1 \cdot P_1^t & P_1 \cdot P_2^t & P_1 \cdot P_3^t \\ P_2 \cdot P_1^t & P_2 \cdot P_2^t & P_2 \cdot P_3^t \\ P_3 \cdot P_1^t & P_3 \cdot P_2^t & P_3 \cdot P_3^t \end{bmatrix}$$

But because the vectors of P are mutually orthogonal, $P_i \cdot P_j = 0$ when $i \neq j$, and $P_i \cdot P_i = \Sigma_j p_{ij}^2$, the sum of the squares of the elements of P_i, the ith row vector of P. Thus

$$\mathbf{PP^t} = \begin{bmatrix} \Sigma_j P_{1j}^2 & 0 & 0 \\ 0 & \Sigma_j P_{2j}^2 & 0 \\ 0 & 0 & \Sigma_j P_{3j}^2 \end{bmatrix}$$

Obviously if we were to postmultiply $\mathbf{PP^t}$ by the matrix

$$\mathbf{A} = \begin{bmatrix} 1/\Sigma_j P_{1j}^2 & 0 & 0 \\ 0 & 1/\Sigma_j P_{2j}^2 & 0 \\ 0 & 0 & 1/\Sigma_j P_{3j}^2 \end{bmatrix}$$

we would obtain the identity matrix, that matrix with ones down the main diagonal and zeroes everywhere else. Therefore $\mathbf{P^{-1}} = \mathbf{P^t A}$. So we have that $\mathbf{b} = \mathbf{V P^{-1}} = \mathbf{V P^t A}$. When we multiply this out we find that $\mathbf{V P^t A}$ is a 1 x 3 row vector in which the ith element is $(\Sigma_j p_{ij} V_j)/\Sigma_j p_{ij}^2$. We see that the first element of $\mathbf{b}$ is $(V_1 + V_2 + V_3)/(1^2 + 1^2 + 1^2) = M$. The second element in $\mathbf{b}$ is $b_1 = \mathbf{C_1 \cdot V}/ \mathbf{C_1 \cdot C_1}$ in which the numerator is the contrast score and the denominator is the sum of the squares of the contrast coefficients for the first contrast. In the example, letting $\mathbf{V}$ be the first subject's three scores [1, 2, 4], $b_1 = [(1)1 + (-1)2 + (0)4]/(1^2 + (-1)^2 + 0^2) = -.5$. Similarly, $b_2 = \mathbf{C_2 \cdot V}/ \mathbf{C_2 \cdot C_2} = [(1)1 + (1)2 + (-2)4]/[1^2 + (1)^2 + (-2)^2] = -.5$.

Now the role of the contrast scores in the vector representation of the data is apparent. They serve as the variable parts of the linear coefficients in the linear combination of orthogonal vectors that equals the subject's set of scores under the several treatments. In each such linear coefficient, the denominator will be the sum of the squares of the corresponding contrast coefficients and therefore will not depend on the data. The numerator, the contrast score, that is, will vary as $\mathbf{V}$, the vector of scores varies.

When we calculate the contrast scores, we convert each subject's scores into a new set that are an equivalent description but indicate the extent to which the variation of the subject's scores from the subject's own mean lies in the various orthogonal one-dimensional spaces spanned by the various vectors of contrast coefficients.

*9.8.1 More on the contrast scores, from a vector point of view. Perhaps it will be helpful toward understanding of the contrast scores to consider the matrix equation

$$
\underset{\mathbf{V}}{\begin{bmatrix} 1 & 2 & 4 \\ 2 & 3 & 5 \\ 3 & 2 & 6 \\ 2 & 1 & 5 \\ 2 & 3 & 6 \\ 1 & 0 & 5 \end{bmatrix}}
=
\underset{\mathbf{V}}{\begin{bmatrix} 1 & 2 & 4 \\ 2 & 3 & 5 \\ 3 & 2 & 6 \\ 2 & 1 & 5 \\ 2 & 3 & 6 \\ 1 & 0 & 5 \end{bmatrix}}
\underset{\mathbf{E}}{\begin{bmatrix} 1 & 0 & 0 \\ 0 & 1 & 0 \\ 0 & 0 & 1 \end{bmatrix}}
=
\underset{\mathbf{b}}{\begin{bmatrix} 7/3 & -1/2 & -5/6 \\ 10/3 & -1/2 & -5/6 \\ 11/3 & 1/2 & -8/6 \\ 8/3 & 1/2 & -7/6 \\ 11/3 & -1/2 & -7/6 \\ 6/3 & 1/2 & -9/6 \end{bmatrix}}
\underset{\mathbf{P}}{\begin{bmatrix} 1 & 1 & 1 \\ 1 & -1 & 0 \\ 1 & 1 & -2 \end{bmatrix}}
$$

Here we see the original collection of data for the Treatments x Subjects design expressed as the matrix **V**. We next note that **V** can be written as **VE**, where **E** is an identity matrix. Let the three rows of **E** be called $\mathbf{E_1}$, $\mathbf{E_2}$, and $\mathbf{E_3}$. Then we see that the first row of **V** is $1\mathbf{E_1} + 2\mathbf{E_2} + 4\mathbf{E_3}$, the second row is $2\mathbf{E_1} + 3\mathbf{E_2} + 5\mathbf{E_3}$, and so on. Obviously $\mathbf{E_1}$, $\mathbf{E_2}$, and $\mathbf{E_3}$ form a basis for three-dimensional space, and the three scores may be thought of as the three linear coefficients in the linear combination of $\mathbf{E_1}$, $\mathbf{E_2}$, and $\mathbf{E_3}$ that gives the vector of scores for a subject. The equation **VE = bP** says that if we change from the basis vectors in **E** to the basis vectors in **P**, the linear coefficients change to the mean and the two contrast scores, each divided by the squared length of the new corresponding basis vector. Take row 1 of **V**, for instance. The new basis vectors in **P** are [1, 1, 1], which lies on the mean line; [1, -1, 0], which is the vector of coefficients for the first contrast; and [1, 1, -2], the vector of coefficients for the second contrast. Then, the first row in **b** is [7/3, -1/2, -5/6]. The first value, 7/3, is the mean of [1,2,4], the first row of **V**, and can also be considered as [1(1) + 1(2) + 1(4)]/($1^2 + 1^2 + 1^2$). The second value, -1/2, is [1(1) + (-1)(2) + 0(4)]/[$1^2 + (-1)^2 + (0)^2$]. And the third value, -5/6, is [1(1) + 1(2) -2(4)]/($1^2 + 1^2 + (-2)^2$].

In fact, we could have chosen as the contrast coefficients the values 1/2, -1/2, 0 for the first contrast and 1/6, 1/6, -2/6 for the second, since these are proportional to the values chosen (and if $1/2\ \mu_1 - 1/2\ \mu_2 = 0$, certainly $\mu_1 - \mu_2 = 0$, etc.). With these values as the contrast coefficients we would have V = VE =

$$
\underset{\mathbf{b_1}}{\begin{bmatrix} 7/3 & -1 & -5 \\ 10/3 & -1 & -5 \\ 11/3 & 1 & -7 \\ 8/3 & 1 & -7 \\ 11/3 & -1 & -7 \\ 6/3 & 1 & -9 \end{bmatrix}}
\underset{\mathbf{P_1}}{\begin{bmatrix} 1 & 1 & 1 \\ 1/2 & -1/2 & 0 \\ 1/6 & 1/6 & -2/6 \end{bmatrix}}
$$

and the contrast scores themselves would now be the linear coefficients. From this perspective we can see that the contrast scores can be thought of as the linear coefficients of the vectors spanning the space in which occur the departures of the treatment scores from the person's mean score.

To see this in one more way, suppose we have a set of scores for subject j that conform perfectly to the two contrast null hypotheses. Then $Y_{1j} - Y_{2j} = 0$ and $Y_{1j} + Y_{2j} - 2Y_{3j} = 0$. So $Y_{1j} = Y_{2j}$ and therefore $Y_{1j} + Y_{2j} - 2Y_{3j} = 2Y_{1j} - 2Y_{3j} = 0$, so $Y_{1j} = Y_{2j} = Y_{3j}$. Hence the vector of scores $[Y_{1j}, Y_{2j}, Y_{3j}]$ would be some multiple of the vector $[1, 1, 1]$, it would be on the line passing through the points $(0, 0, 0)$ and $(1, 1, 1)$, it would therefore not lie in the space spanned by the two vectors of contrast coefficients, and the two contrast scores would therefore be zero. On the other hand, suppose the scores conformed to the first null hypothesis but not to the second. We would have $Y_{1j} = Y_{2j}$ but $2Y_{1j} \neq 2Y_{3j}$ so $Y_{1j} \neq Y_{3j}$. If $Y_{1j} > Y_{3j}$, the contrast score for the second contrast would be $Y_{1j} + Y_{2j} - 2Y_{3j} > 0$. If $Y_{1j} < Y_{3j}$, then it would be $Y_{1j} + Y_{2j} - 2Y_{3j} < 0$. We see that as the data depart from the null hypothesis for a given contrast, the contrast score departs from zero, and when the data exactly conform to the null hypothesis, the contrast score equals zero. Thus a sample of contrast scores can be used to infer the truth or falsity of the null hypothesis by inferring the truth or falsity of the hypothesis that the population mean of the contrast scores is zero.

9.9 Contrast scores can be used to analyze interaction. Suppose that we have a design in which Subjects are nested in Factor B and crossed with Factor A. That is, B is a between-subjects factor and A is a within-subjects factor. The contrast scores for Factor A would test certain null hypotheses about the differences between the overall means for the levels of A. But we can imagine a case where, for a given contrast, this null hypothesis might be true at two levels of B but not at the third. Thus the differences between the means for the levels of Factor A would differ from one level of B to another. This is what we regard as interaction. Consider the data in Table 9.6. There are three degrees of freedom for Factor A so there are three orthogonal contrasts possible. Suppose they correspond to the null hypotheses H_{01}: $(\mu_{1..} + \mu_{2..}) - (\mu_{3..} + \mu_{4..}) = 0$; H_{02}: $\mu_{1..} - \mu_{2..} = 0$; and H_{03}: $\mu_{3..} - \mu_{4..} = 0$, where $M_{i..}$ is the mean for level i of Factor A. We can see that the data for the five subjects nested in level B_1 appear to be compatible with the third hypothesis but not with the first two. The data for the five subjects nested in level B_2 seem consistent with the second and third hypothesis but not with the first, as do the data for the subjects nested in level B_3. It appears, from the inspection, that there is an interaction of Factor A with Factor B but that this interaction is specific to the first and second contrast and not to the third.

We can perform a statistical test for the interaction of each of the three contrasts with Factor B. Let $Y_{ik(j)}$ be the score for Subject k nested in level j of Factor B and receiving level i of Factor A. Then we compute the three sets of contrast scores: $Y_{1k(j)} + Y_{2k(j)} - $

TABLE 9.6 A DESIGN WITH ONE BETWEEN (B) AND ONE WITHIN (A) FACTOR

	A_1	A_2	A_3	A_4
	15	5	5	4
	14	6	4	6
B_1	15	6	5	4
	14	7	5	3
	16	7	3	4
	3	4	10	11
	3	2	9	9
B_2	4	3	8	10
	5	5	10	8
	5	6	11	9
	5	3	9	10
	4	6	10	10
B_3	5	4	11	8
	5	3	11	10
	3	5	9	12

$Y_{3k(j)} - Y_{4k(j)}$; $Y_{1k(j)} - Y_{2k(j)}$; and $Y_{3k(j)} - Y_{4k(j)}$. We will refer to these as the scores under C_1, C_2, and C_3 (for contrasts 1, 2, and 3 corresponding to hypotheses H_{01}, H_{02}, and H_{03}). Thus, for each subject we compute the three contrast scores. These are shown in Table 9.6. Please note that in Table 9.6, C_1, C_2, and C_3 do not denote the levels of some factor but denote the three contrasts for which the contrast scores in the body of the table have been calculated.

To test the hypothesis that there is no interaction of the first contrast with Factor B we simply perform a one-factor ANOVA on the C_1 contrast scores using B as the factor. The sum of the squares of the C_1 contrast scores is $11^2 + 10^2 + 12^2 + 13^2 + 16^2 + (-14)^2 + (-13)^2 + ... + (-13)^2 + (-13)^2 = 2080$, and the totals for the three levels of B are 62, -55, and -57, giving the ANOVA shown for Contrast 1 in Table 9.7. The F-ratio is the usual value for a one-factor design with three levels: $[62^2/5 + (-55)^2/5 + (-57)^2/5 - (-50)^2/15]/2$ as the numerator and $\{11^2 + 10^2 + 12^2 + 13^2 + 16^2 + (-14)^2 + (-13)^2 + ... + (-13)^2 + (-13)^2 -$

$[62^2/5 + (-55)^2/5 + (-57)^2/5]\}/12$ as the denominator. The corresponding analyses of the contrast scores for the other two contrasts are also shown in Table 9.7.

The results of the three analyses of variance of the contrast scores conform to the impressions that the first and second contrasts interact with Factor B but the third does not. The F of 197.55 indicates the difference between the sum of the means for levels A_1 and A_2 and the sum of the means for levels A_3 and A_4 is different at different levels of B. If we let μ_{ij} be the mean for the jth level of B at the ith level of A, then we can infer that $(\mu_{11.} + \mu_{21.} - \mu_{31.} - \mu_{41.})$, $(\mu_{12.} + \mu_{22.} - \mu_{32.} - \mu_{42.})$, and $(\mu_{13.} + \mu_{23.} - \mu_{33.} - \mu_{43.})$ are not all equal. Similarly, we can infer that $\mu_{11.} - \mu_{21.}$, $\mu_{12.} - \mu_{22.}$, and $\mu_{13.} - \mu_{23.}$ are not all equal.

TABLE 9.7 SUMMARY OF THE ANOVAS OF THE THREE SETS OF CONTRAST SCORES

Source	df	SS	MS	F
B x C_1				
Groups	2	1856.93	928.47	197.55
Error	12	56.4	4.70	
B x C_2				
Groups	2	240.93	120.47	55.6
Error	12	26.00	2.17	
B x C_3				
Groups	2	.13	.07	.02
Error	12	43.60	3.63	

9.10 The degrees of freedom in Table 9.7.

Consider the degrees of freedom column in Table 9.7. In all there are 42 degrees of freedom. We should understand where these various degrees of freedom come from. The six degrees of freedom associated with Groups are the six degrees of freedom for the B x A interaction in the original design. The B x A interaction had six = (two for Factor B) times (three for Factor A) degrees of freedom. The sum of squares and degrees of freedom for that interaction have been partitioned into three pieces. Originally, Factor A had four levels and so three df. But those three df were separated into 1 df each for the three contrasts. The interaction of each contrast with Factor B therefore has 1 x 2 df, (one for the contrast) times (two for Factor B).

The 36 df for error come from the interaction of Factor A with Subjects nested in B. These would be the sum of the 3 (df for A) times 4 (df for Subjects) added over the 3 levels

TABLE 9.8 SUBJECTS CROSSED WITH FACTOR A AND NESTED IN B CROSS C

			A_1	A_2	A_3	A_4	A_5
C_1	B_1	S_1 S_2					
	B_2	S_1 S_2					
	B_3	S_1 S_2					
C_2	B_1	S_1 S_2					
	B_2	S_1 S_2					
	B_3	S_1 S_2					
C_3	B_1	S_1 S_2					
	B_2	S_1 S_2					
	B_3	S_1 S_2					

of B, giving 36 df. But now these 36 df have been partitioned so for each of the 3 contrasts there is $12 = 4$ df for subjects at each of 3 levels of B. Each of these pieces of 12 df are the within-groups df in the analysis of variance of the one-factor design containing five contrast scores (for the five subjects) in each of the three cells (levels of B).

9.11 Contrast score analysis of interaction in a design in which Subjects are crossed with Factor A and nested in the cross of Factors B and C. Suppose that Subjects were crossed with Factor A and were nested in the cross of Factors B and C. The design might look like that shown in Table 9.8. Without filling in data and going through all the details, we can still anticipate that there can be four orthogonal contrasts for Factor A, thus four sets of contrast scores. The analysis of each set of contrast scores would involve a 3 x 3 factorial design with Factors B and C as the factors of the design and with two scores per cell, one for each of the two subjects nested in a particular B-C combination. The main effects in one of these factorial designs would test the hypotheses of no interaction of the A contrast with Factor B and with Factor C. The B x C interaction in the factorial design analysis of the contrast scores would test the hypothesis that the differences in the A contrast over levels of B and over levels of C are additive differences. For example, if the contrast is $\mu_{A1} - \mu_{A2}$, then the difference between the mean of A_1 and the mean of A_2 changes from one level of B to another the same amount regardless of which level of C we examine.

As in 9.10 the B and C factors could be partitioned into contrasts, and the interaction of an A contrast with the interaction of a B contrast and a C contrast could be tested. Suppose, for instance, we wanted to test the null hypothesis that a given A contrast's interaction with B x C was all due to the fact that the values of the contrast scores differed from level B_1 to level B_2 more at level C_1 than at level C_2. To perform this test for a given A contrast, take the contrast scores in the 2 x 2 table involving cells B_1-C_1, B_1- C_2, B_2-C_1, and B_2-C_2 and test the significance of the interaction. There would be two scores in each of four cells, and the F-ratio would have 1 and 4 df, 1 for the B x C interaction in this 2 x 2 design and four as the within-cells df in a 2 x 2 design with 2 scores per cell.

9.12 Contrast scores in a more complex design. In this section we will extend the use of contrast scores to a more complex design in which two Within-Subjects factors occur together with one Between-Subjects factor. Suppose Subjects are crossed with the cross of Factors A and B and are nested in Factor C. Let Factor A have four levels, B have three levels, C have three levels, and let four subjects be nested in each level of C. The design is shown in Table 9.9. Suppose we want to do contrasts of the means for Factor A. We can simply ignore Factor B and treat the design as one with one between-subjects factor and one within. The way we ignore Factor B is to sum over its levels.

Thus each subject would have a score at each level of Factor A, which is the sum of the three scores at the three levels of Factor B at that level of Factor A. If $Y_{ijm(k)}$ is the score for Subject m nested in level k of Factor C and at level i of A and j of B, then the four scores for Subject m nested in level k of C would be $\Sigma_j Y_{1jm(k)}$, $\Sigma_j Y_{2jm(k)}$, $\Sigma_j Y_{3jm(k)}$, and

TABLE 9.9 SUBJECTS NESTED IN C AND CROSSED WITH THE CROSS OF A AND B

TABLE 9.10 TWO WITHIN-SUBJECTS FACTORS

	A_1			A_2			A_3			A_4		
	B_1	B_2	B_3	B_1	B_2	B_3	B_1	B_2	B_3	B_1	B_2	B_3
S_1	1	1	2	4	5	5	9	8	7	8	3	3
S_2	2	1	2	5	6	3	10	7	6	7	5	2
S_3	1	2	1	4	4	4	11	7	5	8	4	2
S_4	3	1	1	5	4	4	10	6	4	9	7	3
S_5	2	1	1	3	6	3	11	8	5	9	6	4
S_6	1	3	2	4	4	5	9	7	4	9	5	3
S_7	2	2	2	5	5	4	10	9	6	8	6	4
S_8	1	1	1	3	4	5	11	8	5	9	7	3

$\Sigma_j Y_{4jm(4)}$. For analyzing contrasts of the means for Factor B, we would sum over the levels of A for each subject, giving three scores for Subject m nested in level k of C, which would be $\Sigma_i Y_{i1m(k)}$, $\Sigma_i Y_{i2m(k)}$, and $\Sigma_i Y_{i3m(k)}$. Then we would analyze these data as a design with one between and one within factor.

The introduction of a second within-subjects factor creates an interesting situation. With one within-subjects factor we could escape the problem of lack of homogeneity of the variances of the difference scores by converting to contrast scores. But with two within-subjects factors, even after we convert to contrast scores on one factor, the contrast scores themselves are repeated measurements over the levels of the other within-subjects factor. As you might anticipate, we can use the same approach again. We can create contrast scores at the level of the second within-subjects factor using the contrast scores at the level of the first within-subjects factor. We need an example at this point. And the issue we are discussing now does not depend on the presence or absence of the between-subjects factor, so we will just dispense with the between subjects factor for the example and simply consider the data in Table 9.10. Suppose we were interested in whether the difference between the mean for B_1 and the mean for B_3 differed with different levels of Factor A. The first move would be to convert the data into a set of contrast scores, giving the difference between B_1 and B_3 for each subject at each level of A. These are shown in Table 9.11. We can regard the data in Table 9.11 as a Treatments x Subjects design and analyze them as such. A test of the main effect for A in this table is a test of whether there is an interaction of the B_1 - B_3 contrast with A. This could be performed if homogeneity of the variances of the diffference scores of these contrast scores exists. If not, the usual devices could be used. If a contrast of the Factor A means of these contrast scores were performed, say $(M_{A1} + M_{A2})/2 - (M_{A3} +$

$M_{A4})/2$, the requirement of homogeneity is avoided. This contrast would ask whether the variation of levels of A of the B_1 - B_3 contrast is in part due to the differences between A_1 and A_2 versus A_3 and A_4. We can see that this is a question about a component of the A x B interaction. We can also see that when the contrast of these contrast scores is performed, we will be testing whether the mean of a population is zero; the test will be based on a sample of eight scores, and the degrees of freedom for the F-ratio will naturally be 1 for the numerator and 7 for the denominator.

As a numerical example we do the test of the null hypothesis that the B_1 - B_3 contrast is the same, on the average, at levels A_1 and A_2 as it is, on the average, at levels A_3 and A_4. For each of the eight subjects in Table 9.9, we find the difference between the average score under A_1 and A_2 and the average score under A_3 and A_4. For Subject 1 this difference is $(-1 - 1)/2 - (2 + 5)/2 = -4.5$. The corresponding scores for the remaining seven subjects are -3.5, -6, -4.5, -5, -6.5, -3.5, and -7. Applying the formula $F_{1,N-1} = (T^2/N)/(\Sigma X^2 - T^2/N)/(N-1)$ to these eight scores gives $F_{1,7} = (205)/(217 - 205)/7 = 117$, which is significant at the .05 level.

Note that the one degree of freedom for the numerator is associated with a portion of the sum of squares for the A x B interaction. If we let

$$Y_{ijk} = \mu + A_i + B_j + s_k + AB_{ij} + As_{ik} + Bs_{jk} + ABs_{ijk} + e_{ijk}$$

be the model equation, then the contrast scores in Table 9.11 are the $Y_{i1k} - Y_{i3k}$ scores. The contrast scores for the $(M_{A1} + M_{A2})/2 - (M_{A3} + M_{A4})/2$ contrast would be the $(Y_{11k} - Y_{13k} + Y_{21k} - Y_{23k})/2 - (Y_{31k} - Y_{33k} + Y_{41k} - Y_{43k})/2$ values. Then the sum of squares for the numerator with one degree of freedom is just $\{\Sigma_k[(Y_{11k} - Y_{13k} + Y_{21k} - Y_{23k})/2 - (Y_{31k} - Y_{33k} + Y_{41k} - Y_{43k})/2]\}^2/8$. The remaining contrasts of contrast scores have five degrees of freedom. Since A has three degrees of freedom, there are two other contrasts that can be done with the B_1 - B_3 scores, each on one degree of freedom. Since Factor B has two degrees of freedom, there is another orthogonal contrast of the B scores, say, the $(B_1 + B_3)/2 - B_2$ scores. These can be contrasted in three different ways corresponding to the three degrees of freedom for Factor A. This exhausts the reamining five degrees of freedom. Altogether, the original contrast of the B_1 - B_3 scores together with the five others gives the six degrees of freedom associated with the A x B interaction.

Each of the six possible sets of orthogonal contrast scores will contain eight scores and therefore seven degrees of freedom, for a total of 42 degrees of freedom. These are the 42 degrees of freedom for the A x B x S source. Let C_{ij} be the contrast score for the jth subject on the ith of the six contrasts. Then the sum of squares for error for testing that ith contrast is $SS_{Cij} = [\Sigma_i\Sigma_jC_{ij}^2 - (\Sigma_i\Sigma_jC_{ij})^2/J]/(J - 1)$ where J = 8 in the case described. Each of

**TABLE 9.11 B₁ - B₃
CONTRAST SCORES**

	A_1	A_2	A_3	A_4
S_1	-1	-1	2	5
S_2	0	2	4	5
S_3	0	0	6	6
S_4	2	1	6	6
S_5	1	0	6	5
S_6	-1	-1	5	6
S_7	0	1	4	4
S_8	0	-2	6	6

these sums of squares is a piece of the sum of squares for the A x B x S interaction, and the sum of these sums of squares over all of the orthogonal contrasts gives the sum of squares for the A x B x S interaction.

9.13 Complex analyses are simplified by the use of contrast scores. It is perhaps unnecessary by now to point out that by using contrast scores we are enabled to perform relatively simple, straightforward analyses continually even when we get into tests of fairly complicated hypotheses. Furthermore, the numerators and the denominators of the F-ratios always are obvious, as are the df associated with them just because of the simplicity of the analyses. Master this.

**TABLE 9.12 TWO SETS OF CELL MEANS
FOR A 3 x 3 FACTORIAL DESIGN**

	(a) Factor B 1	2	3	row means	(b) Factor B 1	2	3	row means
Factor A 1	2	8	5	5	22	28	34	28
2	4	10	4	6	16	10	4	10
3	6	12	3	7	26	32	38	32

*9.14 "The contrasts for Factor A have the same value at each level of Factor B" means the same as "the contrasts for Factor A at each level of Factor B equal the contrast of the marginal means of Factor A": namely, no interaction of the contrast with Factor B. We return now to the case of random assignment of subjects to the cells of a factorial design, so that there are no within-subjects factors. We continue to consider using contrasts to analyze interaction. Suppose we have a two-factor design with three levels at each factor. We want to determine whether a contrast of the means for Factor A varies from level to level of Factor B. Consider the cell means shown in Table 9.12. If we are interested in the contrast of the means for Factor A with coefficients -1, 0, 1 for levels 1, 2, and 3, we see that Table 9.12(a) contains means for which the values of the contrast at the three separate levels of Factor B, 6 - 2 = 4, 12 - 8 = 4, and 3 - 5 = -2, are not the same, whereas in Table 9.12(b) the corresponding values all equal 4; 26 - 22, 32 - 28, and 38 - 34. In (a) the contrast interacts with Factor B and in (b) it doesn't. We also note that in (b) the values of all the contrasts at the separate levels of Factor B equal the value of the contrast of the row means, 32 - 28 = 4, whereas this is not the case in (a) where the contrast of the row means is 7 - 5 = 2. This is an alternative way to express the absence versus the presence of interaction of the contrast with Factor B.

*9.14.1 A geometric characterization of the interaction of a Factor A contrast with Factor B. Let's characterize this distinction in one more way: geometrically. For simplicity of presentation we will assume there is one score per cell (although this would never occur in practice since there would be no estimate of error variance). The data vector then will lie in nine-dimensional space and because of the assumption of one score per cell will be the vector of cell means also. The example vector of cell means will be [22, 28, 34, 16, 10, 4, 26, 32, 38]. In general the vector of cell means for the design in question will be as shown on the left side of the equation $M_{ij} = X^t B$ where

$$
M_{ij} =
\begin{bmatrix}
M_{11} \\
M_{12} \\
M_{13} \\
M_{21} \\
M_{22} \\
M_{23} \\
M_{31} \\
M_{32} \\
M_{33}
\end{bmatrix},
\quad
X^t =
\begin{array}{c|cc|cc|cccc}
\text{Mean} & \multicolumn{2}{c|}{A} & \multicolumn{2}{c|}{B} & \multicolumn{4}{c}{A \times B} \\
1 & -1 & 1 & -1 & 1 & 1 & -1 & -1 & 1 \\
1 & -1 & 1 & 0 & -2 & 0 & 2 & 0 & -2 \\
1 & -1 & 1 & 1 & 1 & -1 & -1 & 1 & 1 \\
1 & 0 & -2 & -1 & 1 & 0 & 0 & 2 & -1 \\
1 & 0 & -2 & 0 & -2 & 0 & 0 & 0 & 4 \\
1 & 0 & -2 & 1 & 1 & 0 & 0 & -2 & -2 \\
1 & 1 & 1 & -1 & 1 & -1 & 1 & -1 & 1 \\
1 & 1 & 1 & 0 & -2 & 0 & -2 & 0 & -2 \\
1 & 1 & 1 & 1 & 1 & 1 & 1 & 1 & 1
\end{array},
$$

258 An Introduction to the Analysis of Variance

$$B = \begin{bmatrix} M_{..} \\ (M_{3.} - M_{1.})/2 \\ (M_{1.} - 2M_{2.} + M_{3.})/6 \\ (M_{.3} - M_{.1})/2 \\ (M_{.1} - 2M_{.2} + M_{.3})/6 \\ [(M_{11}+M_{33}) - (M_{13}+M_{31})]/4 \\ (2M_{12}+M_{31}+M_{33}-M_{11}-M_{13}-2M_{32})/12 \\ (M_{13}+2M_{21}+M_{33}-M_{11}+2M_{23}+M_{31})/12 \\ [M_{11}+M_{13}+M_{31}+M_{33}+4M_{22}-2(M_{12}+M_{21}+M_{23}+M_{32})]/36 \end{bmatrix}.$$

There are nine column vectors in X^t. We can see by inspection that these are all mutually orthogonal and that therefore they span the nine-dimensional space in which the vector of cell means, M_{ij}, lies. We recall that this means there is some linear combination of these nine vectors that will give the vector of cell means. The linear coefficients of these nine vectors are given in the column vector B. The coefficient of the first column vector in X^t, the vector of ones labeled Mean, is $M_{..}$; the coefficient of the second column vector in X^t is $(M_{3.} - M_{1.})/2$; and so forth.

We note that the column vectors in X^t are grouped: one labeled Mean; two under the "A" label; two under the "B" label; and four under the "A x B" label. The number of vectors in each group corresponds to the number of degrees of freedom for each of these sources. Let's develop some notation for referring to the column vectors and the elements of B. Let the column vectors in X^t be M, A_1, A_2, B_1, B_2, A_1B_1, A_1B_2, A_2B_1, and A_2B_2, and the elements of B be b_M, b_{A1}, b_{A2}, b_{B1}, b_{B2}, b_{A1B1}, b_{A1B2}, b_{A2B1}, and b_{A2B2}. The notation for referring to the interaction vectors is descriptive of how they are arrived at since for each of the interaction vectors, the element in the kth position of vector A_iB_j is the product of the element in the kth position of A_i and the element in the kth position of B_j.

How the elements of B are obtained. The elements of B are obtained by solving the equation $M = X^tB$. This is done by premultiplying both sides of the equation by the left inverse of X^t to obtain

$$(X^t)^{-1}M = (X^t)^{-1}X^tB = B.$$

It is a simple matter to determine $(X^t)^{-1}$. We just note that if we premultiply X^t by X we obtain a matrix with zeroes off the main diagonal because all of the vectors in X^t are orthogonal to one another and with values on the main diagonal equal to the sums of the squares of the elements in each column vector of X^t. These entries on the main diagonal are, of course, the sums of the squares of the contrast coefficients. So, if we were to premultiply or postmultiply the matrix $\mathbf{X}$ by a matrix that had the reciprocals of these sums of squares on the main diagonal and zeroes elsewhere, that product would be the left inverse of $\mathbf{X^t}$. We should note that in general $\mathbf{X^t}$ will not be a square matrix and therefore will not always have an inverse. Nevertheless, it will always have the left inverse we have described since $\mathbf{XX^t}$ will always be a square diagonal matrix even when $\mathbf{X^t}$ is not square. For the example, this left inverse would be

$$
(\mathbf{X^t})^{-1} = \begin{bmatrix}
1/9 & 0 & 0 & 0 & 0 & 0 & 0 & 0 & 0 \\
0 & 1/6 & 0 & 0 & 0 & 0 & 0 & 0 & 0 \\
0 & 0 & 1/18 & 0 & 0 & 0 & 0 & 0 & 0 \\
0 & 0 & 0 & 1/6 & 0 & 0 & 0 & 0 & 0 \\
0 & 0 & 0 & 0 & 1/18 & 0 & 0 & 0 & 0 \\
0 & 0 & 0 & 0 & 0 & 1/4 & 0 & 0 & 0 \\
0 & 0 & 0 & 0 & 0 & 0 & 1/12 & 0 & 0 \\
0 & 0 & 0 & 0 & 0 & 0 & 0 & 1/12 & 0 \\
0 & 0 & 0 & 0 & 0 & 0 & 0 & 0 & 1/36
\end{bmatrix} \mathbf{X}
$$

The upshot of this is that for any column vector $\mathbf{V}$ of $\mathbf{X^t}$, its coefficient b in $\mathbf{B}$ is $\mathbf{V \cdot M / V \cdot V}$. This means that each of these b's is a contrast of the cell means divided by the sum of the squares of the contrast coefficients, as we can see in the matrix $\mathbf{B}$.

The vector $\mathbf{M}$ spans the space in which the mean vector lies; the vectors $\mathbf{A_1}$ and $\mathbf{A_2}$ span the space in which the vector of the effects of Factor A lies; the vectors $\mathbf{B_1}$ and $\mathbf{B_2}$ span the space in which the vector of the effects of Factor B lies; and the vectors $\mathbf{A_1B_1}$, $\mathbf{A_1B_2}$, $\mathbf{A_2B_1}$, and $\mathbf{A_2B_2}$ span the space in which the vector of the interaction effects lies.

*9.14.2 A useful fact. Note that the vector $\mathbf{A_1}$ is the vector of coefficients for the contrast whose interaction with Factor B we are interested in. Now note that the interaction vectors $\mathbf{A_1B_1}$ and $\mathbf{A_1B_2}$ are the interaction vectors formed by using $\mathbf{A_1}$ with the vectors spanning the space for the Factor B effects. These two vectors $\mathbf{A_1B_1}$ and $\mathbf{A_1B_2}$ span the space in which the interaction of the contrast with Factor B lies. Similarly, if we were interested in how the contrast of the Factor B means represented by the vector $\mathbf{B_2}$ interacts with Factor A, that is, whether the quantities $M_{i1} - 2M_{i2} + M_{i3}$ are equal for all values of i, we would be interested in the vectors $\mathbf{A_1B_2}$ and $\mathbf{A_2B_2}$ since these span the space in which the vector of the interaction of that contrast with Factor A lies. **The first part of the useful fact is that the interaction of any contrast with any factor may be determined in a similar fashion. The second part of the useful fact is that the interaction of any contrast with any portion of a factor represented by any contrast or set of contrasts may also be determined in the same way.**

Thus, for example, the interaction of the contrast represented by A_1 with that by B_2 lies in the space spanned by the vector A_1B_2.

Now the distinction we sought to make in this section was between the case where a contrast interacts with another factor and where it does not. Let A_1 be the vector of coefficients for the contrast in question. let $B_1 ... B_J$ be the vectors for Factor B. Then $A_1B_1, A_1B_2, ..., A_1B_J$ will be the vectors for the interaction of the contrast with Factor B and for this interaction to be zero, all of the b coefficients of vectors $A_1B_1, A_1B_2, ...,$ A_1B_J will theoretically be zero.

**TABLE 9.13 DATA AND CELL MEANS
FOR A TWO-FACTOR DESIGN**

		Factor B				Factor B		
		1	2	3		1	2	3
Factor A	1	1 / 3	7 / 9	4 / 6	1	2	8	5
	2	3 / 5	9 / 11	3 / 5	2	4	10	4
	3	5 / 7	11 / 13	2 / 4	3	6	12	3

*9.14.3 Sums of squares as sums of squared lengths of orthogonal vectors.
We will use the symbol $\|V\|$ to denote the length of a vector V, so that $\|V\|^2$ will denote the squared length of the vector V and will thus be a sum of squares. Using this notation we can write the following identities:

$$SS_{Mean} = \|b_M M\|^2$$

$$SS_A = \|b_{A1}A_1\|^2 + \|b_{A2}A_2\|^2$$

$$SS_B = \|b_{B1}B_1\|^2 + \|b_{B2}B_2\|^2$$

$$SS_{AXB} = \|b_{A1B1}A_1B_1\|^2 + \|b_{A1B2}A_1B_2\|^2 + \|b_{A2B1}A_2B_1\|^2 + \|b_{A2B2}A_2B_2\|^2.$$

Let C_{ij} be the element in a column vector V of X^t that corresponds to the cell mean M_{ij}. We know that the coefficient b of V is $(\Sigma_i\Sigma_jC_{ij}M_{ij})/\Sigma_i\Sigma_jC_{ij}^2$. It is also obvious that any of the terms of the form $\|bV\|^2$ are equal to $b^2\|V\|^2 = b^2\Sigma_i\Sigma_jC_{ij}^2 = [(\Sigma_i\Sigma_jC_{ij}M_{ij})/\Sigma_i\Sigma_jC_{ij}^2]^2(\Sigma_i\Sigma_jC_{ij}^2) = (\Sigma_i\Sigma_jC_{ij}M_{ij})^2/\Sigma_i\Sigma_jC_{ij}^2$. Thus every sum of squares consists of pieces that are of the form $(\Sigma_i\Sigma_jC_{ij}M_{ij})^2/\Sigma_i\Sigma_jC_{ij}^2$—that is, the square of the value of a contrast divided by the sum of the squares of the contrast coefficients. In general, for Factor A with its three levels, $SS_A = nM_1.^2 + nM_2.^2 + nM_3.^2 - 3nM_{..}^2$. For one score per cell as in the example, $SS_A = M_1.^2 + M_2.^2 + M_3.^2 - 3M_{..}^2$. We can easily confirm algebraically that this equals $\|b_{A1}A_1\|^2 + \|b_{A2}A_2\|^2$

$$SS_A = M_1.^2 + M_2.^2 + M_3.^2 - 3M_{..}^2 = M_1.^2 + M_2.^2 + M_3.^2 - 3[(M_1. + M_2.$$

$$+ M_3.)/3]^2 = 2/3(M_1.^2 + M_2.^2 + M_3.^2 + M_1.M_2. + M_2.M_3. + M_1.M_3.),$$

and

$$\|b_{A1}A_1\|^2 + \|b_{A2}A_2\|^2 = (M_3. - M_1.)^2/2 + (M_1. - 2 M_2. + M_3.)^2/6$$

$$= M_3.^2/2 + M_1.^2/2 - M_1.M_3. + (M_1.^2 + 4M_2.^2 + M_3.^2 - 4M_1.M_2. + 2M_2.M_3.$$

$$- 4M_1.M_3.)/6 = 2/3(M_1.^2 + M_2.^2 + M_3.^2 + M_1.M_2. + M_2.M_3. + M_1.M_3.) = SS_A.$$

When certain contrasts used in trend tests (see Chapter 10) are used, the sets of orthogonal vectors are available in tables and could be used to facilitate computations. But with most contrasts that might be selected, the remaining orthogonal vectors of contrast coefficients would have to be computed. This could be done using the Gram-Schmidt process, but it is not an economical procedure. Instead we would use the procedures given in the next section.

9.15 Computing the sum of squares for the interaction of a contrast with a factor. The interaction of a contrast of the A means with Factor B implies that the values of the contrast at the several levels of B are not the same, and therefore do not equal the value of the contrast of the marginal A means, averaged over Factor B. We have seen that when there is one score per cell, the sum of squares for any contrast is just the square of the contrast divided by the sum of the squares of the contrast coefficients. But when there are n scores per cell, then the dimensionality of the vector space is n times greater, there are n times the number of entries in each vector, and consequently the sum of squares is n times the square of the contrast divided by the sum of the squares of the contrast coefficients. The sum of squares for the contrast at the jth level of Factor B is therefore $n(\Sigma_i C_i M_{ij})^2/\Sigma C_i^2$, and the sum of squares that reflects the difference between the contrasts at the several levels of B and the overall average contrast is the sum of the squares for the separate contrasts minus the sum of the squares for the contrast of the average values,

An Introduction to the Analysis of Variance

$$SS_{ContrastXB} = \Sigma_j n(\Sigma_i C_i M_{ij})^2 / \Sigma_i C_i^2 \ - \ Jn(\Sigma_i C_i M_i)^2 / \Sigma_i C_i^2. \tag{9.2}$$

We will do a numerical example using this formula and the contrast of the third level of Factor A with the first level. Then we will confirm that it gives the same value as does $\|b_{A1B1}A_1B_1\|^2 + \|b_{A1B2}A_1B_2\|^2$, the portion of the interaction

TABLE 9.14 DATA FOR A TWO-FACTOR DESIGN

	A_1			A_2			A_3			A_4	
B_1	B_2	B_3	B_1	B_2	B_3	B_1	B_2	B_3	B_1	B_2	B_3
1	1	2	4	5	5	9	8	7	8	3	3
2	1	2	5	6	3	0	7	6	7	5	2
1	2	1	4	4	4	1	7	5	8	4	2
3	1	1	5	4	4	0	6	4	9	7	3
2	1	1	3	6	3	1	8	5	9	6	4
1	3	2	4	4	5	9	7	4	9	5	3
2	2	2	5	5	4	0	9	6	8	6	4
1	1	1	3	4	5	1	8	5	9	7	3
13	12	12	33	38	33	81	60	42	67	43	24

TABLE 9.15 CELL MEANS FOR AN A x B FACTORIAL DESIGN

	A_1	A_2	A_3	A_4
B_1	μ_{11}	μ_{21}	μ_{31}	μ_{41}
B_2	μ_{12}	μ_{22}	μ_{32}	μ_{42}
B_3	μ_{13}	μ_{23}	μ_{33}	μ_{43}

sum of squares that we have seen equals SS_{A1XB}. We will do the example with two scores per cell so that we can see how n enters. The data are shown in Table 9.13. Applying equation 9.2 to the means in Table 9.13 and noting that n = 2 and that the marginal means for Factor A are 5, 6, and 7, we have $SS_{ContrastXB} = 2(6-2)^2/2 + 2(12-8)^2/2 + 2(3-5)^2/2 - 3(2)(7-5)^2/2 = 24$. Using the orthogonal vector approach to the sum of squares we have that $SS_{ContrastXB} = [2(M_{11}+M_{33})-2(M_{13}+M_{31})]^2/8 + [2(2M_{12}+M_{13}+M_{33}) - 2(M_{11}+ M_{13} +2M_{32})]^2/24 = [2(2+3) -2(5+6)]^2/8 + [2(16+6+3)-2(2+5+24)]^2/24 = 144/8 +144/24 = 24$, confirming that in this case $\Sigma_j n(\Sigma_i C_i M_{ij})^2 / \Sigma_i C_i^2 \ - \ Jn(\Sigma_i C_i M_i)^2 / \Sigma_i C_i^2$ gives the same value

TABLE 9.16 TABLE OF CONTRAST COEFFICIENTS

		A_1	A_2	A_3	A_4
		1	-1	0	0
B_1	1	1	-1	0	0
B_2	-1	-1	1	0	0
B_3	0	0	0	0	0

TABLE 9.17 TABLE OF CONTRAST COEFFICIENTS

		A_1	A_2	A_3	A_4
		1/2	-1	1/2	0
B_1	1	1/2	-1	1/2	0
B_2	-1	-1/2	1	-1/2	0
B_3	0	0	0	0	0

as does $\|b_{A1B1}A_1B_1\|^2 + \|b_{A1B2}A_1B_2\|^2$. (It is useful to note that the degrees of freedom for this sum of squares is B - 1. This can be seen by noting that B squared numbers are added and one squared number is subtracted to obtain the sum of squares.)

Consider the data in Table 9.14. Assume A and B are fixed effects and the design is a 4 x 3 factorial design with no repeated measures. Assume the question of interest is whether the contrast $(\mu_{A1} + \mu_{A3})/2 - \mu_{A2}$ interacts with Factor B. The contrast of the sample means at each level of Factor B are given by: B_1: $(1.625 + 10.125)/2 - 4.125 = 1.75$; B_2: $(1.5 + 7.5)/2 - 4.75 = -.25$; and B_3: $(1.5 + 5.25)/2 - 4.125 = -.75$. The marginal means for A_1, A_2, and A_3 are 1.5417, 4.3333, and 7.625, so the marginal value of the contrast $(A_1 + A_3)/2 - A_2$ is $(1.5417 + 7.625)/2 - 4.3333 = .25$. The value of $\Sigma_i C_i^2 = (1/2)^2 + (1/2)^2 + (-1)^2 = 1.5$. Using these values in equation [9.2] gives $SS_{ContrastXB} = [8(1.75)^2 + 8(-.25)^2 + 8(-.75)^2]/1.5 - (3)(8)(.25)^2/1.5 = 18.67$. This component of the A x B interaction has $(1)(3 - 1) = 2$ degrees of freedom so $MS_{Contrast \, X \, B}$ would be 9.33 and would be compared to MS_{error}.

9.16 Computing the sum of squares for the contrast of a contrast without contrast scores. Consider the 4 x 3, A x B factorial design with means μ_{ij}, where i indexes the A level and j, the B level. It is convenient for showing the correspondence between these means and the contrast coefficients to be obtained to display the means in Table 9.15. Suppose we are interested in whether the difference between the effects of levels A_1 and A_2 is different at level B_1 than it is at level B_2. The natural contrast to answer this question is $(\mu_{11} - \mu_{21}) - (\mu_{12} - \mu_{22})$, which equals zero under the null hypothesis that the difference between A_1 and A_2 is the same at both levels of B. We can obtain the appropriate contrast coefficients by assigning to the levels of A the values 1, -1, 0, and 0 (because it is A_1 versus A_2) and to the levels of B the values 1, -1, and 0 (because we are interested in B_1 versus B_2) in the margins of Table 9.16. The entries in each cell of the table are obtained by multiplication of the row entry by the column entry for the row and column of that cell. Note that the coefficients in this table give exactly the correct multipliers of the corresponding entries in the μ_{ij} table above to yield the contrast of interest, $(\mu_{11} - \mu_{21})$ - $(\mu_{12} - \mu_{22})$. If we wanted to know if the average of A_1 and A_3 differed from the value of A_2 differently at level B_1 than at level B_2, the contrast would be $[(\mu_{11} + \mu_{31})/2 - \mu_{21}] - [(\mu_{12} + \mu_{32})/2 - \mu_{22}]$. The contrast coefficients are obtained in the same fashion and are shown in Table 9.17. And if we wanted to ask whether the contrast of the average of A_1 and A_3 with A_2 is different at level 3 of B than it is on the average at levels 1 and 2 of B, we could obtain the appropriate contrast coefficients as the products of 1.2, -1. 1/2. 0 for the A levels and 1/2, 1/2, and -1 for the B levels, giving the coefficients in Table 9.18. Finally, as in the foregoing, let C_A be any contrast of Factor A means with contrast coefficients C_{Ai} and let C_{Bi} be contrast coefficients for Factor B appropriate to asking the question of whether the contrast of the A means differs at one combination of levels of B from the value of the contrast of A means at another combination of levels of B. Then the sum of squares for this contrast of a contrast will be

$$n(\Sigma_i\Sigma_j C_{Ai}C_{Bi}M_{ij})^2 / \Sigma_i\Sigma_j(C_{Ai}{}^2 C_{Bi}{}^2).$$

TABLE 9.18 TABLE OF CONTRAST COEFFICIENTS

	A_1	A_2	A_3	A_4
	1/2	-1	1/2	0
B_1 1/2	1/4	-1/2	1/4	0
B_2 1/2	1/4	-1/2	1/4	0
B_3 -1	-1/2	1	-1/2	0

TABLE 9.19 COEFFICIENTS FOR TESTING THE HYPOTHESIS THAT THE DIFFERENCE BETWEEN THE AVERAGE OF FACTOR A LEVELS 1 AND 2 AND THE AVERAGE OF FACTOR A LEVELS 3 AND 4 IS DIFFERENT AT LEVEL 1 OF FACTOR B THAN IT IS AT THE AVERAGE OF LEVELS 2 AND 3 OF FACTOR B

		A_1	A_2	A_3	A_4
		1/2	1/2	-1/2	-1/2
B_1	1	1/2	1/2	-1/2	-1/2
B_2	-1/2	-1/4	-1/4	1/4	1/4
B_3	-1/2	-1/4	-1/4	1/4	1/4

As an example, using Table 9.14, suppose we want to know if for Factor A the contrast of the average of levels 1 and 2 with the average of levels 3 and 4 is different at level 1 of B than it is at the average of levels 2 and 3 of B. Then the coefficients for the cell means would be as shown in Table 9.19, so the sum of squares, on 1 degree of freedom, for the numerator of the F-ratio would be $8[(1/2)(1.625) + (1/2)(4.125) - (1/2)(10.125) - (1/2)(8.375) - (1/4)(1.5) - (1/4)(4.75) + (1/4)(7.5) + (1/4)(5.375) - (1/4)(1.5) - (1/4)(4.125) + (1/4)(5.25) + (1/4)(3)]^2 / [(1/2)^2 + (1/2)^2 + (-1/2)^2 + (-1/2)^2 + (-1/4)^2 + (-1/4)^2 + (1/4)^2 + (1/4)^2 + (-1/4)^2 + (-1/4)^2 + (1/4)^2 + (1/4)^2] = 8(-4.0625)^2/1.5 = 88.02$.

Consider the sum of squares just obtained for testing the null hypothesis that $(\mu_{11} + \mu_{21})/2 - (\mu_{31} + \mu_{41})/2$

$$= [(\mu_{12} + \mu_{22})/2 - (\mu_{32} + \mu_{42})/2 + (\mu_{13} + \mu_{23})/2 - (\mu_{33} + \mu_{43})/2]/2 \qquad [9.3]$$

TABLE 9.20 CONTRAST COEFFICIENTS FOR TESTING THE NULL HYPOTHESIS THAT THE DIFFERENCE BETWEEN $A_1 - (A_2 + A_3)/2$ AT B_1 AND AT B_2 IS THE SAME WHETHER AT LEVEL C_1 OR AT LEVEL C_2

		C_1			C_2			C_3		
		1			-1			0		
		A_1	A_2	A_3	A_1	A_2	A_3	A_1	A_2	A_3
		1	-1/2	-1/2	1	-1/2	-1/2	1	-1/2	-1/2
B_1	1	1	-1/2	-1/2	-1	1/2	1/2	0	0	0
B_2	-1	-1	1/2	1/2	1	-1/2	-1/2	0	0	0
B_3	0	0	0	0	0	0	0	0	0	0

TABLE 9.21 FICTIONAL DATA FOR A TREATMENTS x TREATMENTS x TREATMENTS x SUBJECTS DESIGN

		A_1			A_2			A_3			A_4		
		B_1	B_2	B_3	B_1	B_2	B_3	B_1	B_2	B_3	B_1	B_2	B_3
C_1	S1	2	5	8	11	11	8	8	2	9	12	9	5
	S2	3	4	7	5	3	4	5	3	6	6	3	5
	S3	3	6	7	11	11	8	9	12	6	10	5	10
	S4	2	5	8	11	5	12	5	12	9	12	9	12
C_2	S1	4	6	7	7	2	4	9	2	8	12	9	12
	S2	4	5	7	7	11	8	8	4	6	12	4	4
	S3	11	6	8	11	5	11	8	5	8	12	3	5
	S4	2	5	2	11	11	4	9	12	6	10	5	10
C_3	S1	3	6	8	8	5	8	6	5	9	12	5	4
	S2	11	5	2	5	5	11	9	4	6	12	5	12
	S3	3	3	3	5	3	4	6	4	6	12	12	4
	S4	4	4	2	10	2	11	10	9	9	10	3	10

that is, for testing the null hypothesis that the difference between the average effect for levels A_1 and A_2 and the average effects for levels A_3 and A_4 is the same at level B_1 as it is, on the average, at levels B_2 and B_3. As indicated above, the contrast coefficients for A are 1/2, 1/2, -1/2 and -1/2, and those for B are 1, -1/2, and -1/2, and the contrast coefficients applied to the cell means are the products of these. Suppose now that instead of the null hypothesis in equation [9.3], we are interested in the null hypothesis that the difference between the effect of level B_1 and the average effect of levels B_2 and B_3 is the same, on the average, at the first two levels of A as it is, on the average, at the second two levels of A. The contrast coefficients for testing this hypothesis would be identical to those for testing equation [9.3]. The sum of squares would therefore also be identical. In fact, there will always be a duality of this sort between one phrasing of a contrast x contrast component of a two-factor interaction and another phrasing. These will always be equivalent statements, which lead to the same sum of squares. This fact is reminiscent of and analogous to the fact that the entire A x B interaction null hypothesis can be couched in two equivalent forms also. That is, we can ask if the differences between the levels of A are the same at each level of B, or we can ask if the differences between levels of B are the same at each level of A.

9.17 Extension to the contrast of a contrast of a contrast, etc. It should be obvious that the idea of a contrast of a contrast can be extended to three or more factors. We will consider just one simple example and leave a more complicated version for the Exercises section. Suppose an A x B x C factorial design with three levels of each factor. The null hypothesis of interest is that the difference between $A_1 - (A_2 + A_13)/2$ at B_1 and at B_2 is the same whether at level C_1 or at level C_2. The contrast coefficients for the cell means are given in Table 9.20. The general formula for the sum of squares for a three-factor contrast of this sort is

$$n(\Sigma_i \Sigma_j \Sigma_k C_{Ai} C_{Bi} C_{Ck} M_{ijk})^2 / \Sigma_i \Sigma_j \Sigma_k (C_{Ai}^2 C_{Bi}^2 C_{Ck}^2).$$

9.18 Confidence intervals for contrasts. A $100(1 - \alpha)$ percent confidence interval for the contrast $\Sigma_i c_i \mu_i$ is given by

$$\Sigma_i c_i M_i - \sqrt{[F_{\alpha,1,dfe} MS_e(\Sigma_i c_i^2/n_i)]} \leq \Sigma_i c_i \mu_i \leq \Sigma_i c_i M_i +$$

$$\sqrt{[F_{\alpha,1,dfe} MS_e(\Sigma_i c_i^2/n_i)]}.$$

This follows immediately from the fact that

$$\Pr\{ [(\Sigma_i c_i M_i - \Sigma_i c_i \mu_i)^2 / \Sigma_i c_i^2/n_i] / MS_e \geq F_{\alpha,1,dfe} \} = \alpha,$$

so $\Pr\{ [(\Sigma_i c_i M_i - \Sigma_i c_i \mu_i)^2 \geq F_{\alpha,1,dfe} \Sigma_i c_i^2/n_i MS_e \} = \alpha,$

which implies that

$$\Pr\{ |\Sigma_i c_i M_i - \Sigma_i c_i \mu_i| \leq \sqrt{[F_{\alpha,1,dfe} \Sigma_i c_i^2/n_i MS_e]} \} = 1 - \alpha.$$

**TABLE 9.22 DATA FROM
EXERCISE 3, CHAPTER 6**

	Professor	
A	B	C
Teaching Asst.	Teaching Asst.	Teaching Asst.
a_A b_A c_A	a_B b_B c_B	a_C b_C c_C
47 49 38	37 42 29	41 37 39
41 45 36	19 49 35	39 33 36
39 50 33	29 38 32	45 36 29
46 42 36	30 39 28	46 35 31
48 45 40	18 37 29	42 42 40

**TABLE 9.23 DATA FROM
EXERCISE 13, CHAPTER 8**

	Subject	1	2	3	4
			Sequence		
Simple	1	211	209	201	220
	2	210	205	208	217
	3	199	219	207	212
	4	204	203	202	215
	5	201	204	223	215
		1	2	3	4
Complex	6	241	229	227	235
	7	238	217	223	248
	8	226	225	248	229
	9	223	232	234	221
	10	239	219	218	240
		1	2	3	4
Compound	11	243	234	229	222
	12	245	234	225	227
	13	225	229	225	223
	14	239	235	231	237
	15	240	239	223	224

For the data set in Table 9.13 we obtain a 95 percent confidence interval for the contrast $\mu_{A3} - \mu_{A1}$ as $(M_{A3} - M_{A1}) \pm \sqrt{(F_{\alpha,1,dfe}(\Sigma C_i/n_i)MS_e)} = (7 - 5) \pm \sqrt{[5.12\{[1^2 + (-1)^2]/6\}(2)]} = 2 \pm 1.8475$ giving the interval from .1525 to 3.8475.

Exercises

1. Using the data in Table 9.10 and assuming fixed effects for A and B, random effects for Subjects:

(a) Test the null hypothesis that $\mu_{A1} - \mu_{A2} = \mu_{A3} - \mu_{A4}$.

(b) Test the null hypothesis that the contrast in exercise #1(a) does not interact with Factor B.

(c) Test the null hypothesis that $(\mu_{B1} - \mu_{B2})/2 = \mu_{B3}$.

(d) Test the null hypothesis that the contrast in exercise 1(c) does not interact with Factor A.

2. The statistic $(\Sigma_i c_i M_i)^2/(\Sigma_i c_i^2/n_i)$ occurs as the numerator of the F-ratio in the test of the null hypothesis that the contrast $\Sigma_i c_i \mu_i = 0$. We expect that as the numerator of an F-ratio it must be a chi-square variable divided by its degrees of freedom, except for a quantity σ_e^2 that cancels out of the denominator against the same quantity that is found in MS_{error}. Since it has only one df, we can conclude that $(\Sigma_i c_i M_i)^2/[(\Sigma_i c_i^2/n_i)\sigma_e^2]$ must be distributed as chi-square when the null hypothesis is true. Prove that this is so. Hint: Show that $\Sigma_i c_i M_i$ is normally distributed, subtract its mean, divide by its variance, and square the result. This should give the square of a standard normal variable, which we have already agreed is distributed as chi-square on 1 df.

3. Using the data in Table 9.21 and assuming fixed effects for A, B, and C, and random effects for Subjects and assuming that A, B, and C are repeated measures variables:

(a) Test the null hypothesis that $(\mu_{A1} + \mu_{A2} + \mu_{A3})/3 - \mu_{A4} = 0$.

(b) Test the null hypothesis that the contrast in exercise 2(a) does not interact with the contrast $(\mu_{B1} + \mu_{B2})/2 - \mu_{B3} = 0$.

(c) Test the null hypothesis that the contrast in #2(a) does not interact with Factor C.

(d) Test the null hypothesis that the interaction of the contrast $(\mu_{A1} + \mu_{A2} + \mu_{A3})/3 - \mu_{A4} = 0$ with the contrast $(\mu_{B1} + \mu_{B2})/2 - \mu_{B3} = 0$ does not interact with the contrast $(\mu_{C1} + \mu_{C2})/2 - \mu_{C3}$.

4. Using the data in Table 9.22 from exercise 3 Chapter 6, and letting μ_A, μ_B, and μ_C be the population means for the populations of scores from which the three different course sections are viewed as samples, test the hypothesis that

$(\mu_A + \mu_B)/2 = \mu_C$ against the alternative of inequality. Use a .05 significance level.

5. Using the data in exercise 4, find a 95 percent confidence interval for $(\mu_A + \mu_B)/2 - \mu_C$.

6. Using the data in exercise 7 Chapter 8, test the following hypotheses:

(a) The average performance during the last three blocks equaled the average performance during the first three blocks.

(b) The average drop in food intake from Block 1 to Block 2 equaled the average drop in food intake from Block 3 to Block 4.

(c) The difference between the drop from Block 1 to Block 2 and the drop from Block 3 to Block 4 was the same for the Tumor groups as for the Control groups.

TABLE 9.24   DATA FROM EXERCISE 10, CHAPTER 8

	Retention Interval													
	2.5 secs.					5.0 secs.					10 secs.			
	Dosage					Dosage					Dosage			
Subject	Sal.	.125	.25	50		Sal.	.125	.25	.50		Sal.	.125	.25	.50
1	.89	.81	.73	.61		.79	.74	.65	.56		.68	.63	.54	.48
2	.90	.79	.75	.60		.80	.75	.65	.57		.69	.65	.56	.49
3	.88	.80	.72	.59		.80	.73	.64	.58		.70	.64	.55	.47
4	.90	.79	.73	.59		.78	.73	.66	.59		.68	.64	.54	.48
5	.88	.80	.75	.60		.80	.75	.65	.56		.70	.64	.54	.48

TABLE 9.25   MEANS FOR EXERCISE 16

		A_1	A_2	A_3
	B_1	5	3	2
C_1	B_2	6	2	4
	B_3	7	1	6
	B_1	9	4	5
C_2	B_2	10	3	7
	B_3	11	2	9
	B_1	12	5	7
C_3	B_2	13	4	9
	B_3	14	3	11

(d) The difference between the drop from Block 1 to Block 2 and the drop from Block 3 to Block 4 was the same for the Tumor group as for the Control group, under the Varied Diet condition.

7. Using the data in Table 9.23 from exercise 13 at the end of Chapter 8, test the hypothesis that the mean reaction time to the Complex stimuli lies exactly midway between the mean reaction time to Simple stimuli and the mean reaction time to Compound stimuli.

8. Find a 95 percent confidence interval for the contrast $(\mu_1 + \mu_2 + \mu_3)/3 - \mu_4$, where μ_i is the population mean reaction time to Sequence i for the data in exercise 7. Use this confidence interval to test the hypothesis that the mean reaction time to the fourth sequence equals the average reaction time to the other three sequences.

9. The text showed that for the data in Table 9.14, the sum of squares for the interaction of B with the contrast $(A_1 + A_3)/2 - A_2$ is 18.67. Since Factor A has three degrees of freedom, there are two other contrasts of the A levels that are mutually orthogonal and are orthogonal to the contrast in the text. Verify that $A_1 - A_3$ and $(A_1 + A_2 + A_3)/3 - A_4$ are two such contrasts. Then, using the data in

Table 9.14, find the sum of squares for the interaction of each of these two

contrasts with Factor B, find the sum of squares for the A x B interaction, and show that the sums of squares for the interactions of these three orthogonal contrasts with B add to give the sum of squares for the interaction of A with B.

10. Using the data in Table 8.21, find a 99 percent confidence interval for the mean difference in looking times between scrambled stimuli and unscrambled stimuli. Use that confidence interval to test, at the .01 significance level, the null hypothesis that there is no such difference.

11. Write out an abbreviated summary table for the analyses of the following data, showing the sources, the degrees of freedom and the expected mean squares:

(a) the design in exercise 4;

(b) the design in exercise 7;

(c) the design in exercise 12.

12. Using the data in Table 9.24 from exercise 10 Chapter 8, test the hypothesis:

(a) that sensitivity under Scopolamine equaled sensitivity under Saline.

(b) that sensitivity under .50 mg/kg was lower than sensitivity under .125 mg/kg.

(c) that sensititivity was no different after a 10-second retention interval than was sensitivity on the average after a 2.5- or 5.0-second retention interval.

(d) that under the 10-second retention interval, there was no difference in sensitivity between the the effect of receiving .25 mg/kg and the effect of receiving .50 mg/kg. Remember this is a component of the Retention Interval x Dosage interaction and so gets tested against the Retention Interval x Dosage x Subjects interaction mean square, unless you use contrast scores, in which case the error term is based on just those contrast scores.

e) that the difference between the effect of receiving .25 mg/kg and the effect of receiving .50 mg/kg was the same at the 10-second retention interval as it was at the 5-second retention interval.

13. Use a contrast score analysis on the data in #12 to test the null hypothesis that the difference between .50 mg/kg and Saline interacted with Retention interval.

14. Continuing with exercise 12, find two more contrasts orthogonal to the contrast between .50 mg/kg and Saline, and, using contrast scores, test whether either of these two contrasts interacted with Retention Interval.

15. State in your own words the difference between a contrast and a contrast score.

16. A contrast in Factor A would not interact with B x C if the change in the contrast over levels of B at levels 2 and 3 of C could be gotten by addition of some constant (possibly different for 2 than for 3) to the values of the contrast at level 1 of C. Using the means in Table 9.25:

(a) Does the contrast $C1 = A_1 - A_2$ appear to interact with B? with C? with B x C?

(b) Graph the $M_{A1} - M_{A2}$ x B interaction.

(c) Graph the $M_{A1} - M_{A2}$ x C interaction.

(d) Does the contrast $C2 = (A_1 + A_2)/2 - A_3$ interact with B? with C? with B x C?

(e) For each contrast C1 and C2, graph the nine values of the contrast at the various levels of B x C.

17. Assume a 4 x 4 x 3 A x B x C factorial design with no repeated measurements. Let i index A, j index B, and k index C. The null hypothesis is that

$$\sum_{j=1}^{2} [(\mu_{1j1} + \mu_{2j1}) - (\mu_{3j1} + \mu_{4j1})] - \sum_{j=3}^{4} [(\mu_{1j1} + \mu_{2j1}) - (\mu_{3j1} + \mu_{4j1})] =$$

$$\sum_{k=2}^{3} \left\{ \sum_{j=1}^{2} [(\mu_{1jk} + \mu_{2jk}) - (\mu_{3jk} + \mu_{4jk})] - \sum_{j=3}^{4} [(\mu_{1jk} + \mu_{2jk}) - (\mu_{3jk} + \mu_{4jk})] \right\}/2$$

(a) State the null hypothesis in words.

(b) Write an expression for the sum of squares for testing the null hypothesis.

18. The null hypothesis is that the difference between the A_1 versus A_2 difference at B_1 and the A_1 versus A_2 difference at B_2 does not change from level C_1 to level C_2.

(a) Write the null hypothesis using μ_{ijk} expressions as in problem exercise 17.

(b) Show the table of contrast coefficients for the M_{ijk}.

10

Trend Tests

10.1 The spacing and order of the values of a qualitative variable along the axis of a graph is arbitrary. Suppose an experiment had been run with students from four high schools as the subjects. Call the schools HS1, HS2, HS3, and HS4. Suppose that the mean scores for the subjects in the four schools turned out to be 8.0, 9.0, 10.0, and 11.0. We might graph the means as shown in Figure 10.1.

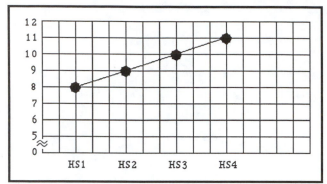

Figure 10.1. Graph of the means for the four high schools.

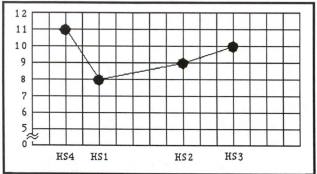

Figure 10.2. Graph of the means for the four high schools.

It would appear that we have found a linear relationship between mean score and high school. But things are not always as they appear. We must ask several questions about the arrangement of symbols in Figure 10.1. What is the meaning of the lines connecting the points? Do they indicate potential other points that simply do not happen to be filled in due to the lack of data? Or are they just a device to lead the eye from one point to the next? Also, why are the High Schools located at the specific points selected along the horizontal axis? And why are they spaced at the distances they are spaced? Consider Figure 10.2.

We see that the order of locating the high schools along the horizontal axis is different, the spacing along that axis is irregular, and as a consequence the formerly linear relationship now appears curvilinear. Is one figure properly drawn and the other improperly? Not at all. We have here an example of the arbitrariness that accompanies the values of a qualitative variable when it comes to drawing graphs. There is nothing about the labels HS1, HS2, HS3, and HS4 that carries order information. The numbers distinguish one high school from another, but the numbers function as names rather than as expressions of some empirical ordering of the high schools. And, of course, if the numbers serve as names, they also do not express some degree of spacing that exists between the high schools on some physical or psychological scale, so the labels can be located arbitrarily along the axis. This means that the appearance of the shape of the lines joining the points is arbitrary and has no significance. In fact, the lines joining the points serve only to guide the eye from one point to another since there is no justification for expecting some other point to be located at any particular place along any line, the locations of the lines being arbitrary.

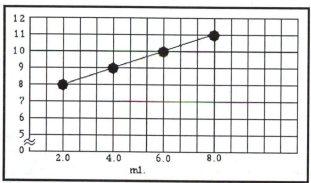

Figure 10.3. Graph of the means for the four dosages.

10.2 With a quantitative variable, the order and spacing are determined. Now suppose that the four groups of scores for which we have graphed the means were instead obtained from four groups of experimental animals that differed by how much of some chemical compound they were given to ingest in their daily food ration. Suppose the amounts were 2.0, 4.0, 6.0, and 8.0 milliliters per cubic centimeter of food. Suppose the graph of the results appeared as in Figure 10.3.

Here we see that the order of the dosage level as graphed corresponds to the order of the amount of the dose. Furthermore, the equal spacing of the values represents the equal differences in the dosage amounts. Thus, the distance between the symbol 2.0 and 4.0 is the same as the distance between 4.0 and 6.0, corresponding to the equality in the differences in amounts, the first difference being 4.0 - 2.0 = 2.0 and the second being 6.0 - 4.0 = 2.0 also. We would find it disorderly and confusing if we were to juggle either the ordering or the spacing (although at least the spacing is sometimes altered when we perform scale transformations such as using the logarithm of the dosage amount rather than the amount itself). Finally, the lines we have drawn connecting the points have a rationale that goes beyond serving as an aid to the eye. The observed linear relationship suggests, but of course does not prove, that if an intermediate dosage such as 3.0 ml had been given, we would observe that the mean score would also fall at the appropriate point on the line, namely, at 8.5.

Here we see a critical difference between our use of qualitative and quantitative variables. With a quantitative variable, the order and spacing of the values of the independent variable are meaningful and may not be trifled with, and the shape, pattern, or configuration of the graphed values has an interpretation and may be used for prediction, both interpolatively to values within the investigated range of the variables and extrapolatively, with greater risk of mistake, to values outside the investigated range. In this chapter we will be concerned with the use of quantitative independent variables and the inferences that can be drawn concerning the shape of the pattern of means when quantitative independent variables are used.

10.3 The effects of sampling error. Because the values that we obtain are subject to sampling error, we rarely find points representing group means lying exactly on a line or exactly on some familiar curve. Often we see a pattern that suggests that the points gradually slope upward or downward as the independent variable increases, but we also see reversals of this general tendency so that we are not sure whether the pattern reflects a systematic relationship or has perhaps occurred due to chance fluctuations of the points above and below a general mean value. In addition, there sometimes appears to be a curvilinear relationship of one sort or another, but here too we are not always confident that we are not reading this into points that have wandered by chance away from the general mean. For example, in Figure 10.3, if the value of 8 at 2.0 ml and the value of 11 at 8.0 ml were each chance deviations from, say, 9.5, due to sampling variability, then the apparently positive slope of the line would be a chance phenomenon. In this chapter we are going to consider a set of orthogonal contrasts that permit us to draw statistically sound conclusions regarding such questions.

10.4. Orthogonal polynomial analysis. There are two standard approaches to determining the shape or pattern taken by the means on the dependent variable. One approach attempts to represent the entire pattern by a single function. The statistical method appropriate to this approach is known as **regression analysis**. The simplest case of this, simple linear regression, is covered in introductory statistics. A second approach attempts to represent the pattern as the linear combination of a set of simple, independent, prototypical patterns involving straight lines and curves. This approach is known as **orthogonal polynomal analysis**. We will take up orthogonal polynomial analysis in this chapter, and then in Chapter 12 we will look a little at regression analysis. Our goal in this chapter is to arrive at a special set of contrasts that will permit us to perform significance tests that statistically evaluate the extent to which the pattern taken by the sample means of the dependent variable is formed by the addition of characteristic patterns or shapes such as straight lines, quadratic curves, and so forth.

We begin by considering a simple example where the means of our dependent variable are associated with three values of the independent variable. We will assume in all of our discussion, until we explicitly change that assumption, that the values of our independent variable are equally spaced, as are the ml values in Figure 10.3. Furthermore, it will be convenient in our example to treat the three means as a vector in three space. The simplest case would be that where all three values of the dependent variable are the same. Suppose those three values are [5,5,5]. This would graph as a horizontal line. We could write it also as 5[1,1,1]. If the three values were [11,11,11] we could write it as 11[1,1,1]. It is obvious that if we have three values that are all some value μ, then we can write them as μ[1,1,1]. This would be the case of no trend. We already know how to conduct the statistical analysis that would demonstrate that all of the means equal a common value μ. It is just the overall analysis of variance. The absence of an effect of the independent variable would indicate that all of the means are the same and that they would therefore graph as a horizontal line.

Suppose, now that there is a positive linear trend to our means. This means that as the values of the independent variable increase, so do the values of the dependent variable and the increase in the dependent variable is proportional to the increase in the independent variable. Suppose the three means are [4,5,6]. We can write this as [4,5,6] = [5,5,5] + ([4,5,6] - [5,5,5]) = [5,5,5] + [-1,0,1] = 5[1,1,1] + 1[-1,0,1]. Now suppose that there is a more pronounced positive trend in the means. Let's say they are [1,5,9]. For each equal increment in the independent variable, the dependent variable increases by four. We can write this as [1,5,9] = 5[1,1,1] + 4[-1,0,1]. We can generalize this observation. Suppose that three means show a positive linear trend. Then they can be written as [m-b, m, m+b], one step in the value of the independent variable producing an increase of b in the value of the dependent variable. But [m-b, m, m+b] = m[1,1,1] + b[-1,0,1]. Naturally a set of means showing a negative linear trend where the means decrease as the independent variable increases could be written in the same way, with b a negative number. So we see that any set of three means that lie on a straight line can be written as a linear combination of the vectors [1,1,1] and [-1,0,1]. We also note that the vectors [1,1,1] and [-1,0,1] are orthogonal to each other. Thus we can say that any vector of three means lying on a straight line can be written as a linear combination of these two orthogonal vectors. We can also note that when m is large relative to b, say m = 100, b = 1, we have a set of means, say [99,100,101], that show a trend but we would say it is slight, perhaps negligible; when m is small relative to b, say m = 1, b = 100, we have, say, [-99,1,101], showing a much more pronounced trend. We can consider that we have analyzed the three means into two components, one having to do with the tendency of the means to be equal and the other having to do with their tendency to lie on a line with a positive or negative slope and therefore not be equal.

We also know that three means can be unequal without lying on a line. Therefore there is a third possible tendency, the tendency of the three means to be unequal and to not lie on a line. We can expect this tendency to be represented by a third vector. To keep these three tendencies independent of each other we will choose as our third vector a vector that is orthogonal to [1,1,1] and [-1,0,1]. Let this vector be [u,v,w]. The first orthogonality requirement is that $[1,1,1] \cdot [u,v,w] = 0$, so $u+v+w = 0$ and the second orthogonality requirement is that $[-1,0,1] \cdot [u,v,w] = 0$, so $w = u$. Combining these we have that $v = -2w = -2u$. We can choose $w = 1$ to obtain $u = w = 1$, $v = -2$ as our third vector. (We have the right to choose $w = 1$ because we have three variables, u, v, and w, but only two constraints; therefore the third is completely arbitrary and can be assigned whatever value we choose.) Thus our third vector can be [1,-2,1] or any multiple of it. For an arbitrary vector of three means $[\mu_1, \mu_2, \mu_3]$ we can write

$$[\mu_1, \mu_2, \mu_3] = \mu[1,1,1] + L\ [-1,0,1] + Q\ [1,-2,1].$$

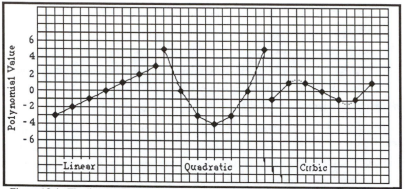

Figure 10.4. The linear, quadratic, and cubic shapes.

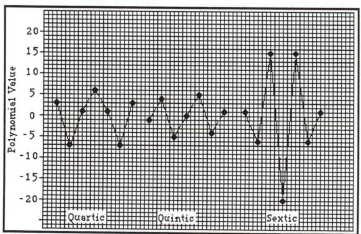

Figure 10.5. The quartic, quintic, and sextic shapes.

(Our use of *L* and *Q* will be clear in a moment.) The values in the vector $\mu[1,1,1]$, when graphed as a function of the independent variable, graph as a horizontal line at the value μ on the vertical axis. The values in $L[-1,0,1]$ graph as a straight line with slope equal to *L*, and the values in $Q[1,-2,1]$ graph as a quadratic function, the values taken by a second-order polynomial of the form $y = ax^2 + bx + c$. For example if we choose $Q = 1$ and x values of -1, 0, and 1, the quadratic function $y = ax^2 + bx + c$ with $a = 3$, $b = 0$, and $c = -2$ would give the values 1, -2, and 1. We can say that the vector $Q[1,-2,1]$ expresses the tendency of the means to lie on a quadratic function rather than on a horizontal line or on a line with slope *L*.

We should note that the three vectors $\mu[1,1,1]$, $L[-1,0,1]$, and $Q[1,-2,1]$ are mutually orthogonal and therefore span three-dimensional space. Thus every vector of three means can be expressed as a linear combination of these three vectors. Every graph of three means will display means that express more or less of the three tendencies: horizontal, linear, and quadratic. Furthermore, as we might expect from our explorations in Chapter 3 into the geometry of ANOVA there is a degree of freedom and a sum of squares associated with each of these three vectors. In fact, the elements of these vectors are used as contrast coefficients, and these degrees of freedom and sums of squares are just those associated with such contrasts. We will return to these contrasts and their df and sums of squares after we consider the situation where there are more than three values of the independent variable.

10.5 The shapes of trend. For each level of the independent variable, there will be a degree of freedom. One of these df will be associated with the tendency of the means to be equal, that is, with a graph that is a horizontal line. The others' df can each be associated with a mode of departure from equality of those means. Each of these modes has a characteristic shape. Each such shape is the shape of a curve described by a polynomial of the form $y = ax^n + bx^{n-1} + cx^{n-2} + ... + dx^3 + ex^2 + fx + g$. Figure 10.4 and Figure 10.5 show these shapes for the first six such shapes. These six shapes correspond to the polynomials with n = 1, 2, ..., 6 respectively. They are known as the **linear, quadratic, cubic, quartic, quintic, and sextic shapes**. Figure 10.4 shows the linear, quadratic and cubic; figure 10.5 shows the quartic, quintic, and sextic. Of course, for all six of these shapes to be relevant, the independent variable factor would require at least seven levels so that there would be six df. For this example of an independent variable with seven levels we have seven means. The means may be thought of as a vector in seven-dimensional space. That seven-dimensional space is spanned by the seven mutually orthogonal vectors [1,1,1,1,1,1,1], [-3,-2,-1,0,1,2,3], [5,0,-3,-4,-3,0,5], [-1,1,1,0,-1,-1,1], [3,-7,1,6,1,-7,3], [-1,4,-5,0,5,-4,1], and [1,-6,15,-20,15,-6,1]. We can say that $[\mu_1, \mu_2, \mu_3, \mu_4, \mu_5, \mu_6, \mu_7] = \mu[1,1,1,1,1,1,1] + L[-3,-2,-1,0,1,2,3] + Q_d[5,0,-3,-4,-3,0,5] + C[-1,1,1,0,-1,-1,1] + Q_r[3,-7,1,6,1,-7,3] + Q_n[-1,4,-5,0,5,-4,1] + S[1,-6,15,-20,15,-6,1]$.

The elements in each of these vectors except the first may be used as contrast coefficients to obtain a contrast of the means. All of the contrasts so obtained will be mutually orthogonal . The elements in these vectors are referred to as **orthogonal polynomial coefficients**. Excluding the mean vector, the vectors are, in order of occurrence, the vectors of orthogonal polynomial coefficients for the linear, quadratic, cubic, quartic, quintic, and sextic components of trend. The coefficients L, C, Q_d, and so on are multipliers that take the value zero if the means do not have a tendency to lie in the corresponding shape and take nonzero values if they do.

10.6 The values of the sums of squares when the group means conform exactly to a single shape. We recall from Chapter 3 that the sum of squares for some source is the squared length of some corresponding vector. When we test the significance of the various contrasts that indicate whether the shape of the means conforms to these linear, quadratic, and other shapes, a sum of squares is obtained for each such contrast. Each such sum of squares is the squared length of a vector such as the ones mentioned in section 10.5. Each such sum of squares has one df and is tested according to the usual procedure for testing a contrast. If the shape of the means is exactly one of the component shapes, then the entire sum of squares for the independent variable factor will exactly equal the sum of squares for that component, and the sum of squares for all other components will be zero. Thus, for example, if the means lie exactly on a straight line with a nonzero slope, then the sum of squares for the linear component will exactly equal the sum of squares for the independent variable.

Note that the sum of squares for the linear component does not include the sum of squares for the mean, and neither does the sum of squares for the independent variable, since the sum of squares for the mean, T^2/N, has been subtracted out. The linear component corresponds to the *effects* of the independent variable. If all of the sum of squares is located in the linear component, the effects for the several levels will plot on a straight line. Thus, with the model equation $Y_{ij} = \mu + A_i + e_{ij}$ the A_i are exactly equal to a constant, L, times the corresponding orthogonal polynomial coefficient. When more than one shape is involved, then the A_i will be the sum of more than one orthogonal polynomial coefficient, each multiplied by the appropriate shape constant.

Consider the following example set of means for some Factor A the levels of which are some equally spaced values of a quantitative independent variable. Suppose each mean is based on three scores. The means are 5, 7, and 9. We can see that the graph of these values would be a straight line with a positive slope. The sum of squares for Factor A would be $SS_A = 3(5^2) + 3(7^2) + 3(9^2) - 9(7^2) = 24$, and the sum of squares for the linear component of the trend would be obtained as the sum of squares for a contrast in which the linear trend coefficients -1, 0, and +1 are used as the contrast coefficients, giving

$SS_{lin} = [(-1)5 + (0)7 + (1)9]^2/[(-1)^2 + (0)^2 + (1)^2]/3 = 16/(2/3) = 24 = SS_A.$

We would expect, therefore, that the sum of squares for the quadratic component of the trend would be zero and that is easily verified:

$SS_{Qd} = [(1)5 + (-2)7 + (1)9]^2/[(1)^2 + (-2)^2 + (1)^2]/3 = 0.$

10.6.1 A relation that holds for each trend component. Recall that in this one-factor design with three scores per cell, the vector in nine-dimensional space that is the vector of group means is $\mu_i = [5, 5, 5, 7, 7, 7, 9, 9, 9]$, the vector on the mean line is $\mu = [7, 7, 7, 7, 7, 7, 7, 7, 7]$, and SS_A is the squared length of the vector $\mu_i - \mu = [5-7, 5-7, 5-7, 7-7, 7-7, 7-7, 9-7, 9-7, 9-7] = [-2, -2, -2, 0, 0, 0, 2, 2, 2]$, which, of course, is the sum of the squares of its elements, 24. The orthogonal polynomial analysis of the components of trend analyzes the vector $\mu_i - \mu$ into the sum of the two orthogonal vectors $L = L[-1, -1, -1, 0, 0, 0, 1, 1, 1]$ and $Q_d = Q_d[1, 1, 1, -2, -2, -2, 1, 1, 1]$. Let C_{lin} be the value of the contrast for the linear component, and let $C_{i,lin}$ be the coefficient of M_i in C_{lin}. Thus, $C_{1,lin} = -1$, $C_{2,lin} = 0$, and $C_{3,lin} = 1$. In our example, $C_{lin} = [(-1)5 + 0(7) + (1)9] = 4$. Then we have that $SS_{lin} = C_{lin}^2/(\Sigma_i C_{i,lin}^2/n)$. But we also know that SS_{lin} equals the squared length of L, which is $L^2(n\Sigma_i C_{i,lin}^2)$ therefore $L^2(n\Sigma_i C_{i,lin}^2) = C_{lin}^2/(\Sigma_i C_{i,lin}^2/n)$ and solving for L we get $L = C_{lin}/(\Sigma_i C_{i,lin}^2)$. A similar result holds for each trend component. Thus $Q_d = C_{quad}/(\Sigma_i C_{i,quad}^2)$, and so on.

*10.6.2 The sketch of a proof. In section 10.6 it says that if the means all lie exactly on a line, then the sum of squares for the linear component will exactly equal the sum of squares for the entire factor. First we will sketch the outline of an algebraic proof of this for an independent variable factor with an odd number, I, of levels and leave the algebraic details for the student to fill in. The proof for I an even number will be left as an exercise. After the algebraic proof we'll consider a more general argument as to why such a result holds not only for the linear component but for all of the components of trend.

Assuming equal spacing on the independent variable, if the group means, the M_i, all lie on a line, we can denote them by a+b, 2a+b, 3a+b, ..., Ia+b. The $C_{i,lin}$ will be $(1-I)/2$, $(3-I)/2$, $(5-I)/2$, ..., $(I-1)/2$. The general mean M will be the average of the first and last mean, assuming an equal number of scores, n, per group, so $M = [(a+b) + (Ia+b)]/2 = (I+1)a/2 + b$. Then

$SS_A = n\Sigma_i M_i^2 - NM^2 = n\Sigma_i(ia + b)^2 - In[(I+1)a/2 + b]^2$

which after some algebraic manipulation reduces to $n[a^2\Sigma_i i^2 - I(I+1)^2 a^2/4]$. Using the fact that the sum of the squares of the first I integers equals $I(I+1)(2I+1)/6$, and juggling terms some more, we finally get $SS_A = na^2 I(I^2 - 1)/12$. We seek to show that SS_{lin} is equal to this value. We have that $SS_{lin} = (\Sigma_i C_{i,lin} M_i)^2 / \Sigma_i C_{i,lin}^2/n$ and that $C_{i,lin} = (1-I)/2 + (i-1) = i - (I+1)/2$. We will show that $(\Sigma_i C_{i,lin} M_i)^2 = a^2 I^2 (I^2 - 1)^2/12^2$ and that $\Sigma_i C_{i,lin}^2/n = I(I^2 - I)/12n$ from which it will follow that $SS_{lin} = (\Sigma_i C_{i,lin} M_i)^2 / \Sigma_i C_{i,lin}^2/n = [a^2 I^2 (I^2 - 1)^2/12^2] / I(I^2 - I)/12n = na^2 I(I^2 - 1)/12 = SS_A$.

First,

$$(\Sigma_i C_{i,lin} M_i)^2 = \{\Sigma_i [i - (I+1)/2](ia + b)\}^2$$

$$= [\Sigma_i i^2 a - I(I+1)^2 a/4]^2 \text{ (since the sum of the first I integers is } I(I+1)/2)$$

$$= [aI(I+1)(2I+1)/6 - I(I+1)^2 a/4]^2 = [aI(I+1)/12]^2 [2(2I+1)-3(I+1)]^2$$

$$= a^2 I^2 (I^2 - 1)^2/12^2.$$

Then,

$$\Sigma_i C_{i,lin}^2/n = \Sigma_i [i - (1+I)/2]^2/n = [\Sigma_i [i^2 - 2i(1+I)/2 + (1+I)^2/4]^2/n$$

$$= [I(I+1)(2I+1)/6 - I(I+1)^2/2 + (1+I)^2/4]/n$$

which after some manipulation reduces to $I(I^2 - 1)/12n$, which is what we set out to show.

As an alternative more general argument, we can say that what we mean by the means all lying in just the shape for a single one of the trend components is that the vector of deviations of the group means from the general mean will exactly equal the vector for just that trend component. (We'll see in a moment that this is equivalent to saying that only the contrast for that component is nonzero.) Let's denote the vectors of orthogonal polynomial coefficients by L, Q_d, C, Q_r, and so on. Then we always have that $\mu_i - \mu = LL + Q_d Q_d + CC + ...$. Now if $\mu_i - \mu$ equals just one of the terms on the right, say, $Q_d Q_d$, then the others, say, $LL + CC + ...$ sum to the zero vector, **0**. Since these others are all mutually orthogonal vectors, no one of them can be a linear combination of the others. Therefore, if they sum to the zero vector, they must all individually be the zero vector. Since they are all the zero vector, their squared lengths are all zero, so the sum of squares for the independent variable factor must be just the sum of squares for, in the example, the quadratic component. The argument is completely general and applies to any component. Furthermore, it is clear that for any of the vectors to equal the zero vector, the coefficient L, Q_d, C, Q_r, and so on must be zero. Therefore we can say that whenever the means all follow a single trend component, the contrasts for all of the other trend components will be zero since if they were not, then the vector coefficient would not be zero (recalling from section 10.6.1 that each such vector coefficient is equal to the contrast value divided by the sum of the squares of the contrast coefficients), and the sum of squares would not be zero. But this would be a contradiction.

TABLE 10.1 FICTIONAL DATA EXHIBITING A TREND

	A_1	A_2	A_3	A_4	
	3	5	8	10	
	3	5	8	12	
	4	6	9	11	
	4	4	9	12	
	6	5	11	15	
Totals	20	25	45	60	150
Means	4	5	9	12	7.5

10.7 An example trend analysis for a one-factor design. In this section we will perform an example trend analysis for a one-factor design with four levels of the experimental variable. We assume that five subjects have been assigned at random to each of the four conditions and that the data in Table 10.1 were obtained. The orthogonal polynomial coefficients for the linear, quadratic, and cubic trend components are -3, -1, 1, 3; 1, -1, -1, 1; and -1, 3,- 3, 1 so the three sums of squares that we need are

$$SS_{lin.} = [(-3)4 + (-1)5 + (1)(9) + (3)12]^2/[(-3)^2 + (-1)^2 + (1)^2 + (3)^2]/5 = 196$$

$$SS_{quad.} = [(1)4 + (-1)5 + (-1)(9) + (1)12]^2/[(1)^2 + (-1)^2 + (-1)^2 + (1)^2]/5 = 5$$

$$SS_{cub.} = [(-1)4 + (3)5 + (-3)(9) + (1)12]^2/[(-1)^2 + (3)^2 + (-3)^2 + (1)^2]/5 = 4.$$

These three quantities exhaust the df and sum of squares for Factor A and should therefore add up to $SS_A = 20^2/5 + 25^2/5 + 45^2/5 + 60^2/5 - 150^2/20 = 1330 - 1125 = 205$, which they do. The sum of the squares of all the scores = $3^2 + 3^2 + ... + 12^2 + 15^2 = 1358$, so the sum of squares for error is $1358 - 1330 = 28$. The resulting ANOVA is shown in Table 10.1. If we were using the .05 significance level, an F-ratio of 4.49 or larger would be required for 1 and 16 degrees of freedom in order to reject the null hypothesis. We would conclude from the results in Table 10.1 that there is a significant linear trend component but no significant quadratic or cubic component.

Figure 10.6 shows the group means, 4, 5, 9, and 12 as the solid circles. It also shows how well these group means are estimated by (1) the general mean shown by the horizontal line of open circles, 7.5, 7.5, 7.5, and 7.5; and (2) the straight line of open squares, which represents the values obtained using $7.5[1,1,1,1] + 1.4[-3,-1,1,3]$, where 1.4 is the sample estimate of L obtained by taking the observed value of the contrast for the linear component, 28, and dividing it by the sum of the squares of the orthogonal polynomial coefficients for the linear component, 20. This gave the values 3.3, 6.1, 8.9, and 11.7. We can see that these are pretty close to the group means, which are 4, 5, 9, and 12. By adding the quadratic component, we can get a little closer. We obtain an estimate of Q in similar fashion by dividing the value of the quadratic contrast, 2, by the sum of the squares of the orthogonal polynomial coefficients for the quadratic component, 4, giving .5 as our estimate of Q. We then have $7.5[1,1,1,1] + 1.4[-3,-1,1,3] + .5[1,-1,-1,1] = 3.8, 5.6, 8.4,$ and 12.2. The estimate of C is obtained in the same fashion and is $(-4)/20 = -.2$. The degrees of freedom being exhausted, the obtained means are equal to the general mean plus the linear, quadratic, and cubic components,

$$[4, 5, 9, 12] = 7.5[1,1,1,1] + 1.4[-3,-1,1,3] + .5[1,-1,-1,1] + (-.2)[-1,3,-3,1]$$

$$= [7.5, 7.5, 7.5, 7.5] + [-4.2, -1.4, 1.4, 4.2] + [.5, -.5, -.5, .5] + [.2, -.6, .6, -.2].$$

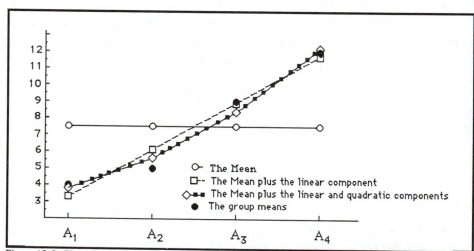

Figure 10.6. The group means are shown with their estimates using just the overall mean, using the overall mean together with the linear component, and the overall mean together with the linear and the quadratic components. (Using all three components plus the overall mean would reproduce the group means exactly.)

**TABLE 10.2 ANOVA OF THE
TREND COMPONENTS**

Source	df	SS	MS	F
Factor A	3	205	68.33	39.05
linear	1	196	196	112.00
quadratic	1	5	5	2.86
cubic	1	4	4	2.29
Error	16	28	1.75	

The various sums of squares in Table 10.2 can be related to these vectors if we take into account that each of the means is based on five scores. Recall that those sums of squares were 205 for Factor A, equaling the sum of the linear, quadratic, and cubic sums of squares, 196, 5, and 4. The value 205 is $5[(4 - 7.5)^2 + (5 - 7.5)^2 + (9 - 7.5)^2 + (12 - 7.5)^2]$. This is the sum of the squares of the deviations of the group means from the general mean. The sum of squares for linear, 196, is $5\{[4 - 7.5 - .5 -. 2]^2 + [5 - 7.5 - (-.5) - (-.6)]^2 + [9 - 7.5 - (-.5) - .6]^2 + [12 - 7.5 - .5 - (-.2)]^2\}$, which is the sum of the squares of the deviations of the group means from the values predicted using the general mean, the quadratic component, and the cubic component. Similarly, the sum of squares for the quadratic component, 5, is the sum of the squares of the deviations of the group means from the values predicted by using the general mean, the linear component, and the cubic component. What would you expect the sum of the squares of the deviations to be if we predicted the group means using the general mean and the linear component? What vector is $5[(4 - 7.5)^2 + (5 - 7.5)^2 + (9 - 7.5)^2 + (12 - 7.5)^2]$ the squared length of? What is the dimensionality of that vector? (hint: it is not 4) What vector is $5\{[4 - 7.5 - .5 - .2]^2 + [5 - 7.5 - (-.5) - (-.6)]^2 + [9 - 7.5 - (-.5) - .6]^2 + [12 - 7.5 - .5 - (-.2)]^2\}$ the squared length of?

We can see from this analysis of the sums of squares for the various trend components that the sum of squares for each component "measures" the adequacy of the mean plus all of the other components to describe the location of the group means. The smaller is the sum of squares for a given component, the better does the mean and the other components describe the group means; the larger is the sum of squares for a given component, the less well does the mean and the other components describe the group means. Therefore, the larger is the sum of squares for a given component, the stronger is the case for requiring the given component in the description of the group means.

TABLE 10.3   LINEAR x LINEAR AND LINEAR x QUADRATIC CONTRAST COEFFICIENTS FOR A 3 x 3 FACTORIAL DESIGN

	Table of Cell Means				Linear$_A$ X Linear$_B$				Linear$_A$ X Quadratic$_B$		
	B_1	B_2	B_3		-1	0	1		1	-2	1
A_1	M_{11}	M_{12}	M_{13}	-1	1	0	-1	-1	-1	2	-1
A_2	M_{21}	M_{22}	M_{23}	0	0	0	0	0	0	0	0
A_3	M_{31}	M_{32}	M_{33}	1	-1	0	1	1	1	-2	1
	(a)				(b)				(c)		

10.8   The shape of trend interaction components. We will now consider the shape of trend interaction components, first for two-factor designs and then a few examples for three-factor designs. We should note that our device for finding the contrast coefficients for interaction components (by multiplying corresponding elements in the vectors of coefficients for the orthogonal components that are interacting, given in 9.14.1), of course, applies to the trend interaction contrasts. Furthermore, since the arrangement of cell means in A x B factorial designs is customarily in an A x B table of means, it will be useful to note that a corresponding table of interaction contrast coefficients can be created by using a method that is equivalent to the multiplication of corresponding elements.

Consider Tables 10.3(a), 10.3(b), and 10.3(c). Table 10.3(a) shows the cell means for a 3 x 3 factorial design. Table 10.3(b) shows the contrast coefficients for the linear x linear component of the interaction. The entry in each cell of Table 10.3(b) is obtained as the following product: the contrast coefficient for the linear component of Factor A that would multiply the mean in the corresponding cell of Table 10.3(a) times the contrast coefficient for the linear component of Factor B that would multiply that mean. These values entering into the product are shown in the left-hand and top margins of Table 10.3(b). Similarly, the contrast coefficients for the linear x quadratic component are obtained as the products of the values in the left-hand and top margins of Table 10.3(c), which respectively are the contrast coefficients for the linear component
of Factor A and the quadratic component of Factor B. How would you find the contrast coefficients for the quadratic X linear component of the A x B interaction? The quadratic x quadratic?

We recall that that an A x B interaction requires that the three rows of means be nonparallel. **The various trend components of the A x B interaction are prototypical shapes that nonparallelism might follow.** Figure 10.7 shows the

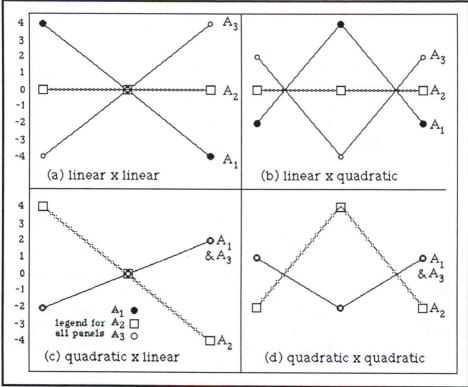

Figure 10.7. The shapes for the (a) linear x linear, (b) linear x quadratic, (c) quadratic x linear, and (d) quadratic x quadratic components of interaction in a 3 x 3 factorial design.

four prototypical shapes that the orthogonal polynomial trend analysis proposes for the manner in which the three rows of three means in Table 10.3(a) might be nonparallel. These four shapes are the linear x linear, the linear x quadratic, the quadratic x linear, and the quadratic x quadratic shapes. Consider panel (a) of Figure 10.7. The slope of the line connecting the solid dots, the means at level A_1, is negative, the slope of the line connecting the squares, the A_2 means, is zero, and the slope of the line connecting the empty dots, the A_3 means, is positive. If the successive values of the quantitative variable denoted by the levels of B differed by one unit, these slopes would be -4, 0, and +4. What we have is three lines differing in their slopes and the three slopes themselves falling on a line. In the designation "linear x linear," the second "linear" denotes the fact that the means at each level fall on a straight line. The first "linear" denotes the fact that the slopes themselves fall on a line. Compare this to panel (c) of Figure 10.7. In panel (c) all three sets of means at the levels of A also fall on straight lines. The slopes for these lines are 2 for A_1, -4 for A_2, and 2 for A_3. Thus the slopes fall in the quadratic pattern 2, -4, 2, reminiscent of the quadratic

TABLE 10.4 LINEAR x LINEAR MEANS

	B_1	B_2	B_3	Means	Effects
A_1	2	4	6	4	-4
A_2	4	8	12	8	0
A_3	6	12	18	12	4
Means	4	8	12	8	
Effects	-4	0	4		

TABLE 10.5 MEANS FROM TABLE 10.4 MINUS THE EFFECTS AND THE MEAN

	B_1	B_2	B_3
A_1	2	0	-2
A_2	0	0	0
A_3	-2	0	2

TABLE 10.6 INTERACTION MEANS

	B_1	B_2	B_3
A_1	6	8	-2
A_2	12	16	8
A_3	6	12	6

contrast coefficients, 1, -2, 1. The "quadratic x linear" expression indicates that the means at each level of A are described by lines and that the graph of the slopes of those lines would follow a quadratic shape.

In panels (b) and (d) the three means at each level of A follow a quadratic shape. This might seem inappropriate as a description of the means for A_2 in Panel (b), but those means can be considered as following a "quadratic" pattern with a zero slope (multiplier). Let us consider the means at each level of A in Panel (b). They are -2, 4, -2 at A_1, 0,0, and 0 at A_2, and 2, -4, and 2 at A_3. We can think of these as -2(1, -2, 1), 0(1, -2, 1), and 2(1, -2, 1). The 1, -2, 1 part is the basic quadratic shape and the multipliers -2, 0, and 2 are the "slopes" of those quadratic shapes. Those "slopes" follow the linear pattern -1, 0, 1 but are multiplied by 2. Thus, we see that in panel (b), the basic shape of the three levels of A is quadratic, with the slopes varying in a linear fashion from level to level of A, hence the name linear x quadratic. From the foregoing discussion, we can anticipate that the means in panel (d) lie in quadratic shapes at each level of A and that the "slopes" of those quadratic shapes themselves follow a quadratic pattern. This is the case. The "slopes" turn out to be 1, -2, and 1.

Let's be explicit regarding these slopes for the linear shapes and "slopes" for the quadratic shapes. They are nothing other than contrasts divided by the sum of the squares of the contrast coefficients. Thus, for example, in panel (d) of Figure 10.7, the means for level A_2 are -2, 4, -2. If we apply the quadratic contrast coefficients to these means, we get $(1)(-2) + (-2)(4) + (1)(-2) = -12$. Dividing this by the sum of the squares of the contrast coefficients, $1^2 + (-2)^2 + 1^2 = 6$, we get $-12/6 = -2$, the "slope" of the quadratic shape for A_2 in panel (d).

10.9 More on interaction trend component shapes. The patterns shown in Figure 10.7 are the shapes that the means take solely as a result of the specific component of interaction indicated for a particular panel. When the effects of these components combine with the main effects of Factor A and Factor B, the shapes we observe will not follow the exact patterns we have seen. For example, the entire A x B interaction might be of the linear x linear type and yet at no level of A would there be a line joining the means that had a negative slope. Table 10.4 shows a set of means for a 3 x 3 factorial design. Obviously the graph of these means will consist of three straight lines with different slopes. *All of the slopes will be positive.* Yet if we subtract from each cell mean the appropriate one of the row effects, which are -4, 0, and +4, the appropriate one of the column effects which are also -4, 0, and +4, and also subtract the general mean which is 8, then we obtain the values in Table 10.5, which are obviously an instance of the linear x linear shape. What interaction component is displayed by the means in Table 10.6?

Recognition of the various interaction components comes with experience, but it can be hastened somewhat by taking a table of interaction effects for a particular interaction component, such as Table 10.5 for the linear x linear component and adding different combinations of general mean, row effects, and column effects to it to get patterns of means that have the underlying interaction component of interest. In this way you can see how the various row and column effects affect the interaction pattern.

Another useful exercise is to take two different interaction components and add them together to see what a pattern of means would look like if there were not only, say, a linear x linear component but also, say, a quadratic x linear component affecting the cell means.

Although it is standard in the literature to refer to these components as the linear x linear, linear x quadratic, and so on, what we have seen is that it would be more explicit if the terminology were something like a "linearly shaped pattern of slopes for the linear shapes at each level of Factor A" or a "quadratic pattern of slopes for the linear shapes."

10.10   Trend components in three-factor designs. Obviously since factorial designs can have more than two factors, we can analyze for trend components in interactions involving more than two factors. We'll consider an example from a three-factor design here and leave the student to devise an example using more than three factors. Consider an A x B x C factorial design in which Factors A and C have three levels and Factor B has four. From this information we know immediately that Factors A and C can each be analyzed in terms of a linear and a quadratic component and that Factor B can be analyzed in terms of a linear, a quadratic, and a cubic component. We know from this that the A x B interaction can be analyzed in terms of the components formed by crossing linear and quadratic with linear, quadratic, and cubic, giving the linear x linear, linear x quadratic, linear x cubic, quadratic x linear, quadratic x quadratic, and quadratic x cubic components. Similarly the B x C interaction can be analyzed in terms of the linear x linear, quadratic x linear, cubic x linear, linear x quadratic, quadratic x quadratic, and cubic x quadratic. And the A x C

TABLE 10.7 ORTHOGONAL POLYNOMIAL CONTRAST COEFFICIENTS FOR THE LINEAR x LINEAR x LINEAR, LINEAR x CUBIC x QUADRATIC, AND QUADRATIC x CUBIC x LINEAR COMPONENTS OF THE A x B x C INTERACTION

Linear x Linear x Linear

$A_1(-1)$

	C_1	C_2	C_3
	-1	0	1
B_1 -3	-3	0	3
B_2 -1	-1	0	1
B_3 1	1	0	-1
B_4 3	3	0	-3

$A_2(0)$

	C_1	C_2	C_3
	-1	0	1
B_1 -3	0	0	0
B_2 -1	0	0	0
B_3 1	0	0	0
B_4 3	0	0	0

$A_3(1)$

	C_1	C_2	C_3
	-1	0	1
B_1 -3	3	0	-3
B_2 -1	1	0	-1
B_3 1	-1	0	1
B_4 3	-3	0	3

Linear x Cubic x Quadratic

$A_1(-1)$

	C_1	C_2	C_3
	1	-2	1
B_1 -1	1	-2	1
B_2 3	-3	6	-3
B_3 -3	3	-6	3
B_4 1	-1	2	-1

$A_2(0)$

	C_1	C_2	C_3
	1	-2	1
B_1 -1	0	0	0
B_2 3	0	0	0
B_3 -3	0	0	0
B_4 1	0	0	0

$A_3(1)$

	C_1	C_2	C_3
	1	-2	1
B_1 -1	-1	-2	-1
B_2 3	3	-6	3
B_3 -3	-3	6	-3
B_4 1	1	-2	1

Quadratic x Cubic x Linear

$A_1(1)$

	C_1	C_2	C_3
	-1	0	1
B_1 -1	1	0	-1
B_2 3	-3	0	3
B_3 -3	3	0	-3
B_4 1	-1	0	1

$A_2(-2)$

	C_1	C_2	C_3
	-1	0	1
B_1 -1	-2	0	2
B_2 3	6	0	-6
B_3 -3	-6	0	6
B_4 1	2	0	-2

$A_3(1)$

	C_1	C_2	C_3
	-1	0	1
B_1 -1	1	0	-1
B_2 3	-3	0	3
B_3 -3	3	0	-3
B_4 1	-1	0	1

interaction can of course be analyzed in terms of the linear x linear, linear x quadratic, quadratic x linear and quadratic x quadratic components. Finally, the A X B X C three factor interaction can be analyzed in terms of its trend components. We find these components by crossing the components with A with the cross of the components of B with C. We expect 2 X 3 X 2 = 12 such components. Letting l, q, and c, stand for linear,

**TABLE 10.8 DATA
FOR A TREATMENTS
x SUBJECTS DESIGN**

	A_1	A_2	A_3	A_4	A_5
S_1	1	3	7	11	13
S_2	0	3	8	10	12
S_3	1	4	8	12	14
S_4	0	3	7	12	15
S_5	1	3	6	10	13
S_6	0	5	8	12	16

quadratic, and cubic, these 12 components are: l x l x l; l x l x q; l x q x l; l x q x q; l x c x l; l x c x q; q x l x l; q x l x q; q x q x l; q x q x q; q x c x l; and q x c x q.

The sum of squares for each of these components is found in the usual fashion as the square of a contrast divided by the sum of the squares of the contrast coefficients divided by the number of scores per cell. The contrast coefficients are found as products of the orthogonal polynomial contrast coefficients for the corresponding levels of the interacting factors. Table 10.7 shows the contrast coefficients for the linear x linear x linear, the linear x cubic x quadratic, and the quadratic x cubic x linear components of the A x B x C interaction. **Notice that the cell entries, which are the contrast coefficients, are the product of three values, these three values being the corresponding orthogonal polynomial contrast coefficients for the levels of Factors A, B, and C that combine to determine the cell in question.**

10.11 Trend tests with repeated measures. We have seen that the trend tests using orthogonal polynomial coefficients are just a particular variety of orthogonal contrasts. In section 9.7 we introduced the use of contrast scores to provide a simple and familiar way to obtain F-statistics that are exactly distributed as F even when nonhomogeneity of the variances of the difference scores occurs. That procedure carries over exactly to the tests of trend. We can test the linear component against its own exact error term, the quadratic against its own exact error term, and so on. In this section we will perform trend tests for a Treatments x Subjects design using the contrast score procedure. We assume that the levels of Factor A represent a quantitative variable with equally spaced values. We will also assume that on the basis of previous knowledge the experimental interest lies in the linear and quadratic components of trend, so that the remaining components will be untested and their sums of squares will be combined into an untested pooled residual. Table 10.8 shows the data for six fictitious subjects. The orthogonal polynomial coefficients for the linear trend component with five groups are -2, -1, 0, 1, and 2, and those for the quadratic trend component are 2, -1, -2, -1, 2. We can obtain for each subject an L-score (a contrast score using the linear coefficients). Let Y_{ij} be the score for Subject J at Level I of Factor A. Let L_i and Q_i be the linear and quadratic coefficient for Level i of Factor A. Then we will define the L-score and the Q-score for Subject i to be $\Sigma_i L_i Y_{ij}$ and $\Sigma_i Q_i Y_{ij}$, respectively. Thus, the L-score for Subject 1 is (-2)1 + (-1)3 + (0)7 +1(11) + 2(13) = 32 and the Q-score for Subject 1 is (2)1 + (-1)3 + (-2)7 + (-1)11 + (2)13 = 0. A little arithmetic shows that the complete sample of L-scores for the six subjects is 32, 31, 34, 39, 31, and 39; and the complete sample of Q-scores is 0, -5, -2, 1, 3, and -1. To test for the significance of the linear trend component we simply test the hypothesis that the L-scores are sampled from a normal distribution with a mean of zero. This is just the significance test for the mean but applied now to a sample of L-scores. Since this is a test of whether the mean is zero, our F-ratio for the test of this hypothesis is by now familiar: the numerator is the squared total of the scores (the L-scores, of course) divided by the number of L-scores, and the denominator is a fraction, the numerator of which is {the sum of the squared L-scores} minus {the squared total of the

TABLE 10.9 L x Q COEFFICIENTS FOR THE DRUG A x DRUG B INTERACTION IN TABLE 10.10

		Q		
		1	-2	1
L	-1	-1	2	-1
	0	0	0	0
	1	1	-2	1

scores divided by the number of L-scores}, and the denominator of which is {the number of L-scores minus one}. That is

F_{linear} =   [(32+31+34+39+31+39)^2/6]/ [(32^2 + 31^2 + 34^2 + 39^2 + 31^2 + 39^2) -

(32 + 31 + 34 + 39 + 31 + 39)^2/6]/(6 - 1)

= [2062/6]/[7144 - 2062/6]/5 = 7072.67/(7144-7072.67)/5 = 495.75.

Following the same procedure for testing the quadratic component against its own error term, we obtain

$$F_{quadratic} = [0+(-5)+(-2)+1+3+(-1)]^2/6 \ / \ \{[0^2+(-5)^2+(-2)^2+1^2+3^2+(-1)^2]$$

$$- [0+(-5)+(-2)+1+3+(-1)]^2/6 \ / \ (6-1)\} = .36.$$

It should be mentioned that in other textbooks there are other formulas for arriving at this same value of the F-ratio. Generally, in these other formulas, the numerator and the denominator will both differ from the quantities obtained here by a factor equal to the sum of the squares of the contrast coefficients. Since this factor multiplies both numerator and denominator, it cancels out, and the same F-ratio is obtained.

The L-scores and the Q-scores and any of the higher-order trend component scores are perfectly legitimate scores to be used in the analysis of a within-subjects design. If the design were mixed, with a between-subjects and a within-subjects factor, an L-score, say, could be computed for each subject, and these L-scores would form a one-factor design (the one factor being the between-subjects factor). An analysis of this one-factor design would include a test for the overall mean and a test for Groups. A significant F-ratio for the overall mean would indicate a significant linear trend in the within-subjects factor means, averaged over Groups. A significant effect for Groups in the analysis of the L-scores would indicate that the linear trend component in the within-subjects factor interacted with the between-subjects factor. That is, the slopes of the lines varied from group to group.

These interpretations become easy to use as we realize that the L-scores are direct measures of the linear trend at the level of the individual subject (the L-score for a subject is proportional to the slope of the best-fitting straight line fitted to that subject's scores on the within-subjects variable), and analyses of these L-scores over subjects and groups show the nature of the linear trend over subjects and groups. Similar remarks apply not only to the analysis of Q-scores in mixed designs but to analysis of L x L-scores, L x Q-scores, and others that could be computed in designs with more than one within-subjects factor. Analyses of such L x L scores carried out as described in this section would ensure that each interaction trend component would be tested against an exact error term and that the F-ratio would be exactly distributed as F, under the appropriate null hypothesis.

10.11.1 An example of using trend component scores in a mixed design. To be sure that the use of analyses of L x L scores, L x Q scores, etc. is clear, let's consider a small example. Suppose an investigation of appetite suppression by two drugs given in combination to rats from either of two hereditary strains (Groups). Suppose Drug A is administered in doses of 10, 20, or 30 units and Drug B is administered in doses of 5, 10, or 15 units. Suppose there are five rats in each hereditary strain group and each rat receives all nine possible combinations of the two drugs, the order of receiving the different combinations being a different random order for each rat. Assume also that sufficient time is allowed between treatments so that there are no carryover effects from one drug combination to another. Suppose that previous research has indicated a quadratic component to the effects of Drug B in this range of values and the investigator wished to test whether this component varies in a linear fashion with changes in the level of Drug A. This can be done by calculating an L x Q score for each rat in each group and testing whether the overall mean of the L x Q scores differs from zero. In addition, the investigator has reason to believe that this linear change in the quadratic component may differ for the two strains of rats. This can be tested by testing for an effect of Groups on the L x Q scores. Suppose the data are as shown in Table 10.10. The L x Q coefficients are shown in Table 10.9. Multiplying these values by the corresponding values in Table 10.10 and summing, the five L x Q scores for the rats in Group 1 are -5, -2, -2, -2, and -4. The five values for the rats in Group 2 are -4, -2, -4, -2, and -3. Since the means for the two groups are identical, there is no possibility of a significant effect due to strains. The sum of squares for error is 12 with 8 df, giving a mean square of 1.5. The sum of squares for the mean is $NM^2 = 10(-3)^2 = 90$ on 1 df. Hence $F = 90/1.5 = 60$. The magnitude of this F ratio indicates that the L x Q scores are significantly different from 0, indicating that there is a significant component of the Drug A x Drug B interaction, resulting in a linear change in the quadratic component of B associated with change in Drug A. The lack of an effect due to Groups indicates that this finding is uniform over the two Groups.

10.12 On testing the various trend components. Sophisticated researchers tend to avoid testing for the significance of higher order trend components such as the cubic and quartic, even when these can be tested. The situation is similar to testing third- and fourth-order interactions. Even after the significant statistic is found, there is usually little one can do in interpreting the result. But this is largely a matter of style. I, for example, like to search exhaustively through a set of data, finding what ever I can, and worrying later about what can be interpreted and what cannot. What doesn't make sense to me today may well make a lot of sense two or three experiments from now, or may make perfect sense to someone else who reads my results. Gathering data is usually expensive; analyzing data is relatively cheap. It seems economical, once one has gone to the expense of data gathering, to see, analyze, and hopefully interpret as much of what one has gathered as one can.

In discussing this matter, another author (Keppel, 1982, pp. 139-140) indicates that usually interest does not go beyond the linear and quadratic component but that if a theory predicted the significance of a higher-order component we would test it. Then he goes on to suggest a different way of proceeding. He suggests that when there is no theory to guide

TABLE 10.10 THE FICTIONAL DATA FOR FIVE RATS FROM EACH OF TWO STRAINS RECEIVING ALL COMBINATIONS OF THREE LEVELS OF EACH OF TWO DRUGS

Group 1

			Subject												
		1			2			3			4			5	
		Drug B			Drug B			Drug B			Drug B			Drug B	
Drug A		10 15 20			10 15 20			10 15 20			10 15 20			10 15 20	
	5	1 2 1			2 3 1			1 3 2			3 5 4			2 4 2	
	10	2 5 3			3 5 4			2 6 4			5 7 6			3 6 3	
	15	3 7 4			4 6 3			3 6 4			7 9 6			4 8 4	

Group 2

		1			2			3			4			5	
		Drug B			Drug B			Drug B			Drug B			Drug B	
Drug A		10 15 20			10 15 20			10 15 20			10 15 20			10 15 20	
	5	1 3 2			2 3 1			2 4 2			3 5 4			1 2 1	
	10	3 5 4			3 6 3			5 7 6			2 6 4			2 5 3	
	15	3 7 4			7 9 6			4 8 4			4 6 3			3 6 4	

analysis and we are interested in discovering the trend components that will describe the data, we first perform an overall (omnibus) F-test for the factor of interest and if this is significant, the linear trend component be tested and a test of the residual sum of squares be done using the residual degrees of freedom. Then, if the residual is significant, a test of the quadratic component be performed and a test of the new residual sum of squares consisting of the sum of squares for the factor minus the sum of squares for the linear and the quadratic components, using the new residual degrees of freedom—and so on through the various components and residuals until a nonsignificant residual is found or until the degrees of freedom are exhausted. The reason given for testing the residual sum of squares each time is that since we have no particular hypotheses, we should first see if there is any variation in the means to worry about. I would like to suggest an alternative view of the matter.

In my view there is no need for the overall omnibus F-test or for tests of any of the residuals. Since we do have the notion that the trend components may describe the data, we are not without hypotheses. In any case, there would be no rationale for testing the linear component first, and then the quadratic, if we were completely without hypotheses. Furthermore, the components are orthogonal to one another. Whether any one is significant has nothing to do with whether or not any other one is significant. Therefore there can be no basis for testing them in any particular sequence. If, in our state of relative ignorance, we are going to test them, we may as well test all of them.

There may be some concern that we will inflate our chances of making a Type I error by testing all of the components that can be tested. This is a legitimate concern and can be protected against in legitimate ways. But the omnibus test and the tests of the residuals are fraught with their own error rate problems. A real linear trend might well be missed by the overall F-test. A real quadratic trend might be obscured by the rest of the residual but might have shown through loud and clear if tested alone. It is simple to confirm that an overall F-test can miss a significant component. Consider a one-factor design with three subjects in each of three groups. In Group I the scores for the three subjects are 1, 2, and 3; in Group II, they are 2, 3, and 4; and in Group III, 3, 4, and 5. Analysis of variance of these data gives an F-ratio of 3 on two and six degrees of freedom, which is nonsignificant at the .05 level. A test of the linear component, however, yields a significant F of 6 on one and six df.

It is easy to understand how this can happen. Consider the fact that whenever the Group means lie exactly on a line, the sum of squares for Groups will exactly equal the sum of squares for the linear component. But the mean square for the linear component will always be $(J - 1)$ times the mean square for Groups when the design has J Groups. Therefore, depending on the size of the error mean square, it is always possible for there to be a significant linear component without a significant overall F. Even if the means do not fall exactly on a line, a similar situation can exist, although in less extreme form.

I recommend that when there is enough interest in the possible appropriateness of the various trend components for one to envision sequentially testing all of them, instead of using the overall test and the test of each of the components and the residuals, **the overall F-test should be omitted, the tests of the residuals should be omitted, and the tests of all of the various independent trend components that one was prepared to consider be carried out and considered independently of one another**; simultaneously, sotospeak, rather than sequentially. In the light of the orthogonality of the trend components, this seems perfectly appropriate to me.

The student has just been introduced to the idea that authors and researchers can disagree on the most appropriate way to proceed in the analysis of data. This is not a weakness of the field but a strength. It is through such disagreement and the discussion it generates that the various ideas are submitted to scrutiny and consensus develops as to how we should proceed.

10.13   Calculating orthogonal polynomial contrast coefficients. For balanced designs the orthogonal polynomial contrast coefficients orthogonal polynomial contrast coefficients:calculation of such as -1, 0, 1 and 1, -2, 1, can be found in standard tables (e.g., Fisher & Yates, 1948). In this section we will give a simple method for calculating these coefficients in the absence of such tables. Furthermore, the standard tabled values are for equally spaced values of the independent variable. The formulas we will present will enable the student to calculate the appropriate contrast coefficients for unequally spaced values and also for the case where the design is not balanced.

We start by noting the forms of the linear, quadratic, cubic, and other coefficients. Let there be I levels of the independent variable, and let the known measured quantitative values for these levels be $X_1, X_2, ..., X_i, ..., X_I$. Let $L_i, Q_{di}, C_i, Q_{ri}, ...$ be the linear, quadratic, cubic, quartic, etc. coefficient for level i. Then

$$L_i = a_L + X_i; \quad Q_{di} = a_{Qd} + b_{Qd}X_i + X_i^2; \quad C_i = a_C + b_CX_i + c_CX_i^2 + X_i^3;$$

$$Q_{ri} = a_{Qr} + b_{Qr}X_i + c_{Qr}X_i^2 + d_{Qr}X_i^3 + X_i^4, \quad \text{etc.}$$

The coefficients $a_L, a_{Qd}, b_{Qd}, ...$ remain to be determined subject to two orthogonality requirements. The first is that the vectors of coefficients be orthogonal to one another. That is, $\Sigma_i n_i L_i Q_{di} = 0$, $\Sigma_i n_i L_i C_i = 0$, and so forth. The second is that they be orthogonal to the vector containing all ones so that they will be contrast coefficients. If there are different numbers of scores at each level, this fact must be taken into account in determining such orthogonalities. We will assume that at level i of the quantitative factor, there are n_i scores. Then the first orthogonality requirement can be expressed by equations of the form

$$\Sigma_i n_i L_i Q_{di} = \Sigma_i n_i (a_L + X_i)(a_{Qd} + b_{Qd}X_i + X_i^2) = 0,$$

$$\Sigma_i n_i L_i C_i = \Sigma_i n_i (a_L + X_i)(a_C + b_CX_i + c_CX_i^2 + X_i^3) = 0,$$

$$\Sigma_i n_i L_i Q_{ri} = \Sigma_i n_i (a_L + X_i)(a_{Qr} + b_{Qr}X_i + c_{Qr}X_i^2 + d_{Qr}X_i^3 + X_i^4) = 0,$$

$$\Sigma_i n_i Q_{di} C_i = \Sigma_i n_i (a_{Qd} + b_{Qd}X_i + X_i^2)(a_C + b_CX_i + c_CX_i^2 + X_i^3) = 0,$$

$$\Sigma_i n_i Q_{di} Q_{ri} = \Sigma_i n_i (a_{Qd} + b_{Qd}X_i + X_i^2)(a_{Qr} + b_{Qr}X_i + c_{Qr}X_i^2 + d_{Qr}X_i^3 + X_i^4) =$$

$$0,$$

$$\Sigma_i n_i C_i Q_{ri} = \Sigma_i n_i (a_C + b_CX_i + c_CX_i^2 + X_i^3)(a_{Qr} + b_{Qr}X_i + c_{Qr}X_i^2 + d_{Qr}X_i^3 +$$

$$X_i^4) = 0,$$

and the second orthogonality requirement is satisfied by equations of the form

$$\Sigma_i n_i L_i = \Sigma_i n_i (a_L + X_i) = 0, \qquad \Sigma_i n_i Q_{di} = \Sigma_i n_i (a_{Qd} + b_{Qd}X_i + X_i^2) = 0,$$

$\Sigma_i n_i C_i = \Sigma_i n_i(a_C + b_C X_i + c_C X_i^2 + X_i^3) = 0,$

$\Sigma_i n_i Q_{ri} = \Sigma_i n_i(a_{Qr} + b_{Qr} X_i + c_{Qr} X_i^2 + d_{Qr} X_i^3 + X_i^4) = 0,$ etc.

These two sets of equations jointly permit solving for the coefficients a_L, a_{Qd}, b_{Qd}, ... which completely determine the values of the L_i, Q_{di}, C_i, Q_{ri}, ... at each level of i. As it turns out, these equations are solved very easily because all of the X_i are known values.

TABLE 10.11 ORTHOGONAL POLYNOMIALS: UNEQUAL SPACING

Level:	1	2	3	4	5
X_i:	2	4	5	6	8
n_i:	4	3	4	6	3
$n_i X_i$:	8	12	20	36	24
$n_i X_i^2$:	16	48	100	216	192
$n_i X_i^3$:	32	192	500	1296	1536

$\Sigma_i n_i = 20$

$\Sigma_i n_i X_i = 100$

$\Sigma_i n_i X_i^2 = 572$

$\Sigma_i n_i X_i^3 = 3556$

Let us take a numerical example and work through it as we work through the formulas. Suppose we have a design with five levels and the measurements of the X_i's and the sample sizes, together with some other values we will need given in Table 10.11. We first solve for a_L using the equation $\Sigma_i n_i(a_L + X_i) = 0$. This gives us $\Sigma_i n_i(a_L + X_i) = a_L \Sigma_i n_i + \Sigma_i n_i X_i = a_L(20) + 100 = 0$, so $a_L = -5$. Inserting this into the equation $L_i = a_L + X_i$ gives the L_i shown in the first row of Table 10.12.

The next step is to solve for a_{Qd} and b_{Qd}. To do this we use the equation

$\Sigma_i n_i L_i Q_{di} = \Sigma_i n_i(a_L + X_i)(a_{Qd} + b_{Qd} X_i + X_i^2) = 0,$

inserting the value -5 in for a_L, and the equation

$\Sigma_i n_i Q_{di} = \Sigma_i n_i(a_{Qd} + b_{Qd} X_i + X_i^2) = 0.$

The first equation gives us

$\Sigma_i n_i (-5 + X_i)(a_{Qd} + b_{Qd}X_i + X_i^2)$

$= -5 \Sigma_i n_i (a_{Qd} + b_{Qd}X_i + X_i^2) + \Sigma_i n_i X_i (a_{Qd} + b_{Qd}X_i + X_i^2) = 0,$

which, using the second equation, reduces to

$\Sigma_i n_i X_i (a_{Qd} + b_{Qd}X_i + X_i^2) = 0.$

Combining this with the second equation we have

$a_{Qd} \Sigma_i n_i X_i + b_{Qd} \Sigma_i n_i X_i^2 + \Sigma_i n_i X_i^3 = 0$

$a_{Qd} \Sigma_i n_i + b_{Qd} \Sigma_i n_i X_i + \Sigma_i n_i X_i^2 = 0$

which is a system of two equations in two unknowns that is easily solved by inserting the known quantities to get $100 a_{Qd} + 572 b_{Qd} + 3556 = 0$ and $20 a_{Qd} + 100 b_{Qd} + 572 = 0$, which, multiplying the second equation by 5 and subtracting it from the first equation, gives $72 b_{Qd} + 696 = 0$, so $b_{Qd} = -696/72 = -9.67$, and substituting this back into either of the two equations gives $a_{Qd} = -76.93$. Using these two values of a_{Qd} and b_{Qd} in the equation $Q_{di} = a_{Qd} + b_{Qd}X_i + X_i^2$ gives the second row of Table 10.12. A simpler set of Q_{di} results if we make them smaller. In this case dividing them by 100 produces a reasonably

TABLE 10.12 ORTHOGONAL POLYNOMIAL COEFFICIENTS FOR THE NUMERICAL EXAMPLE

Level:	1	2	3	4	5
L_i:	-3	-1	0	1	3
Q_{di}:	-92.27	-99.61	-100.28	-98.95	-90.29

nice set. What to divide or multiply by is a matter of judgment with each set of coefficients. The idea is to keep the computations manageable. The student should confirm that multiplication of all of the Q_{di} by a constant preserves all of the orthogonality requirements that determined them.

To find the C_i, we use the three equations

$\Sigma_i n_i L_i C_i = \Sigma_i n_i (a_L + X_i)(a_C + b_C X_i + c_C X_i^2 + X_i^3) = 0,$

$$\Sigma_i n_i Q_{di} C_i = \Sigma_i n_i (a_{Qd} + b_{Qd} X_i + X_i^2)(a_C + b_C X_i + c_C X_i^2 + X_i^3) = 0,$$

and

$$\Sigma_i n_i C_i = \Sigma_i n_i (a_C + b_C X_i + c_C X_i^2 + X_i^3) = 0,$$

giving three equations in the three unknowns, a_C, b_C, and c_C. The quartic coefficients require solution of four equations, and so on.

Exercises

1. Find the cubic coefficients for the example values.
2. Find the quartic coefficients.
3. Find the linear, quadratic, and cubic coefficients for the case where the n_i are all equal and the X_i are equally spaced at 1, 2, 3, 4, and 5.
4. Do exercise 3 again but this time using X_i that are an arbitrary linear transformation of the X_i in exercise 3: that is, using X_i of a + b, 2a + b, 3a + b, 4a + b, and 5a + b. Show that the same linear, quadratic, and cubic coefficients are obtained. What do you infer about the coefficients for all equally spaced X_i with equal n_i?
5. Using the data in Table 10.10, test the following hypotheses:
(a) That the slope of the linear trend in Drug B varies linearly as Drug A varies (there is a nonzero L x L component
(b) That there is a difference in the variation in part 5(a) due to difference in strain of rats
c) That the quadratic trend in Drug B varies in a quadratic manner as Drug A varies (that there is a nonzero quadratic x quadratic component;
d) That there is a difference in the the variation in part 5c due to difference in strain of rats.
6. Recall the data in Table 10.13 relating to the Spencer et al. experiment on drug dosage effects on rats' memory for brightness of light displays presented at the end of Chapter 9. Assign the Saline condition a Scopolamine hydrobromide value of 0, calculate the appropriate contrast coefficients for trend tests for the linear components of both Drug Dosage and Retention Interval, and perform the test of the linear x linear component of the Drug Dosage x Retention Interval interaction.
7. Assume that the levels of Factor A for the data in Table 10.7 were unequally spaced, having values of 2, 4, 5, 7, and 10 at A_1, A_2, A_3, A_4, and A_5. Determine the appropriate linear trend coefficients, use these to obtain an L-score for each subject, and test the hypothesis of no linear trend by testing the hypothesis that the mean of the L-scores is zero.

TABLE 10.13 DATA RELATING TO THE SPENCER ET AL. EXPERIMENT, CHAPTER 9

			Retention Interval									
	2.5 secs.				5.0 secs.				10 secs.			
	Dosage				Dosage				Dosage			
Subject	Sal.	.125	.25	.50	Sal.	.125	.25	.50	Sal.	.125	.25	.50
1	.89	.81	.73	.61	.79	.74	.65	.56	.68	.63	.54	.48
2	.90	.79	.75	.60	.80	.75	.65	.57	.69	.65	.56	.49
3	.88	.80	.72	.59	.80	.73	.64	.58	.70	.64	.55	.47
4	.90	.79	.73	.59	.78	.73	.66	.59	.68	.64	.54	.48
5	.88	.80	.75	.60	.80	.75	.65	.56	.70	.64	.54	.48

TABLE 10.14 AVERAGE AREA RESPONSES TO THE 27 TYPES OF STIMULUS CONDITIONS

Height	Times 1			Times 2			Times 3		
	Width			Width			Width		
	4	6	8	4	6	8	4	6	8
	9.64	13.70	19.67	16.14	26.13	36.96	27.76	37.23	54.08
	16.43	25.52	35.59	35.34	51.05	68.63	52.95	76.63	102.45
	25.76	37.29	48.40	53.50	71.52	96.42	72.05	112.22	139.98

8. Sixteen undergraduate psychology students were shown rectangles and asked to produce a square equal to one, two, or three times the area of the stimulus rectangle. The heights of the stimuli were 2, 4, or 6, cm and the widths were 4, 6, or 8 cm. Thus, there were 27 types of trials composed of the three heights x three widths x three multipliers. Each subject responded to each type of trial three times, giving 81 responses in all. A different random sequence of trials was used with each subject. The averages over the subjects and replications are given in Table 10.14.

(a) Write the model equation for this design

(b) Write the sources and their degrees of freedom.

9. For the data in Table 10.13:

(a) Make up a numerical value for the Height x Subjects sum of squares so that the Linear component of Height is significant but the residual is not

(b) Make up a numerical value for the Height x Width x Subjects sum of squares so that the Linear x Linear component of the Height x Width interaction is significant, but each of the other components of the residual is not.

10. Make up a numerical value for the Height x Width x Multiplier x Subjects sum of squares so that the Linear x Linear x Linear component of the Height x Width x Multiplier interaction is significant but each of the other components of the residual is not.

11. Assume that the data in Table 10.15 came from one of the subjects in the experiment in exercise 8.

(a) Calculate the L and Q scores for Height, for Width, and for Multiplier for this subject

TABLE 10.15　FICTIONAL DATA FOR A SUBJECT IN THE EXPERIMENT OF EXERCISE 8

	Times 1			Times 2			Times 3		
	4	6	8	4	6	8	4	6	8
2	3.2	8.0	14.4	8.8	17.2	26.5	13.2	26.9	41.3
4	9.2	17.6	27.3	16.8	36.1	52.1	26.9	53.3	79.0
6	12.8	26.5	39.3	27.3	52.3	79.0	39.7	78.6	119.9

(b) Calculate the L x L score for Height x Width;

(c) Calculate the L x L x L score.

12. A theory of stimulus preference asserts that there is some optimal level of stimulation on a given stimulus dimension that results in the highest preference by a subject, but that on either side of this optimal level stimulus, preference should decline. What component of trend would you expect to describe the shape of the preference function?

13. A theory of performance in a learning situation predicts that the performance should improve with increasing opportunities for experience and then taper off to a maximal level of performance. What components of trend would you expect to be significant in the analysis of performance as a function of experience?

14. A theory of performance in problem tasks that require the subject to switch from a simpler approach to the problem to a more complex approach predicts that performance will rise during the first stage of the task, suffer a setback when the subject must learn to switch, and then will rise to a higher level than before. What shape component would you expect to be significant in the analysis of performance as a function of time on the problem?

15. What would be an example of a hypothesis being tested by a contrast of contrast scores? See, for example, Table 9.8.

11

Multiple Comparisons

11.21   *Comparison of the procedures and recommendations*

Exercises

11.1 The effective Type I error rate with multiple significance tests. When we test a null hypothesis there are four possible <u>outcomes</u>:

1.   The null hypothesis is true, and we correctly decide that it is true
2.   The null hypothesis is true, but we incorrectly decide that it is false (we make a Type I error)
3.   The null hypothesis is false, but we incorrectly decide that it is true (we make a Type II error)
4.   The null hypothesis is false, and we correctly decide that it is false.

We refer to the <u>probability</u> of rejecting the null hypothesis when it is actually true as the significance level, α. When this value is set in advance by the researcher, usually at .05 or .01, and the test is conducted, the test is analogous to the flip of a coin. When the null hypothesis is true and the significance level is set at .05, then the "flip" of the experiment will result in the experiment "coming up" reject-the-null-hypothesis with a probability of .05 and "coming up" accept-the-null-hypothesis with a probability of .95. The test is analogous to flipping a biased coin.

Consider a coin that comes up Heads with probability α and Tails with probability $1 - \alpha$. If we flip that coin twice, then the possible joint outcomes for two flips of the coin are HH, HT, TH, and TT . Assuming the flips are independent of one another, the probabilities of occurrence for these four possible joint outcomes are α^2, $\alpha(1 - \alpha)$, $(1 - \alpha)\alpha$, and $(1 - \alpha)^2$. Three of the four possible joint outcomes involve at least one Heads. Only TT has no Heads. So, the probability of no Heads in two independent flips of the coin is the probability of TT, $(1 - \alpha)^2$. Since TT is the complement of at least one head occurring, the probability of at least one Head occurring is $1 - (1 - \alpha)^2 = \alpha^2 + \alpha(1 - \alpha) + (1 - \alpha)\alpha$.

In completely analogous fashion, if we conduct independent tests of two <u>true</u> null hypotheses and if we take α to be the significance level for each test, then the probability of incorrectly rejecting <u>at least one</u> of the two true null hypotheses is $1 - (1 - \alpha)^2$. If the significance level for each single test is .05, this turns out to be $1 - (1 - .05)^2 = .0975$. Notice that even though we are using a significance level of .05 for each individual test, the probability of at least one false rejection of a true null hypothesis has risen to .0975 because we are performing two tests. Similarly, with three flips of a coin, the probability of no Heads would be $(1 - \alpha)^3$, and in general, with n flips the probability of no Heads in n flips would be $(1 - \alpha)^n$. Thus, the probability of at least one Head would be $1 - (1 - \alpha)^n$. From our analogy it follows that in testing n null hypotheses with each test independently conducted at the .05 significance level, the probability of at least one incorrect rejection of a null hypothesis in those n tests would be $1 - (1 - .05)^n = 1 - .95^n$. As n increases, $.95^n$ approaches zero, and the probability of at least one false rejection therefore approaches one.

It is customary to distinguish between the significance level for any single test, usually referred to as the **nominal significance level**, and the probability of making at least one Type I error in the entire collection oF-tests. The latter is referred to either as the **experimentwise significance level or error rate** in the earlier literature and more recently by some as the **familywise significance level or error rate.** The term "familywise" acknowledges that most investigators in analyzing a multifactor design attempt to control the overall error rate for comparisons performed within each source rather than over the entire experimental design (although sources need not be the definition of family). More generally it indicates that choice of the group of null hypotheses for which the overall Type I error rate is to be controlled is arbitrary and in the hands of the experimenter. It may or may not be the entire set of F-tests to be conducted for a given experiment or for a given source.

We saw in Chapters 9 and 10 that even in a one-factor design we could conduct as many orthogonal tests of null hypotheses as there were degrees of freedom for Groups. A one-factor design with I Groups would have I - 1 degrees of freedom for Groups; therefore I - 1 orthogonal tests could be conducted. If all of the null hypotheses were true and a significance level equal to .05 were used with each test, the probability of falsely rejecting at least one of the null hypotheses would be approximately $1 - .95^{I-1}$—approximately because the tests are usually not all independent of each other since the same estimate of error variance may be used in all of them. (Furthermore, it is possible to conduct many more than I - 1 tests if contrasts that are not all mutually independent are admitted.) From a certain point of view a problem exists in that although the .05 significance level has been adopted for the individual tests, the overall probability of making at least one false rejection of a true hypothesis, when all of the null hypotheses are true, is not .05 but is a function of the number oF-tests conducted and approaches one as the number oF-tests increases. The purpose of this chapter is to consider some of the ways that have been proposed to deal with this problem.

The fundamental issue hinges on the fact that the Type I error rate for the individual tests of hypotheses within a family of hypotheses is related to the familywise Type I error rate. If the familywise Type I error rate is to be held to a chosen value, call it α_f, then the Type I error rates or significance levels for the members of the family, call them the α_i, are also constrained. Let's go back to our coin-flipping model of testing two hypotheses. Again assume we are testing a family of two true null hypotheses, H_{01} and H_{02}. If we let α_1 and α_2 be their respective Type I error rates, then the probability of not making any Type I error will be $(1 - \alpha_1)(1 - \alpha_2)$, and therefore the probability of at least one Type I error will be $1 -$

$(1 - \alpha_1)(1 - \alpha_2)$. The familywise Type I error rate is therefore $\alpha_f = 1 - (1 - \alpha_1)(1 - \alpha_2)$. We have already seen above that if we choose $\alpha_1 = \alpha_2 = .05$, then $\alpha_f = 1 - .95^2 = 1 - .9025 = .0975$. But suppose we want to hold the familywise error rate down to $\alpha_f = .05$, keeping $\alpha_1 = \alpha_2$. Then $(1- \alpha_1)(1 - \alpha_2)$ will have to equal .95. Letting α be the common value of α_1 and α_2, we have that $(1 - \alpha)^2 = .95$ so $1 - \alpha = (.95)^{.5}$ and $\alpha = 1 - (.95)^{.5} = .0253$. Thus, in order to hold the familywise error rate down to .05, we must test each of the two hypotheses in the family at a significance level of .0253. (Of course, we could have chosen the two significance levels to be unequal, in which case one could have exceeded .0253 but the other would have had to have been even smaller.)

Because the power of each of the individual tests decreases as the significance level of each test decreases, a dilemma can arise. If there are many hypotheses in the family, holding α_f at a desirable level can reduce the power of the tests of the individual hypotheses so much that there is little point to conducting the experiment. Consider a one-factor design with 11 groups. Suppose the experimenter wants to test 10 orthogonal contrasts and wants the familywise Type I error rate to be .05. Then the error rates for the 10 individual tests, assuming they are to be kept equal, will have to be about .0051 since $1 - (1 - .0051)^{10}$ is approximately .05. To simplify the argument about how power decreases, we can assume that the standard error of the difference between two sample means is known and equals $\sigma^2_{Mi - Mi'} = 1$. Then, under the null hypothesis that $\mu_i = \mu_{i'}$, it follows that $(M_i - M_{i'})/\sigma_{Mi - Mi'} = M_i - M_{i'}$ has the standard normal distribution. A value of $| M_i - M_{i'} | \geq 2.8$ would therefore occur with a probability of about .0051 so 2.8 can be used as the critical value against which we compare $M_i - M_{i'}$ in order to test this null hypothesis. Suppose now that for two of the experimental groups, call them groups A and B, the null hypothesis is actually false, although, of course the experimenter does not know this. Suppose, in fact, that the null hypothesis is false in exactly this way: $\mu_B - \mu_A = 1.96$. We can compute the probability that $M_B - M_A$ will exceed 2.8 since $M_B - M_A$ is a normally distributed variable with a mean of 1.96 and a standard deviation of 1. This probability is just the probability that a standard normal variable will exceed the value $(2.8 - 1.96)/1$ and is equal to approximately .20. (We can ignore the probability that $M_B - M_A \leq -2.8$ since that is zero to four decimal places.) Thus, the probability that the experimenter will reject the null hypothesis that $\mu_A = \mu_B$ when $\mu_B - \mu_A = 1.96$ is about .20 and this is by definition the power of the test. But if the experiment had consisted of only the two groups, A and B, instead of the 11 groups, the familywise error rate would have been the error rate for the one contrast $M_B - M_A$ and therefore the .05 level could have been used for the single contrast. This would have given a critical value of 1.96, and the power of the test would have been equal to the probability that a standard normal variable would exceed $(1.96 - 1.96)/1 = 0$, which is, of course, equal to .5. We see, then, that because the other nine groups were included and the familywise error rate based on 10 contrasts was held to .05, the power of the specific contrast M_B - M_A was reduced in this example from .50 to about .20.

This trade-off of familywise Type I error protection against Type II error protection is the fundamental problem that the various multiple comparison procedures address. The great variety of multiple comparison procedures that have arisen vary in their different approaches to dealing with, on the one hand, not letting the familywise error rate get out of hand, while on the other hand attempting to maintain the power of the individual tests at adequately high levels.

11.2 The Box, Hunter, and Hunter method: Using a reference distribution.

The variety of methods for performing multiple contrasts or comparisons is remarkable. The methods range from the simple and intuitively appealing to at least one method by Peritz (Peritz, 1970; Begun & Gabriel, 1981), which in some contexts appears to be the best available but is sufficiently complex in both its logic and its procedure that Einot and Gabriel (1975) did not recommend it because they considered the procedures impractically complicated. The method to be considered in this section is among the simplest and is arguably the most intuitively appealing of all. Box, Hunter, and Hunter (1978, Chapter 6) propose this method in the context of certain difficulties (p. 206) that they see with using the more formal procedures that we will consider in the following sections. Seeing the significance level as a measure of our uncertainty, they ask how exact should we be about uncertainty. They raise the question of how much difference it makes to know if a particular probability is exactly .04, .05, or .06. They also note that significance levels are chosen arbitrarily. In addition, they indicate that in some methods for performing multiple comparisons "The subtleties are not easy to understand, and the experimenter may find himself provided with an exact measure of the uncertainty of a proposition he does not fully comprehend." (p. 206).

Box, Hunter & Hunter propose using a reference distribution to compare group means. They first note that I group means, M_1, M_2, ..., M_I, based on samples of size n_i from normal distributions with means μ_i and the same variance σ^2 would each be distributed normally about its mean μ_i with a variance σ^2/n_i. If the μ_i were all equal to μ , then the sample means would distribute themselves about μ in a nearly normal distribution (not exactly normal because of the different sample sizes). They then argue that if we construct such a normal distribution, we should be able to slide it along the number line so as to locate a position such that the I sample means would appear to be random samples from it. To approximate this normal distribution, Box, Hunter & Hunter suggest we use the t distribution. To scale the t distribution to the expected spread of the sample means, they

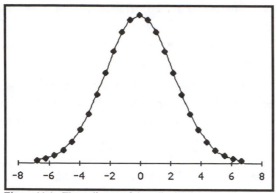

Figure 11.1. The ordinates of the t distribution as a function of
2.236 times t, 2.236 being the scale factor (MSe/n).5. The values
of t range from -3.00 to 3.00 in steps of .25.

suggest that a scale factor equal to the square root of MS_e/n be used where MS_e is mean square for error and n is the average sample size, $\sum_i n_i/I$.

To illustrate their procedure, we will assume that a one-factor design with seven groups having sample sizes 17, 18, 20, 27, 18, 20, and 20 produced corresponding means of 37, 40, 53, 55, 58, 63, and 65. We will assume that MS_e turned out to be 100. With the indicated sample sizes, df for error is 133 and the average of the n_i is 20. The scale factor is therefore $2.236 = (100/20)^{.5}$, and using the error df of 133, the tabled ordinates of the t distribution for t ranging from -3.00 to +3.00 in increments of .25 are given in Table 11.1 together with the values of t multiplied by the scale factor 2.236. (Note that the ordinate values depend upon the degrees of freedom.) A graph of the resulting reference distribution is shown in Figure 11.1.

The next step is to graph the means together with the reference distribution. This is shown in Figure 11.2.

The next step is to determine which means might have been sampled from the same reference distribution. This is accomplished by sliding, or imagining sliding, the reference distribution to determine which means appear to have possibly come from a single distribution. In Figure 11.3 we see that some investigators would conclude that the largest five means could have been drawn from the same reference distribution and would not conclude that they have been sampled from populations having different means.

From Figure 11.4 Box, Hunter & Hunter would conclude that it is implausible that the means of 40 and 53 arose by sampling from a single population. And of course the other means that are separated by greater numerical distances are even less likely to have come from the same population.

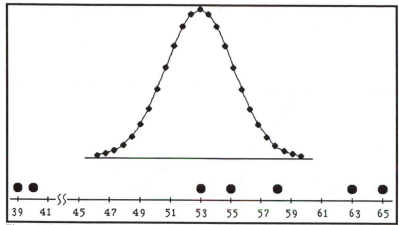

Figure 11.2. The group means graphed together with the reference distribution.

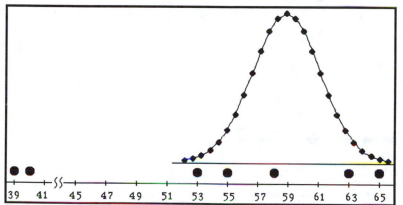

Figure 11.3. The largest five means could have been drawn from the same reference distribution.

It is interesting to note that for Box, Hunter & Hunter the distance between two means relative to the reference distribution is not the sole deciding feature in reaching a conclusion about whether two sample means came from the same population. They indicate that if the gap between two means that are barely encompassed by the reference distribution, such as is the case for 40 and 53 in Figure 11.4, is filled with many sample means, then it becomes increasingly plausible that the entire collection came from a single population, the two extreme ones being more likely in a large collection of sample means. Figure 11.5 shows a case where the interval between 40 and 53 is filled with many means and Box, Hunter & Hunter (Box1978, pp. 192-193) would conclude that the sample means of 40 and 53 simply

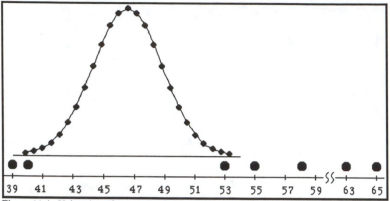

Figure 11.4. Using the reference distribution indicates the implausibility of the group means of 40 and 53 having been sampled from a single population.

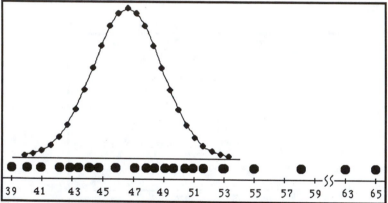

Figure 11.5. The many means between 40 and 53 make it more plausible that 40 and 53 are simply the extreme values of a large collection of means that all came from the same population.

constitute the extreme values of a large collection of sample means that all came from the same population.

Although the reference distribution procedure is simple to use and intuitively appealing in that it refers the conclusions back to the fundamental concept of the sampling distribution of sample means, it does leave a degree of subjectivity to the decision that is reminiscent of fitting a line to a scatterplot by holding a string to it and eyeballing it for the line of best fit. Different investigators, given the same data, will reach different conclusions. Not everyone, looking at Figure 11.3, would decide that the means of 53 and 65 were likely to have come from the same distribution. On the other hand, this amount of subjectivity in the inferential process is perhaps no worse than exists now with different investigators choosing different formal procedures from the great variety that are available. Jaccard, Becker, and Wood

(1984) noted that of 49 randomly sampled articles that specified a procedure for differences between pairs of means, "37% used the Newman-Keuls test, 27%used multiple *t* tests or Fisher's least significant difference test, 10%used Duncan's multiple-range test, 8% used Scheffés general multiple comparison procedure, 8% used the Bonferroni/Dunn test, and 8% used Tukey's honest significant difference (HSD) test." Of course, with any formal procedure, each investigator should reach the same conclusion given the same set of data. But this is scarcely to the point if investigators in fact do not use the same procedure.

TABLE 11.2 POWER OF THE RYAN AND THE PERITZ MULTIPLE COMPARISON PROCEDURES AGAINST THE HYPOTHESIS THAT $\mu_1 = \mu_2$ FOR DIFFERENT VALUES OF *d* WHEN $\mu_1 = 10 + d$ AND $\mu_2 = 12$

d	Ryan	Peritz
2.0	.010	.050
1.8	.025	.092
1.6	.084	.224
1.4	.218	.437
1.2	.429	.670
1.0	.663	.851
.8	.846	.950
.6	.947	.988
.4	.987	.998
.2	.998	.9997
.0	.9997	.9999

But another more forceful concern regarding the use of reference distributions is that sometimes the differences in error rates between different procedures are not as slight as Box, Hunter & Hunter imply but instead can be quite sizable. Furthermore, differences in power (the probability of rejecting the null hypothesis when it is false) can be quite substantial. For example, Begun and Gabriel (1981) compared the power of two procedures that we will present in detail below, Ryan's multiple comparison procedure (Ryan, 1959) and Peritz's procedure (Peritz, 1970; Begun & Gabriel, 1981). Begun and Gabriel considered the case where large differences existed among all of 10 population means except possibly between μ_1 and μ_2. They let μ_1 be $10 + d$ where $d < 2$, and let the other means μ_i = $10 + 2(i - 1)$ for i = 2, ..., 10, so the other means took the values 12, 14, ..., 28. They assumed that unknown to the investigator, $\sigma^2 = 1$. Then, assuming an experimentwise significance level of .05 for both procedures they were able to show that as d varied, the differences between the two procedures in the probability that the hypothesis that $\mu_1 = \mu_2$ would be rejected could be substantial. Table 11.2, taken from Begun and Gabriel (1981), shows for each procedure the probability of rejecting that hypothesis for various values of d. We can see in Table 11.2 that the differences in power between the two procedures can be substantial. These procedures will be compared in more detail below.

11.3 The various multiple comparison procedures vary in many ways. Multiple comparison procedures differ in whether the tests of hypotheses are conducted simultaneously or in stages. They differ regarding the type of contrast they are intended for. They differ in the assumptions regarding the sample sizes and the equality of the variances of the sampled populations. They differ in their treatment of α_i and α_f. They differ in regard to the test statistics they use and the theoretical distribution that provides the critical value. They differ in whether they provide a confidence interval as well as a test of a hypothesis. They differ in their strengths and weaknesses. In this chapter we will consider some of the most commonly used and what are generally considered the best of a very large number of methods but space will not permit an exhaustive treatment of all of the procedures that at one time or another have been recommended (the interested student can begin to pursue the topic with Duncan, 1955; Ryan, 1959, 1960; Miller, 1981; Games, 1971; Games, Keselman & Rogan, 1981; Begun & Gabriel, 1981; Jaccard, Becker & Wood, 1984; Zwick & Marascuilo, 1984).

11.4 The studentized range distribution. Before beginning our review of some of the methods, we must introduce one more sampling distribution. With the exception of Dunnett's procedure for contrasting I - 1 treatment groups with a control group, all of the procedures that we will consider use the t distribution, the F distribution, or the **studentized range distribution**. We have considered t and F. The studentized range will be briefly indicated here. Let R be the difference between the largest and the smallest of r independent unit normal variables (variables with a mean of zero and a standard deviation of one); R is the range. Let χ^2_v be a chi-square variable with v degrees of freedom, and let χ^2_v be independent of the r unit normal variables. Then the variable

$$q_{r,v} = R/(\chi^2_v/v)$$

has the studentized range distribution with parameters r and v. The upper 100α percentage point, $q_{\alpha,r,v}$, of this distribution has been tabled for various values of r and v and for values of α = .05 and .01 (Harter, 1960; also in Miller, 1971, pp. 234-237) and are included here as Statistical Table 5.

11.5 Multiple t-tests on all pairs of means. In a one-factor design with I levels, the overall null hypothesis is that the scores sampled at each level are samples from normal distributions having the same mean, that is, $\mu_1 = \mu_2 = ... = \mu_I$. The multiple t-test procedure on all pairs of means approaches this null hypothesis by contrasting each group mean with every other group mean. With I levels there are $I(I - 1)/2$ different pairs of means that can be contrasted. For $I \geq 3$, this will exceed the I - 1 orthogonal contrasts that can be made. The multiple t-test procedure simultaneously tests each of the $I(I - 1)/2$ contrasts of two means at a significance level equal to α and lets α_f increase as I increases. Customarily, it is assumed that the populations have the same variance. Let $t_{\alpha,dfe}$ denote the critical value of a t-statistic with df_e degrees of freedom for a two-tailed α-level significance test. That is, let $t_{\alpha,dfe}$ be the upper $100(1 - \alpha/2)$ percentage point of the t distribution with df_e degrees of freedom. Then the null hypothesis that $\mu_i = \mu_{i'}$ is rejected if

$$| M_i - M_{i'} |/[MS_e(1/n_i + 1/n_{i'})]^{.5} \geq t_{\alpha,dfe}.$$

The familywise error rate for the $I(I - 1)/2$ tests will be

$$\alpha_f = Pr[q_{I-1,dfe} > t_{\alpha,dfe} (2)^{.5}].$$

Games (1971, p. 541) describes how to use the Harter, Clemens, and Guthrie (1959) tables of the studentized range to solve for α_f.

A $100(1 - \alpha)$ percent confidence interval for the difference between μ_i and $\mu_{i'}$ is given by

$$Pr[(M_i - M_{i'}) - CP \leq (\mu_i-\mu_{i'}) \leq (M_i-M_{i'}) + CP] = 1 - \alpha,$$

where $CP = t_{\alpha,dfe}[MS_e(1/n_i +1/n_{i'})]^{.5}$. The probability that all of the true differences between pairs of means simultaneously fall in the confidence intervals so constructed is $1 - \alpha_f$.

The **strength** of the multiple t-test procedure lies in its **familiarity**, its **simplicity** and its **power**. Everyone who uses any procedure to test such hypotheses will know how to do a t-test (or as Miller,1981, puts it, "Everyone is born knowing the t distribution"). The computations even for unequal group n's are simple and straightforward. For equal n's, it is only necessary to compare each absolute difference between two sample means with the value $[MS_e(2/n)]^{.5} t_{\alpha,dfe}$. The procedure is more powerful than any of the other procedures in use but pays a heavy price in familywise error rate for this greater power. The **weakness** is an **unacceptably large familywise error rate** even for moderately large values of I unless α is chosen sufficiently small. For the researcher interested in controlling familywise error rate, attention to the choice of α is essential.

Games (1971) points out that while the multiple t-test procedure is usually considered inadequate by those concerned with α_f, it is formally equivalent to Tukey's WSD procedure (considered below) which is considered generally acceptable. The two procedures differ only in whether α_i is determined first and α_f is left to increase with I or α_f is determined first and α_i is left to become as small as necessary.

TABLE 11.3   VALUES OF α_f FOR I - 1 ORTHOGONAL t-TESTS AND FOR t-TESTS   ON ALL POSSIBLE PAIRS OF MEANS

I	3	5	7	9	15
$\alpha = .01$					
$1 - (1 - \alpha)^{I-1}$	.0199	.0394	.0585	.0772	.1312
$I(I-1)/2$ t's	.0268	.0735	.1299	.1904	.3880
$\alpha = .05$					
$1-(1 - \alpha)^{I-1}$	.0975	.1855	.2649	.3366	.5123
$I(I-1)/2$ t's	.1216	.2821	.4328	.5603	.8059

11.6 Simultaneous t-tests for h orthogonal contrasts, $h \le I - 1$. This procedure addresses the same general situation as that addressed by the multiple-t test procedure, but the t-tests are constrained to a set of h orthogonal contrasts from among the I - 1 possible orthogonal contrasts for I levels of a factor. The sample sizes need not be equal at each level. The variances of the I sampled populations are usually assumed to be equal. The null hypothesis that the contrast $\Sigma_i c_i \mu_i = 0$ is rejected if

$$\Sigma_i c_i M_i / [MS_e(\Sigma_i c_i^2 / n_i)]^{.5} \ge t_{\alpha, dfe}.$$

The Type I error rate for each test is α, and the familywise Type I error rate is

$$\alpha_f = 1 - (1 - \alpha)^h.$$

A $100(1 - \alpha)$ percent confidence interval for the contrast $\Sigma_i c_i \mu_i$ is given by

$$Pr\{\Sigma_i c_i M_i - t_{\alpha,dfe}[MS_e(\Sigma_i c_i^2/n_i)]^{.5} \leq \Sigma_i c_i \mu_i \leq \Sigma_i c_i M_i + t_{\alpha,dfe}[MS_e(\Sigma_i c_i^2/n_i)]^{.5}\}$$

$$= 1 - \alpha.$$

The probability that all of the h contrasts are contained within their confidence intervals is $(1 - \alpha)^h$.

TABLE 11.4 COMPARISON OF APPROXIMATE WITH EXACT UPPER 100α PERCENT POINTS IN THE t DISTRIBUTION USING THE APPROXIMATION $t_{\alpha,v} = z_\alpha + (z_\alpha^3 + z_\alpha)/4v$

df		α:	.40	.25	.10	.05	.025	.01
5	approx.		.266	.723	1.451	1.949	2.434	3.072
	exact		.267	.727	1.476	2.015	2.571	3.365
20	approx.		.256	.686	1.324	1.721	2.079	2.512
	exact		.257	.687	1.325	1.725	2.086	2.528
60	approx.		.255	.682	1.310	1.696	2.039	2.450
	exact		.254	.679	1.296	1.671	2.000	2.390
z_α			.253	.674	1.282	1.645	1.960	2.326

The **strengths** of this procedure are **familiarity, simplicity of computation, and ease of computation of the** α_f. Duncan (1955, pp. 14-16) has argued strongly for allowing α_f to increase with the increased number of independent tests permitted by increased degrees of freedom, although on other grounds he favors multiple range or multiple F-tests (see below). But many other workers still find a **weakness** in this procedure in that that **the increase in $1 - (1 - \alpha)^h$ as h increases becomes unacceptable**. Table 11.3, following Games (1971, p. 541), shows the increase in α_f as h increases and compares the values of α_f when I-1 orthogonal t tests are performed versus when the entire set of $I(I-1)/2$ t tests for all possible pairs of means are performed. One natural approach to the unacceptable increase in $1 - (1 - \alpha)^h$ as h increases is to constrain it in advance. This is done in the following procedure.

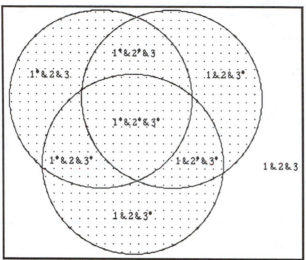

Figure 11.6a. The areas corresponding to the probabilities of rejecting
the starred hypothesis and not rejecting the unstarred hypothesis.

11.7 Simultaneous t-tests for h orthogonal contrasts with α_f held at α. This procedure differs from the preceding one only in setting α_f equal to α and letting the α_i be reduced accordingly rather than setting the α_i to α and letting α_f increase. The α_i can all take the same value or can be assigned different values. If they all take the same value, that value will be $1 - (1 - \alpha)^{1/h}$. The null hypothesis that the contrast $\Sigma_i c_i \mu_i = 0$ is rejected if

$$\Sigma_i c_i M_i / [MS_e(\Sigma_i c_i^2/n_i)]^{.5} \geq t_{1-(1-\alpha)^{1/h}, dfe}.$$

The Type I error rate for each test is $1 - (1 - \alpha)^{1/h}$, and the familywise Type I error rate is $\alpha_f = \alpha$. A $100(1 - \alpha)^{1/h}$ percent confidence interval for the contrast $\Sigma_i c_i \mu_i$ is given by

$$Pr\{\Sigma_i c_i M_i - t_{1-(1-\alpha)^{1/h}, dfe}[MS_e(\Sigma_i c_i^2/n_i)]^{.5} \leq \Sigma_i c_i \mu_i \leq \Sigma_i c_i M_i +$$

$$t_{1-(1-\alpha)^{1/h}, dfe}[MS_e(\Sigma_i c_i^2/n_i)]^{.5}\} = (1 - \alpha)^{1/h}.$$

The probability that all of the h contrasts are contained within their confidence intervals is $(1 - \alpha)$.

The **strength** of this method lies in its **holding the familywise Type I error rate to a selected value** α. The first **weakness** is that the procedure **rapidly becomes too conservative, using very low power tests for large h unless the value of** α_f

is chosen large. For example, with h = 5 and $\alpha_f = .05$, the α_i are down to .01. The second **weakness** is that the

critical values of t are not tabled and will have to be calculated. Linear or curvilinear interpolation may be used in the standard t tables, or the approximation, due to Peiser (1943),

$$t_{\alpha,v} = z_\alpha + (z_\alpha^3 + z_\alpha)/4v$$

may be used in which v is the degrees of freedom for t and z_α is the upper 100α percent point in the standard normal distribution. Table 11.4 shows a comparison of the approximate with the exact values of t for some selected degrees of freedom and values of α. If this approximation is not satisfactory, exact values may be obtained by using the fact that t_v^2 is equivalent to $F_{1,v}$ and $F_{1,v}/(1 + F_{1,v})$ is equivalent to a generic beta variable with the same degrees of freedom as $F_{1,v}$. Hence the cumulative distribution function of $(t_v^2/v)/[1 + t_v^2/v]$ will be the incomplete beta function with parameters p = .5 and q = v/2 (Miller, 1971, p. 70).

11.8 Bonferroni t-tests on h contrasts. Suppose, again in analogy to the testing of a family of three true null hypotheses H_{01}, H_{02}, and H_{03}, we are flipping three coins. A heads on coin i is equivalent to rejecting the null hypothesis H_{0i} and a tails to accepting it. Assume that for coin i the probability

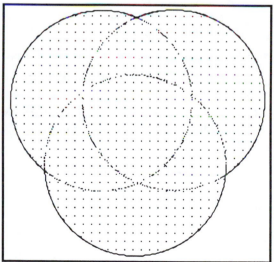

Figure 11.6b. The area corresponding to the probability of rejection of at least one of the three hypotheses. That is, the probability of rejecting H_{01} or rejecting H_{02} or rejecting H_{03} (the inclusive "or").

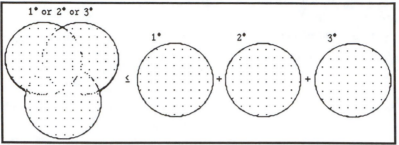

Figure 11.6c. The value of α_f is always less than or equal to $\alpha_1 + \alpha_2 + \alpha_3$.

of a heads, and therefore a false rejection, is α_i, $i = 1, 2, 3$. If the coins are independent, the probability of no false rejections is $(1 - \alpha_1)(1 - \alpha_2)(1 - \alpha_3)$. It is easy to show that $1 - (\alpha_1 + \alpha_2 + \alpha_3) \le (1 - \alpha_1)(1 - \alpha_2)(1 - \alpha_3) = \Pr\{\text{no false rejections}\} = 1 - \alpha_f$. Therefore α_f will always be less than $(\alpha_1 + \alpha_2 + \alpha_3)$. That is, the familywise error rate will always be less than or equal to the sum of the individual error rates. If the coins are not independent, we ordinarily cannot give a simple expression for the probability of no false rejections, but we can still show that $1 - (\alpha_1 + \alpha_2 + \alpha_3) \le \Pr\{\text{no false rejections}\} = 1 - \alpha_f$ and therefore α_f will always be less than or equal to $(\alpha_1 + \alpha_2 + \alpha_3)$. Figure 11.6a shows a Venn diagram in which the areas represent the probabilities of rejecting the three hypotheses separately, pairwise, or all three at once. In the diagram an i*

denotes rejection of hypothesis i and an i denotes its acceptance. Thus, for example, 1*&2*&3* labels the area corresponding to the probability of rejecting all three hypotheses. Figure 11.6b shows the area corresponding to α_f, the probability of rejecting at least one of the three hypotheses. Figure 11.6c shows the area corresponding to the probability $(\alpha_1 + \alpha_2 + \alpha_3)$. It is evident that α_f will always be less than or equal to $(\alpha_1 + \alpha_2 + \alpha_3)$. This, then, exemplifies the Bonferroni inequality applied to the case of testing three null hypotheses. The inequality applies regardless of the number of hypotheses so that for h hypotheses, α_f is always greater than or equal to $\alpha_1 + \alpha_2 + ... + \alpha_h$. This means that by choosing the α_i such that $\alpha_1 + \alpha_2 + ... + \alpha_h = \alpha$, the value of α_f can be held to a value no greater than α.

The Bonferroni t-tests assume equal population variances, but the sample sizes may be unequal. This procedure differs from the preceding one only in choosing the α_i so that they sum to α. The α_i can all take the same value or can be assigned different values. If they all take the same value, that value will be α/h. The null hypothesis that the gth contrast $\Sigma_i c_{gi} \mu_i = 0$ is rejected if $\Sigma_i c_{gi} M_i / [MS_e(\Sigma_i c_{gi}^2/n_i)]^{.5} \ge t_{\alpha g, dfe}$. The Type I error rate for each test is α_i and the familywise Type I error rate is $\alpha_f \le \alpha$. A greater than $100(1 - \alpha)$ percent confidence interval for the entire set of contrasts $\Sigma_i c_{gi} \mu_i$, $g = 1, 2, ..., h$, is given by

TABLE 11.5 SCORES FOR FIVE EXPERIMENTAL GROUPS

	Group			
1	2	3	4	5
15	11	20	19	10
15	16	3	9	17
10	15	10	16	13
13	15	12	17	16
14	16	15	14	18
11	16	11	19	24
10	14	9	6	10
11	17	13	14	14
6	21	12	15	20
3	11	4	15	19
9	17	11	11	26
9	4	14	16	10
11	18	14	9	18
6	18	16	11	13
7	14	13	12	14
Totals 150	223	177	203	242
Means 10.00	14.87	11.80	13.53	16.13
$\Sigma_j Y_{ij}^2$ 1670	3535	2347	2949	4236
$\Sigma_i \Sigma_j Y_{ij}^2 = 14{,}737$				

$$Pr\{\Sigma_i c_{gi} M_i - t_{\alpha g, dfe}[MS_e(\Sigma_i c_{gi}^2/n_i)]^{.5} \leq \Sigma_i c_{gi}\mu_i \leq \Sigma_i c_{gi} M_i +$$

$$t_{\alpha g, dfe}[MS_e(\Sigma_i c_{gi}^2/n_i)]^{.5}, g = 1,2, ..., h\} \geq 1 - \alpha,$$

where for equal α_i the value of $t_{\alpha g}$ in the previous two expressions is $t_{\alpha/h}$.

The **strength** of Bonferroni t-tests lies in **holding α_f less than α whether or not the contrasts are orthogonal.** This is very useful in that often the investigator wants to test two or more nonorthogonal contrasts. The method is usually superior to Scheffé's method (section 11.13) except when the number of contrasts is considerably greater than the degrees of freedom for the source in question. It is the preferred method for contrasts on repeated measurement factors and within-subject factors (see the section on comparison of methods). Its **weakness** lies in its being **wastefully conservative in that** α_f **is truly less than** α by an unknown amount and also in the **need for special tables or use of special formulas to obtain critical values of t**.

In the event that the investigator wishes to test only orthogonal contrasts, an improved Bonferroni inequality is available (Kimball, 1951; Miller, 1981, pp. 101-102). Kimball showed that in the case where p independent numerator mean squares are being compared with the same denominator mean square (which is independent of all of the numerators), forming a family of hypotheses, with α_1, α_2, ..., α_p being the error rates for each test, the familywise error rate would be $\alpha_f \leq 1 - (1 - \alpha_1)(1 - \alpha_2) ... (1 - \alpha_p)$, which is less than or equal to $1 - (\alpha_1 + \alpha_2 + ... + \alpha_p)$. In the case of orthogonal contrasts, any concern about the lack of independence due to the use of the same denominator mean square should be alleviated by Kimball's limit on the familywise error rate.

TABLE 11.6 ANOVA FOR THE DATA IN TABLE 11.5

Source	df	SS	MS
Groups	4	13,555.4	3388.85
Error	70	1181.6	16.88

TABLE 11.7 COEFFICIENTS FOR FOUR ORTHOGONAL CONTRASTS

	Groups				
	1	2	3	4	5
C_{1i}	-1	0	1	0	0
C_{2i}	0	1	0	-1/2	-1/2
C_{3i}	0	0	0	-1	1
C_{4i}	-1.5	1	-1.5	1	1

11.9 A numerical example of the four simultaneous methods that use the t distribution to obtain critical values. The four methods described so far all share the use of the t distribution for determining the critical value of the test statistic. It is convenient to interrupt the description of the various methods to illustrate how these four procedures are alike and how they differ by applying them to the same set of data. Consider the scores for five different experimental groups shown in Table 11.5. The design is a one-factor design with 15 subjects per level. Table 11.6 shows the summary of the analysis of variance from which MS_e is obtained. It should be mentioned that although the analysis of variance provides MS_e for the test statistics, **there is no requirement that the overall (omnibus) F-test be performed prior to using any of the methods that are about to be demonstrated.** There is a staged analysis, Fisher's LSD procedure, which requires an overall F-test before using t-tests to test the differences between all pairs of means, but this procedure will be discussed below.

For the **multiple t-tests on all pairs of means,** using a two-tailed significance test with $\alpha = .05$, the critical value of $t_{.05,70} = 1.995$. The tests can be performed by comparing the absolute difference between any two means with the value

$$[MS_e(1/n_i + 1/n_{i'})]^{.5} \, t_{\alpha,dfe} = [16.88(1/15 + 1/15)]^{.5}(1.995) = 2.99.$$

If the difference between the two means exceeds 2.99, it is a significant difference.

Consider the following convenient way to represent the results of these tests (Duncan, 1955):

1	3	4	2	5
10.00	11.80	13.53	14.87	16.13

We display the group means in order from low to high and draw an unbroken line beneath those means that are not significantly different. We read the following display as indicating that the difference between 10.00 and 11.80 is not significant; the difference between 11.80 and 13.53 is not significant; 13.53, 14.87, and 15.13 do not significantly differ from one another, but all other differences are significant.

The next procedure to be exemplified is the case of **t-tests for h orthogonal contrasts with h ≤ I - 1 all conducted at $\alpha_i = \alpha$ with $\alpha_f = 1 - (1 - \alpha)^h$.** In this case $I - 1 = 4$ and we will choose $h = 4$ as well. The value of α is .05. As the four orthogonal contrasts permitted by the four degrees of freedom for Groups, we will use the contrasts involving the sets of contrast coefficients in Table 11.7. The critical value of $t_{.05,70}$ for a two-tailed test is 1.995. The values of $\Sigma_i c_i M_i / [MS_e(\Sigma_i c_i^2/n_i)]^{.5}$ for the four contrasts are

C_1: $(11.80 - 10.00)/[16.88(1/15 + 1/15)]^{.5} = 1.20$

C_2: $[14.87 - (.5)13.53 - (.5)16.13]/\{16.88[1/15 + (.5^2)/15 + (.5^2)/15]\}^{.5} = .03$

C_3: $(16.13 - 13.53)/[16.88(1/15 + 1/15)]^{.5} = 1.73$

C_4: $[14.87 + 11.80 + 16.13 - (1.5)10.00 - (1.5)11.80]/ \{16.88[1/15 + 1/15 + 1/15 + (1.5^2)/15 +$

$(1.5^2)/15]\}^{.5} = 10.98$

Only the fourth contrast is significant by this method.

We next apply to the same four contrasts the method of **t-tests for h orthogonal contrasts with h $\leq$ I - 1, all conducted at $\alpha_i = 1 - (1 - \alpha)^{1/h}$, holding $\alpha_f = \alpha$,** using $\alpha = .05$ and two-tailed tests. For h = 4, $\alpha_i = 1 - (1 - .05)^{1/4} = .0127$. The value in the standard normal distribution, which has .0127/2 of the distribution above it, is approximately 2.4922. Using Peiser's formula $t_{\alpha,v} = z_\alpha + (z_\alpha^3 + z_\alpha)/4v = [(4v + 1)z_\alpha + z_\alpha^3]/4v$ to approximate the required critical value gives $t_{.0127,70} = 2.56$. Using this larger critical value of t still results in only the fourth contrast being significant.

TABLE 11.8 COEFFICIENTS FOR TWO NONORTHOGONAL CONTRASTS

		Groups			
	1	2	3	4	5
C_{5i}	1/2	-1	1/2	0	0
C_{6i}	0	1	0	-1	0

To exemplify the **Bonferroni t-tests on h not necessarily orthogonal contrasts,** we will consider two cases, one with selected nonorthogonal contrasts and the second with contrasts on all possible pairs of means. In the first case the investigator tests the four contrasts considered in the two previous procedures but also tests two additional contrasts with the coefficients given in Table 11.8. Holding $\alpha_f < \alpha$ in this case means choosing $\alpha_i = \alpha/6$. For a two-tailed .05 value of α, $\alpha_i = .0083$. The approximate value of $t_{.0083,70}$ is $2.6433 + (2.6433^3 + 2.6433)/280 = 2.72$ (the value of 2.6433 was obtained by linear interpolation in the standard normal distribution), an even larger value than in the preceding cases. The first three contrasts are still not significant, the fourth still is significant, C_5: $[(.5)10.00 + (.5)13.53 - 11.80]/ \{16.88[(.5^2)/15 + (.5^2)/15 + 1/15]\}^{.5} = -.027$ is not significant, and C_6: $(11.80 - 14.87)/ \{16.88[(1)/15 + (1)/15]\}^{.5} = -.79$ is not significant.

In the second case, **applying Bonferroni-t tests to all possible pairs of means**, involves $I(I - 1)/2 = 10$ contrasts; therefore $\alpha_i = .05/10 = .005$. The approximate value of $t_{.005,70}$ is $2.8087 + (2.8087^3 + 2.8087)/280 = 2.90$. Using a critical t value of 2.90 gives a critical difference between two means of $2.90[16.88(1/15 + 1/15)]^{.5} = 4.35$. The results of the 10 contrasts are summarized in the following display.

1	3	4	2	5
10.00	11.80	13.53	14.87	16.13

We see that with the Bonferroni procedure the mean for Group 1 differs significantly from the means for Groups 2 and 5, but there are no significant differences among the other four Group means. This result differs substantially from that found with the multiple t-test procedure applied to all pairs of means.

We now take up some procedures that use the studentized range statistic.

11.10   Tukey's Wholly Significant Difference (WSD) test applied to all possible pairs of means. The WSD procedure, proposed by Tukey (1952, 1953; see also Miller, 1981, pp. 37-48) requires equal numbers of scores in each group as well as the same variance in each of the sampled populations. The value of α_f is α. The α_i all take the same value which is $Pr\{t_{dfe} \geq q_{\alpha,I,dfe}/2^{.5}\}$. The null hypothesis that $\mu_i - \mu_{i'} = 0$ is rejected if

$$|M_i - M_{i'}|/(MS_e/n)^{.5} \geq q_{\alpha,I,dfe}.$$

A $100(1 - \alpha)$ percent confidence interval for $I(I-1)/2$ contrasts $\mu_i - \mu_{i'}$, $i,i' = 1,2, ..., I$, is given by

$\Pr\{ \ |(M_i - M_{i'}) - (\mu_i - \mu_{i'})|/(MS_e/n)^{.5} \leq q_{\alpha, I, dfe}, \ i,i' = 1,2, ..., I\} \ = 1 - \alpha.$

The **strength** of Tukey's WSD procedure lies in **holding α_f equal to α for contrasts of all pairs of means; it is a simple procedure, and it is always more powerful than the Bonferroni procedure applied to all pairs of means given equal sample sizes and equal variances.** The requirement of equal sample sizes is not actually a weakness in that the **Tukey-Kramer generalization** (Kramer, 1956), which uses the test statistic

$|M_i - M_{i'}|/[MS_e(1/n_i + 1/n_{i'})/2]^{.5}$

when the sample sizes for group i and group i' are not equal, is available. To avoid distortion of the Type I error rate, it is important that the equal variances assumption be met when equal sample sizes do not exist. The Tukey WSD and the Tukey-Kramer generalization are preferred by many researchers for tests involving between-subjects factors (Jaccard, Becker, & Wood, 1984; Dunnett, 1980). The WSD procedure can be applied to more general contrasts (Miller, 1981) but it is inferior to a variety of other procedures such as that of Scheffé and the Bonferroni procedure.

Games' (1971) observation that the WSD method is completely equivalent to the use of the multiple t procedure at a more stringent (smaller) signficance level deserves repeating. Games points out that there is no intrinsic difference between the two methods and that the claim that the WSD method is superior to using multiple t-tests (Petrinovich & Hardyck, 1969) is spurious. The practical difference between the two is that the WSD procedure allows easy control of α_f but α_i is more difficult to specify, while the multiple t procedure provides for easy control of α_i with α_f slightly more difficult to specify. Since $t = q/\sqrt{2}$, we can determine what critical value of t would correspond to a critical value of q and then approximate the value of α that would have to be used in the multiple t procedure for equivalence. For 30 or 60 degrees of freedom for error, as the number of groups takes the values 2, 4, 6, and 8, the value of α for multiple t that would be equivalent to using .05 for α_f in the WSD test takes the values .05, about .01, about .005, and about .003. Thus, while WSD and multiple t are formally equivalent, as the number of groups increases they increasingly differ in their severity so far as individual contrast Type I error rates are concerned.

11.11 The Games and Howell procedure. Games and Howell (1976) provided a procedure that can be used with unequal sample sizes and unequal population variances. The available evidence (Games, Keselman & Rogan, 1981) indicates that the value of α_f

stays quite close to α, although it can slightly exceed α. The α_i are unknown. The null hypothesis that $\mu_i - \mu_{i'} = 0$ is rejected if

$$|M_i - M_{i'}|/[.5(s_i^2/n_i + s_{i'}^2/n_{i'})]^{.5} \geq q_{\alpha,I,df*},$$

where s_i^2 is the usual unbiased estimate of a population variance and df* are obtained using the Welch (1938) solution for error df,

$$df* = (s_i^2/n_i + s_{i'}^2/n_{i'})^2/[\ (s_i^4/n_i^2(n_i - 1)\ +\ s_{i'}^4/n_{i'}^2(n_{i'} - 1)\ ].$$

The **strength** of the Games and Howell procedure is that it is **more powerful than the alternatives** that have been proposed. Its two **weaknesses** are that the value of α_f can exceed α, and the computations are cumbersome if not done with a computer since the difference between two means is compared to a different value for each pair and the df have to be computed separately for each pair as well. In the next section we will apply the WSD and the Games and Howell procedures to the example data.

11.12 Application of the WSD and the Games and Howell procedures to the example data. According to the WSD procedure, the critical difference between two means is $(MS_e/n)^{.5}\ q_{\alpha,I,dfe} = [(16.88/15)^{.5}]\ (3.967) = 4.21$, requiring a somewhat smaller difference than the Bonferroni procedure. The results are summarized by the display

1	3	4	2	5
10.00	11.80	13.53	14.87	16.13

giving a significant difference between the means for Groups 3 and 5 that was not indicated by the Bonferroni t procedure. **In the fixed-effects, between-subjects situation with equal sample sizes and equal population variances, the WSD procedure will always be more powerful than the Bonferroni procedure** (Ury, 1976) and the Bonferroni method is therefore "not recommended" in that context (Jaccard, Becker & Wood, 1984, p. 591).

The Games and Howell procedure requires computation of a different denominator and a different value of the degrees of freedom for each test statistic. The values of the s_i^2/n_i are involved in both these computations. For the example data, these values are

Group	1	2	3	4	5
s_i^2/n_i	.8095	1.0463	1.2305	.9606	1.5797

To provide the student with a check on procedure, the test statistic denominator for the contrast of the means for Groups 1 and 2 is

$$[.5(.8095 + 1.0463)]^{.5} = .9633,$$

the degrees of freedom are

$$(.8095 + 1.0463)^2 / (.8095^2/14 + 1.0463^2/14) = 27.5514,$$

the value of the test statistic is $(10 - 14.8667)/.9633 = -5.0521$, and the value of $q_{.05,5,27.5514}$, obtained by linear interpolation in the tables of the percentage points of the studentized range, is 4.1281, indicating a significant difference between the means for Group 1 and Group 2. Table 11.9 summarizes the values of the test statistics, the degrees of freedom, and the interpolated values of q for the contrasts of all pairs of means and the results of the contrasts are summarized by the display

1	3	4	2	5
10.00	11.80	13.53	14.87	16.13

11.13 Scheffé's method for testing all contrasts. Scheffé's method is appropriate to any contrast of means. The sample sizes may be unequal, but the population variances are assumed to be equal. The null hypothesis that the contrast $\Sigma_i c_i \mu_i = 0$ is rejected if the test statistic

$$(\Sigma_i c_i M_i)^2/[MS_e(\Sigma_i c_i^2/n_i)]$$

is greater than the critical value $(I-1)F_{\alpha,I-1,df_e}$ (or alternatively if $(\Sigma_i c_i M_i)^2 \geq [MS_e(\Sigma_i c_i^2/n_i)](I-1)F_{\alpha,I-1,df_e}$). The familywise error rate, α_f, is held to a value less than

α, and the individual contrast Type I error rate is $\alpha_i = \Pr\{|t| \geq [(I-1)F_{\alpha,I-1,dfe}]^{.5}\}$. A $100(1-\alpha)$ percent confidence interval is provided for the one-factor design by

$\Pr\{$ For all sets of c_i, $i = 1, ..., I$, such that $\Sigma_i c_i = 0$:

$$\Sigma_i c_i M_i - MS_e(\Sigma_i c_i^2/n_i) [(I-1)F_{\alpha,I-1,dfe}]^{.5} \leq \Sigma_i c_i \mu_i \leq \Sigma_i c_i M_i +$$

$$MS_e(\Sigma_i c_i^2/n_i) [(I-1)F_{\alpha,I-1,dfe}]^{.5} \} = 1 - \alpha.$$

TABLE 11.9 TEST STATISTICS, ESTIMATED DEGREES OF FREEDOM, AND LINEARLY INTERPOLATED q VALUES FOR GAMES AND HOWELL'S PROCEDURE

Test Statistics	2	3	4	5
1	-5.0521	-1.7823	-3.7557	-5.6116
2		2.8742	1.3310	-1.1054
3			-1.6560	-3.6557
4				-2.3070
df	2	3	4	5
1	27.5514	26.8565	27.7974	25.3644
2		27.8181	27.9490	26.8908
3			27.5817	27.5742
4				26.4304
q	2	3	4	5
1	4.1281	4.1355	4.1255	4.1514
2		4.1253	4.1239	4.1352
3			4.1278	4.1279
4				4.1401

It has sometimes been stated (Hays, 1973) that the overall F-test must be performed and a significant F-statistic obtained prior to the use of Scheffé's method, but this is not true. The familywise error rate is held at less than α without any such prior overall F-test.

The **strength** of the Scheffé procedure is its **very great generality**. An **unlimited number of contrasts may be tested at the α_f familywise error rate.** The **method generalizes not only to many-factor fixed-effects models but also to regression models (see Chapter 12).** It is highly recommended for data

snooping where the investigator has not planned the contrasts in advance but is trying to find whatever might be lying in the bushes. It is often the most powerful procedure for the specific tests to which it is applied. On the other hand, its **weakness** is that because it is so general, there are **often more specialized techniques that are more powerful for answering specific questions**. For example, the WSD method is more powerful than Scheffé's for testing all differences between pairs of means, while Scheffé's method is more powerful than WSD for contrasts involving more than two means (Scheffé, 1959; Miller, 1981). Also, because the familywise error rate applies to all possible contrasts, the Scheffé procedure is likely to be unnecessarily conservative since all contrasts, or even a complete set of orthogonal contrasts, are often not of interest.

We now apply Scheffé's method to the six contrasts to which the Bonferroni t-tests were applied in section 11.9 and to the remaining contrasts of pairs of means not included in those six. The same critical value $(I-1)F_{\alpha,I-1,dfe} = 4F_{.05,4,70} = 15.92$ is used for all of the contrasts. The test statistics for the three contrasts involving more than two means are C_2: $[14.87 - (.5)13.53 - (.5)16.13]^2/\{16.88[1/15 + (.5^2)/15 + (.5^2)/15]\} = .0009$, not significant; C_4: $[14.87 + 11.80 + 16.13 - (1.5)10.00 - (1.5)11.80]^2/\{16.88[1/15 + 1/15 + 1/15 + (1.5^2)/15 + (1.5^2)/15]\} = 12.09$, not significant; and C_5: $[(.5)10.00 + (.5)13.53 - 11.80]^2/\{16.88[(.5^2)/15 + (.5^2)/15 + 1/15]\} = .0007$, not significant. The difference $M_i - M_{i'}$ is significant if $(M_i - M_{i'})^2 \geq [MS_e(\Sigma_i c_i^2/n_i)](I-1)F_{\alpha,I-1,dfe} = 16.88(2/15)(15.92) = 35.83$, which means that two means are significantly different if they are separated by $\sqrt{35.83} = 5.99$ or more. Only the difference between M_1 and M_5 is that great, so the result of applying the highly conservative Scheffé method to the contrasts of all the pairs of means is given by the display

1	3	4	2	5
10.00	11.80	13.53	14.87	16.13

11.14 Stage tests. In the simultaneous tests, the difference between a pair of means is significant if that difference exceeds some given value. **In the stage tests, the difference between a pair of means is significant provided that each subset of means containing that pair of means is significant by some test depending upon the procedure.** In the case of multiple range tests on a group of I means, two means are significantly different if the range of each and every subset of p means containing that pair of means is significant according to an α_p-level studentized range test. With a multiple F-test procedure on a group of I means, two means are significantly different if the F-test of each and every subset of p means containing that pair of means is significant according to an α_p-level F-test.

The most common exception to this characteristic of stage tests is **Fisher's Least Significant Difference (LSD) test**, which is identical in procedure to the multiple t-test procedure except that it requires that at stage I the overall α-level F-test in the analysis of variance be significant prior to proceding to stage II wherein α-level t-tests are performed on all of the pairs of means. The **strengths** of Fisher's LSD lie in its **great familiarity and the simplicity of the procedure, plus the good power of the overall F-test**. It is nice to be able to depend on the F-test to know that there is a difference and then to be able to follow up that F-test with t-ests to try to locate which means are contributing to the significant F. Also, except for the multiple F-test, it is the only stage procedure we will consider that can be used with different sample sizes in the different groups. But there are **weaknesses**. Games (1971) points out that with $I = 6$ and certain situations with small degrees of freedom, **a significant F can be found but with no significant t for any pair of means**. The significant F indicates that there is a significant contrast of the means and therefore that the means are not all equal,but it does not indicate what that contrast is. Since the nonsignificant t's do not detect that difference, a Type II error will occur.

Another way in which Type II errors can proliferate is in a situation where there is a significant linear component (see Chapter 10) but where the means at each level do not differ very much from the means at adjacent levels. **The overall F-test can be nonsignificant and prevent the finding of the significant linear component that would have been detected had the overall F-test been omitted.**

Another problem with the LSD procedure, indicated by Games, is exemplified by a one-factor design with seven levels in which two of the groups have similar means but these two means are much larger than the other five, which are also similar to each other. The overall F-test will detect the difference between the two means and the five others, but then the $(7)(6)/2 = 21$ pairs of means will be tested by t-tests, possibly resulting in a **very high familywise Type I error rate**. The sudden shift from the overall test to tests of the pairs of means is avoided by the other stage methods, to which we now turn.

11.15 Duncan's multiple range test. Duncan's (1955) multiple range test requires equal sample sizes and equal variances. Two means are significantly different if the range of every subset of p means in the I-group one-factor design is significant at the α_p level, where $\alpha_p = 1 - (1-\alpha)^{p-1}$. For each set of p means, the test statistic is $|M_{max} - M_{min}|/(MS_e/n)^{.5}$, where M_{max} is the largest of the p means and M_{min} is the smallest. The critical value for a p level range is $q_{1-(1-\alpha)^{p-1},p,df_e}$ and these critical values have been tabled by Duncan (1955) and are given here as Statistical Table 8.

To test the means in the example data, we will need the values for p = 2, 3, 4, and 5. Using Duncan's table and linearly interpolating for 70 degrees of freedom, we obtain as the values of $q_{1-(1-.05)^{p-1},p,70}$ the values

p:	2	3	4	5
q:	2.82	2.97	3.07	3.14

Let's focus on the difference between the means for Groups 1 and 2. If the difference between the means for Groups 1 and 2 is to be significant, then the range of the entire group of five means (p = 5) must be significant using the critical value 3.14; the range of each of the three groups of four means (p = 4) that include Groups 1 and 2 (1,2,3,4; 1,2,3,5; and 1,2,4,5) must be significant using the critical value 3.07; the range of each of the three groups of three means that include Groups 1 and 2 (1,2,3; 1,2,4; 1,2,5) must be significant using the critical value 2.97; and the range for Groups 1 and 2 must be significant using the critical value 2.82.

Since the denominator of the test statistic will always be $(MS_e/n)^{.5} = (16.88/15)^{.5} = 1.06$, it is simpler to compare each p-level range, $|M_{max} - M_{min}|$, with the quantity $(MS_e/n)^{.5} q_{1-(1-.05)^{p-1},p,70}$ which for the different values of p takes the values

p:	2	3	4	5
$(MS_e/n)^{.5} q$	2.99	3.15	3.25	3.33

The example means were

1	2	3	4	5
10.00	14.87	11.80	13.53	16.13

If the difference between 10.00 and 14.87 is to be significant, then for p = 5 (Groups 1,2,3,4,5), 16.13 - 10.00 must exceed 3.33; for p = 4 (Groups1,2,3,4; Groups 1,2,3,5; Groups 1,2,4,5) 16.13 - 10.00 and 13.53 - 10.00 must exceed 3.25, for p = 3

(Groups 1,2,3; Groups 1,2,4; Groups 1,2,5) , 16.13 - 10.00 and 14.87 - 10.00 must exceed 3.15, and for p = 2 (1,2) , 14.87 - 10.00 must exceed 2.99. Since all these conditions are satisfied, the means for Groups 1 and 2 are significantly different. The steps of the complete multiple range test are given in Table 11.10 and summarized by the display

1	3	4	2	5
10.00	11.80	13.53	14.87	16.13

TABLE 11.10   THE DUNCAN MULTIPLE RANGE TEST FOR THE EXAMPLE DATA

p = 5	16.13 - 10.00 = 6.13 > 3.33; draw no line
p = 4	14.87 - 10.00 = 4.87 > 3.25; draw no line
	16.13 - 11.80 = 4.33 > 3.25; draw no line
p = 3	16.13 - 13.53 = 2.60 < 3.15; draw a line
	14.87 - 11.80 = 3.07 < 3.15; draw a line
	3.53 - 10.00 = 3.53 > 3.15; draw no line
p = 2	11.80 - 10.00 = 1.80 < 2.99; draw a line
	13.53 - 11.80 = 1.73 < 2.99; draw a line
	14.87 - 13.53 = 1.34 < 2.99; draw a line
	16.13 - 14.87 = 1.26 < 2.99; draw a line

The student should go through the motions of performing the test since various shortcuts become immediately apparent, circumventing the necessity for performing all of the comparison of the ranges to the $(MS_e/n)^{.5}$ q values. Once the difference between 10.00 and 14.87 is shown to exceed 3.25, there is no need to go through the motions of comparing the difference between 10.00 and 16.13 to 3.25, and so forth.

Duncan's test is as lenient with α_f " as any other test seriously advocated in the literature, and more lenient than most writers advocate" (Games, 1971). Because of this leniency toward Type I errors, Duncan's procedure is always more powerful than Tukey's WSD and more powerful than the next method to be considered, that of Newman (1939) and Keuls (1952). In support of this leniency Duncan (1955) argues that the significance level for a p-level range test should depend on the degrees of freedom for that many levels, p - 1. If p - 1 independent α-level tests for p - 1 separate hypotheses are performed, the overall Type I error rate will be $1 - (1 - \alpha)^{p-1}$. Duncan's position is that this is not fundamentally different from the p - 1 independent contrasts (except for the use of the same denominator) that could be performed with p - 1 degrees of freedom even though there are $p(p - 1)/2$ pairwise contrasts in all. Therefore, he argues, for a p-level range test, the significance level should be $1 - (1 - \alpha)^{p-1}$. Duncan's (1955) argument is much longer and deserves reading.

Miller (1981) replied that as long as the hypotheses are independent, Duncan's argument for a $1 - (1 - \alpha)^{p-1}$ error rate is acceptable, but if the hypotheses were not unrelated, as might well be the case in testing numerous contrasts in a family of contrasts, Miller would prefer an error rate that offered protection to the combined hypotheses. "The degree of protection should be based on the relatedness of the null hypotheses and their need for protection, and not on the probabilistic dependence or independence of the test statistics" (Miller, 1981, p. 89).

11.16 The Newman-Keuls multiple range test. The only difference between the Newman-Keuls procedure and the Duncan procedure is that where Duncan allows the significance level to depend on p, the Newman-Keuls procedure holds $\alpha_p = \alpha$. The critical values, q_{α,p,df_e}, are therefore obtained from the tables of the percentage points of the studentized range rather than from Duncan's tables. For the example data, the critical values of q, obtained by linear interpolation, are

p:	2	3	4	5
q:	2.82	3.39	3.73	3.97

Again it is simpler to compare each p-level range, $|M_{max} - M_{min}|$, with the quantity $(MS_e/n)^{.5}$ $q_{\alpha,p,70}$, which for the different values of p takes the values

p:	2	3	4	5
$(MS_e/n)^{.5}$ q	2.99	3.59	3.95	4.21

The exact same procedure now follows comparing the appropriate p-level sample ranges to these values of $(MS_e/n)^{.5}$ q, which increasingly diverge from the corresponding Duncan values of 2.99, 3.15, 3.25, and 3.33. As a consequence, the summary of the Newman-Keuls analysis of the data is

1	3	4	2	5
10.00	11.80	13.53	14.87	16.13

and the steps are given in Table 11.11.

TABLE 11.11 THE NEWMAN-KEULS MULTIPLE RANGE TEST FOR THE EXAMPLE DATA

$p = 5$ $16.13 - 10.00 = 6.13 > 4.21$; draw no line
$p = 4$ $14.87 - 10.00 = 4.87 > 3.95$; draw no line
          $16.13 - 11.80 = 4.33 > 3.95$; draw no line
$p = 3$ $16.13 - 13.53 = 2.60 < 3.59$; draw a line
          $14.87 - 11.80 = 3.07 < 3.59$; draw a line
          $13.53 - 10.00 = 3.53 < 3.59$; draw a line
$p = 2$ $11.80 - 10.00 = 1.80 < 2.99$; draw a line
          $13.53 - 11.80 = 1.73 < 2.99$; draw a line
          $14.87 - 13.53 = 1.34 < 2.99$; draw a line
          $16.13 - 14.87 = 1.26 < 2.99$; draw a line

Although the Newman-Keuls method appears to be, by one sample (Jaccard, Becker & Wood, 1984), the most popular method used for pairwise multiple comparisons in articles published by the American Psychological Association (in 1982), it is less popular among those who compare the various available methods. One reason is that there are situations for which the experimentwise Type I error rate exceeds α (Hartley, 1955). An example, given by Begun and Gabriel (1981, p. 244), is where there are 10 populations with pairs of identical group means separated from one another by amounts large enough so that almost certainly the Newman-Keuls procedure will reach the stage of testing all of the pairs, having found all of the three-level and higher-level ranges significant. Furthermore, all of the range tests for pairs will almost certainly be found to be significant except for the pairs arising from the pairs of populations that have identical means. Each of these pairs will be tested at the α significance level, and since they are independent, their familywise Type I error rate will be $1 - (1 - \alpha)^5$, which is greater than α.

11.17 Ryan's method for multiple range tests. Ryan's method is identical to Duncan's and to Newman-Keuls's except that the p-level significance value is taken as $1 - (1 - \alpha)^{p/I}$. This procedure does maintain the experimentwise error rate at less than or equal to α. It is simpler than the Peritz procedure, considered in section 11.18, but it is not as powerful. Because the tables of the studentized range are usually limited to α values of .05 and .01, it is necessary to interpolate. Following Begun and Gabriel (1981) we will linearly interpolate in the logarithms of the significance values. Let $\alpha_p = 1 - (1 - \alpha)^{p/I}$. To interpolate linearly in $\ln \alpha_p$ for $q_{\alpha p, p, dfe}$, we set

$$(\ln \alpha_p - \ln.05)/(\ln.01 - \ln.05) = (q_{\alpha p, p, dfe} - q_{.05, p, dfe})/(q_{.01, p, dfe} - q_{.05, p, dfe})$$

which gives

$$q_{\alpha p, p, dfe} = (q_{.01, p, dfe} - q_{.05, p, dfe})(\ln \alpha_p - \ln.05)/(\ln.01 - \ln.05) + q_{.05, p, dfe}.$$

TABLE 11.12 THE RYAN MULTIPLE RANGE TEST FOR THE EXAMPLE DATA

p = 5	16.13 - 10.00 = 6.13 > 4.21; draw no line
p = 4	14.87 - 10.00 = 4.87 > 4.08; draw no line
	16.13 - 11.80 = 4.33 > 4.08; draw no line
p = 3	16.13 - 13.53 = 2.60 < 3.88; draw a line
	14.87 - 11.80 = 3.07 < 3.88; draw a line
	13.53 - 10.00 = 3.53 < 3.88; draw a line
p = 2	11.80 - 10.00 = 1.80 < 3.83; draw a line
	13.53 - 11.80 = 1.73 < 3.83; draw a line
	14.87 - 13.53 = 1.34 < 3.83; draw a line
	16.13 - 14.87 = 1.26 < 3.83; draw a line

The values (by linear interpolation) for $q_{.05, p, dfe}$ and $q_{.01, p, dfe}$ are

p:	2	3	4	5
$q_{.05,p,70}$:	2.82	3.39	3.73	3.97
$q_{.01,p,70}$:	3.75	4.27	4.58	4.80

giving

p:	2	3	4	5
$q_{1-(1-\alpha)^{p/5},p,70}$:	3.61	3.66	3.85	3.97

which in turn results in critical values of

p:	2	3	4	5
$(MS_e/n)^{.5} q_{1-(1-\alpha)^{p/5},p,70}$:	3.83	3.88	4.08	4.21

giving the steps in Table 11.12 and the summary in the display

1	3	4	2	5
10.00	11.80	13.53	14.87	16.13

Table 11.13 provides a comparison of the $(MS_e/n)^{.5} q$ values used in the Duncan, Newman-Keuls, and Ryan multiple range tests, indicating that the ordering from most tolerant of Type I errors and most powerful to least tolerant and least powerful is Duncan, Newman-Keuls, and then Ryan.

11.18 The Peritz closure of the Newman-Keuls procedure. The Peritz procedure is a method for modifying the Newman-Keuls procedure so that α_f remains less than or equal to α (Einot & Gabriel, 1975; Marcus, Peritz & Gabriel, 1976; Begun & Gabriel, 1981). Let us use H_{12345} to denote the hypothesis that the population means for the set of five groups in our example are equal, that is, $\mu_1 = \mu_2 = \mu_3 = \mu_4 = \mu_5$; H_{1234} to denote $\mu_1 = \mu_2 = \mu_3 = \mu_4$; and so on. We will refer to these as hypotheses of homogeneity of group means, or simply **homogeneity hypotheses**.

TABLE 11.13   EXAMPLE DUNCAN, NEWMAN-KEULS AND RYAN VALUES OF $(MS_e/n)^{.5}$ q

p:	2	3	4	5
Duncan:	2.99	3.15	3.25	3.33
Newman-Keuls	2.99	3.59	3.95	4.21
Ryan	3.83	3.88	4.08	4.21

For an experiment with five groups, there is one homogeneity hypothesis for the set of all five means, H_{12345}; five homogeneity hypotheses for sets of four means, H_{1234}, H_{1235}, H_{1245}, H_{1345}, and H_{2345}, and, as shown in Table 11.14, 10 for sets of three means, and 10 for sets of two means. Both the hypotheses and the sets they refer to are shown in Table 11.14.

The Peritz procedure begins by expanding the collection of hypotheses by including in it the set intersection of certain hypotheses. This new, expanded set of hypotheses contains all of the old hypotheses and also all of the intersections of **"partition" hypotheses**. Two hypotheses are partition hypotheses if the means they refer to form two mutually exclusive and exhaustive subsets of the entire group of five means. Thus, the pair H_{12} and H_{345} are partition hypotheses, as is the pair H_{35} and H_{124}. Therefore the new set would include all of the hypothesis intersections such as $H_{12} \cap H_{345}$ and $H_{35} \cap H_{124}$. These are shown in Table 11.14. (For the purposes of the Peritz procedure, the partitions in which one of the two subsets contains only one mean, such as H_1 and H_{2345}, are not presented in the table but they are regarded as partition hypotheses and so treated.)

Next, the hypotheses are tested in stepwise fashion, starting with the hypothesis for the entire set of $I = 5$ means and proceeding succesively through smaller sets. **The nonintersection hypotheses are tested using the Newman-Keuls critical values. The intersection hypotheses are tested and rejected if either of the two hypotheses in the intersection is rejected using the Ryan critical values.** When one of the homogeneity hypotheses in an intersection is a hypothesis for a single mean, it is trivially accepted; therefore unless the other is Ryan rejected, the intersection is accepted. If an intersection hypothesis is accepted, then according to the **"acceptance by**

TABLE 11.14 DECISIONS OF THE NEWMAN-KEULS, PERITZ, AND RYAN PROCEDURE

Hypothesis	Range	$(MS_e/n)^{.5}q$ N-K	Ryan	Test N-K	Peritz	Ryan	Decision N-K	Peritz	Ryan
H_{12345}	8.00	4.29	4.57	CR	CR	CR	RJ	RJ	RJ
H_{1234}	6.00	3.95	4.43	CR	CR	CR	RJ	RJ	RJ
H_{1235}	8.00	3.95	4.43	CR	CR	CR	RJ	RJ	RJ
H_{1245}	8.00	3.95	4.43	CR	CR	CR	RJ	RJ	RJ
H_{1345}	8.00	3.95	4.43	CR	CR	CR	RJ	RJ	RJ
H_{2345}	6.00	3.95	4.43	CR	CR	CR	RJ	RJ	RJ
H_{123}	6.00	3.59	4.21	CR	CR	N	RJ	A	A
H_{124}	6.00	3.59	4.21	CR	CR	CR	RJ	RJ	RJ
H_{125}	8.00	3.59	4.21	CR	CR	CR	RJ	RJ	RJ
H_{134}	6.00	3.59	4.21	CR	CR	CR	RJ	RJ	RJ
H_{135}	8.00	3.59	4.21	CR	CR	CR	RJ	RJ	RJ
H_{145}	8.00	3.59	4.21	CR	CR	CR	RJ	RJ	RJ
H_{234}	4.00	3.59	4.21	CR	CR	N	RJ	RJ	A
H_{235}	6.00	3.59	4.21	CR	CR	CR	RJ	RJ	RJ
H_{245}	6.00	3.59	4.21	CR	CR	CR	RJ	RJ	RJ
H_{345}	4.00	3.59	4.21	CR	CR	N	RJ	A	A
$H_{123} \cap H_{45}$						N			A
$H_{124} \cap H_{35}$					CR			RJ	
$H_{125} \cap H_{34}$					CR			RJ	
$H_{134} \cap H_{25}$						CR			RJ
$H_{135} \cap H_{24}$					CR			RJ	
$H_{145} \cap H_{23}$					CR			RJ	
$H_{234} \cap H_{15}$					CR			RJ	
$H_{235} \cap H_{14}$					CR			RJ	
$H_{245} \cap H_{13}$					CR			RJ	
$H_{345} \cap H_{12}$					N			A	
H_{12}	2.00	3.24	4.15	N	N	N	A	A	A
H_{13}	4.00	3.24	4.15	CR	CR	N	RJ	RJ	A
H_{14}	6.00	3.24	4.15	CR	CR	CR	RJ	RJ	RJ
H_{15}	8.00	3.24	4.15	CR	CR	CR	RJ	RJ	RJ
H_{23}	2.00	3.24	4.15	N	N	N	A	A	A
H_{24}	4.00	3.24	4.15	CR	CR	N	RJ	RJ	A
H_{25}	6.00	3.24	4.15	CR	CR	CR	RJ	RJ	RJ
H_{34}	2.00	3.24	4.15	N	N	N	A	A	A
H_{35}	4.00	3.24	4.15	CR	CR	N	RJ	RJ	A
H_{45}	2.00	3.24	4.15	N	N	N	A	A	A

Note: CR means critical; N means noncritical; RJ means reject; A means accept.

implication rule" both of the hypotheses in the intersection are accepted. **If the intersection hypothesis is rejected, then <u>both</u> hypotheses in the intersection are tested using the Newman-Keuls critical values.**

For an example of this, consider H_{13} in Table 11.14. It is a part of $H_{245} \cap H_{13}$, which is rejected because H_{245} is critical by the Ryan procedure; therefore it is tested using the

Newman-Keuls critical value and preliminarily rejected. This does not finish the story for H_{13}, however. Because the Peritz procedure accepts H_{123}, and because H_{123} implies H_{13}, H_{13} is ultimately accepted. This is because the "acceptance by implication" rule requires the acceptance of any hypothesis implied by an accepted hypothesis. A first homogeneity hypothesis implies a second if all of the means in the second are contained in the first. Or, putting it another way, a homogeneity hypothesis for a given set of means is rejected only if the homogeneity hypothesis for <u>every</u> set of means containing that given set is rejected (Gabriel, 1969, p. 229; Begun & Gabriel, 1981, pp. 241-242).

The example data used thus far do not display well the differences in conclusions that can be reached by the Newman-Keuls, Ryan, and Peritz procedures. We will leave application of the Peritz procedure to the example data as an exercise and instead assume that the data resulted in sample means of 10.00, 12.00, 14.00, 16.00, and 18.00, with $(MS_e/n)^{.5} = 1.15$. This gives the values of $(MS_e/n)^{.5}q$ shown in Table 11.14. The preliminary results of the Peritz procedure for these values are shown in Table 11.14. Combining these results with the "acceptance by implication rule" gives the final results summarized in the display

Peritz

1	2	3	4	5
10.00	12.00	14.00	16.00	18.00

which can be compared with the following two displays that summarize the results of applying the Newman-Keuls and Ryan procedures to the same values.

Newman-Keuls

1	3	4	2	5
10.00	11.80	13.53	14.87	16.13

Ryan

1	3	4	2	5
10.00	11.80	13.53	14.87	16.13

Begun and Gabriel (1981, pp. 243-244) have recognized that the stepwise fashion for carrying out the Peritz procedure described above can be formidable and have provided a simplifying algorithm for obtaining the accept/reject decisions on all of the subsets. To follow their algorithm, begin by running both the Newman-Keuls and Ryan procedures. Then (closely paraphrasing Begun and Gabriel):

I. Accept homogeneity for all sets that are Newman-Keuls accepted;

II. Reject the homogeneity for all sets for which the homogeneity hypotheses are Ryan rejected; and

III. Classify as contentious the hypotheses for those sets that are accepted by Ryan but rejected by Newman-Keuls.

Proceed stepwise from the largest to the smallest of the **contentious sets**. Accept the homogeneity hypothesis for a contentious set P:

Ia If P is contained in another set for which the homogeneity hypothesis is accepted, or

Ib If the homogeneity hypothesis for P is Ryan noncritical and there is some subset Q of the complement of P such that the homogeneity hypothesis for Q is also Ryan noncritical.

Conversely, reject the hypothesis for a contentious set P:

IIa If P is not contained in any set for which a contentious hypothesis has been accepted, and

IIb If the homogeneity hypothesis for P is Ryan critical or, for each subset of two or more means in the complement of P, the homogeneity hypothesis for that subset is Ryan critical.

For a contentious set of I - 1 means, the hypothesis can always be tested at the Newman-Keuls critical value for I - 1 means, α, and will therefore be accepted, since its complement is trivially accepted as homogeneous (see rule Ib) (Ramsey, 1978; Shaffer, 1979, cited in Begun & Gabriel, 1981).

The **Peritz procedure** will always accept every hypothesis that the Newman-Keuls procedure does, but it will sometimes accept more. It will reject every hypothesis that the Ryan procedure rejects but it will sometimes reject more. Its **strengths** are therefore that **it is more powerful than the Ryan procedure and, unlike the Newman-Keuls procedure, it will hold the familywise error rate at less than or equal to** α. Computer simulations (Ramsey, 1978) have shown that the increase in power is particularly notable when the population means are equally and well spread apart. Its major **weakness** is the **complexity** of the testing method, although a FORTRAN computer program is available from Begun and Gabriel. There is also a **considerably nonintuitive or even counterintuitive aspect** to the Peritz procedure in that **the decision on a subset of the means can depend on the test for its complement.** Consider the hypotheses H_{12} and H_{345}. Suppose that H_{12} is Newman-Keuls critical but not Ryan critical. If H_{345} is Ryan critical, then $H_{12} \cap H_{345}$ will be rejected and H_{12} will be tested using the Newman-Keuls critical value and rejected. But if H_{345} is not Ryan critical, then $H_{12} \cap H_{345}$ will be accepted and, by implication, H_{12} will be accepted. In general, a hypothesis is more likely to be rejected by the Peritz procedure if its complement is heterogeneous than if it is homogeneous!

11.19 Multiple F-tests. Multiple F-tests differ from multiple range tests in that the test statistic is an F-ratio rather than a range. Also, multiple F-tests can be done with unequal sample sizes, but the equal variance assumption is still made. Multiple F-tests can use any of the schemes proposed by Duncan, Newman-Keuls, Ryan, or Peritz for setting the value of α_i and controlling α_f. (In fact, Duncan (1955) recommended multiple F-tests when the interest is in contrasts other than that between pairs of means.) **The basic rule for multiple F-tests is that the difference between any two means in a set of I means is significant provided that the between-groups variance for each and every subset of means which contains the given means is significant according to an** α_p**-level F-test where p is the number of means in the subset and** α_p **is determined according to some scheme.** Duncan recommended $\alpha_p = 1 - (1 - \alpha)^{p-1}$, but as Miller (1981) points out, the α_p can be chosen in any fashion, as, for example, $\alpha_p = \alpha$, à la Newman-Keuls. For technical reasons, which we will not go into here (see Miller, 1981, pp. 97-98), the p-mean significance level for multiple F-tests is not necessarily α_p, although this is the case for multiple range tests. Instead, in general it is less than or equal to α_p.

As an example we will perform multiple F-tests on the means of 10.00, 14.87, 11.80, 13.53, and 16.13 for groups 1, 2, 3, 4, and 5, using Ryan's scheme for setting α_p. In the light of the equal variance assumption, it is natural to use $MS_e = 16.88$ as the denominator of each F-ratio. The F-tests were not performed for sets of group means which were ruled out by a previous decision to draw a line for a set of means containing the excluded set. For example, since the F-test for Groups 1, 3, and 4 was not significant, the tests for Groups 1 and 3, Groups 1 and 4, and Groups 3 and 4 were omitted.

Table 11.15 shows the results, which are summarized in the display
Ryan Multiple F-tests

1	3	4	2	5
10.00	11.80	13.53	14.87	16.13

The critical values of F in Table 11.14 were linearly interpolated using ln α values for $\alpha =$ .01, .05, and the desired α value.

The **strengths** of the multiple F-test are its **familiarity and the fact that it can be applied to any one-factor design**. The weaknesses are the **amount of computation if the computations are being done by hand**, in which case they become unacceptable. The need to determine **oddball critical values** of F is also annoying but only a few moments work.

11.20 Dunnett's many-one test. Dunnett's many-one test is for comparing the means of some treatment groups with that of a control. Let μ_i be the population mean for the ith of I treatment groups, each having n scores, and let μ_0 be the population mean of a single control group, also having n scores (but see Miller's discussion of unequal sample sizes [1981, p. 77]). The null hypothesis tested by Dunnett's many-one test is that $\mu_i = \mu_0$ for i = 1, 2, ..., I. One-sided and two-sided alternatives to this null hypothesis will be considered here. In each case Dunnett's procedure holds the familywise error rate to α.

For the **two-sided alternative** that some of the treatment group means do not equal the control group mean, **the null hypothesis is rejected if** $|M_i - M_0| \geq (2MS_e/n)^{.5}$ $|d|_{\alpha, I, df_e}$, where $df_e = (I + 1)(n - 1)$, and $|d|_{\alpha, I, df_e}$ is the upper 100α percent point of a

TABLE 11.15   THE MULTIPLE F-TEST FOR THE EXAMPLE DATA

Groups	$MS_{between}$	df	$F = MS_b/MS_e$	$F_{critical}$	Decision
1,2,3,4,5	88.73	4	5.26	2.50	Draw no line
1,2,3,4	67.04	3	3.97	2.92	Draw no line
1,2,3,5	117.87	3	6.98	2.92	Draw no line
1,2,4,5	104.87	3	6.21	2.92	Draw no line
1,3,4,5	102.22	3	6.06	2.92	Draw no line
2,3,4,5	51.64	3	3.06	2.92	Draw no line
1,2,3	90.95	2	5.39	3.69	Draw no line
1,2,4	94.93	2	5.62	3.69	Draw no line
1,2,5	157.20	2	9.31	3.69	Draw no line
1,3,4	46.73	2	2.77	3.69	Draw a line
1,3,5	148.91	2	8.82	3.69	Draw no line
1,4,5	141.99	2	8.41	3.69	Draw no line
2,3,4	35.53	2	2.11	3.69	Draw a line
2,3,5	74.40	2	4.41	3.69	Draw no line
2,4,5	25.36	2	1.50	3.69	Draw a line
3,4,5	71.25	2	4.22	3.69	Draw no line
1,2	177.88	1	10.54	5.68	Draw no line
1,5	281.83	1	16.70	5.68	Draw no line
3,5	140.62	1	8.33	5.68	Draw no line

distribution tabled by Dunnett (1955, 1964) for two-tailed tests and reproduced in Statistical Table 7. The probability is $1 - \alpha$ that all of the intervals

$$M_i - M_0 \pm (2MS_e/n)^{.5} |d|_{\alpha,I,dfe} \quad \text{for } i = 1, 2, ..., I$$

contain their respective $\mu_i - \mu_0$.

For the **one-sided alternative** that one or more of the treatment group means is larger than the control group mean, **the null hypothesis is rejected if** $M_i - M_0 \geq$ $(2MS_e/n)^{.5} d_{\alpha,I,dfe}$, where $d_{\alpha,I,dfe}$ is the upper 100α percent point of a distribution tabled by Dunnett (1955, 1964) for one-tailed tests and reproduced in Statistical Table 7. The probability is $1 - \alpha$ that all of the

$$\mu_i - \mu_0 \geq M_i - M_0 - (2MS_e/n)^{.5} |d|_{\alpha,I,dfe} \quad \text{for } i = 1, 2, ..., I.$$

Miller (1981, p. 77) points out that the confidence intervals and hypothesis testing procedures can be extended to include one- or two-sided comparisons of weighted averages of the μ_i with μ_0 for $i = 1, ..., I$. For example, the two-sided version would reject the null hypothesis that $(\Sigma_i w_i \mu_i) = \mu_0$ if $(\Sigma_i w_i M_i) - M_0 \geq (2MS_e/n)^{.5} |d|_{\alpha, I, dfe}$, where $w_i \geq 0$ and $\Sigma_i w_i = 1$.

The **strength** of Dunnett's procedure is that it is **just about the most powerful procedure** for the specific tasks to which it is applied. Only the Marcus, Peritz, and Gabriel (1976) extension of the Peritz closure procedure to Dunnett's procedure gives a more powerful method, although it does not provide a confidence interval. Miller (1981) suggests that the Dunnett procedure should be applied in a multiple-stage fashion analogously to converting the Tukey procedure to a multiple range test such as Duncan or Ryan. Its **"weakness"** is that because it is a **specialized procedure, it is not suited to any of the more general classes of questions.**

11.21 Comparison of the procedures and recommendations. There are many positions on various issues and many variables that will influence the choice of a procedure. Not necessarily in order of importance, some of these are: Is it important to control the familywise error rate and if so, how much? Will confidence intervals be required, or is the investigation limited only to hypothesis testing? Are the contrasts limited to pairs of means, or will they involve more than two means? Are the assumptions of equal variance and normality tenable? Is the design balanced? If there are within-subject factors, is the assumption of homogeneity of the variance of the difference scores tenable? Will there be many contrasts or few? Are the treatments all compared to a single control group, or are other contrasts of interest? Is the investigator interested in data snooping to find whatever may be there, or are the contrasts all planned in advance? Are the contrasts all orthogonal? Are specific contrasts so important that each one should not be allowed to depend on the configuration of means other than those involved in that contrast? How important is it to protect that part of the overall null hypothesis that may still be true after the entire null hypothesis has been rejected? How important are small gains in power compared to ease and familiarity? How important is it that the logic of the test be completely clear and intuitively appealing?

There do not appear to be many, if any, universally accepted choices of procedures for specific positions with respect to these various issues. In this section we will try to make some recommendations that make some sense and that usually are shared by at least some others in the field. The student is encouraged to read broadly in the literature to get a fair and more complete appreciation of the many different positions that have been taken in this regard.

If there is no concern with holding the familywise error rate down, multiple t tests should be used for reasons of familiarity, ease, and power. Such lack of concern might occur when one is searching for a way to enter an uncharted area
and is more concerned with finding alternatives to the null hypothesis that may be

TABLE 11.16   FICTIONAL DATA FOR EXERCISE 1

A_1	A_2	A_3
15	18	19
17	17	19
16	16	21
14	20	23
12	20	27
	24	22
		24

true than with the risk of falsely rejecting that null hypothesis, or perhaps in preliminary research where one is more concerned with convincing oneself than with publishing results that will convince others. However, note well: self-deception is rarely without cost. Also, one can imagine many situations where concluding that there is no effect when there actually is can be far more costly than concluding that there is an effect when there really isn't, as, say, in studies involving toxic effects such as those of radioactivity, controlled substances, and various pharmaceutical agents. Finally, one might be willing to regard the several contrasts as fundamentally independent of one another, and the procedure as equivalent to running separate experiments, only more efficient in estimating error variance. In that case each contrast constitutes its own family, and an α-level t-test can be used for each. Naturally, libertinism is to be avoided in making such cases, but it is also fair to note that, as Miller has pointed out, setting acceptable error rates and defining what constitutes a family properly belongs in the hands of the investigator and is not a matter for legislation.

For within-subjects factors in repeated measurement designs, when the assumption of homogeneity of variances of difference scores is untenable, Bonferroni t-tests are recommended both for pairwise contrasts and for contrasts involving more than two means. (Jaccard, Becker & Wood, 1984; Keselman, Rogan, & Games, 1981; Myers, 1979). For homogeneous variances of difference scores or when tests using contrast scores are performed, the recommendations below apply.

For between-subjects factors, when interest is limited to all possible pairwise contrasts and the variances are homogeneous, then decide if the test of a particular pair of means should depend on the configuration of means not involved in that test. If not, use Tukey's WSD method if the groups have equal sample sizes, or for more than one factor, if the design is balanced. For unequal sample sizes but homogeneous variances, use the Tukey-Kramer procedure. For heterogeneous variances, known or suspected, use the Games and Howell procedure, but note that α_f can exceed α although apparently only slightly. If extra power is worth the price of letting the pairwise tests depend on the configuration of means not involved in the tests, then for balanced designs use Ryan's procedure for simplicity (I, personally, have never been impressed by arguments for simplicity in statistical analysis simply because, compared to the rest of the work in a scientific investigation, the statistical analysis is a relatively small part, and adding a little to that effort to give the whole undertaking a better chance of being fruitful seems effort well spent), or, ignoring simplicity, use the Peritz procedure to get the last drop of power out. For unequal sample sizes, use multiple F-tests with the Ryan or Peritz assignment of critical values. If there is genuine concern with holding α_f down, Newman-Keuls should be avoided, especially where the means are in clusters. For many-one tests, use Dunnett's procedure in a stagewise fashion to avoid unnecessary conservatism or use the Peritz closure of the Dunnett procedure for somewhat more power.

When there is interest in contrasts involving more than two means, the choice of procedure will be between Scheffé's method and Bonferroni t tests. Use Scheffé's method except where the number of contrasts is fairly close to the degrees of freedom for the set of contrasts to which the method is to be applied, in which case use Bonferroni t-tests. To be precise, use Bonferroni t-tests if $t_{\alpha/h, dfe} < [(I-1)F_{\alpha, I-1, dfe}]^{.5}$.

Exercises

1. Use the Games and Howell procedure with the data in Table 11.16 to test the hypotheses that $A_1 = A_2$, $A_2 = A_3$, $A_1 = A_3$.

2. Use the Newman-Keuls multiple range test to analyze the means for the Blocks of 3 Days variable for the data in exercise 7 at the end of Chapter 8.

3. Apply Ryan's multiple range test to the Blocks of 3 days variable using the data in Table 8.19.

4. Use multiple F-tests to analyze the effects of Blocks of 3 Days using the data in Table 8.19. Use Ryan's scheme for setting α_p, holding the experimentwise Type I error rate at .05.

5. For the same data as in exercise 4, assume the first block of trials is a "control" block, and use Dunnett's many-one test to compare performance on each of the reamining blocks of 3 Days with performance on that first block. Hold the familywise Type I error rate to .05.

6. Using the data of Table 5.9, use .05 level multiple t-tests on all pairs of means for the stimulus variable.

(a) Which pairs of stimulus conditions are significantly different?

(b) What is the familywise error rate for these tests?

(c) Give a 95 percent confidence interval for the difference between $\mu_{picture}$ and $\mu_{scrambled\ picture}$. Does this interval overlap zero? How does this relate to your answer to part (a)?

7. For the data in exercise 6, suppose you had planned to ask only three questions of the data by testing the following three null hypotheses: (1) $\mu_{picture} = \mu_{diagram}$; (2) $\mu_{scrambled\ picture} = \mu_{scrambled\ diagram}$. and (3) $(\mu_{picture} + \mu_{diagram})/2 = (\mu_{scrambled\ picture} + \mu_{scrambled\ diagram})/2$.

(a) Are these contrasts mutually orthogonal?

(b) Test each hypothesis with a .05 level t test. What are the results?

(c) What is the familywise Type I error rate for the three tests in (b)?

(d) Find a 95 percent confidence interval for each contrast.

(e) Could you have tested one more contrast orthogonal to the ones you tested in (b)? Why or why not?

(f) Find a 95 percent confidence interval for the mean of each stimulus condition.

8. a) Use t tests to test the same hypotheses as in exercise 7 but hold the familywise Type I error rate to .05

b) Find the corresponding confidence intervals for the three contrasts and compare their lengths to the lengths of those you obtained in exercise 2(d).

9. Use Peiser's approximation to find $t_{.01,20}$.

10. Use Bonferroni t-tests to test the differences between all possible pairs of means and to test the three contrasts in exercise 7. Assume equal α values for each of the nine tests and hold the familywise error rate less than or equal to .05.

11. Use Bonferroni t's and the improved Bonferroni inequality to test the three orthogonal contrasts in exercise 7, holding $\alpha_f \le .05$.

12. Find 95 percent confidence intervals for all of the pairwise contrasts of the Stimulus variable means in the data in exercise 6, using Tukey's WSD procedure. Use the intervals to test the hypotheses tested in exercise 1.

13. Use the data in Table 6.5 and Tukey's WSD procedure to test the hypotheses that $A_1 = A_2$, $A_2 = A_3$, $A_1 = A_3$.

14. Using the data in exercise 13, use Scheffé's to test the following contrasts of the levels of D:

(a) $[\mu_{D1(1,1)} + \mu_{D2(1,1)}]/2 = \mu_{D3(1,1)}$

(b) $[\mu_{D1(1,2)} + \mu_{D2(1,2)}]/2 = \mu_{D3(1,2)}$

(c) $[\mu_{D1(1,1)} + \mu_{D2(1,1)}]/2 - \mu_{D3(1,1)} = [\mu_{D1(2,1)} + \mu_{D2(2,1)}]/2 - \mu_{D3(2,1)}$

(d) $[\mu_{D1(1,1)} + \mu_{D2(1,1)}]/2 = [\mu_{D1(2,2)} + \mu_{D2(2,2)}]/2$

15. Apply Fisher's LSD test and Duncan's multiple range test to the means of the levels of D for the data in exercise 9. How do the results of the two procedures compare?

16. You are going to perform an experiment with only between-subject factors, expect heterogeneity of variance, and are not too concerned if the familywiseType I error rate goes slightly above .05, but you do want to hold it close to that value. Assume a balanced design. What method for testing pairwise differences would you use?

17. You expect to test many contrasts, most of which will involve more than two means. The number of contrasts is one less than the degrees of freedom for the set of contrasts you are interested in. What method would you use? Suppose that you decided that the data deserved lots of snooping around, searching for significant contrasts other than the original group you envisioned testing. What method would you switch to?

18. You are interested in testing some within-subjects trend components for a single factor. You have good reason to expect heterogeneity of the variances of the difference scores. How would you hold the familywise Type I error rate down to less than or equal to .05?

19. Using Tukey's WSD method with the data in Table 11.5, find a 95 percent confidence interval for the difference between the population means for Group 2 and Group 4.

20. Tukey's WSD method allows for contrast of all possible pairs of means. For I groups there are $I(I-1)/2$ such contrasts. Assume the same number of contrasts are done with Bonferroni t-tests. Compare the Bonferroni confidence interval for the difference between the Group 2 and Group 4 means in Table 11.5 to the confidence interval you found in exercise 19.

21. Explain how the result in exercise 20 relates to the claim in the text that the WSD procedure is always more powerful than the Bonferroni method given equal sample sizes and equal variances.

Supplementary Readings

Games, P. A. (1971) Multiple comparison of means. *American Educational Research Journal, 8,* 531-565.

Jaccard, J., Becker, M. A., & Wood, G. (1984) Pairwise multiple comparison procedures: A review. *Psychological Bulletin, 96,* 589-596.

Miller, R. J., Jr. (1981) *Simultaneous statistical inference* 2nd ed. New York: Springer-Verlag.

Tukey, J. W. (1991). The philosophy of multiple comparisons. *Statistical Science, 6,* 100-116.

12

Regression, ANOVA, and the General Linear Model

12.1 Simple linear regression. This chapter shows how ANOVA is related to regression analysis. We will look at a more general regression model than was considered in introductory statistics where only simple linear regression was taken up. Simple linear regression is applied to a situation where scores are collected in pairs, such as an IQ score and a Graduate Record Exam score for each of a group of people. If the relationship between these two variables is approximately linear, we expect that plotting each pair of scores as a point in a two-dimensional coordinate system will result in a scattering of points that fall more or less on a straight line (see Figure 12.1).

In introductory statistics we learned that a quantitative dependent variable Y could be related to a quantitative independent variable X according to the linear equation $Y = b + mX$, but that because of errors of various sorts, the sample (X,Y)-points would not fall exactly on a straight line. Instead it was necessary to write the expression $Y_i = b + mX_i + e_i$, where e_i is the error associated with the pair (X_i, Y_i). Throughout this chapter we will assume that the errors are independently normally distributed with a mean of zero and a variance σ^2. Because our sampling is subject to the effects of error, we estimate the slope, m, and the intercept, b, of the line relating X and Y. The estimation method chooses values b_{est} and m_{est} that minimize the value of $\Sigma_i(Y'_i - Y_i)^2$ where $Y' = b_{est} + m_{est}X$. This estimation procedure is the method of least-squares. The sum of squares minimized by this method is the sum of the squares of the deviations of the actual Y value that went with a given X value from the Y' value predicted as going with that X value by the equation $Y' = b_{est} + m_{est}X$. We can think of b_{est} and m_{est} as that particular choice of a b and an m that results in $\Sigma_i(Y'_i - Y_i)^2$ being smaller than it would be with any other choice of a b and an m. It can be shown that $b_{est} = M_y - m_{est}M_x$ and $m_{est} = (\Sigma_i X_i Y_i - IM_x M_y)/(\Sigma_i X^2 - IM_x^2)$ where I is the number of X,Y pairs.

Figure 12.1 shows a scatterplot of four X,Y pairs of values (filled circles) together with the predicted X,Y' values (empty circles) lying on the regression line or line of best fit defined by the equation $Y' = b_{est} + m_{est}X$. An alternative geometric perspective would be

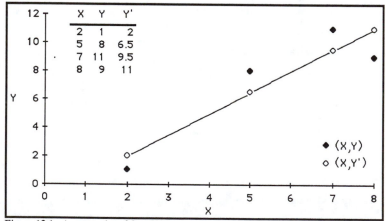

Figure 12.1. A scatterplot of four X,Y pairs of scores (filled circles), together with the least-squares regression line (empty circles) for those pairs.

to consider the collections of X scores and Y scores as two vectors that in the example case would lie somewhere in a four-dimensional space. The vector equation corresponding to the equation $Y' = b_{est} + m_{est}X$ would then be $\mathbf{Y'} = b_{est}\mathbf{1} + m_{est}\mathbf{X_1}$, where $\mathbf{1}$ is a vector of ones, $\mathbf{X_1}$ is the vector of X scores, and $\mathbf{Y'}$ is that vector lying in the two-dimensional space spanned by the vectors $\mathbf{1}$ and $\mathbf{X_1}$ that is closest to the vector $\mathbf{Y}$, the vector of Y scores. Choosing $\mathbf{Y'}$ as that vector closest to $\mathbf{Y}$, of course, minimizes the length of the vector $\mathbf{Y}$-$\mathbf{Y'}$, which is equivalent to minimizing the sum of squared deviations, $\Sigma_i (Y_i - Y'_i)^2 = (\mathbf{Y}$-$\mathbf{Y'})^t(\mathbf{Y}$-$\mathbf{Y'})$. We can also think of the $Y_i - Y'_i$ value as an estimate of the error e_i so that the least-squares method is a method that minimizes the sum of the squares of the error estimates.

12.1.1 The normal equations. To solve for the estimates of b and m that minimize the sum of the squared error estimates, we can set $e_{i,est} = Y_i - b_{est} - m_{est}X_i$ so that $\Sigma_i(e_{i,est})^2 = \Sigma_i(Y_i - b_{est} - m_{est}X_i)^2$. If we were to set up a Cartesian coordinate system on a plane on which the values on one axis are the possible values of b_{est} and those on the other are the possible values of m_{est}, and then we were to graph each value of the quantity $\Sigma_i(Y_i - b_{est} - m_{est}X_i)^2$ as the height of a surface above that plane for each choice of a b_{est} and an m_{est}, the surface would have the shape of a bowl. The point (b_{est}, m_{est}) in the plane directly beneath the lowest point in that bowl would have the coordinate values that minimize $\Sigma_i(Y_i - b_{est} - m_{est}X_i)^2$ and therefore would be our least-squares estimates of b and m. The solution for this pair of values is usually obtained using calculus, by taking the partial derivatives of $\Sigma_i(Y_i - b_{est} - m_{est}X_i)^2$ with respect to b_{est} and with respect to m_{est}, setting both expressions equal to zero, and solving for b_{est} and m_{est}. This standard method gives the same result as we get using the matrix methods we developed for least-squares estimation. The resulting equations are called the **normal equations**.

*Using calculus, taking the two partial derivatives and setting them equal to zero gives

$$\partial/\partial \, b_{est}\{\Sigma_i(Y_i - b_{est} - m_{est}X_i)^2\} = -2\Sigma_i(Y_i - b_{est} - m_{est}X_i) = 0$$

$$\partial/\partial \, m_{est}\{\Sigma_i(Y_i - b_{est} - m_{est}X_i)^2\} = -2\Sigma_i(X_iY_i - b_{est}X_i - m_{est}X_i^2) = 0.$$

Solving these two equations for b_{est} and m_{est} gives

$$b_{est} = M_y - m_{est} M_x \quad \text{and} \quad m_{est} = (\Sigma_iX_iY_i - IM_xM_y)/(\Sigma_iX^2 - IM_x^2).$$

To use the matrix approach, consider the vector $\mathbf{Y}$ of Y scores as residing in an I-dimensional space and $\mathbf{Y'}$, the vector of Y' or predicted Y scores, as residing in a two-dimensional subspace (the plane) spanned by the vectors $\mathbf{1}$ and $\mathbf{X_1}$. To locate $\mathbf{Y'}$, that linear combination of **1** and $\mathbf{X_1}$ which is closest to **Y**, we drop a perpendicular from **Y** to the plane. That perpendicular is the vector **Y-Y'**, and it must be perpendicular to **Y'**, therefore,

$$(\mathbf{Y'})^{t\cdot}(\mathbf{Y\text{-}Y'}) \; = \; \mathbf{0}.$$

Let $\mathbf{X} = [\mathbf{1} \; \mathbf{X_1}]$, let $\beta^t = [b \; m]$, and let $\beta_{est}{}^t = [b_{est} \; m_{est}]$. Then, $\mathbf{Y'} = \mathbf{X}\beta_{est}$ and the perpendicularity requirement may be written $(\mathbf{X}\beta_{est})^{t\cdot}(\mathbf{Y} - \mathbf{X}\beta_{est}) = \mathbf{0}$ giving $\beta_{est}{}^t\mathbf{X^t Y} - \beta_{est}{}^t\mathbf{X^t X}\beta_{est} = \mathbf{0}$, which gives, assuming β_{est} is not the zero vector, the normal equations

$$\mathbf{X^t Y} \; = \; \mathbf{X^t X}\,\beta_{est}.$$

Provided that the inverse of $\mathbf{X^t X}$ exists, these equations can be solved to give

$$\beta_{est} = (\mathbf{X^t X})^{-1}\,\mathbf{X^t Y}.$$

For our example, $(\mathbf{X^t X}) =$

$$\begin{bmatrix} \mathbf{1}^t \\ \mathbf{X_1}^t \end{bmatrix} \begin{bmatrix} \mathbf{1} & \mathbf{X_1} \end{bmatrix} \; = \; \begin{bmatrix} I & \sum_{i=1}^{I} X_i \\ \sum_{i=1}^{I} X_i & \sum_{i=1}^{I} X_i^2 \end{bmatrix}$$

so that

$$(\mathbf{X^t X})^{-1} \; = \; \frac{1}{I\sum_{i=1}^{I} X_i^2 - (\sum_{i=1}^{I} X_i)^2} \begin{bmatrix} \sum_{i=1}^{I} X_i^2 & -\sum_{i=1}^{I} X_i \\ -\sum_{i=1}^{I} X_i & I \end{bmatrix}$$

Since

$$\mathbf{X^t Y} = \begin{bmatrix} \sum_{i=1}^{I} Y_i \\ \sum_{i=1}^{I} X_i Y_i \end{bmatrix}$$

we have that

$$(\mathbf{X^t X})^{-1} \mathbf{X^t Y} = \begin{bmatrix} \dfrac{\sum_{i=1}^{I} X_i^2 \sum_{i=1}^{I} Y_i - \sum_{i=1}^{I} X_i \sum_{i=1}^{I} X_i Y_i}{I \sum_{i=1}^{I} X_i^2 - (\sum_{i=1}^{I} X_i)^2} \\[3ex] \dfrac{I \sum_{i=1}^{I} X_i Y_i - \sum_{i=1}^{I} X_i Y_i}{I \sum_{i=1}^{I} X_i^2 - (\sum_{i=1}^{I} X_i)^2} \end{bmatrix} = \begin{bmatrix} b_{est} \\ m_{est} \end{bmatrix}$$

The interested student should show that these estimators are the same as those obtained by the methods of calculus and that in each case the least-squares estimates for the example data are $b_{est} = -1$ and $m_{est} = 1.5$.

12.2 Multiple linear regression. Simple linear regression expresses a linear relationship between one dependent variable Y and one independent variable X. It is often desirable to consider the case where there are more than one independent variable, so that with two independent variables the model equation is

$$Y_i = b + m_1 X_{1i} + m_2 X_{2i} + e_i,$$

and in general, with p-1 independent variables, the model equation is

$$Y_i = b + m_1 X_{1i} + m_2 X_{2i} + \ldots + m_{p-1} X_{(p-1)i} + e_i.$$

Figure 12.2 shows a possible regression plane for regression of Y on X_1 and X_2 in a case where m_1 is positive and m_2 is negative. The value b is the Y value at which the plane intercepts the Y axis, that is, where X_1 and X_2 are both zero. Panel b of Figure 12.2 shows a three-dimensional scatterplot of a possible sample of (X_1, X_2, Y) points that might have come from the population of values described by this model. We will assume that p < I.

For the general case, the vector of predicted values, $\mathbf{Y'}$, lies in the p-dimensional subspace

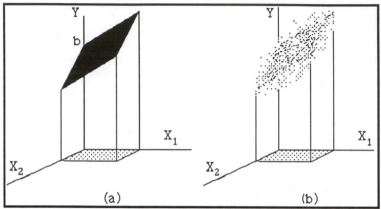

Figure 12.2. Panel (a) shows a possible regression plane for the model $Y_i = b + m_1 X_{1i} + m_2 X_{2i} + e_i$, and panel (b) shows a scatterplot of (X_1, X_2, Y) points that might have been sampled from the population characterized by the regression plane in panel (a).

spanned by the vectors $\mathbf{1}, \mathbf{X_1}, \mathbf{X_2}, ..., \mathbf{X_{p-1}}$, where $\mathbf{X_n}$ is the vector of X_{ni} values, n = 1, 2, ..., p, and the vectors $\mathbf{1}, \mathbf{X_1}, \mathbf{X_2}, ..., \mathbf{X_{p-1}}$ are p linearly independent vectors. If we let $\mathbf{X}$ be the I x p matrix the columns of which are $\mathbf{1}, \mathbf{X_1}, \mathbf{X_2}, ..., \mathbf{X_{p-1}}$, let β be the p x 1 vector of parameters b, m_1, m_2, ..., m_{p-1}, and e be the I x 1 vector of errors, the general model may be expressed as

$$\mathbf{Y} = \mathbf{X}\beta + \mathbf{e}$$

and the least-squares solution for the parameter estimates is

$$\beta_{est} = (\mathbf{X^t X})^{-1} \mathbf{X^t Y}.$$

For $(\mathbf{X^t X})^{-1}$ to exist, the matrix $\mathbf{X}$ must be of rank p. That is, no column vector of $\mathbf{X}$ may be a linear combination of the other column vectors of $\mathbf{X}$. Since the matrix $\mathbf{X}$ has p columns, the largest rank it can have is p, and when it does, we say that it is of full rank. Thus, we often say for $(\mathbf{X^t X})^{-1}$ to exist, the matrix $\mathbf{X}$ must be of full rank.

The statistic β_{est} has the multivariate normal distribution with mean vector β and variance-covariance matrix $\sigma^2 (\mathbf{X^t X})^{-1}$. The standard estimate for σ^2 is

$$s^2 = \mathbf{Y^t} (\mathbf{I} - \mathbf{X}(\mathbf{X^t X})^{-1} \mathbf{X^t}) \mathbf{Y} / (I - p),$$

where I is the $I \times I$ identity matrix. The statistic $(I - p)s^2/\sigma^2$ has the chi-square distribution with $I - p$ degrees of freedom.

12.3 Confidence bands and confidence intervals for the multiple regression model. In Chapter 11 we saw various methods for obtaining confidence intervals for means or for linear combinations of means in the ANOVA. We used sample means or sample contrasts plus information about the variability of the data to determine upper and lower values for those confidence intervals. In simple linear regression instead of a group mean or a contrast of group means, we obtain a sample regression line. The sample regression line is completely analogous to a group mean or a contrast of means. We can obtain a "confidence interval" for the regression line. Because it is a line rather than a single value, we obtain a band of values around the sample regression line that define a region within which we can be $100(1 - \alpha)$ percent confident that the true or population regression line lies (the confidence as usual being placed in the process of generating such a band, rather than in the particular band in hand). For regression models with more than one independent variable, instead of a prediction line we obtain a prediction surface. The $100(1 - \alpha)$ percent confidence band for the general model is

$$b_{est} + \Sigma_i m_{est,i} x_i \pm (pF_{\alpha,p,I-p})^{.5} s (X^t (X^t X)^{-1} X)^{.5}.$$

(In all of the preceding, for a regression model without the additive constant b it is only necessary to remove b and the vector **1**, leaving everything else the same except that the range of the indices on the **X**-vectors should now be from 1 to p.) For the case of simple linear regression, the confidence band formula reduces to

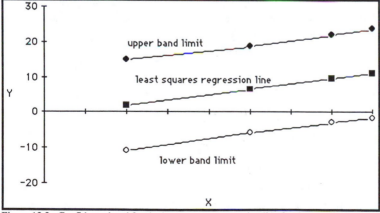

Figure 12.3. Confidence band for the least-squares regression line for the sample data.

TABLE 12.1 SUMMARY OF THE REGRESSION ANALYSIS

Source	df	Mean square	F
Regression	p	$(\beta_{est})^t X^t Y/p$	$[(\beta_{est})^t X^t Y/p]/[Y^t Y - (\beta_{est})^t X^t Y]/(I-p)$
Error	I - p	$[Y^t Y - (\beta_{est})^t X^t Y]/(I-p)$	
Total	I	$Y^t Y$	

$$b_{est} + m_{est}x \pm (2F_{\alpha,2,I-2})^{.5} s [1/I + (x - M_x)^2/\Sigma_i(x_i - M_x)^2]^{.5}$$

where the formula for s^2 reduces to

$$s^2 = \{\Sigma_i Y_i^2 - I M_y^2 - b_{est}[\Sigma_i(Y_i - M_y)(X_i - M_x)]\}/(I - 2).$$

Obtaining the various values and inserting them gives for the example data the confidence band

$$-1 + 1.5X \pm (3.7256)(6.6427)[.25 + (X - 5.5)^2/441]^{.5}$$

which is shown in Figure 12.3 together with the least-squares regression line which is the same as in Figure 12.1. For additional details the reader can start with Chapter 3 in Miller (1981).

12.4 Hypothesis testing in regression. We are going to look at hypothesis testing with an eye toward the topic of this chapter, which is to show some of the parallels between ANOVA models and regression ANOVA models and regression models:parallels between regression models. With this in mind we can consider three levels of hypotheses. The largest hypothesis is that all of the independent variables play a significant part in the value of the dependent variables. That is, $Y_i = m_1 X_{1i} + m_2 X_{2i} + ... + m_p X_{pi} + e_i$. (This equation covers the case of $Y_i = b + m_1 X_{1i} + m_2 X_{2i} + ... + m_{p-1} X_{(p-1)i} + e_i$ also if for the first term we let $b = m_1$, $X_{1i} = 1$, $i = 1, ..., I$, and for the remaining terms we increment their first index by one.) The smallest hypothesis is that none of the independent variables plays a part, in which case all of the $m_n = 0$, $n = 1,...,p$, and $Y_i = e_i$. The third level of hypothesis is that some but not all of the p variables play a part.

It can be shown that under any of these three levels of hypotheses, $[Y^t Y - (\beta_{est})^t X^t Y]/\sigma^2$ is distributed as chi-square with I - p degrees of freedom. It can also be shown that when the smallest hypothesis is true, $(\beta_{est})^t X^t Y/\sigma^2$ is distributed as chi-square with p degrees of freedom, and that these two chi-square variables are independent. Therefore, under the null hypothesis that all of the elements of β are zero,

$$\{[(\beta_{est})^t X^t Y / \sigma^2]/p]\} \, / \{[(Y^t Y - (\beta_{est})^t X^t Y)/\sigma^2]/(I-p)\} \; =$$

$$F_{p,(I-p)} = \{[(\beta_{est})^t X^t Y]/p\}/ \; \{[Y^t Y - (\beta_{est})^t X^t Y]/(I-p)\}$$

has the F distribution with p and (I-p) degrees of freedom. The results of a significance test of the smallest hypothesis against the largest might be reported in a summary table such as that shown in Table 12.1. In this test of the smallest model against the largest, a statistically significant F would provide inferential evidence in favor of the largest model.

12.4.1 The geometry. The geometric understanding of this test of a multiple regression model is the same as that for the geometry of fixed-effects analyses of variance. The dependent variable vector, Y, is viewed as the sum of two orthogonal vectors: a vector $X\beta$ which is the systematic, lawful component of Y, and a vector e, which is the error component. The vector $X\beta$ lies somewhere in the subspace spanned by the column vectors of X and is estimated by dropping a perpendicular from Y to that subspace. This gives the vector Y' lying in that subspace and closest to the vector Y, as the estimate $X\beta_{est}$, and the perpendicular dropped from Y as the error estimate $Y - X\beta_{est}$. In the analysis of variance we measured the vector of systematic effects against the vector of error effects to see if the systematic effects were significant. We used the squared lengths of the vectors divided by their respective degrees of freedom. In regression we do the same. The squared length of $X\beta_{est}$ is $(X\beta_{est})^t X\beta_{est} = \beta_{est}^t X^t X \beta_{est} = Y^t X (X^t X)^{-1} X^t X (X^t X)^{-1} X^t Y = Y^t X (X^t X)^{-1} X^t Y = \beta_{est}^t X^t Y$. And the squared length of $Y - Y'$ = $Y - X\beta_{est}$ is $(Y - X\beta_{est})^t (Y - X\beta_{est}) = (Y^t - \beta_{est}^t X)(Y - X\beta_{est}) = Y^t Y - \beta_{est}^t X^t Y - Y^t X \beta_{est} + \beta_{est}^t X^t X \beta_{est} = Y^t Y - \beta_{est}^t X^t Y$. (It is left as an exercise for the student to show that $- Y^t X\beta_{est} + \beta_{est}^t X^t X\beta_{est} = 0$. Recall that $(X^t X)^{-1}$ is symmetric so that it is its own transpose.) Table 12.2 summarizes these results.

12.5 Testing submodels. In analysis of variance, when we analyze a two-factor experimental design, for example, we usually test the significance of the row effects, the column effects, and the interaction effects. When we test the interaction effects we are asking whether the model without interaction effects, does virtually as good a job of describing the data as does the model with interaction effects. We are comparing a smaller model with fewer parameters to a larger model with more parameters. In regression analysis we can do the same. We can ask whether a regression model that excludes r of the p independent variables does virtually as good a job of describing the data as does the full model with p independent variables. We have already written the largest model as $Y = X\beta$ + e where X is I x p and β is p x 1. We can write the smaller model as

TABLE 12.2 SUMMARY OF SOME VECTOR PROPERTIES IN REGRESSION

Vector	Dimensionality	Squared Length
$X\beta_{est}$	p	$\beta_{est}^t X^t Y$
$Y - X\beta_{est}$	I - p	$Y^t Y - \beta_{est}^t X^t Y$
Y	I	$Y^t Y$

$$Y = X_s\beta_s + e$$

where X_s is an I x (p - r) matrix whose columns are the vectors of values of the variables that Y is assumed to be related to, and β_s is (p - r) x 1. For example, suppose that the data in Table 12.3 have been collected. Assume that the larger hypothesis is the quadratic relationship

$$Y_i = b + m_1X_i + m_2X_i^2 + e_i.$$

(Note that the second independent variable here consists of the squares of the first independent variable. The sense of independence here is linear independence. This type of regression model is a case of what is known as polynomial regression. A model with cubes and higher powers of X could also be used.) Assume that the smaller hypothesis is the simple linear relationship $Y_i = b + m_1X_i + e_i$. Then the larger model can be written as

$$
\begin{bmatrix} 29 \\ 30 \\ 72 \\ 137 \\ 157 \\ 169 \\ 204 \\ 230 \end{bmatrix}
=
\begin{bmatrix} 1 & 2 & 4 \\ 1 & 3 & 9 \\ 1 & 5 & 25 \\ 1 & 7 & 49 \\ 1 & 8 & 64 \\ 1 & 8 & 64 \\ 1 & 9 & 81 \\ 1 & 10 & 100 \end{bmatrix}
\begin{bmatrix} b \\ m_1 \\ m_2 \end{bmatrix}
+ e
$$

and the smaller model as

$$
\mathbf{Y} \qquad\qquad \mathbf{X}_g \qquad \boldsymbol{\beta}_g
$$

$$
\begin{bmatrix} 29 \\ 30 \\ 72 \\ 137 \\ 157 \\ 169 \\ 204 \\ 230 \end{bmatrix} = \begin{bmatrix} 1 & 2 \\ 1 & 3 \\ 1 & 5 \\ 1 & 7 \\ 1 & 8 \\ 1 & 8 \\ 1 & 9 \\ 1 & 10 \end{bmatrix} \begin{bmatrix} b \\ m_1 \end{bmatrix} + e
$$

TABLE 12.3 A SINGLE INDEPENDENT AND DEPENDENT VARIABLE

Y	X
29	2
30	3
72	5
137	7
157	8
169	8
204	9
230	10

TABLE 12.4 SUMMARY TABLE OF THE REGRESSION ANALYSIS

Source	df	Sums of squares
H_{larger}	p	$(\beta_{est})^t \mathbf{X}^t \mathbf{Y}$
$H_{smaller}$	p - r	$(\beta_{sest})^t \mathbf{X}_s{}^t \mathbf{Y}$
The model difference	r	$(\beta_{est})^t \mathbf{X}^t \mathbf{Y} - (\beta_{sest})^t \mathbf{X}_s{}^t \mathbf{Y}$
Error	I - p	$[\mathbf{Y}^t \mathbf{Y} - (\beta_{est})^t \mathbf{X}^t \mathbf{Y}]$
Total	I	$\mathbf{Y}^t \mathbf{Y}$

In this case r = 1 since the one column of squared values of X has been deleted under the smaller hypothesis. To test the null hypothesis that the quadratic equation does no better at describing the data than does the simple linear equation, we obtain the least-squares estimates of the predicted vector under each hypothesis, $\mathbf{Y}' = \mathbf{X}\beta_{est}$ under the larger and

$\mathbf{Y'_s} = \mathbf{X_s}\beta_{sest}$ under the smaller hypothesis. If the smaller model does about as well as the larger, we expect that the difference between these two predicted vectors should be small compared to

error. In Table 12.4 the sums of squares and the df are obtained for testing the null hypothesis by comparing the squared length of $\mathbf{Y'} - \mathbf{Y'_s}$ with the squared

length of the error vector under the larger hypothesis.

If the null hypothesis is true, the statistic

$$F = \{[(\beta_{est})^t\mathbf{X}^t\mathbf{Y} - (\beta_{sest})^t\mathbf{X_s}^t\mathbf{Y}]/r\}/\{[[\mathbf{Y}^t\mathbf{Y} - (\beta_{est})^t\mathbf{X}^t\mathbf{Y}]]/(I-p)\}$$

is distributed as F with r and I - p degrees of freedom. A significant F statistic provides inferential evidence for rejecting the null hypothesis and concluding that the larger model does a better job of describing the data than does the smaller model. It should be obvious that the notation is sufficiently general to apply to every case of a smaller hypothesis being tested against a larger one. Applying this procedure to the fictitious data in Table 12.3 gives the results shown in Table 12.5. Using a significance level of .05 would result in the F of 11.10 being significant and the conclusion that the quadratic model does a better job of describing the data than does the linear model.

In the analysis of variance, the estimates of the row or column effects did not depend upon whether the model included interaction effects or omitted them. In regression the parameter estimates in general will change with a change in the model. Thus, for the sample data, the values under the quadratic equation model for b, m_1, and m_2 were 1.79, 6.87, and 1.66. Under the linear equation model, the estimates of b and m_1 were -42.85 and 26.36. This fact is preserved in the notation by the distinction between β and β_s.

12.6 The analysis of variance in the form $\mathbf{Y} = \mathbf{X}\beta + \mathbf{e}$. analysis of variance:in the

form $\mathbf{Y} = \mathbf{X}\beta + \mathbf{e}$ We now want to show that the analyses of variance for fixed-effects models that we have looked at in previous chapters can all be expressed in the same form as a regression model. Let us take a simple case as our example. It will be obvious how things generalize. Our simple case will be a 2 x 2 factorial design with two scores per cell and the model equation $Y_{ijk} = \mu + a_i + b_j + c_{ij} + e_{ijk}$. We can represent the left side of the equation by a vector $\mathbf{Y}$ with eight elements. The error portion of the right side can also be represented by a vector of eight elements. The elements of $\mathbf{X}$ and β must be chosen so that the appropriate effects are added for each element of $\mathbf{Y}$. This can be accomplished by using indicator variables as the elements of $\mathbf{X}$ and the effects as the elements of β. For each effect in β, there will be an indicator variable whose values will be the entries in a column of $\mathbf{X}$. In row i of $\mathbf{X}$ each indicator variable will take the value 1 if the effect it indicates is a component of the score in row i of **Y**. For our 2 x 2 factorial design with interaction, this would look as follows.

$$
\begin{array}{cccc}
\mathbf{Y} & \mathbf{X} & \boldsymbol{\beta} & \mathbf{e}
\end{array}
$$

$$
\begin{bmatrix} Y_{111} \\ Y_{112} \\ Y_{121} \\ Y_{122} \\ Y_{211} \\ Y_{212} \\ Y_{221} \\ Y_{222} \end{bmatrix}
=
\begin{bmatrix}
1 & 1 & 0 & 1 & 0 & 1 & 0 & 0 & 0 \\
1 & 1 & 0 & 1 & 0 & 1 & 0 & 0 & 0 \\
1 & 1 & 0 & 0 & 1 & 0 & 1 & 0 & 0 \\
1 & 1 & 0 & 0 & 1 & 0 & 1 & 0 & 0 \\
1 & 0 & 1 & 1 & 0 & 0 & 0 & 1 & 0 \\
1 & 0 & 1 & 1 & 0 & 0 & 0 & 1 & 0 \\
1 & 0 & 1 & 0 & 1 & 0 & 0 & 0 & 1 \\
1 & 0 & 1 & 0 & 1 & 0 & 0 & 0 & 1
\end{bmatrix}
\begin{bmatrix} \mu \\ a_1 \\ a_2 \\ b_1 \\ b_2 \\ c_{11} \\ c_{12} \\ c_{21} \\ c_{22} \end{bmatrix}
+
\begin{bmatrix} e_{111} \\ e_{112} \\ e_{121} \\ e_{122} \\ e_{211} \\ e_{212} \\ e_{221} \\ e_{222} \end{bmatrix}
$$

The student should multiply one of the row vectors of **X** by the column vector β to be satisfied that this formulation does in fact give the appropriate values of the model equation for each Y_{ijk} score.

It is obvious that **X** is not of full rank. The first column is the sum of the second and third columns, as well as being the sum of the fourth and fifth and the sum of the sixth through ninth. We know from our understanding of the geometry of the analysis of variance that the rank of **X** is in fact only 4 since in a 2 x 2 design there is one df for the mean, one for rows, one for columns, and one for interaction. In order to solve for the least-squares estimate of β, we must introduce the side conditions of section 4.3.1. For this model equation the side conditions are $a_1 + a_2 = b_1 + b_2 = c_{11} + c_{12} = c_{21} + c_{22} = c_{11} + c_{21} = c_{12} + c_{22} = 0$. We can state the side conditions in the matrix form $H\beta = 0$ where for our example

$$
\begin{array}{cc}
\mathbf{H} & \boldsymbol{\beta}
\end{array}
$$

$$
\mathbf{H}\boldsymbol{\beta} =
\begin{bmatrix}
0 & 1 & 1 & 0 & 0 & 0 & 0 & 0 & 0 \\
0 & 0 & 0 & 1 & 1 & 0 & 0 & 0 & 0 \\
0 & 0 & 0 & 0 & 0 & 1 & 1 & 0 & 0 \\
0 & 0 & 0 & 0 & 0 & 0 & 0 & 1 & 1 \\
0 & 0 & 0 & 0 & 0 & 1 & 0 & 1 & 0 \\
0 & 0 & 0 & 0 & 0 & 0 & 1 & 0 & 1
\end{bmatrix}
\begin{bmatrix} \mu \\ a_1 \\ a_2 \\ b_1 \\ b_2 \\ c_{11} \\ c_{12} \\ c_{21} \\ c_{22} \end{bmatrix}
= \mathbf{0}
$$

If we append the matrix **H** to the bottom of the matrix **X** we obtain a 14 x 9 matrix which is of full rank (see Scheffé, 1959, pp. 15-19 for details). Premultiplying this matrix by its transpose gives the matrix $X^tX + H^tH$, and it can be shown that the vector $(X^tX + H^tH)^{-1}X^tY$ is the unique unbiased estimate of β satisfying the side conditions and in fact consists of just the very same estimates of the general mean and the effects we obtain in the usual way in the analysis of variance.

As a simple numerical example suppose the scores for the above 2 x 2 design are

2	5
3	8
7	17
9	21

Then the elements of **Y** are 2, 3, 5, 8, 7, 9, 17, 21, and it is easy to tabulate the elements of $X^tX + H^tH$, which turns out to be

$$
\begin{bmatrix}
8 & 4 & 4 & 4 & 4 & 2 & 2 & 2 & 2 \\
4 & 5 & 1 & 2 & 2 & 2 & 2 & 0 & 0 \\
4 & 1 & 5 & 2 & 2 & 0 & 0 & 2 & 2 \\
4 & 2 & 2 & 5 & 1 & 2 & 0 & 2 & 0 \\
4 & 2 & 2 & 1 & 5 & 0 & 2 & 0 & 2 \\
2 & 2 & 0 & 2 & 0 & 4 & 1 & 1 & 0 \\
2 & 2 & 0 & 0 & 2 & 1 & 4 & 0 & 1 \\
2 & 0 & 2 & 2 & 0 & 1 & 0 & 4 & 1 \\
2 & 0 & 2 & 0 & 2 & 0 & 1 & 1 & 4
\end{bmatrix}
$$

The inverse of $X^tX + H^tH$ is

$$
\begin{bmatrix}
.6875 & -.2500 & -.2500 & -.2500 & -.2500 & -.0625 & -.0625 & -.0625 & -.0625 \\
-.2500 & .5000 & 0 & 0 & 0 & -.1250 & -.1250 & .1250 & .1250 \\
-.2500 & 0 & -.5000 & 0 & 0 & .1250 & .1250 & -.1250 & -.1250 \\
-.2500 & 0 & 0 & -.5000 & 0 & -.1250 & .1250 & -.1250 & .1250 \\
-.2500 & 0 & 0 & 0 & -.5000 & .1250 & -.1250 & .1250 & -.1250 \\
-.0625 & -.1250 & .1250 & -.1250 & .1250 & .4375 & -.0625 & -.0625 & -.0625 \\
-.0625 & -.1250 & .1250 & .1250 & -.1250 & -.0625 & .4375 & -.0625 & -.0625 \\
-.0625 & .1250 & -.1250 & -.1250 & .1250 & -.0625 & -.0625 & .4375 & -.0625 \\
-.0625 & .1250 & -.1250 & .1250 & -.1250 & -.0625 & -.0625 & -.0625 & .4375
\end{bmatrix}
$$

It is then easy to calculate $(X^tX + H^tH)^{-1}X^tY$, which turns out to be

$$\begin{bmatrix} 9.0 \\ -4.5 \\ 4.75 \\ -3.75 \\ 3.75 \\ 1.75 \\ -1.75 \\ -1.75 \\ 1.75 \end{bmatrix}$$

TABLE 12.5 REGRESSION ANALYSIS:
TEST OF QUADRATIC VERSUS LINEAR

Source	df	SS	MS	F
Quadratic Equation	3	173,105	57,702	
Linear Equation	2	172,406	86,203	
Difference	1	699	699	11.10
Error	5	315	63	
Total	8	173,420		

The student should verify that these estimates of the analysis of variance model parameters for the example data are just the estimates that are obtained in the standard way using the cell means, row marginal means, column marginal means, and grand mean.

There is a simpler alternative method of introducing the side conditions into the equation $Y = X\beta + e.$

12.7 Regression and analysis of variance. We have seen that the structure of the fixed-effects analysis of variance is the same as that for regression. In regression and in the analysis of variance, the predicted data vector lies in the space spanned by the column vectors of X and is found by the method of least-squares, that is, by dropping a perpendicular from the data vector to that space. In regression the column vectors of X contain quantitative variables, and in analysis of variance, they contain qualitative values indicating which effects are added to obtain the score.

In the analysis of variance model with the same number of scores per cell, the row effects, column effects, and interaction effects are orthogonal to one another. This means that the

**TABLE 12.6   FICTIONAL X AND Y
SCORES FOR FIVE SUBJECTS IN
EACH OF THREE GROUPS**

GROUP 1		GROUP 2		GROUP 3	
X	Y	X	Y	X	Y
33	165	28	136	34	128
31	140	27	130	33	120
31	141	26	115	35	140
31	143	26	116	36	155
29	122	25	100	36	154

decision concerning the significance of any one of the three is not influenced by any of the others or by the order in which we test the three. Whether we decide that the row effects are significant is not determined either by whether the interaction effects are significant or by whether we test the interaction effects before the row effects or after them. This is not the case in regression, however, because the independent variables ordinarily are not orthogonal to one another. Thus, if we want to determine which of 10 independent variables significantly contribute to the value of the dependent variable, they might fall into a natural grouping of three, three, and four variables. Call these packages of variables A, B, and C. Let H_{ABC} be the hypothesis that all three packages of variables influence the dependent variable. Let H_{AB}, H_{AC}, and H_{BC} be, respectively, the hypotheses that C, B, and A have no influence. Then deciding whether A influences the dependent variable may depend upon whether we first test H_{AB} against H_{ABC} or instead test H_{BC} against H_{ABC}. The details of this problem and how it is coped with in various contexts, such as whether there is a natural order to test the hypotheses in or not, are beyond the scope of this text (see Cohen & Cohen, 1975).

12.8 The analysis of covariance. We have seen that the model $Y = X\beta + e$ covers the case where the independent variables are quantitative and where they are qualitative. It seems reasonable to suppose that the model might also cover the case where some of the independent variables are qualitative and others are quantiative. This would yield an X matrix with some columns of quantitative variables and some columns of qualitative variables. The analysis in such a case would proceed as before but is referred to as an **analysis of covariance**. The traditional example of an analysis of covariance is the case where an analysis of variance is to be performed upon a set of data and the experimenter has also measured a single quantitative independent variable. For example, suppose a one-factor design has been used and the experimenter wants to demonstrate an effect due to groups.

Suppose also that the value of the dependent variable is a linear function of the quantitative independent variable. A model equation for this situation would be

$$Y_{ij} = G + a_i + mx_{ij} + e_{ij}$$

which asserts that the jth score in Group i is the sum of a general effect G, an effect a_i specific to Group i, the value of the quantititative independent variable x for the jth score in group i multiplied by a slope m, and an error e_{ij}. It might be that as a result of chance or due to factors that could not be controlled or randomized, the subjects in the different groups had substantially different values of x. Then the results might be as shown in Figure 12.4. We see that the scores for the three experimental groups differ considerably, and we expect that a simple analysis of variance would produce a significant F-statistic for the Groups effect. But we also see that the subjects' Y scores appear to be very strongly associated with their X scores. Since the subjects in the different groups differ in their X score values, we suspect

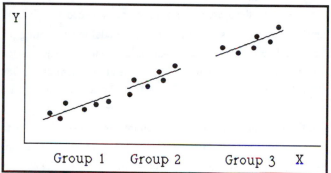

Figure 12.4. The Y scores for three experimental groups, plotted as a function of the covariate X. The relationship between Y and X appears to account for the differences between groups.

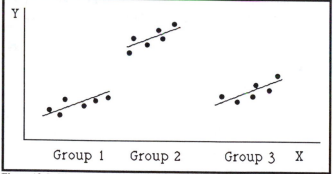

Figure 12.5. The Y scores for three experimental groups, plotted as a function of the covariate X. The relationship between Y and X does not appear to account completely for the differences between groups.

that it may be the relationship between X and Y rather than effects of the experimental treatments that are producing the group differences. Contrast Figure 12.4 with Figure 12.5, where we see that there is still a strong relationship between Y and X, but this does not appear to account totally for the differences between the scores in the three groups.

The data shown in Figure 12.4 conform to the model equation $Y_{ij} = G + a_i + mx_{ij} + e_{ij}$ under the case where all of the a_i equal zero. The model equation reduces to $Y_{ij} = G + mx_{ij} + e_{ij}$ In this case the three lines of best fit have the same slope and the same intercept. We would say that the three groups differ in their average Y score but only as a result of the regression of Y on X and not as a result of different effects due to the three different experimental treatments. In Figure 12.5 the three lines still have the same slope but have different intercepts, one for each group. This is in accord with the model equation $Y_{ij} = G + a_i + mx_{ij} + e_{ij}$ assuming that the a_i take different values. Here we would say that the three groups differ in their average Y score due to regression of Y on X and also due to differences in the effects of the experimental treatments.

To test the experimental hypothesis that the a_i are not all zero, we can proceed as we would to test whether a smaller regression model does as well as a larger model in accounting for the dependent variable. We formulate the two models, calculate the sums of squares for each, and compare the difference between those two sums of squares to the sum of squares for error in the usual way. (Of course, the side conditions on the a_i will have to be included.) We divide the difference sum of squares and the error sum of squares by their degrees of freedom and treat the ratio of these two mean squares as an F-statistic. The degrees of freedom for error will be the usual IJ - I with one more degree of freedom subtracted for the regression coefficient, m, giving df for error equal to IJ - I - 1. The df for the test of the Groups effect will be the same I - 1 as in the analysis of variance.

To perform the computations we can use the matrix equations for regression or a set of formulas specifically set up for this analysis of covariance. We will do both here for comparison. Consider the fictional set of X and Y scores in Table 12.6 obtained for five

TABLE 12.7 ANALYSIS OF COVARIANCE OF DATA IN TABLE 12.6

Source	df	SS	MS	F
Error: larger model	11	57.39	5.22	
Error: smaller model	13	1982.51	152.50	
The difference	2	1925.11	962.56	184.40

subjects in each of three experimental conditions. In matrix notation we can formulate the larger model as

$$
\begin{array}{cccc}
\mathbf{Y} & \mathbf{X} & \boldsymbol{\beta} & \mathbf{e}
\end{array}
$$

$$
\begin{bmatrix}
165 \\
140 \\
141 \\
143 \\
122 \\
136 \\
130 \\
115 \\
116 \\
100 \\
128 \\
120 \\
140 \\
155 \\
154
\end{bmatrix}
=
\begin{bmatrix}
1 & 1 & 0 & 0 & 33 \\
1 & 1 & 0 & 0 & 31 \\
1 & 1 & 0 & 0 & 31 \\
1 & 1 & 0 & 0 & 31 \\
1 & 1 & 0 & 0 & 29 \\
1 & 0 & 1 & 0 & 28 \\
1 & 0 & 1 & 0 & 27 \\
1 & 0 & 1 & 0 & 26 \\
1 & 0 & 1 & 0 & 26 \\
1 & 0 & 1 & 0 & 25 \\
1 & 0 & 0 & 1 & 34 \\
1 & 0 & 0 & 1 & 33 \\
1 & 0 & 0 & 1 & 35 \\
1 & 0 & 0 & 1 & 36 \\
1 & 0 & 0 & 1 & 36
\end{bmatrix}
\begin{bmatrix}
G \\
a_1 \\
a_2 \\
a_3 \\
m
\end{bmatrix}
+
\begin{bmatrix}
e_{11} \\
e_{12} \\
e_{13} \\
e_{14} \\
e_{15} \\
e_{21} \\
e_{22} \\
e_{23} \\
e_{24} \\
e_{25} \\
e_{31} \\
e_{32} \\
e_{33} \\
e_{34} \\
e_{35}
\end{bmatrix}
$$

subject to the side condition

$$
\begin{array}{ccc}
\mathbf{H} & \boldsymbol{\beta} & \mathbf{0}
\end{array}
$$

$$
\begin{bmatrix}
0 & 1 & 1 & 1 & 0
\end{bmatrix}
\begin{bmatrix}
G \\
a_1 \\
a_2 \\
a_3 \\
m
\end{bmatrix}
=
\begin{bmatrix}
0 \\
0 \\
0 \\
0 \\
0
\end{bmatrix}
$$

and the smaller model as

$$
\begin{array}{cccc}
\mathbf{Y} & \mathbf{X}_s & \boldsymbol{\beta}_s & \mathbf{e}_s
\end{array}
$$

$$
\begin{bmatrix}
165 \\
140 \\
141 \\
143 \\
122 \\
136 \\
130 \\
115 \\
116 \\
100 \\
128 \\
120 \\
140 \\
155 \\
154
\end{bmatrix}
=
\begin{bmatrix}
1 & 33 \\
1 & 31 \\
1 & 31 \\
1 & 31 \\
1 & 29 \\
1 & 28 \\
1 & 27 \\
1 & 26 \\
1 & 26 \\
1 & 25 \\
1 & 34 \\
1 & 33 \\
1 & 35 \\
1 & 36 \\
1 & 36
\end{bmatrix}
\begin{bmatrix}
G \\
m
\end{bmatrix}
+
\begin{bmatrix}
e_{11} \\
e_{12} \\
e_{13} \\
e_{14} \\
e_{15} \\
e_{21} \\
e_{22} \\
e_{23} \\
e_{24} \\
e_{25} \\
e_{31} \\
e_{32} \\
e_{33} \\
e_{34} \\
e_{35}
\end{bmatrix}
$$

To perform the analysis we need the sum of squares for error under the smaller model, the sum of squares for error under the larger model, and the difference between these two sums of squares. Let Ω represent the larger model, and ω represent the smaller model. Then $SS_{\Omega e} = Y^tY - [(X^tX + H^tH)^{-1}X^tY]^tX^tY = 57.39$, $SS_{\omega e} = Y^tY - [(X_s^tX_s)^1X_s^tY]^tX_s^tY = 1982.51$, and $SS_{\omega e} - SS_{\Omega e} = [(X^tX + H^tH)^{-1}X^tY]^tX^tY - [(X_s^tX_s)^{-1}X_s^tY]^tX_s^tY = 1925.11$. The results of the analysis are shown in Table 12.7. It is interesting to compare the results of this analysis with the results of the ordinary analysis of variance that would be applied to the Y scores if the investigator had no knowledge of the X covariate. This is given in Table 12.8. We can see that the analysis of variance detects no significant differences between the three groups. This is because all of the within-groups variation contributes to the estimate of error variance here, whereas in the covariance analysis, a substantial portion of that within-groups variation was attributed to regression of Y on X within the groups and therefore not treated as error variance.

12.9 The "adjusted" sums of squares. In the earliest and most familiar treatments of the analysis of covariance, the primary interest was in performing an analysis of variance to test group treatment effects. The relationship of the dependent variable Y to some covariate X was viewed as something to be taken into account in order to reduce the estimate of error variance and thereby increase the power of the test. The fact that the sums of squares used in the final test were not the same as those that would have been used had the analysis of variance been performed without taking the covariate into account was referred to as an adjustment of the analysis of variance sums of squares. Furthermore, the standard computational procedure to obtain the new sums of squares involved

TABLE 12.8 ANOVA OF THE DATA IN TABLE 12.6

Source	df	SS	MS	F
Groups	2	1546.13	773.07	3.44
Error	12	2693.20	224.43	
Total		14	4239.33	

subtracting quantities from the analysis of variance sums of squares, so this too justified referring to the new sums of squares as the adjusted sums of squares. In fact, however, when we view the analysis of covariance as the comparison of a larger model with a smaller model, there is nothing to adjust. And nothing is actually adjusted. The sums of squares that are used are just the right ones to compare the two models. Still, the terminology of "adjusted sums of squares" is so pervasive that we should consider both that terminology and the formulas for performing those "adjustments." In this section we will obtain the formulas for the adjusted sums of squares in the analysis of covariance for a one-factor design, but we will show how they arise out of the logic of comparing the larger and the smaller models.

We will again denote the larger model by Ω and the smaller by ω. Under ω: all of the Y_{ij} fall on a single straight line, therefore $Y_{ij} = \mu_y + \beta_T(X_{ij} - \mu_X) + e_{ij}$. It is easy to show that the least-squares estimates of μ_X, μ_y and β_T are M_X, M_Y, and $b_T = [\Sigma_i\Sigma_j(X_{ij} - M_X)(Y_{ij} - M_Y)]/\Sigma_i\Sigma_j(X_{ij} - M_X)^2$. The predicted value of Y_{ij} under ω is therefore $Y_{ij\omega}' = M_Y + b_T(X_{ij} - M_X)$, the error of prediction under ω is $Y_{ij} - Y_{ij\omega}' = Y_{ij} - M_Y - b_T(X_{ij} - M_X)$, and the sum of the squares of the errors of prediction is $\Sigma_i\Sigma_j[Y_{ij} - M_Y - b_T(X_{ij} - M_X)]^2$. Let us introduce the following notation:

$$SS_{TY} = \Sigma_i\Sigma_j(Y_{ij} - M_Y)^2 \quad \text{("Y sum of squares, total"),}$$

$$SP_T = \Sigma_i\Sigma_j(X_{ij} - M_X)(Y_{ij} - M_Y) \quad \text{("sum of products, total"),}$$

$$SS_{TX} = \Sigma_i\Sigma_j(X_{ij} - M_X)^2 \qquad \text{("X sum of squares, total").}$$

It is left as an exercise for the student to show that the sum of the squares of the errors of prediction under ω is

$$SS_{e\omega} = \Sigma_i\Sigma_j[Y_{ij} - M_Y - b_T(X_{ij} - M_X)]^2 = SS_{TY} - SP_T^2/SS_{TX}.$$

This quantity $SS_{e\omega} = SS_{TY} - SP_T^2/SS_{TX}$ is the so-called "adjusted sum of squares for Y, total".

The predicted value of Y_{ij} under Ω is

$$Y_{ij\Omega}' = M_{i,Y} + b_w(X_{ij} - M_{i,X}),$$

where $M_{i,Y}$ is the mean of the Y scores in Group i and $M_{i,X}$ is the mean of the X scores in Group i, and $b_w = [\Sigma_i\Sigma_j(X_{ij} - M_{i,X}) (Y_{ij} - M_{i,Y})]/\Sigma_i\Sigma_j(X_{ij} - M_{i,X})^2$, which is the least-squares estimate of the common slope of the I different regression lines, which differ only in their intercept.

The error of prediction under Ω is

$$Y_{ij} - Y_{ij\Omega}' = Y_{ij} - M_{i,Y} - b_w(X_{ij} - M_{i,X}),$$

and the sum of the squares of the errors of prediction are

$$SS_{e\Omega} = \Sigma_i\Sigma_j[Y_{ij} - M_{i,Y} - b_w(X_{ij} - M_{i,X})]^2.$$

Let us now introduce the additional notation:

$$SS_{wY} = \Sigma_i\Sigma_j(Y_{ij} - M_{i,Y})^2 \qquad \text{("Y sum of squares within groups")}$$

$$SP_w = \Sigma_i\Sigma_j(X_{ij} - M_{i,X})(Y_{ij} - M_{i,Y}) \quad \text{("sum of products within groups")}$$

$$SS_{wX} = \Sigma_i\Sigma_j(X_{ij} - M_{i,X})^2 \qquad \text{("X sum of squares within groups")}.$$

To save the student from another exercise we will show that

$$SS_{e\Omega} = \Sigma_i\Sigma_j[Y_{ij} - M_{i,Y} - b_w(X_{ij} - M_{i,X})]^2 = SS_{wY} - (SP_w^2/SS_{wX})$$

which is the "adjusted sum of squares within." Performing the indicated squaring and summing we have

$$SS_{e\Omega} = \Sigma_i\Sigma_j(Y_{ij} - M_{i,Y})^2 - 2b_w \Sigma_i\Sigma_j(X_{ij} - M_{i,X})(Y_{ij} - M_{i,Y}) + b_w^2 \Sigma_i\Sigma_j(X_{ij} -$$

$$M_{i,X})^2.$$

At this point the desired result is obtained immediately by noting that $SS_{wY} = \Sigma_i\Sigma_j(Y_{ij} - M_{i,Y})^2$ and that $b_w = [\Sigma_i\Sigma_j(X_{ij} - M_{i,X})(Y_{ij} - M_{i,Y})]/\Sigma_i\Sigma_j(X_{ij} - M_{i,X})^2 = SP_w/SS_{wX}$.

The difference between the sum of squares for error under ω and the sum of squares for error under Ω measures the extent to which the larger model fits the data better than the smaller model. This difference is

$$SS_{e\omega} - SS_{e\Omega} = (SS_{TY} - SP_T^2/SS_{TX}) - [SS_{wY} - (SP_w^2/SS_{wX})]$$

$$= (SS_{TY} - SS_{wY}) - (SP_T^2/SS_{TX} - SP_w^2/SS_{wX})$$

$$= SS_{GY} - (SP_T^2/SS_{TX} - SP_w^2/SS_{wX}) = SS_{GY,adj.}$$

which we call the adjusted sum of squares for groups. The adjusted sum of squares for groups has $I - 1$ degrees of freedom. We compare the adjusted sum of squares for groups to the sum of squares for error under the larger model. We summarize the adjusted sums of squares in Table 12.9.

Each of these sums of squares is the squared length of a vector and all of our previous geometric discussions carry over to this situation directly.

12.9.1 The vectors Y'_ω and Y'_Ω. The vector Y'_ω is the projection of the Y in the space spanned by 1 and X. This is a two-dimensional space. The vector Y'_Ω is the projection of Y in the space spanned by 1, X, and the I vectors of indicator values (1's or 0's) that specify which intercept goes with which Y-score on the basis of which group it belongs to—that is, the last I column vectors of the X-matrix under the larger hypothesis. Since the I vectors of indicator variables add to give 1, the space spanned by the vectors of this matrix is $(I + 1)$-dimensional.

12.10   Contrasts in the standard analysis of covariance. In the case of a one-factor design with a single covariate, the adjusted group means are

$$M_{Yi,adj.} = M_{Yi} - b_w M_{Xi}.$$

A contrast of the I adjusted means, $\Sigma_i c_i\, M_{Yi,adj.}$ can be tested using

$$F_{1,I(J-1)-1} = (\Sigma_i c_i\, M_{Yi,adj.})^2 / \{\, MS_{wadj.}\{(\Sigma_i c_i^2/J) +$$

$$[(\Sigma_i c_i M_{Xi})^2/\Sigma_i\Sigma_j(X_{ij} - M_{Xi})^2]\}\} \,.$$

For multiple contrasts, Scheffé's method can be applied such that with probability $1 - \alpha$

$$\Sigma_i c_i\, M_{Yi,adj.} - R \;\leq\; \Sigma_i c_i \mu_{Yi} \;\leq\; \Sigma_i c_i\, M_{Yi,adj.} + R$$

where

$$R = [\, (I-1)F_{\alpha,1,I(J-1)-1}\, MS_{wadj.}\{(\Sigma_i c_i^2/J) + [(\Sigma_i c_i M_{Xi})^2/\Sigma_i\Sigma_j(X_{ij} - M_{Xi})^2]\} \,]^{.5}.$$

12.11   Other analyses of covariance. The extension of the analysis of covariance to multifactor designs with or without mixed designs can be found in standard textbooks (Myers, 1979; Winer, 1971). In this section and the next, we will consider some extensions that are not so widely presented. Our first example will be some cases where our interest does not lie in whether there are Group effects. We will assume that we already know or are confident that there are Group effects. Our primary interest is instead in the presence or

TABLE 12.9 ANALYSIS OF COVARIANCE

Source	df	SS
Within Groups adjusted	$I(J-1) - 1$	$SS_{wY} - (SP_w{}^2/SS_{wX})$
Total adjusted	$IJ - 2$	$SS_{TY} - SP_T{}^2/SS_{TX}$
Groups adjusted	$I - 1$	$SS_{GY} - (SP_T{}^2/SS_{TX} - SP_w{}^2/SS_{wX})$

absence of a linear regression of our dependent variable Y on a covariate X. Here if we were inclined to use the terminology of "adjustment" it would be the sum of squares for regression that requires "adjustment" for the effects of Groups rather than the sum of squares for Groups requiring "adjustment" for the effects of regression of Y on X.

We will list three cases as three models with their model equations:

$$\omega \quad : \quad Y_{ij} = \mu_Y + \alpha_i + e_{ij}$$

$$\pi \quad : \quad Y_{ij} = \mu_Y + \alpha_i + \beta_w(X_{ij} - \mu_{X_i}) + e_{ij}$$

$$\xi \quad : \quad Y_{ij} = \mu_Y + \alpha_i + \beta_i(X_{ij} - \mu_{X_i}) + e_{ij}. \qquad (\xi \text{ is "zi" and rhymes with "pie"})$$

The model ω is just the ordinary analysis of variance model. We can also think of it as the case of I different "regressions" of Y on X where for each group there is a different intercept but a zero slope. The model π is the case where the regression line for each group has a different intercept but the same slope. The model ξ is the largest model in that it permits each of the groups to have a different intercept and a different slope. We can imagine that in the case of the model ξ we might be dealing with a dependent variable that is linearly related to a covariate but the slope and intercept are affected by an experimental treatment that differs for different values of i, the level of the treatment factor. The rate of information processing might be one such slope. The psychophysical law relating perceived line length to physical line length (Bogartz, 1980) might be another.

We will do the test of π versus ω and leave the other such tests between pairs of models as exercises. The least-squares estimates of Y'_{ij} under the two models are

$$Y'_{ij\omega} = M_{Y_i}$$

$$Y'_{ij\pi} = M_{Y_i} + b_w(X_{ij} - M_{X_i})$$

and the corresponding sums of squares for error under the two models are

$$SS_{error\omega} = \Sigma_i\Sigma_j(Y_{ij} - Y'_{ij\omega})^2 = \Sigma_i\Sigma_j(Y_{ij} - M_{Yi})^2 = SS_{wY}$$

$$SS_{error\pi} = \Sigma_i\Sigma_j(Y_{ij} - Y'_{ij\pi})^2 = \Sigma_i\Sigma_j[Y_{ij} - b_w(X_{ij} - M_{Xi})]^2 = SS_{wY} -$$

$$SP_w^2/SS_{wX}.$$

The sum of squares for measuring whether the within-groups regression of Y on X reduces the error of prediction beyond that reduced by estimation of the group effects is, as usual, the sum of squares for error under the smaller model minus the sum of squares for error under the larger model, giving

$$SS_{error\omega} - SS_{error\pi} = SS_{wY} - (SS_{wY} - SP_w^2/SS_{wX}) = SP_w^2/SS_{wX}$$

which has one degree of freedom and is tested against the error sum of squares under the larger model,

$$SS_{error\pi} = SS_{wY} - SP_w^2/SS_{wX}$$

which has $I(J - 1) - 1$ degrees of freedom. The summary of the analysis is shown in Table 12.10.

12.12   Multiple linear and nonlinear regression and the analysis of covariance. It should be apparent that since the analysis of covariance is nothing more than testing a larger model against a smaller model, there is nothing that necessarily limits the regression portion of the models to simple linear regression. There might be more than one covariate, in which case we would have multiple regression of the dependent variable on the independent variables. "Adjustment" for the effects of multiple covariates follows the same logic as that for a single variable. Similarly, the regression on one or more covariates might involve powers of the covariates such as squares or cubes, in which case in general we might have an analysis of covariance with multiple polynomial regression involved. Here the powers of the covariate are functioning in the role of additional covariates.

   Alert. The student should be warned that the expression "analysis of covariance" is used in a broad sense and in a narrow sense. We have so far used it in the broad sense to indicate the situation where a regression analysis is being performed in which both qualitative and quantitative variables are involved. The narrow sense is that of the first case we considered: simple linear regression of Y on a single covariate, homogeneous within-group regression

TABLE 12.10 THE ANALYSIS OF COVARIANCE

Source	df	SS	F
Model π	$I(J-1)-1$	$SS_{wY} - SP_w^2/SS_{wX}$	
Model ω	$I(J-1)$	SS_{wY}	
$\omega - \pi$	1	SP_w^2/SS_{wX}	$\dfrac{SP_w^2/SS_{wX}}{(SS_{wY} - SP_w^2/SS_{wX})/\,[I(J-1)-1]}$

coefficients, with interest centered on the presence or absence of group effects. When "analysis of covariance" is used in this narrow sense, the student will find remarks such as the following: "... analyses of covariance require a number of specialized statistical assumptions. ... the most stringent is the assumption of homogeneous within-group regression coefficients. ... the analysis of covariance [is] sensitive only to the linear relationship between X and Y ..." (Keppel, 1982, p. 513). These remarks are true for the analysis of covariance in the narrow sense, but in general, there is no requirement of homogeneous within-group regression coefficients, nor is it required that only a linear relationship between X and Y be structured into the analysis of covariance. The covariance analysis will be sensitive to whatever relationships have been built into the matrix of independent variables.

12.13 The general linear model. We have seen in this chapter that fixed-effects analyses of variance, simple and multiple linear and nonlinear regression, and various forms of the analysis of covariance are all cases of the same structure. To gain some closure now, we can consider that structure in its general form. With respect to the testing of a particular null hypothesis, the data vector is viewed as comprising two parts if the null hypothesis is true or three parts if it is not. Under the larger model, Ω,

$$\mathbf{Y} = \mathbf{X}_1 \boldsymbol{\beta}_{\Omega 1} + \mathbf{X}_2 \boldsymbol{\beta}_{\Omega 2} + \mathbf{e}$$

and under the smaller model, ω,

$$\mathbf{Y} = \mathbf{X}_1 \boldsymbol{\beta}_{\omega 1} + \mathbf{e}.$$

For example, in the case of a one-factor analysis of variance, the larger model would look like this:

$$
\begin{bmatrix} Y_{11} \\ Y_{12} \\ Y_{13} \\ Y_{21} \\ Y_{22} \\ Y_{23} \\ Y_{31} \\ Y_{32} \\ Y_{33} \end{bmatrix} = \mathbf{X_1 \beta_{\Omega 1}} + \mathbf{X_2 \beta_{\Omega 2}} + \mathbf{e} = \begin{bmatrix} 1 \\ 1 \\ 1 \\ 1 \\ 1 \\ 1 \\ 1 \\ 1 \\ 1 \end{bmatrix} \begin{bmatrix} \mu \end{bmatrix} + \begin{bmatrix} 1 & 0 & 0 \\ 1 & 0 & 0 \\ 1 & 0 & 0 \\ 0 & 1 & 0 \\ 0 & 1 & 0 \\ 0 & 1 & 0 \\ 0 & 0 & 1 \\ 0 & 0 & 1 \\ 0 & 0 & 1 \end{bmatrix} \begin{bmatrix} \alpha_1 \\ \alpha_2 \\ \alpha_3 \end{bmatrix} + \mathbf{e}
$$

and the smaller model would look like this:

$$
\begin{bmatrix} Y_{11} \\ Y_{12} \\ Y_{13} \\ Y_{21} \\ Y_{22} \\ Y_{23} \\ Y_{31} \\ Y_{32} \\ Y_{33} \end{bmatrix} = \mathbf{X_1 \beta_{\Omega 1}} + \mathbf{e} = \begin{bmatrix} 1 \\ 1 \\ 1 \\ 1 \\ 1 \\ 1 \\ 1 \\ 1 \\ 1 \end{bmatrix} \begin{bmatrix} \mu \end{bmatrix} + \mathbf{e}
$$

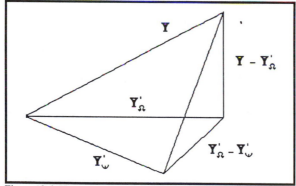

Figure 12.6 The vector space for the analysis of covariance.

(Of course in the former case, the side condition $\Sigma_j \alpha_j = 0$ would have to be included in matrix form.) In the case of analysis of covariance, in each model the $\mathbf{X_1}$ matrix would have a vector of X-values included and each β_1 vector would have a regression coefficient in addition to μ. The geometry in all of these cases is as in Figure 12.6. The general form of

TABLE 12.11   ANALYSIS OF THE GENERAL LINEAR MODEL

Source	df	SS	MS	F
The model Ω	p	SS_Ω	$SS_{S\Omega}/p$	
The model ω	p - r	SS_ω	$SS_\omega/(p - r)$	
The difference	r	$SS_\Omega - SS_\omega$	$(SS_\Omega - SS_\omega)/r$	$\dfrac{(SS_\Omega - SS_\omega)/r}{(Y^tY - SS_\Omega)/(N-p)}$
Error	N - p	$Y^tY - SS_\Omega$	$(Y^tY - SS_\Omega)/(N-p)$	

the summary table for the analysis is as shown in Table 12.10. We assume there are p - r linearly independent column vectors in X_1, r linearly independent column vectors in X_2, and N Y-scores in all.   It should be noted that Table 12.10 presents the sums of squares under the two models as the squared lengths of the vectors of least-squares estimates of the predicted Y values. When we have compared the sums of squares for errors of prediction under the two models, we have been comparing $Y^tY - SS_\Omega$, the sum of squares for error under Ω, with $Y^tY - SS_\omega$, the sum of squares for error under the smaller model. Since the latter is always greater than or equal to the former, we have looked at ($Y^tY - SS_w$) - ($Y^tY - SS_\Omega$), and compared it to the sum of squares under the larger model. This, of course, gives the same sum of squares for the numerator of the F test as in Table 12.11.

What we now have in hand is an integration of fixed-effects analyses of variance, regression models, and covariance models. Basically each is tested in the same way, although, as we have seen, the particular details of the different approaches can get fairly elaborate.

Exercises

1. Assume the multiple linear regression model $Y_i = b + m_1X_1 + m_2X_2 + m_3X_3 + e_i$ applies to the data in Table 12.12.
(a) Find the vector of least-squares parameter estimates.
(b) Find the 95 percent confidence band for Y when $X_1 = 4$, $X_2 = 10$, and $X_3 = 3$.
(c) Test the hypothesis that Y is independent of X_1, X_2, and X_3.
(d) Test the hypothesis that $Y_i = b + m_1X_1 + m_2X_2 + e_i$ describes the data as well as does $Y_i = b + m_1X_1 + m_2X_2 + m_3X_3 + e_i$.

TABLE 12.12 DATA FOR MULTIPLE LINEAR REGRESSION EXERCISES

Y	X_1	X_2	X_3
2.4	4	11	2
2.7	5	8	3
2.1	4	9	2
3.2	7	5	4
3.5	9	4	5
3.7	10	3	2
3.3	10	4	4
4.1	12	2	3
4.2	14	1	4
2.5	9	7	2

2. Using the data in Table 12.12, test the hypothesis that $Y_i = b + m_1 X_1 + m_2 X_1^2 + e_i$ does no better than $Y_i = b + m_1 X_1 + e_i$ in describing the population from which these data were sampled.

3. Write the **X** matrix and the **H** matrix for a 2 x 3 factorial design with three scores per cell.

4. Write the **X** matrix and the **H** matrix for a 3 x 2 x 2 factorial design with two scores per cell.

5. Write the analysis of covariance model for a design with three levels of Factor A and one covariate, assuming homogeneity of regression slopes over all levels of Factor A.

6. Using the same conditions as in exercise 5 except that the regression slopes may vary from level to level of Factor A, write the analysis of covariance model equation.

7. Using the data in Table 12.6, test the model in exercise 6 against the model in exercise 5.

8. Assume the model in exercise 5 applies to the data in Table 12.6, and, to test the hypothesis of no difference between the adjusted means for Groups 1 and 2, find

(a) the degrees of freedom for the F ratio for that contrast

(b) the value of the contrast of the adjusted sample means.

9. Consider Figure 12.6. Show that:

(a) $Y'_\Omega - Y'_\omega$ is orthogonal to Y'_ω;

(b) $Y - Y'_\Omega$ is orthogonal to Y'_Ω.

10. Describe the appropriate decomposition of the IJ-dimensional space in Figure 12.6, and indicate the dimensionality of each of the subspaces.

11. Show that the adjusted sum of squares for groups is the sum of the squared deviations of the predicted values for Y_{ij} under ω from the predicted values for Y_{ij} under Ω. That is, that

$$SS_{Gy,adj.} = \Sigma_i\Sigma_j(Y'_{ij\omega} - Y'_{ij\Omega})^2.$$

12. (a) Suppose some question existed concerning the assumption that the I groups all had regression lines with the same slope. Formulate the model, ζ ("zeta"), in matrix form that assigns a possibly different slope to each group. How would you test ω, the hypothesis that all I slopes were equal, against ζ, the model that in general they are different?

(b) Write a computational formula for the least-squares estimate of the slope of the regression line for Group i assuming model ζ.

(c) Write a computational formula for the predicted value of Y_{ij} assuming a different slope for each group. Let $Y'_{ij\zeta}$ be that predicted value. Write a computational formula for the sum of squares for error under the model ζ.

(d) What would the degrees of freedom be for the error sum of squares under model ζ?

(e) Write the F-ratio for testing ζ vs. ω. The numerator mean square will be (the error sum of squares under ω minus the error sum of squares under ζ) divided by the difference in their degrees of freedom. What will the denominator degrees of freedom be?

13. (a) State in words the additional reduction in error of prediction that model π provides beyond that provided by the analysis of variance model ω.

(b) Do the same for model ξ relative to model π.

TABLE 12.13 FICTIONAL DATA FOR AN AREA JUDGMENT TASK

Height	Width	Perimeter	Diagonal	ln Perimeter	ln Diagonal	ln Jgd. area	Jgd. area
1	3	8	3.16	2.0794415	1.1512925	1.94	7
2	3	10	3.61	2.3025851	1.2824747	2.15	9
3	3	12	4.24	2.4849066	1.4451859	2.30	10
4	3	14	5.00	2.6390573	1.6094379	2.42	11
1	4	10	4.12	2.3025851	1.4166067	2.11	8
2	4	12	4.47	2.4849066	1.4978661	2.28	10
3	4	14	5.00	2.6390573	1.6094379	2.42	11
4	4	16	5.66	2.7725887	1.732868	2.53	13
1	5	12	5.10	2.4849066	1.6290483	2.24	9
2	5	14	5.39	2.6390573	1.6836479	2.40	11
3	5	16	5.83	2.7725887	1.7631803	2.52	12
4	5	18	6.40	2.8903718	1.856786	2.62	14
1	6	14	6.08	2.6390573	1.805459	2.36	11
2	6	16	6.32	2.7725887	1.8444397	2.50	12
3	6	18	6.71	2.8903718	1.9033312	2.61	14
4	6	20	7.21	2.9957323	1.9756219	2.70	15

14. Write out the summary table for the covariance analysis that compares model ξ with model π. Do the same for model ξ versus model ω.

15. Use the data in Table 12.6 to perform each of the analyses of covariance mentioned in exercise 2.

16. Consider a theory of area judgment that proposes that the subject judges the area of a rectangle by subjectively computing a power function of the perimeter times a power function of the diagonal. That is,

Judged area = (Perimeter)^a(diagonal)^b,
which would imply that

ln(Judged area) = a ln(Perimeter) + b ln(diagonal).

An alternative model proposes that

Judged area = c(Perimeter)^a(diagonal)^b,

which would imply that

ln(Judged area) = a ln(Perimeter) + b ln(diagonal) + ln c.

(a) Estimate the model parameters for each theory, and
(b) test the first theory against the second theory, using the data in Table 12.13..

Supplementary Reading

Maxwell, C., & Cramer, E. M. (1975) A note on analysis of covariance. *Psychological Bulletin, 82,* 187-190.

13

Some Fine Points

13.1 A brief review of the concept of power. In this chapter we will consider briefly some fine points in the analysis of variance. The first is power. Power is a very simple idea that somehow seems to get very complicated in the explaining of it. The basic question is: Suppose I am testing a null hypothesis and it isn't true. What is the probability that I will reject this false null hypothesis? The answer is the power of the test, usually symbolized by $1 - \beta$. The complications for the student seem to arise in that sentence, "Suppose I am testing a null hypothesis and it isn't true." If the null hypothesis isn't true, then some other hypothesis must be the true one. But the process of testing the null hypothesis involves choosing a critical region for the test and basing that critical region on the assumption that the null hypothesis is true. The student appears to undergo some distress in trying to keep straight the fact that the test procedure is based on assuming H_0 is true, but the determining of the power of the test is based on assuming it is false in some specified way. Let's be more concrete.

Recall the coin-flipping example in Chapter 1. We discussed flipping a coin 10 times to decide if the null hypothesis that it is a fair coin is true. We said that if it was a fair coin it would hardly ever come up 0, 1, 9, or 10 heads in 10 flips. On this basis we decided that we would reject H_0 if it did come up 0, 1, 9, or 10 heads in 10 flips. Now suppose we happen to select a coin that is not a fair coin or we use a flipping process that is not fair. What is the probability that we will reject H_0? That is, what is the power of the test? Obviously we need more information to answer this question. Specifically, we need to know the probability that flipping this coin 10 times will result in 0, 1, 9, or 10 heads. Assuming that the flips are independent, it would suffice if we knew the probability of a heads occurring on each flip. Assuming that this probability on each flip, call it P, remains the same on each flip, we could use the binomial distribution to determine the probability of 0, 1, 9, or 10 heads.

This is where things always seem to get a little confusing in introductory statistics. "If we know P and we know that it is not .5," the student wonders, "why would we test a null hypothesis that it is .5? And if, on the other hand, we do not know P, how can we calculate the probability of 0,1,9, or 10 heads when P does not equal .5?" It is vital for the student to keep foremost the idea that we never know what the probability of a heads is when we are testing the null hypothesis. The null hypothesis is just that, a hypothesis, not a fact. There would be no problem if we were to consider the null hypothesis that P = .5, then consider that instead it equals .6; then consider that it equals .3, and so on. The student can mentally switch from one hypothesis to another. But in thinking about power, we do something slightly more complicated. We say to ourselves, "Suppose that I go through the entire test procedure of testing one hypothesis, the null hypothesis, and that in fact a different hypothesis is true." That is, suppose that I choose my test statistic (the number of heads in 10 flips), find the sampling distribution of this statistic (binomial, N = 10, P = .5), determine the rejection region (0, 1, 9, or 10 heads), flip the coin 10 times, and decide whether to accept or reject the null hypothesis while in fact I am working with a coin for which P is not equal to .5. Then what will the probability be that I will obtain a value of 0, 1, 9, or 10 heads and therefore reject the null hypothesis? Here I am working with two hypotheses at once: the null hypothesis that I am testing and that I use to determine the rejection region, and the alternative hypothesis that I suppose, for the moment, is the truth. What am I up to here?

Recall that usually when we test a null hypothesis, it is with the purpose of inferentially demonstrating that it is false. It is only natural for us to wonder and be concerned whether, in designing the experiment, we have created a procedure that will serve that purpose. If the null hypothesis is false, does this experimental procedure have a good chance of resulting in rejecting it? **If we reflect for a moment, we realize that answering this question requires that we use the sampling distribution of the test statistic but that we incorporate the information about the null hypothesis not being true.** In the case of the coin-flipping experiment, if we assume that the flips are independent and that the probability of a heads remains constant from flip to flip, then we know that whatever P is, the probability of 0, 1, 9, or 10 heads is

$$\Pr(0,1,9,\text{or } 10 \text{ heads}) = 10!/(0!10!)P^0(1\text{-}P)^{10} + 10!/(1!9!)P^1(1\text{-}P)^9 +$$

$$10!/(9!1!)P^9(1\text{-}P)^1 + 10!/(10!0!)P^{10}(1\text{-}P)^0. \qquad\qquad [13.1]$$

We chose 0, 1, 9, and 10 heads as the rejection region because when P = .5, the probability of 0, 1, 9, and 10 heads was suitably small, so we would hold the type I error rate down to a desirable value. Now we can ask what the probability is of getting 0, 1, 9, or 10 heads if P = .7 by simply substituting .7 for P in equation [13.1]. For P = .7 this value is .1494. We see that with the experimental design, P could be as large as .7 and the probability of rejecting the null hypothesis that P = .5 would only be about .15. Even when P = .75, the probability of rejecting the null hypothesis is still about .24. For some purposes we might not be happy with an experiment that would miss detecting so unfair a coin 76 percent of the time. We would say that the experiment is not powerful enough for our purposes.

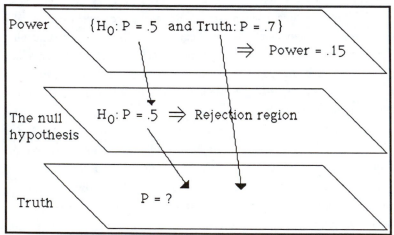

Figure 13.1. The null hypothesis is a reflection on the unknown true value of the parameter P. Power is a reflection on the implications of choosing a null hypothesis that is different from the truth. Since we never know the true value of P, we explore these implications by holding the null hypothesis value constant while conceptually varying the possible values that might be the truth. Each different candidate for the truth coupled with the null hypothesis value gives a different value of power.

Let us view this way of thinking as comprising three levels: the level of truth, the level of the null hypothesis, and the level of power considerations. Figure 13.1 shows these three levels.

The bottom level in Figure 13.1 indicates that we never know what the truth is. The next level is the level at which we reflect upon what the truth might be, this reflection taking the form of a null hypothesis. It is at this level that we

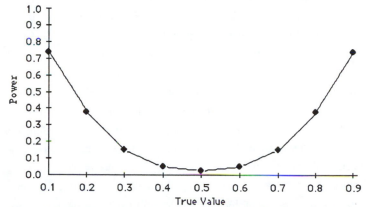

Figure 13.2. The power of the test of the null hypothesis, P = .5, as a function of the true value of P.

deduce the implications of the choice of the null hypothesis. At this level we derive a critical region for a test of the selected null hypothesis, and we perform the statistical test. All of this can be done with no consideration of power at all (and often has been in the research literature) and therefore no use is made of the top level. At the top level we are reflecting upon the bottom and middle levels taken together. We consider that the null hypothesis can be false, and we ask what actions at the middle level will lead us to decide about the null hypothesis if the truth is not the null hypothesis but some alternative that we select for consideration. **Notice that in selecting an alternative true value, we are not disposing of the null hypothesis. Quite the contrary. We are asking how the test of the selected null hypothesis is affected by the truth being this alternative we are now considering.** Specifically, we are asking what the probability is that we will reject the selected null hypothesis if the truth is a particular alternative value, say .7.

We realize that for every different alternative true value we choose, there will in general be a different value of power and that we could plot those values as a function of the choice of the alternative, giving a power function for the given null hypothesis. Figure 13.2 is such a plot. We notice that as the true value departs from the null hypothesis value of .5, the probability of correctly rejecting the null hypothesis increases. We also notice that when the true value equals the null hypothesis value, then the power is exactly equal to the significance level.

All of these considerations that we have raised concerning power in the case of the test of the value of P in the binomial distributution for N = 10 carry over directly to the case of the analysis of variance. The null hypothesis will be different, pertaining to the mean of a normal distribution or to a collection of means of normal distributions, the test statistic will be an F-statistic now rather than the number of successes, and the sampling distribution of the test statistic when the null hypothesis is false will either be a new distribution that we have not considered yet, called the **noncentral F distribution**, or it will be our old friend the F distribution, but the logic of the situation will all be exactly the same.

13.2   The noncentral chi-square and noncentral F distributions.   With a fixed-effects model, if the null hypothesis is false, then the distribution of the test statistic F will not belong to the F family of distributions but instead will be distributed according to a different family known as the **noncentral F distribution**. Let the variables $y_1, y_2, ..., y_I$ be independently normally distributed with means $\mu_1, \mu_2, ..., \mu_I$, and all have the same variance $\sigma^2 = 1$. Then the random variable $U = \Sigma_i Y_i^2$ has the **noncentral chi-square distribution** with I degrees of freedom. (Tables for the noncentral chi-square distribution exist in the statistical literature.) The quantity $\delta = (\Sigma \mu_i^2)$ is the noncentrality parameter of the distribution of U. For $\delta = 0$, which can only be the case if all of the μ_i are zero, the distribution of U is the ordinary or central chi-square distribution that we have discussed before.

If U_1 and U_2 are independent random variables, U_1 is a noncentral chi-square variable with r degrees of freedom and noncentrality parameter δ, and U_2 is a central chi-square variable with s degrees of freedom, then the variable $(U_1/r)/(U_2/s)$ has the **noncentral F distribution** with r and s degrees of freedom and noncentrality parameter δ. All three quantities r, s, and δ are needed to enter tables or charts in order to find the probability of rejecting the null hypothesis when the test statistic has the noncentral F distribution.

13.3 Power. Consider the case where we wish to test the null hypothesis that the mean of a normal distribution, μ, equals zero. The test statistic is

$$F = (NM^2/\sigma^2)/\{\Sigma(Y_i - M)^2/(N-1) \sigma^2\}$$

on 1 and N-1 degrees of freedom. We know that the denominator of this fraction is a central chi-square variable divided by its degrees of freedom. Also, when $\mu = 0$, $NM^2/\sigma^2 = (M - \mu)^2/(\sigma^2/N)$ is a central chi-square divided by its degrees of freedom (1 df), but when $\mu \neq 0$, then $NM^2/\sigma^2 = M^2/(\sigma^2/N)$ is a noncentral chi-square variable divided by its degrees of freedom. This follows because the sample mean, M, is normally distributed with mean μ and variance σ^2/N; therefore $M/(\sigma/\sqrt{N})$ is $N(\mu,1)$ so $M^2/(\sigma^2/N)$ has the noncentral chi-square distribution with noncentrality parameter $\delta = [\mu^2/(\sigma^2/N)]^{.5} = [N\mu^2/\sigma^2]^{.5}$. Therefore

$$F = (NM^2/\sigma^2)/\{\Sigma(Y_i - M)^2/(N-1)\sigma^2\} = NM^2/\{\Sigma(Y_i - M)^2/(N-1)\}$$

has the noncentral F distribution with 1 and N-1 degrees of freedom and with noncentrality parameter $\delta = [N\mu^2/\sigma^2]^{.5}$. Suppose that the sample size is N = 10, a significance level of .05 is used, the true value of μ is actually 10, and $\sigma = 5$. Then $\delta^2 = 10(100)/25 = 40$. We can determine the power of this test by using the Pearson and Hartley charts in the Statistical Tables and Charts section (Appendix 3). To enter these charts we need α, r, s, and the quantity $\phi = [\delta^2/(r+1)]^{.5}$, which in this case is $(40/2)^{.5} = 4.47$.

Entering the first Pearson and Hartley chart (note that the Pearson and Hartley Chart uses v_1 and v_2 where we are using r and s) with r = 1, s = 9, in the α = .05 section of the chart and locating ϕ = 4.47 along the bottom margin in the α = .05 layer, we find that the power of the test is approximately .81. About 81 percent of the time we will reject the null hypothesis that μ = 0 when we sample 10 scores from a normal distribution with a mean of 10 and a standard deviation of 5.

For fixed-effects models in general, the noncentrality parameter δ for a statistic F can always easily be calculated by replacing each score y_i in the numerator sum of squares formula by its expected value under the larger hypothesis. This resulting sum of squares will always equal $\sigma^2\delta^2$. To exemplify this, let us assume that you are performing an analysis of a one-factor design with 100 scores at each of four levels or experimental conditions. You are interested in knowing what the power of the overall F-test for conditions will be if the first three of the conditions have the same mean μ_1 but the fourth has a mean that is greater than μ_1 by two standard errors of a condition mean; that is, by $2(\sigma/10)$ = $\sigma/5$. The formula for the numerator sum of squares is $\Sigma_i 100(M_i - M)^2$. Let the common true mean for the first three groups be μ_1, and the mean for the fourth group will therefore be $\mu_1 + \sigma/5$. The general mean will therefore be $\mu_1 + \sigma/20$. Replacing each quantity in the sum of squares formula by its expected value we have

$$\delta^2\sigma^2 = \Sigma 100(\mu_i - \mu)^2 = 3\{100[\mu_1 - (\mu_1 + \sigma/20)]^2\} + 100[(\mu_1 + \sigma/5) - (\mu_1 +$$

$$\sigma/20)]^2 = 3\sigma^2,$$

so $\delta = 3^{.5}$. Since r = 3, $\phi = \delta(r+1)^{-.5} = 3^{.5}(4)^{-.5} = 3.46$. Entering the Pearson and Hartley chart with α = .05 and s = 96 we see that the power is approximately .99. About half the time a design such as this would fail to reject the null hypothesis when three of the four means were equal and the fourth was two standard errors of the mean away from those three.

13.4   Power in random-effects designs. We have seen in Chapter 7 that in a one-factor random-effects model with I groups and J scores per group, we use the test statistic

$$F = MS_A/MS_e = (1 + J\sigma^2_A/\sigma^2_e)F_{I-1,I(J-1)}.$$

This means that for any $\sigma^2_A \neq 0$, we can answer a power question of the form, "What is the probability we will reject the null hypothesis if σ^2_A/σ^2_e is so large as η?" For example, suppose we wanted to know the power of the test if σ^2_A is twice as large as σ^2_e so that $\eta = 2$. Then the test statistic would be distributed as $(1 + 2J)F_{I-1,I(J-1)}$. Since we will reject the null hypothesis if MS_A/MS_e is greater than $F_{\alpha,I-1,I(J-1)}$, and since this will happen with the probability that $(1 + 2J)F_{I-1,I(J-1)} \geq F_{\alpha,I-1,I(J-1)}$, it follows that the power is equal to

$$Pr[F_{I-1,I(J-1)} \geq F_{\alpha,I-1,I(J-1)} / (1 + 2J)]. \qquad [13.2]$$

Because binomial distribution tables are more accessible than extensive tables of the F distribution, it can be useful to use a binomial distribution approximation to the F distribution in calculating probabilities such as [13.2] (see Hays, 1973, p. 449).

13.5   The efficiency of blocking relative to a completely randomized design. A second topic we will briefly consider is whether the introduction of a blocking factor into an experimental design is advantageous. Consider a one-factor design with IJK subjects (or other experimental units) assigned at random to I experimental conditions under the restriction that there be exactly JK subjects in each condition. As an example, these might be K = 10 children from each of J = 3 grades assigned to each of I = 5 experimental conditions. The primary concern lies in the effects of the five experimental conditions. We realize also that if there is substantial variability due to an effect of school grade, this variability will show up within the five cells of the design and will be reflected in the estimate of error variance. We could remove such variability from the error estimate by changing the design to include a Grades factor with three levels. In this design the IJK subjects are assigned at random to the IJ cells of an I Treatments x J Blocks (Grades) design with the constraint that exactly K subjects are assigned to each cell. Table 13.1 shows an example of the former **completely randomized design** and the latter **randomized blocks design**.

TABLE 13.1 COMPLETELY RANDOMIZED DESIGN AND RANDOMIZED BLOCKS DESIGN USING THE SAME NUMBER OF SUBJECTS BUT BLOCKING THEM AT THREE LEVELS OF THE GRADES FACTOR

		Treatment Condition				
		1	2	3	4	5
Completely Randomized Design		n = 30	n = 30	n = 30	n = 30	n = 30

		Treatment Condition				
		1	2	3	4	5
Randomized Blocks Design	Grade 1	n = 10	n = 10	n = 10	n = 10	n = 10
	Grade 2	n = 10	n = 10	n = 10	n = 10	n = 10
	Grade 3	n = 10	n = 10	n = 10	n = 10	n = 10

On the one hand, by treating Grades as a factor in the design, we remove any variance due to the effect of Grades from the within-cell variability that we use to estimate error variance. This will reduce the denominator of the F-ratio and therefore increase the power of the F-test. On the other hand, in the completely randomized design we have $I(JK - 1) = IJK - I$ degrees of freedom for error, but in the randomized blocks design, we have $IJ(K - 1) = IJK - IJ$ degrees of freedom for error. We have lost $I(J - 1)$ degrees of freedom for error, and this will decrease the power of the F-test. Suppose that actually there is no effect of Grades. Then we will have lost the $I(J - 1)$ error degrees of freedom but there will have been no reduction in the within-cell variability. In this case, blocking on the Grades variable would produce a loss in power rather than a gain. Even if there is a Grades effect, it could be so small that there would be a net loss in power due to blocking.

Interest lies, then, in whether the reduction in error variance is large. The greater the reduction in error variance due to blocking, the greater is the **relative efficiency** of the randomized blocks design relative to the completely randomized design. The first measure of relative efficiency that we could use would simply compare the estimates of error variance for the two designs. For both designs, these estimates would be the mean squares for within-cells variation. In the completely randomized design, this would be $MS_{er} = \Sigma_i\Sigma_j\Sigma_k(Y_{ijk} - M_{i.})^2/I(JK-1)$. In the randomized blocks design, it would be $MS_{eb} = \Sigma_i\Sigma_j\Sigma_k(Y_{ijk} - M_{ij.})^2/IJ(K-1)$. The relative efficiency of the randomized blocks design relative to the completely randomized design could then be defined as

$$RelEff = MS_{er}/MS_{eb}$$

$$= [\Sigma_i\Sigma_j\Sigma_k(Y_{ijk} - M_{i.})^2/I(JK-1)]/\Sigma_i\Sigma_j\Sigma_k(Y_{ijk} - M_{ij.})^2/IJ(K-1).$$

The smaller the randomized blocks design error variance estimate is relative to the error variance estimate for the completely randomized design, the greater is the relative efficiency of blocking.

In an attempt to adjust this measure for the difference in degrees of freedom for error in the two designs, Fisher (1952) proposed using the measure

$$\{[IJ(K-1) + 1][I(JK - 1) + 3]\}/\{[IJ(K - 1) + 3][IJ(K - 1) + 1]\}\text{RelEff}.$$

Fisher's correction is worth bothering with only in the rare case of a design with a very small number of scores. Even a randomized blocks design with two levels of the treatment, two levels of the blocking variable, and six scores per cell gives a value of .99RelEff, and with more levels of treatment or blocks or with more scores per cell, the value increases rapidly to virtual identity with RelEff.

13.6 Selecting the number of levels for the blocking factor. It is obvious from the discussion in section 13.5 that the greater the number of levels for the blocking factor, the more df for error will be lost and the greater is the potential gain in power from reduction of within-cells variability. It is also obvious that if there is no relationship between the blocking variable and the dependent variable, then blocking will not reduce within-cell variability. A very large correlation between the blocking variable and the dependent variable would mean that much within-cell variability would be removed by blocking, and so more levels of the blocks factor should be used, with less concern for loss of degrees of freedom. A weaker correlation would dictate fewer Blocks levels. The relationship between the correlation, the number of treatment conditions, the number of scores in the experimental design, and the optimal number of levels for the Blocks factor has been studied by Feldt (1958) and suggested optimal values are given. Hornbeck and Alf (1972) extended these results to blocking on the basis of ranks. Myers (1979, pp. 150-156) reproduces some of Feldt's tables and gives a useful discussion of the matter, as well as an important caution against using the values of the dependent variable itself as the basis for blocking.

In the event that a continuous concomitant variable (covariate) is available, use of this variable to perform an analysis of covariance as well as to assign subjects to experimental conditions may be superior to blocking. Maxwell, Delaney, and Dill (1984) indicate that while most experimental design texts follow Feldt (1958) in suggesting that the correlation between the covariate and the dependent variable should be considered in deciding between blocking and ANACOVA, their results indicate that the two most important factors are whether scores on the concomitant variable are available for all subjects prior to assigning any subjects to treatment conditions and whether the relationship of the dependent and concomitant variables is linear. Even in the event of nonlinearity, they favor ANACOVA based on generalized regression with higher-order powers of the continuous covariate where the form of the nonlinearity can be specified. The researcher anticipating deciding between blocking and ANACOVA is advised to consult their paper first.

13.7 Estimating the proportion of the total variance accounted for by treatment effects. Because the power of the F-test increases as the degrees of freedom for error increases, it is possible to obtain a statistically significant F-statistic when the null hypothesis is only slightly false. In fact, no matter how small the effects are so long as they are not all zero, the probability of correctly rejecting the null hypothesis can be made as close to one as we like by using sufficiently many observations. This has disturbed some researchers who have felt that microscopic effects, significant or not, are usually not of interest to the general research community, whether or not the statistical test yields a significant result. The result may be statistically significant, but it is probably not scientifically significant. (This is a clear case where confidence intervals provide a different emphasis than does hypothesis testing. The confidence intervals for the group means will display their virtual identity, whereas the hypothesis test will emphasize the significance of their very small difference.) You perhaps recall a similar argument from your introductory study of correlation. When you learned to test the significance of a Pearson product-moment correlation coefficient, you were probably also told about squaring the coefficient and using the square as a measure of the proportion of the variance in the Y variable that was accounted for by the relationship between the Y variable and the X variable. For the fixed-effects analysis of variance models, a similar measure of the proportion of variance accounted for by a factor has also been suggested. It is called ω^2 ("omega-squared"). For the one-factor design with model equation $Y_{ij} = M + A_i + e_{ij}$, we define the variance of the A_i to be

$$\sigma^2_A = \Sigma_i[A_i - E(A_i)]^2/I = \Sigma_i A_i^2/I$$

since $E(A_i) = 0$, and we define

$$\omega^2 = \sigma^2_A / \sigma^2_Y$$

where σ^2_Y is the total population variance of the Y scores. We will use σ^2_e to denote the error variance. Then obviously $\sigma^2_Y = \sigma^2_A + \sigma^2_e$.

We can use MS_e to estimate σ^2_e. In exercise 1 at the end of Chapter 2 you showed that $E(SS_A) = (I - 1)\sigma^2_e + J\Sigma_i A_i^2$. Substituting SS_A for $E(SS_A)$ and using MS_e to estimate σ^2_e we obtain $SS_A = (I - 1) MS_e + J\Sigma_i A_i^2$, which we can manipulate to obtain

$\Sigma_i A_i^2/I = [SS_A - (I - 1) MS_e]/IJ.$ [13.3]

We will use the right side of equation [13.3] as $\sigma^2_{A,est}$, the estimate of σ^2_A. Then, the estimate of ω^2 will be $\omega^2_{est} = \sigma^2_{A,est}/(\sigma^2_{A,est} + \sigma^2_{e,est}) = \{[SS_A - (I - 1) MS_e]/IJ\}/\{[SS_A - (I - 1) MS_e]/IJ + MS_e\}$ which with a little manipulation can be rewritten as

$\omega^2_{est} = [SS_A - (I - 1) MS_e]/(SS_{Total} + MS_e).$

It is possible for this value to be negative, in which case it is set equal to zero.

Consider the ANOVA summary in Table 13.2. The F is significant at the .05 level. The estimate of ω^2 is $\omega^2_{est} = [153 - 3(19.03)]/(3959 + 19.03) = .024$. Thus the effect of the A factor is statistically significant but it accounts for only an estimated 2.4 percent of the variance in the dependent variable.

Despite the urging of textbook writers, few researchers bother much with estimating the proportion of variance accounted for in an analysis of variance. Also, while the estimation procedure can be used in a multifactor design by estimating the proportion of variance accounted for by each factor and by each interaction, it is not completely obvious what to do with these estimates after you have them. In a three-factor design there can be three main effects, three two-factor interactions and a three-factor interaction. Suppose each of these seven sources accounts for an estimated 10 percent of the total variance. Should we be pleased that the systematic sources account for 70 percent of the total variance or dismayed that none of the sources of variance that we have manipulated accounts for more than 10 percent. Obviously with more factors, this question can become more confusing.

TABLE 13.2   ANOVA SUMMARY

Source	df	SS	MS	F
A	3	153	51	2.68
Error	200	3806	19.03	
Total	203	3959		

TABLE 13.3 SCORES FOR TWO TREATMENT CONDITIONS IN A ONE-FACTOR DESIGN

	Y		$\sqrt{Y}$	
	Cond. 1	Cond. 2	Cond. 1	Cond. 2
	.77	2.66	.88	1.63
	.83	2.76	.91	1.66
	1.32	3.61	1.15	1.90
	1.66	4.16	1.29	2.04
	2.99	6.15	1.73	2.48
	3.72	7.18	1.93	2.68
	3.84	7.34	1.96	2.71
	4.00	7.56	2.00	2.75
	4.33	8.01	2.08	2.83
	4.71	8.53	2.17	2.92
	4.80	8.64	2.19	2.94
	5.43	9.49	2.33	3.08
	7.18	11.76	2.68	3.43
	7.34	11.97	2.71	3.46
	9.86	15.13	3.14	3.89
	10.18	15.52	3.19	3.94
	12.60	18.49	3.55	4.30
	13.25	19.27	3.64	4.39
	14.21	20.43	3.77	4.52
	14.82	21.16	3.85	4.60
	15.05	21.44	3.88	4.63
	17.89	24.80	4.23	4.98
	22.37	30.03	4.73	5.48
	22.94	30.69	4.79	5.54
	28.73	37.33	5.36	6.11

Also, suppose we estimate that a main effect accounts for twice as much variance as does some interaction. It is not obvious what to do with such a finding.

It seems to me that estimating proportion of variance accounted for is a primitive approach to determining whether the magnitude of the experimental results with respect to some treatment is of scientific significance. I believe that such a determination must occur within a theoretical and empirical context where the obtained magnitudes are compared to other related values of the same variable and of other related variables. The size and the importance of an effect become increasingly comprehensible as we know about a body of phenomena. To the extent that we are ignorant of such a context, estimating proportion of variance accounted for will not be very informative. I suppose that in some preliminary, more or less blind, shotgun approach to a new area, where little or no previous knowledge exists, one might use proportion of variance accounted for to direct the choice of variables to follow up, but I believe that even in such a context (if one ever really exists), there are better ways to decide how to proceed than to use proportions of variance accounted for.

13.8 Transforming the data to satisfy distribution assumptions. The decision to use the F-ratio as the test statistic for fixed-effects designs rested upon its having a known distribution, the F distribution, which we could use to determine the risk of a Type I error. If the null hypothesis is true, the F-ratio is distributed according to the F distribution provided that the population distributions of error effects for all of the cells in the design are normal, the variances of those normal distributions of errors are homogeneous (all equal), and the errors are all independent of one another. A natural question that arises is how we should proceed if we suspect that one or more of these assumptions has been violated.

A **robust** statistical procedure with respect to some assumption is one in which the violation of that assumption does not seriously invalidate the inferences that are drawn when using the procedure. In the case of nonnormality of the error distributions, the F-test is a robust procedure so far as the significance level is concerned. The significance level is not seriously affected by violation of the normality assumption. There are some recent results that indicate that power may be affected seriously when the null hypothesis is false, however. In the case of heterogeneity of variance, the F-test is also robust when the numbers of scores per cell are equal (e.g. Scheffé, 1959, Chapter 10). When there are unequal numbers of scores per cell or when the distributions of the errors vary from cell to cell, then violation of the homogeneity of variance assumption can result in an actual signficance level that is substantially smaller or larger than the level adopted by the researcher (see Scheffé's Table 10.4.2 or its original source in Box,1954a, p. 299). In most designs the maintaining of equal numbers of scores per cell is within the control of the experimenter and should be adopted as the standard procedure (see Chapter 15 for exceptions). We have already dealt with the lack of independence in repeated measurement designs. In designs without repeated measures, ordinary experimental care coupled with random assignment of subjects or experimental material to experimental conditions should avoid problems of independence.

It sometimes happens that scores are distributed according to a family of distributions in which the mean and the variance are related. The Poisson distribution is an example where the mean equals the variance and in the binomial distribution the mean is Np and the variance is $Np - Np^2$. In such instances it is often the case that a transformation can be found to homogenize the variances. Bartlett (1947) has provided various transformations appropriate for various relationships between the mean and the variance. We will look at one example of such a transformation and its results and then provide the entire collections of transformation provided by Bartlett.

Consider the Y score data shown in the left half of Table 13.3 for two levels of a one-factor fixed-effects design. The scores are arranged in order from low to high. We can readily see that the distributions are skewed to the right by comparing the difference between the low score and the median to the difference between the high score and the median. In Condition 1 these differences are about 6 and 21, and in Condition 2 they are about 9 and 26. The variances for the two conditions are 56.32 and 86.92. When we perform the F test to test the null hypothesis that the means for the two conditions are equal, we find an F of 3.81 on 1 and 48 df, which is not significant at the .05 level.

Now suppose that we transform the Y scores by taking their square root, giving the scores in the right half of Table 13.3. We notice that the scores are now normally distributed, the variances of the two distributions are equal, and the corresponding F ratio is now 4.43 on 1 and 48 df which is significant at the .05 level. In this obviously contrived example, the square root transformation produces normality, homogeneity of variance, and a significant F ratio. We cannot always expect such total vitually divine beneficence from a transformation, but it may sometimes help to homogenize the variances, especially if we find an appropriate relationship between the sample means and sample variances.

One procedure to try to find the right transformation is to plot the sample variances as a function of the sample means. Where the sample variances are equal to or proportional to the sample means, use a square root transformation on the original scores, as in Table 13.3. If the scores are small integers, Bartlett recommends using $\sqrt{(Y + .5)}$. Where the variances are proportional to the square of the sample mean, Bartlett recommends the logarithmic transformation, using as the new scores the logarithms of the original scores. If there are scores equal to zero, take logarithms of $Y+1$. If the sample variances are proportional to $M - M^2$, Bartlett recommends using $\log_e Y/(1 - Y)$ or taking the inverse sine of the square root of Y. (The inverse sine of $\sqrt{Y}$ is the angle the sine of which equals $\sqrt{Y}$.) If the sample variances are proportional to $M^2(1 - M)^2$ use $\log_e Y/(1 - Y)$. For still other recommended transformations the student is referred to Bartlett (1947); for discussion of the theory see Bartlett (1947) and Scheffé(1959, section 10.7).

The square root transformation is of the form $Y_{new} = (Y_{old})^a$ where $a = .5$ and is therefore just a special case of the general power transformation. A more general procedure than just assuming $a = .5$ would be to estimate a. Box and Cox (1964) present a maximum likelihood procedure for estimating a. Box, Hunter, and Hunter (1978) illustrate this procedure for finding a power transformation Y^a. To estimate the exponent a they substitute various values of a into the expression

$$Y^{(a)} = (Y^a - 1)/(a\,G^{a-1})$$ [13.4]

where G is the geometric mean of all the data (the antilog of the average of of the logarithms of all of the scores) and where $Y^{(0)}$ is G ln Y. (In [13.4] the expression $Y^{(a)}$ denotes the transformation $(Y^a - 1)/(a\,G^{a-1})$ for the value of a in the parenthesized superscript. Each choice of a in the superscript denotes a different member of the family of transformations $(Y^a - 1)/(a\,G^{a-1})$.) For each value of a they compute the error sum of squares and choose that value of a that minimizes the error sum of squares.

Exercises

1. State in your own words the distinctions between the three levels of discussion in considering the power of a test.

TABLE 13.4 DATA AS COMPLETELY RANDOMIZED DESIGN (a) OR AS RANDOMIZED BLOCKS DESIGN (b)

(a) Conditions

1	2	3
12	10	18
14	12	20
16	14	22
4	2	10
6	4	12
8	6	14

(b) Conditions

	1	2	3
Boys	12	10	18
	14	12	20
	16	14	22
Girls	4	2	10
	6	4	12
	8	6	14

2. Assume you are testing the null hypothesis that the mean of a normal distribution is $\mu = 80$ using a significance level of .05 and that you know that the standard deviation is 20. Your sample size is 25, and you use the standard normal distribution as the sampling distribution of the mean. Under the null hypothesis, this sampling distribution will have a mean of 80 and a standard deviation of $20/5 = 4$. Plot a power function similar to that in Figure 13.1 by considering possible true values of μ ranging from 72 to 88 in steps of 2.

3. (a) Plot a power function for the test that the mean of a normal distribution is zero assuming that your sample size is 10, $\sigma = 5$, and your significance level is .05. Consider alternative true values of the mean ranging from -16 to + 16 in steps of 4.

(b) Do the same thing as in (a) but assume N = 20.

(c) Do the same thing as in (a) but assume $\sigma = 1$.

4. Plot the power function for the test of the null hypothesis that the means of four normally distributed populations are the same when in fact three of the means are the same and one of them differs from the others by x standard errors of the mean, where x ranges from .25 to 2.00 in steps of .25. Assume a sample of 25 scores for each of the four groups and a significance level of .05.

5. You have gathered a set of decision times from Boy and Girl subjects under three experimental conditions. The data are shown in Table 13.4 either as a completely randomized design or as a randomized blocks design with Gender as the blocking variable. Estimate the relative efficiency of the randomized blocks design relative to the completely randomized design.

6. (a) Use the data for the completely randomized design in exercise 5 to estimate ω^2 for the effect of conditions.

(b) Do the same as in (a) but using the data in the randomized blocks design of exercise 5.

7. Why are the two values for ω^2 in exercise 6 different?

8. What is the relationship between relative efficiency and power?

9. (a) Using the completely randomized design in exercise 5, using $MS_{e)}$ to estimate σ^2, and using M_i to estimate μ_i, estimate the noncentrality parameter δ and the probability that the completely randomized design would produce a significant conditions effect F-ratio if the experiment were replicated.

(b) What would be the benefit of using an analysis such as on published data before deciding whether to attempt a replication of an experiment published in the literature.

10. What is the relationship between the number of blocks that should be used in a randomized blocks design and the correlation between the blocking variable and the dependent variable?

Supplementary Reading

Koele, P. (1982) Calculating power in analysis of variance. *Psychological Bulletin,92,*
   513-516.

14

Some Advanced Applications

14.1   The ANOVA model coordinated with a substantive theoretical model.
In most experimentation in my field, which is psychology, there is virtually no reason to choose between a design model that includes interaction effects and one that assumes additivity. This is because, while the researchers are usually confident that the various design factors will have significant effects, there is rarely a theoretical basis for deciding whether these effects will combine additively. Still less frequently is there a basis for predicting the presence or absence of some particular component of interaction such as the linear x linear trend component. There have been some noteworthy exceptions, however, and the purpose of this chapter is to consider some of them and to familiarize the student with some of the features of theory testing that become of interest when such specific predictions can be made.

Predictions of such specific effects become possible when the terms in the analysis of variance model are coordinated with the terms in some substantive theoretical model. As an example, consider the following judgment task. The subject is asked to listen to two tones

and to judge how long the average of the durations of the two tones is. Somehow the subject has to take the information about the duration of the first tone and combine it with the information about the second tone to reach a judgment about the average of those two durations. Curtis and Rule (1977) proposed a model for relating judgment of the average duration to the physical measurements of the two time durations. We'll add a little color to their approach by describing their model as if the processes take place in stages. Let d_i and d_j be the physical measurements of the duration of the first and second tone for some first tone i and some second tone j. Curtis and Rule assume that psychological judgment of the duration of a tone is related to the physical measure by a power law of the form

$$J_i = d_i{}^k.$$

Thus, after hearing the two tones i and j, there are two available pieces of information, $d_i{}^k$ and $d_j{}^k$. The subject then averages these two values by assigning a positive weight to each of them such that the two weights add to one. This results in a subjective value

$$wd_i{}^k + (1-w)d_j{}^k.$$

The reason for the possibly different values of w and 1-w is that the stimuli were delivered sequentially and the impression of the second stimulus might be given greater weight than the impression of the first stimulus (this is called a recency effect) or give it less weight (this is called a primacy effect). Curtis and Rule assumed that the subject converts the subjective impression to a numerical response by first raising that impression to some power m and then obtaining some linear function of the result. First this results in

$$[wd_i{}^k + (1-w)d_j{}^k]^m$$

and then as the final numerical response,

$$J_{ij} = a[wd_i{}^k + (1-w)d_j{}^k]^m + b,$$

where J_{ij} is the observed judgment by the subject, a and b are the slope and intercept of the linear function, d_i and d_j are the physical measurements of the durations of intervals i and j, w and 1-w are the weights in the weighted averaging process, k is the exponent in the power function of each of the physical durations, and m is the exponent in the power function of the weighted average of the two power functions of the physical stimuli.

Now suppose that in the Curtis and Rule model, the value of m is one. Then their model becomes

TABLE 14.1 A FACTORIAL DESIGN OF STIMULUS PRESENTATIONS

Second Stimulus

		4	5	6
First Stimulus	4			
	5			
	6			

TABLE 14.2 THE PREDICTED JUDGMENT VAUES FROM EQUATION [14.1]

	4	5	6
4	$a[w4^k + (1-w)4^k] + b$	$a[w4^k + (1-w)5^k] + b$	$a[w4^k + (1-w)6^k] + b$
5	$a[w5^k + (1-w)4^k] + b$	$a[w5^k + (1-w)5^k] + b$	$a[w5^k + (1-w)6^k] + b$
6	$a[w6^k + (1-w)4^k] + b$	$a[w6^k + (1-w)5^k] + b$	$a[w6^k + (1-w)6^k] + b$

$$J_{ij} = a[wd_i^k + (1-w)d_j^k] + b. \qquad\qquad [14.1]$$

Suppose further that three different intervals 4, 5, and 6 seconds are used as the first stimulus and the same three intervals are used as the second stimulus and that all possible pairs of first stimulus with second stimulus are presented. We can then assign the different stimulus pairs being presented in the experiment to the cells in the design in Table 14.1.

If we substitute the pair of physical values for each cell into the right side of expression [14.1] we can obtain the predicted judgment value for each cell in this factorial design. They are given in Table 14.2. The first thing that we notice about these predicted judgments is that there is a prediction of no interaction. In any column the difference between the cell value for the i second first stimulus interval and the cell value for the j second first stimulus interval is predicted to be $aw(i^k - j^k)$ for i, j = 4, 5, 6. Thus the differences between row means are constant from column to column and this is sufficient for there to be no interaction. **The test of the null hypothesis of no First Stimulus x Second Stimulus interaction becomes a test of the theoretical model because the model directly predicts no interaction.**

14.1.1 A simple transformation to remove the interaction when m ≠ 1. The prediction of no interaction holds only if the parameter m equals one. If it does not, the data may be transformed so that the test of no interaction will still apply (Bogartz, 1980). We first note that when the first and second stimulus intervals are the same, then the predicted value is

$$J_{ii} = a[wd_i^k + (1-w)d_i^k]^m + b = ad_i^{km} + b.$$

Let u stand for the exponent product km. We could do a simple computer search for the value of u_{est} that maximizes the Pearson correlation of the J_{ii} with the d_i. We could then use the methods of simple linear regression to find the slope and the intercept of the regression line

$$J_{ii} = ad_i^{uest} + b.$$

The slope and intercept would be the estimates a_{est} and b_{est}. We could then transform the J_{ij} to

$$K_{ij}^m = (J_{ij} - B_{est})/a_{est} = [wd_i^k + (1-w)d_j^k]^m.$$

Finally, we could do another computer search for that value of m_{est} that minimizes the interaction in the table of values

TABLE 14.3 ANOVA TESTING THE NULL HYPOTHESIS THAT THE SET OF ROW MEANS EQUALS THE SET OF COLUMN MEANS, ASSUMING NO ROW x COLUMN INTERACTION

Source	df	SS	MS	F
H_A	2I-1	$(\Sigma_i T_{i..}^2 + \Sigma_i T_{.i.}^2 - T^2/I)/IK$		
H_0	I	$[\Sigma_i(T_{i..} + T_{.i.})^2 - T^2/I)]/IK$		
H_A vs. H_0	I-1	$SS_A - SS_0$	$(SS_A - SS_0)/(I-1)$	$MS_{A\,vs.0}$

Error	$I^2K-2I+1$	$\Sigma_i\Sigma_j\Sigma_k Y_{ijk}^2 - SS_A$	SS_{error}/df_{error}	MS_{error}
Total	I^2K	$\Sigma_i\Sigma_j\Sigma_k Y_{ijk}^2$		

Note: $T = \Sigma_i\Sigma_j\Sigma_k Y_{ijk}$; $T_{i..} = \Sigma_j\Sigma_k Y_{ijk}$; $T_{.j.} = \Sigma_i\Sigma_k Y_{ijk}$; H_0: *The row means equal the column means;* H_A: *the row means do not equal the column means.*

$$[(J_{ij} - B_{est})/a_{est}]^{1/mest} = \{[wd_i^k + (1-w)d_j^k]^{mest}\}^{1/mest} = wd_i^k + (1-w)d_j^k$$

which should then give a nonsignificant interaction in the analysis of variance. We will discuss this tactic of transforming the data to remove some interaction more in section 14.8.

14.2   Testing the null hypothesis that the row means equal the column means. Another feature of the predicted data in the factorial design is that if the subjects give equal weight to the first and second interval, then $w = 1 - w = .5$. It then follows that so long as the design uses the same stimulus sets for the first and second stimuli, the row mean for Stimulus i will equal the column mean for Stimulus j whenever $i = j$. There exists an analysis of variance that explicitly tests the hypothesis that the row means equal the column means assuming that there is no row xcolumn interaction (Bogartz, 1980, p. 289) in a design with I rows, I columns, and K scores per cell. Table 14.3 gives the summary of that analysis.

14.3 Functional measurement. Sometimes we judge some situation or event in terms of more than one aspect. In the Curtis and Rule experiment for judging the average tone duration, information from the two stimulus events was used. When we judge the desirability of someone as a friend or business partner, we no doubt use more than one aspect. The quality of a meal may be judged in terms of the separate dishes, how they went together, who we ate with, and other factors. **Information integration theory** (Anderson, 1982) is an approach to understanding how we combine the information from various aspects of a situation or event to arrive at a single judgment. **Functional measurement** is a set of general assumptions and methods for solving certain problems that arise in determining how people perform this information integration.

According to the theory of functional measurement, physical stimuli S_1, S_2, ... are transformed to subjective stimulus values by the application of some **valuation function** V, giving subjective values s_1, s_2, ... These subjective values are integrated by an **integration function**, I, to yield a subjective response value, r. Then an **output function** M transforms the subjective response r into the overt observed response, R. If M is a linear function, then R is said to be a linear or equal interval scale for r. These steps in the information integration process are shown in Figure 14.1.

We could look back at the Curtis and Rule equation

$$J_{ij} = a[wd_i^k + (1-w)d_j^k]^m + b$$

to exemplify these different steps. The valuation function V could be said to be the power function that raises the physical stimulus $S_i = d_i$ to the kth power, giving the subjective

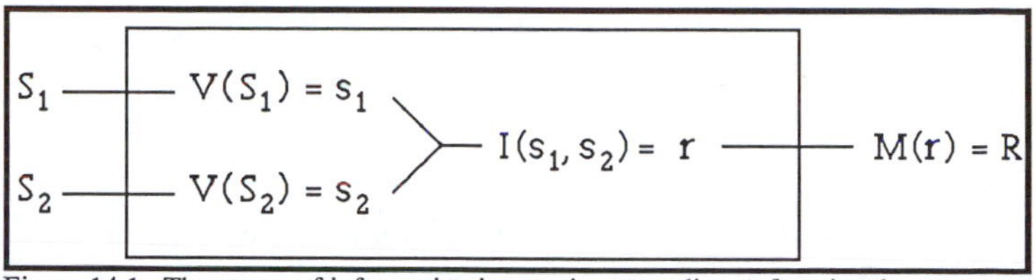

Figure 14.1. The stages of information integration according to functional measurement theory.

stimulus value $s_i = d_i^k$. The integration rule would be the weighted averaging of the subjective values to give $r = wd_i^k + (1-w)d_j^k$, and the output function M would be the linear function of the mth power of r, giving $R = a[wd_i^k + (1-w)d_j^k]^m + b$.

Functional measurement addresses the three problems of determining I, V, and M: the integration rule, the valuation rule, and the output function. The primary consideration in the study of information integration is the nature of the integration function, I. The psychologist is primarily interested in the form of the law governing how diverse information is put together to arrive at a unitary judgment. In a vast array of theoretical and empirical research Anderson (1974a, 1974b, 1976, 1980, 1982) has shown the efficacy of assuming that simple algebraic rules such as addition, multiplication, and averaging are often sufficient to express the form of the integration function, I. The additional questions of the form of the valuation function V and the output function M are considered secondary and are approached in that light. The integration function is viewed as forming the base and frame for determining V and M. The standard approach is to use factorial stimulus designs and a numerical rating response.

Suppose the row levels of a 3 x 3 factorial design are three adjectives S_1, S_2, and $S3$ describing an applicant for admission to graduate school, and the column levels are three other adjectives T_1, T_2, and T_3 describing that candidate. Each cell in the design then corresponds to a stimulus pair (S_i, T_j). Suppose judges are asked to rate the likelihood that an applicant characterized by the pair of adjectives (S_i, T_j) will be admitted. Assume that the integration rule is that each judge averages his or her subjective stimulus values $s_i = V(S_i)$ and $t_j = V(T_j)$ according to the simple averaging rule $r_{ij} = (s_i + t_j)/2$. Then, if the observed rating response R_{ij} is a linear function of r_{ij}, it follows that the cell means for the factorial design will plot as a set of parallel curves and that the Row x Column interaction should be nonsignificant. This is the case for any adding-type model.

Anderson formalized this prediction as the **Parallelism Theorem: Suppose (a) that the integration process follows an adding-type model, and (b) the overt measured response is a linear scale. Then (a) the factorial plot of the data will be a set of parallel curves, and (b) the row (column) means of the data table will be linear scales (i.e., some linear transformation) of the subjective values of the row (column) stimuli.** This latter deduction results from the fact that

$R_{i.} = a(s_i + t_.) + b$

$R_{.j} = a(s_. + t_j) + b$

where $R_{i.}$ is the ith row mean, $R_{.j}$ is the jth column mean, $s_.$ is the mean of the row subjective stimulus values, and $t_.$ is the mean of the column subjective stimulus values, and a and b are the slope and intercept of the linear output function M. See Table 14.4. The prediction that the data will plot as a set of parallel curves follows from the fact that in any column j, the difference between the mean for Row i and the mean for Row i' will be

$$R_{ij} - R_{i'j} = [a(s_i + t_j)/2 + b] - [a(s_{i'} + t_j)/2 + b] = (a/2)(s_i - s_{i'})$$

which is a constant from column to column since it does not depend on the choice of the column index, j. The fact that the parallelism theorem predicts no interaction permits the direct use of the analysis of variance as an instrument for testing the specific psychological assumption concerning the form of the integration function. A significant interaction would be direct evidence against the averaging model for information integration in this task.

If the additive or averaging integration assumption were correct but the output function were not linear, the observed response values theoretically would display an interaction even though at the psychological level of the subjective responses, the r's, there is no interaction. For example, if the output function were

$$R_{ij} = r^2 = [(s_i + t_j)/2]^2$$

then in any column j, the difference between the mean for Row i and the mean for Row i' will be

$$R_{ij} - R_{i'j} = [(s_i + t_j)/2]^2 - [(s_{i'} + t_j)/2]^2 = (s_i^2 - s_{i'}^2)/4 + t_j(s_i - s_{i'})/2 .$$

Since this difference is not constant from column to column because it depends on j, the differences between the means will vary from column to column, and therefore there will be an interaction.   Clearly, if the researcher finds a significant interaction, it may not be immediately clear whether the interaction results from a nonlinear output function or from an integration function that is nonadditive. But the researcher is not helpless in the face of this ambiguity. There is a strategy that can be adopted to determine the source of the interaction.

If the interaction is due to a nonlinear but monotone output function (a monotone increasing transformation R = M(r) is one such that if $r_i > r_j$ then $M(r_i) > M(r_j)$; a monotone

TABLE 14.4 SUBJECTIVE r VALUES RESULTING FROM SIMPLE AVERAGING OF SUBJECTIVE STIMULI, OBSERVED R VALUES AS A LINEAR FUNCTION OF r VALUES, AND THE ROW AND COLUMN MARGINAL MEANS AS LINEAR FUNCTIONS OF THE SUBJECTIVE STIMULUS VALUES

The r values

$(s_1 + t_1)/2$	$(s_1 + t_2)/2$	$(s_1 + t_3)/2$
$(s_2 + t_1)/2$	$(s_2 + t_2)/2$	$(s_2 + t_3)/2$
$(s_3 + t_1)/2$	$(s_3 + t_2)/2$	$(s_3 + t_3)/2$

The R values

$a(s_1 + t_1)/2 + b$	$a(s_1 + t_2)/2 + b$	$a(s_1 + t_3)/2 + b$	$a(s_1 + t_.)/2 + b$
$a(s_2 + t_1)/2 + b$	$a(s_2 + t_2)/2 + b$	$a(s_2 + t_3)/2 + b$	$a(s_2 + t_.)/2 + b$
$a(s_3 + t_1)/2 + b$	$a(s_3 + t_2)/2 + b$	$a(s_3 + t_3)/2 + b$	$a(s_3 + t_.)/2 + b$
$a(s_. + t_1)/2 + b$	$a(s_. + t_2)/2 + b$	$a(s_. + t_3)/2 + b$	

decreasing transformation is one such that if $r_i > r_j$ then $M(r_i) < M(r_j)$), then there is a transformation that can be performed on the R values to remove the interaction. This transformation would be the inverse of the output function. For our example, $R_{ij} = r^2 = [(s_i + t_j)/2]^2$, we would use $\sqrt{R}$ as the inverse function that would remove the observed interaction. The technical literature contains a number of approaches to determining the appropriate transformation that will remove the interaction (Bogartz & Wackwitz, 1971; de Leeuw, Young & Takane, 1976; Kruskal, 1965; Weiss, 1973).

Anderson also formulated the **Linear Fan Theorem** for the case of a multiplying integration function such as $r_{ij} = as_i t_j + b$. **If the integration process follows a multiplying model and if the output function is linear, then if the levels of the factors are arranged in increasing order, the factorial plot of the means will form a linear fan of diverging straight lines, and the row (column) means of the data will be linear scales of the subjective values of the row (column) stimuli.** For example, suppose that subjects are asked to judge the likelihood of a person being hired for a management position in a small corporation and the candidates are described by a pair of stimulus words that are the combination of an adjective modified by an adverb. Suppose the stimulus adjectives were Effective, Ambitious, Goodnatured, and Introverted, and the adverbs were Somewhat, Unusually, and Clearheadedly. Let s_i be the subjective stimulus value of the ith adverb and t_j be the subjective stimulus values of the jth adjective. A reasonable integration rule might be $r_{ij} = s_i t_j$, which says that the effect of the adverb is to multiply the adjective. Suppose further that the output function is linear so that

$$R_{ij} = ar_{ij} + b = as_i t_j + b.$$

Figure 14.2 shows the predicted values for the observed response, assuming that the subjective values for the adjectives Effective, Ambitious, Goodnatured, and Introverted are 6, 3, 4, 2, the subjective values for the adverbs Somewhat, Unusually, and Clearheadedly were 2, 5, and 3, and a = 2, b = 1. The stimuli have been arranged in increasing order. The values in Figure 14.2 are plotted as if we actually knew the subjective stimulus values for the adjectives and the linear output function. In practice this would not be the case. We would use the observed column means to estimate the spacing of the values on the X axis.

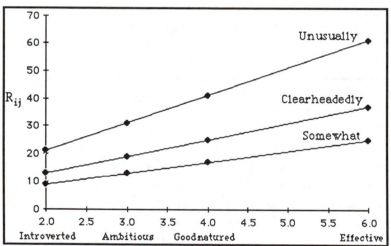

Figure 14.2. An example of the linear fan for the multiplication model.

In Table 14.5 the observed column means are shown. In Figure 14.3 the graph of the linear fan that would occur in practice is shown.

The correspondence of information integration models to analysis of variance models extends to more complex models that use adding and multiplying models as their building blocks (Anderson, 1974a, p. 264). Thus, for example, we can imagine a task in which a subject gives a numerical response that is intended to represent the average area of two

TABLE 14.5 CELL, ROW, AND COLUMN MEANS FOR THE LINEAR FAN IN FIGURE 14.5

	The R values			row means
9	13	17	25	16
13	19	25	37	23.5
21	31	41	61	38.5
col. means 14.33	21	27.67	41	26

stimulus rectangles presented sequentially. The integration law for each subjective rectangle area might be

$$a_i = h_i w_i$$

where a_i, the perceived subjective area of the ith rectangle, is the mental product of the subjective height, h_i, times the subjective width, w_i. Assume that a subjective weighted averaging of the two subjective areas takes place to yield the subjective response and the integration model takes the form

$$r = fa_1 + (1-f)a_2 = f h_1 w_1 + (1-f) h_2 w_2 ,$$

where f and 1-f are the weights assigned to the first and second stimulus rectangles.

We can now imagine a four-factor experimental design in which the factors are the heights and widths of the first and second stimulus rectangles. For example, the design diagram in Table 14.6 shows a 3 x 3 x 3 x 3 factorial stimulus design with all possible combinations of a first rectangle with heights 2, 4, or 6 cm and widths of 3, 5, or 7 cm with a second rectangle with heights 4, 6, or 8 cm and widths of 4, 5, or 6 cm. The integration law $r = f h_1 w_1 + (1-f) h_2 w_2$ predicts that in this experimental design there will be no interaction between any factors except a linear x linear interaction of Height 1 with Width 1 and a linear x linear interaction of Height 2 with Width 2. The analysis of variance of the four-factor design thus provides an exacting, precise, and powerful test of the specific integration model.

14.4 The meaningfulness of statistical interactions. Whether we take an interaction to be meaningful will depend upon two matters: our interpretation of the observed values of the means and the form of the observed interaction. Sometimes the researcher is

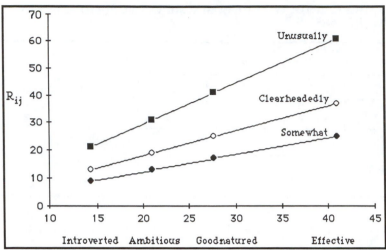

Figure 14.3. The graph of the linear fan using the observed column means to determine the spacing on the horizontal (X) axis.

only interested in the observed means and the population means they are assumed to estimate. Other times the observed means are assumed to be some function of some underlying value or values. It is these underlying values that are of central concern. For example, in classical or Pavlovian conditioning we can measure the amount of appetitive conditioning in a dog by measuring the amount of saliva released when the conditioned

TABLE 14.6   THE DESIGN DIAGRAM FOR AN EXPERIMENTAL TEST OF THE INTEGRATION MODEL $r = fa_1 + (1-f)a_2 = f h_1 w_1 + (1-f) h_2 w_2$ **FOR JUDGMENT OF THE AVERAGE AREA OF TWO RECTANGLES**

		Height 2			Height 2			Height 2		
		4	4	4	6	6	6	8	8	8
		Width 2			Width 2			Width 2		
Height 1	Width 1	4	5	6	4	5	6	4	5	6
2	3									
2	5									
2	7									
4	3									
4	5									
4	7									
6	3									
6	5									
6	7									

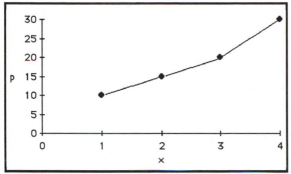

Figure 14.4. A monotone function relating the observed variable p
to an underlying variable x.

stimulus is presented, and we can measure the amount of conditioning by measuring the
number of unreinforced trials required to extinguish the conditioned response. We draw a
distinction between the observed performance measures and the presumed underlying
amount of conditioning. Generally, in the study of learning, psychologists distinguish
between observed performance measures and a presumed underlying variable taken to be
amount of learning. Because fatigue, boredom, and other such variables can diminish
performance presumably without reducing the amount learned, this distinction has been very
useful. It is usually assumed that other things being equal, a given performance measure is
some monotonic function of the amount of learning. Sometimes the monotone function is
specified in more detail, sometimes not. When our concern is with an underlying variable
such as amount learned, and we are using the observed variable such as trials to extinction to
draw inferences about the underlying variable, then great care is required when it comes to
inferring the presence or absence of interaction at the level of the underlying variable. We
will consider this matter here briefly but the student is referred to Bogartz (1976; 1990a,
1990b) and Loftus (1978) for a more complete treatment.

Loftus (1978, p. 318) put it well when he said "that a dependent variable such as response
probability is not intrinsically interesting. Rather it is only interesting because of what it
reflects about a component of some theory. Getting from the dependent variable back to the
theoretical component may well involve a transformation on the dependent variable. If this
transformation is nonlinear, then one is limited in fairly specifiable ways when interpreting
data involving the original dependent variable." He considered in detail the case where the
observed dependent variable, call it p = Drops of Saliva to Conditioned Stimulus, is a
monotone function of an underlying dependent variable, call it x = Strength of Conditioning,
and two independent variables form a 2 x 2 factorial design of treatment conditions. Call
these two independent variables A = Number of Conditioning Trials and B= Number of

Hours of Food Deprivation. Let their values be A_1 and A_2 and B_1 and B_2. Suppose the values for p shown in the following display are observed:

	B_1	B_2
A_1	10	15
A_2	20	30

Suppose also that all of the differences are statistically significant. What can we infer about the presence or absence of interaction in the underlying variable x given that there is a clear indication of interaction in the observed variable p? The fact is that we cannot draw any conclusions about presence or absence of interaction in x. Why is this? Because in this specific case the monotone function relating p to x might be as shown in Figure 14.4. If we recover the underlying x values for each p value, then we obtain the values in the following display:

	B_1	B_2
A_1	1	2
A_2	3	4

We see that at the level of the x values there is no interaction even though there is one at the level of the p values.

Does this mean that no interaction at the level of p can be interpreted as implying an interaction at the level of x? The answer is no. A **crossover interaction** such as that shown in Figure 14.5 implies an interaction at the level of x because there is no monotone transformation of x that could produce a crossover in p if there were no crossover in x. Why is this? It is because a monotone transformation is an order-preserving transformation but not necessarily difference preserving. If $p_i = f(x_i)$ and f is monotone increasing, then we know that if $x_1 < x_2$, then $p_1 < p_2$. Thus the order of the two values is the same for the two variables, although the differences might not be equal. That is, $x_1 - x_2$ is not necessarily equal to $p_1 - p_2$. In a crossover interaction, the ordering of the values at B_1 and B_2 changes from A_1 to A_2. To be precise, let p_{ij} be the value of p at A_i and B_j. Then a crossover interaction means that if $p_{11} < p_{12}$, then $p_{21} > p_{22}$. But this could not occur if there is no interaction at the level of the x variable since in that case, $x_{11} - x_{12} = x_{21} - x_{22}$. Two possibilities exist. Either $x_{11} - x_{12} > 0$ or $x_{11} - x_{12} < 0$. If $x_{11} - x_{12} > 0$, then $x_{11} > x_{12}$ and therefore $x_{21} > x_{22}$. But the monotonicity of f implies that $p_{11} > p_{12}$ and $p_{21} > p_{22}$. Therefore no crossover interaction is permitted. The case where $x_{11} - x_{12} < 0$ is left for the student to argue through.

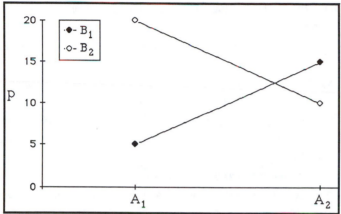

Figure 14.5. A crossover interaction in p could not occur if p is a monotone function of an underlying variable x for which no crossover interaction exists.

14.5 The meaning of statistical interactions. In the previous section we considered whether an observed interaction could be used as the basis for inferring an interaction in an underlying variable. I call this the question of whether an observed interaction is meaningful. (Loftus, 1978, uses the word "interpretable.") Another question that can be directed to an observed interaction is, "What does it mean?" The psychological research literature is awash with intuitive or incomplete theoretical analyses used to "predict" the presence or absence of interactions. Observed interactions are then taken to confirm or infirm these intuitions. In fact, "... the prediction of the presence or absence of statistical interaction is often a rather subtle matter, sometimes resulting in highly counterintuitive results." (Bogartz, 1976). In this section I will briefly recapitulate an analysis of one such case. For a more complete treatment, the student is referred to Bogartz (1976).

Hale and Stevenson (1974) presented 5-year-old and 8-year-old children with a task in which the children were shown a group of stimuli, each in a certain position. Then they were shown one of the stimuli and had to indicate in which position that stimulus was presented. The children made 12 such responses on each of six blocks of trials. On four of the six blocks, visual or auditory distractors were also presented. Hale and Stevenson found that on the average, without distraction the 8-year-olds made 6.43 correct responses per block but with distraction they made 5.65 correct responses per block. The 5-year-olds made 3.94 correct responses with no distraction and 2.88 with distraction. An analysis of variance found no significant age by distraction condition interaction.

Hale and Stevenson "predicted" that greater distractability for the 5-year-olds than for the 8-year-olds would result in an age x distraction condition interaction and that equality of distractability would result in no interaction, but they did not make explicit any theoretical model upon which such a prediction was based. To illustrate how such intuitive predictions can go astray, Bogartz (1976) formulated the following model based on three process hypotheses and two developmental hypotheses.

Hypothesis 1. On each opportunity to respond, the subject remembers the correct stimulus location with a probability p *and forgets it with probability* 1 - p.

Hypothesis 2. If the subject remembers the correct location, she makes a correct response; if not, she guesses and is correct with a guessing probability, g.

Hypothesis 3. The effect of distraction is to reduce the probability of remembering from p to a quantity rp, *where* r *is a positive value less than or equal to 1 and may be interpreted as the subject's resistance to distraction.*

Hypothesis 4. The probability of remembering increases with age.

Hypothesis 5. Let r_8 *and* r_5 *be the resistance to distraction parameters for the 8 and 5-year-olds. Then the experimental null hypothesis is that* $r_8 = r_5$. *The experimental alternative hypothesis is that* $r_8 > r_5$.

The implications of this model for the Hale and Stevenson study are apparent if we arrange the predicted probability of a correct response for the 2 x 2 design with two age conditions and two distraction conditions. This would be

	No Distraction	Distraction
8 years	$p_8 + (1 - p_8)g$	$r_8 p_8 + (1 - r_8 p_8)g$
5 years	$p_5 + (1 - p_5)g$	$r_5 p_5 + (1 - r_5 p_5)g$

The interaction effect is the difference between the two age levels under No Distraction minus the difference between the two age levels under Distraction, which is

$$I = \{[p_8 + (1 - p_8)g] - [p_5 + (1 - p_5)g]\} - \{[r_8 p_8 + (1 - r_8 p_8)g] - [r_5 p_5 +$$

$$(1 - r_5 p_5)g]\}$$

$$= (1 - g)[(1 - r_8)p_8 - (1 - r_5)p_5].$$

Under the experimental null hypothesis that $r_8 = r_5 = r$, the interaction effect $I = (1 - g)(1 - r)(p_8 - p_5)$ cannot be negative and can only be zero if $g = 1$, $r = 1$, or $p_8 = p_5$. But if $g = 1$ there would be no errors. If $r = 1$ there would be no effect of distraction and that effect was found. And $p_8 = p_5$ violates hypothesis 4. Therefore the null hypothesis that distraction is the same at both age levels predicts that there will be a positive age x distraction condition interaction. When the two age levels have the same resistance to distraction, the performance level of the older children will decline more than that of the younger children.

14.6 Transforming the data to satisfy model assumptions. In section 14.3 we described the functional measurement approach to determining psychological laws. This approach admits the possibility that both the dependent and the independent variables as measured are functionally related to the underlying psychological values and that a rescaling of all of these variables may be necessary to determine the nature of the underlying psychological laws. In this section we will demonstrate a complete rescaling of such variables and an analysis of variance this rescaling leads to. A more extensive treatement of the problem and its motivation is presented elsewhere (Bogartz, 1990a).

For reasons relating to a dispute between Loftus (1985a, 1985bb) and Slamecka (1983, 1985), Bogartz (1990) proposed a reanalysis of data gathered by Hellyer (1962). The part of the dispute we will consider here concerned whether rate of forgetting depends upon amount of original learning. Hellyer measured proportion of items correctly recalled at recall delay

intervals of T = 3, 9, 18, and 27 seconds following O = 1, 2, 4, or 8 presentations. Hellyer's data are presented in Table 14.7.

Bogartz proposed that a functional measurement approach to the combination of recall delay interval and number of presentations could be taken along the lines

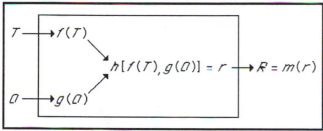

Figure 14.6. A functional measurement diagram for Hellyer's experiment. The observed measures are T = recall delay interval, O = number of presentations, and R = proportion of items correctly recalled. The underlying variables are f(T) = psychological time, g(O) = amount originally learned, and r = h[f(T), g(O)] = the amount of information retained about the item. The function h determines how the amount originally learned and psychological time combine to determine the amount of information retained, and the function m is a monotone increasing function relating R to r.

of Figure 14.6. In Figure 14.6 the observed measures are T = recall delay interval, O = number of presentations, and R = proportion of items correctly

recalled. The underlying variables are f(T) = psychological time, g(O) = amount originally learned, and r = h[f(T), g(O)] = the amount of information retained about the item. The function h determines how the amount originally learned and psychological time combine to determine the amount of information retained. Bogartz assumed that f(T) was some monotonic increasing function of T, g(O) was some monotonic increasing function of O,

TABLE 14.7   HELLYER'S DATA

Number of Presentations	Recall Delay Interval (secs.)			
	3	9	18	27
8	.99	.89	.74	.66
4	.94	.73	.56	.46
2	.92	.54	.31	.22
1	.89	.38	.21	.14

TABLE 14.8   UNDERLYING r_{ij} VALUES PREDICTED FOR HELLYER'S DATA

	$e^{-f(T)}$			
$g(0)$	$e^{-f(3)}$	$e^{-f(9)}$	$e^{-f(18)}$	$e^{-f(27)}$
$g(8)$	$g(8)\,e^{-f(3)}$	$g(8)\,e^{-f(9)}$	$g(8)\,e^{-f(18)}$	$g(8)\,e^{-f(27)}$
$g(4)$	$g(4)\,e^{-f(3)}$	$g(4)\,e^{-f(9)}$	$g(4)\,e^{-f(18)}$	$g(4)\,e^{-f(27)}$
$g(2)$	$g(2)\,e^{-f(3)}$	$g(2)\,e^{-f(9)}$	$g(2)\,e^{-f(18)}$	$g(2)\,e^{-f(27)}$
$g(1)$	$g(1)\,e^{-f(3)}$	$g(1)\,e^{-f(9)}$	$g(1)\,e^{-f(18)}$	$g(1)\,e^{-f(27)}$
Means	$M_g e^{-f(3)}$	$M_g e^{-f(9)}$	$M_g e^{-f(18)}$	$M_g e^{-f(27)}$

Note: $M_g = [g(1) + g(2) + g(4) + g(8)]/4$.

and that $r_{ij} = g(O_i)e^{-f(T_j)}$, $i = 1, 2, 4, 8$; $j = 3, 9, 18, 27$. Thus if we could measure the r_{ij} we should find them conforming to the pattern in Table 14.8.   We particularly want to notice that each row of values in Table 14.8 is proportional to the row of column means. Thus, examining row 1 we find that each entry in row 1 divided by its column mean gives the same constant, $g(8)/M_g$. Each entry in the second row divided by its column mean gives $g(4)/M_g$. And so forth. This means that if we were to plot the first row of values as a function of the column means the values would plot as a straight line with slope $g(8)/M_g$. The second row plotted as a function of the column means would plot as another straight line with slope $g(4)/M_g$. And so forth. Consequently the plot of the entire set of r_{ij} values, plotted as a function of the marginal column means, would be a diverging fan of lines. The linear fan theorem would apply and the interaction in a two-factor analysis of variance

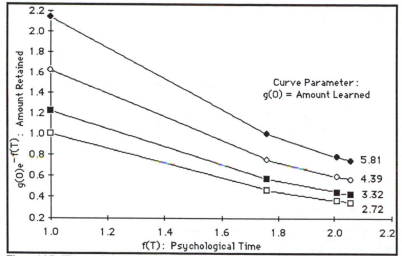

Figure 14.7. The rescaled response values plotted as a function of the rescaled independent variables.

should all be concentrated in the linear x linear component. This would all apply if we knew $g(O)$, $f(T)$, and could measure the r_{ij}. The details of the required rescaling are given in section 14.6.1.

Figure 14.7 shows the rescaled response values plotted as a function of the rescaled independent variables. If instead of using the values of $f(T)$ to space along the horizontal axis we instead use the marginal column means we obtain the graph shown in Figure 14.8 displaying the complete concentration of the interaction in the linear x linear component. These results demonstrate that with rescaling of the variables, the analysis of variance can be brought to bear upon testing the validity of the theoretical assumptions concerning the relationship of original learning and rate of forgetting. The test of the theory rests in showing that the predicted linear x linear component is significant and that the remaining components of the interaction are not significant. In a repeated measurements design these components such as the linear by quadratic, quadratic x quadratic, and so on, would be tested separately, each on its single numerator degree of freedom.

*14.6.1 The technical details of rescaling Hellyer's data. The transformation $r = m^{-1}(R) = g(O)e^{-f(T)}$ for Hellyer's data must satisfy the three requirements that g, f, and m^{-1} are each monotone increasing functions. It follows that r will be a monotone-increasing function of O and monotone-decreasing functions of T. Let O_i, $i = 1$ to 4 and T_j, $j = 1$ to 4, be the observed values of the dependent variable, where $O_i > O_{i'}$ if $i >$ i' and $T_j > T_{j'}$ if $j < j'$. Since $\ln r$ is a monotone-increasing function of r, if we find values of $\ln r = \ln [g(O)e^{-f(T)}]$ that satisfy the required conditions, then r will also satisfy those conditions.

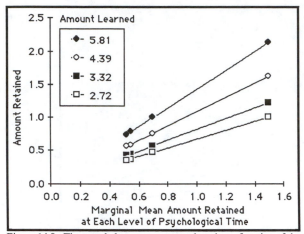

Figure 14.8. The rescaled mean responses plotted as a function of the marginal column means and the scaled values for Amount Learned. The data points fall exactly on a diverging fan of lines indicating conformance to the theory and complete concentration of the interaction in the linear x linear component.

Let R_{ij} be the observed R mean for O_i and T_j. Table 14.3 shows these R_{ij}. We observe in Table 14.3 the relation

$$R_{41} > R_{31} > R_{21} > R_{11} = R_{42} > R_{43} > R_{32} > R_{44} >$$

$$R_{33} > R_{22} > R_{34} > R_{12} > R_{23} > R_{24} > R_{13} > R_{14} .$$
$$[14.2]$$

We require that the r_{ij} and therefore the $\ln r_{ij} = \ln g(O_i) - f(T_j)$ stand in the same relation. Because f and g are monotone, we already have that $r_{ij} > r_{ij'}$ if $j < j'$ and $r_{ij} > r_{i'j}$ if $i > i'$. For example, we know that $r_{41} > r_{31}$ for any proper choice of f and g, as do we know that $r_{33} > r_{34}$. Therefore that part of the relation in [14.2] which indicates this redundant information can be eliminated leaving us with the requirement that:

$$r_{11} = r_{42}; \quad r_{43} > r_{32} > r_{44} > r_{33} > r_{22} > r_{34} > r_{12} > r_{23} > r_{14}.$$
$$[14.3]$$

Hence,

$$\ln r_{11} = \ln r_{42}; \quad \ln r_{43} > \ln r_{32} > \ln r_{44} > \ln r_{33} > \ln r_{22} > \ln r_{34} > \ln r_{12} > \ln r_{23} >$$

$$\ln r_1 .$$
$$[14.4]$$

**TABLE 14.9 RESCALING OF
THE HELLYER DATA**

Amount Learned	Subjective Time			
	1.00	1.76	2.01	2.06
5.81	2.14	1.00	0.78	0.74
4.39	1.62	0.76	0.59	0.56
3.32	1.22	0.57	0.44	0.42
2.72	1.00	0.47	0.36	0.35

Note. Amount Learned = $g(O_i)$, Subjective
Time = $f(T_j)$, and the values in the body of
the table are the $r_{ij} = g(O_i)e^{f(T_j)}$.

By substituting $\ln g(O_i) - f(T_j)$ for $\ln r_{ij}$ for all i and j in [14.4] we obtain a set of expressions such as

$$\ln g(O_4) - f(T_3) > \ln g(O_3) - f(T_2).$$

These can be manipulated so that the $\ln g(O_i)$ values are on one side of the equality or inequality sign and the $f(T_j)$ values are on the other side. This gives an ordering containing expressions such as

$$\ln g(O_4) - \ln g(O_3) > f(T_3) - f(T_2).$$

It is convenient to introduce the notation $a_{ij} = \ln g(O_i) - \ln g(O_j)$ and $b_{ij} = f(T_i) - f(T_j)$. It is also useful to note identities such as that $a_{43} + a_{32} = a_{42}$ and $b_{32} + b_{21} = b_{31}$. Then the entire set of relations in the Hellyer data required for establishing the required transformations can be expressed by the partial ordering shown in Figure 14.9.

Numerical assignment was begun by arbitrarily assigning 1.00 to $r_{41} = r_{12}$. This required that $\ln g(O_1) = f(T_1)$ and that $\ln g(O_4) = f(T_2)$. Next the additional arbitrary assignment $\ln g(O_1) = f(T_1) = 1$ was made. From here on numbers were assigned to satisfy the various orderings and equalities in Figure 14.9. This begins by assigning $b_{43} = .05$, $a_{21} = .20$, $b_{32} = .25$, and $a_{32} = a_{43} = .28$, thus satisfying the ordering at the bottom of the figure. These choices and the equalities in the partial ordering then determined that $b_{42} = .30$, $a_{31} = .48$, $a_{41} = .76$, and $b_{31} = 1.01$. Then, recalling that $a_{ij} = \ln g(O_i) - \ln g(O_j)$ and $b_{ij} = f(T_i) - f(T_j)$, it followed that $\ln g(O_2) = 1.20$, $\ln g(O_3) = 1.48$, and $\ln g(O_4) = 1.76$, so that $g(O_1) = $

2.72, $g(O_2)$ = 3.32, $g(O_3)$ = 4.39, and   Figure 14.9 The ordering of the $a_{ij} = \ln g(O_i) - \ln g(O_j)$
$g(O_4)$ = 5.81. Similarly, since $f(T_1) = 1$ and $b_{ij} = f(T_i) - f(T_j)$ imposed by the relation [14.4].

and $b_{21} = a_{41} = .76$, we have $f(T_2) = 1.76$. Since $b_{31} = 1.01$, $f(T_3) = 2.01$, and since $b_{43} = .05$, $f(T_4) = 2.06$. This completes the scaling, giving the $g(O_i)$, the $e^{-f(T_j)}$, and the $r_{ij} = g(O_i)e^{-f(T_j)}$. The numerical values to two decimal places are given in Table 14.9.

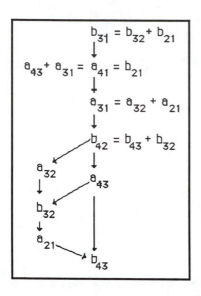

The three functions relating the observed variables to the underlying variables are shown in Figure 14.10, 14.11, and 14.12.

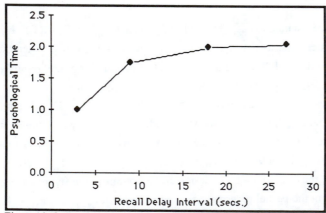

Figure 14.10. Psychological Time as a function of Recall Delay Interval.

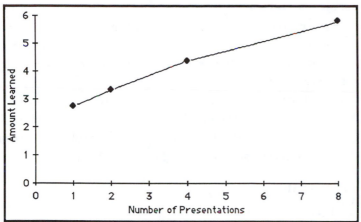

Figure 14.11. The function g relating Amount Learned to Number of Presentations.

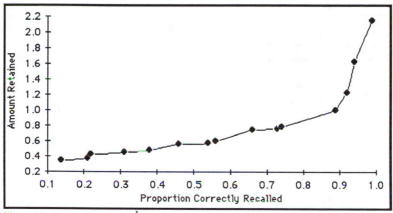

Figure 14.12. The function m^{-1} relating Amount Retained to Proportion Correctly Recalled.

Exercises

1. For each of the following 2 x 2 designs, assume that these are the true p values uncontaminated by error variance and that p is a monotone function of an underlying variable x. Decide whether the p values do or do not imply an interaction at the level of x.

(a) $p_{11} = p_{12}$; $p_{21} > p_{22}$

(b) $p_{11} = 10$, $p_{12} = 8$; $p_{21} = 8$, $p_{22} = 10$

(c) $p_{11} = p_{22}$; $p_{21} = p_{12}$

2. Suppose that a theory requires that the observed variable p is related to the underlying variable x by the function $p = 1 - .5^x$. Which of the following sets of observed values of p require an interaction at the level of x?

(a) $p_{11} = 10$, $p_{12} = 20$; $p_{21} = 30$, $p_{22} = 35$

(b) $p_{11} = 10$, $p_{12} = 15$; $p_{21} = 30$, $p_{22} = 40$

3. Suppose that in the model of section 14.5 the experimental alternative hypothesis is true and that $r_8 > r_5$. Show that the interaction can be zero, negative, or positive.

4. In regard to the previous question, what experimental results would allow deciding between the null hypothesis and the alternative?

5. Assume the average time judgment data in Table 14.10 are described by the model $R_{ijm} = wd_i^k + (1 - w)d_j^k$ where d_i is the ith row stimulus, d_j is the jth column stimulus, and R_{ijm} is the mth response by the subject to the combination of d_i and d_j, the combinations being presented in random order. (Note this is analysis of a single subject's data.)

**TABLE 14.10 FICTIONAL
AVERAGE TIME JUDGMENTS
FOR A SINGLE SUBJECT**

	2	4	6	8
2	2.5	4.1	6.1	7.8
	2.2	3.8	5.9	8.2
	2.4	4.0	5.8	7.9
4	3.6	5.4	7.3	9.1
	3.4	5.3	7.0	9.4
	3.4	5.2	7.2	9.2
5	4.8	6.7	8.6	10.4
	5.0	6.7	8.4	10.6
	5.2	6.8	8.6	10.8
6	6.2	8.3	10.2	12.0
	6.5	8.2	10.1	12.3
	6.4	8.4	10.1	12.1

(a) Show why the ith row mean equals the ith column mean if $w = 1 - w$.

(b) Test the hypothesis that $w = 1 - w$ by testing the hypothesis that the row means equal the column means.

(c) How might you estimate w if $w \neq 1 - w$?

6. Suppose subjects judge the area of a rectangle by determining a subjective height and a subjective width, subjectively multiplying them, and then responding with an overt area judgment that is a power function of the subjective product. That is, the subject's overt area judgment is

$$R_{ij} = (h_i w_j)^k,$$

where h_i is the subjective height corresponding to a physical height H_i and w_j is the subjective width corresponding to a physical width W_j. Assume a factorial stimulus design where Heights are crossed with Widths.

(a) Under what circumstances would you expect the data to plot as a linear fan?

(b) Is there some transformation that will produce a linear fan?

(c) Is there some transformation that will remove the interaction producing parallelism?

7. Explain in your own words why the presence or absence of interaction depends on the response scale.

8. Why does a monotone transformation not remove a crossover interaction?

9. Choose another set of values for transforming Hellyer's data, using the relations in Figure 14.9. Then plot the figures analogous to Figures 14.7, 14.8, 14.9, 14.10, and 14.11.

15

Nonorthogonal Designs

15.1 Nonorthogonality: A simple example. So far we have considered only designs in which the same number of scores occurs in each cell of the design. Because we have assumed that a corresponding equality of frequency occurs in the various populations from which these cell scores have been sampled, we have dealt with only orthogonal designs, those in which the subspaces spanned by the vectors for the various sources are mutually orthogonal. Our interest now turns to fixed effects models where designs occur, by plan or by accident, in which nonorthogonality occurs. Usually, but not always, this nonorthogonality results from unequal cell n's. Cell n's differ sometimes because the experimenter has planned such differences, as when the experimenter assigns more subjects to a control group because several experimental groups will be compared with it and the experimenter wants greater precision for this group that will enter into numerous contrasts. At other times the inequality of cell n's occurs as a result of randomly missing data, as when a subject fails to show up for the experiment or asks to discontinue participation before completion of the task. In the case of planned or randomly occurring inequality of cell n's, it is likely that the population n's for these cells are assumed to be equal, and as a result a nonorthogonal design occurs. In other cases the number of scores in each cell can be equal but because the experimenter believes that this is not true of the population, a nonorthogonal design results.

With designs in which the cell n's differ, a new set of issues arise that gradually have been clarified through a lengthy debate occurring in the *Psychological Bulletin* beginning in 1969 (Overall & Spiegel, 1969). To try to understand the issues and the positions that have been taken, we first look at the **nonorthogonality** that results from unequal cell n's. We will consider a two-factor design with I rows, J columns, and n_{ij} scores in cell ij. The simplest case we can use to see this is a 2 x 2 factorial design in which we assume no interaction and use the minimal number of scores per cell needed to make the necessary points. The minimal number with equal n's is one score per cell, and to get a design with unequal n's we will add one score to one cell. But first we will introduce the **matrix of full rank**.

With one score per cell the design is

	B_1	B_2
A_1	Y_{11}	Y_{12}
A_2	Y_{21}	Y_{22}

for which our model equation is $Y_{ij} = \mu + \alpha_i + \beta_j + e_{ij}$, which we can write in matrix form as $\mathbf{Y} = \mathbf{X}\beta + \mathbf{e}$, that is,

$$\begin{bmatrix} Y_{11} \\ Y_{12} \\ Y_{21} \\ Y_{22} \end{bmatrix} = \begin{bmatrix} 1 & 1 & 0 & 1 & 0 \\ 1 & 1 & 0 & 0 & 1 \\ 1 & 0 & 1 & 1 & 0 \\ 1 & 0 & 1 & 0 & 1 \end{bmatrix} \begin{bmatrix} \mu \\ \alpha_1 \\ \alpha_2 \\ \beta_1 \\ \beta_2 \end{bmatrix} + \begin{bmatrix} e_{11} \\ e_{12} \\ e_{21} \\ e_{22} \end{bmatrix} \qquad [15.1]$$

with the side conditions that $\alpha_1 + \alpha_2 = \beta_1 + \beta_2 = 0$. Our next step is to use the side conditions to rewrite the model in a form so that the column vectors of the $\mathbf{X}$ matrix are linearly independent. (When the column vectors of $\mathbf{X}$ are linearly independent, the matrix $\mathbf{X}$ is said to be of full rank, and the model is referred to as a full-rank model. We will always use models of full rank (see Scheffé, 1959; Carlson and Timm, 1974; and Speedand Hocking 1976, for discussion of advantages of full-rank models. The most important reason is that the hypotheses being tested in nonorthgonal designs become more comprehensible.) Since $\alpha_2 = -\alpha_1$ and $\beta_2 = -\beta_1$ we can write

$$
\begin{bmatrix} Y_{11} \\ Y_{12} \\ Y_{21} \\ Y_{22} \end{bmatrix} = \begin{bmatrix} 1 & 1 & 1 \\ 1 & 1 & -1 \\ 1 & -1 & 1 \\ 1 & -1 & -1 \end{bmatrix} \begin{bmatrix} \mu \\ \alpha_1 \\ \beta_1 \end{bmatrix} + \begin{bmatrix} e_{11} \\ e_{12} \\ e_{21} \\ e_{22} \end{bmatrix} \qquad [15.2]
$$

We can see at a glance that all of the column vectors of X are mutually orthogonal.

Now, suppose we add one more score to cell A_2B_2. The model in matrix form, again incorporating the side conditions, becomes

$$
\begin{bmatrix} Y_{111} \\ Y_{121} \\ Y_{211} \\ Y_{221} \\ Y_{222} \end{bmatrix} = \begin{bmatrix} 1 & 1 & 1 \\ 1 & 1 & -1 \\ 1 & -1 & 1 \\ 1 & -1 & -1 \\ 1 & -1 & -1 \end{bmatrix} \begin{bmatrix} \mu \\ \alpha_1 \\ \beta_1 \end{bmatrix} + \begin{bmatrix} e_{111} \\ e_{121} \\ e_{211} \\ e_{221} \\ e_{222} \end{bmatrix} \qquad [15.3]
$$

We see that the column vectors of X in [15.3] are not mutually orthogonal.

Nonorthogonality produces several problems for the analysis of variance. The least of these is that the computational algorithms for calculating sums of squares, expected mean squares, and so forth, from the model equation no longer work. More serious is the fact that our partitioning of the total sum of squares into orthogonal and therefore independent components no longer works.

For the orthogonal case we could say

$$
Y = \mu_{est}X_\mu + \alpha_{est}X_\alpha + \beta_{est}X_\beta + e_{est}
$$

where X_μ, X_α, and X_β are the column vectors of X, and therefore the total sum of squares can be partitioned as

$$
Y^T Y = \mu_{est}{}^2 X_\mu{}^T X_\mu + \alpha_{est}{}^2 X_\alpha{}^T X_\alpha + \beta_{est}{}^2 X_\beta{}^T X_\beta + e_{est}{}^T e_{est}. \qquad [15.4]
$$

But with nonorthogonal vectors, the cross-product terms do not in general drop out (are not zero) and

$$
Y^T Y = \mu_{est}{}^2 X_\mu{}^T X_\mu + \alpha_{est}{}^2 X_\alpha{}^T X_\alpha + \beta_{est}{}^2 X_\beta{}^T X_\beta + e_{est}{}^T e_{est}
$$

$$
+ 2[\mu_{est}X_\mu{}^T(\alpha_{est}X_\alpha + \beta_{est}X_\beta + e_{est}) + \alpha_{est}X_\alpha{}^T(\beta_{est}X_\beta + e_{est})
$$

$$
+ \beta_{est}X_\beta e_{est})]
$$

which, because $\mathbf{e}_{est}$ is chosen as orthogonal to the space spanned by $\mathbf{X}_\mu$, $\mathbf{X}_\alpha$, and $\mathbf{X}_\beta$ so long as we are using the method of least squares, reduces to

$$\mathbf{Y}^\mathbf{T}\mathbf{Y} = \mu_{est}^2\mathbf{X}_\mu^\mathbf{T}\mathbf{X}_\mu + \alpha_{est}^2\mathbf{X}_\alpha^\mathbf{T}\mathbf{X}_\alpha + \beta_{est}^2\mathbf{X}_\beta^\mathbf{T}\mathbf{X}_\beta + \mathbf{e}_{est}^\mathbf{T}\mathbf{e}_{est}$$

$$+ 2[\mu_{est}\alpha_{est}\,\mathbf{X}_\mu^\mathbf{T}\,\mathbf{X}_\alpha + \mu_{est}\beta_{est}\,\mathbf{X}_\mu^\mathbf{T}\,\mathbf{X}_\beta + \alpha_{est}\beta_{est}\mathbf{X}_\alpha^\mathbf{T}\mathbf{X}_\beta]. \qquad [15.5]$$

Obviously, if $\mathbf{X}_\mu$, $\mathbf{X}_\alpha$, and $\mathbf{X}_\beta$ were mutually orthogonal, the terms in the bracketed section would each equal the zero vector and [15.5] would reduce to the orthogonal case, [15.4].

To see more clearly how nonorthogonality produces lack of independence between the row sums of squares and the column sums of squares, consider a 2 x 2 design in which all the scores are either in cell A_1B_1 or in A_2B_2. This is an extreme case of nonorthogonality. Notice that the sum of squares for A will equal the sum of squares for B, no matter what the scores are. If the row means are equal, the column means must be equal. The discrepancy of the row means from the general mean must exactly equal the discrepancy of the column means from the general mean. The two factors in the design are completely confounded, and no conclusion can be drawn about one factor that is independent of the conclusion drawn about the other factor. With most of the scores in these two cells but with a few in cells A_2B_1 and A_1B_2, the confounding is imperfect, the lack of independence is relaxed a little, but it still remains.

15.2 Multiple regression and nonorthogonality. An approach to the problem of nonorthogonality came with the recognition that analyses of variance could be cast as instances of general linear regression. There is no requirement that the independent variables in linear regression be mutually orthogonal. Furthermore, standard techniques exist in regression analysis for estimating and testing the effect of one independent variable on the dependent variable adjusted for the contribution or effect of one or more other correlated independent variables. But casting the analysis in the form of multiple regression gave rise to a new issue. For a two factor design without interaction (again only for simplification) we can write four hypotheses:

H_1: $\quad Y_{ijk} = \mu + e_{ijk}$

H_2: $\quad Y_{ijk} = \mu + \alpha_i + e_{ijk}$

H_3: $\quad Y_{ijk} = \mu + \beta_j + e_{ijk}$

H_4: $Y_{ijk} = \mu + \alpha_i + \beta_j + e_{ijk}$

(The equations that omit μ are also possible but we will ignore them.) In an analysis of variance with orthogonal factors, the test of the hypothesis that all of the α_i are equal could be performed by testing H_1 versus H_2 or by H_3 versus H_4. For either case, let Ω be the more general (larger) model and ω be the more restricted (smaller) model. The F-statistic would in each case be

$$F = [(SS_{e\omega} - SS_{e\Omega})/df_{(\omega-\Omega)}]/SS_e/df_e .$$

In either case the numerator of F would be $SS_A/(I - 1)$. This follows because **with orthogonality the sum of squares associated with α_i does not depend on any of the other parameters**. From the vector perspective, the sum of squares for the α_i is the squared length of the projection of the data vector into the space spanned by those vectors in the **X** matrix that indicate which value of α_i is associated with each score. Since that space is orthogonal to the spaces spanned by the other vectors in **X**, the same projection will result regardless of which of the other vectors (and therefore subspaces) are included in the model.

But when the vectors of **X** are not orthogonal, as in the case of the unbalanced design, the different tests give different results. Furthermore, for the two-factor design, investigators rarely exclude interaction, as we have done in our example. This results in even more possible models and possible tests which do not give the same results. For the two factor design with interaction we could write

H_1: $Y_{ijk} = \mu + e_{ijk}$
H_2: $Y_{ijk} = \mu + \alpha_i + e_{ijk}$
H_3: $Y_{ijk} = \mu + \alpha_j + e_{ijk}$
H_4: $Y_{ijk} = \mu + \alpha_i + \beta_j + e_{ijk}$
H_5: $Y_{ijk} = \mu + \gamma_{ij} + e_{ijk}$
H_6: $Y_{ijk} = \mu + \alpha_i + \gamma_{ij} + e_{ijk}$
H_7: $Y_{ijk} = \mu + \beta_j + \gamma_{ij} + e_{ijk}$
H_8: $Y_{ijk} = \mu + \alpha_i + \beta_j + \gamma_{ij} + e_{ijk}$

assuming $\Sigma_i\alpha_i = \Sigma_i\beta_j = \Sigma_i\gamma_{ij} = \Sigma_j\gamma_{ij} = 0$, for all i and j. (We should note here that although this set of side conditions is fairly standard, it is not the only set that could be chosen and the hypotheses being tested depend upon the choice of side conditions [Speed & Hocking, 1976]). Unless otherwise indicated we will always be using these side conditions.) Now we can test H_α: $\alpha_i = 0$ by testing H_1 versus H_2, H_3 versus H_4, H_5 versus H_6, or H_7 versus H_8.

Let us consider in some detail the test of H_3: $Y_{ijk} = \mu + \beta_j + e_{ijk}$ versus H_4: $Y_{ijk} = \mu + \alpha_i + \beta_j + e_{ijk}$. This test can be viewed as answering the question whether the model with the addition of the α_i terms produces a significant reduction in the discrepancy between predicted and observed Y score values. Under model H_3 the predicted Y scores would be

$$
\mathbf{Y}_{pred\,3} =
\overset{\mathbf{X}_3}{\begin{bmatrix} 1 & 1 \\ 1 & -1 \\ 1 & 1 \\ 1 & -1 \\ 1 & -1 \end{bmatrix}}
\overset{\boldsymbol{\beta}_{est3}}{\begin{bmatrix} \mu_{est3} \\ \beta_{est3} \end{bmatrix}}
=
\begin{bmatrix} \mu_{est3} & + & \beta_{est3} \\ \mu_{est3} & - & \beta_{est3} \\ \mu_{est3} & + & \beta_{est3} \\ \mu_{est3} & - & \beta_{est3} \\ \mu_{est3} & - & \beta_{est3} \end{bmatrix}
$$

and the squared length of this vector of predicted scores would be the sum of squares for regression under model H_3,

$$ SS_{reg3} = 2(\mu_{est3} + \beta_{est3})^2 + 3(\mu_{est3} - \beta_{est3})^2 , $$

where 2 and 3 are $\Sigma_i n_{i1}$ and $\Sigma_i n_{i2}$, respectively. Under model H_4 the predicted Y scores would be

$$
\mathbf{Y}_{pred\,3} =
\overset{\mathbf{X}_4}{\begin{bmatrix} 1 & 1 & 1 \\ 1 & 1 & -1 \\ 1 & -1 & 1 \\ 1 & -1 & -1 \\ 1 & -1 & -1 \end{bmatrix}}
\overset{\boldsymbol{\beta}_{est4}}{\begin{bmatrix} \mu_{est4} \\ \alpha_{est4} \\ \beta_{est4} \end{bmatrix}}
=
\begin{bmatrix} \mu_{est4} & + & \alpha_{est4} & + & \beta_{est4} \\ \mu_{est4} & + & \alpha_{est4} & - & \beta_{est4} \\ \mu_{est4} & - & \alpha_{est4} & + & \beta_{est4} \\ \mu_{est4} & - & \alpha_{est4} & - & \beta_{est4} \\ \mu_{est4} & - & \alpha_{est4} & - & \beta_{est4} \end{bmatrix}
$$

and the sum of squares for regression under model H_4 would be

$$ SS_{reg4} = \mathbf{Y}_{pred4}{}^T \cdot \mathbf{Y}_{pred4} = (\mu_{est4} + \alpha_{est4} + \beta_{est4})^2 + (\mu_{est4} + \alpha_{est4} $$

$$ - \beta_{est4})^2 + (\mu_{est4} - \alpha_{est4} + \beta_{est4})^2 + 2(\mu_{est4} - \alpha_{est4} - \beta_{est4})^2 $$

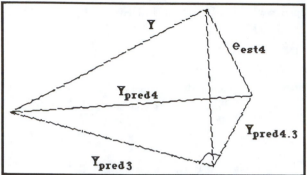

Figure 15.1. The vector $Y_{pred4.3}$ as the projection of the data vector Y into the space $W_4 - W_3$ which is the orthogonal complement of W_3 relative to W_4. The vector $Y_{pred4.3}$ is orthogonal to Y_{pred3}, measures the difference between Y_{pred4} and Y_{pred3}, and its squared length furnishes a measure of the extent to which H_4 fits Y better than H_3.

Let Ω_4 be the space spanned by the column vectors of X_4 and ω_3 be the space spanned by the column vectors of X_3. The vector $Y_{pred4.3} = Y_{pred4} - Y_{pred3}$ is the projection of the data vector on that subspace of Ω_4 orthogonal to the space ω_3. Call that subspace $\Omega_4 - \omega_3$. We can think of Ω_4 as partitioned into two orthogonal subspaces, ω_3 and $\Omega_4 - \omega_3$. The vector Y_{pred4} lies in Ω_4, Y_{pred3} lies in ω_3, and $Y_{pred4.3}$ lies in $\Omega_4 - \omega_3$. The vector $Y_{pred4.3}$ measures the difference between the best fitting vector according to H_4 and that according to H_3. This is displayed graphically in Figure 15.1.

If model H_3 is true, then $Y_{pred4.3}$ can only be a measure of error. We can test the significance of the α_i term by using the squared length of $Y_{pred4.3}$ as a sum of squares associated with the α_i term, dividing by its degrees of freedom, which is the dimensionality of the space $\Omega_4 - \omega_3$, $I - 1$, to obtain a mean square, and dividing this mean square by an error mean square to obtain an F-ratio. A significant F indicates that model H_4 is a significant improvement over model H_3 in fitting the data vector. Because Y_{pred3} and $Y_{pred4.3}$ form a right angle

$$SS_{reg4.3} = SS_{reg4} - SS_{reg3}.$$

We can find SS_{reg4} and SS_{reg3} by doing a regression analysis for each model, and then we can obtain $SS_{reg4.3}$ as the difference between the two sums of squares due to regression. Our F-ratio would then be $F = [(SS_{reg4} - SS_{reg3})/(I - 1)]/(SS_{error}/df_{error})$. The SS_{error} will always be $Y^TY - SS_{reg\ max}$, where $SS_{reg\ max}$ is the sum of squares for regression for the largest model which we are willing to consider as possibly true when we conduct the test. We would report the results of this analysis in a summary table such as Table 15.1.

15.3 Interchangeability of R^2 and SS. Some textbooks and statistical literature follow the above lines of discussion, treating the analysis of regression in terms of sums of squares. Others treat it in terms of R^2, the square of the multiple correlation coefficient. These two treatments differ only in notation and emphasis since every sum of squares of interest is equal to an R^2 times the adjusted total sum of squares, $Y^TY - NM^2$. Thus, $R^2_{Y.\beta} = SS_{reg3}/SS_{total}$, $R^2_{Y.\alpha\beta} = SS_{reg4}/SS_{total}$, and $R^2_{Y(\alpha.\beta)} = (SS_{reg4} - SS_{reg3})/SS_{total}$. The student will often find the F-ratio in a form such as $F = [R^2_{Y(\alpha.\beta)}/(I - 1)]/[(1 - R^2_{\alpha\beta\gamma})/(N - IJ)]$. The term $(1 - R^2_{\alpha\beta\gamma})$ is just $(SS_{total} - SS_{reg8})/SS_{total} = SS_{error}/SS_{total}$, assuming that the appropriate sum of squares for error is $SS_{total} - SS_{reg8}$. In this chapter the appropriate results will be presented in R^2 and in SS notation, or you will be asked to convert from one to the other.

15.4 Which model, which method, which error term? Overall and Spiegel (1969) noted that different regression analyses lead to different solutions in the nonorthogonal case and that these were only superficially similar to the analysis of variance for the orthogonal case. The purpose of their article was to consider three different regression methods and to decide which method was the correct or proper generalization of the orthogonal analysis of variance to the case of nonorthogonality. The three methods they proposed were:

TABLE 15.1 REGRESSION ANALYSIS TESTING H_4 VERSUS H_3

Source	df	SS	MS	F
H_4	$I + J - 1$	SS_{reg4}	$SS_{reg4} / (I + J - 1)$	
H_3	J	SS_{reg3}	SS_{reg3} / J	
$H_4 - H_3$	$I - 1$	$SS_{reg4} - SS_{reg3}$	$SS_{reg4} - SS_{reg3} / (I - 1)$	MS_{H4-H3}/MS_{error}
Error	$N - IJ$	$SS_{total} - SS_{reg8}$		

Method I: adjust each effect for every other effect in the largest model under consideration,

Method II: use the hierarchy of main effects and interactions, and adjust each effect for all other effects at the same or a lower level in the hierarchy,

Method III: use an a priori ordering of the terms in the model, and adjust each effect for those preceding it in the ordering.

(Keep in mind that "adjusting for an effect" means including that effect in the null hypothesis model.) Thus, in the two-factor design with interaction, using Method I we would test the effect of α_i by testing H_7 versus H_8. According to this method the β_j and γ_{ij} effects are included in the null hypothesis model, H_7, when we test for the effect of α_i. Similarly, we would test β_j by testing H_6 versus H_8, and test the interaction by H_4 versus H_8.

Using Method II we would test α_i by testing H_3 versus H_4, β_j by testing H_2 versus H_4, and γ_{ij} by testing H_4 versus H_8. Using Method III and assuming that the a priori ordering is γ_{ij}, α_i, β_j, we would test γ_{ij} by H_4 versus H_8; α_i by H_2 versus H_6, and β_j by H_6 versus H_8. Notice that while the interaction effect would be tested by H_4 versus H_8 in each method, the α_i would be tested by H_7 versus H_8, H_3 versus H_4, or H_2 versus H_6, depending on the method used.

Overall and Spiegel recommended Method II as the proper generalization of analysis of variance to nonorthogonal designs but indicated that in special circumstances the other methods might be more appropriate. A controversy over the proper method developed and by 1975 Overall, Spiegel and Cohen (1975) were arguing for Method I, adopting a criterion that ANOVA for nonorthogonal designs, using regression methods, should estimate the same parameters and test the same hypotheses as tested in a balanced design involving the same factors.

Gradually, in a series of papers by Carlson and Timm (1974), Lewis and Keren (1977), Herr and Gaebelein (1978) and others, it became increasingly clear that the question, "Which method is the proper generalization of the ANOVA for balanced designs?" was not as useful a question as, "What are the implications of different methods (including but not limited to the three proposed by Overall and Speigel), and to which situations do the different methods best apply?" To this, Lewis and Keren (1977) added the additional important question, "What are the implications of a choice of method for the choice of error terms?"

There now seems to be general agreement that in a two-factor design, unless interaction is ruled out a priori, it should be tested first using H_4 versus H_8. There is also general agreement that when the design is unbalanced due to random loss of scores that is unrelated to the treatment conditions, the correct approach is Method I. Such disagreement as still remains seems to relate to the issue of whether one should ignore in later tests an effect that has been found nonsignificant in an earlier test. Thus, if we have tested the interaction effects using model H_4 versus H_8 and found that the interaction effects are nonsignificant, some authors suggest that we should now use H_4 as our largest model, so that the test of α or β, whichever comes next, should be made against model H_4. The opposition argues that this pools any interaction effects into the estimate of error variance and therefore tends to bias the error term if we are wrong in our rejection of H_8. The advocates rejoin that we should be consistent: having rejected H_8, we should act accordingly. The opposition asserts that rejecting H8 is not equivalent to proving that H_8 is false; therefore, we should still be cautious and use an error term we can depend on. I consider both positions defensible. I personally lean toward the opposition position and except for extraordinary circumstances would refrain from pooling.

Now let's analyze a small set of example data from the standpoint of Method I to see how the numerical methods work. We will use a 2 x 3 factorial design with the example scores given in Table 15.2. Assuming $\Sigma_i\alpha_i = \Sigma_j\beta_j = \Sigma_j\gamma_{1j} = \Sigma_j\gamma_{2j} = \Sigma_i\gamma_{i1} = \Sigma_i\gamma_{i2} = \Sigma_i\gamma_{i3} = 0$, to test the interaction we find the sum of squares for regression under the models H_4 and H_8. Under H_8, $\mathbf{Y} = \mathbf{X_8}\beta + \mathbf{e}$. That is,

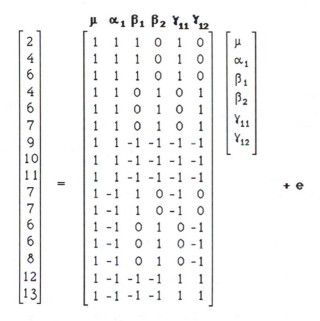

$$
\begin{bmatrix} 2 \\ 4 \\ 6 \\ 4 \\ 6 \\ 7 \\ 9 \\ 10 \\ 11 \\ 7 \\ 7 \\ 6 \\ 6 \\ 8 \\ 12 \\ 13 \end{bmatrix}
=
\begin{bmatrix}
\mu & \alpha_1 & \beta_1 & \beta_2 & \gamma_{11} & \gamma_{12} \\
1 & 1 & 1 & 0 & 1 & 0 \\
1 & 1 & 1 & 0 & 1 & 0 \\
1 & 1 & 1 & 0 & 1 & 0 \\
1 & 1 & 0 & 1 & 0 & 1 \\
1 & 1 & 0 & 1 & 0 & 1 \\
1 & 1 & 0 & 1 & 0 & 1 \\
1 & 1 & -1 & -1 & -1 & -1 \\
1 & 1 & -1 & -1 & -1 & -1 \\
1 & 1 & -1 & -1 & -1 & -1 \\
1 & -1 & 1 & 0 & -1 & 0 \\
1 & -1 & 1 & 0 & -1 & 0 \\
1 & -1 & 0 & 1 & 0 & -1 \\
1 & -1 & 0 & 1 & 0 & -1 \\
1 & -1 & 0 & 1 & 0 & -1 \\
1 & -1 & -1 & -1 & 1 & 1 \\
1 & -1 & -1 & -1 & 1 & 1
\end{bmatrix}
\begin{bmatrix} \mu \\ \alpha_1 \\ \beta_1 \\ \beta_2 \\ \gamma_{11} \\ \gamma_{12} \end{bmatrix}
+ \mathbf{e}
$$

TABLE 15.2 EXAMPLE SCORES FOR METHOD I

	B₁	B₂	B₃
	2	4	9
A₁	4	6	10
	6	7	11
	7	6	12
A₂	7	6	13
	8		

TABLE 15.3   THE INTERACTION, ROW, AND COLUMN EFFECTS FOR THE DESIGN IN TABLE 15.2

(a)

	B_1	B_2	B_3
A_1	Y_{11}	Y_{12}	$-Y_{11} - Y_{12}$
A_2	$-Y_{11}$	$-Y_{12}$	$Y_{11} + Y_{12}$

(b)

A_1	α_1	α_1	α_1
A_2	$-\alpha_1$	$-\alpha_1$	$-\alpha_1$

(c)

A_1	β_1	β_2	$-(\beta_1 + \beta_2)$
A_2	β_1	β_2	$-(\beta_1 + \beta_2)$

Note the labels of the column vectors in the X_8 matrix. It will be convenient to use them to define the X matrices for the other models of interest. The student should also fastidiously examine each column of X_8 to determine why each entry takes the value it does. To encourage this I will go through the vector for γ_{12}. Consider the diagram in Table 15.3a showing the assignment of interaction effects to each cell. Note that this is the assignment that satisfies all of the side conditions. The sum of the interaction effects in each row is zero, and the sum in each column is zero. Now as we examine the entries in the vector γ_2, we first find three zeroes. These zeroes are assigned to the first three scores, 2, 4, and 6, because they are in cell$_{11}$ and γ_{12} does not occur in cell$_{11}$. Next we find three ones in γ_2 because the next three scores, 4, 6, and 7, occur in cell$_{12}$ and γ_{12} is the interaction effect in cell$_{12}$. The next three values are -1 because the next three Y scores, 9, 10, and 11, are in cell$_{13}$ and $-\gamma_{12}$ is a part of the interaction effect for cell$_{13}$. And so it goes for the remaining scores. Two scores occur in cell$_{21}$ and two zeroes occur in γ_2 since γ_{12} does not occur in cell$_{21}$, the next three scores are in cell$_{22}$ and get -1 in γ_2 because the cell$_{21}$ interaction effect is $-\gamma_{12}$, and the final two scores get plus one in γ_2 because the interaction effect for cell$_{23}$

contains γ_{12}. The student should use the diagrams in Tables 15.3b and 15.3c to check the entries in the column vectors α_1, β_1, and β_2.

We continue now with the analysis of the example data in the 2 x 3 design. For model H_8 the sum of squares for regression is $\beta_{est}{}^T X_8{}^T Y$ where $\beta_{est} = (X_8{}^T X_8)^{-1} X_8{}^T Y$ so SS_{reg8} $= Y^T X_8 (X_8{}^T X_8)^{-1} X_8{}^T Y$ which turns out to be 988.1667. The total sum of squares of all the scores is $Y^T Y = 1006$, so $SS_{error} = 1006 - 988.1667 = 17.8333$. Model H_4 has $SS_{reg4} = Y^T X_4 (X_4{}^T X_4)^{-1} X_4{}^T Y = 985.1897$, where $X_4 = [\mu \ \alpha_1 \ \beta_1 \ \beta_2]$, the matrix consisting of the first four column vectors of X_8. We see that X_4 is obtained from the matrix X_8 by deletion of the column vectors for the interaction effects. The X matrix for each of the remaining models is formed in corresponding fashion by including the column vectors from X_8 for the parameters in the model of interest and excluding the vectors for the parameters excluded from the model. Thus the matrices for the remaining models are

$$X_1 = [\mu]$$
$$X_2 = [\mu \ \alpha_1]$$
$$X_3 = [\mu \ \beta_1 \ \beta_2]$$
$$X_5 = [\mu \ \gamma_1 \ \gamma_2]$$
$$X_7 = [\mu \ \beta_1 \ \beta_2 \ \gamma_1 \ \gamma_2] .$$

The sums of squares for regression under the eight models are

Model	SS_{reg}
H_1	870.25
H_2	884.06
H_3	968.37
H_4	985.19
H_5	876.13
H_6	890.81
H_7	970.06
H_8	988.17

Table 15.4 shows the various sums of squares, mean squares, and F-ratios for testing the various effects by comparison of models from the perspective of Method 1.

15.5 Nonorthogonality with equal n's: unequal population sizes. It is easy to think of many cases where the population sizes of various populations are unequal. For example, an investigator might wish to study the learning ability of university students who are either male or female and in either a nursing or an engineering program. It might be an

**TABLE 15.4   METHOD 1 REGRESSION ANALYSIS
OF THE SAMPLE NONORTHOGONAL DESIGN**

Effect	Model comparison	df	SS	MS	F
α_i	H_7 vs. H_8	1	918.17 - 970.06	18.11	10.17
β_j	H_6 vs. H_8	2	918.17 - 890.81	48.68	27.35
γ_{ij}	H_4 vs. H_8	2	918.17 - 985.19	1.49	.84
Error		10	1006 - 918.17	1.78	
Total		16	1006		

easy matter to get 20 persons from each group to serve as subjects in a 2 x 2 factorial design with equal cell n's. But if our generalizations are to the population from which these subjects are assumed to be sampled, we may wish to take the population sizes into account. At the University of Massachusetts Amherst campus in the undergraduate engineering programs there are about 80 percent men and 20 percent women. In the nursing program there are about 10 percent men and 90 percent women. Let us assume that in the population of men and women majoring in engineering or nursing, the proportions of persons in the four possible categories are as given in Table 15.5. Let us use α_1 and α_2 to be the effects of being male and female, respectively, and let β_1 and β_2 be the effects of being an engineering and nursing major, respectively. We further assume for simplicity that there are no interaction effects. Then our model for an individual's score is

$$Y_{ijk} = \mu + \alpha_i + \beta_j + e_{ijk}.$$

**TABLE 15.5   PROPORTIONS OF
PERSONS IN FOUR CATEGORIES**

	Engineering	Nursing	
Men	.32	.05	.37
Women	.08	.55	.63
	.40	.60	

We can see in the diagram above that in the population there will be 37 percent α_1's and 63 percent α_2's; 40 percent β_1's and 60 percent β_2's. If we assume that the sum of the α_i's over the entire population is zero, then $.37 \alpha_1 + .63 \alpha_2 = 0$ and therefore $\alpha_2 = (-.37/.63)$

**TABLE 15.6 SAMPLE SIZES
PROPORTIONAL TO A
POPULATION
NONORTHOGONALITY**

	Engineering	Nursing
Men	32	2
Women	8	18

α_1. Similarly, assuming that the sum of the β_j's over the entire population is zero, then $.40\beta_1 + .60\beta_2 = 0$ and therefore $\beta_2 = (-.40/.60)\ \beta_1$. **The nonorthogonality in the population is dealt with by using the population sizes to restrict the parameter values (the α_i, β_j, etc.) and the restrictions then dictate the proper values to insert in the X matrix of full rank.** When we use the side conditions in creating the column vectors of the X matrix, we get nonorthogonal column vectors even for an equal n design. For one score per cell we would have

$$\mathbf{X} = \begin{bmatrix} 1 & 1 & 1 \\ 1 & 1 & -.40/.60 \\ 1 & -.37/.63 & 1 \\ 1 & -.37/.63 & -.40/.60 \end{bmatrix}$$

in which the column vectors are obviously nonorthogonal. Of course, with 20 scores per cell, a comparable nonorthogonality occurs.

The investigator can take the unequal population sizes into account and create an orthogonal design by using sample sizes for the various cells of the design that are proportional to the population cell frequencies or relative frequencies. Thus, for example, a design with the cell frequencies shown in Table 15.6 would result in an orthogonal design. Notice that the cell frequency for Male Nursing majors is only 2. To raise this frequency to a modest size of 10, say, the frequency for Male Engineering majors would have to also be multiplied by 5, giving 160 subjects required in that group. Most investigators faced with the alternative of having very small or very large cell sizes and an orthogonal design versus nicely sized cell frequencies and a nonorthogonal design would choose the nonorthogonal design.

Exercises

1. Satisfy yourself that the matrix $\mathbf{X}\beta$ in [15.1] equals the matrix $\mathbf{X}\beta$ in [15.2].

2. Persuade yourself that for a 2 x 2 factorial design with n scores per cell, n > 1, the column vectors of the appropriate $\mathbf{X}$ matrix would be mutually orthogonal. State why.

TABLE 15.7 A 3 x 3 FACTORIAL DESIGN WITH UNEQUAL CELL FREQUENCIES

	B_1	B_2	B_3
A_1	2 4 3	5 7	4 1
A_2	3 3	2 2 4 2	3 3
A_3	3 3 1	4 4 5	7 7 8

3. Extend exercise 2 to a 3 x 4 factorial design. (Hint: use orthogonal contrast coefficients or orthogonal polynomial coefficients to form the column vectors, or else set $\alpha_I = -(\alpha_1 + \alpha_2 + ... + \alpha_{I-1}$ and $\beta_J = -(\beta_1 + \beta_2 + ... + \beta_{J-1})$. Then persuade yourself that orthogonality holds for any r x c factorial design with n scores per cell.

4. Write a model with unequal cell n's in which the column vectors in $\mathbf{X}$ are not mutually orthogonal.

5. Write the model corresponding to [15.3] for which there is one score in cells A_1B_1 and A_2B_2 and two scores in A_1B_2 and A_2B_1. Are the column vectors of $\mathbf{X}$ orthogonal?

6. Write the model corresponding to [15.3] for which there are two scores in cells A_1B_1 and A_1B_2 and one score in A_2B_1 and A_2B_1. Are the column vectors of $\mathbf{X}$ orthogonal? Compare this result with that of exercise 2. Write the two design diagrams for the two models. Compare them. What do you conclude?

7. Write the matrix model equation and draw the design diagram for a 3 x 4 factorial design where all cells in the first row have two scores, all in the second row have one score, and all in the third have three scores. Are the column vectors mutually orthogonal? Now switch the

contents of any cell in row 1 with any cell in row 2. What do you conclude about unequal cell sizes and orthogonality?

8. Write the full rank $\mathbf{X}_8$ for the design in Table 15.7.

9. Examine the three diagrams of effects in the text for the 2 x 3 design. Explain the relationship between the degrees of freedom for a source and the number of parameters for that source in a full rank model. Does this relationship hold for the 3 x 3 design in Table 15.7?

10. Apply the three methods to the data in Table 15.7.

Supplementary Readings

Carlson, J. E., & Timm, N. H. (1974) Analysis of nonorthogonal fixed-effects designs. *Psychological Bulletin,* 81, 563-570.

Herr, D. G., & Gaebelein, J. (1978) Nonorthogonal two-way analysis of variance. *Psychological Bulletin*, 85, 207-216.

Horst, P., & Edwards, A. L. (1982) Analysis of nonorthogonal designs: The 2^k factorial experiment. *Psychological Bulletin*, 91, 190-192.

Keren, G., & Lewis, C. (1976) Nonorthgonal designs: Sample versus population. *Psychological Bulletin*, 83, 817-826.

Pedhazur, E. J. (1977) Coding subjects in repeated measures designs. *Psychological Bulletin*, 84, 298-305.

16

Experimental Design

16.1 Introduction. In the preceding chapters we have considered various aspects of the analysis of variance, analysis of covariance, and multiple regression as they apply to the analysis of experimental data. We have used a variety of experimental designs to illustrate the breadth and depth of ANOVA procedures. But we have said very little about how such experimental designs were arrived at. The subject of experimental design is vast. We cannot hope to cover it in a single book, much less a single chapter. Instead, we will introduce here some of the important principles of experimental design and exemplify them with sample designs. In my vision of statistical training, a one-semester course on experimental design using a book like Kirk's (1982) or Cochran and Cox (1957) would follow a course using this book. The student is referrred to these sources for a more detailed and extensive treatment of experimental design.

TABLE 16.1 THE A x B x C FACTORIAL DESIGN WITH THREE LEVELS AT EACH FACTOR

	C_1				C_2				C_3		
	B_1	B_2	B_3		B_1	B_2	B_3		B_1	B_2	B_3
A_1				A_1				A_1			
A_2				A_2				A_2			
A_3				A_3				A_3			

The Big Ideas of experimental design are **Precision, Accuracy, Control**, and **Economy** (a good PACE to keep up with). We desire our estimators of effects to be accurate so that our conclusions concerning hypotheses will be accurate. In this context **inaccuracy means bias**. An adequate design will avoid biasing the estimators or at least provide an estimate of the amount of bias whereby some correction can be made. Precision differs from accuracy in that precision refers to repeatability of the measurement process, to reducing variability in the estimators. We can use estimation of the population variance to distinguish between the concepts of precision and accuracy. The estimator $\sigma^2_{est1} = \Sigma_i(X_i - M)^2/N$ is inaccurate because it is biased. But as N gets larger and larger, σ^2_{est1} becomes more and more precise. (Actually it becomes less and less biased also.) The estimator $\sigma^2_{est2} = \Sigma_i(X_i - M)^2/(N - 1)$ is unbiased and therefore as accurate as it can be. As N increases it becomes increasingly precise but no more accurate.

    Control in the broad sense refers to the standardization and repeatability of our experimental conditions, our sampling process, our measuring process, and even our data analysis procedures. The experimental variables that we control remain constant or vary in a known way that we can take into account in determining their effects on our experiment. The experimental variables that we do not control influence our experiment in unknown ways, contributing to error variance or to bias or both. Similarly, our control or lack of control of the measuring process determines the contribution of measurement error to variability and to bias. If we use a measuring instrument that is not reliable, such as a rubber ruler that stretches a different unknown amount each time we use it, we get different values even when we measure the same object or the same behavior. To be sure, a certain amount of this is unavoidable. Our goal is to hold it to a practical minimum. If we use a measuring process that systematically distorts or interacts with the measured material or subjects, then we can expect bias. For example, some have claimed that standardized intelligence tests produce biased results because their items favor one subgroup, middle-class whites, over others such as various minority groups with different cultural backgrounds and traditions. Control of the data analysis procedures primarily involves using procedures that are as free from computational and other procedural errors as possible. Even computers can make errors. And when they don't, they still analyze only the data we provide. Therefore care in the input of data and checking of the results of the analysis is another form of control.

Economy refers to the fact that performing an experiment entails a cost in time, in money, in resources, in energy, in attention. Given our commitment to an investigation of some question, we want to keep its cost to a minimum. At the same time we do not want to skimp so much that our experiment lacks enough power to reveal the existence of effects of the variables we are manipulating. This would be like planting expensive trees but saving money by not watering them. The results would be fruitless. **The issue of economy is therefore the confrontation between matters of frugality and matters of power.**

In our everyday experience we discover that when we have only a limited amount of time to inspect something, we get better results if we know which aspects to direct our attention to and which to ignore. We call this **focus**. In experimental design it is often possible to focus our attention on a limited number of possible effects while ignoring others. This permits us to husband our resources, for example, use fewer subjects, and yet keep the power of our tests up. The price that we pay is in the lack of information concerning the ignored effects and, in some cases, in the possible confounding of the ignored effects with those we have attended to. In what follows we will see this theme repeated.

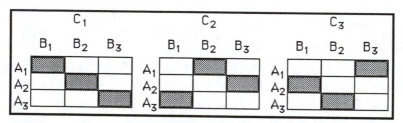

Figure 16.1. A latin square design based on a 3 x 3 x 3 factorial design.

16.2 Latin squares. Consider an experiment in which the subject's response may be sensitive to time of day—some measure of perceptual vigilence or alertness, or perhaps some emotional response or mood response. Suppose also that the subjects are being run individually in different rooms by different experimenters, the same experimenter always working in the same room. For reasons that will be clear in a moment, assume that the number of levels of the primary experimental independent variable of interest, call it Factor C, equals both the number of rooms (Factor A) and the number of times of day at which subjects can be run (Factor B). As an experimenter you would certainly not want to assign all the subjects at level C_1 to room A_1, and run them at one time of day, B_1, or do the same with the other levels of C, say C_2 in room A_2 at time B_2, and so on. This would confound

**TABLE 16.2 A
LATIN SQUARE**

	B_1	B_2	B_3
A_1	C_1	C_2	C_3
A_2	C_3	C_1	C_2
A_3	C_2	C_3	C_1

the effects of primary concern, the effects of Factor C, with the effects of two variables that could affect the response level but are not of primary concern. Some experimenters call such uninteresting secondary variables "nuisance variables" since they must be attended to even though they are not of interest—just like any other nuisance.

One way to cope would be to assign all levels of the treatment variable C to all rooms and all times of day. This would result in, say, the A x B x C factorial design shown in Table 16.1, assuming three levels for each factor.

To have even one score per cell requires that we run 27 subjects. This is obviously a tremendous investment of resources such as time and perhaps money to control for two variables that are not of primary interest to us.

Suppose we have good reason to believe that there are no interaction effects among any of these three factors. Then our model equation would be

$$Y_{ijk} = \mu + \alpha_i + \beta_j + \gamma_k + e_{ijk}.$$

In this case we can use only one-third of the treatment combinations in order to assess the effects of Factor C and control the effects of Factors A and B. Suppose we use only the shaded cells in Figure 16.1. We have reduced our design from 27 cells to only 9 cells. We can arrange the selected cells in Table 16.2. This diagram is called a **latin square**. **Its fundamental property is that each level of C occurs exactly once in each row and exactly once in each column.** Thus each level of C occurs equally often with each of the three levels of each of the other two factors, A and B. There are many other rearrangements of the levels of the C factor within the cells of this A x B diagram that would satisfy the latin square property. In fact any permutation of the rows and/or columns of the latin square shown above would also be a latin square, as would any permutation of the levels of the square variable (C in this case). Three examples are shown in Table 16.3. In Table 16.3, in (1) the first two rows of the original square were permuted. In (2) the first two columns were permuted. How was (3) obtained? Usually when experimenters set up a

TABLE 16.3 PERMUTATIONS OF THE LATIN SQUARE IN TABLE 16.2

	(1)				(2)				(3)		
	B_1	B_2	B_3		B_1	B_2	B_3		B_1	B_2	B_3
A_1	C_3	C_1	C_2	A_1	C_1	C_3	C_2	A_1	C_3	C_2	C_1
A_2	C_1	C_2	C_3	A_2	C_3	C_2	C_1	A_2	C_2	C_1	C_3
A_3	C_2	C_3	C_1	A_3	C_2	C_1	C_3	A_3	C_1	C_3	C_2

TABLE 16.4 A FOUR LEVEL LATIN SQUARE

	B_1	B_2	B_3	B_4
A_1	C_1	C_2	C_3	C_4
A_2	C_4	C_1	C_2	C_3
A_3	C_3	C_4	C_1	C_2
A_4	C_2	C_3	C_4	C_1

latin square they will start with one they make up or get from a source of such plans, such as Cochran and Cox (1957), and then use a random number table to permute randomly the rows and columns of the initial square to obtain the square they will use in the experiment.

If there had been four levels of each factor we could have produced the latin square shown in Table 16.4. Latin squares exist for all possible numbers of levels provided always that the number of levels is the same for all three factors.

The result of exercise 2 shows that even though 18 of the 27 cells in the factorial design are empty, this latin square fraction of that design will result in orthogonal sums of squares for the three factors. For a latin square design with n scores per cell, we would perform the analysis shown in Table 16.5.

The sum of squares for the square residual is a measure of error if all of the interactions that have been assumed to be zero are in fact zero. Different researchers take different positions toward conducting a significance test of the square residual. Some argue there is no need to test the square residual since you had good reason to assume no interaction or you would not have adopted a latin square design. To test the residual now would be to open the design up to the occasional Type I error that comes along. They suggest leaving the residual untested. Some even endorse pooling the sum of squares with the error sum of

TABLE 16.5 SUMMARY TABLE OF THE LATIN SQUARE DESIGN

Source	df	Sum of squares
A	$I - 1$	$\Sigma_i T_{Ai}^2/In - T^2/I^2n$
B	$I - 1$	$\Sigma_j T_{Bj}^2/In - T^2/I^2n$
C	$I - 1$	$\Sigma_k T_{Ck}^2/In - T^2/I^2n$
Square residual	$(I - 2)(I - 1)$	$\Sigma_i\Sigma_j T_{AiBj}^2/n - (\Sigma_i T_{Ai}^2/In$
		$+ \Sigma_j T_{Bj}^2/In + \Sigma_k T_{Ck}^2/In) + 2\, T^2/I^2$
Error	$N - I^2$	$\Sigma_i\Sigma_j\Sigma_k Y_{(Ai)(Bj)k}^2 - \Sigma_i\Sigma_j T_{AiBj}^2/n$

Note: There are I levels of each factor; T_{Ai} is the total of all scores in the design at level i of Factor A; T_{Bj} is the total of all scores in the design at level j of Factor B; T_{Ck} is the total of all scores in the design at level k of Factor C; and T_{AiBj} is the total of all scores at level i of Factor A and level j of Factor B.

squares and pooling the degrees of freedom. Others, from a more conservative position, argue that you can always be wrong in assuming no interaction and since the information is available, it is better to test and to know than to leave it untested and have ignorance as an ally. They argue further that if there are interaction effects, they will be confounded with the main effects in the design. Any indication of such interactions should cause us to be concerned about the meaning of a significant main effect. I lean toward the more conservative view. Where one is certain that interaction effects are zero, I would say pool with error and thereby have an error term with more degrees of freedom. But such certainty will be rare, and if you are not certain enough to pool it with error, then test the square residual.

We will now analyze an example set of data for a latin square design. The data are given in Table 16.6. The row and column totals and the grand total are given in the table. The totals for the C factor are $T_{C1} = 58$, $T_{C2} = 23$, $T_{C3} = 36$ and the sum of the squares of all the scores is 603. For the sums of squares we have then

$$SS_A = (40^2 + 38^2 + 39^2)/9 - 117^2/27 = .22$$

$$SS_B = (44^2 + 37^2 + 36^2)/9 - 117^2/27 = 4.22$$

$$SS_C = (58^2 + 23^2 + 36^2)/9 - 117^2/27 = 69.56$$

$$SS_{sq.\ res.} = (11^2 + 11^2 + 18^2 + 20^2 + 6^2 + 12^2 + 13^2 + 20^2 + 6^2)/3 - [\,(40^2 + 37^2 + 39^2)/9 + (44^2 + 37^2 + 36^2)/9 + (58^2 + 23^2 + 36^2)/9\,] + 2(117)^2/27$$

TABLE 16.6 A LATIN SQUARE DESIGN

	B_1	B_2	B_3	
A_1	C_2 2 4 5 $T_{A_1B_1} = 11$	C_3 4 4 3 $T_{A_1B_2} = 11$	C_1 5 6 7 $T_{A_1B_3} = 18$	40
A_2	C_1 6 7 7 $T_{A_2B_1} = 20$	C_2 3 1 2 $T_{A_2B_2} = 6$	C_3 3 5 4 $T_{A_2B_3} = 12$	38
A_3	C_3 4 3 6 $T_{A_3B_1} = 13$	C_1 6 7 7 $T_{A_3B_2} = 20$	C_2 2 1 3 $T_{A_3B_3} = 6$	39
	44	37	36	117

$= 583.67 - [507.22 + 511.22 + 576.56] + 2(507) = 2.67$

$SS_{error} = 603 - (11^2 + 11^2 + 18^2 + 20^2 + 6^2 + 12^2 + 13^2 + 20^2 + 6^2)/3$

$= 603 - 583.67 = 19.33.$

The summary of the ANOVA is given in Table 16.7. For additional treatment of latin squares the student is referred to the books by Kirk and by Cochran and Cox and also to Grant (1948).

TABLE 16.7 ANOVA FOR THE LATIN SQUARE DESIGN

Source	df	SS	MS	F
A	2	.22	.11	.10
B	2	4.22	2.11	1.97
C	2	69.56	34.78	32.50
Sq. Res.	2	2.67	1.34	1.25
Error	18	19.33	1.07	

16.3 Graeco-latin squares. We will not go into these designs in any detail but just mention that it is possible to assign a second variable within the cells of a latin square in such a way that each level of the second variable not only conforms to the latin square property with respect to the rows and columns but also each level of this second variable occurs exactly once with each level of the first square variable. Table 16.8 shows a 3 x 3 Graeco-latin square. They can be formed for a design with any number of levels, each factor again, of course, having the same number of levels. The sums of squares are obtained in the same way as in the latin square and the ANOVA is performed in the obvious fashion. All of the factors, A, B, C, and D, are orthogonal to each other if the design is balanced (equal n's in each cell).

16.4 Confounding. In the split-plot design we saw that effects due to differences between groups of subjects were confounded with the Between-Groups variable effects. We choose to use such a design because crossing with Subjects all of the factors, including those we used as the Between-Groups factor, may be too costly, take too much time per subject, or simply be impossible because of the nature of the variables. Assigning subjects to groups at random when possible enables us to cope with this confounding. The point is that confounding is intentional because it is economical or experimentally necessary or both. In this section we will consider briefly intentional confounding of the Blocking factor in a randomized blocks design.

**TABLE 16.8 A 3 x 3
GRAECO-LATIN SQUARE**

	B_1	B_2	B_3
A_1	C_1 D_1	C_2 D_3	C_3 D_2
A_2	C_3 D_3	C_1 D_2	C_2 D_1
A_3	C_2 D_2	C_3 D_1	C_1 D_3

Suppose we have two experimental variables of primary interest, each having three levels, and we decide that a substantial reduction in error variance can be achieved by blocking on a third variable. For example, suppose you are interested in the effects of Diet and Amount of Sleep on Visual Acuity, and you also believe that blocking on Time of Day of Vision Test

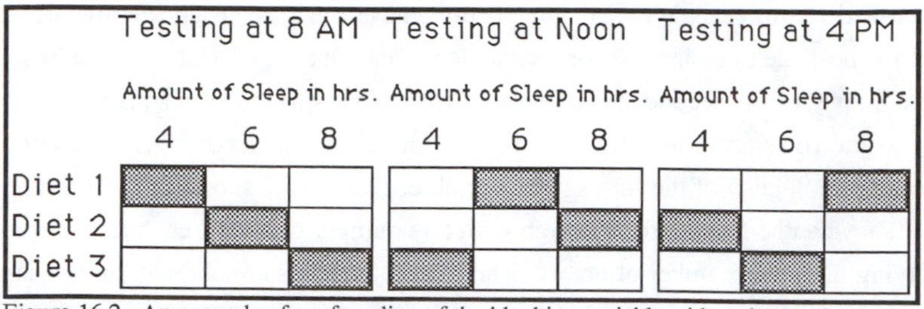

Testing at 8 AM			Testing at Noon			Testing at 4 PM		
Amount of Sleep in hrs.			Amount of Sleep in hrs.			Amount of Sleep in hrs.		
4	6	8	4	6	8	4	6	8
Diet 1 ▓				▓				▓
Diet 2	▓				▓	▓		
Diet 3		▓	▓				▓	

Figure 16.2. An example of confounding of the blocking variable with an interaction. In this case, confounding of the Time of Testing with the Diet x Amount of Sleep interaction.

TABLE 16.9 A 3 x 3 x 3 FACTORIAL DESIGN

Testing at 8 AM			Testing at Noon			Testing at 4 PM		
Amount of Sleep in hrs.			Amount of Sleep in hrs.			Amount of Sleep in hrs.		
4	6	8	4	6	8	4	6	8
Diet 1								
Diet 2								
Diet 3								

would substantially reduce error variance. If you are concerned with possible carryover effects from one test to another and it will be hard to get one subject to go through nine different tests, you might decide to avoid repeated measures and use different subjects in each combination of treatments. The design might look like that shown in Table 16.9. You would need 27 subjects just to have one score per cell and 54 subjects to have a balanced design with some degrees of freedom for error. This large number of subjects might be prohibitive.

One strategy that has been found useful when it can be assumed that the interaction effects for the primary variables are negligible is to confound the Blocking Factor with a portion of that interaction. In the example, we would confound Time of Testing with the interaction of Diet and Amount of Sleep. We could do this by using only the shaded cells in Figure 16.2. This diagram in Figure 16.2 can be rewritten as the diagram in Table 16.10 or in Table 16.11.

*It is in Table 16.11 that we can see how Blocks are confounded with a portion of the Diet x Amount of Sleep interaction. Consider the following full-rank model equation for this design assuming one score per cell, letting μ be the grand mean, α_i be the Diet effect, β_j be the Amount of Sleep effect, γ_k be the Blocks effect, and assume that $\Sigma_i \alpha_i = \Sigma_j \beta_j = \Sigma_k \gamma_k = 0$.

$$
\begin{bmatrix} Y_{11} \\ Y_{12} \\ Y_{13} \\ Y_{21} \\ Y_{22} \\ Y_{23} \\ Y_{31} \\ Y_{32} \\ Y_{33} \end{bmatrix}
=
\begin{bmatrix}
1 & 1 & 0 & 1 & 0 & 1 & 0 \\
1 & 1 & 0 & 0 & 1 & 0 & 1 \\
1 & 1 & 0 & 1 & 1 & 1 & 1 \\
1 & 0 & 1 & 1 & 0 & 1 & 1 \\
1 & 0 & 1 & 0 & 1 & 1 & 0 \\
1 & 0 & 1 & 1 & 1 & 0 & 1 \\
1 & 1 & 1 & 1 & 0 & 0 & 1 \\
1 & 1 & 1 & 0 & 1 & 1 & 1 \\
1 & 1 & 1 & 1 & 1 & 1 & 0
\end{bmatrix}
\begin{bmatrix} \mu \\ \alpha_1 \\ \alpha_2 \\ \beta_1 \\ \beta_2 \\ \gamma_1 \\ \gamma_2 \end{bmatrix}
+ \; e
$$

TABLE 16.10 ALTERNATIVE FORM OF THE DESIGN IN FIGURE 16.2

Groups in Blocks

Block	1	2	3
8	D_1, 4	D_2, 6	D_3, 8
12	D_1, 6	D_2, 8	D_3, 4
4	D_1, 8	D_2, 4	D_3, 6

We see that the last two vectors in the **X** matrix, the γ-vectors, are orthogonal to both α-vectors and both β-vectors. This means that these γ-vectors lie in the Diet x Amount of Sleep interaction space. Since there are two linearly independent γ-vectors, they span a two-dimensional subspace of the interaction space. This means they are associated with two degrees of freedom. Those two degrees of freedom are the same two degrees of freedom associated with the three levels of Blocks. The γ-vectors may be viewed as both the vectors of coefficients for two nonorthogonal contrasts of the means for the Blocks levels or as the vectors of coefficients for two nonorthogonal contrasts on the interaction of Diet with Amount of Sleep. The nonorthogonality of the two γ-vectors is inconsequential. We could just as easily have used $\gamma_2^T = [-2\ 1\ 1\ 1\ -2\ 1\ 1\ 1\ -2]$ as the second vector to make this point. In this case both γ_1 and γ_2 are orthogonal to each other and to both α-vectors and both β-vectors. The γ-vectors now are the coefficients of two orthogonal contrasts of the Blocks levels and also of two orthogonal contrasts that define components of the Diet x Amount of Sleep interaction.

What is important here is that by confounding the Blocks factor with a part of the interaction, the design has been reduced from 27 cells to only 9 cells. This economizing might well mean the difference between an experiment's being feasible or not. Of course,

TABLE 16.11 ALTERNATIVE FORM OF THE DESIGN IN FIGURE 16.2

Amount of Sleep

	4	6	8
D_1	8	12	4
Diet D_2	4	8	12
D_3	12	4	8

you do not get something for nothing. You have paid the price of being unable to test for a portion of the interaction.

You may wonder about the other two degrees of freedom for interaction, those associated with the components of interaction that are not confounded with Blocks. These degrees of freedom still exist together with their associated sums of squares, which can be used to test the significance of the unconfounded portion of the interaction. This test seems like a good idea. It allows the investigator to assess the interaction at least partially . There is a very simple device in this case to determine the remaining two vectors of contrast coefficients to obtain

$$
X\beta = \begin{bmatrix}
1 & 1 & 0 & 1 & 0 & 1 & 0 & 1 & 0 \\
1 & 1 & 0 & 0 & 1 & 0 & 1 & 0 & 1 \\
1 & 1 & 0 & -1 & -1 & -1 & -1 & -1 & -1 \\
1 & 0 & 1 & 1 & 0 & -1 & -1 & 0 & 1 \\
1 & 0 & 1 & 0 & 1 & 1 & 0 & -1 & -1 \\
1 & 0 & 1 & -1 & -1 & 0 & 1 & 1 & 0 \\
1 & -1 & -1 & 1 & 0 & 0 & 1 & -1 & -1 \\
1 & -1 & -1 & 0 & 1 & -1 & -1 & 1 & 0 \\
1 & -1 & -1 & -1 & -1 & 1 & 0 & 0 & 1
\end{bmatrix}
\begin{bmatrix}
\mu \\ \alpha_1 \\ \alpha_2 \\ \beta_1 \\ \beta_2 \\ \gamma_1 \\ \gamma_2 \\ \gamma_3 \\ \gamma_4
\end{bmatrix}
\qquad [16.1]
$$

We note that in Figure 16.11 the Blocks levels are located as if they were a latin square factor. We have already seen that in a Graeco-latin square, the Greeks and the Latins are orthogonal to each other, as well as to the row and column factors. All we need to do to find the two vectors of coefficients that span the space orthogonal to the space spanned by the μ, α_1, α_2, β_1, β_2, and γ_1 and γ_2 vectors is to let a fictional Greek variable take the values G_1,

TABLE 16.12 UNCONFOUNDED PORTION OF THE INTERACTION AS A "GREEK" VARIABLE

Amount of Sleep

	4	6	8
D_1	8 G_1	12 G_2	4 G_3
Diet D_2	4 G_2	8 G_3	12 G_1
D_3	12 G_3	4 G_1	8 G_2

G_2, and G_3, and assign it to the square, giving the design in Table 16.12. Now if we let γ_3 be the "effect" of G_1, γ_4 be the effect of G_2, and $-(\gamma_3 + \gamma_4)$ be the "effect" of G_3, then the vectors γ_3 and γ_4 in the $\mathbf{X}$ matrix above immediately follow. We note that γ_3 and γ_4 are both orthogonal to γ_1 and γ_2, as well as to α_1, α_2, β_1 and β_2.

To exemplify the analysis of variance we will use the small set of contrived visual acuity scores shown in Table 16.13. The Block totals are $T_8 = 71$, $T_{12} = 39$, $T_4 = 32$. The sums of squares for rows, columns, and blocks are obtained in the usual fashion.

$$SS_{Diet} = (48^2 + 32^2 + 62^2)/6 - 142^2/18,$$

$$SS_{Hours} = (34^2 + 53^2 + 55^2)/6 - 142^2/18,$$

$$SS_{Time} = (71^2 + 39^2 + 32^2)/6 - 142^2/18.$$

Let T_{ij} be the cell total for cell$_{ij}$. Then $SS_{error} = \Sigma_i\Sigma_j\Sigma_k Y_{ijk}^2 - \Sigma_i\Sigma_j T_{ij}^2/2$ and SS_{DxH} is most easily obtained as the residual

$$\Sigma_i\Sigma_j\Sigma_k Y_{ijk}^2 - T^2/N - SS_{Diet} - SS_{Hours} - SS_{Time} - SS_{error}.$$

Alternatively the sum of squares for the interaction components can be obtained as sums of squares for contrasts using the contrast coefficients in γ_3 and γ_4. These would be

$$SS_{\gamma3} = [(1)(20) + (0)(15) + (-1)(13) + (0)(1) + (-1)(20) + (1)(11) + (-1)(13) +$$

$$(1)(18) + (0)(31)]^2/[1^2 + 0^2 + (-1)^2 + 0^2 + (-1)^2 + 1^2 + (-1)^2 + 1^2 + 0^2]$$

TABLE 16.13 FICTIONAL DATA FOR THE CONFOUNDED DESIGN

Hours of Sleep

		4		8		12		
Diet	1	8 AM	9 11	12 Noon	7 8	4 PM	6 7	48
		Total	20	Total	15	Total	13	
	2	4 PM	1 0	8 AM	9 11	12 Noon	5 6	32
		Total	1	Total	20	Total	11	
	3	12 Noon	6 7	4 PM	8 10	8 AM	16 15	62
		Total	13	Total	18	Total	31	
		34		53		55	142	

$SS_{\gamma 4} = [(0)(20) + (1)(15) + (-1)(13) + (1)(1) + (-1)(20) + (0)(11) + (-1)(13) +$

$(0)(18) + (1)(31)]^2/[0^2 + 1^2 + (-1)^2 + 1^2 + (-1)^2 + 0^2 + (-1)^2 + 0^2 + 1^2].$

Then $SS_{\text{Diet x Hours}} = SS_{\gamma 3} + SS_{\gamma 4}$. The summary table of the ANOVA is given in Table 16.14.

**TABLE 16.14 ANOVA FOR THE
DESIGN WITH DIET x AMOUNT
OF SLEEP INTERACTION
CONFOUNDED WITH BLOCKS**

Source	df	SS	MS	F
Diet	2	75.11	37.55	37.55
Sleep	2	44.78	22.39	22.39
Time	2	144.11	72.06	72.06
D X S	2	.78	.39	.39
Error	9	9.00	1.00	

If the investigator is uncomfortable about getting a look at only part of the interaction, a scheme for confounding Blocks with interaction can be used in which both parts of the interaction can be looked at, but some economy can still be introduced. In this scheme, half the design is devoted to confounding Blocks with the first part of the interaction and testing the second part, and the other half of the design is devoted to testing the first part of the interaction and confounding Blocks with the second part. This design is shown in Table 16.15. The assessment of each portion of the interaction is only one-half as precise as it would be if we had tested only one portion and

confounded the other, but in this design we have balanced the confounding and not loaded it all on one part of the interaction. Notice this design has 18 cells, so it takes twice as many cells as our first confounded design but only two thirds of the 27 cell in the completely crossed design of Blocks x Diet x Amount of Sleep.

TABLE 16.15 DESIGN FOR ASSESSING BOTH PORTIONS OF THE CONFOUNDED INTERACTION

Diet	Amount of Sleep			Diet	Amount of Sleep		
	4	6	8		4	6	8
D_1	8	12	4	D_1	8	12	4
D_2	4	8	12	D_2	12	4	8
D_3	12	4	8	D_3	4	8	12

16.5   Fractional replication. In this section we will exemplify a design for an investigation where subjects are in such short supply or the cost of running them is so great that we can not even get one subject for each cell of the design. Consider an experiment in which the investigator wants to study the communication between mothers and their infants as a function of several variables. Of interest is (1) whether the mother is hard of hearing, (2) whether the infant is hard of hearing, (3) whether the child was born prematurely, (4) the gender of the infant, and (5) the age of the infant. Let us suppose that the experimenter uses only two values of each of these five variables. The full factorial design would require the $2^5 = 32$ cells shown in Table 16.16. It might be very hard to locate enough hard-of-hearing mothers and/or infants to fill in this design even with one subject per cell. A solution to this difficulty can be achieved by using only a fraction of the design. To illustrate this, we will need some additional notation and concepts, which I have freely borrowed from Cochran

TABLE 16.16 A DESIGN SUGGESTING FRACTIONAL REPLICATION

		Age of Infant			
		4 Months		10 Months	
		Premature Infant	Full Term Infant	Premature Infant	Full Term Infant
	Mother	Hard of Hearing / Normal	Hard of Hearing / Normal	Hard of Hearing / Normal	Hard of Hearing / Normal
Male	Hard of Hearing				
	Normal				
Fem.	Hard of Hearing				
	Normal				

TABLE 16.17 CELL NOTATION FOR THE 2^5 FACTORIAL DESIGN

		E_1				E_2			
		C_1		C_2		C_1		C_2	
		B_1	B_2	B_1	B_2	B_1	B_2	B_1	B_2
D_1	A_1	(1)	b	c	bc	e	be	ce	bce
	A_2	a	ab	ac	abc	ae	abe	ace	abce
D_2	A_1	d	bd	cd	bcd	de	bde	cde	bcde
	A_2	ad	abd	acd	abcd	ade	abde	acde	abcde

and Cox (1957).

16.5.1 Cell label notation. We can denote each cell in the 2^5 factorial design described above if we denote the five factors by the uppercase letters A, B, C, D, and E, and denote level 2 of each of these factors by the presence of the lowercase letters a, b, c, d, and e. We denote level 1 of each of the factors by the absence of the corresponding lower case letter. When we are at level 1 of all of the factors, we will denote it by (1). With this notation, the cells of the design are labeled as in Table 16.17. We will use these cell labels to denote cell means or cell totals, whichever we need.

16.5.2 Using cell label notation to define contrasts. We can use a handy device to specify any contrast of interest. Consider the expression

$$(a - 1)(b - 1)(c + 1)(d + 1)(e + 1)$$

which defines the contrast for the AB interaction if we let the cell notation stand for cell means in this context. Notice that a minus sign is used with a and b since A and B are the factors involved in the contrast of interest, and a plus sign is used with c, d, and e since C, D, and E are the factors not involved in that contrast. If we multiply this expression out, we get the contrast

abcde + abcd + abce + abde + abc + abd + abe + cde + ab + cd + ce + de + c + d

+ e + (1) - acde - bcde - acd - ace - ade - bcd - bde - bce - ac - ad - ae - bc - bd -

be - a - b.

The linear combination of cell means defining any other contrast is obtained in the same fashion using a minus sign if the factor is in the contrast and a plus sign if it is not. Thus the contrast for the effect of Factor A would be
$(a - 1)(b + 1)(c + 1)(d + 1)(e + 1)$ and that for the BCDE interaction would be
$(a + 1)(b - 1)(c - 1)(d - 1)(e - 1)$.

16.5.3 The defining contrast for the fractional replication. Each contrast divides the cell means into two groups: the ones that are added in the contrast and the ones that are subtracted. We can select any contrast and by using only the cells the means of which are added in the contrast, we thereby divide the design in half. If we use only those cells in our experimental design, we have created a design that is only one-half the original design. With one subject in each cell we have a **fractional replication design**. Almost always the contrast defining the highest-order interaction is used to create the fractional design when the object is to create a design with one-half the treatment combinations that occurred in the original design. This is because **no information will be obtained about the contrast used to divide the cells**, and the contrast for the highest-order interaction is usually the contrast of least interest. We will do this here, using the contrast for the ABCDE interaction $(a - 1)(b - 1)(c - 1)(d - 1)(e - 1)$. The cells with means having a

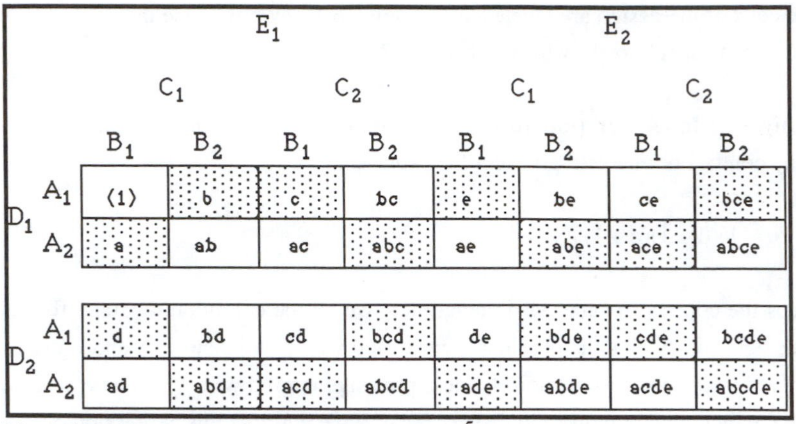

Figure 16.3. The shaded cells are the one-half of the 2^5 factorial design to be used in a fractional replication. The are defined by the ABCDE interaction contrast. See text.

plus sign in this contrast are the cells with one, three, or five letters in the cell label—that is: a, b, c, d, e, abc, abd, abe, acd, ace, ade, bcd, bce, bde, cde, and abcde.

16.5.4 Aliases in a half replicate of a 2^5 factorial design.

Let us consider the diagram of the 2^5 factorial design in Figure 16.3 in which we have shaded the cell to be used in the one-half of the design that will be our fractional replication. Suppose we wanted to perform the contrast for the effect of Factor A. Our intuition would suggest that the contrast should be a + abc + abe + ace + abd + acd + ade + abcde - b - c - e - bce - d - bcd - bde - cde, that is, a contrast of the cells with level 2 of Factor A versus the cells with level 1 of Factor A. And this would, of course, be the correct contrast.

Now suppose we wanted to perform the contrast for the BCDE interaction in this same fractional replication design. Our intuition might guide us as follows. We inspect the diagram for the BC interaction contrast at level 1 of D and level 1 of E, using only the shaded cells, of course. We would see that it is (a - b) - (c - abc). At level 2 of D and 1 of E it is (d - abd) - (acd - bcd). The difference [(a - b) - (c - abc)] - [(d - abd) - (acd - bcd)] is the BCD interaction contrast at level a of E. By similar reasoning we could determine that the BCD interaction contrast at level 2 of E is [(e - abe) - (ace - bce)] - [(ade - bde) - (cde - abcde)]. The difference between the BCD interaction contrast at level 1 of E and the BCD interaction contrast at level 2 of E is the BCDE interaction contrast {[(a - b) - (c - abc)] - [(d - abd) - (acd - bcd)]} - {[(e - abe) - (ace - bce)] - [(ade - bde) - (cde - abcde)]}.

If we compare the BCDE contrast with that for Factor A, we find that they are identical. Two such contrasts that are for different effects but are identical are referred to as **aliases**. The same contrast can go by two different names. Every contrast in our fractional replication design has an alias. **We can find the alias for any contrast by cancelling the factors in that contrast out of the expression ABCDE.** Thus, the alias for the AB contrast would be the CDE contrast. For the entire fractional replication we have

Contrast	Alias
A	BCDE
B	ACDE
C	ABDE
D	ABCE
E	ABCD
AB	CDE
AC	BDE
AD	BCE
AE	BCD
BC	ADE
BD	ACE
BE	ACD
CD	ABE
CE	ABD
DE	ABC

TABLE 16.18 FICTIONAL DATA FOR A FRACTIONAL REPLICATION

		Age of Infant							
		4 Months				10 Months			
		Premature Infant		Full Term Infant		Premature Infant		Full Term Infant	
	Mother	Hard of Hearing	Normal	Hard of Hearing	Normal	Hard of Hearing	Normal	Hard of Hearing	Normal
Male	Hard of Hearing		6	7		15			17
	Normal	4			8		23	12	
Fem.	Hard of Hearing	5			9		22	14	
	Normal		6	8		16			19

As we see, each contrast involving a single factor has an alias that is the contrast for a four-factor interaction. **Each single factor contrast is perfectly confounded with**

TABLE 16.19 ANOVA FOR THE ONE-HALF 2^5 FRACTIONAL REPLICATION DESIGN

Source	df	SS	MS	F
A	1	5.06	5.06	.43
B	1	52.56	52.56	4.48
C	1	.56	.56	.05
D	1	3.06	3.06	.26
E	1	451.56	451.56	38.47
AB	1	.56	.56	.05
AC	1	.56	.56	.05
AD	1	.56	.56	.05
AE	1	.56	.56	.05
BC	1	1.56	1.56	.13
BD	1	.56	.56	.05
BE	1	22.56	22.56	1.92
Error	3	35.22	11.74	

the contrast for its four-factor alias. Similarly, each two-factor contrast is perfectly confounded with its alias contrast, which in each case is a three-factor contrast. Therefore, in order to interpret a contrast as solely due to the effects of the factors in its label, it will always be necessary to assume that the contrast for its alias is zero.

We are now prepared to return to the analysis of our experiment on the communication between mothers and their infants.

16.6 Analyzing the fractional replication. Suppose somehow we managed to complete our fractional replication and the data are as shown in Table 16.18. Suppose also that we are willing to assume that Age of Infant (Factor E) does not interact with Gender of Infant (Factor D) or with Pregnancy Duration (Factor C). Nor does C interact with D. And the CDE interaction effects are also assumed to be zero. We also assume that no pair of these factors interacts with any other factor in the design and that all of the triple interaction effects are zero. Then we can perform and interpret the contrasts that test the effects of A, B, C, D, E, AB, AC, AD, AE, BC, BD, and BE, where A is Mother's Hearing Condition and B is Infant's Hearing Condition. We have three degrees of freedom that we can use for error. These are the degrees of freedom associated with CD (alias ABE), CE (alias ABD), and DE (alias ABC), (alias all of which we have assumed to be equal to zero and therefore will provide us with an estimate of error variance.

The sums of squares for the various sources are computed as the sums of squares for contrasts of the cell means. Since all of the sources of interest here are main effects or two-factor interactions, the values of the contrasts can be obtained virtually by inspection. Looking at the data, we see immediately that the

contrast for Factor E is $(4 + 6 + 7 + 8 + 5 + 6 + 8 + 9) - (15 + 23 + 12 + 17 + 16 + 22 + 14 + 19)$ just by assigning $+1$ as the coefficient for all the scores under E_1 and -1 for the others. For a two-factor interaction, say, AC, we assign $+1$ to all scores in A_1C_1 and A_2C_2 and -1 to the others. Thus $SS_{AC} = \{[(6 + 15 + 5 + 22) - (7 + 17 + 9 + 14)] - [(4 + 23 + 6 + 16) - (8 + 12 + 8 + 19)]\}^2/16 = .06$. The SS_{error} can then be obtained as a residual by subtracting the sums of squares for all of the various sources to be tested from $\Sigma_i\Sigma_j\Sigma_k\Sigma_l\Sigma_m Y_{ijklm}^2 - T^2/N = 2,855 - (191)^2/16 = 574.94$. The ANOVA for the sample data is shown in Table 16.19. No doubt we are disappointed to find only the Age of Infant to be a significant effect but this is unfortunately the usual fate of studies with very little power due to small numbers of degrees of freedom for error.

Exercises

1. Randomly permute the rows, columns, and levels of C in the 4 x 4 latin square diagram above. Verify that the latin square property is maintained.

2. For the case of one score per cell write out the X matrix of full rank using the model for the latin square as $Y_{ijk} = \mu + \alpha_i + \beta_j + \gamma_k + e_{ijk}$ with the restrictions that $\alpha_3 = -(\alpha_1 + \alpha_2)$, $\beta_3 = -(\beta_1 + \beta_2)$, and $\gamma_3 = -(\gamma_1 + \gamma_2)$. Verify that the spaces spanned by the column vectors for the three factors are mutually orthogonal.

3. Suppose you design a repeated measures experiment in which the subjects are to receive a sequence of four treatments, C_1, C_2, C_3, and C_4 on four consecutive trials. Suppose there are six Motivation Level groups of eight subjects. You want to assign two subject to every sequence. You also want the sequences for a given group to form a latin square and no more than two subjects in the experiment to receive the same sequence. This means you will need a different latin square for each group, and no sequence in any latin square may be the same as any sequence in any other latin square. The design will use all possible sequences of the stimuli, and those sequences will be partitioned into six groups of four, each group of four forming a latin square. We have Sequences nested in Motivation Level Groups and Subjects nested in Sequences. Motivation Level Groups, Sequences, and Subjects are crossed with Trials.

(a) Write out the six latin squares.

(b) Write the model equation and the ANOVA summary table showing Sources, df, sums of squares, and F-ratios.

4. Which variables are confounded in exercise 1?

5. What are the advantages and disadvantages of confounding in fractional replication?

6. What is the fundamental property of a latin square?

7. Write out the row, column, and cell level combinations for a Graeco-latin square involving four levels of four factors. Suggest an experiment in which such a design might be used.

Supplementary Readings

Cochran, W. G., & Cox, G. (1957). *Experimental designs*. (2nd ed.). New York: John Wiley

Keppel, G. (1991). *Design and analysis: A researcher's handbook* (3rd ed.). Englewood Cliffs, N. J.: Prentice-Hall.

Kirk, R. E. (1982). *Experimental designs: Procedures for the behavioral sciences* (2nd ed.). Monterey, Calif.: Brooks/Cole.

Answers to Exercises

CHAPTER 1

1. Experimental control reduces the noise level.

2. It relegates to a systematic source variation that would function as error.

3. More noise and possible confounding of extraneous variable with experimental variable.

4. All of the uncontrolled systematic and random effects in the experiment.

5. If the confounding is known, no conclusions can be drawn about the effect of the experimental variable. If the confounding is not known, the wrong conclusions may be drawn.

6. Because sequences would be confounded with all other individual difference variables.

7. They argue there is no obvious reason why the handy sample should differ from a random sample, or that other things being equal, the results would generalize to the population in mind.

8. (a) The sample variances are 0,1,4,1,0,1,4,1, and 0. They average to 12/9, but the population variance is 24/9.

(b) These values are 0,2,8,2,0,2,8,2, and 0, and they average to 24/9, the population variance.

(c) The standard deviation of the population is 1.633, but the average over all samples of the square root of the unbiased estimator of the population variance is 1.035. It is a biased estimator of the population standard deviation.

9. Yes. Because a very large sample will closely approximate the population in all of its characteristics except perhaps size.

10. $z = (31-25)/5 = 1.2$, which is not significant since a two-tailed .05 test requires a z of 1.96 or larger in absolute value.

11. $z = (30.75-25)/5/\sqrt{4} = 2.3 > 1.96$ is significant. Reject.

12. Let N be the number of scores in each population. Then $\mu_D = \Sigma D_j/N = \Sigma(Y_{1j} - Y_{2j})/N$ $= \Sigma Y_{1j}/N - \Sigma Y_{2j}/N = \mu_1 - \mu_2$. If $\mu_1 = \mu_2$ then $\mu_D = \mu_1 - \mu_2 = 0$.

15. The possible samples have 0, 1, 2, or 3 1's together with 3, 2, 1, or 0 2's. These give possible sample means of 6/3, 5/3, 4/3, or 3/3, which occur with probabilities 1/27, 6/27, 12/27, and 8/27. Hence the mean and variance of the sampling distribution are 1.33 and .074. The population distribution is 1,1,2; an example of a sample distribution is 1,1,1; and the sampling distribution of the mean assigns probabilities to the possible values of the sample mean: 3/3, 4/3, 5/3, and 6/3.

16. When the population variance is unknown. Because it provides the correct sampling distribution of the test statistic.

21. Section 1.26 gives $t = [(M_1 - M_2) - (\mu_1 - \mu_2)]/\sqrt{[\sigma^2_{est}(1/N_1 + 1/N_2)]}$ and substituting this into the form for the confidence interval in section 1.40 gives $Pr\{ (M_1 - M_2) - t_{critical}\sqrt{[\sigma^2_{est}(1/N_1 + 1/N_2)]} < \mu_1 - \mu_2 < (M_1 - M_2) + t_{critical}\sqrt{[\sigma^2_{est}(1/N_1 + 1/N_2)]} \} = .95$.

22. Reject the hypothesis if the confidence interval does not overlap zero.

23. (d) The sampling distribution of the sample mean will assign probabilities to different values but the variances of the sample mean for the two distributions will be the same.

24. (a) The possible values of X_{max} are 1, 2, 3 with probabilities 1/9, 3/9, and 5/9, respectively.

(b) 22/9

(c) $(58/9) - (22/9)2 = .469$

25. (a) X_{min} is 0 in every one of the nine possible samples except the one with all ones so the values are 0 and 1 with probabilities 8/9 and 1/9, respectively.

(b) 1/9

(c) $1/9 - (1/9)2 = 8/81$

26. (a) The two possible values of the sample variance are 0 and 1/4, and their probabilities of occurrence are each .5.

(b) 1/8

27. (a) The possible values of the sample range are 0, 1, 2, 3, and they occur, respectively, with probabilities 3/9, 2/9, 2/9, 2/9.

(b) 1.33

(c) $28/9 - (12/9)2 = 1.33$

28.   The confidence interval is $2 \pm 2.262(1.826)/\sqrt{10}$: .694 to 3.306. Since the interval does not overlap the value zero, the hypothesis that μ = zero is rejected at the .05 level.

29. $(3.667 - 8.375) \pm 2.131[1.64 (1/9 + 1/8)].5$ gives the confidence interval -6.034 to -3.382. Reject the hypothesis since the value 10 is not included in the interval.

CHAPTER 2

1. $E(SS_G) = E[\Sigma_i N_i(M_i - M)^2] = E[\Sigma_i(N_i M_i^2 + N_i M^2 - 2N_i M_i M)]$
$= E[\Sigma_i N_i M_i^2 + \Sigma_i N_i M^2 - 2M\Sigma_i N_i M_i] = E[\Sigma_i N_i M_i^2 + NM^2 - 2NM^2]$
$= E[\Sigma_i N_i M_i^2 - NM^2] = \Sigma_i N_i E(M_i^2) - NE(M^2)$. But $E(M_i^2) = \sigma^2/N_i + (\mu + \alpha_i)^2$ and $E(M^2)$
$= \sigma^2/N + \mu^2$ so we have $\Sigma_i N_i E(M_i^2) - NE(M^2) = \Sigma_i N_i[\sigma^2/N_i + (\mu + \alpha_i)^2] - N[\sigma^2/N + \mu^2] =$
$I\sigma^2 + \Sigma_i N_i(\mu + \alpha_i)^2 - \sigma^2 - N\mu^2] = (I - 1)\sigma^2 + \Sigma_i N_i(\mu^2 + 2\mu\alpha_i + \alpha_i^2) - N\mu^2 = (I - 1)\sigma^2 +$
$\Sigma_i N_i \alpha_i^2)$ since $\Sigma_i N_i \alpha_i = 0$.

2. $Y_{ij} = \mu + \alpha_i + e_{ij}$. (a) $\mu = 0$; (b) $\alpha_1 = \alpha_2 = \alpha_3$.

3. $(X - 15)^2/10$ or $\Sigma_i(X_i - 15)^2/10$.

4. The values are .889, .921, and .947. The greater are the denominator degrees of freedom, the greater is the probability that an obtained F statistic will be less than some chosen value.

5. For 10 degrees of freedom in the denominator and 2, 4, and 6 degrees of freedom in the numerator, the probability that F is less than 4 is .947, .966, and .974 respectively.

7. $F = 62.5/(50.5/9) = 11.139$.

8. The expected value is $N - 1$, which is the degrees of freedom for error. The variable SS_E/σ^2 is a chi-square variable, so its expected value is its degree of freedom.

10. (a) $Y_{ij} = \mu + \alpha_i + e_{ij}$; (b) $\alpha_1 = \alpha_2 = \alpha_3 = \alpha_4$; (c) df for drugs = 3, df for error = 16; mean square for drugs = 16,445, mean square for error = 360. $F = 45.68$ and $F_{critical} = 3.24$ so we reject the null hypothesis that the effect of each drug dosage is the same.

11. The critical value of t for 16 degrees of freedom is 2.120. We use Mean Square for error as σ^2_{est}. The confidence interval is therefore $(M10 - M20) - (M30 - M40) \pm 2.120\sqrt{[360(1/5 + 1/5 + 1/5 + 1/5)]} = -2 \pm 2.120\sqrt{288}$, giving the interval -37.96 to 33.96. Since this confidence interval includes zero, we do not reject the hypothesis that the difference $(\mu_{10} - \mu_{20})$ is equal to the difference $(\mu_{30} - \mu_{40})$.

16. See if the value of the statistic $\Sigma_i(Y_i - M)2/10$ is an improbable value for $\chi^2(N-1)$ using the table of the chi-square distribution.

17. We are given that $Pr(F < F_{critical}) = .95$, so, letting $MS_e = \Sigma_i(Y_i - M)^2/(N-1)$ we have
$Pr[N(M - \mu)^2/MS_e < F_{critical}] = .95$, so that
$Pr[(M - \mu)^2 < MS_e F_{critical}(1/N)] = Pr\{|(M - m)| < \sqrt{[MS_e F_{critical}(1/N)]}\} = .95$.
Hence, $Pr\{|(M - \sqrt{[MS_e F_{critical}(1/N)]} < \mu < M + \sqrt{[MS_e F_{critical}(1/N)]}\} = .95$.

18. NM^2 would increase to $N(M + 5)^2$ and the other terms would stay the same.

21. (a) $Y_i = e_i$; (b) $Y_i = \mu + e_i$.

22. Divide it by σ^2.

23. $52 + 30/10 = 28$.

25. $(4.7 - 8.1) \pm 2.101\sqrt{[(67/18)(1/10 + 1/10)]}$ gives the interval -5.21 to -1.59.

26. $SS_M = 426.67$, $SS_G = 10.7440$, $SS_E = 14.5893$.

27. (a) less than zero; (b) in between

28. You may reject, at the .05 significance level, the hypothesis that $\mu_1 - \mu_2 = 0$.

29. Error variance should be reduced, thereby reducing the denominator of the F-ratio and so increasing the size of F.

30. $E(X) = .5(10) + .5(5) = 7.5$; $E(Y) = .5(3) + .5(1) = 2$; $E(X)/E(Y) = 7.5/2 = 3.75$. $E(X/Y) = .25(10/3) + .25(10/1) + .25(5/3) + .25(5/1) = .25(20) = 5 \neq 3.75$.

CHAPTER 3

1. $\mathbf{X} + \mathbf{Y} = [3, 5, 6]$

2. $\mathbf{X} + \mathbf{Y} = [3, 5, 6, 8, 10]$

4. $-\mathbf{X} = [-1, -3, -5]$

5. $-\mathbf{X} = [-2, -4, 5, -6, 1]$

6. $\mathbf{0}$. A vector of zeroes.

7. (a) [8, 17, 19]; (b) [-4, -1, -11]; (c) [-2, -18, -2]; (d) [6, 14, 14]

8. (a) [4, -3, 25, -10, -11]; (b) [4, -9, -5, 14, -5];
    (c) [-12, 21, -15, -18, 21]; (d) [4, -4, 20, -6, -10].

9. 35

10. 27

11. 8

12. It will not. The vectors must be orthogonal.

13. 79

14. 45

15. 34

16. $79 \neq 20 + 39$

17. 0

18. 0

19. [0, 0, 0].

20. The zero vector

21. E.g., [-1, 0, 1]

24. $\mathbf{M} = [5, 5]$, $\mathbf{D} = [1, -1]$. $\mathbf{M}\cdot\mathbf{D} = [0, 0]$ so $\mathbf{M}$ and $\mathbf{D}$ are orthogonal.

27. Their sum must equal zero.

29. (a) $VAR(Y_i) = VAR(\mu + e_i) = VAR(\mu) + VAR(e_i) = 0 + \sigma^2$
    (b) $E(NM^2) = NE(M^2) = N(\mu^2 + \sigma^2/N) = Nm^2 + \sigma^2$

(c) $E\Sigma(Y_i - M)^2 = E\Sigma(Y_i^2 - 2Y_iM + M^2) = E(\Sigma Y_i^2 - 2NM^2 + NM^2) = E(\Sigma Y_i^2 - NM^2) =$
$\Sigma E(Y_i^2) - NE(M^2) = \Sigma(\mu^2 + \sigma^2) - NE(\mu^2 + \sigma^2/N) = N\mu^2 + N\sigma^2 - N\mu^2 - \sigma^2 = (N - 1)\sigma^2$

30. The expectation is over both i and j. $E(Y_{ij}) = \mu$ so $E[Y_{ij} - E(Y_{ij})]^2 =$
$E[\mu + \alpha_i + e_{ij} - \mu]^2 = E[\alpha_i + e_{ij}]^2 = E[\alpha_i^2 + 2\alpha_i e_{ij} + e_{ij}^2]$. The term drops out since the
α_i and the e_{ij} are independent of each other so that the expected value of their product is just
the product of their expected values, which is zero. Thus $E[\alpha_i^2 + 2\alpha_i e_{ij} + e_{ij}^2] = E[\alpha_i + e_{ij}]$
$= E(\alpha_i^2) + E(e_{ij}^2)$. The expected value of the α_i^2 is just the weighted average of the α_i^2,
$\Sigma N_i \alpha_i^2/N$ and $E(e_{ij}^2) = \sigma^2$ since the expected value of e_{ij} is zero.

31. A little algebra reduces $E[\Sigma_i\Sigma_j(M_i - M)^2]$ to $E[\Sigma_i N_i M_i^2 - NM^2]$. $E(M_i^2) = E(\mu + \alpha_i +$
$\Sigma_j e_{ij}/N_i)^2$. Since every cross-product involving an e_{ij} has an expectation of zero, this
becomes $E(\mu + \alpha_i)^2 + E(\Sigma_j e_{ij}^2/N_i) = (\mu + \alpha_i)^2 + \sigma^2/N_i$, using the fact that $E(e_{ij}^2) = \sigma^2$.
Therefore $E(\Sigma_i N_i M_i^2) = \Sigma_i N_i[(\mu + \alpha_i)^2 + \sigma^2/N_i] = \Sigma_i N_i(\mu + \alpha_i)^2 + I\sigma^2$. By similar
reasoning, $E(M^2) = \mu^2 + \sigma^2/N$. Combining these results algebraically and recalling that
$\Sigma_i N_i \alpha_i = 0$ gives the desired result.

32. $E[\Sigma_i\Sigma_j(Y_i - M_i)^2] = E\{\Sigma_i\Sigma_j[(\mu + \alpha_i + e_{ij} - (\mu + \alpha_i + \Sigma_j e_{ij}/N_i)]^2\} =$
$E\{\Sigma_i\Sigma_j[e_{ij} - \Sigma_j e_{ij}/N_i)]^2\} = E\{\Sigma_i\Sigma_j e_{ij}^2 - \Sigma_i N_i(\Sigma_j e_{ij}/N_i)^2]\} = (N - I)\sigma^2$.

33. The average α_i is zero since $\Sigma_i N_i \alpha_i = 0$. Since the variance of a variable is the average
square of the variable minus the square of the mean of the variable, we have immediately that
$Var(\alpha) = \Sigma_i N_i \alpha_i^2/N - 0 = \Sigma_i N_i \alpha_i^2/N$.

34. (a) N - 1. $V_1 = V_2 = ... = V_{N1} = V_{N1+1} = ... = V_{N1 + N2}$
(b) $N_1 - 1 + N_2 - 1$. $V_1 = V_2 = ... = V_{N1}, V_{N1+1} = ... = V_{N1 + N2}$
(c) 1. $\mathbf{D}\cdot\mathbf{\mu} = \mathbf{0}$

39. All the scores in Group 1 are equal and all the scores in Group 2 are equal.

40. (a) N; (b) 1; (c) N - 1; (d) N - 1; (e) N

41. 9. The vectors are linearly independent.

42. $a[1, 2, 2, 1] + b[2, 0, -2, 1]$

45. We know that the dimensionality of the space is N - 1 = 2 and that therefore at least N -
1 = 2 independent vectors are required to span the space.

46. For the first part, see the answer to exercise 45. We know that a vector of 1's is a
multiple of the vector **M** which is orthogonal to **D** and therefore cannot be a linear
combination of the vectors spanning **D** and is therefore independent of the vectors spanning
D.

48. Let the elements of the vector be V_1 to V_N. Then $M\Sigma_i V_i = 0$ is the equation.

CHAPTER 4

2. (a) 4.5, 6.5, 6.17, 8.83

(b) 5.88, 6.62, 7.00

(c) 3, 4, 6.5

  8, 7, 4.5

  5.5, 6, 7

  7, 9.5, 10

d) -2, 0, -.33, 2.33

(e) -.625, .125, .50

(f) -.875, -.625, 1.5

  2.125, .375, -2.5

  -.045, -.295, .33

  -1.21, .54, .67

3. -.5 and .5

4. A constant added to a curve of means simply displaces the curve upward or downward.

5. $\Sigma_i A_i = \Sigma_j B_j = \Sigma_i AB_{ij} = \Sigma_j AB_{ij} = 0$

$\Sigma_i A_i = \Sigma_j B_j = \Sigma_k C_k = \Sigma_i AB_{ij} = \Sigma_j AB_{ij} = \Sigma_i AC_{ik} = \Sigma_k AC_{ik} = \Sigma_j BC_{jk}$

$= \Sigma_k BC_{jk} =$

$\Sigma_i ABC_{ijk} = \Sigma_j ABC_{ijk} = \Sigma_k ABC_{ijk} = \Sigma_i \Sigma_j ABC_{ijk} = \Sigma_i \Sigma_k ABC_{ijk} = \Sigma_j \Sigma_k ABC_{ijk} = 0.$

6 (e) $BCD_{jkl} = \mu_{.jkl} - [\mu_{....} + (\mu_{.j..} - \mu_{....}) + (\mu_{..k.} - \mu_{....}) + (\mu_{...l} - \mu_{....}) + (\mu_{.jk.} - \mu_{.j..} - \mu_{..k.} + \mu_{....}) + (\mu_{.j.l} - \mu_{.j..} - \mu_{...l} + \mu_{....}) + (\mu_{..kl} - \mu_{..k.} - \mu_{...l} + \mu_{....})]$

7. μ_{ijk}.

8. (a) Yes; (b) Yes.

9. IJK - IJ - IK - JK + I + J + K - 1

11. The two-factor interactions at the several levels of the third factor average to a zero two-factor interaction.

13. 11.17 -[4.80 + (5.28 - 4.80) + (9.50 - 4.80)] = 1.19

20. (a) 6.83; (b) -.695; (c) 6.5 - (7.53 -.695 -1.61) = -.12; (d) 1.47

23. They should all be the same.

28. The part showing the Class effects.

29. The part showing the interaction effects.

CHAPTER 5

1. (a) The sum of squares is a squared length of a given vector and the degrees of freedom is the dimensionality of the space in which that vector is constrained to lie. A sum of squares composed of several pieces is the squared length of the sum of orthogonal vectors, and the degrees of freedom for those several pieces are the dimensionalities of the spaces in which those mutually orthogonal vectors lie, and the sum of those several degrees of

freedom is the dimensionality of the space in which the vector, which is the sum of the orthogonal vectors, lies.

(b) Subtraction of one sum of squares from another corresponds to subtraction of one vector from another that is orthogonal to it. The resulting vector must lie in a space smaller than the original space and orthogonal to the space in which the subtracted vector lies.

6. Girls:

Source	df	SS	MS	F
Age	1	21.025	21.025	7.22
Stimulus	3	918.275	306.092	105.10
A x S	3	390.875	130.292	44.74
Error	32	93.2		2.91

Boys:

Source	df	SS	MS	F
Age	1	38.025	38.025	19.75
Stimulus	3	1222.275	407.425	211.65
A x S	3	535.875	178.625	92.79
Error	32	61.6	1.92	

(a) Both the magnitude of the effects and the within-cells estimates of error variance differ between the two genders so the F-ratios do not turn out to be the same.

(b) A test of the Gender effect and of the interaction of gender with the other experimental variables.

7. (a) $IJKL - IJK - IJL - IKL - JKL + IJ + IK + IL + JK + JL + KL - I - J - K - L + 1$ degrees of freedom corresponds to the T-dot term $\Sigma_i\Sigma_j\Sigma_k\Sigma_l T2_{ijkl}/M - \Sigma_i\Sigma_j\Sigma_k T2_{ijk.}/LM - \Sigma_i\Sigma_j\Sigma_l T2_{ij.l}/KM - \Sigma_i\Sigma_k\Sigma_l T2_{i.kl}/JM - \Sigma_j\Sigma_k\Sigma_l T2_{.jkl}/IM + \Sigma_i\Sigma_j T2_{ij..}/KLM + \Sigma_i\Sigma_k T2_{i.k.}/JLM + \Sigma_i\Sigma_l T2_{i..l}/JKM + \Sigma_j\Sigma_k T2_{.jk.}/IK + \Sigma_j\Sigma_l T2_{.j.l}/IKM + \Sigma_k\Sigma_l T2_{..kl}/IJM - \Sigma_i T2_{i...}/JKLM - \Sigma_j T2_{.j..}/IKLM - \Sigma_k T2_{..k.}/IJLM - \Sigma_l T2_{...l}/IJKM + T2/IJKLM$

(b) $I(J - 1)$ corresponds to $\Sigma_i\Sigma_j T2_{ij.}/K - \Sigma_i T2_{i..}/JK$

9.

Model Term	Source	df	SS	MS	F
μ	Mean	1	4440.83	4440.83	1352.54
$\mu_{i..}-\mu_{i..}$	Word Type	1	140.83	140.83	42.89
$\mu_{i..}-\mu_{i..}$	List Length	2	88.47	44.23	13.47
$\mu_{ij.}-\mu_{i..}-\mu_{.j.}+\mu$	Type x Length	2	4.07	2.03	.62
$Y_{ijk}-\mu_{ij.}$	Error	24	78.80	3.28	
Y_{ijk}	Total	30	4753		

11.

Model Term	Source	df	SS	MS	F

μ	Mean	1	4161.60	4161.6	1140.16
$\mu_{i..}-\mu_{i..}$	Age	1	6.4	6.4	1.75
$\mu_{i..}-\mu_{i..}$	Stimulus	3	224.60	74.87	20.51
$\mu_{ij.}-\mu_{i..}-\mu_{.j.}+\mu$	Age x Stimulus	3	384.60	128.2	35.12
$Y_{ijk}-\mu_{ij.}$	Error	32	116.80	3.65	
Y_{ijk}	Total	40	4894		

12. (a) IJ, $\Sigma_i\Sigma_j T^2_{ij.}/K$

(b) I, $\Sigma_i T^2_{i..}/JK$

(c) 1, T^2/IJK (assuming a two-factor design)

(d) IJK, $\Sigma_i\Sigma_j\Sigma_k T^2_{ijk..}/MN$

(e) IK, $\Sigma_i\Sigma_k T^2_{i.k.}/JM$

13. $SS_A = 4.17$, $SS_C = 9.77$, $SS_{AB} = .33$, $SS_{AC} = 1.52$, $SS_{ABC} = 1.48$

14. The sum of the squares of all of the scores.

15. $T_{1...} = 153$, $T_{.3..} = 77$, $T_{23..} = 36$, $T_{223.} = 12$

16. (a) IJKM - IJK - IJM - IKM - JKM + IJ + IK + IM + JK + JM + KM - I - J - K - M + 1, etc.

(b) IJKMN - IJKM - IJKN - IJMN - JKMN - IKMN + IJK + IJM + IJN + IKM + IKN + JKM + JKN + KMN + IMN + JMN - IJ - IK - IM - IN - JK - JM - JN - KM - KN - MN +I + J + K + M + N - 1

17. $\Sigma_i\Sigma_j\Sigma_k\Sigma_m T^2_{ijkm.}/N - \Sigma_i\Sigma_j\Sigma_k T^2_{ijk..}/MN - \Sigma_i\Sigma_j\Sigma_m T^2_{ij.m.}/KN - \Sigma_i\Sigma_k\Sigma_m T^2_{i.km.}/JN - \Sigma_j\Sigma_k\Sigma_m T^2_{.jkm.}/IN + \Sigma_i\Sigma_j T^2_{ij...}/KMN \ \Sigma_i\Sigma_k T^2_{i.k..}/JMN + \Sigma_i\Sigma_m T^2_{i..m.}/JKN + \Sigma_j\Sigma_k T^2_{.jk..}/IMN + \Sigma_j\Sigma_m T^2_{.j.m.}/IKN + \Sigma_k\Sigma_m T^2_{..km.}/IJN \ \Sigma_i T^2_{i....}/JKMN - \Sigma_j T^2_{.j...}/IKMN - \Sigma_k T^2_{..k..}/IJMN - \Sigma_m T^2_{...m.}/IJKN + T^2/IJKMN$

CHAPTER 6

1. (a) $Y_{ijkm} = \mu + T_i + A_{j(i)} + S_k + TS_{ik} + AS_{j(i)k} + e_{ijkm}$

(b)

Mean	1	$T^2/IJKM$
Teaching Method	I - 1	$\Sigma_i T^2_{i...}/JKM - T^2/IJKM$
Age	I(J - 1)	$\Sigma_i\Sigma_j T^2_{ij..}/KM - \Sigma_i T^2_{i...}/JK$
Sex	K - 1	$\Sigma_k T^2_{..k.}/IJM - T^2/IJKM$
TM x S	IK - I - K + 1	$\Sigma_i\Sigma_k T^2_{i.k.}/JM - \Sigma_i T^2_{i...}/JKM$
		$- \Sigma_k T^2_{..k.}/IJM + T^2/IJKM$
A x S	IJK - IJ - IK + I	$\Sigma_i\Sigma_j\Sigma_k T^2_{ijk.}/M - \Sigma_i\Sigma_j T^2_{ij..}/KM$
		$-\Sigma_i\Sigma_k T^2_{i.k.}/JM + \Sigma_i T^2_{i...}/JKM$
Error	IJKM - IJK	$\Sigma_i\Sigma_j\Sigma_k\Sigma_m Y^2_{ijkm} - \Sigma_i\Sigma_j\Sigma_k T^2_{ijk.}/M$
Total	IJKM	$\Sigma_i\Sigma_j\Sigma_k\Sigma_m Y^2_{ijkm}$

3.

Mean	1	63996	63996	3341
Professor	2	694.04	347	18.12
TA	6	969.60	161.6	8.44
Error	36	689.60	19.16	
Total	45	66349		

5. No possibility of assessing the interaction since it is completely confounded with the Teaching Assistants effect.

6. IJKM, 1, I - 1, I(J - 1), IJ(K - 1), M - 1, (I - 1)(M - 1), I(J - 1)(M - 1), IJ(K - 1)(M - 1), 0

7. The model equation is: $Y_{ijkmno} = \mu + A_i + B_j + C_k + D_{m(i,j,k)} + E_{n(i,j,k,m)} + AB_{ij} + AC_{ik} + BC_{jk} + ABC_{ijk} + e_{ijkmno}$. The df are: IJKMNO, 1, I - 1, J - 1, K - 1, IJK(M - 1), IJKM(N - 1), (I -1)(J - 1), (I - 1)(K - 1), (J - 1)(K - 1), (I - 1)(J - 1)(K - 1), and IJKMNO - IJKMN.

8. The model equation is: $Y_{ijkmno} = \mu + A_i + B_j + C_{k(i,j)} + D_m + E_{n(m)} + AB_{ij} + AD_{im} + BD_{jm} + CD_{k(i,j)m} + AE_{in(m)} + BE_{jm} + CE_{k(i,j)n(m)} + ABD_{ijm} + ABE_{ijn(m)} + e_{ijkmno}$. The df are: IJKMNO, 1, I - 1, J - 1, IJ(K - 1), M - 1, M(N - 1), (I - 1)(J - 1), (I - 1)(M - 1), (J - 1)(M - 1), IJ(K - 1)(M - 1),M(I - 1)(N - 1), (J - 1)(M - 1), IJM(K - 1)(N - 1), (I - 1)(J - 1)(M - 1),

M(I - 1)(J - 1)(N - 1), IJKMNO - IJKMN.

11. (a) A is crossed with B, C, D and E. B is crossed with C and D. D is nested in C. E is nested in C and in D.

(b) B is nested in A, C is nested in A and B, D is nested in A, B, and C.

(c) B is nested in A, A is crossed with C and B is crossed with C.

(d) A is crossed with C and with D, B is nested in A, D is nested in C, B is crossed with C, and B is crossed with D.

13. (a) $Y_{ijk} = \mu + T_i + L_{j(i)} + e_{ijk}$

14 (a) See the model equation in question 11(d).

(b)

Mean	1
A	2
B	3
C	1
D	4
AC	2
AD	8
BC	3
BD	12
Error	108

Total 144

15. Crossed with.

17. B is nested in A, C is nested in E, A is crossed with C, D and E, B is crossed with C, D, and E, C is crossed with D and D is crossed with E.

18.

Mean	1
A	I - 1
B	I(J - 1)
C	N(K - 1)
D	M - 1
E	N - 1
AC	N(I - 1)(K - 1)
AD	(I - 1)(M - 1)
AE	(I - 1)(N - 1)
BC	IN(J - 10(K - 1)
BD	I(J - 1)(M - 1)
BE	I(J - 1)(N - 1)
CD	N(K - 1)(M - 1)
DE	(M - 1)(N - 1)
ACD	N(I - 1)(K - 1)(M - 1)
ADE	(I - 1)(M - 1)(N - 1)
BCD	IN(J - 1)(K - 1)(M - 1)
BDE	I(J - 1)(M - 1)(N - 1)
ACDE	N(I - 1)(K - 1)(M - 1)(N - 1)
BCDE	IN(J - 1)(K - 1)(M - 1)(N - 1)
Error	IJKMNO - IJKMN

CHAPTER 7

2.

Source	E(MS)
A	$JKMN\sigma^2 A + JMN\sigma^2 AC + N\sigma^2 AD + \sigma^2_e$
B	$IKMN\sigma^2 B + IN\sigma^2 D + IMN\sigma^2 BC + \sigma^2_e$
C	$IJMN\sigma^2 C + IN\sigma^2 D + \sigma^2_e$
D	$IN\sigma^2 D + \sigma^2_e$
AB	$KMN\sigma^2 AB + N\sigma^2 AD + MN\sigma^2 ABC + \sigma^2_e$
AC	$JMN\sigma^2 AC + N\sigma^2 AD + \sigma^2_e$
AD	$N\sigma^2 AD + \sigma^2_e$
BC	$IMN\sigma^2 BC + IN\sigma^2 D + \sigma^2_e$
ABC	$MN\sigma^2 ABC + N\sigma^2 AD + \sigma^2_e$

Error σ^2_e

3. Source   E(MS)

Source	E(MS)
A	$JKM\sigma^2_A + KM\sigma^2_{AB} + JM\sigma^2_{AC} + \sigma^2_e$
B	$IKM\sigma^2_B + IM\sigma^2_{BC} + \sigma^2_e$
C	$IJM\sigma^2_C + IM\sigma^2_{BC} + \sigma^2_e$
AB	$KM\sigma^2_{AB} + M\sigma^2_{ABC} + \sigma^2_e$
AC	$JM\sigma^2_{AC} + M\sigma^2_{ABC} + \sigma^2_e$
BC	$IM\sigma^2_{BC} + \sigma^2_e$
ABC	$M\sigma^2_{ABC} + \sigma^2_e$
Error	σ^2_e

4. Source   E(MS)

Source	E(MS)
A	$JKM\sigma^2_A + \sigma^2_e$
B	$IKM\sigma^2_B + KM\sigma^2_{AB} + \sigma^2_e$
C	$IJM\sigma^2_C + JM\sigma^2_{AC} + \sigma^2_e$
AB	$KM\sigma^2_{AB} + \sigma^2_e$
AC	$JM\sigma^2_{AC} + \sigma^2_e$
BC	$IM\sigma^2_{BC} + M\sigma^2_{ABC} + \sigma^2_e$
ABC	$M\sigma^2_{ABC} + \sigma^2_e$
Error	σ^2_e

5. (a) 120

(b) $Y_{ijk} = \mu + L_i + d_{j(i)} + s_{k(i,j)}$

(c)

Source	E(MS)
Learning tasks (L)	$JK\sigma^2_L + K\sigma^2_D + \sigma^2_S$
Drugs in Tasks(D)	$K\sigma^2_D + \sigma^2_S$
Subjects	σ^2_S

(d) Mean Square for Drugs nested in Learning Tasks

(e) Mean Square for Subjects nested in Drugs

6. Mean Square for the B x C interaction

7.

Source	F-Ratio
A	$MS_A/(MS_{AB} + MS_{AC} - MS_{ABC})$;
B	$MS_B/(MS_{AB} + MS_{BC} - MS_{ABC})$;
C	$MS_C/(MS_{AC} + MS_{BC} - MS_{ABC})$;

D	MS_D/MS_{AD}
AB	MS_{AB}/MS_{ABC}
AC	MS_{AC}/MS_{ABC}
AD	MS_{AD}/MS_e
BC	$MS_{BC}/(MS_{ABC} + MS_{AD} - MS_e)$;
ABC	MS_{ABC}/MS_{AD}

8.

Source	df	SS	MS	F
Gender	1	42.05	42.05	6.69
Age	1	57.80	57.80	.19
Stimulus	3	2121.70	707.20	292.4
GxA	1	1.25	1.25	.17
GxS	3	18.85	6.28	2.60
AxS	3	904.30	301.40	124.60
GxAxS	3	22.45	7.48	3.09
Error	64	154.80	2.42	
Total	80	14652		

9. (a)

Source	df	SS	MS	F	Test
A	2	15.19	7.60	14.78	A vs. AD
B	1	48.35	48.35	12.57	B vs. D
C	1	42.01	42.01	10.92	C vs. D
D	8	30.78	3.85	2.45	D vs. error
AB	2	15.53	7.76	15.11	AB vs AD
AC	2	6.03	3.01	5.86	AC vs. AD
AD	16	8.22	.51	.33	AD vs. error
BC	1	.68	.68	.18	BC vs. D
ABC	2	.36	.18	.12	ABC vs. error
Error	36	56.50	1.57		
Total	72	2347			

(b)

Source	E(MS)
A	$JKMN\sigma^2_A + N\sigma^2_{AD} + \sigma^2_e$
B	$IKMN\sigma^2_B + IN\sigma^2_D + \sigma^2_e$
C	$IJMN\sigma^2_C + IN\sigma^2_D + \sigma^2_e$
D	$IN\sigma^2_D + \sigma^2_e$

AB	$KMN\sigma^2_{AB} + N\sigma^2_{AD} + \sigma^2_e$
AC	$JMN\sigma^2_{AC} + N\sigma^2_{AD} + \sigma^2_e$
AD	$N\sigma^2_{AD} + \sigma^2_e$
BC	$IMN\sigma^2_{BC} + IN\sigma^2_D + \sigma^2_e$
ABC	$MN\sigma^2_{ABC} + \sigma^2_e$
Error	σ^2_e

10. (a) Grades are fixed effects; Schools, Classroom nested in Grades, and Children are random effects.

(b) Grades are crossed with Schools; Classrooms are nested in Grades and in Schools, and Children are nested in Classrooms and therefore in Grades and Schools as well.

(c) Let P represent schools; G, Grades; C, Classrooms, and S, Children. $Y_{ijkm} = \mu + p_j + c_{k(i,j)} + s_{m(i,j,k)} + pG_{ij} + e_{ijkm}$.

11.

Source	df	SS	MS	F	Test
Type	2	6329.23	3164.62	24.86	Type vs. Sequence
Sequence	9	1145.90	127.32	2.42	Sequence vs. Subjects
Subjects	48	2525.60	52.62		
Total	60	3014292			

12.

Source	df	SS	MS	F	Test
Sequence	11	7475.13	679.56	12.92	Sequence vs. Subjects
Subjects	48	2525.60	52.62		
Total	60	3014292			

Inspection of the ANOVAs in exercise 11 and this problem shows that the sum of squares for Sequence in this problem contains both SS_{Type} and $SS_{Sequence}$ used in exercise 11. The df are also combined.

CHAPTER 8

1. In [8.1], Subjects are Between and the rest are Within. In [8.2], Subjects and D are Between, the rest are Within. In [8.3], Subjects, D, E, and DxE are Between, the rest are Within.

2. $Y_{ijkmn} = \mu + D_k + E_m + DE_{km} + s_{n(k,m)} + A_i + AD_{ik} + AE_{im} + ADE_{ikm} + As_{in(k,m)} + B_j + BD_{jk} + BE_{jm} + BDE_{jkm} + Bs_{jn(k,m)} + + AB_{ij} + ABD_{ijk} + ABE_{ijm} + ABDE_{ijkm} + ABs_{ijn(k,m)} + e_{ijkmn}$. Subjects, D, E, and DxE are Between, the rest are Within.

4.

Source	E(MS)
D	$IJKNP\sigma^2_D + IJK\sigma^2_S + \sigma^2_e$
E	$IJKMP\sigma^2_E + IJK\sigma^2_S + \sigma^2_e$
DE	$IJP\sigma^2_{DE} + IJK\sigma^2_S + \sigma^2_e$
S	$IJK\sigma^2_S + \sigma^2_e$
A	$JKMNP\sigma^2_A + JK\sigma^2_{AS} + \sigma^2_e$
AD	$JKNP\sigma^2_{AD} + JK\sigma^2_{AS} + \sigma^2_e$
AE	$JKMP\sigma^2_{AD} + JK\sigma^2_{AS} + \sigma^2_e$
ADE	$JKP\sigma^2_{ADE} + JK\sigma^2_{AS} + \sigma^2_e$
AS	$JK\sigma^2_{AS} + \sigma^2_e$
B	$IKMNP\sigma^2_B + IK\sigma^2_{BS} + \sigma^2_e$
BD	$IKNP\sigma^2_{BD} + IK\sigma^2_{BS} + \sigma^2_e$
BE	$IKMP\sigma^2_{DB} + IK\sigma^2_{BS} + \sigma^2_e$
BDE	$IKP\sigma^2_{BDE} + IK\sigma^2_{BS} + \sigma^2_e$
BS	$IK\sigma^2_{BS} + \sigma^2_e$
C	$IJMNP\sigma^2_C + IJ\sigma^2_{CS} + \sigma^2_e$
CD	$IJNP\sigma^2_{CD} + IJ\sigma^2_{CS} + \sigma^2_e$
CE	$IJMP\sigma^2_{CD} + IJ\sigma^2_{CS} + \sigma^2_e$
CDE	$IJP\sigma^2_{CDE} + IJ\sigma^2_{CS} + \sigma^2_e$
CS	$IJ\sigma^2_{CS} + \sigma^2_e$
AB	$KMNP\sigma^2_{AB} + K\sigma^2_{ABS} + \sigma^2_e$
ABD	$KNP\sigma^2_{ABD} + K\sigma^2_{ABS} + \sigma^2_e$
ABE	$KMP\sigma^2_{ABD} + K\sigma^2_{ABS} + \sigma^2_e$
ABDE	$KP\sigma^2_{ABDE} + K\sigma^2_{ABS} + \sigma^2_e$
ABS	$K\sigma^2_{ABS} + \sigma^2_e$
AC	$JMNP\sigma^2_{AC} + J\sigma^2_{ACS} + \sigma^2_e$
ACD	$JNP\sigma^2_{ACD} + J\sigma^2_{ACS} + \sigma^2_e$
ACE	$JMP\sigma^2_{ACD} + J\sigma^2_{ACS} + \sigma^2_e$
ACDE	$JP\sigma^2_{ACDE} + J\sigma^2_{ACS} + \sigma^2_e$
ACS	$J\sigma^2_{ACS} + \sigma^2_e$
ABC	$MNP\sigma^2_{ABC} + \sigma^2_{ABCS} + \sigma^2_e$
ABCD	$NP\sigma^2_{ABCD} + \sigma^2_{ABCS} + \sigma^2_e$
ABCE	$MP\sigma^2_{ABCD} + \sigma^2_{ABCS} + \sigma^2_e$
ABCDE	$P\sigma^2_{ABCDE} + \sigma^2_{ABCS} + \sigma^2_e$

ABCS	$\sigma^2_{ABCS} + \sigma^2_e$
ERROR	σ^2_e

5.

Source	df
D	M - 1
E	N - 1
DE	(M - 1)(N - 1)
S	MN(P - 1)
A	(I - 1)
AD	(I - 1)(M - 1)
AE	(I - 1)(N - 1)
ADE	(I - 1)(M - 1)(N - 1)
AS	MN(I - 1)(P - 1)
B	(J - 1)
BD	(J - 1)(M - 1)
BE	(J - 1)(N - 1)
BDE	(J - 1)(M - 1)(N - 1)
BS	MN(J - 1)(P - 1)
C	(K - 1)
CD	(K - 1)(M - 1)
CE	(K - 1)(N - 1)
CDE	(K - 1)(M - 1)(N - 1)
CS	MN(K - 1)(P - 1)
AB	(I - 1)(J - 1)
ABD	(I - 1)(J - 1)(M - 1)
ABE	(I - 1)(J - 1)(N - 1)
ABDE	(I - 1)(J - 1)(M - 1)(N - 1)
ABS	MN(I - 1)(J - 1)(P - 1)
AC	(I - 1)(K - 1)
ACD	(I - 1)(K - 1)(M - 1)
ACE	(I - 1)(K - 1)(N - 1)
ACDE	(I - 1)(K - 1)(M - 1)(N - 1)
ACS	MN(I - 1)(K - 1)(P - 1)
ABC	(I - 1)(J - 1)(K - 1)
ABCD	(I - 1)(J - 1)(K - 1)(M - 1)
ABCE	(I - 1)(J - 1)(K - 1)(N - 1)
ABCDE	(I - 1)(J - 1)(K - 1)(M - 1)(N - 1)

ABCS $MN(I - 1)(J - 1)(K - 1)(P - 1)$

7. (a) $Y_{ijkm} = \mu + A_i + B_j + C_k + s_{m(j,k)} + AB_{ij} + AC_{ik} + BC_{jk} + ABC_{ijk} + As_{im(j,k)} + e_{ijkm}$

(b) B, C, BC and Subjects are Between. The rest are Within.

(c) The answer is actually quite complex and a case can be made for each of several choices. The Diet x Tumor Condition interaction in Block 6 could be used. Slope scores (see Chapter 10) could be used but the different initial levels complicate this. On the other hand, inspection of the data suggests a clear effect o diet on the Tumor rats.

(d) A test of the linear trend in the Blocks variable (see Chapter 10). Until you get to that chapter your best bet is the test of the Blocks effect, but see part (f) for a problem here.

(f) The order of the two food types is confounded with Block number. Yes. Perhaps the question is best addressed by using only the C-21 Control subjects to test whether food intake declined.

8. (a) 2.2   .95   -.6

     .95   1.7   -.1

     -.6   -.1   1.3

(b) 2,8 and 1,4

(c) 1.63 and 6.54 so use 1 and 6.

10. (a) $Y_{ijk} = \mu + A_i + B_j + s_k + AB_{ij} + As_{ik} + Bs_{jk} + ABs_{ijk} + e_{ijkm}$

(b)

Source	df	SS	MS	F
Mean	1	27.57		
Subjects	4	27.57		
R	2	.28	.14	2031
RxS	8	.00055	.000069	
D	3	.49	.16	3796
DxS	12	.00052	.000043	
RxD	6	.012	.0020	17.33
RxDxS	24	.0028	.00011	

11. (a) $Y_{ijkmn} = \mu + G_i + A_j + GA_{ij} + s_{n(i,j)} + D_k + GD_{ik} + AD_{jk} + GAD_{ijk} + C_m + GC_{im} + AC_{jm} + GAC_{ijm} + Cs_{mn(i,j)} + DC_{km} + GDC_{ikm} + ADC_{jkm} + GADC_{ijkm} + DCs_{kmn(i,j)} + e_{ijkmn}$

(b) - (f) Bowey collected 4 scores for each of the 96 subjects giving 384 scores. Your various answers should conform to the following ANOVA table except that you may have chosen to omit the Mean as a source:

Source	df	SS	MS	F
Between	96			
Mean	1	44.00		
Grade(G)	1	2.34	2.34	6.55
Skill(A)	1	12.23	12.23	34.28
GxA	1	.56	.56	1.57
Within	288			
Difficulty(D)	1	.15	.15	72.79
GxD	1	.77	.77	4.14
AxD	1	3.16	3.16	16.93
GxAxD	1	.03	.03	14.67
DxS	92	.19	.002	
Context(C)	1	.28	.28	2.27
GxC	1	.15	.15	1.21
AxC	1	.50	.50	4.11
GxAxC	1	.15	.15	1.21
CxS	92	11.2	.12	
DxC	1	.15	.15	1.68
GxDxC	1	.00088	.00088	.01
AxDxC	1	.15	.15	1.68
GxAxDxC	1	.033	.033	.38
DxCxS	92	8.06	.088	

12. (a) Subjects are nested in the cross of Gender with Age. All other relations between factors are crosses.

(b) Subjects, Gender, Age, and Gender x Age are Between Subjects factors; the rest are Within.

(c)

Source	df	SS	MS	F
Between	19			
Gender(G)	1	42.05	42.05	13.17
Age(A)		57.80	57.80	18.10
GxA	1	1.25	1.25	.39
Subjects(S)	16	51.10	3.19	
Within	60			
Stimulus(D)	3	2121.70	707.23	327.36
GxD	3	18.85	6.28	2.91
AxD	3	904.30	301.43	139.53
GxAxD	3	22.45	7.48	3.46

DxS	48	103.70	2.16
Total	80	14652	

(d) This design uses only one-fourth the number of subjects used in the Chapter 7, exercise 8 design. Also it is more sensitive to stimulus effects since these effects are compared within subjects.

13. (a) Subjects are nested in Stimulus Types.

(b) Sequences are crossed with Stimulus Types.

(c) Subjects are crossed with Sequences.

(d) Subjects and Stimulus Types are Between; the others are within.

(e) $Y_{ijk} = \mu + A_i + s_{j(i)} + B_k + AB_{ik} + Bs_{kj(i)} + e_{ijk}$.

(f)

Source	df	SS	MS	F
Between	15			
Condition(C)	2	6329.23	3165	106.8
Subjects(S)	12	355.50	29.63	
Within	45			
Sequence(Q)	3	211.80	70.60	1.01
QxC	6	934.10	155.70	2.22
QxCxS	36	2525.60		
Total	60	3014292		

14. (a) $Y_{ijkmn} = \mu + B_j + C_k + BC_{jk} + D_{m(j,k)} + A_i + AB_{ij} + AC_{ik} + ABC_{ijk} + AD_{im(j,k)} + e_{ijkmn}$

(b)

Source	df	SS	MS	F	Test
Between					
B	1	48.35	48.35	12.57	B vs. D
C	1	42.01	42.01	10.92	C vs. D
BC	1	.68	.68	.18	BC vs. D
D	8	30.78	3.85	2.45	D vs. error
Within					
A	2	15.19	7.60	14.78	A vs. AD
AB	2	15.53	7.76	15.11	AB vs AD
AC	2	6.03	3.01	5.86	AC vs. AD
ABC	2	.36	.18	.35	ABC vs. AD
AD	16	8.22	.51	.33	AD vs. error

Error   36   56.50   1.57

Total   72   2347

15. (a) Let A be Instruction Sets, B be Conditions, C be Treatments, D be Motivation Level, and S be Subjects. $Y_{ijkmn} = \mu + A_i + B_j + D_m + AB_{ij} + BD_{jm} + AD_{im} + ABD_{ijm} + S_{n(i,j,m)} + C_k + AC_{ik} + BC_{jk} + CD_{km} + ABC_{ijk} + ACD_{ikm} + BCD_{jkm} + ABCD_{ijkm} + CS_{kn(i,j,m)}$

(b) - (d) follow straightforwardly from the model equation.

16. (a) $Y_{ijkmno} = \mu + B_j + C_k + BC_{jk} + D_{m(j,k)} + A_i + AB_{ij} + AC_{ik} + ABC_{ijk} + AD_{im(j,k)} + T_n + TB_{nj} + TC_{nk} + TBC_{njk} + TD_{nm(j,k)} + AT_{in} + ATB_{nj} + ATC_{ink} + ATBC_{injk} + ATD_{inm(j,k)} + e_{ijkmno}$

(b)

Source	df
Between	
B	1
C	1
BC	1
D	8
Within	
A	2
AB	2
AC	2
ABC	2
AD	16
T	1
TB	1
TC	1
TBC	1
TD	8
AT	2
ATB	2
ATC	2
ATBC	2
ATD	16
Error	72
Total	144

17. (a) $Y_{ijk} = \mu + T_i + L_j + TL_{ij} + s_k + Ts_{ik} + Ls_{jk} + TLs_{ijk} + e_{ijk}$

(b)

Source	df	SS	MS	F
Subjects(S)	4	6.00		
Type(T)	1	140.80	140.80	30.18
TxS	4	18.67	4.67	
Length(L)	2	88.47	44.23	7.34
LxS	8	48.20	6.02	
TxL	2	4.07	2.03	
TxLxS	8	5.93	.74	
Total	30	4753.00		

CHAPTER 9

(Note that some of the answers given were calculated based on terms taken to more decimal places than the constituent terms shown, so that the given answer will not precisely agree with the calculation based on the parts shown to only two decimal places.)

1. (a) Using for each subject the total under A_1 and A_4 minus the total under A_2 and A_4 and testing the mean of these contrast scores gives $F = 1682/(1784 - 1682)/7 = 115$ on 1 and 7 df.

(b) Obtaining a contrast score at each level of B and testing for the B effect gives

Source	df	SS	MS	F
Subjects	7	34		
B	2	5.08	2.54	1.26
BxS	14	28.25	2.02	
Total	24	628		

(c) $\{ [(-4.25 -5.38)/2 - (-4.88)]2 - 0\}/[2.02(1/4 + 1/4 + 1)] = .0014 = F.$

(d) Obtaining a contrast score at each level of A and testing for the A effect gives

Source	df	SS	MS	F
Subjects	7	10.49		
A	3	100.40	33.50	39.51
AxS	21	17.79	.85	
Total	32	250.75		

3. (a) The four subjects have mean contrast scores of -.33, .60, .69, and .36. The ANOVA is

Source	df	SS	MS	F
Mean	1	.44	.44	2.03
Error	3	.65	.22	

Total	4	1.09	

(b) Analyzing the contrast scores of the contrast scores gives

Source	df	SS	MS	F
Mean	1	7.72	7.72	.76
Error	3	30.39	10.13	
Total	4	38.10		

(c) Testing the C effect for the contrast scores gives

Source	df	SS	MS	F
C	2	2.94	1.47	.28
S	3	1.94	.65	
CxS	6	31.09	5.18	
Total	12	37		

(d) The four contrast x contrast x contrast scores are .25, -7.92, 11.25, and -2.58. The ANOVA is

Source	df	SS	MS	F
Mean	1	.25	.25	.004
Error	3	195.72	65.24	
Total	4	195.970		

4. $F = [(42.33 + 32.73)/2 - 38.07]2/[19.16(1.5)/15] = .15$ on 1 and 36 df

5. Using linear interpolation between $F_{1,30,.05}$ and $F_{1,40,.05}$ to get $F_{1,36,.05} = 4.12$, the interval is $-.53 \pm \sqrt{[4.12(1.5/15)19.16]}$ giving -3.34 to 2.28.

6. (a) $F_{1,80} = 3.032/[1.24(6/9)/20] = 222.42$

(b) $F_{1,80} = 5.252/[1.24(4/4)/20] = 445.16$

(c) $F_{1,80} = \{[(18.4 - 10) - (9.0 - 9.1)] - [(21.5 - 20.2) - (19.3 - 20.0)]\}^2/[1.24(8/10)] = 42.65$

(d) $F_{1,80} = \{[(18.0 - 11.8) - (12.8 - 13.0)] - [(20.0 - 19.2) - (18.8 - 21.8)]\}^2/[1.24(8/5)] = 3.41$

7. Obtaining one score per subject by summing over sequences we get the following ANOVA:

Source	df	SS	MS	F
Stimuli	2	25316.93	12658	
Error	12	1422	118.5	

The test of the contrast is $F_{1,12} = [(209.25 + 231.45)/2 - 230.6]2/[(1.5/20)118.50] = 11.82$.

8. The mean square for Sequence x Subjects is the appropriate denominator for a test of Sequences so the confidence interval is $(225.60 + 222.20 + 221.60)/3 - 225.67 \pm \sqrt{[4.12(1.33/15)60.28]} = -2.53 \pm 4.69$ giving -7.23 to 2.16. Since zero is contained in the confidence interval, the hypothesis is not rejected.

9. The sum of squares for the interaction of $A_1 - A_3$ with B is 45.17 and that for the interaction of $(A_1 + A_2 + A_3)/3 - A_4$ with B is 42.02.

10. Linearly interpolating for F gives $F_{1,48,.01} = 7.218$. The confidence interval is $20.4 \pm \sqrt{[7.218(2.16)(4/20)]}$ giving the interval 18.63 to 22.17. The interval does not contain zero, so reject the hypothesis.

12. (a) $F_{1,12} = [.79 - (.73 + .64 + .55)]2/[.000043(1.33/15)] = 5984.01$

(b) $F_{1,12} = (.73 - .55)2/[.000043(2/15)] = 5395.82$

(c) $F_{1,8} = [(.76 + .69) - .59]2/[.000069(1.5/20)] = 3521.74$ (with less rounding a more precise answer is $F = 3422.76$)

(d) $F_{1,24} = (.55 - .48)2/[.00011(2/5)] = 94.92$

(e) $F_{1,24} = [(.65 - .57) - (.55 - .48)]2/[.00011(4/5)] = 1.57$

13. Obtaining the Saline - .50 mg/kg contrast scores for each subject in each retention interval and doing a Retention Interval x Subjects ANOVA on them gives $F_{2,8} = .0098/.00032 = 31.13$ for the Retention effect indicating an interaction of the contrast with Retention Interval.

16. (a) With C but not with B or B x C

(d) With B and with C but not with B x C

17. (a) At Level 1 of C, the difference between the first two levels of A and the second two levels of A, summed over the first two levels of B, from that same difference between the pairs of levels of A summed over the second two levels of B, equals the difference between those differences averaged over Levels 2 and 3 of C.

(b) This is just tedious, not difficult. You need a contrast of the 48 means, assigning the appropriate coefficients. The rest is as usual. The coefficients of M_{111}, M_{211}, M_{121}, M_{221}, M_{331}, M_{431}, M_{341}, and M_{441}, are all 1; those for M_{311}, M_{411}, M_{321}, M_{421}, M_{131}, M_{231}, M_{141}, and M_{241} are -1; the rest are +1/2 or -1/2 depending on the sign in the expression stating the problem.

18. $(\mu_{111} - \mu_{211}) - (\mu_{121} - \mu_{221}) = (\mu_{112} - \mu_{212}) - (\mu_{122} - \mu_{222})$

CHAPTER 10

1. 40, 156, 259, 400, 820

2. $L_i = -3, -1, 0, 1, 3$; $QD_i = 4.40, -2.93, -3.60, -2.27, 6.40$; $C_i = -2.35, 8.56, 1.65, -5.52, 3.40$; $Qr_i = .34, -4.11, 5.48, -2.06, .46.3$

3. L_i = -2, -1, 0, 1, 2; QD_i = 2, -1, -2, -1, 2; C_i = -1, 2, 0, -2, 1

4. They are the same except for multiplication by a constant.

5. (a, b) Get an L x L score for each rat and test the mean and groups effects. The test for the mean gives $F_{1,8}$ = .33; the test for Groups gives $F_{1,8}$ = 0.

(c, d) The test for the mean gives $F_{1,8}$ = .03; the test for Groups gives $F_{1,8}$ = 0.

6. For Dosage, A_1 = -.21875 and the Linear coefficients are -.21875, -.09375, .03125, .28125; for Retention Interval, A_1 = -5.8333 and the Linear coefficients are 2.28125, 4.78125, and 9.78125. Obtaining L x L scores for each subject gave -1.03, -1.04, -1.09, -.99, -1.09 and an ANOVA of these L x L scores permitted rejecting the null hypothesis that they came from a population with μ = 0: $F_{1,4}$ = 5.516/.002 = 3046.

7. The linear coefficients are -3.6, -1.6, -.6, 1.4, 4.4. The test of the L-scores gives an $F_{1,5}$ = 438.

8. $Y_{ijkmn} = \mu + A_i + B_j + C_k + s_m + AB_{ij} + AC_{ik} + As_{im} + BC_{jk} + Bs_{jm} + Cs_{km} + ABC_{ijk} + ABs_{ijm} + ACs_{ikm} + BCs_{jkm} + ABCs_{ijkm} + e_{ijkmn}$

11.(a) Height L score = 315.9, Height Q score = -1.7

Width L score = 320.9, Width Q score = 3.7

Multiplier L score = 320.5, Multiplier Q score = 4.9

(b) L x L for H x W = -101

(c) -36.8

12. Quadratic

13. Linear and quadratic

14. Cubic

CHAPTER 11

1. For the Games and Howell procedure:

A_1 - A_2: the difference is -4.37 and the critical difference is 8.67

A_2 - A_3: the difference is -2.98 and the critical difference is 8.56

A_1 - A_3: the difference is -7.34 and the critical difference is 8.36.

None of the differences is significant.

2. There are six levels of Blocks. The df for B x Ss is 80, so we use $q_{.05,2,80}$ through $q_{.05,6,80}$. These are, approximately, 2.819, 2.966, 3.064, 3.134, and 3.189. Multiplying each of these by $(MS_{BxSs}/20)^{.5}$ gives .702, .738, .762, .780, .794 for the critical values at 2, 3, 4, 5, 6. The result is: 12.6   12.95   14.15   14.55   <u>15.1   19.95</u>

3. Using Ryan's method, $\alpha_p = 1 - (1 - \alpha)^{P/I}$, thus $\alpha_2 = 1 - (1 - \alpha)^{2/6}$. The following gives the linear interpolation for the $q_{.05,p}$ values and the $q_{.01,p}$ values and the logarithmic interpolations for the $q_{\alpha p,p,df_e}$ values.

α_p	$q_{.05,p}$	$q_{.01,p}$	$q_{\alpha p,p},df_e$	$q_{\alpha p,p,df_e}(MS_e/n)^{.5}$
.017	2.819	2.883	2.862	.712
.025	2.966	3.010	2.985	.743
.034	3.064	3.100	3.073	.765
.042	3.134	3.167	3.138	.781
.05	3.189	3.227	3.189	.794

This gives the result: <u>12.6</u> <u>12.95</u> <u>14.15</u> <u>14.55</u> <u>15.1</u> 19.95.

4. The answer to exercise 13 gives Ryan's α_p values.

	F	Fcritical	Decision
1,2,3,4	5.08	2.76	No line
1,2,3	6.73	3.15	No line
1,2,4	6.14	3.15	No line
1,3,4	7.30	3.15	No line
2,3,4	.16	3.15	Draw a line
1,2	8.18	4.00	No line
1,3	11.69	4.00	No line
1,4	10.14	4.00	No line
2,3	Not necesary		
2,4	Not necesary		
3,4	Not necesary		

Result: 1   2   3   4

6. (a) All except the two scrambled stimuli.

(b) 1 - .879 = .121

(c) 11.35 ± .98

7. (a) Yes

(b)   1) t = 4.07, significant

         2) t = -.61, not significant

         3) t = 29.33, significant

(c) .143

(d)   1) 1.016 to 2.984

         2) -1.28 t0 .684

3) 9.504 to 10.896

(e) No. Three df for Stimulus implies at most three orthogonal contrasts.

(f) $M_i \pm t.05,64(2.419/20).5$ gives 17.30 to 18.70, 15.30 to 16.60, 5.95 to 7.35, and 6.25 to 7.65.

8. (a) $\alpha = .017$, $z = 2.12085$, $t = 2.17$ using Peiser

(b)   1) .933 to 3.067

       2) -1.37 to .767

       3) 9.445 to 10.955

9. 2.2656

10. $\alpha = .05/9 = .00556$, $1 - \alpha/2 = .99444$, $z = 2.77654$. Using Peiser gives $t = 2.871$ for the various tests.

11. $1 - .9833 = .05$, $1 - .983 = .017$, $1 - .017/2 = .9915$, $z_{.9915} = 2.38814$, $t_{64, .017/2} = 2.45$

12. Using a critical value of $q = 3.737$ (3.72 is more precise) and $(MS_e/n)^{.5} = .348$, we get $M_i - M_j \pm (3.737)(.348)$ giving the intervals: $.7 \leq M_1 - M_2 \leq 3.3$, $10.05 \leq M_1 - M_3 \leq 12.65$, $9.75 \leq M_1 - M_4 \leq 12.35$, $8.05 \leq M_2 - M_3 \leq 10.65$, $7.75 \leq M_2 - M_4 \leq 10.35$, $-1.6 \leq M_3 - M_4 \leq 1.0$.

13. $MS_e = 1.569$, $q_{.05,3,36} = 4.940$, $n = 24$. The critical difference is 1.26 and none of the pairwise differences between the means are significant.

14. The confidence interval for each contrast is $\Sigma_i C_i Mi \pm MS_e \Sigma_i (c_i^2/n_i)[(I - 1)F_{\alpha,I-1,df_e}]$. Reject the null hypothesis if the interval does not overlap zero. The intervals are:

(a) -3.16 to 2.49

(b) -3.66 to 1.99

(c) -3.49 to 4.49

(d) -5.06 to -.44

Only (d) is significant.

15. Fisher's LSD requires the F for the D effects to be significant. It is not so no further testing is done. Using df = 30 in Duncan's Table, the critical difference for an adjacent pair is 2.888. None of the pairs differ by this much so all further testing is stopped. Results of Fisher's LSD and Duncan's Range Test agree for this set of data: no significant differences.

15. The critical difference is 3.87 and all of the group means differ from Group 1 significantly.

19. $df_{error} = 70$, $I = 5$, $n = 15$. $MS_{error} = 16.88$ (see Table 11.6), and $q_{.05,5,70} = 3.967$. The interval is $(14.87 - 13.53) \pm (16.88/15).5(3.967)$, -2.87 to 5.55.

20. The Bonferroni interval for a two-tailed test is $(14.87 - 13.53) \pm [16.88(2/15)]^{.5}t_{.005/2}$, where $z_{.9975}$ is 2.81131, giving a Peiser approximation to t of 2.90908. The confidence interval is -3.02 to 5.70. The Bonferroni interval is longer than the Tukey interval.

21. When the null hypothesis is false, the longer interval is more likely to include the null hypothesis parameter value, leading to more Type II errors, hence less power.

CHAPTER 12

1. (a) $\beta^T = Y^T X^T (X^T X)^{-1} = [.246, .076, .218]$.

(b) $2.4 \pm (3.435)^{.5}(.412)(1.732)$ gives -.18 to 4.98.

(c)

Source	df	SS	MS	F
X 3		104.04	34.68	204
Y - Xβ 7		97.79		
Y 10		105.23		

(d)

Source	df	SS	MS	F
X1,X2,X3	3	104.04		
X1,X2	2	97.79		
Difference	1	6.25	6.25	36.76
Error	7	1.19	.17	
Total	10	105.23		

Model 1,2 does not fit the data as well as model 1,2,3.

2.

Source	df	SS	MS	F
XLarge	2	103.66		
Xsmaller	1	101.16		
Difference	1	2.50	2.50	12.76
Error	8	1.57	.196	
Total	10	105.23		

7.

Source	df	SS	MS	F
3 reg. coefs.	6	272,191.04		
1 reg. coef.	4	272,183.61		
Difference	2	7.43	3.72	<1
Error	9	49.97	5.55	
Total	15	272,241		

8. (a) 1

(b) $b_w = 85.08/20$; the two adjusted means are $142.2 - 85.08/20(31)$ and $119.4 - 85.08/20(26.4)$, $MS_{w,adj.} = 211.9154$, $SS_{w,Y} = 2693$, $SP_w^2 = 85.08$, and $SS_{w,X} = 20$. So the test statistic equals .03.

12. π vs. ξ: $[(57.39 - 49.97)/2]/(49.97/9) = .67$;

ω vs. ξ: $[(2693.2 - 49.97)/3]/(49.97/9) = 158.69$;

16.

Source	df	SS	MS	F
Ω	3	91.35431876		
ω	2	91.354318201		
Difference	1	.00000056	.00000056	.0896
Error	13	.00008124	.00000624923	
Total	16	91.3544		

CHAPTER 13

5. RelEff $= MS_r/MS_b = 22.4/4 = 5.6$

6. (a) .057

(b) .07

9. $MS_e = \sigma^2_{est} = 22.4$, the M_i are 10, 8, and 16. $\delta^2\sigma^2_{est} = 6[(10 - 11.33)2 + (8 - 11.33)2 + (16 - 11.33)2]$ so $\delta = 3.047$.

CHAPTER 14

1. (a) Do; (b) Do; (c) Do not. All could be equal. But do if $p_{11} \neq p_{21}$.

2. (a) Interaction (b) Interaction.

4. A negative interaction effect.

5. (b)

Source	df	SS	MS	F
HA	7	2734.6	390.70	
H0	4	2727.2	681.80	
HA vs. H0	3	7.41	2.47	126.6
Error	41	.8	.02	
Total	48	2735.4		

(c) One way would be to average the $R_{i.}/R_{.i}$, set the average equal to $w/(1-w)$, and solve for w.

6. (a) If $k = 1$

(b) $R_{ij'} = (R_{ij})^{1/k}$

c) $R_{ij'} = \ln(R_{ijk}) = k\ln(R_{ij}) = k[\ln(h_i) + \ln(w_j)]$

CHAPTER 15

10. $SS_1 = 337.50$, $SS_2 = 353.07$, $SS_3 = 352.18$, $SS_4 = 368.61$, $SS_5 = 382.87$, $SS_6 = 395.02$, $SS_7 = 393.05$, $SS_8 = 406.50$. $SS_{error} = 15.5$.

Method	Parameter	F
1	α	6.94
	β	5.92
	γ	9.78
2	α	8.48
	β	8.02
	γ	9.78
3	α	6.27
	β	5.92
	γ	9.78

Appendix 1

Random Variables
and Their Expectations

A1.1 Definition of a random variable. A **random variable** is a variable that takes its values probabilistically. Suppose we defined a variable that took its values depending upon the outcome of the flip of a fair coin. We might decide that the variable, call it X, equals 1 if the coin comes up heads and 0 if the coin comes up tails. Then, because the coin outcomes occur probabilistically, so do the values of X. Or suppose that we define a variable Y that takes as its values the number of dots on the upward face of a fair die after the die has been rolled. Then Y would take the values 1, 2, 3, 4, 5, or 6, probabilistically. We would call Y a random variable. As a third example, consider a variable W that takes as its value the numerical value of a score that is randomly sampled from a normal distribution with a mean of 50 and a standard deviation of 10. Because W takes its values probabilistically it is a random variable.

The random variables X and Y differ from the random variable W in that X and Y are **discrete random variables** but W is a **continuous random variable**. (We are concerned only with real variables.) A discrete variable is one for which the possible values can be put into one-to-one correspondence with the positive integers. As with the integers, between any two adjacent values there is a gap in which possible values do not occur. A real continuous variable has no such gap. Given any two possible values of the continuous variable there is always another real value between those two. In fact, every real value between those two must be a possible value. Thus, for example, if the numbers 1 and 2 are possible values of a continuous variable, then 1.5 must be a possible value. And between 1.5 and 2 there will be a possible value, say 1.75—and between 1.75 and 2, and so on. By an odd quirk of mathematical truth (or definition), it can be said that in fact there are as many possible values of this continuous variable between 1.75 and 2 as there are between 1 and 2. Further pursuit of the oddities of continuity is left to the student's own devices.

A1.2   The probability distribution of a discrete random variable. In the case of each of the random variables we have defined a **probabilistic experiment**, the coin flip, the die roll, or the random sampling procedure, and assigned numerical values to the outcome of the probabilistic experiment. This assignment of values to the outcomes of the probabilistic experiment indirectly assigns probabilities to the values of the random variable. (The assignment procedure is technically different for a continuous random variable because probabilities are assigned to intervals of possible values and this will be considered below. The big idea is that assignment of probabilities to the outcomes of the probabilistic experiment induces an assignment of probabilities on the values of the random variable and this big idea is the same for discrete and continuous random variables.) In the case of the discrete random variable X, because $Pr(\text{Heads}) = Pr(\text{Tails}) = 1/2$, we have $Pr(X{=}1) = Pr(X{=}0) = 1/2$. Similarly, with the fair die, since $Pr(\text{the die comes up } 4) = 1/6$, this determines that $Pr(Y{=}4) = 1/6$, etc. In the discrete case we say that such an assignment of probabilities to the various possible values of the random variables is the **probability distribution of the discrete random variable.**

A1.3   Expectation of a discrete random variable. The intuitive meaning of the expectation of a random variable is the long-run average of the numerical values of the random variable that would occur as a result of the repeated performance of the probabilistic experiment. To illustrate how this intuitive meaning slides easily into the formal definition, consider a die roll experiment in which the die is not necessarily a fair die. It may be a loaded (biased) die such that not all of the surfaces have the same long-run relative frequency of landing upward. Let f_i be the frequency with which $Y = i$ in any N rolls of this die. Note

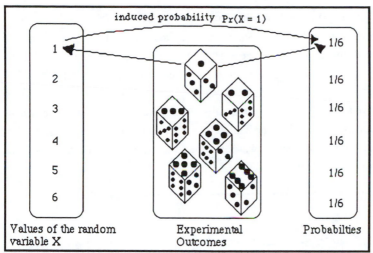

Values of the random variable X — Experimental Outcomes — Probabilties

Figure A1.1. The assignment of the probability 1/6 to the outcome of a one on the die and the assignment of the value of 1 on the random variable when the die comes up one determines that the probability of the random variable equaling 1 is 1/6, assuming that the random variable does not take the value 1 when any of the other surfaces of the die comes up.

that $N = \Sigma_i f_i$. Then the average value of Y would certainly be

$$M_Y = (1f_1 + 2f_2 + 3f_3 + 4f_4 + 5f_5 + 6f_6)/N \; = \; \Sigma_i if_i/N$$

because this simply adds up all the different values that Y takes and divides by the total number of values. We can rewrite this expression as

$$M_Y = [1(f_1/N) + 2(f_2/N) + 3(f_3/N) + 4(f_4/N) + 5(f_5/N) + 6(f_6/N)] \; = \; \Sigma_i i(f_i/N),$$

which is a sum of six products, each one being the product of a possible value of Y with the relative frequency of that value's occurrence in the N trials of the probabilistic experiment. The mean of Y is a weighted sum of the possible values of Y, the weight for each value being the relative frequency of occurrence of that value.

Now if, following the frequentist perspective on probability, we define the probability that Y= i to be the limiting value (assuming such a value exists) of f_i/N as N increases without limit, then we see that as N increases without limit, the quantity M_Y approaches the limiting value

$$1Pr(Y = 1) + 2Pr(Y = 1) + 3Pr(Y = 1) + 4Pr(Y = 1) + 5Pr(Y = 1) + 6Pr(Y = 1)$$

which equals = $\Sigma_i iPr(Y = i)$.   We define this limiting weighted sum of the various values of Y, each weighted by its probability of occurrence, to be the expected value of the random variable Y, and we denote it by E(Y).   In general, let X be any discrete random variable that takes the value x with probability Pr(X = x), then the expected value of X is defined as E(X) = $\Sigma xPr(X=x)$, where the summation is over all possible values of X.

Suppose we have a jar containing five red balls, three yellow balls and two green balls. Our experiment consists of drawing one ball out at random and we will assumes that each ball has an equal probability of being drawn.   Let X be a random variable that takes the value 10 if a red ball is drawn, 20 if a yellow ball

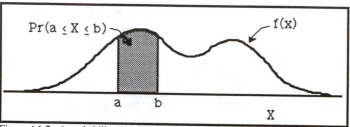

Figure A1.2. A probability density function f(x). The shaded area is the probability that the random variable X takes a value between a and b.

is drawn, and 30 if a green ball is drawn.   Then E(X) = (.5)10 + (.3)20 + .2(30) = 17.

A1.4   A probability density function determines the probability distribution of a continuous random variable. In the case of a continuous variable, a probability distribution is created by a rule that assigns a probability to every possible interval of values of the variable. This is done by a function called the **probability density function f(x)**, which is defined over the range of possible values taken by the continuous random variable and is equal to zero everywhere else. Figure A1.2 shows such a function. The probability assigned to an interval of possible values of the random variable is then defined to be the area under the probability density curve, f(x), over the given interval. The area under the entire curve is equal to one. Figure A1.2 shows an interval on the X axis from the value a to the value b and an area under the probability density curve, over that interval, which is the probability that $a \leq X \leq b$.

The area bounded by the X axis, two vertical lines, and the curve f(x) is expressed as the integral

$$\int_a^b f(x)\ dx.$$

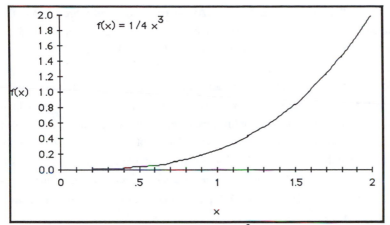

Figure A1.3. The probability density curve $f(x) = 1/4\ x^3$, $0 \le x \le 2$, $f(x) = 0$ everywhere else.

This integral can be defined as the limiting value of a sum of the areas of rectangles. Let the interval from a to b be exhaustively partitioned into n nonoverlapping subintervals, with the ith subinterval having a width Δx_i. Then if we choose any point x_i within the ith interval and let the value $f(x_i)$ be the height of a rectangle having Δx_i as its base, the area of that rectangle will be $f(x_i)\Delta x_i$ and will approximate the area under the density curve over the subinterval Δx_i. The sum $\Sigma_i\, f(x_i)\Delta x_i$ will approximate the area under the density curve and over the interval from a to b. If this sum approaches a limiting value as n increases without limit, then the integral is defined to equal that limiting value of the sum.

Figure A1.3 shows a probability density curve that we can use to illustrate the notion of the integral as a limiting value of a sum of rectangular areas. For convenience as our point x_i in the interval with width Δx_i, we will always use the midpoint of the interval. Also we will always choose the Δx_i to be of equal length. Let's first observe what happens to the sum $\Sigma_i f(x_i)\Delta x_i$ as we let n start at one and increase. For n = 1 we have one interval of length Δx_1 = 2, the midpoint of that interval is at $x_1 = 1$, and $f(x_i) = (1/4)1^3 = .25$. So, $\Sigma_i f(x_i)\Delta x_i = .25(2) = .5$. For n = 2 we have two intervals, the first from 0 to 1 and the second from 1 to 2. The value of Δx_i is 1 in each case, the two interval midpoints are $x_1 = .5$ and $x_2 = 1.5$, and the values of f(x) are $f(x_1) = (1/4).5^3 = .03125$ and $f(x_2) = (1/4)1.5^3 = .84375$. Therefore $\Sigma_i f(x_i)\Delta x_i = [(.03125 + .84375)]1 = .875$. For n = 4, the intervals would run from 0 to .5, .5 to 1, 1 to 1.5 and 1.5 to 2. The value of Δx_i is .5 in each case; the four interval midpoints are $x_1 = .25$ and $x_2 = .75$, $x_3 = 1.25$ and $x_4 = 1.75$; and the values of f(x) are $f(x_1) = (1/4).25^3 = ..00391$, $f(x_2) = (1/4).75^3 = .07031$, $f(x_3) = (1/4)1.25^3 = .48828$, $f(x_2) = (1/4)1.75^3 = 1.33984$. Therefore $\Sigma_i f(x_i)\Delta x_i = [(.00391 + .07031 + .48828 + 1.33984)].5 = .95117$. As n increases the value of $\Sigma_i f(x_i)\Delta x_i$ approaches the value one.

What is happening is that as n increases and the Δx_i become more and more narrow, the rectangles with base Δx_i and height $f(x_i)$ become increasingly closer approximations to the area under the piece of curve over Δx_i. If the student sketches these rectangles for two different values of n, this improvement of approximation will be apparent.

The student may wonder how a proof of the approach of $\Sigma_i f(x_i)\Delta x_i$ to a limiting value is done. This is reasonably simple for the example we have chosen. First we note that with n subintervals the length of each subinterval will be the length of the whole interval, 2, divided by the number of subintervals, n, giving a subinterval length of $\Delta x_i = 2/n$. Also, since we have let x_i be located at the center of each subinterval, we can see that the value of x_i will always be $(2i - 1)/n$. Thus with four intervals the values of x_1, x_2, x_3, and x_4 are $[2(1) - 1]/4 = .25$, $[2(2) - 1]/4 = .75$, $[2(3) - 1]/4 = 1.25$, and $[2(4) - 1]/4 = 1.75$ as we saw above. This means that we can write

$$\Sigma_i f(x_i)\Delta x_i = \Sigma_i (1/4)[(2i-1)/n]^3(2/n) = \Sigma_i [(2i-1)]^3/(2n^4)$$

$$= \Sigma_i (8i^3 - 6i^2 + 6i - 1)/(2n^4).$$

Now if we want to see how $\Sigma_i f(x_i)\Delta x_i$ behaves as n --> ∞, we perform the summation and then examine its behavior as n increases without limit. To perform the summation it will be helpful to know that the sum of the first n integers is $n(n+1)/2$, the sum of the squares of the first n integers is $n(n+1)(2n+1)/6$, and the sum of the cubes of the first n integers is $n^2(n+1)^2/4$. (The student who does not wish to take these formulas on faith can prove them by mathematical induction, which is a relatively simple procedure discussed in most introductory algebra books.) Applying these formulas we obtain

$$\Sigma_i (8i^3 - 6i^2 + 6i - 1)/(2n^4) = (8\Sigma_i i^3 - 6\Sigma_i i^2 + \Sigma_i i - \Sigma_i 1)/2n^4$$

$$= \{8[n^2(n+1)^2/4] - 6[n(n+1)(2n+1)/6] + 6[n(n+1)/2] - n\}/2n^4$$

which after some algebraic manipulation reduces to

$$(2n^4 + 2n^3 + 2n^2 + n)/2n^4 = 1 + (1/n) + (1/n^2) + (1/2n^3).$$

Now, as n increases without limit the quantities $(1/n)$, $(1/n^2)$, and $(1/2n^3)$ all approach zero. We can say then that the limiting value, as n --> ∞, is

$$\lim \Sigma_i f(x_i)\Delta x_i = \lim \Sigma_i (1/4)[(2i-1)/n]^3(2/n)$$

$\lim [1 + (1/n) + (1/n^2) + (1/2n^3)] = 1.$

This, of course, is what we expected since we had chosen our function and its range of application to give us a probability density function, and the area under a probability density curve over its entire range must equal one.

A1.5 The expected value of a continuous random variable. We recall that for a discrete random variable, $E(X) = \Sigma x Pr(X=x)$. If we think of $f(x)dx$ in the integral playing the role of $Pr(X=x)$ in the summation, then we might expect that for a continuous random variable X we would have

$$E(X) = \int x \, f(x) \, dx$$

where the integration is performed over the entire range of X. For our example we would have

$$E(X) = \int_{0}^{2} x \,(1/4)x^3 \, dx \;\; = \;\; 1/4 \int_{0} x^4 \, dx$$

which is shown in introductory calculus books to equal 1.6. We would expect this to be approximated by $\Sigma_i x_i f(x_i)\Delta x_i = [.25(.00391) + .75(.07031) + 1.25(.48828) + 1.75(1.33984)].5$, which turns out to equal 1.50439. We will not pursue further examples of continuous random variables since these would require the techniques of integral calculus, which the reader is not expected to be familiar with. When we indicate an expected value, we will simply use the $E(X)$ notation without necessarily spelling out in detail the ranges of summation or integration or even indicating in the notation whether we are dealing with a discrete or continuous random variable. All of the statements that we will make below apply to both discrete and continuous random variables. To exemplify the proofs of some of these we will use the discrete case.

A1.6 The variance and the covariance as expectations. The variance of a random variable is an expectation. It is the expected value of the squared deviation of a random variable from its own expected value. That is,

$$VAR(X) = E\{ [X - E(X)]^2 \} = E[X^2 - 2XE(X) + E^2(X)]$$

where $E^2(X) = E(X)E(X)$. Using certain properties of the expected value operator covered in the next section we obtain

$$E[\ X^2 - 2XE(X) + E^2(X)\ ] \ = \ E(X^2) - 2E(X)E(X) + E^2(X) \ = E(X^2) \ - \ E^2(X).$$

Thus we have that the variance of a random variable is the long-run average value of the square of that variable minus the square of the long-run average value of that random variable—in short, the expected value of X-squared minus the square of the expected value of X. This conforms to the fact that in the case of the sample variance,

$$S^2 \ = \ \Sigma_i(X_i - M)^2/N \ = \ \Sigma_i X_i^2/N \ - \ M^2,$$

which is the average squared X minus the squared average X.

The covariance of two random variables, X and Y, is also an expectation. We can describe this expectation in two ways. It is the expected value of the product of the deviation of X from its expected value times the deviation of the corresponding Y value from its expected value. By "corresponding" we simply mean that the X and Y values occur in pairs, a generic pair being X_i and Y_i. Thus

$$COV(XY) = E\{[(X - E(X)][Y - E(Y)]\}.$$

With some additional manipulation to be shown in the next section we can also find that

$$COV(XY) = E(XY) - E(X)E(Y).$$

In words, the covariance of X with Y is the expected value of their product minus the product of their expected values. As an example, consider the following X,Y pairs and their probabilities of occurrence:

X	Y	Pr(X & Y)	XY
1	2	.3	2
2	0	.3	0
3	1	.4	3

The product of X times Y is given in the fourth column. The $E(XY) = .3(2) + .3(0) + .4(3) = 1.8$. Since $E(X) = .3(1) + .3(2) + .4(3) = 2.1$ and $E(Y) = .3(2) + .3(0) + .4(1) = 1.0$, the $COV(XY) = 1.8 - (2.1)(1) = -.3$. According to the first definition of covariance this should also equal $.3(1 - 2.1)(2 - 1.0) + .3(2 - 2.1)(0 - 1.0) + .4(3 - 2.1)(1 - 1.0) = -.33 + .03 + 0 =$ $-.3$.

A1.7 The properties of the expected value operator. In this section some useful properties of the expected value operator will be indicated. Obviously, the long-run average value of a constant will be that constant. So, if c is any constant,

$E(c) = c$.

If a new random variable is created by adding a constant to every value of an old random variable, the long-run average value of the new variable will obviously be greater than that of the old by just the value of the constant. Thus,

$E(X + c) = E(X) + c$.

As an example of how we would prove such a statement, we assume X is a discrete random variable and resort to the definition of the expected value of a discrete random variable:

$E(X + c) = \Sigma_i(x_i + c)Pr[x_i + c]$.

Now certainly $X + c$ will take the value $x_i + c$ with the same probability that X takes the value x_i. So

$E(X + c) = \Sigma_i(x_i + c)Pr[x_i + c] = \Sigma_i(x_i + c)Pr(x_i)$

$= \Sigma_i[x_iPr(x_i) + cPr(x_i)] = \Sigma_i x_iPr(x_i) + \Sigma_i cPr(x_i)$

$= E(X) + c\,\Sigma_iPr(x_i) = E(X) + c$

since $\Sigma_iPr(x_i) = 1$. The proof is essentially the same for a continuous variable. Also the proofs for the remaining properties of the expected values follow similar lines so we will omit proving most of them.

The expected value of a constant times a random variable equals the constant times the expected value of the random variable.

$E(cX) = cE(X)$.

Since c could be a fraction less than one, we have the equivalent property that

$$E(X/c) \quad = \quad (1/c)E(X).$$

The long-run average value of the sum of two or more random variables equals the sum of their long-run average values. Thus

$$E(X + Y) \quad = \quad E(X) + E(Y).$$

To show this for a discrete random variable we observe that

$$E(X + Y) = \Sigma_x \Sigma_y (x+y)\Pr(X=x \text{ and } Y=y)$$

$$= \Sigma_x \Sigma_y x \Pr(X=x \text{ and } Y=y) + \Sigma_x \Sigma_y y \Pr(X=x \text{ and } Y=y)$$

$$= \Sigma_x x \Sigma_y \Pr(X=x \text{ and } Y=y) + \Sigma_y y \Sigma_x \Pr(X=x \text{ and } Y=y).$$

But $\Sigma_y \Pr(X=x \text{ and } Y=y) = \Pr(X=x)$ and $\Sigma_x \Pr(X=x \text{ and } Y=y) = \Pr(Y=y)$. Substituting we get

$$E(X + Y) = \Sigma_x x \Sigma_y \Pr(X=x \text{ and } Y=y) + \Sigma_y y \Sigma_x \Pr(X=x \text{ and } Y=y)$$

$$= \Sigma_x x \Pr(X=x) + \Sigma_y y \Pr(Y=y) \quad = E(X) + E(Y).$$

Similarly,

$$E(X + Y + Z) \quad = \quad E(X) + E(Y) + E(Z)$$

and so forth. If we let N random variables be denoted by $X_1, X_2, ..., X_N$ we can write

$$E(\Sigma_i X_i) \quad = \quad E(X_1) + E(X_2) + ... + E(X_N) \quad = \Sigma_i E(X_i).$$

You should notice how the expected value operator may be run through an expression that is the sum of random variables and applied to each of them. We say that it may be distributed over the expression. Similarly, if the random variables are multiplied by constants, the expected value operator may be run through the expression, giving

$$E(aX + bY) \; = \; E(aX) + E(bY) \; = \; aE(X) + bE(Y),$$

and so on.

The expected value of the product of two random variables is equal to the product of their expected values if the two random variables are independent. That is,

$$E(XY) = E(X)E(Y) \quad \text{when } X \text{ and } Y \text{ are independent.}$$

This follows because $E(XY) = \Sigma_x \Sigma_y xy \, \Pr(X=x \text{ and } Y=y)$ and when X and Y are independent, $\Pr(X=x \text{ and } Y=x) = \Pr(X=x)\Pr(Y=y)$. Therefore,

$$E(XY) \; = \; \Sigma_x \Sigma_y xy \, \Pr(X=x \text{ and } Y=y) = \Sigma_x \Sigma_y xy \, \Pr(X=x \,)\Pr(Y=y)$$

$$= \; [\, \Sigma_x x \, \Pr(X=x \,) \,] \, [\, \Sigma_y y \, \Pr(Y=y)] \; = \; E(X)E(Y).$$

since $x \, \Pr(X=x)$ is a constant with respect to summation over y and can therefore be factored out of that summation.

A.1.8   The algebra of the variance operator.   Since the variance is an expected value, the algebra of the expected value operator reveals how the variance of the sums and differences of random variables behave. The variance of the sum of two random variables, $X + Y$, is by definition

$$VAR(X + Y) = E[(X + Y)^2] - E^2(X + Y) = E[(X^2 + Y^2 + 2XY] - [E(X) + E(Y)]^2$$

$$= E(X^2) + E(Y^2) + 2E(XY) - E^2(X) - E^2(Y) - 2E(X)E(Y) = VAR(X) + VAR(Y)$$

$$+ \, 2COV(XY).$$

The variance of the sum of two random variables is the variance of one plus the variance of the other plus twice the covariance of the two. In similar fashion it can be shown that

$$VAR(X_1 + X_2 + ... + X_N) \; = \; \Sigma_i VAR(X_i) + 2\Sigma_i \Sigma_{j \neq i} COV(X_i X_j)$$

and that

$$VAR(a_1 X_1 + a_2 X_2 + ... + a_N X_N) = \Sigma_i a_i^2 VAR(X_i) + 2\Sigma_i \Sigma_{j \neq i} a_i a_j COV(X_i X_j).$$

If the X_i are all independent of one another, then all of the covariances are zero, and we have that the variance of the sum of independent random variables is just the sum of the variances of those variables and the variance of a linear combination of independent random variables is just the sum of the variances of those variables after each variance is multiplied by the square of the coefficient of the variable in the linear combination, that is, by a_i^2.

Appendix 2

Vectors and Matrices

A2.1 Vectors. A vector is an ordered collection of components or elements. In this book the elements are real numbers. A vector is written algebraically by writing the elements in their order, separated by commas, and containing the collection within brackets. The elements can be written as a column of numbers or as a row of numbers and are correspondingly referred to as column vectors or row vectors. Thus, a vector might be [1], [1, 2, 5], or [4, 3, 5, 6, 8]. We identify a vector with a line emanating from the origin of a Cartesian coordinate system. The coordinate system has exactly as many orthogonal axes as the vector has elements. (For three or fewer dimensions we can draw a representation of the coordinate system in which we include the axes. For four or more we can draw the vectors but exclude the axes.) If the vector has only one number, there is only one axis. The line emanates from zero on that one axis to the point on the axis corresponding to the number in the vector. We can call the number the coordinate of the point to which the vector reaches. So, [3] reaches to the point (3).

We envision the set of all such one-number vectors that we could create by inserting one real number between brackets and we call that set the one-dimensional vector space, V_{1r}. (The 1 is for 1-dimensional and the r is for real numbers.) In V_{1r} there is a vector corresponding to every point on the line, and to every vector in V_{1r} there corresponds a point on the line. This correspondence of the vectors with the points they reach to gives a feeling of a spatial sense to the collection of all such vectors. When we call the set of vectors a vector space, we can think of the line as densely covered with all the possible vectors reaching out from the origin.

For a vector with two numbers such as [3, 5], we can use a coordinate system with two axes. We draw the vector [3, 5] as a line emanating from the origin reaching to the point (3, 5). The set of all possible vectors having two real elements we call the vector space V_{2r} and similarly for vectors with three or more components. A vector with n real components would in general be written $[x_1, x_2, ..., x_n]$ and we think of it drawn as a line from the origin of an n-dimensional coordinate system to the point $(x_1, x_2, ..., x_n)$ in n-dimensional space. We call the set of all such n-dimensional vectors the vector space V_{nr}.

We can coordinate a vector with any specific collection of real numbers. A sample of n scores can be coordinated with a vector in V_{nr} emanating from the origin to the point with coordinates equal to the values of the scores in the sample. Significant properties of samples of scores are expressible in terms of properties of vectors, relations between vectors, and so forth. As we discover and use these, we also experience a subtle shift in thought where a sample of scores changes from a collection of objects to a single object, the sample vector or the data vector. Similarly, a whole collection of parameters can be thought of as a single entity, a parameter vector. The same is true for collections of errors, parameter estimates, and error estimates. All of these collections can now be thought of as unitary objects. This plays a remarkable simplifying effect on our thinking about such collections. It is analogous to the unifying and simplifying effect produced by seeing a string of letters as a single word. We now consider some of the properties of vectors.

A2.2 Vector algebra. In arithmetic we learned how to operate on numbers to obtain new numbers by adding, subtracting, multiplying, dividing, squaring, reciprocalizing, and so forth. In algebra we learned the abstract properties of those arithmetic operations. Vectors are collections of numbers, and vector algebra informs us of the abstract rules governing operating on vectors to get either new vectors or numbers.

To add two vectors they must both belong to the same vector space (have the same number of elements). Then if $A = [x_1, x_2, ..., x_n]$ and $B = [y_1, y_2, ..., y_n]$, the **sum of two vectors** is defined as

$$A + B = [x_1, x_2, ..., x_n] + [y_1, y_2, ..., y_n] = [x_1 + y_1, x_2 + y_2, ..., x_n + y_n].$$

That is, we add the corresponding elements in the two vectors to obtain the sum. Hence, [4, 2, 3, 1] + [1, 2, 5, 3] = [5, 4, 8, 4] but [4, 2, 3, 1] + [1, 2, 5] is not defined. (See Chapter 3, section 3.7 and Figure 3.3.)

Two vectors $A = [x_1, x_2, ..., x_n]$ and $B = [y_1, y_2, ..., y_n]$ are **equal** if for every i, $x_i = y_i$.

The **additive inverse** of a vector $A = [x_1, x_2, ..., x_n]$ is $-A = [-x_1, -x_2, ..., -x_n]$. The **0** vector in V_{nr} is a vector containing n zeroes. The vector **0** is an **additive identity element** since for any vector A, $A + 0 = 0 + A = A$. The sum of a vector and its additive inverse is always the zero vector. This is completely analogous to the role that zero plays in arithmetic.

Vector subtraction is defined as $A - B = A + (-B) = [x_1 - y_1, x_2 - y_2, ..., x_n - y_n]$. (See section 3.8 and Figure 3.5.) Thus [4, 2, 3, 1] - [1, 2, 5, 3] = [3, 0, -2, -2], and [4, 2, 3, 1] + [-4, -2, -3, -1] = [0, 0, 0, 0]. In short, for vector addition or subtraction we just use ordinary arithmetic on the elements, one position at a time.

Vector addition is **associative** in that $A + (B + C) = (A + B) + C$ and it is commutative in that $A + B = B + A$. This just says that when we add vectors it doesn't matter how we group them or in what order we add them.

Scalar multiplication is defined as the multiplication of a vector by a real number. The rule is that $a[x_1, x_2, ..., x_n] = [ax_1, ax_2, ..., ax_n]$. Thus, 5[4, 2, 3, 1] = [20, 10, 15, 5]. Geometrically, the effect of scalar multiplication of a vector is to lengthen it or shorten it depending upon whether the scalar multiplier is greater than one or less than one. Scalar multiplication is associative and commutative. That is $t(uA) = (tu)A$ and $tA = At$. It also obeys the two distributive laws $t(A + B) = tA + tB$ and $(t + u)A = tA + uA$.

The transpose of a vector. We can subscript a vector to denote the number of rows and columns in that vector. A row vector A having one row and n columns will be denoted by A_{1xn}, and a column vector A having n rows and one column will be denoted by A_{nx1}. To transpose a row vector is to change it to a column vector having the same elements and to transpose a column vector is to change it to a row vector having the same elements. The **transpose** of the vector A_{1xn} is denoted by A_{1xn}' or sometimes by $A_{1xn}{}^t$ and it is an n x 1 column vector. Thus

$$[2, 3, 4, 5]^{\cdot} = \begin{bmatrix} 2 \\ 3 \\ 4 \\ 5 \end{bmatrix}$$

The transpose of the transpose of a vector A is again the vector A.

Let A be a row vector $[a_1, a_2, ..., a_n]$ and B be a column vector $[b_1, b_2, ..., b_n]'$. The **inner product** of A and B is $A \cdot B = \Sigma_i a_i b_i$. For example, if $A = [1, 2, 4]$ and $B = [4, 5, 9]$, then $A \cdot B = (1)(4) + (2)(5) + (4)(9)$. It follows that $A' \cdot A = \Sigma_i a_i a_i = \Sigma_i a_i^2$. The sum of the squares of the elements of a column vector are obtained by premultiplying it by its own transpose. (Vector multiplication is a special case of matrix multiplication, which is treated in section A2.6).

A2.3 Vector properties and relations. The **length** of a vector A is defined as the square root of $A' \cdot A$. It is often denoted by the symbol $||A||$. Thus, the length of the vector $[3, 4]$ is $(9 + 16)^{.5} = 5$. From this definition it is apparent why scalar multiplication of a vector by a constant lengthens or shorten the vector by a factor equal to the constant. That is, the length of cA is $||cA|| = [(cA)' \cdot (cA)]^{.5} = [\Sigma_i (ca_i)(ca_i)]^{.5} = c[\Sigma_i (a_i)(a_i)]^{.5} = c||A||$, which is c times the length of A.

The **distance between two vectors** $X = [x_1, x_2, ..., x_n]$ and $Y = [y_1, y_2, ..., y_n]$ is defined to be the length of the difference between them. Thus it is $||X - Y|| = [\Sigma_i (x_i - y_i)^2]^{.5}$. That is, it is the square root of the sum of the squares of the differences between the components on each of the n dimensions.

Two vectors A and B are **orthogonal** if their inner product is zero. Thus, the vectors $[-1, 0, 1]$ and $[1, -2, 1]$ are orthogonal to each other and are orthogonal to the vector $[1, 1, 1]$. Two vectors being orthogonal means that the angle between them is a right angle, an angle of 90 degrees. The top and the side of this page are orthogonal to each other, and a line coming straight up out of the page would be orthogonal to both of them. With more than three vectors, we seem to be unable to visualize mutual orthogonality, but the algebraic definition continues to hold. We can draw more than three vectors and denote which pairs are mutually orthogonal without being able to draw four mutually orthogonal axes. (See Chapter 3).

The **projection of X on Y** is a vector that has the same direction as Y and has length equal to the length of Y times the inner product of X with Y divided by the inner product of Y with itself. Thus the projection of X on Y is $(X'Y/Y'Y)Y$. The projection of X on Y is found by dropping a perpendicular from X to Y. This is shown in Figure A2.1.

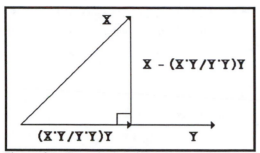

Figure A2.1. The projection of **X** on **Y** is a perpendicular dropped from **X** to **Y**. The projection is a vector with the same direction as **Y** but with length equal to $(\mathbf{X'Y}/\mathbf{Y'Y})\|\mathbf{Y}\|$.

A2.4 Linear combinations of vectors. A linear combination of the vectors $\mathbf{X}_1$, $\mathbf{X}_2$, ..., $\mathbf{X}_n$ is a vector of the form $c_1\mathbf{X}_1 + c_2\mathbf{X}_2 + ... + c_n\mathbf{X}_n$. The vectors $\mathbf{X}_1$, $\mathbf{X}_2$, ..., $\mathbf{X}_n$ are **linearly independent** if no one of them is equal to a linear combination of the others. Otherwise, they are **linearly dependent**. If the vectors $\mathbf{X}_1$, $\mathbf{X}_2$, ..., $\mathbf{X}_n$ are linearly dependent, then there exists a set of c_i not all equal to zero such that $c_1\mathbf{X}_1 + c_2\mathbf{X}_2 + ... + c_n\mathbf{X}_n = 0$.

A set of vectors **S** is said to **span** a vector space if every vector in that space can be written as a linear combination of the vectors in **S**. A set of linearly independent vectors **S** that spans a vector space **V** is called a **basis** for **V**. If **S** is a basis for **V**, then it is always possible to find a new set of vectors, **O**, each of which is a linear combination of the vectors in **S**, such that all of the vectors in **O** are mutually orthogonal. If each of these vectors is divided by its length, so that each now has a length of one, this new set is referred to as an **orthonormal basis** for the vector space **V**. Standard texts describe the Gram-Schmidt process for finding such an orthonormal basis.

If the number of vectors in an orthonormal basis is r, and r is less than n, the number of elements in each of the vectors in **V**, then it is always possible to rotate rigidly the axes of the coordinate system so that each vector in **V** will be represented in the new, rotated coordinate system by a set of coordinates such that only the first r can take nonzero values. All of the last n - r will always be zero. This means that all of the information in the original set of scores that required n dimensions can in fact be expressed by new scores, which only require n - r dimensions. This reduction in dimensions reflects the lack of linear independence of the original vectors in **V**.

A2.5 Matrices. A **matrix** is a rectangular array of numbers consisting of m rows and n columns. We denote a matrix by boldface capital letters and the elements of that matrix by the corresponding lowercase letters with indices to indicate the row and column. Thus the element in row i and column j of matrix **A** is denoted by a_{ij}.

The **transpose** of a matrix **A** is denoted by **A'** and the element in row i, column j of **A'** is a_{ji}, the element in row j and column i of **A**. Putting it another way, the transpose of **A** is that matrix which has as its rows the columns of **A** and has as its columns the rows of **A**.

$$\text{If } \mathbf{A} = \begin{bmatrix} 1 & 3 & 4 \\ 2 & 5 & 6 \end{bmatrix}, \text{ then } \mathbf{A'} \begin{bmatrix} 1 & 2 \\ 3 & 5 \\ 4 & 6 \end{bmatrix}.$$

If m = n the matrix is a **square matrix**. If not, it is **rectangular**.
If **A** is a square matrix and **A'** = **A**, then **A** is called **symmetric**.

$$\text{Thus } \begin{bmatrix} 1 & 5 & 6 \\ 5 & 8 & 2 \\ 6 & 2 & 9 \end{bmatrix} \text{ is symmetric but } \begin{bmatrix} 6 & 5 & 5 \\ 5 & 2 & 6 \\ 3 & 2 & 1 \end{bmatrix} \text{ is not.}$$

A row vector is just a matrix with one row. A column vector is just a matrix with one column. All the rules applying to matrices also apply to vectors. Some books refer to scalars as matrices with one row and one column. This usage is consistent with the rules of matrix operations.

The **main or principal diagonal** of a square matrix extends from the upper left corner to the lower right corner of the matrix. A matrix with all elements off the main diagonal equal to zero is called a **diagonal matrix**.

A2.6 Matrix operations. Matrix addition and **matrix subtraction** are performed just as with vectors, by the addition of corresponding elements. Thus **A** + **B** = **C**, if and only if $c_{ij} = a_{ij} + b_{ij}$. As with vectors, **scalar multiplication of a matrix** by a scalar results in multiplication of each element in the matrix by that scalar. The **matrix product AB** is defined only if the number of columns in **A** equals the number of rows in **B**. That is, if **A** has m rows and n columns (we can write this as $\mathbf{A}_{mxn}$) and **B** has r rows and c columns, then we can multiply **A** times **B** only if n = r, in which case the product, **AB**, will be an m x c matrix. Then, if ab_{ij} is the element in the ith row and j column of **AB**, then $ab_{ij} = \Sigma_k a_{ik} b_{kj}$. That is, ab_{ij} is the inner product of the vector in the ith row of **A** and the vector in the jth column of **B**. For example,

$$\begin{bmatrix} 2 & 4 & 6 \\ 3 & 5 & 7 \end{bmatrix}_{2x3} \begin{bmatrix} 2 & 1 & 1 \\ 3 & 1 & 2 \\ 5 & 2 & 1 \end{bmatrix}_{3x3} = \begin{bmatrix} 46 & 18 & 16 \\ 56 & 22 & 20 \end{bmatrix}_{2x3}$$

Matrix multiplication is **not commutative** in that **AB** is not necessarily equal to **BA**. In fact, **AB** may exist and **BA** may not even be defined, as in the case where $\mathbf{A}_{mxn}\mathbf{B}_{nxc}$ exists but because $c \neq m$, $\mathbf{B}_{nxc}\,\mathbf{A}_{mxn}$ is not defined. However the following rules do apply:

A(BC) = (AB)C	(associativity)
(A + B)C = AB + AC	(distribution)
A(B + C) = AB + AC	(distribution)

The **transpose of the product of matrices** is equal to the product of the transposes of the separate matrices taken in reverse order. Thus, **(AB)' = B'A'** and **(ABC)' = C'B'A'**. From this it follows that **A'A = (A'A)'** and therefore the product of a matrix times its transpose is always a symmetric matrix.

A2.7 Determinants. The determinant of a square matrix **A** is a real number usually denoted by | **A** |. We will define it recursively as follows. If **A** is the 2 x 2 matrix with elements a_{ij}, then $| \mathbf{A} | = a_{11}a_{22} - a_{21}a_{12}$. If **A** is n x n, define the cofactor associated with element a_{ij} as the signed determinant of the matrix obtained by deleting the ith row and jth column of **A**, with the sign being $(-1)^{i+j}$. We will denote this cofactor by $\text{cof}_{ij}(\mathbf{A})$. For example, if

$$\mathbf{A} = \begin{bmatrix} 2 & 3 & 4 \\ 1 & 2 & 1 \\ 5 & 3 & 6 \end{bmatrix}, \text{ then } \text{cof}_{13}(\mathbf{A}) = (-1)^{(1+3)}\begin{vmatrix} 1 & 2 \\ 5 & 3 \end{vmatrix} = (+1)(3 - 10) = -7$$

Then, $| \mathbf{A} | = \Sigma_j a_{ij}\text{cof}_{ij}(\mathbf{A}) = \Sigma_i a_{ij}\text{cof}_{ij}(\mathbf{A})$. That is, we can choose any row (column) of **A** and add the products of each element in that row (column) times the cofactor associated with that element to obtain the determinant of **A**. For the example, using the elements in the first row, $| \mathbf{A} | = 2(1)(12 - 3) + 3(-1)(6 - 5) + 4(1)(3 - 10) = -13$ which is also equal to, say, using the elements in the second column, $3(-1)(6 - 5) + 2(1)(12 - 20) + 3(-1)(2 - 4) = -13$. For matrices larger than 3 x 3 we can repeatedly perform this process (it is known as the Laplace development). Thus, for a 4 x 4 matrix, we would proceed across some row (down some column) obtaining the sum of the products of each element in that row (column) times the 3 x 3 determinant which is that cofactor of that element. Each such 3 x 3 determinant would then be reduced as we have just done. Computers are well suited for such tasks when n gets bigger than three or four. There are also simplified methods for symmetric matrices such as the Doolittle method. And for a nonsymmetric matrix **A**, the Doolittle method can be applied to $\mathbf{A'A}$, and then the determinant of $\mathbf{A}$ will be the square root of the determinant of $\mathbf{A'A}$.

A2.8   Rank and singularity of a matrix.   A matrix is called **singular** if its determinant equals zero. Otherwise it is called **nonsingular**. If a matrix is singular, then not all of its row vectors or column vectors are linearly independent. If a matrix is nonsingular and has r rows and c columns, then its **rank** is the smaller of r and c.   If a matrix is singular, then its rank is the number of linearly independent rows or columns of that matrix. If a matrix is r x r and its determinant is nonzero, then its rank is r. Otherwise it is less than r.   The rank of $\mathbf{AB}$ is the smaller of the ranks of $\mathbf{A}$ and $\mathbf{B}$.   The rank of $\mathbf{AA'}$ equals the rank of $\mathbf{A'A}$ equals the rank of $\mathbf{A}$.

A2.9   The inverse of a matrix.   If $\mathbf{A}$ is an r x r matrix of rank r, that is, $\mathbf{A}$ is a square, nonsingular matrix, then there exists a unique matrix called $\mathbf{A^{-1}}$ ("A-inverse") such that $\mathbf{A^{-1}A = AA^{-1} = I}$, where $\mathbf{I}$ is the identity matrix consisting of 1's on the main diagonal and zeroes everywhere else.

The inverse of a matrix functions in matrix multiplication the way the reciprocal of a number functions in arithmetic multiplications. A number times its reciprocal, for example $(1/2)2 = 2(1/2)$, always equals one, which is the identity element in arithmetic multiplication because for any x, $x(1) = 1(x) = x$. Similarly, for any matrix $\mathbf{B}$, the identity matrix is such that $\mathbf{BI = IB = B}$. We see that the matrix inverse in matrix multiplication is the analog of the reciprocal in ordinary arithmetic multiplication, since when we multiply a matrix by its inverse, we get the identity element of matrix multiplication, the identity matrix. For example,

$$\text{the inverse of } \begin{bmatrix} 1 & 3 \\ 4 & 2 \end{bmatrix} \text{ is } \begin{bmatrix} -.2 & .3 \\ .4 & -.1 \end{bmatrix}.$$

When we multiply these two matrices we obtain the 2 x 2 identity matrix. If we multiply either of these, or any other 2 x 2 matrix by that identity matrix we get the matrix we multiplied. Thus,

$$\begin{bmatrix} 1 & 3 \\ 4 & 2 \end{bmatrix}\begin{bmatrix} -.2 & .3 \\ .4 & -.1 \end{bmatrix} = \begin{bmatrix} 1 & 0 \\ 0 & 1 \end{bmatrix} \text{ and } \begin{bmatrix} 1 & 0 \\ 0 & 1 \end{bmatrix}\begin{bmatrix} 1 & 3 \\ 4 & 2 \end{bmatrix} = \begin{bmatrix} 1 & 3 \\ 4 & 2 \end{bmatrix}.$$

The inverse of a product of matrices is equal to the product of the inverses of those matrices taken in reverse order. Thus $(ABC)^{-1} = C^{-1}B^{-1}A^{-1}$. Also, the inverse of the transpose of a matrix is equal to the transpose of the inverses of that matrix.

The process of inverting a large matrix is best left to a computer. But for small matrices, up to say 4 x 4, or 5 x 5 for the hardier, can be inverted by the following procedures, among others. The first method is to find the inverse of the matrix **A** by finding $1/|A|$ and multiplying it by the matrix formed by by transposing **A** and replacing every element in **A'** by its cofactor. Thus, the inverse of the matrix **A** =

$$\begin{bmatrix} 1 & 2 & 3 \\ 2 & 1 & 2 \\ 1 & 1 & 3 \end{bmatrix}$$

is found by obtaining its determinant, $1(1) -2(4) +3(1) = -4$ and then multiplying $-1/4$ by the matrix obtained by transposing the original matrix an replacing each element by its cofactor, giving

$$(-1/4)\begin{bmatrix} 1 & -3 & 1 \\ -4 & 0 & 4 \\ 1 & 1 & -3 \end{bmatrix} = \begin{bmatrix} -1/4 & 3/4 & -1/4 \\ 1 & 0 & -1 \\ -1/4 & -1/4 & 3/4 \end{bmatrix}$$

which is equal to the inverse of **A**.

A second procedure, known as Gauss's method, involves creating an augmented matrix by appending to the matrix to be inverted an identity matrix of the same size. Thus, for our example matrix we would create the augmented matrix

$$\begin{bmatrix} 1 & 2 & 3 & \vdots & 1 & 0 & 0 \\ 2 & 1 & 2 & \vdots & 0 & 1 & 0 \\ 1 & 1 & 3 & \vdots & 0 & 0 & 1 \end{bmatrix}$$

To find the desired inverse, we now merely operate on the augmented matrix in order to transform the left half into the identity matrix. In the process, the right half will be transformed into the inverse of **A**. Let V_i and V_j be any two row vectors of A and let r be any nonzero real number. Then the permissible operations which we may use are: replacement of any V_i by r V_i; replacement of any V_i by V_i + r V_j; and interchanging V_i with V_j. In the case of the example augmented matrix, the inverse is obtained by the following sequence of steps: change row 3 to row 3 - row 1; change row 1 to row 1 + 2 times row 3; change row 2 to row 2 minus 2 times row 1; change row 3 to row 3 plus row 2; change row 3 to (-1/4) times row 3; change row 2 to row 2 plus 4 times row 3; and finally change row 1 to row 1 minus three times row 3. These successive steps result in the following augmented matrices:

1	2	3	1	0	0
2	1	2	0	1	0
0	-1	0	-1	0	1

1	0	3	-1	0	2
2	1	2	0	1	0
0	-1	0	-1	0	1

1	0	3	-1	0	2
0	1	-4	2	1	-4
0	-1	0	-1	0	1

1	0	3	-1	0	2
0	1	-4	2	1	-4
0	-1	0	-1	0	1

1	0	3	-1	0	2
0	1	-4	2	1	-4
0	0	-4	1	1	-3

1	0	3	-1	0	2
0	1	-4	2	1	-4
0	0	1	-1/4	-1/4	3/4

1	0	3	-1	0	2
0	1	0	1	0	-1
0	0	1	-1/4	-1/4	3/4

1	0	0	-1/4	3/4	-1/4
0	1	0	1	0	-1
0	0	1	-1/4	-1/4	3/4

This results in the identity matrix on the left side of the augmented matrix and the desired inverse of $\mathbf{A}$ on the right side. Since the inverse of a matrix is unique when it exists, this inverse must equal the inverse obtained by the previous method and, as can be seen, it does.

A2.10 Solution of a system of linear equations. Suppose we have a system of linear equations

$$x_{11}b_1 + x_{12}b_2 + ... + x_{1J}b_J = Y_1$$
$$x_{21}b_1 + x_{22}b_2 + ... + x_{2J}b_J = Y_2$$

...

$$x_{I1}b_1 + x_{I2}b_2 + ... + x_{IJ}b_J = Y_I.$$

We can write this as the matrix equation $\mathbf{Xb} = \mathbf{Y}$, where $\mathbf{X}$ is an I x J matrix of elements x_{ij}, $\mathbf{b}$ is the J x 1 vector of b_j's, and $\mathbf{Y}$ is the I x 1 vector of Y_i's. If I = J so that $\mathbf{A}$ is square, and if $\mathbf{X}$ is nonsingular, then there exists a unique solution for the b_i's given by the equation $\mathbf{b} = \mathbf{X^{-1}Y}$. This follows since we can multiply each side of the equation $\mathbf{Xb} = \mathbf{Y}$ by the quantity $\mathbf{X^{-1}}$ to obtain $\mathbf{X^{-1}Xb} = \mathbf{X^{-1}Y}$, which can be rewritten as $\mathbf{b} = \mathbf{X^{-1}Y}$ since $\mathbf{X^{-1}X}$ is just the identity matrix.

A2.11 Least-squares estimation. Let $\mathbf{Y}$ be a data vector and let $\mathbf{Y} = \mathbf{X}\beta + \mathbf{e}$ be a case of the general linear model where the e_i are independently normally distributed. Let $\mathbf{X}$ be an r x c matrix of independent variables of rank c (of full rank). Let β_{est} be the least-squares estimate of β. This means that the squared distance between $\mathbf{Y}$ and the vector of predicted Y values, $\mathbf{X}\beta_{est}$, is smaller for this estimate of β than for any other. For this to be true, the vector $\mathbf{Y} - \mathbf{X}\beta_{est}$ must be orthogonal to the vector $\mathbf{X}\beta_{est}$. Hence $(\mathbf{X}\beta_{est})'(\mathbf{Y} - \mathbf{X}\beta_{est}) = 0$, which implies that $\beta_{est}'\mathbf{X'Y} - \beta_{est}'\mathbf{X'X}\,\beta_{est} = 0$, from which it follows that $\mathbf{X'Y} - \mathbf{X'X}\,\beta_{est} = 0$, and therefore $\mathbf{X'Y} = \mathbf{X'X}\,\beta_{est}$. Since $\mathbf{X'X}$ is a c x c matrix of rank c, it is square and nonsingular. Therefore its inverse exists. Multiplying both sides of the equation from the left by that inverse, we obtain $(\mathbf{X'X})^{-1}\mathbf{X'Y} = (\mathbf{X'X})^{-1}\mathbf{X'X}\beta_{est}$, which reduces to $(\mathbf{X'X})^{-1}\mathbf{X'Y} = \beta_{est}$ since $(\mathbf{X'X})^{-1}\mathbf{X'X} = (\mathbf{X'X})^{-1}(\mathbf{X'X})$ is the identity matrix. Thus, the least-squares estimator of the parameter vector β is given by $(\mathbf{X'X})^{-1}\mathbf{X'Y}$. Since the predicted values of Y are given by the vector $\mathbf{X}\beta_{est}$, it follows that they are $\mathbf{X}(\mathbf{X'X})^{-1}\mathbf{X'Y}$.

In this general linear model, since $\mathbf{X}\beta_{est}$ and $\mathbf{Y} - \mathbf{X}\beta_{est}$ are orthogonal, they form the base and height of a right triangle of which the data vector $\mathbf{Y}$ is the hypotenuse. It follows that the squared lengths of $\mathbf{X}\beta_{est}$ and $\mathbf{Y} - \mathbf{X}\beta_{est}$ sum to the squared length of $\mathbf{Y}$, which is the sum of the squares of the elements in $\mathbf{Y}$. The squared lengths of $\mathbf{X}\beta_{est}$ is

$$(X\beta_{est})'X\beta_{est} = \beta_{est}'X' \ X\beta_{est} = [(X'X)^{-1}X'Y]' \ X'X \ (X'X)^{-1}X'Y$$

$$= \ Y'X(X'X)^{-1} \ X'X \ (X'X)^{-1}X'Y \ = \ Y'X(X'X)^{-1}X'Y$$

and the squared length of $Y - X\beta_{est}$ is

$$(Y - X\beta_{est})' \ (Y - X\beta_{est}) = (Y' - \beta_{est}'X')(Y - X\beta_{est})$$

$$= Y'Y - \beta_{est}'X'Y - Y'X\beta_{est} + \beta_{est}'X'X\beta_{est}$$

$$= Y'Y - \beta_{est}'X'Y - Y'X\beta_{est} + \beta_{est}'X'X \ (X'X)^{-1}X'Y$$

$$= Y'Y - \beta_{est}'X'Y - Y'X\beta_{est} + \beta_{est}'X'Y = Y'Y - Y'X\beta_{est}$$

$$= Y'Y - Y'X(X'X)^{-1}X'Y.$$

The quantity $Y'X(X'X)^{-1}X'Y$ is the estimated portion of the Y sum of squares attributable to the linear relationship between Y and the X variables, and $Y'Y - Y'X(X'X)^{-1}X'Y$ is the estimated portion of the Y sum of squares due to error.

A2.12 Partitioning the sum of squares. For the linear model $Y = X\beta + e$, where X is of full rank, let $X = [X_1, X_2, ...X_i, ..., X_I]$, where each X_i is a submatrix of independent variables. Then

$$Y = [X_1, X_2, ..., X_I] \begin{bmatrix} \beta_1 \\ \beta_2 \\ \vdots \\ \beta_I \end{bmatrix} + e$$

where the β_i are subvectors of parameters associated with the independent variables in X_i. Then the least-squares estimates of the β_i are $\beta_{iest} = (X_i'X_i)^{-1}X_iY$. The predicted value for Y may be written as

$$Y_{pred} = X_1\beta_{1est} + X_2\beta_{2est.} + ...X_i\beta_{iest} + ... + X_I\beta_{Iest}.$$

The total sum of squares, that is the squared length of the data vector Y, is then

$$Y_{pred}' Y_{pred} + (Y - Y_{pred})'(Y - Y_{pred})$$

where the right hand term is the error sum of squares. The left hand term, which is the sum of squares associated with the independent variables in X, is equal to

$$Y_{pred}' Y_{pred} =$$

$$(X_1\beta_{1est} + X_2\beta_{2est} + ...X_i\beta_{iest} + ... + X_I\beta_{Iest})' (X_1\beta_{1est}$$

$$+ X_2\beta_{2est} + ...X_i\beta_{iest} + ... + X_I\beta_{Iest})$$

$$= \beta_{1est}'X_1'X_1\beta_{1est} + ... + \beta_{Iest}'X_I'X_I\beta_{Iest}.$$

But for each i,

$$\beta_{iest}'X_i'X_i\beta_{iest} = [(X_i'X_i)^{-1}X_i Y]'X_i'X_i(X_i'X_i)^{-1}X_i' Y$$

$$= Y'X_i(X_i'X_i)^{-1}(X_i'X_i)(X_i'X_i)^{-1}X_i'Y = Y'[X_i(X_i'X_i)^{-1}X_i']Y$$

$$= Y'A_i Y$$

(where $A_i = [X_i(X_i'X_i)^{-1}X_i']$).

Thus $Y_{pred}'Y_{pred} = \Sigma_i Y'A_i Y$, where each $Y'A_i Y$ is a part of the sum of squares and is associated with the independent variables in X_i. The degrees of freedom associated with this sum of squares is equal to the number of column vectors in X_i.

As a numerical example take the following data from a one-factor design:

A_1	A_2	A_3
1	4	5
2	5	7

The model equation $Y = Xb + e$ is written in matrix form as

$$
\begin{array}{cccc}
\mathbf{Y} & \mathbf{X_1} & \mathbf{X_2} & \beta
\end{array}
$$

$$
\begin{bmatrix} 1 \\ 2 \\ 4 \\ 5 \\ 5 \\ 7 \end{bmatrix}
=
\begin{bmatrix} 1 & 1 & 0 \\ 1 & 1 & 0 \\ 1 & 0 & 1 \\ 1 & 0 & 1 \\ 1 & -1 & -1 \\ 1 & -1 & -1 \end{bmatrix}
\begin{bmatrix} \mu \\ \alpha_1 \\ \alpha_2 \end{bmatrix} + \mathbf{e}
$$

where the $\mathbf{X}$ matrix is of full rank. The total sum of squares is $\mathbf{Y'Y} = 120$. The systematic portion is equal to $SS_{mean} = \mathbf{Y'[X_1(X_1'X_1)^{-1}X_1']Y}$ plus SS_{groups} $\mathbf{Y'[X_2(X_2'X_2)^{-1}X_2']Y}$. Now $(\mathbf{X_1'X_1})$ is just the 1 x 1 matrix [6], so $(\mathbf{X_1'X_1})^{-1}$ is the 1 x 1 matrix [1/6] and $\mathbf{X_1(X_1'X_1)^{-1}X_1'}$ is the 6 x 6 matrix

$$
\begin{bmatrix} 1 \\ 1 \\ 1 \\ 1 \\ 1 \\ 1 \end{bmatrix}
\begin{bmatrix} 1/6 \end{bmatrix}
\begin{bmatrix} 1 & 1 & 1 & 1 & 1 & 1 \end{bmatrix}
=
\begin{bmatrix}
1/6 & 1/6 & 1/6 & 1/6 & 1/6 & 1/6 \\
1/6 & 1/6 & 1/6 & 1/6 & 1/6 & 1/6 \\
1/6 & 1/6 & 1/6 & 1/6 & 1/6 & 1/6 \\
1/6 & 1/6 & 1/6 & 1/6 & 1/6 & 1/6 \\
1/6 & 1/6 & 1/6 & 1/6 & 1/6 & 1/6 \\
1/6 & 1/6 & 1/6 & 1/6 & 1/6 & 1/6
\end{bmatrix}
$$

Therefore $SS_{mean} = \mathbf{Y'[X_1(X_1'X_1)^{-1}X_1']Y} =$

$$
\begin{bmatrix} 1 & 2 & 4 & 5 & 5 & 7 \end{bmatrix}
\begin{bmatrix}
1/6 & 1/6 & 1/6 & 1/6 & 1/6 & 1/6 \\
1/6 & 1/6 & 1/6 & 1/6 & 1/6 & 1/6 \\
1/6 & 1/6 & 1/6 & 1/6 & 1/6 & 1/6 \\
1/6 & 1/6 & 1/6 & 1/6 & 1/6 & 1/6 \\
1/6 & 1/6 & 1/6 & 1/6 & 1/6 & 1/6 \\
1/6 & 1/6 & 1/6 & 1/6 & 1/6 & 1/6
\end{bmatrix}
\begin{bmatrix} 1 \\ 2 \\ 4 \\ 5 \\ 5 \\ 7 \end{bmatrix}
$$

which equals $(\Sigma Y_i)^2/6$ or $6M_Y^2$, which is exactly what we expect from our formula for the sum of squares for the mean, IJM^2.

To find $SS_{groups} = \mathbf{Y'[X_2(X_2'X_2)^{-1}X_2']Y}$ we first find $(\mathbf{X_2'X_2}) =$

$$\begin{bmatrix} 1 & 1 & 0 & 0 & -1 & -1 \\ 0 & 0 & 1 & 1 & -1 & -1 \end{bmatrix} \begin{bmatrix} 1 & 0 \\ 1 & 0 \\ 0 & 1 \\ 0 & 1 \\ -1 & -1 \\ -1 & -1 \end{bmatrix} = \begin{bmatrix} 4 & 2 \\ 2 & 4 \end{bmatrix}$$

and its inverse

$$(1/12) \begin{bmatrix} 4 & -2 \\ -2 & 4 \end{bmatrix} = \begin{bmatrix} 1/3 & -1/6 \\ -1/6 & 1/3 \end{bmatrix}$$

Then, $[X_2(X_2'X_2)^{-1}X_2'] =$

$$\begin{bmatrix} 1 & 0 \\ 1 & 0 \\ 0 & 1 \\ 0 & 1 \\ -1 & -1 \\ -1 & -1 \end{bmatrix} \begin{bmatrix} 1/3 & -1/6 \\ -1/6 & 1/3 \end{bmatrix} \begin{bmatrix} 1 & 1 & 0 & 0 & -1 & -1 \\ 0 & 0 & 1 & 1 & -1 & -1 \end{bmatrix}$$

$$= \begin{bmatrix} 1/3 & 1/3 & -1/6 & -1/6 & -1/6 & -1/6 \\ 1/3 & 1/3 & -1/6 & -1/6 & -1/6 & -1/6 \\ -1/6 & -1/6 & 1/3 & 1/3 & -1/6 & -1/6 \\ -1/6 & -1/6 & 1/3 & 1/3 & -1/6 & -1/6 \\ -1/6 & -1/6 & -1/6 & -1/6 & 1/3 & 1/3 \\ -1/6 & -1/6 & -1/6 & -1/6 & 1/3 & 1/3 \end{bmatrix}$$

Finally, $Y'[X_2(X_2'X_2)^{-1}X_2']Y =$

$$
\begin{bmatrix} 1 & 2 & 4 & 5 & 5 & 7 \end{bmatrix}
\begin{bmatrix}
1/3 & 1/3 & -1/6 & -1/6 & -1/6 & -1/6 \\
1/3 & 1/3 & -1/6 & -1/6 & -1/6 & -1/6 \\
-1/6 & -1/6 & 1/3 & 1/3 & -1/6 & -1/6 \\
-1/6 & -1/6 & 1/3 & 1/3 & -1/6 & -1/6 \\
-1/6 & -1/6 & -1/6 & -1/6 & 1/3 & 1/3 \\
-1/6 & -1/6 & -1/6 & -1/6 & 1/3 & 1/3
\end{bmatrix}
\begin{bmatrix} 1 \\ 2 \\ 4 \\ 5 \\ 5 \\ 7 \end{bmatrix}
$$

which equals 21 and is the same value that we get using the usual anova computational formula $3^2/2 + 9^2/2 + 12^2/2 - 24^2/6$.

A2.13 Vector populations and vector samples. Consider the model $Y = X\beta + e$, where the elements Y are our data sample, the elements of $X\beta$ are their expected values, and the elements of e are independently $N(0, \sigma^2)$ distributed errors. We can think of repeatedly drawing a sample of Y scores as repeatedly sampling a Y vector from a population of such vectors, each of which is composed of a fixed, invariant component $X\beta$ and a random component e. The random component e is a vector that has as its expected value the zero vector, 0, and has an expected squared length of $N\sigma^2$. The vector $X\beta$ never varies from sample to sample. The vector e in general is different from sample to sample.

We can think of all of these vectors as located somewhere in the N-dimensional data space, which is the vector space V_{Nr}, the space of all possible Y vectors. The number of linearly independent column vectors in X, call it p, determines the dimensionality of the subspace V_p in which $X\beta$ is located. We call this subspace the **parameter space**, and the vectors in this space we call **parameter vectors**. Its dimensionality is the degrees of freedom for systematic sources in the fixed-effects analysis of variance models. The orthogonal complement of V_p is the space V_{N-p}, which contains all and only those vectors orthogonal to every vector in V_p. We call this subspace the **error space**, and the vectors in this space are called the error vectors. The dimensionality of the error space is N - p, which is the degrees of freedom for error in the fixed-effects analysis of variance. The process of least-squares estimation is the process of finding that parameter vector closest to the data vector. Since the difference between the data vector and the parameter vector will be an error vector, least-squares estimation finds that error vector which is the shortest. The values in the selected parameter vector are the least-squares estimates of the elements in $X\beta$, and the elements in the selected error vector are the error estimates for each score.

The possible inhabitants of this N-dimensional space, then, are the possible data vectors, the vector $X\beta$, the vector e, the possible parameter vectors that estimate $X\beta$, and the possible error vectors that equal the difference between the data vector and the parameter vector. For a given data vector, the parameter vector and the error vector form the base and the height of a right triangle, the hypotenuse of which is the data vector.

In hypothesis testing, two or more different models are compared. In the analysis of variance, one model, the smaller model, is a special case of a more general, larger model. Algebraically, the column vectors in X are sorted into two groups, X_r and X_{p-r}. Under the smaller model, $Y = X_r\beta_r + e$; under the larger model, $Y = X_r\beta_r + X_{p-r}\beta_{p-r} + e$. Geometrically this means that the p-dimensional space spanned by the vectors of X is partitioned into two mutually orthogonal subspaces, the space V_r spanned by the vectors of X_r and the space V_{p-r} spanned by the vectors of X_{p-r}. Under the smaller model V_r is the parameter space and least-squares estimation locates linear combination of the vectors in X_r which are closest to Y. Under the larger model the parameter space is that spanned by $X = [X_r X_{p-r}]$. The test of the smaller model versus the larger model is based on a comparison of the lengths of the error estimate vectors under the two models. If the error estimate vector under the smaller model is substantially longer than the error estimate vector under the larger model, the smaller model is rejected. But if the difference between the lengths of the two error estimate vectors is within the range of differences that would be likely to occur by chance if the smaller model were true, then the larger model is rejected. The comparison of the two lengths is based on an F test. These vectors are shown in Figure A2.2.

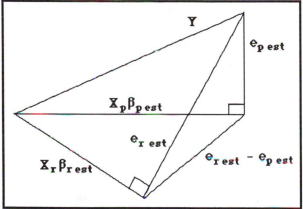

Figure A2.2. The model $Y = Xb + e$ versus the smaller model $Y = X_r b_r + e$ is tested by finding the least squares estimates under each model and comparing the lengths of the error estimates under the two models. Under the null hypothesis that $Y = X_r b_r + e$, the statistic $\{[(e_{r\ est} - e_{p\ est})'(e_{r\ est} - e_{p\ est})]/(p - r)\}/\{[e_p'e_p]/(N - p)\}$ is distributed as F on p - r and N - p degrees of freedom.

Appendix 3

Statistical Tables and Charts

TABLE 1 THE NORMAL CUMULATIVE PROBABILITY DISTRIBUTION

z	F(z)	z	F(z)	z	F(z)	z	F(z)
.00	.500000	.50	.691462	1.00	.841345	1.50	.933193
.01	.503989	.51	.694974	1.01	.843752	1.51	.934478
.02	.507978	.52	.698468	1.02	.846136	1.52	.935744
.03	.511966	.53	.701944	1.03	.848495	1.53	.936992
.04	.515953	.54	.705402	1.04	.850830	1.54	.938220
.05	.519939	.55	.708840	1.05	.853141	1.55	.939429
.05	.523922	.56	.712260	1.06	.855428	1.56	.940620
.07	.527903	.57	.715661	1.07	.857690	1.57	.941792
.08	.531881	.58	.719043	1.08	.859929	1.58	.942947
.09	.535856	.59	.722405	1.09	.862143	1.59	.944083
.10	.539828	.60	.725747	1.10	.864334	1.60	.945201
.11	.543795	.61	.729069	1.11	.866500	1.61	.946301
.12	.547758	.62	.732371	1.12	.868643	1.62	.947384
.13	.551717	.63	.735653	1.13	.870762	1.63	.948449
.14	.555670	.64	.738914	1.14	.872857	1.64	.949497
.15	.559618	.65	.742154	1.15	.874928	1.65	.950528
.16	.563560	.66	.745373	1.16	.876976	1.66	.951543
.17	.567495	.67	.748571	1.17	.879000	1.67	.952540
.18	.571424	.68	.751748	1.18	.881000	1.68	.953521
.19	.575345	.69	.754903	1.19	.882977	1.69	.954486
.20	.579260	.70	.758036	1.20	.884930	1.70	.955434
.21	.583166	.71	.761148	1.21	.886861	1.71	.956367
.22	.587064	.72	.764238	1.22	.888768	1.72	.957284
.23	.590954	.73	.767305	1.23	.890651	1.73	.958185
.24	.594835	.74	.770350	1.24	.892512	1.74	.959070
.25	.598706	.75	.773373	1.25	.894350	1.75	.959941
.26	.602568	.76	.776373	1.26	.896165	1.76	.960796
.27	.606420	.77	.779350	1.27	.897958	1.77	.961636
.28	.610261	.78	.782305	1.28	.899727	1.78	.962462
.29	.614092	.79	.785236	1.29	.901475	1.79	.963273
.30	.617911	.80	.788145	1.30	.903200	1.80	.964070
.31	.621720	.81	.791030	1.31	.904902	1.81	.964852
.32	.625516	.82	.793892	1.32	.906582	1.82	.965620
.33	.629300	.83	.796731	1.33	.908241	1.83	.966375
.34	.633072	.84	.799546	1.34	.909877	1.84	.967116
.35	.636831	.85	.802338	1.35	.911492	1.85	.967843
.36	.640576	.86	.805106	1.36	.913085	1.86	.968557
.37	.644309	.87	.807850	1.37	.914656	1.87	.969258
.38	.648027	.88	.810570	1.38	.916207	1.88	.969946
.39	.651732	.89	.813267	1.39	.917736	1.89	.970621
.40	.655422	.90	.815940	1.40	.919243	1.90	.971283
.41	.659097	.91	.818589	1.41	.920730	1.91	.971933
.42	.662757	.92	.821214	1.42	.922196	1.92	.972571
.43	.666402	.93	.823814	1.43	.923642	1.93	.973197
.44	.670031	.94	.826391	1.44	.925066	1.94	.973810
.45	.673645	.95	.828944	1.45	.926471	1.95	.974412
.46	.677242	.96	.831472	1.46	.927855	1.96	.975002
.47	.680822	.97	.833977	1.47	.929219	1.97	.975581
.48	.684386	.98	.836457	1.48	.930563	1.98	.976148
.49	.687933	.99	.838913	1.49	.931888	1.99	.976704
.50	.691462	1.00	.841345	1.50	.933193	2.00	.977250

TABLE 1 (continued) THE NORMAL CUMULATIVE PROBABILITY DISTRIBUTION

z	F(z)	z	.F(z)	z	F(z)	z	F(z)
2.00	.977250	2.50	.993790	3.00	.998650	3.50	.999767
2.01	.977784	2.51	.993963	3.01	.998694	3.51	.999776
2.02	.978308	2.52	.994132	3.02	.998736	3.52	.999784
2.03	.978822	2.53	.994297	3.03	.998777	3.53	.999792
2.04	.979325	2.54	.994457	3.04	.998817	3.54	.999800
2.05	.979818	2.55	.994614	3.05	.998856	3.55	.999807
2.06	.980301	2.56	.994766	3.05	.998893	3.56	.999815
2.07	.980774	2.57	.994915	3.07	.998930	3.57	.999822
2.08	.981237	2.58	.995060	3.08	.998965	3.58	.999828
2.09	.981691	2.59	.995201	3.09	.998999	3.59	.999835
2.10	.982136	2.60	.995339	3.10	.999032	3.60	.999841
2.11	.982571	2.61	.995473	3.11	.999065	3.61	.999847
2.12	.982997	2.62	.995604	3.12	.999096	3.62	.999853
2.13	.983414	2.63	.995731	3.13	.999126	3.63	.999858
2.14	.983823	2.64	.995855	3.14	.999155	3.64	.999864
2.15	.984222	2.65	.995975	3.15	.999184	3.65	.999869
2.16	.984614	2.66	.996093	3.16	.999211	3.66	.999874
2.17	.984997	2.67	.996207	3.17	.999238	3.67	.999879
2.18	.985371	2.68	.996319	3.18	.999264	3.68	.999883
2.19	.985738	2.69	.996427	3.19	.999289	3.69	.999888
2.20	.986097	2.70	.996533	3.20	.999313	3.70	.999892
2.21	.986447	2.71	.996636	3.21	.999336	3.71	.999896
2.22	.986791	2.72	.996736	3.22	.999359	3.72	.999900
2.23	.987126	2.73	.996833	3.23	.999381	3.73	.999904
2.24	.987454	2.74	.996928	3.24	.999402	3.74	.999908
2.25	.987776	2.75	.997020	3.25	.999423	3.75	.999912
2.26	.988089	2.76	.997110	3.26	.999443	3.76	.999915
2.27	.988396	2.77	.997197	3.27	.999462	3.77	.999918
2.28	.988696	2.78	.997282	3.28	.999481	3.78	.999922
2.29	.988989	2.79	.997365	3.29	.999499	3.79	.999925
2.30	.989276	2.80	.997445	3.30	.999517	3.80	.999928
2.31	.989556	2.81	.997523	3.31	.999534	3.81	.999930
2.32	.989830	2.82	.997599	3.32	.999550	3.82	.999933
2.33	.990097	2.83	.997673	3.33	.999566	3.83	.999936
2.34	.990358	2.84	.997744	3.34	.999581	3.84	.999938
2.35	.990613	2.85	.997814	3.35	.999596	3.85	.999941
2.36	.990862	2.86	.997882	3.36	.999610	3.86	.999943
2.37	.991106	2.87	.997948	3.37	.999624	3.87	.999946
2.38	.991344	2.88	.998012	3.38	.999638	3.88	.999948
2.39	.991576	2.89	.998074	3.39	.999650	3.89	.999950
2.40	.991802	2.90	.998134	3.40	.999663	3.90	.999952
2.41	.992024	2.91	.998193	3.41	.999675	3.91	.999954
2.42	.992240	2.92	.998250	3.42	.999687	3.92	.999956
2.43	.992451	2.93	.998305	3.43	.999698	3.93	.999958
2.44	.992656	2.94	.998359	3.44	.999709	3.94	.999959
2.45	.992857	2.95	.998411	3.45	.999720	3.95	.999961
2.46	.993053	2.96	.998462	3.46	.999730	3.96	.999962
2.47	.993244	2.97	.998511	3.47	.999740	3.97	.999964
2.48	.993431	2.98	.998559	3.48	.999749	3.98	.999966
2.49	.993613	2.99	.998605	3.49	.999758	3.99	.999967
2.50	.993790	3.00	.998650	3.50	.999767	4.00	.999968

TABLE 2   PERCENTAGE POINTS OF THE t DISTRIBUTION

v	Q = .4	.25	.10	.05	.025	.01	.005	.0025	.001	.0005
	2Q =.8	.50	.20	.10	.050	.02	.010	.0050	.002	.0010
1	.325	1.000	3.078	6.314	12.706	31.821	63.657	127.320	318.310	636.620
2	.289	.816	1.886	2.920	4.303	6.965	9.925	14.089	22.327	31.598
3	.277	.765	1.638	2.353	3.182	4.541	5.841	7.453	10.214	12.924
4	.267	.741	1.533	2.132	2.776	3.747	4.604	5.598	7.173	8.610
5	.265	.727	1.476	2.015	2.571	3.365	4.032	4.773	5.893	6.869
6	.263	.718	1.440	1.943	2.447	3.143	3.707	4.317	5.208	5.959
7	.262	.711	1.415	1.895	2.365	2.998	3.499	4.029	4.785	5.408
8	.261	.706	1.397	1.860	2.306	2.896	3.355	3.883	4.501	5.041
9	.260	.703	1.383	1.833	2.262	2.821	3.250	3.690	4.297	4.781
1 0	.260	.700	1.372	1.812	2.228	2.764	3.169	3.581	4.144	4.587
1 1	.259	.697	1.363	1.796	2.201	2.718	3.106	3.497	4.025	4.437
1 2	.259	.695	1.356	1.782	2.179	2.681	3.055	3.428	3.930	4.318
1 3	.258	.694	1.350	1.771	2.160	2.650	3.012	3.372	3.852	4.221
1 4	.258	.692	1.345	1.761	2.145	2.624	2.977	3.326	3.787	4.140
1 5	.258	.691	1.341	1.753	2.131	2.602	2.947	3.286	3.733	4.073
1 6	.257	.690	1.337	1.746	2.120	2.583	2.921	3.252	3.686	4.015
1 7	.257	.689	1.333	1.740	2.110	2.567	2.898	3.222	3.646	3.965
1 8	.257	.688	1.330	1.734	2.101	2.552	2.878	3.197	3.610	3.922
1 9	.257	.688	1.328	1.729	2.093	2.539	2.861	3.174	3.579	3.883
2 0	.257	.687	1.325	1.725	2.086	2.528	2.845	3.153	3.552	3.850
2 1	.257	.686	1.323	1.721	2.080	2.518	2.831	3.135	3.527	3.819
2 2	.256	.686	1.321	1.717	2.074	2.508	2.819	3.119	3.505	3.792
2 3	.256	.685	1.319	1.714	2.069	2.500	2.807	3.104	3.485	3.767
2 4	.256	.685	1.318	1.711	2.064	2.492	2.797	3.091	3.467	3.745
2 5	.256	.684	1.316	1.708	2.060	2.485	2.787	3.078	3.450	3.725
2 6	.256	.684	1.315	1.706	2.056	2.479	2.779	3.067	3.435	3.707
2 7	.256	.684	1.314	1.703	2.052	2.473	2.771	3.057	3.421	3.690
2 8	.256	.683	1.313	1.701	2.048	2.467	2.763	3.047	3.408	3.674
2 9	.256	.683	1.311	1.699	2.045	2.462	2.756	3.038	3.396	3.659
3 0	.256	.683	1.310	1.697	2.042	2.457	2.750	3.030	3.385	3.646
4 0	.255	.681	1.303	1.684	2.021	2.423	2.704	2.971	3.307	3.551
6 0	.254	.679	1.296	1.671	2.000	2.390	2.660	2.915	3.232	3.460
1 2 0	.254	.677	1.289	1.658	1.980	2.358	2.617	2.860	3.160	3.373
∞	.253	.674	1.282	1.645	1.960	2.326	2.576	2.807	3.090	3.291

Q is the upper-tail area of the distribution, v degrees of freedom For a two-tail test use 2Q.

Reproduced from E. S. Pearson and H. O. Hartley (Eds.) 1970. *Biometrika tables for statisticians* Vol I, 3rd edition by kind permission of the Biometrika Trustees.

Appendix 3

TABLE 3   PERCENTAGE POINTS OF THE χ^2 DISTRIBUTION

Q / ν	.995	.990	.975	.950	.900	.750	.500
1	$392704 \cdot 10^{-10}$	$157088 \cdot 10^{-9}$	$982069 \cdot 10^{-9}$	$393214 \cdot 10^{-8}$	.0157908	.1015308	.454936
2	.010025	.0201007	.0506356	.102587	.210721	.575364	1.38629
3	.071722	.114832	.215795	.351846	.584374	1.212534	2.36597
4	.206989	.297109	.484419	.710723	1.063623	1.92256	3.35669
5	.411742	.554298	.831212	1.145476	1.61031	2.67460	4.35146
6	.675727	.872090	1.23734	1.63538	2.20413	3.45460	5.34812
7	.989256	1.239043	1.68987	2.16735	2.83311	4.25485	6.34581
8	1.34441	1.64650	2.17973	2.73264	3.48954	5.07064	7.34412
9	1.73493	2.08790	2.70039	3.32511	4.16816	5.89883	8.34283
10	2.15586	2.55821	3.24697	3.94030	4.86518	6.73720	9.34182
11	2.60322	3.05348	3.81575	4.57481	5.57778	7.58414	10.3410
12	3.07382	3.57057	4.40379	5.22603	6.30380	8.43842	11.3403
13	3.56503	4.10692	5.00875	5.89186	7.04150	9.29907	12.3398
14	4.07467	4.66043	5.62873	6.57063	7.78953	10.1653	13.3393
15	4.60092	5.22935	6.26214	7.26094	8.54676	11.0365	14.3389
16	5.14221	5.81221	6.90766	7.96165	9.31224	11.9122	15.3385
17	5.69722	6.40776	7.56419	8.67176	10.0852	12.7919	16.3382
18	6.26480	7.01491	8.23075	9.39046	10.8649	13.6753	17.3379
19	6.84397	7.63273	8.90652	10.1170	11.6509	14.5620	18.3377
20	7.43384	8.26040	9.59078	10.8508	12.4426	15.4518	19.3374
21	8.03365	8.89720	10.28293	11.5913	13.2396	16.3444	20.3372
22	8.64272	9.54249	10.9823	12.3380	14.0415	17.2396	21.3370
23	9.26043	10.19567	11.6886	13.0905	14.8480	18.1373	22.3369
24	9.88623	10.8564	12.4012	13.8484	15.6587	19.0373	23.3367
25	10.5197	11.5240	13.1197	14.6114	16.4734	19.9393	24.3366
26	11.1602	12.1981	13.8439	15.3792	17.2919	20.8434	25.3365
27	11.8076	12.8785	14.5734	16.1514	18.1139	21.7494	26.3363
28	12.4613	13.5647	15.3079	16.9279	18.9392	22.6572	27.3362
29	13.1211	14.2565	16.0471	17.7084	19.7677	23.5666	28.3361
30	13.7867	14.9535	16.7908	18.4927	20.5992	24.4776	29.3360
40	20.7065	22.1643	24.4330	26.5093	29.0505	33.6603	39.3353
50	27.9907	29.7067	32.3574	34.7643	37.6886	42.9421	49.3349
60	35.5345	37.4849	40.4817	43.1880	46.4589	52.2938	59.3347
70	43.2752	45.4417	48.7576	51.7393	55.3289	61.6983	69.3345
80	51.1719	53.5401	57.1532	60.3915	64.2778	71.1445	79.3343
90	59.1963	61.7541	65.6466	69.1260	73.2911	80.6247	89.3342
100	67.3276	70.0649	74.2219	77.9295	82.3581	90.1332	99.3341

TABLE 3 (continued)   PERCENTAGE POINTS OF THE χ^2 DISTRIBUTION

Q	.250	.100	.050	.025	.010	.005	.001
ν							
1	1.32330	2.70554	3.84146	5.02389	6.63490	7.87944	10.828
2	2.77259	4.60517	5.99146	7.37776	9.21034	10.5966	13.816
3	4.10834	6.25139	7.81473	9.34840	11.3449	12.8382	16.266
4	5.38527	7.77944	9.48773	11.1433	13.2767	14.8603	18.467
5	6.62568	9.23636	11.0705	12.8325	15.0863	16.7496	20.515
6	7.84080	10.6446	12.5916	14.4494	16.8119	18.5476	22.458
7	9.03715	12.0170	14.0671	16.0128	18.4753	20.2777	24.322
8	10.2189	13.3616	15.5073	17.5345	20.0902	21.9550	26.125
9	11.3888	14.6837	16.9190	19.0228	21.6660	23.5894	27.877
10	12.5489	15.9872	18.3070	20.4832	23.2093	25.1882	29.588
11	13.7007	17.2750	19.6751	21.9200	24.7250	26.7568	31.264
12	14.8454	18.5493	21.0261	23.3367	26.2170	28.2995	32.909
13	15.9839	19.8119	22.3620	24.7356	27.6882	29.8195	34.528
14	17.1169	21.0641	23.6848	26.1189	29.1412	31.3194	36.123
15	18.2451	22.3071	24.9958	27.4884	30.5779	32.8013	37.697
16	19.3689	23.5418	26.2962	28.8454	31.9999	34.2672	39.252
17	20.4887	24.7690	27.5871	30.1910	33.4087	35.7185	40.790
18	21.6049	25.9894	28.8693	31.5264	34.8053	37.1565	42.312
19	22.7178	27.2036	30.1435	32.8523	36.1909	38.5823	43.820
20	23.8277	28.4120	31.4104	34.1696	37.5662	39.9968	45.315
21	24.9348	29.6151	32.6706	35.4789	38.9322	41.4011	46.797
22	26.0393	30.8133	33.9244	36.7807	40.2894	42.7957	48.268
23	27.1413	32.0069	35.1725	38.0756	41.6384	44.1813	49.728
24	28.2412	33.1962	36.4150	39.3641	42.9798	45.5585	51.179
25	29.3389	34.3816	37.6525	40.6465	44.3141	46.9279	52.618
26	30.4346	35.5632	38.8851	41.9232	45.6417	48.2899	54.052
27	31.5284	36.7412	40.1133	43.1945	46.9629	49.6449	55.476
28	32.6205	37.9159	41.3371	44.4608	48.2782	50.9934	56.892
29	33.7109	39.0875	42.5570	45.7223	49.5879	52.3356	58.301
30	34.7997	40.2560	43.7730	46.9792	50.8922	53.6720	59.703
40	45.6160	51.8051	55.7585	59.3417	63.6907	66.7660	73.402
50	56.3336	63.1671	67.5048	71.4202	76.1539	79.4900	86.661
60	66.9815	74.3970	79.0819	83.2977	88.3794	91.9517	99.607
70	77.5767	85.5270	90.5312	95.0232	100.425	104.215	112.317
80	88.1303	96.5782	101.879	106.629	112.329	116.321	124.839
90	98.6499	107.565	113.145	118.136	124.116	128.299	137.208
100	109.141	118.498	124.342	129.561	135.807	140.169	149.449

For $n > 100$ take $\chi^2 = v\{1 - [2/(9v)] + z\sqrt{[2/(9v)]}\}^{23}$ or $\chi^2 = .5\{z + \sqrt{(2v - 1)}\}^2$ where z is the standard normal deviate corresponding to $1 - Q$.

Reproduced from E. S. Pearson and H. O. Hartley (Eds.) 1970. *Biometrika tables for statisticians* Vol I, 3rd edition by kind permission of the Biometrika Trustees.

TABLE 4 PERCENTAGE POINTS OF THE F DISTRIBUTION: UPPER 10 PERCENT POINTS

v_2 \ v_1	1	2	3	4	5	6	7	8	9	10	12	15	20	24	30	40	60	120	∞
1	39.86	49.00	53.59	55.83	57.24	58.20	58.91	59.44	59.86	60.19	60.71	61.22	61.74	62.00	62.26	62.53	62.79	63.06	63.33
2	8.53	9.00	9.16	9.24	9.29	9.33	9.35	9.37	9.38	9.39	9.41	9.42	9.44	9.45	9.46	9.47	9.47	9.48	9.49
3	5.54	5.46	5.39	5.34	5.31	5.28	5.27	5.25	5.24	5.23	5.22	5.20	5.18	5.18	5.17	5.16	5.15	5.14	5.13
4	4.54	4.32	4.19	4.11	4.05	4.01	3.98	3.95	3.94	3.92	3.90	3.87	3.84	3.83	3.82	3.80	3.79	3.78	3.76
5	4.06	3.78	3.62	3.52	3.45	3.40	3.37	3.34	3.32	3.30	3.27	3.24	3.21	3.19	3.17	3.16	3.14	3.12	3.10
6	3.78	3.46	3.29	3.18	3.11	3.05	3.01	2.98	2.96	2.94	2.90	2.87	2.84	2.82	2.80	2.78	2.76	2.74	2.72
7	3.59	3.26	3.07	2.96	2.88	2.83	2.78	2.75	2.72	2.70	2.67	2.63	2.59	2.58	2.56	2.54	2.51	2.49	2.47
8	3.46	3.11	2.92	2.81	2.73	2.67	2.62	2.59	2.56	2.54	2.50	2.46	2.42	2.40	2.38	2.36	2.34	2.32	2.29
9	3.36	3.01	2.81	2.69	2.61	2.55	2.51	2.47	2.44	2.42	2.38	2.34	2.30	2.28	2.25	2.23	2.21	2.18	2.16
10	3.29	2.92	2.73	2.61	2.52	2.46	2.41	2.38	2.35	2.32	2.28	2.24	2.20	2.18	2.16	2.13	2.11	2.08	2.06
11	3.23	2.86	2.66	2.54	2.45	2.39	2.34	2.30	2.27	2.25	2.21	2.17	2.12	2.10	2.08	2.05	2.03	2.00	1.97
12	3.18	2.81	2.61	2.48	2.39	2.33	2.28	2.24	2.21	2.19	2.15	2.10	2.06	2.04	2.01	1.99	1.96	1.93	1.90
13	3.14	2.76	2.56	2.43	2.35	2.28	2.23	2.20	2.16	2.14	2.10	2.05	2.01	1.98	1.96	1.93	1.90	1.88	1.85
14	3.10	2.73	2.52	2.39	2.31	2.24	2.19	2.15	2.12	2.10	2.05	2.01	1.96	1.94	1.91	1.89	1.86	1.83	1.80
15	3.07	2.70	2.49	2.36	2.27	2.21	2.16	2.12	2.09	2.06	2.02	1.97	1.92	1.90	1.87	1.85	1.82	1.79	1.76
16	3.05	2.67	2.46	2.33	2.24	2.18	2.13	2.09	2.06	2.03	1.99	1.94	1.89	1.87	1.84	1.81	1.78	1.75	1.72
17	3.03	2.64	2.44	2.31	2.22	2.15	2.10	2.06	2.03	2.00	1.96	1.91	1.86	1.84	1.81	1.78	1.75	1.72	1.69
18	3.01	2.62	2.42	2.29	2.20	2.13	2.08	2.04	2.00	1.98	1.93	1.89	1.84	1.81	1.78	1.75	1.72	1.69	1.66
19	2.99	2.61	2.40	2.27	2.18	2.11	2.06	2.02	1.98	1.96	1.91	1.86	1.81	1.79	1.76	1.73	1.70	1.67	1.63
20	2.97	2.59	2.38	2.25	2.16	2.09	2.04	2.00	1.96	1.94	1.89	1.84	1.79	1.77	1.74	1.71	1.68	1.64	1.61
21	2.96	2.57	2.36	2.23	2.14	2.08	2.02	1.98	1.95	1.92	1.87	1.83	1.78	1.75	1.72	1.69	1.66	1.62	1.59
22	2.95	2.56	2.35	2.22	2.13	2.06	2.01	1.97	1.93	1.90	1.86	1.81	1.76	1.73	1.70	1.67	1.64	1.60	1.57
23	2.94	2.55	2.34	2.21	2.11	2.05	1.99	1.95	1.92	1.89	1.84	1.80	1.74	1.72	1.69	1.66	1.62	1.59	1.55
24	2.93	2.54	2.33	2.19	2.10	2.04	1.98	1.94	1.91	1.88	1.83	1.78	1.73	1.70	1.67	1.64	1.61	1.57	1.53
25	2.92	2.53	2.32	2.18	2.09	2.02	1.97	1.93	1.89	1.87	1.82	1.77	1.72	1.69	1.66	1.63	1.59	1.56	1.52
26	2.91	2.52	2.31	2.17	2.08	2.01	1.96	1.92	1.88	1.86	1.81	1.76	1.71	1.68	1.65	1.61	1.58	1.54	1.50
27	2.90	2.51	2.30	2.17	2.07	2.00	1.95	1.91	1.87	1.85	1.80	1.75	1.70	1.67	1.64	1.60	1.57	1.53	1.49
28	2.89	2.50	2.29	2.16	2.06	2.00	1.94	1.90	1.87	1.84	1.79	1.74	1.69	1.66	1.63	1.59	1.56	1.52	1.48
29	2.89	2.50	2.28	2.15	2.06	1.99	1.93	1.89	1.86	1.83	1.78	1.73	1.68	1.65	1.62	1.58	1.55	1.51	1.47
30	2.88	2.49	2.28	2.14	2.05	1.98	1.93	1.88	1.85	1.82	1.77	1.72	1.67	1.64	1.61	1.57	1.54	1.50	1.46
40	2.84	2.44	2.23	2.09	2.00	1.93	1.87	1.83	1.79	1.76	1.71	1.66	1.61	1.57	1.54	1.51	1.47	1.42	1.38
60	2.79	2.39	2.18	2.04	1.95	1.87	1.82	1.77	1.74	1.71	1.66	1.60	1.54	1.51	1.48	1.44	1.40	1.35	1.29
120	2.75	2.35	2.13	1.99	1.90	1.82	1.77	1.72	1.68	1.65	1.60	1.55	1.48	1.45	1.41	1.37	1.32	1.26	1.19
∞	2.71	2.30	2.08	1.94	1.85	1.77	1.72	1.67	1.63	1.60	1.55	1.49	1.42	1.38	1.34	1.30	1.24	1.17	1.00

TABLE 4 (continued) PERCENTAGE POINTS OF THE F DISTRIBUTION: UPPER 5 PERCENT POINTS

v_2 \ v_1	1	2	3	4	5	6	7	8	9	10	12	15	20	24	30	40	60	120	∞
1	161.4	199.5	215.7	224.6	230.2	234.0	236.8	238.9	240.5	241.9	243.9	245.9	248.0	249.1	250.1	251.1	252.2	253.3	254.3
2	18.51	19.00	19.16	19.25	19.30	19.33	19.35	19.37	19.38	19.40	19.41	19.43	19.45	19.45	19.46	19.47	19.48	19.49	19.5
3	10.13	9.55	9.28	9.12	9.01	8.94	8.89	8.85	8.81	8.79	8.74	8.70	8.66	8.64	8.62	8.59	8.57	8.55	8.53
4	7.71	6.94	6.59	6.39	6.26	6.16	6.09	6.04	6.00	5.96	5.91	5.86	5.80	5.77	5.75	5.72	5.69	5.66	5.63
5	6.61	5.79	5.41	5.19	5.05	4.95	4.88	4.82	4.77	4.74	4.68	4.62	4.56	4.53	4.50	4.46	4.43	4.40	4.36
6	5.99	5.14	4.76	4.53	4.39	4.28	4.21	4.15	4.10	4.06	4.00	3.94	3.87	3.84	3.81	3.77	3.74	3.70	3.67
7	5.59	4.74	4.35	4.12	3.97	3.87	3.79	3.73	3.68	3.64	3.57	3.51	3.44	3.41	3.38	3.34	3.30	3.27	3.23
8	5.32	4.46	4.07	3.84	3.69	3.58	3.50	3.44	3.39	3.35	3.28	3.22	3.15	3.12	3.08	3.04	3.01	2.97	2.93
9	5.12	4.26	3.86	3.63	3.48	3.37	3.29	3.23	3.18	3.14	3.07	3.01	2.94	2.90	2.86	2.83	2.79	2.75	2.71
10	4.96	4.10	3.71	3.48	3.33	3.22	3.14	3.07	3.02	2.98	2.91	2.85	2.77	2.74	2.70	2.66	2.62	2.58	2.54
11	4.84	3.98	3.59	3.36	3.20	3.09	3.01	2.95	2.90	2.85	2.79	2.72	2.65	2.61	2.57	2.53	2.49	2.45	2.40
12	4.75	3.89	3.49	3.26	3.11	3.00	2.91	2.85	2.80	2.75	2.69	2.62	2.54	2.51	2.47	2.43	2.38	2.34	2.30
13	4.67	3.81	3.41	3.18	3.03	2.92	2.83	2.77	2.71	2.67	2.60	2.53	2.46	2.42	2.38	2.34	2.30	2.25	2.21
14	4.60	3.74	3.34	3.11	2.96	2.85	2.76	2.70	2.65	2.60	2.53	2.46	2.39	2.35	2.31	2.27	2.22	2.18	2.13
15	4.54	3.68	3.29	3.06	2.90	2.79	2.71	2.64	2.59	2.54	2.48	2.40	2.33	2.29	2.25	2.20	2.16	2.11	2.07
16	4.49	3.63	3.24	3.01	2.85	2.74	2.66	2.59	2.54	2.49	2.42	2.35	2.28	2.24	2.19	2.15	2.11	2.06	2.01
17	4.45	3.59	3.20	2.96	2.81	2.70	2.61	2.55	2.49	2.45	2.38	2.31	2.23	2.19	2.15	2.10	2.06	2.01	1.96
18	4.41	3.55	3.16	2.93	2.77	2.66	2.58	2.51	2.46	2.41	2.34	2.27	2.19	2.15	2.11	2.06	2.02	1.97	1.92
19	4.38	3.52	3.13	2.90	2.74	2.63	2.54	2.48	2.42	2.38	2.31	2.23	2.16	2.11	2.07	2.03	1.98	1.93	1.88
20	4.35	3.49	3.10	2.87	2.71	2.60	2.51	2.45	2.39	2.35	2.28	2.20	2.12	2.08	2.04	1.99	1.95	1.90	1.84
21	4.32	3.47	3.07	2.84	2.68	2.57	2.49	2.42	2.37	2.32	2.25	2.18	2.10	2.05	2.01	1.96	1.92	1.87	1.81
22	4.30	3.44	3.05	2.82	2.66	2.55	2.46	2.40	2.34	2.30	2.23	2.15	2.07	2.03	1.98	1.94	1.89	1.84	1.78
23	4.28	3.42	3.03	2.80	2.64	2.53	2.44	2.37	2.32	2.27	2.20	2.13	2.05	2.01	1.96	1.91	1.86	1.81	1.76
24	4.26	3.40	3.01	2.78	2.62	2.51	2.42	2.36	2.30	2.25	2.18	2.11	2.03	1.98	1.94	1.89	1.84	1.79	1.73
25	4.24	3.39	2.99	2.76	2.60	2.49	2.40	2.34	2.28	2.24	2.16	2.09	2.01	1.96	1.92	1.87	1.82	1.77	1.71
26	4.23	3.37	2.98	2.74	2.59	2.47	2.39	2.32	2.27	2.22	2.15	2.07	1.99	1.95	1.90	1.85	1.80	1.75	1.69
27	4.21	3.35	2.96	2.73	2.57	2.46	2.37	2.31	2.25	2.20	2.13	2.06	1.97	1.93	1.88	1.84	1.79	1.73	1.67
28	4.20	3.34	2.95	2.71	2.56	2.45	2.36	2.29	2.24	2.19	2.12	2.04	1.96	1.91	1.87	1.82	1.77	1.71	1.65
29	4.18	3.33	2.93	2.70	2.55	2.43	2.35	2.28	2.22	2.18	2.10	2.03	1.94	1.90	1.85	1.81	1.75	1.70	1.64
30	4.17	3.32	2.92	2.69	2.53	2.42	2.33	2.27	2.21	2.16	2.09	2.01	1.93	1.89	1.84	1.79	1.74	1.68	1.62
40	4.08	3.23	2.84	2.61	2.45	2.34	2.25	2.18	2.12	2.08	2.00	1.92	1.84	1.79	1.74	1.69	1.64	1.58	1.51
60	4.00	3.15	2.76	2.53	2.37	2.25	2.17	2.10	2.04	1.99	1.92	1.84	1.75	1.70	1.65	1.59	1.53	1.47	1.39
120	3.92	3.07	2.68	2.45	2.29	2.17	2.09	2.02	1.96	1.91	1.83	1.75	1.66	1.61	1.55	1.50	1.43	1.35	1.25
∞	3.84	3.00	2.60	2.37	2.21	2.10	2.01	1.94	1.88	1.83	1.75	1.67	1.57	1.52	1.46	1.39	1.32	1.22	1.00

TABLE 4 (continued) PERCENTAGE POINTS OF THE F DISTRIBUTION: UPPER 2.5 PERCENT POINTS

v_2 \ v_1	1	2	3	4	5	6	7	8	9	10	12	15	20	24	30	40	60	120	∞
1	647.8	799.5	864.2	899.6	921.8	937.1	948.2	956.7	963.3	968.6	976.7	984.9	993.1	997.2	1001	1006	1010	1014	1018
2	38.51	39.00	39.17	39.25	39.30	39.33	39.36	39.37	39.39	39.40	39.41	39.43	39.45	39.46	39.46	39.47	39.48	39.49	39.50
3	17.44	16.04	15.44	15.10	14.88	14.73	14.62	14.54	14.47	14.42	14.34	14.25	14.17	14.12	14.08	14.04	13.99	13.95	13.90
4	12.22	10.65	9.98	9.60	9.36	9.20	9.07	8.98	8.90	8.84	8.75	8.66	8.56	8.51	8.46	8.41	8.36	8.31	8.26
5	10.01	8.43	7.76	7.39	7.15	6.98	6.85	6.76	6.68	6.62	6.52	6.43	6.33	6.28	6.23	6.18	6.12	6.07	6.02
6	8.81	7.26	6.60	6.23	5.99	5.82	5.70	5.60	5.52	5.46	5.37	5.27	5.17	5.12	5.07	5.01	4.96	4.90	4.85
7	8.07	6.54	5.89	5.52	5.29	5.12	4.99	4.90	4.82	4.76	4.67	4.57	4.47	4.42	4.36	4.31	4.25	4.20	4.14
8	7.57	6.06	5.42	5.05	4.82	4.65	4.53	4.43	4.36	4.30	4.20	4.10	4.00	3.95	3.89	3.84	3.78	3.73	3.67
9	7.21	5.71	5.08	4.72	4.48	4.32	4.20	4.10	4.03	3.96	3.87	3.77	3.67	3.61	3.56	3.51	3.45	3.39	3.33
10	6.94	5.46	4.83	4.47	4.24	4.07	3.95	3.85	3.78	3.72	3.62	3.52	3.42	3.37	3.31	3.26	3.20	3.14	3.08
11	6.72	5.26	4.63	4.28	4.04	3.88	3.76	3.66	3.59	3.53	3.43	3.33	3.23	3.17	3.12	3.06	3.00	2.94	2.88
12	6.55	5.10	4.47	4.12	3.89	3.73	3.61	3.51	3.44	3.37	3.28	3.18	3.07	3.02	2.96	2.91	2.85	2.79	2.72
13	6.41	4.97	4.35	4.00	3.77	3.60	3.48	3.39	3.31	3.25	3.15	3.05	2.95	2.89	2.84	2.78	2.72	2.66	2.60
14	6.30	4.86	4.24	3.89	3.66	3.50	3.38	3.29	3.21	3.15	3.05	2.95	2.84	2.79	2.73	2.67	2.61	2.55	2.49
15	6.20	4.77	4.15	3.80	3.58	3.41	3.29	3.20	3.12	3.06	2.96	2.86	2.76	2.70	2.64	2.59	2.52	2.46	2.40
16	6.12	4.69	4.08	3.73	3.50	3.34	3.22	3.12	3.05	2.99	2.89	2.79	2.68	2.63	2.57	2.51	2.45	2.38	2.32
17	6.04	4.62	4.01	3.66	3.44	3.28	3.16	3.06	2.98	2.92	2.82	2.72	2.62	2.56	2.50	2.44	2.38	2.32	2.25
18	5.98	4.56	3.95	3.61	3.38	3.22	3.10	3.01	2.93	2.87	2.77	2.67	2.56	2.50	2.44	2.38	2.32	2.26	2.19
19	5.92	4.51	3.90	3.56	3.33	3.17	3.05	2.96	2.88	2.82	2.72	2.62	2.51	2.45	2.39	2.33	2.27	2.20	2.13
20	5.87	4.46	3.86	3.51	3.29	3.13	3.01	2.91	2.84	2.77	2.68	2.57	2.46	2.41	2.35	2.29	2.22	2.16	2.09
21	5.83	4.42	3.82	3.48	3.25	3.09	2.97	2.87	2.80	2.73	2.64	2.53	2.42	2.37	2.31	2.25	2.18	2.11	2.04
22	5.79	4.38	3.78	3.44	3.22	3.05	2.93	2.84	2.76	2.70	2.60	2.50	2.39	2.33	2.27	2.21	2.14	2.08	2.00
23	5.75	4.35	3.75	3.41	3.18	3.02	2.90	2.81	2.73	2.67	2.57	2.47	2.36	2.30	2.24	2.18	2.11	2.04	1.97
24	5.72	4.32	3.72	3.38	3.15	2.99	2.87	2.78	2.70	2.64	2.54	2.44	2.33	2.27	2.21	2.15	2.08	2.01	1.94
25	5.69	4.29	3.69	3.35	3.13	2.97	2.85	2.75	2.68	2.61	2.51	2.41	2.30	2.24	2.18	2.12	2.05	1.98	1.91
26	5.66	4.27	3.67	3.33	3.10	2.94	2.82	2.73	2.65	2.59	2.49	2.39	2.28	2.22	2.16	2.09	2.03	1.95	1.88
27	5.63	4.24	3.65	3.31	3.08	2.92	2.80	2.71	2.63	2.57	2.47	2.36	2.25	2.19	2.13	2.07	2.00	1.93	1.85
28	5.61	4.22	3.63	3.29	3.06	2.90	2.78	2.69	2.61	2.55	2.45	2.34	2.23	2.17	2.11	2.05	1.98	1.91	1.83
29	5.59	4.20	3.61	3.27	3.04	2.88	2.76	2.67	2.59	2.53	2.43	2.32	2.21	2.15	2.09	2.03	1.96	1.89	1.81
30	5.57	4.18	3.59	3.25	3.03	2.87	2.75	2.65	2.57	2.51	2.41	2.31	2.20	2.14	2.07	2.01	1.94	1.87	1.79
40	5.42	4.05	3.46	3.13	2.90	2.74	2.62	2.53	2.45	2.39	2.29	2.18	2.07	2.01	1.94	1.88	1.80	1.72	1.64
60	5.29	3.93	3.34	3.01	2.79	2.63	2.51	2.41	2.33	2.27	2.17	2.06	1.94	1.88	1.82	1.74	1.67	1.58	1.48
120	5.15	3.80	3.23	2.89	2.67	2.52	2.39	2.30	2.22	2.16	2.05	1.94	1.82	1.76	1.69	1.61	1.53	1.43	1.31
∞	5.02	3.69	3.12	2.79	2.57	2.41	2.29	2.19	2.11	2.05	1.94	1.83	1.71	1.64	1.57	1.48	1.39	1.27	1.00

TABLE 4 (continued) PERCENTAGE POINTS OF THE F DISTRIBUTION: UPPER 1 PERCENT POINTS

v_2 \ v_1	1	2	3	4	5	6	7	8	9	10	12	15	20	24	30	40	60	120	∞
1	4052	5000	5403	5625	5764	5859	5928	5981	6022	6056	6106	6157	6209	6235	6261	6287	6313	6339	6366
2	98.50	99.00	99.17	99.25	99.30	99.33	99.36	99.37	99.39	99.40	99.42	99.43	99.45	99.46	99.47	99.47	99.48	99.49	99.50
3	34.12	30.82	29.46	28.71	28.24	27.91	27.67	27.49	27.35	27.23	27.05	26.87	26.69	26.60	26.50	26.41	26.32	26.22	26.13
4	21.20	18.00	16.69	15.98	15.52	15.21	14.98	14.80	14.66	14.55	14.37	14.20	14.02	13.93	13.84	13.75	13.65	13.56	13.46
5	16.26	13.27	12.06	11.39	10.97	10.67	10.46	10.29	10.16	10.05	9.89	9.72	9.55	9.47	9.38	9.29	9.20	9.11	9.02
6	13.75	10.92	9.78	9.15	8.75	8.47	8.26	8.10	7.98	7.87	7.72	7.56	7.40	7.31	7.23	7.14	7.06	6.97	6.88
7	12.25	9.55	8.45	7.85	7.46	7.19	6.99	6.84	6.72	6.62	6.47	6.31	6.16	6.07	5.99	5.91	5.82	5.74	5.65
8	11.26	8.65	7.59	7.01	6.63	6.37	6.18	6.03	5.91	5.81	5.67	5.52	5.36	5.28	5.20	5.12	5.03	4.95	4.86
9	10.56	8.02	6.99	6.42	6.06	5.80	5.61	5.47	5.35	5.26	5.11	4.96	4.81	4.73	4.65	4.57	4.48	4.40	4.31
10	10.04	7.56	6.55	5.99	5.64	5.39	5.20	5.06	4.94	4.85	4.71	4.56	4.41	4.33	4.25	4.17	4.08	4.00	3.91
11	9.65	7.21	6.22	5.67	5.32	5.07	4.89	4.74	4.63	4.54	4.40	4.25	4.10	4.02	3.94	3.86	3.78	3.69	3.60
12	9.33	6.93	5.95	5.41	5.06	4.82	4.64	4.50	4.39	4.30	4.16	4.01	3.86	3.78	3.70	3.62	3.54	3.45	3.36
13	9.07	6.70	5.74	5.21	4.86	4.62	4.44	4.30	4.19	4.10	3.96	3.82	3.66	3.59	3.51	3.43	3.34	3.25	3.17
14	8.86	6.51	5.56	5.04	4.69	4.46	4.28	4.14	4.03	3.94	3.80	3.66	3.51	3.43	3.35	3.27	3.18	3.09	3.00
15	8.68	6.36	5.42	4.89	4.56	4.32	4.14	4.00	3.89	3.80	3.67	3.52	3.37	3.29	3.21	3.13	3.05	2.96	2.87
16	8.53	6.23	5.29	4.77	4.44	4.20	4.03	3.89	3.78	3.69	3.55	3.41	3.26	3.18	3.10	3.02	2.93	2.84	2.75
17	8.40	6.11	5.18	4.67	4.34	4.10	3.93	3.79	3.68	3.59	3.46	3.31	3.16	3.08	3.00	2.92	2.83	2.75	2.65
18	8.29	6.01	5.09	4.58	4.25	4.01	3.84	3.71	3.60	3.51	3.37	3.23	3.08	3.00	2.92	2.84	2.75	2.66	2.57
19	8.18	5.93	5.01	4.50	4.17	3.94	3.77	3.63	3.52	3.43	3.30	3.15	3.00	2.92	2.84	2.76	2.67	2.58	2.49
20	8.10	5.85	4.94	4.43	4.10	3.87	3.70	3.56	3.46	3.37	3.23	3.09	2.94	2.86	2.78	2.69	2.61	2.52	2.42
21	8.02	5.78	4.87	4.37	4.04	3.81	3.64	3.51	3.40	3.31	3.17	3.03	2.88	2.80	2.72	2.64	2.55	2.46	2.36
22	7.95	5.72	4.82	4.31	3.99	3.76	3.59	3.45	3.35	3.26	3.12	2.98	2.83	2.75	2.67	2.58	2.50	2.40	2.31
23	7.88	5.66	4.76	4.26	3.94	3.71	3.54	3.41	3.30	3.21	3.07	2.93	2.78	2.70	2.62	2.54	2.45	2.35	2.26
24	7.82	5.61	4.72	4.22	3.90	3.67	3.50	3.36	3.26	3.17	3.03	2.89	2.74	2.66	2.58	2.49	2.40	2.31	2.21
25	7.77	5.57	4.68	4.18	3.85	3.63	3.46	3.32	3.22	3.13	2.99	2.85	2.70	2.62	2.54	2.45	2.36	2.27	2.17
26	7.72	5.53	4.64	4.14	3.82	3.59	3.42	3.29	3.18	3.09	2.96	2.81	2.66	2.58	2.50	2.42	2.33	2.23	2.13
27	7.68	5.49	4.60	4.11	3.78	3.56	3.39	3.26	3.15	3.06	2.93	2.78	2.63	2.55	2.47	2.38	2.29	2.20	2.10
28	7.64	5.45	4.57	4.07	3.75	3.53	3.36	3.23	3.12	3.03	2.90	2.75	2.60	2.52	2.44	2.35	2.26	2.17	2.06
29	7.60	5.42	4.54	4.04	3.73	3.50	3.33	3.20	3.09	3.00	2.87	2.73	2.57	2.49	2.41	2.33	2.23	2.14	2.03
30	7.56	5.39	4.51	4.02	3.70	3.47	3.30	3.17	3.07	2.98	2.84	2.70	2.55	2.47	2.39	2.30	2.21	2.11	2.01
40	7.31	5.18	4.31	3.83	3.51	3.29	3.12	2.99	2.89	2.80	2.66	2.52	2.37	2.29	2.20	2.11	2.02	1.92	1.80
60	7.08	4.98	4.13	3.65	3.34	3.12	2.95	2.82	2.72	2.63	2.50	2.35	2.20	2.12	2.03	1.94	1.84	1.73	1.60
120	6.85	4.79	3.95*	3.48	3.17	2.96	2.79	2.66	2.56	2.47	2.34	2.19	2.03	1.95	1.86	1.76	1.66	1.53	1.38
∞	6.63	4.61	3.78	3.32	3.02	2.80	2.64	2.51	2.41	2.32	2.18	2.04	1.88	1.79	1.70	1.59	1.47	1.32	1.00

TABLE 5 PERCENTAGE POINTS OF THE STUDENTIZED RANGE, $q = (x_n - x_1)/s_y$:

Upper 5 percent points

v \ n	2	3	4	5	6	7	8	9	10	11	12	13	14	15	16	17	18	19	20
1	17.97	26.98	32.82	37.08	40.41	43.12	45.40	47.36	49.07	50.59	51.96	53.20	54.33	55.36	56.32	57.22	58.04	58.83	59.56
2	6.08	8.33	9.80	10.88	11.74	12.44	13.03	13.54	13.99	14.39	14.75	15.08	15.38	15.65	15.91	16.14	16.37	16.57	16.77
3	4.50	5.91	6.82	7.50	8.04	8.48	8.85	9.18	9.46	9.72	9.95	10.15	10.35	10.52	10.69	10.84	10.98	11.11	11.24
4	3.93	5.04	5.76	6.29	6.71	7.05	7.35	7.60	7.83	8.03	8.21	8.37	8.52	8.66	8.79	8.91	9.03	9.13	9.23
5	3.64	4.60	5.22	5.67	6.03	6.33	6.58	6.80	6.99	7.17	7.32	7.47	7.60	7.72	7.83	7.93	8.03	8.12	8.21
6	3.46	4.34	4.90	5.30	5.63	5.90	6.12	6.32	6.49	6.65	6.79	6.92	7.03	7.14	7.24	7.34	7.43	7.51	7.59
7	3.34	4.16	4.68	5.06	5.36	5.61	5.82	6.00	6.16	6.30	6.43	6.55	6.66	6.76	6.85	6.94	7.02	7.10	7.17
8	3.26	4.04	4.53	4.89	5.17	5.40	5.60	5.77	5.92	6.05	6.18	6.29	6.39	6.48	6.57	6.65	6.73	6.80	6.87
9	3.20	3.95	4.41	4.76	5.02	5.24	5.43	5.59	5.74	5.87	5.98	6.09	6.19	6.28	6.36	6.44	6.51	6.58	6.64
10	3.15	3.88	4.33	4.65	4.91	5.12	5.30	5.46	5.60	5.72	5.83	5.93	6.03	6.11	6.19	6.27	6.34	6.40	6.47
11	3.11	3.82	4.26	4.57	4.82	5.03	5.20	5.35	5.49	5.61	5.71	5.81	5.90	5.98	6.06	6.13	6.20	6.27	6.33
12	3.08	3.77	4.20	4.51	4.75	4.95	5.12	5.27	5.39	5.51	5.61	5.71	5.80	5.88	5.95	6.02	6.09	6.15	6.21
13	3.06	3.73	4.15	4.45	4.69	4.88	5.05	5.19	5.32	5.43	5.53	5.63	5.71	5.79	5.86	5.93	5.99	6.05	6.11
14	3.03	3.70	4.11	4.41	4.64	4.83	4.99	5.13	5.25	5.36	5.46	5.55	5.64	5.71	5.79	5.85	5.91	5.97	6.03
15	3.01	3.67	4.08	4.37	4.59	4.78	4.94	5.08	5.20	5.31	5.40	5.49	5.57	5.65	5.72	5.78	5.85	5.90	5.96
16	3.00	3.65	4.05	4.33	4.56	4.74	4.90	5.03	5.15	5.26	5.35	5.44	5.52	5.59	5.66	5.73	5.79	5.84	5.90
17	2.98	3.63	4.02	4.30	4.52	4.70	4.86	4.99	5.11	5.21	5.31	5.39	5.47	5.54	5.61	5.67	5.73	5.79	5.84
18	2.97	3.61	4.00	4.28	4.49	4.67	4.82	4.96	5.07	5.17	5.27	5.35	5.43	5.50	5.57	5.63	5.69	5.74	5.79
19	2.96	3.59	3.98	4.25	4.47	4.65	4.79	4.92	5.04	5.14	5.23	5.31	5.39	5.46	5.53	5.59	5.65	5.70	5.75
20	2.95	3.58	3.96	4.23	4.45	4.62	4.77	4.90	5.01	5.11	5.20	5.28	5.36	5.43	5.49	5.55	5.61	5.66	5.71
24	2.92	3.53	3.90	4.17	4.37	4.54	4.68	4.81	4.92	5.01	5.10	5.18	5.25	5.32	5.38	5.44	5.49	5.55	5.59
30	2.89	3.49	3.85	4.10	4.30	4.46	4.60	4.72	4.82	4.92	5.00	5.08	5.15	5.21	5.27	5.33	5.38	5.43	5.47
40	2.86	3.44	3.79	4.04	4.23	4.39	4.52	4.63	4.73	4.82	4.90	4.98	5.04	5.11	5.16	5.22	5.27	5.31	5.36
60	2.83	3.40	3.74	3.98	4.16	4.31	4.44	4.55	4.65	4.73	4.81	4.88	4.94	5.00	5.06	5.11	5.15	5.20	5.24
120	2.80	3.36	3.68	3.92	4.10	4.24	4.36	4.47	4.56	4.64	4.71	4.78	4.84	4.90	4.95	5.00	5.04	5.09	5.13
∞	2.77	3.31	3.63	3.86	4.03	4.17	4.29	4.39	4.47	4.55	4.62	4.68	4.74	4.80	4.85	4.89	4.93	4.97	5.01

TABLE 5 (continued) PERCENTAGE POINTS OF THE STUDENTIZED RANGE, $q = (x_n - x_1)/s_\nu$:

Upper 1 percent points

n \ ν	2	3	4	5	6	7	8	9	10	11	12	13	14	15	16	17	18	19	20
1	90.03	135.0	164.3	185.6	202.2	215.8	227.2	237.0	245.6	253.2	260.0	266.2	271.8	277.0	281.8	286.3	290.4	294.3	298.0
2	14.04	19.02	22.29	24.72	26.63	28.20	29.53	30.68	31.69	32.59	33.40	34.13	34.81	35.43	36.00	36.53	37.03	37.50	37.95
3	8.26	10.62	12.17	13.33	14.24	15.00	15.64	16.20	16.69	17.13	17.53	17.89	18.22	18.52	18.81	19.07	19.32	19.55	19.77
4	6.51	8.12	9.17	9.96	10.58	11.10	11.55	11.93	12.27	12.57	12.84	13.09	13.32	13.53	13.73	13.91	14.08	14.24	14.40
5	5.70	6.98	7.80	8.42	8.91	9.32	9.67	9.97	10.24	10.48	10.70	10.89	11.08	11.24	11.40	11.55	11.68	11.81	11.93
6	5.24	6.33	7.03	7.56	7.97	8.32	8.61	8.87	9.10	9.30	9.48	9.65	9.81	9.95	10.08	10.21	10.32	10.43	10.54
7	4.95	5.92	6.54	7.01	7.37	7.68	7.94	8.17	8.37	8.55	8.71	8.86	9.00	9.12	9.24	9.35	9.46	9.55	9.65
8	4.75	5.64	6.20	6.62	6.96	7.24	7.47	7.68	7.86	8.03	8.18	8.31	8.44	8.55	8.66	8.76	8.85	8.94	9.03
9	4.60	5.43	5.96	6.35	6.66	6.91	7.13	7.33	7.49	7.65	7.78	7.91	8.03	8.13	8.23	8.33	8.41	8.49	8.57
10	4.48	5.27	5.77	6.14	6.43	6.67	6.87	7.05	7.21	7.36	7.49	7.60	7.71	7.81	7.91	7.99	8.08	8.15	8.23
11	4.39	5.15	5.62	5.97	6.25	6.48	6.67	6.84	6.99	7.13	7.25	7.36	7.46	7.56	7.65	7.73	7.81	7.88	7.95
12	4.32	5.05	5.50	5.84	6.10	6.32	6.51	6.67	6.81	6.94	7.06	7.17	7.26	7.36	7.44	7.52	7.59	7.66	7.73
13	4.26	4.96	5.40	5.73	5.98	6.19	6.37	6.53	6.67	6.79	6.90	7.01	7.10	7.19	7.27	7.35	7.42	7.48	7.55
14	4.21	4.89	5.32	5.63	5.88	6.08	6.26	6.41	6.54	6.66	6.77	6.87	6.96	7.05	7.13	7.20	7.27	7.33	7.39
15	4.17	4.84	5.25	5.56	5.80	5.99	6.16	6.31	6.44	6.55	6.66	6.76	6.84	6.93	7.00	7.07	7.14	7.20	7.26
16	4.13	4.79	5.19	5.49	5.72	5.92	6.08	6.22	6.35	6.46	6.56	6.66	6.74	6.82	6.90	6.97	7.03	7.09	7.15
17	4.10	4.74	5.14	5.43	5.66	5.85	6.01	6.15	6.27	6.38	6.48	6.57	6.66	6.73	6.81	6.87	6.94	7.00	7.05
18	4.07	4.70	5.09	5.38	5.60	5.79	5.94	6.08	6.20	6.31	6.41	6.50	6.58	6.65	6.73	6.79	6.85	6.91	6.97
19	4.05	4.67	5.05	5.33	5.55	5.73	5.89	6.02	6.14	6.25	6.34	6.43	6.51	6.58	6.65	6.72	6.78	6.84	6.89
20	4.02	4.64	5.02	5.29	5.51	5.69	5.84	5.97	6.09	6.19	6.28	6.37	6.45	6.52	6.59	6.65	6.71	6.77	6.82
24	3.96	4.55	4.91	5.17	5.37	5.54	5.69	5.81	5.92	6.02	6.11	6.19	6.26	6.33	6.39	6.45	6.51	6.56	6.61
30	3.89	4.45	4.80	5.05	5.24	5.40	5.54	5.65	5.76	5.85	5.93	6.01	6.08	6.14	6.20	6.26	6.31	6.36	6.41
40	3.82	4.37	4.70	4.93	5.11	5.26	5.39	5.50	5.60	5.69	5.76	5.83	5.90	5.96	6.02	6.07	6.12	6.16	6.21
60	3.76	4.28	4.59	4.82	4.99	5.13	5.25	5.36	5.45	5.53	5.60	5.67	5.73	5.78	5.84	5.89	5.93	5.97	6.01
120	3.70	4.20	4.50	4.71	4.87	5.01	5.12	5.21	5.30	5.37	5.44	5.50	5.56	5.61	5.66	5.71	5.75	5.79	5.83
∞	3.64	4.12	4.40	4.60	4.76	4.88	4.99	5.08	5.16	5.23	5.29	5.35	5.40	5.45	5.49	5.54	5.57	5.61	5.65

Reproduced from E. S. Pearson and H. O. Hartley (Eds.) 1970. *Biometrika tables for statisticians* Vol. I 3rd Edition by kind permission of the Biometrika Trustees.

Appendix 3

TABLE 6 PERCENTAGE POINTS OF THE BONFERRONI t STATISTIC FOR K CONTRASTS WITH THE INDICATED DF

$\alpha = .05$

K \ df	5	7	10	12	15	20	24	30	40	60	120	∞
2	3.17	2.84	2.64	2.56	2.49	2.42	2.39	2.36	2.33	2.30	2.27	2.24
3	3.54	3.13	2.87	2.78	2.69	2.61	2.58	2.54	2.50	2.47	2.43	2.39
4	3.81	3.34	3.04	2.94	2.84	2.75	2.70	2.66	2.62	2.58	2.54	2.50
5	4.04	3.50	3.17	3.06	2.95	2.85	2.80	2.75	2.71	2.66	2.62	2.58
6	4.22	3.64	3.28	3.15	3.04	2.93	2.88	2.83	2.78	2.73	2.68	2.64
7	4.38	3.76	3.37	3.24	3.11	3.00	2.94	2.89	2.84	2.79	2.74	2.69
8	4.53	3.86	3.45	3.31	3.18	3.06	3.00	2.94	2.89	2.84	2.79	2.74
9	4.66	3.95	3.52	3.37	3.24	3.11	3.05	2.99	2.93	2.88	2.83	2.77
10	4.78	4.03	3.58	3.43	3.29	3.16	3.09	3.03	2.97	2.92	2.86	2.81
15	5.25	4.36	3.83	3.65	3.48	3.33	3.26	3.19	3.12	3.06	2.99	2.94
20	5.60	4.59	4.01	3.80	3.62	3.46	3.38	3.30	3.23	3.16	3.09	3.02
25	5.89	4.78	4.15	3.93	3.74	3.55	3.47	3.39	3.31	3.24	3.16	3.09
30	6.15	4.95	4.27	4.04	3.82	3.63	3.54	3.46	3.38	3.30	3.22	3.15
35	6.36	5.09	4.37	4.13	3.90	3.70	3.61	3.52	3.43	3.34	3.27	3.19
40	6.56	5.21	4.45	4.20	3.97	3.76	3.66	3.57	3.48	3.39	3.31	3.23
45	6.70	5.31	4.53	4.26	4.02	3.80	3.70	3.61	3.51	3.42	3.34	3.26
50	6.86	5.40	4.59	4.32	4.07	3.85	3.74	3.65	3.55	3.46	3.37	3.29
100	8.00	6.08	5.06	4.73	4.42	4.15	4.04	3.90	3.79	3.69	3.58	3.48
250	9.68	7.06	5.70	5.27	4.90	4.56	4.4*	4.2*	4.1*	3.97	3.83	3.72

$\alpha = .01$

K \ df	5	7	10	12	15	20	24	30	40	60	120	∞
2	4.78	4.03	3.58	3.43	3.29	3.16	3.09	3.03	2.97	2.92	2.86	2.81
3	5.25	4.36	3.83	3.65	3.48	3.33	3.26	3.19	3.12	3.06	2.99	2.94
4	5.60	4.59	4.01	3.80	3.62	3.46	3.38	3.30	3.23	3.16	3.09	3.02
5	5.89	4.78	4.15	3.93	3.74	3.55	3.47	3.39	3.31	3.24	3.16	3.09
6	6.15	4.95	4.27	4.04	3.82	3.63	3.54	3.46	3.38	3.30	3.22	3.15
7	6.36	5.09	4.37	4.13	3.90	3.70	3.61	3.52	3.43	3.34	3.27	3.19
8	6.56	5.21	4.45	4.20	3.97	3.76	3.66	3.57	3.48	3.39	3.31	3.23
9	6.70	5.31	4.53	4.26	4.02	3.80	3.70	3.61	3.51	3.42	3.34	3.26
10	6.86	5.40	4.59	4.32	4.07	3.85	3.74	3.65	3.55	3.46	3.37	3.29
15	7.51	5.79	4.86	4.56	4.29	4.03	3.91	3.80	3.70	3.59	3.50	3.40
20	8.00	6.08	5.06	4.73	4.42	4.15	4.04	3.90	3.79	3.69	3.58	3.48
25	8.37	6.30	5.20	4.86	4.53	4.25	4.1*	3.98	3.88	3.76	3.64	3.54
30	8.68	6.49	5.33	4.95	4.61	4.33	4.2*	4.13	3.93	3.81	3.69	3.59
35	8.95	6.67	5.44	5.04	4.71	4.39	4.3*	4.26	3.97	3.84	3.73	3.63
40	9.19	6.83	5.52	5.12	4.78	4.46	4.3*	4.1*	3.89	3.89	3.77	3.66
45	9.41	6.93	5.60	5.20	4.84	4.52	4.3*	4.2*	4.1*	3.93	3.80	3.69
50	9.68	7.06	5.70	5.27	4.90	4.56	4.4*	4.2*	4.1*	3.97	3.83	3.72
100	11.04	7.80	6.20	5.70	5.20	4.80	4.7*	4.4*	4.5*		4.00	3.89
250	13.26	8.83	6.9*	6.3*	5.8*	5.2*	5.0*	4.9*	4.8*			4.11

TABLE 7 PERCENTAGE POINTS OF DUNNETT'S MANY-ONE t STATISTIC

Table of t for two-sided comparisons between p treatments and a control for a familywise error rate of .05.

p = number of treatment means (including the control)

df	2	3	4	5	6	7	8	9	10	11	12	13	16	21
5	2.57	3.03	3.29	3.48	3.62	3.73	3.82	3.90	3.97	4.03	4.09	4.14	4.26	4.42
6	2.45	2.86	3.10	3.26	3.39	3.49	3.57	3.64	3.71	3.76	3.81	3.86	3.97	4.11
7	2.36	2.75	2.97	3.12	3.24	3.33	3.41	3.47	3.53	3.58	3.63	3.67	3.78	3.91
8	2.31	2.67	2.88	3.02	3.13	3.22	3.29	3.35	3.41	3.46	3.50	3.54	3.64	3.76
9	2.26	2.61	2.81	2.95	3.05	3.14	3.20	3.26	3.32	3.36	3.40	3.44	3.53	3.65
10	2.23	2.57	2.76	2.89	2.99	3.07	3.14	3.19	3.24	3.29	3.33	3.36	3.45	3.57
11	2.20	2.53	2.72	2.84	2.94	3.02	3.08	3.14	3.19	3.23	3.27	3.30	3.39	3.50
12	2.18	2.50	2.68	2.81	2.90	2.98	3.04	3.09	3.14	3.18	3.22	3.25	3.34	3.45
13	2.16	2.48	2.65	2.78	2.87	2.94	3.00	3.06	3.10	3.14	3.18	3.21	3.29	3.40
14	2.14	2.46	2.63	2.75	2.84	2.91	2.97	3.02	3.07	3.11	3.14	3.18	3.26	3.36
15	2.13	2.44	2.61	2.73	2.82	2.89	2.95	3.00	3.04	3.08	3.12	3.15	3.23	3.33
16	2.12	2.42	2.59	2.71	2.80	2.87	2.92	2.97	3.02	3.06	3.09	3.12	3.20	3.30
17	2.11	2.41	2.58	2.69	2.78	2.85	2.90	2.95	3.00	3.03	3.07	3.10	3.18	3.27
18	2.10	2.40	2.56	2.68	2.76	2.83	2.89	2.94	2.98	3.01	3.05	3.08	3.16	3.25
19	2.09	2.39	2.55	2.66	2.75	2.81	2.87	2.92	2.96	3.00	3.03	3.06	3.14	3.23
20	2.09	2.38	2.54	2.65	2.73	2.80	2.86	2.90	2.95	2.98	3.02	3.05	3.12	3.22
24	2.06	2.35	2.51	2.61	2.70	2.76	2.81	2.86	2.90	2.94	2.97	3.00	3.07	3.16
30	2.04	2.32	5.47	2.58	2.66	2.72	2.77	2.82	2.86	2.89	2.92	2.95	3.02	3.11
40	2.02	2.29	2.44	2.54	2.62	2.68	2.73	2.77	2.81	2.85	2.87	2.90	2.97	3.06
60	2.00	2.27	2.41	2.51	2.58	2.64	2.69	2.73	2.77	2.80	2.83	2.86	2.92	3.00
120	1.98	2.24	2.38	2.47	2.55	2.60	2.65	2.69	2.73	2.76	2.79	2.81	2.87	2.95
∞	1.96	2.21	2.35	2.44	2.51	2.57	2.61	2.65	2.69	2.72	2.74	2.77	2.83	2.91

TABLE 7 (continued) PERCENTAGE POINTS OF DUNNETT'S MANY-ONE t STATISTIC

Table of t for two-sided comparisons between p treatments and a control for a familywise error rate of .01.

p = number of treatment means (including the control)

df	2	3	4	5	6	7	8	9	10	11	12	13	16	21
5	4.03	4.63	4.98	5.22	5.41	5.56	5.69	5.80	5.89	5.98	6.05	6.12	6.30	6.52
6	3.71	4.21	4.51	4.71	4.87	5.00	5.10	5.20	5.28	5.35	5.41	5.47	5.62	5.81
7	3.50	3.95	4.21	4.39	4.53	4.64	4.74	4.82	4.89	4.95	5.01	5.06	5.19	5.36
8	3.36	3.77	4.00	4.17	4.29	4.40	4.48	4.56	4.62	4.68	4.73	4.78	4.90	5.05
9	3.25	3.63	3.85	4.01	4.12	4.22	4.30	4.37	4.43	4.48	4.53	4.57	4.68	4.82
10	3.17	3.53	3.74	3.88	3.99	4.08	4.16	4.22	4.28	4.33	4.37	4.42	4.52	4.65
11	3.11	3.45	3.65	3.79	3.89	3.98	4.05	4.11	4.16	4.21	4.25	4.29	4.39	4.52
12	3.05	3.39	3.58	3.71	3.81	3.89	3.96	4.02	4.07	4.11	4.16	4.19	4.29	4.41
13	3.01	3.33	3.52	3.65	3.74	3.82	3.89	3.94	3.99	4.04	4.08	4.11	4.20	4.32
14	2.98	3.29	3.47	3.59	3.69	3.76	3.83	3.88	3.93	3.97	4.01	4.05	4.13	4.24
15	2.95	3.25	3.43	3.55	3.64	3.71	3.78	3.83	3.88	3.92	3.95	3.99	4.07	4.18
16	2.92	3.22	3.39	3.51	3.60	3.67	3.73	3.78	3.83	3.87	3.91	3.94	4.02	4.13
17	2.90	3.19	3.36	3.47	3.56	3.63	3.69	3.74	3.79	3.83	3.86	3.90	3.98	4.08
18	2.88	3.17	3.33	3.44	3.53	3.60	3.66	3.71	3.75	3.79	3.83	3.86	3.94	4.04
19	2.86	3.15	3.31	3.42	3.50	3.57	3.63	3.68	3.72	3.76	3.79	3.83	3.90	4.00
20	2.85	3.13	3.29	3.40	3.48	3.55	3.60	3.65	3.69	3.73	3.77	3.80	3.87	3.97
24	2.80	3.07	3.22	3.32	3.40	3.47	3.52	3.57	3.61	3.64	3.68	3.70	3.78	3.87
30	2.75	3.01	3.15	3.25	3.33	3.39	3.44	3.49	3.52	3.56	3.59	3.62	3.69	3.78
40	2.70	2.95	3.09	3.19	3.26	3.32	3.37	3.41	3.44	3.48	3.51	3.53	3.60	3.68
60	2.66	2.90	3.03	3.12	3.19	3.25	3.29	3.33	3.37	3.40	3.42	3.45	3.51	3.59
120	2.62	2.85	2.97	3.06	3.12	3.18	3.22	3.26	3.29	3.32	3.35	3.37	3.43	3.51
∞	2.58	2.79	2.92	3.00	3.06	3.11	3.15	3.19	3.22	3.25	3.27	3.29	3.35	3.42

Reproduced from C. W. Dunnett (1964). New tables for multiple comparisons with a control. Biometrics, 20, 482-491 with the kind permission from The Biometric Society.

TABLE 8 CRITICAL VALUES FOR DUNCAN'S NEW MULTIPLE RANGE TEST

Protection level $P = (.95)^{p-1}$; Significance level $a = .05$

v \ p	2	3	4	5	6	7	8	9	10	11	12	13	14	15	16	17	18	19
1	17.97	17.97	17.97	17.97	17.97	17.97	17.97	17.97	17.97	17.97	17.97	17.97	17.97	17.97	17.97	17.97	17.97	17.97
2	6.085	6.085	6.085	6.085	6.085	6.085	6.085	6.085	6.085	6.085	6.085	6.085	6.085	6.085	6.085	6.085	6.085	6.085
3	4.501	4.516	4.516	4.516	4.516	4.516	4.516	4.516	4.516	4.516	4.516	4.516	4.516	4.516	4.516	4.516	4.516	4.516
4	3.927	4.013	4.033	4.033	4.033	4.033	4.033	4.033	4.033	4.033	4.033	4.033	4.033	4.033	4.033	4.033	4.033	4.033
5	3.635	3.749	3.797	3.814	3.814	3.814	3.814	3.814	3.814	3.814	3.814	3.814	3.814	3.814	3.814	3.814	3.814	3.814
6	3.461	3.587	3.649	3.680	3.694	3.697	3.697	3.697	3.697	3.697	3.697	3.697	3.697	3.697	3.697	3.697	3.697	3.697
7	3.344	3.477	3.548	3.588	3.611	3.622	3.626	3.626	3.626	3.626	3.626	3.626	3.626	3.626	3.626	3.626	3.626	3.626
8	3.261	3.399	3.475	3.521	3.549	3.566	3.575	3.579	3.579	3.579	3.579	3.579	3.579	3.579	3.579	3.579	3.579	3.579
9	3.199	3.339	3.420	3.470	3.502	3.523	3.536	3.544	3.547	3.547	3.547	3.547	3.547	3.547	3.547	3.547	3.547	3.547
10	3.151	3.293	3.376	3.430	3.465	3.489	3.505	3.516	3.522	3.525	3.526	3.526	3.526	3.526	3.526	3.526	3.526	3.526
11	3.113	3.256	3.342	3.397	3.435	3.462	3.480	3.493	3.501	3.506	3.509	3.510	3.510	3.510	3.510	3.510	3.510	3.510
12	3.082	3.225	3.313	3.370	3.410	3.439	3.459	3.474	3.484	3.491	3.496	3.498	3.499	3.499	3.499	3.499	3.499	3.499
13	3.055	3.200	3.289	3.348	3.389	3.419	3.442	3.458	3.470	3.478	3.484	3.488	3.490	3.490	3.490	3.490	3.490	3.490
14	3.033	3.178	3.268	3.329	3.372	3.403	3.426	3.444	3.457	3.467	3.474	3.479	3.482	3.484	3.484	3.485	3.485	3.485
15	3.014	3.160	3.250	3.312	3.356	3.389	3.413	3.432	3.446	3.457	3.465	3.471	3.476	3.478	3.480	3.481	3.481	3.481
16	2.998	3.144	3.235	3.298	3.343	3.376	3.402	3.422	3.437	3.449	3.458	3.465	3.470	3.473	3.477	3.478	3.478	3.478
17	2.984	3.130	3.222	3.285	3.331	3.366	3.392	3.412	3.429	3.441	3.451	3.459	3.465	3.469	3.473	3.475	3.476	3.476
18	2.971	3.118	3.210	3.274	3.320	3.356	3.383	3.405	3.421	3.435	3.445	3.454	3.460	3.465	3.470	3.472	3.474	3.474
19	2.960	3.107	3.199	3.264	3.311	3.347	3.375	3.397	3.415	3.429	3.440	3.449	3.456	3.462	3.467	3.470	3.472	3.473
20	2.950	3.097	3.190	3.255	3.303	3.339	3.368	3.391	3.409	3.424	3.436	3.445	3.453	3.459	3.464	3.467	3.470	3.472
24	2.919	3.066	3.160	3.226	3.276	3.315	3.345	3.370	3.390	3.406	3.420	3.432	3.441	3.449	3.456	3.461	3.465	3.469
30	2.888	3.035	3.131	3.199	3.250	3.290	3.322	3.349	3.371	3.389	3.405	3.418	3.430	3.439	3.447	3.454	3.460	3.466
40	2.858	3.006	3.102	3.171	3.224	3.266	3.300	3.328	3.352	3.373	3.390	3.405	3.418	3.429	3.439	3.448	3.456	3.463
60	2.829	2.976	3.073	3.143	3.198	3.241	3.277	3.307	3.333	3.355	3.374	3.391	3.406	3.419	3.431	3.442	3.451	3.460
120	2.800	2.947	3.045	3.116	3.172	3.217	3.254	3.287	3.314	3.337	3.359	3.377	3.394	3.409	3.423	3.435	3.446	3.457
∞	2.772	2.918	3.017	3.089	3.146	3.193	3.232	3.265	3.294	3.320	3.343	3.363	3.382	3.399	3.414	3.428	3.442	3.454

TABLE 8 (continued) CRITICAL VALUES FOR DUNCAN'S NEW MULTIPLE RANGE TEST

Protection level $P = (.95)^{p-1}$; Significance level $a = .05$

p \ v	20	22	24	26	28	30	32	34	36	38	40	50	60	70	80	90	100
1	17.97	17.97	17.97	17.97	17.97	17.97	17.97	17.97	17.97	17.97	17.97	17.97	17.97	17.97	17.97	17.97	17.97
2	6.085	6.085	6.085	6.085	6.085	6.085	6.085	6.085	6.085	6.085	6.085	6.085	6.085	6.085	6.085	6.085	6.085
3	4.516	4.516	4.516	4.516	4.516	4.516	4.516	4.516	4.516	4.516	4.516	4.516	4.516	4.516	4.516	4.516	4.516
4	4.033	4.033	4.033	4.033	4.033	4.033	4.033	4.033	4.033	4.033	4.033	4.033	4.033	4.033	4.033	4.033	4.033
5	3.814	3.814	3.814	3.814	3.814	3.814	3.814	3.814	3.814	3.814	3.814	3.814	3.814	3.814	3.814	3.814	3.814
6	3.697	3.697	3.697	3.697	3.697	3.697	3.697	3.697	3.697	3.697	3.697	3.697	3.697	3.697	3.697	3.697	3.697
7	3.626	3.626	3.626	3.626	3.626	3.626	3.626	3.626	3.626	3.626	3.626	3.626	3.626	3.626	3.626	3.626	3.626
8	3.579	3.579	3.579	3.579	3.579	3.579	3.579	3.579	3.579	3.579	3.579	3.579	3.579	3.579	3.579	3.579	3.579
9	3.547	3.547	3.547	3.547	3.547	3.547	3.547	3.547	3.547	3.547	3.547	3.547	3.547	3.547	3.547	3.547	3.547
10	3.526	3.526	3.526	3.526	3.526	3.526	3.526	3.526	3.526	3.526	3.526	3.526	3.526	3.526	3.526	3.526	3.526
11	3.510	3.510	3.510	3.510	3.510	3.510	3.510	3.510	3.510	3.510	3.510	3.510	3.510	3.510	3.510	3.510	3.510
12	3.499	3.499	3.499	3.499	3.499	3.499	3.499	3.499	3.499	3.499	3.499	3.499	3.499	3.499	3.499	3.499	3.499
13	3.490	3.490	3.490	3.490	3.490	3.490	3.490	3.490	3.490	3.490	3.490	3.490	3.490	3.490	3.490	3.490	3.490
14	3.485	3.485	3.485	3.485	3.485	3.485	3.485	3.485	3.485	3.485	3.485	3.485	3.485	3.485	3.485	3.485	3.485
15	3.481	3.481	3.481	3.481	3.481	3.481	3.481	3.481	3.481	3.481	3.481	3.481	3.481	3.481	3.481	3.481	3.481
16	3.478	3.478	3.478	3.478	3.478	3.478	3.478	3.478	3.478	3.478	3.478	3.478	3.478	3.478	3.478	3.478	3.478
17	3.476	3.476	3.476	3.476	3.476	3.476	3.476	3.476	3.476	3.476	3.476	3.476	3.476	3.476	3.476	3.476	3.476
18	3.474	3.474	3.474	3.474	3.474	3.474	3.474	3.474	3.474	3.474	3.474	3.474	3.474	3.474	3.474	3.474	3.474
19	3.474	3.474	3.474	3.474	3.474	3.474	3.474	3.474	3.474	3.474	3.474	3.474	3.474	3.474	3.474	3.474	3.474
20	3.473	3.474	3.474	3.474	3.474	3.474	3.474	3.474	3.474	3.474	3.474	3.474	3.474	3.474	3.474	3.474	3.474
24	3.471	3.475	3.477	3.477	3.477	3.477	3.477	3.477	3.477	3.477	3.477	3.477	3.477	3.477	3.477	3.477	3.477
30	3.470	3.477	3.481	3.484	3.486	3.486	3.486	3.486	3.486	3.486	3.486	3.486	3.486	3.486	3.486	3.486	3.486
40	3.469	3.479	3.486	3.492	3.497	3.500	3.503	3.504	3.504	3.504	3.504	3.504	3.504	3.504	3.504	3.504	3.504
60	3.467	3.481	3.492	3.501	3.509	3.515	3.521	3.525	3.529	3.531	3.534	3.537	3.537	3.537	3.537	3.537	3.537
120	3.466	3.483	3.498	3.511	3.522	3.532	3.541	3.548	3.555	3.561	3.566	3.585	3.596	3.600	3.601	3.601	3.601
∞	3.466	3.486	3.505	3.522	3.536	3.550	3.562	3.574	3.584	3.594	3.603	3.640	3.668	3.690	3.708	3.722	3.735

TABLE 8 (continued) CRITICAL VALUES FOR DUNCAN'S NEW MULTIPLE RANGE TEST

Protection level $P = (.95)^{p-1}$; Significance level $a = .01$

v \ p	2	3	4	5	6	7	8	9	10	11	12	13	14	15	16	17	18	19
1	90.03	90.03	90.03	90.03	90.03	90.03	90.03	90.03	90.03	90.03	90.03	90.03	90.03	90.03	90.03	90.03	90.03	90.03
2	14.04	14.04	14.04	14.04	14.04	14.04	14.04	14.04	14.04	14.04	14.04	14.04	14.04	14.04	14.04	14.04	14.04	14.04
3	8.261	8.321	8.321	8.321	8.321	8.321	8.321	8.321	8.321	8.321	8.321	8.321	8.321	8.321	8.321	8.321	8.321	8.321
4	6.512	6.677	6.740	6.756	6.756	6.756	6.756	6.756	6.756	6.756	6.756	6.756	6.756	6.756	6.756	6.756	6.756	6.756
5	5.702	5.893	5.989	6.040	6.065	6.074	6.074	6.074	6.074	6.074	6.074	6.074	6.074	6.074	6.074	6.074	6.074	6.074
6	5.243	5.439	5.549	5.614	5.655	5.680	5.694	5.701	5.703	5.703	5.703	5.703	5.703	5.703	5.703	5.703	5.703	5.703
7	4.949	5.145	5.260	5.334	5.383	5.416	5.439	5.454	5.464	5.470	5.472	5.472	5.472	5.472	5.472	5.472	5.472	5.472
8	4.746	4.939	5.057	5.135	5.189	5.227	5.256	5.276	5.291	5.302	5.309	5.314	5.316	5.317	5.317	5.317	5.317	5.317
9	4.596	4.787	4.906	4.986	5.043	5.086	5.118	5.142	5.160	5.174	5.185	5.193	5.199	5.203	5.205	5.206	5.206	5.206
10	4.482	4.671	4.790	4.871	4.931	4.975	5.010	5.037	5.058	5.074	5.088	5.098	5.106	5.112	5.117	5.120	5.122	5.124
11	4.392	4.579	4.697	4.780	4.841	4.887	4.924	4.952	4.975	4.994	5.009	5.021	5.031	5.039	5.045	5.050	5.054	5.057
12	4.320	4.504	4.622	4.706	4.767	4.815	4.852	4.883	4.907	4.927	4.944	4.958	4.969	4.978	4.986	4.993	4.998	5.002
13	4.260	4.442	4.560	4.644	4.706	4.755	4.793	4.824	4.850	4.872	4.889	4.904	4.917	4.928	4.937	4.944	4.950	4.956
14	4.210	4.391	4.508	4.591	4.654	4.704	4.743	4.775	4.802	4.824	4.843	4.859	4.872	4.884	4.894	4.902	4.910	4.916
15	4.168	4.347	4.463	4.547	4.610	4.660	4.700	4.733	4.760	4.783	4.803	4.820	4.834	4.846	4.857	4.866	4.874	4.881
16	4.131	4.309	4.425	4.509	4.572	4.622	4.663	4.696	4.724	4.748	4.768	4.786	4.800	4.813	4.825	4.835	4.844	4.851
17	4.099	4.275	4.391	4.475	4.539	4.589	4.630	4.664	4.693	4.717	4.738	4.756	4.771	4.785	4.797	4.807	4.816	4.824
18	4.071	4.246	4.362	4.445	4.509	4.560	4.601	4.635	4.664	4.689	4.711	4.729	4.745	4.759	4.772	4.783	4.792	4.801
19	4.046	4.220	4.335	4.419	4.483	4.534	4.575	4.610	4.639	4.665	4.686	4.705	4.722	4.736	4.749	4.761	4.771	4.780
20	4.024	4.197	4.312	4.395	4.459	4.510	4.552	4.587	4.617	4.642	4.664	4.684	4.701	4.716	4.729	4.741	4.751	4.761
24	3.956	4.126	4.239	4.322	4.386	4.437	4.480	4.516	4.546	4.573	4.596	4.616	4.634	4.651	4.665	4.678	4.690	4.700
30	3.889	4.056	4.168	4.250	4.314	4.366	4.409	4.445	4.477	4.504	4.528	4.550	4.569	4.586	4.601	4.615	4.628	4.640
40	3.825	3.988	4.098	4.180	4.244	4.296	4.339	4.376	4.408	4.436	4.461	4.483	4.503	4.521	4.537	4.553	4.566	4.579
60	3.762	3.922	4.031	4.111	4.174	4.226	4.270	4.307	4.340	4.368	4.394	4.417	4.438	4.456	4.474	4.490	4.504	4.518
120	3.702	3.858	3.965	4.044	4.107	4.158	4.202	4.239	4.272	4.301	4.327	4.351	4.372	4.392	4.410	4.426	4.442	4.456
∞	3.643	3.796	3.900	3.978	4.040	4.091	4.135	4.172	4.205	4.235	4.261	4.285	4.307	4.327	4.345	4.363	4.379	4.394

TABLE 8 (continued) CRITICAL VALUES FOR DUNCAN'S NEW MULTIPLE RANGE TEST

Protection level P = (.95)$^{p-1}$; Significance level a = .01

p / v	20	22	24	26	28	30	32	34	36	38	40	50	60	70	80	90	100
1	90.03	90.03	90.03	90.03	90.03	90.03	90.03	90.03	90.03	90.03	90.03	90.03	90.03	90.03	90.03	90.03	90.03
2	14.04	14.04	14.04	14.04	14.04	14.04	14.04	14.04	14.04	14.04	14.04	14.04	14.04	14.04	14.04	14.04	14.04
3	8.321	8.321	8.321	8.321	8.321	8.321	8.321	8.321	8.321	8.321	8.321	8.321	8.321	8.321	8.321	8.321	8.321
4	6.756	6.756	6.756	6.756	6.756	6.756	6.756	6.756	6.756	6.756	6.756	6.756	6.756	6.756	6.756	6.756	6.756
5	6.074	6.074	6.074	6.074	6.074	6.074	6.074	6.074	6.074	6.074	6.074	6.074	6.074	6.074	6.074	6.074	6.074
6	5.703	5.703	5.703	5.703	5.703	5.703	5.703	5.703	5.703	5.703	5.703	5.703	5.703	5.703	5.703	5.703	5.703
7	5.472	5.472	5.472	5.472	5.472	5.472	5.472	5.472	5.472	5.472	5.472	5.472	5.472	5.472	5.472	5.472	5.472
8	5.317	5.317	5.317	5.317	5.317	5.317	5.317	5.317	5.317	5.317	5.317	5.317	5.317	5.317	5.317	5.317	5.317
9	5.206	5.206	5.206	5.206	5.206	5.206	5.206	5.206	5.206	5.206	5.206	5.206	5.206	5.206	5.206	5.206	5.206
10	5.124	5.124	5.124	5.124	5.124	5.124	5.124	5.124	5.124	5.124	5.124	5.124	5.124	5.124	5.124	5.124	5.124
11	5.059	5.061	5.061	5.061	5.061	5.061	5.061	5.061	5.061	5.061	5.061	5.061	5.061	5.061	5.061	5.061	5.061
12	5.006	5.010	5.011	5.011	5.011	5.011	5.011	5.011	5.011	5.011	5.011	5.011	5.011	5.011	5.011	5.011	5.011
13	4.960	4.966	4.970	4.972	4.972	4.972	4.972	4.972	4.972	4.972	4.972	4.972	4.972	4.972	4.972	4.972	4.972
14	4.921	4.929	4.935	4.938	4.940	4.940	4.940	4.940	4.940	4.940	4.940	4.940	4.940	4.940	4.940	4.940	4.940
15	4.887	4.897	4.904	4.909	4.912	4.914	4.914	4.914	4.914	4.914	4.914	4.914	4.914	4.914	4.914	4.914	4.914
16	4.858	4.869	4.877	4.883	4.887	4.890	4.892	4.892	4.892	4.892	4.892	4.892	4.892	4.892	4.892	4.892	4.892
17	4.832	4.844	4.853	4.860	4.865	4.869	4.872	4.873	4.874	4.874	4.874	4.874	4.874	4.874	4.874	4.874	4.874
18	4.808	4.821	4.832	4.839	4.846	4.850	4.854	4.856	4.857	4.858	4.858	4.858	4.858	4.858	4.858	4.858	4.858
19	4.788	4.802	4.812	4.821	4.828	4.833	4.838	4.841	4.843	4.844	4.845	4.845	4.845	4.845	4.845	4.845	4.845
20	4.769	4.784	4.795	4.805	4.813	4.818	4.823	4.827	4.830	4.832	4.833	4.833	4.833	4.833	4.833	4.833	4.833
24	4.710	4.727	4.741	4.752	4.762	4.770	4.777	4.783	4.788	4.791	4.794	4.802	4.802	4.802	4.802	4.802	4.802
30	4.650	4.669	4.685	4.699	4.711	4.721	4.730	4.738	4.744	4.750	4.755	4.772	4.777	4.777	4.777	4.777	4.777
40	4.591	4.611	4.630	4.645	4.659	4.671	4.682	4.692	4.700	4.708	4.715	4.740	4.754	4.761	4.764	4.764	4.764
60	4.530	4.553	4.573	4.591	4.607	4.620	4.633	4.645	4.655	4.665	4.673	4.707	4.730	4.745	4.755	4.761	4.765
120	4.469	4.494	4.516	4.535	4.552	4.568	4.583	4.596	4.609	4.619	4.630	4.673	4.703	4.727	4.745	4.759	4.770
∞	4.408	4.434	4.457	4.478	4.497	4.514	4.530	4.545	4.559	4.572	4.584	4.635	4.675	4.707	4.731	4.756	4.776

TABLE 8 (continued) CRITICAL VALUES FOR DUNCAN'S NEW MULTIPLE RANGE TEST

Protection level P = (.95)$^{p-1}$; Significance level a = .005

p / v	2	3	4	5	6	7	8	9	10	11	12	13	14	15	16	17	18	19
1	180.1	180.1	180.1	180.1	180.1	180.1	180.1	180.1	180.1	180.1	180.1	180.1	180.1	180.1	180.1	180.1	180.1	180.1
2	19.93	19.93	19.93	19.93	19.93	19.93	19.93	19.93	19.93	19.93	19.93	19.93	19.93	19.93	19.93	19.93	19.93	19.93
3	10.55	10.63	10.63	10.63	10.63	10.63	10.63	10.63	10.63	10.63	10.63	10.63	10.63	10.63	10.63	10.63	10.63	10.63
4	7.916	8.126	8.210	8.238	8.238	8.238	8.238	8.238	8.238	8.238	8.238	8.238	8.238	8.238	8.238	8.238	8.238	8.238
5	6.751	6.980	7.100	7.167	7.204	7.222	7.228	7.228	7.228	7.228	7.228	7.228	7.228	7.228	7.228	7.228	7.228	7.228
6	6.105	6.334	6.466	6.547	6.600	6.635	6.658	6.672	6.679	6.682	6.682	6.682	6.682	6.682	6.682	6.682	6.682	6.682
7	5.699	5.922	6.057	6.145	6.207	6.250	6.281	6.304	6.320	6.331	6.339	6.343	6.345	6.345	6.345	6.345	6.345	6.345
8	5.420	5.638	5.773	5.864	5.930	5.978	6.014	6.042	6.064	6.080	6.092	6.101	6.108	6.113	6.116	6.118	6.119	6.119
9	5.218	5.430	5.565	5.657	5.725	5.776	5.815	5.846	5.871	5.891	5.907	5.920	5.930	5.938	5.944	5.949	5.952	5.955
10	5.065	5.273	5.405	5.498	5.567	5.620	5.662	5.695	5.722	5.744	5.762	5.777	5.790	5.800	5.809	5.816	5.821	5.826
11	4.945	5.149	5.280	5.372	5.442	5.496	5.539	5.574	5.603	5.626	5.646	5.663	5.678	5.690	5.700	5.709	5.716	5.722
12	4.849	5.048	5.178	5.270	5.341	5.396	5.439	5.475	5.505	5.532	5.552	5.570	5.585	5.599	5.610	5.620	5.629	5.636
13	4.770	4.966	5.094	5.186	5.256	5.312	5.356	5.393	5.424	5.450	5.472	5.492	5.508	5.523	5.535	5.546	5.556	5.564
14	4.704	4.897	5.023	5.116	5.185	5.241	5.286	5.324	5.355	5.382	5.405	5.425	5.442	5.458	5.471	5.483	5.494	5.503
15	4.647	4.838	4.964	5.055	5.125	5.181	5.226	5.264	5.297	5.324	5.348	5.368	5.386	5.402	5.416	5.429	5.440	5.450
16	4.599	4.787	4.912	5.003	5.073	5.129	5.175	5.213	5.245	5.273	5.298	5.319	5.338	5.354	5.368	5.381	5.393	5.404
17	4.557	4.744	4.867	4.958	5.027	5.084	5.130	5.168	5.201	5.229	5.254	5.275	5.295	5.311	5.327	5.340	5.352	5.363
18	4.521	4.705	4.828	4.918	4.987	5.043	5.090	5.129	5.162	5.190	5.215	5.237	5.256	5.274	5.289	5.303	5.316	5.327
19	4.488	4.671	4.793	4.883	4.952	5.008	5.054	5.093	5.127	5.156	5.181	5.203	5.222	5.240	5.256	5.270	5.283	5.295
20	4.460	4.641	4.762	4.851	4.920	4.976	5.022	5.061	5.095	5.124	5.150	5.172	5.193	5.210	5.226	5.241	5.254	5.266
24	4.371	4.547	4.666	4.753	4.822	4.877	4.924	4.963	4.997	5.027	5.053	5.076	5.097	5.116	5.133	5.148	5.162	5.175
30	4.285	4.456	4.572	4.658	4.726	4.781	4.827	4.867	4.901	4.931	4.958	4.981	5.003	5.022	5.040	5.056	5.071	5.085
40	4.202	4.369	4.482	4.566	4.632	4.687	4.733	4.772	4.806	4.837	4.864	4.888	4.910	4.930	4.948	4.965	4.980	4.995
60	4.122	4.284	4.394	4.476	4.541	4.595	4.640	4.679	4.713	4.744	4.771	4.796	4.818	4.838	4.857	4.874	4.890	4.905
120	4.045	4.201	4.308	4.388	4.452	4.505	4.550	4.588	4.622	4.652	4.679	4.704	4.726	4.747	4.766	4.784	4.800	4.815
∞	3.970	4.121	4.225	4.303	4.365	4.417	4.461	4.499	4.532	4.562	4.589	4.614	4.636	4.657	4.676	4.694	4.710	4.726

TABLE 8 (continued) CRITICAL VALUES FOR DUNCAN'S NEW MULTIPLE RANGE TEST

Protection level $P = (.95)^{p-1}$; Significance level $a = .005$

p / v	20	22	24	26	28	30	32	34	36	38	40	50	60	70	80	90	100
1	180.1	180.1	180.1	180.1	180.1	180.1	180.1	180.1	180.1	180.1	180.1	180.1	180.1	180.1	180.1	180.1	180.1
2	19.93	19.93	19.93	19.93	19.93	19.93	19.93	19.93	19.93	19.93	19.93	19.93	19.93	19.93	19.93	19.93	19.93
3	10.63	10.63	10.63	10.63	10.63	10.63	10.63	10.63	10.63	10.63	10.63	10.63	10.63	10.63	10.63	10.63	10.63
4	8.238	8.238	8.238	8.238	8.238	8.238	8.238	8.238	8.238	8.238	8.238	8.238	8.238	8.238	8.238	8.238	8.238
5	7.228	7.228	7.228	7.228	7.228	7.228	7.228	7.228	7.228	7.228	7.228	7.228	7.228	7.228	7.228	7.228	7.228
6	6.682	6.682	6.682	6.682	6.682	6.682	6.682	6.682	6.682	6.682	6.682	6.682	6.682	6.682	6.682	6.682	6.682
7	6.345	6.345	6.345	6.345	6.345	6.345	6.345	6.345	6.345	6.345	6.345	6.345	6.345	6.345	6.345	6.345	6.345
8	6.119	6.119	6.119	6.119	6.119	6.119	6.119	6.119	6.119	6.119	6.119	6.119	6.119	6.119	6.119	6.119	6.119
9	5.956	5.957	5.957	5.957	5.957	5.957	5.957	5.957	5.957	5.957	5.957	5.957	5.957	5.957	5.957	5.957	5.957
10	5.829	5.834	5.836	5.836	5.836	5.836	5.836	5.836	5.836	5.836	5.836	5.836	5.836	5.836	5.836	5.836	5.836
11	5.727	5.735	5.740	5.743	5.744	5.744	5.744	5.744	5.744	5.744	5.744	5.744	5.744	5.744	5.744	5.744	5.744
12	5.642	5.653	5.660	5.665	5.668	5.670	5.670	5.670	5.670	5.670	5.670	5.670	5.670	5.670	5.670	5.670	5.670
13	5.571	5.583	5.593	5.600	5.605	5.608	5.610	5.611	5.611	5.611	5.611	5.611	5.611	5.611	5.611	5.611	5.611
14	5.511	5.525	5.535	5.544	5.550	5.555	5.559	5.561	5.563	5.563	5.563	5.563	5.563	5.563	5.563	5.563	5.563
15	5.459	5.474	5.486	5.495	5.503	5.509	5.514	5.518	5.520	5.522	5.523	5.523	5.523	5.523	5.523	5.523	5.523
16	5.413	5.429	5.442	5.453	5.462	5.469	5.475	5.479	5.483	5.485	5.488	5.489	5.489	5.489	5.489	5.489	5.489
17	5.373	5.390	5.404	5.416	5.425	5.433	5.440	5.445	5.450	5.453	5.456	5.461	5.461	5.461	5.461	5.461	5.461
18	5.338	5.355	5.370	5.383	5.393	5.402	5.409	5.415	5.420	5.425	5.428	5.436	5.436	5.436	5.436	5.436	5.436
19	5.306	5.325	5.340	5.353	5.364	5.374	5.382	5.388	5.395	5.399	5.403	5.414	5.415	5.415	5.415	5.415	5.415
20	5.277	5.296	5.313	5.326	5.338	5.348	5.357	5.364	5.370	5.376	5.380	5.394	5.397	5.397	5.397	5.397	5.397
24	5.187	5.209	5.226	5.242	5.255	5.267	5.278	5.287	5.295	5.302	5.308	5.329	5.340	5.343	5.343	5.343	5.343
30	5.098	5.120	5.140	5.157	5.172	5.186	5.198	5.209	5.218	5.227	5.235	5.264	5.281	5.292	5.297	5.298	5.298
40	5.008	5.032	5.054	5.072	5.089	5.104	5.118	5.130	5.141	5.151	5.160	5.197	5.221	5.238	5.249	5.257	5.261
60	4.919	4.944	4.967	4.987	5.005	5.021	5.036	5.050	5.062	5.074	5.084	5.128	5.159	5.182	5.199	5.213	5.223
120	4.830	4.856	4.880	4.901	4.920	4.937	4.953	4.968	4.982	4.995	5.007	5.056	5.094	5.123	5.146	5.166	5.182
∞	4.740	4.767	4.792	4.813	4.833	4.852	4.869	4.885	4.899	4.913	4.956	4.981	5.024	5.059	5.088	5.114	5.136

Reproduced from H. L. Harter (1960). Critical values for Duncan's new multiple range test. *Biometrics, 16*, 671-685 by kind permission from the Biometric Society.

TABLE 9 ORTHOGONAL POLYNOMIAL COEFFICIENTS

I =	3		4			5				6				
	1	2	1	2	3	1	2	3	4	1	2	3	4	5
X_1	-1	1	-3	1	-1	-2	2	-1	1	-5	5	-5	1	-1
X_2	0	-2	-1	-1	3	-1	-1	2	-4	-3	-1	7	-3	5
X_3	1	1	1	-1	-3	0	-2	0	6	-1	-4	4	2	-10
X_4			3	1	1	1	-1	-2	-4	1	-4	-4	2	10
X_5						2	2	1	1	3	-1	-7	-3	-5
X_6										5	5	5	1	1
Σc_i^2	2	6	20	4	20	10	14	10	70	70	84	180	28	252

I =	7						8					
	1	2	3	4	5	6	1	2	3	4	5	6
X_1	-3	5	-1	3	-1	1	-7	7	-7	7	-7	1
X_2	-2	0	1	-7	4	-6	-5	1	5	-13	23	-5
X_3	-1	-3	1	1	-5	15	-3	-3	7	-3	-17	9
X_4	0	-4	0	6	0	-20	-1	-5	3	9	-15	-5
X_5	1	-3	-1	1	5	15	1	-5	-3	9	15	-5
X_6	2	0	-1	-7	-4	-6	3	-3	-7	-3	17	9
X_7	3	5	1	3	1	1	5	1	-5	-13	-23	-5
X_8							7	7	7	7	7	1
Σc_i^2	28	84	6	154	84	924	168	168	264	616	2184	264

Additional values may be calculated using the rules at the end of Chapter 10 and much more extensive tables are given in E. S. Pearson and H. O. Hart.ley (Eds.) 1970. Biometric tables for statisticians *Vol I, 3rd Edition.*

CHARTS 1 - 8 PEARSON AND HARTLEY CHARTS FOR THE POWER OF THE F TEST

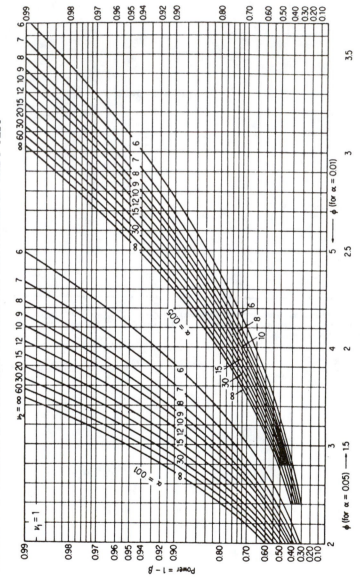

Reproduced from E. S. Pearson and H. O. Hartley in Biometrika, 1951, 38, 115-122 with the kind permission of the Trustees of Biometrika

CHARTS 1 - 8 PEARSON AND HARTLEY CHARTS FOR THE POWER OF THE F TEST

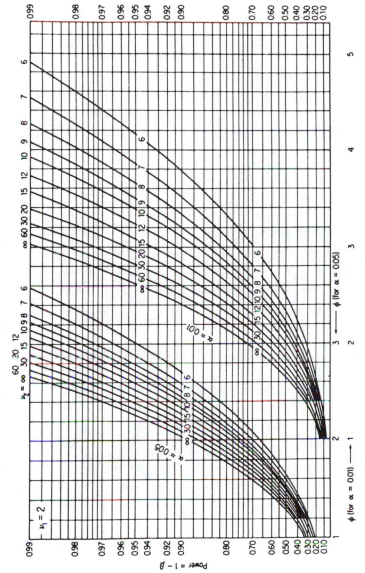

Reproduced from E. S. Pearson and H. O. Hartley in Biometrika, 1951, 38, 115-122 with the kind permission of the Trustees of Biometrika

CHARTS 1 - 8 PEARSON AND HARTLEY CHARTS FOR THE POWER OF THE F TEST

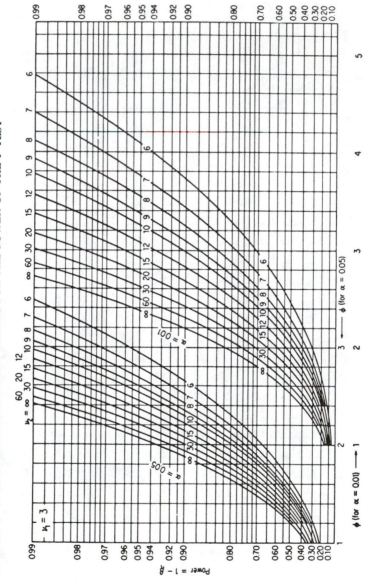

Reproduced from E. S. Pearson and H. O. Hartley in Biometrika, 1951, 38, 115-122
with the kind permission of the Trustees of Biometrika

CHARTS 1 - 8 PEARSON AND HARTLEY CHARTS FOR THE POWER OF THE F TEST

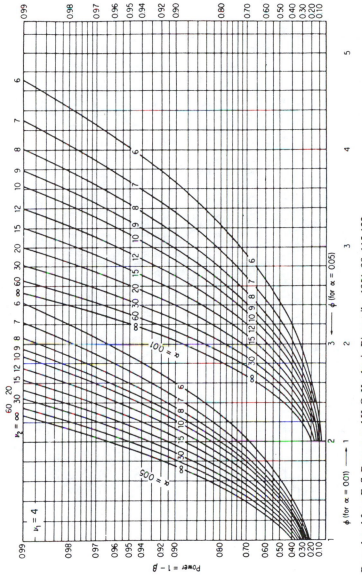

CHARTS 1 - 8 PEARSON AND HARTLEY CHARTS FOR THE POWER OF THE F TEST

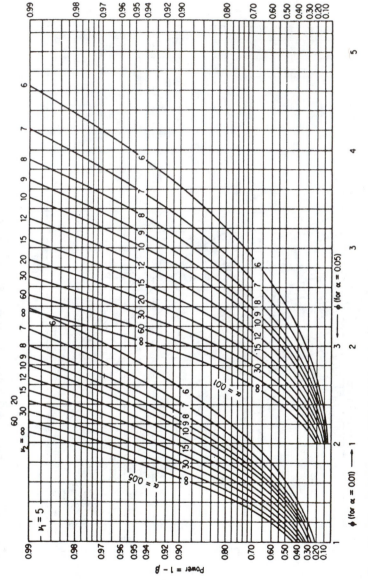

Reproduced from E. S. Pearson and H. O. Hartley in Biometrika, 1951, 38, 115-122
with the kind permission of the Trustees of Biometrika

CHARTS 1 - 8 PEARSON AND HARTLEY CHARTS FOR THE POWER OF THE F TEST

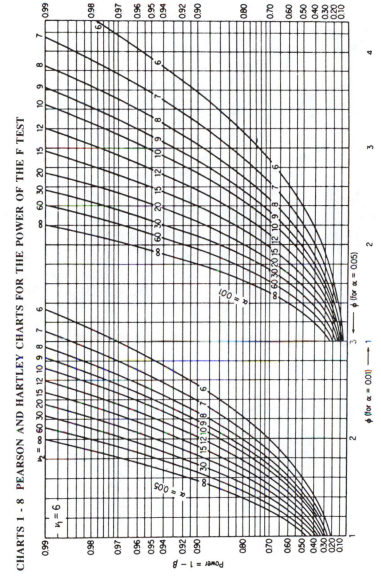

CHARTS 1 - 8 PEARSON AND HARTLEY CHARTS FOR THE POWER OF THE F TEST

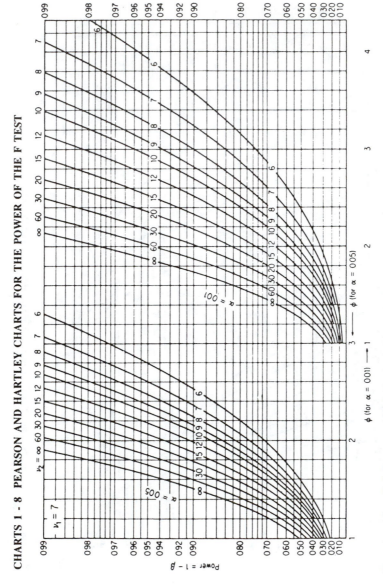

Reproduced from E. S. Pearson and H. O. Hartley in Biometrika, 1951, 38, 115-122
with the kind permission of the Trustees of Biometrika

542

CHARTS 1 - 8 PEARSON AND HARTLEY CHARTS FOR THE POWER OF THE F TEST

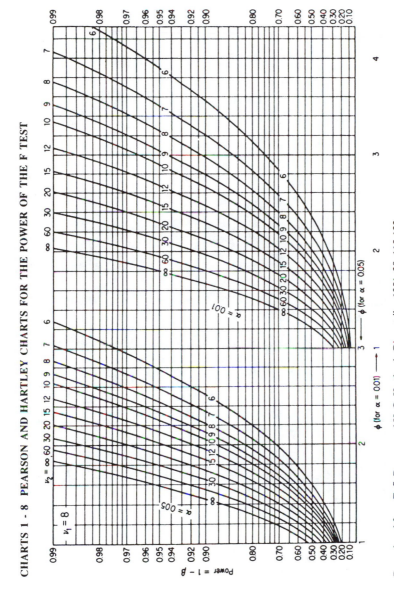

Reproduced from E. S. Pearson and H. O. Hartley in Biometrika, 1951, 38, 115-122
with the kind permission of the Trustees of Biometrika

References

Anderson, N. H. (1974a). Algebraic models in perception. In E. C. Carterette & M. P. Friedman (Eds.), *Handbook of perception (Vol. 2)*. New York: Academic Press.

Anderson, N. H. (1974b). Cognitive algebra. In L. Berkowitz (Ed.) *Advances in experimental social psychology (Vol. 7)*. New York: Academic Press.

Anderson, N. H. (1976). How functional measurement can yield validated interval scales of mental quantities. *Journal of Applied Psychology, 61*, 677-692.

Anderson, N. H. (1980). Information integration theory in developmental psychology. In F. Wilkening, J. Becker & T. Trabasso (Eds.), *Information integration by children*. Hillsdale, N.J.: Erlbaum.

Anderson, N. H. (1982). *Foundations of information integration theory*. New York: Academic Press.

Bartlett, M. S. (1947). The use of transformations. *Biometrics, 3*, 39-52.

Begun, J. M., & Gabriel, K. R. (1981). Closure of the Newman-Keuls multiple comparisons procedure. *Journal of the American Statistical Association, 76*, 241-245.

Bernstein, I. L., Treneer, C. M., Goehler, L. E., & Murowchick, E. (1985). Tumor growth in rats: conditional suppression of food intake and preference. *Behavioral Neuroscience, 99*, 818-830.

Bogartz, R. S. (1976). On the meaning of statistical interactions. *Journal of Experimental Child Psychology, 22*, 178-183.

Bogartz, R. S. (1980). Some functional measurement procedures for determining the psychophysical law. *Perception and Psychophysics, 27*, 284-294.

Bogartz, R. S. (1982). Proportional effects in experimental designs. *Psychological Bulletin, 91*, 666-672.

Bogartz, R. S. (1990a). Evaluating forgetting curves psychologically. *Journal of Experimental Psychology: Learning, Memory & Cognition, 16*, 138-148.

Bogartz, R. S. (1990b). Learning-forgetting rate independence defined by forgetting function parameters or forgetting function form: Reply to Loftus and Bamber and to Wixted. *Journal of Experimental Psychology: Learning, Memory & Cognition, 16*, 936-945.

Bogartz, R. S., & Wackwitz, J. H. (1971). Polynomial response scaling and functional measurement. *Journal of Mathematical Psychology, 8*, 418-443.

Bowey, J. A. (1985). Contextual facilitation in children's oral reading in relation to grade and decoding skill. *Journal of Experimental Child Psychology, 40*, 23-48.

Box, G. E. P. (1954a). Some theorems on quadratic forms applied in the study of analysis of variance problems, I: Effects of inequality of variance in the one-way classification. *Annals of Mathematical Statistics, 25*, 290-302.

Box, G. E. P. (1954b). Some theorems on quadratic forms applied in the study of analysis of variance problems, II: Effects of inequality of variance and of correlations between errors in the two-way classification. *Annals of Mathematical Statistics, 25*, 484-498.

Box, G. E. P., & Cox, D. R. (1964). An analysis of transformations. *Journal of the Royal Statistical Society, Series B, 26*, 211.

Box, G. E. P., Hunter, W. G., & Hunter, J. S. (1978). Statistics for experimenters. New York: Wiley.

Carlson, J. E., & Timm, N. H. (1974). Analysis of nonorthogonal fixed-effects designs. *Psychological Bulletin, 81*, 563-570.

Christensen, L. B. (1977). *Experimental methodology.* Boston: Allyn & Bacon.

Cochran, W. G., & Cox, G. M. (1957). *Experimental Designs.* New York: Wiley.

Cohen, J., & Cohen, P. (1975). *Applied multiple regression/correlation analysis for the behavioral sciences.* Hillsdale, N.J.: Erlbaum.

Collier, R. O., Baker, F. D., Mandeville, G. K., & Hayes, T. F. (1967). Estimates of test size for several test procedures based on conventional variance ratios in the repeated measures design. *Psychometrika, 32*, 339-353.

Consul, P. C. (1967). On the exact distribution of the criterion W for testing sphericity in a p-variate normal distribution. *Annals of Mathematical Statistics, 11*, 204-209.

Consul, P. C. (1969). The exact distribution of likelihood criteria for different hypotheses. *Multivariate analysis (Vol. 2).* New York: Academic Press.

Curtis, D. W., & Rule, S. J. (1977). Judgment of duration relations: Simultaneous and sequential presentations. *Perception and Psychophysics, 22*, 578-584.

de Leeuw, J., Young, F. W., & Takane, Y. (1976). Additive structure in qualitative data: An alternating least squares method with optimal scaling features. *Psychometrika, 41*, 471-503.

Duncan, D. B. (1955). Multiple range and multiple F tests. *Biometrics, 11*, 1-42.

Dunn, O. J. (1961). Multiple comparisons among means. *Journal of the American Statistical Association, 56*, 52-64.

Dunnett, C. W. (1955). A multiple comparisons procedure for comparing several treatments with a control. *Journal of the American Statistical Association, 50,* 1096-1121.

Dunnett, C. W. (1964). New tables for multiple comparisons with a control. *Biometrics, 20,* 482-491.

Dunnett, C. W. (1980). Pairwise multiple comparisons in the homogeneous variance, unequal sample size case. *Journal of the American Statistical Association, 75,* 789-795.

Einot, I., & Gabriel, K. R. (1975). A study of the powers of several methods of multiple comparisons. *Journal of the American Statistical Association, 70,* 574-583.

Feldt, L. S. (1958). A comparison of the precision of three experimental designs employing a concomitant variable. *Psychometrika, 23,* 335-354.

Fisher, R. A. (1952). *Statistical methods for research workers (12th ed.).* London: Oliver & Boyd.

Fisher, R. A., & Yates, F. (1948). *Statistical tables for biological, agricultural, and medical research.* Edinburgh: Oliver & Boyd, Ltd.

Gabriel, K. R. (1969). Simultaneous test procedures—some theory of multiple comparisons. *Annals of Mathematical Statistics, 40,* 224-250.

Games, P. A. (1971). Multiple comparisons of means. *American Educational Research Journal, 8,* 531-565.

Games, P. A., & Howell, J. F. (1976). Pairwise multiple comparison procedures with unequal n's and/or variances: A Monte Carlo study. *Journal of Educational Statistics, 1,* 113-125.

Games, P. A., Keselman, H. J., & Rogan, J. C. (1981). Simultaneous pairwise multiple comparison procedures for means when sample sizes are unequal. *Psychological Bulletin, 90,* 594-598.

Grant, D. A. (1948). The latin square principle in the design and analysis of psychological experiments. *Psychological Bulletin, 45,* 427-442.

Greenhouse, S. W., and Geisser, S. (1959). On methods in the analysis of profile data. *Psychometrika, 24,* 95-112.

Grier, J. (1971). Nonparametric indexes for sensitivity and bias: Computing formulas. *Psychological Bulletin, 75,* 424-429.

Hale, G. A., and Stevenson, E. E., Jr. (1974). The effects of auditory and visual distractors on children's performance in a short-term memory task. *Journal of Experimental Child Psychology, 18,* 280-292.

Harter, H. L. (1960). Tables of range and studentized range. *Annals of Mathematical Statistics, 31,* 1122-1147.

Harter, H. L., Clemens, D. S., & Guthrie, E. H. (1959). *The probability integrals of the range and of the studentized range—probability integral and percentage points of the studentized range; critical values for Duncan's new multiple range test.* Wright Air Development Center Technical Report, Wright-Patterson AFB, Ohio.

Hartley, H. O. (1955). Some recent developments in analysis of variance. *Communications on Pure and Applied Mathematics, 8,* 47-74.

Hays, W. L. (1973). *Statistics for the social sciences (2nd ed.).* New York: Holt, Rinehart, and Winston.

Hellyer, S. (1962). Frequency of stimulus presentation and short-term decrement in recall. *Journal of Experimental Psychology, 64,* 650.

Herr, D. G., & Gaebelein, J. (1978). Nonorthogonal two-way analysis of variance. *Psychological Bulletin, 85,* 207-216.

Hornbeck, F. W., & Alf, E. F. (1972). *Precision of the treatments-by-blocks analysis of variance.* Paper presented at Fifth Annual Meeting in Mathematical Psychology, La Jolla, California, August 10, 1972.

Horst, P., & Edwards, A. L. (1982). Analysis of nonorthogonal designs: The 2^k factorial experiment. *Psychological Bulletin, 91,*190-192.

Huynh, H. (1978). Some approximate tests for repeated measurement designs. *Psychometrika, 43,* 161-175.

Huynh, H., & Feldt, L. S. (1970). Conditions under which mean square ratios in repeated measurement designs have exact F-distributions. *Journal of the American Statistical Association, 65,* 1582-1589.

Huynh, H., & Feldt, L. S. (1976). Estimation of the Box correction for degrees of freedom from sample data in randomized block and split-plot designs. *Journal of Educational Statistics, 1,* 69-82.

Huynh, H., & Mandeville, G. K. (1979). Validity conditions in repeated measures designs. *Psychological Bulletin, 86,* 964-973.

Jaccard, J., Becker, M. A., & Wood, G. (1984). Pairwise multiple comparison procedures: A review. *Psychological Bulletin, 96,* 589-596.

Kenny, D. A., & Judd, C. M. (1986). Consequences of violating the independence assumption in analysis of variance. *Psychological Bulletin, 99,* 422-431.

Keppel, G. (1982). *Design and analysis: A researcher's handbook (2nd ed.)* .Englewood Cliffs, NJ: Prentice-Hall.

Keppel, G. (1991). *Design and analysis: A researcher's handbook* (3rd ed.). Englewood Cliffs, N. J.: Prentice-Hall.

Keren, G., & Lewis, C. (1976). Nonorthogonal designs: Sample versus population. *Psychological Bulletin, 83,* 817-826.

Keselman, H. J., Rogan, J. C., Mendoza, J. L., & Breen, L. J. (1980). Testing the validity conditions of repeated measures F tests. *Psychological Bulletin, 87,* 479-481.

Keuls, M. (1952). The use of the "studentized range" in connection with an analysis of variance. *Euphytics, 1,* 112-122.

Kimball, A. W. (1951). On dependent tests of significance in the analysis of variance. *Annals of Mathematical Statistics, 22,* 600-602.

Kirk, R. E. (1982). *Experimental design: Procedures for the behavioral sciences (2nd ed.).* Belmont, Calif.: Brooks/Cole.

Koele, P. (1982). Calculating power in analysis of variance. *Psychological Bulletin, 92*, 513-516.

Korin, B. P. (1969). On testing the equality of k covariance matrices. *Biometrika, 56*, 216-218.

Kramer, C. Y. (1956). Extension of multiple range test to group means with unequal numbers of replications. *Biometrics, 12*, 307-310.

Kruskal, J. B. (1965). Analysis of factorial experiments by estimating monotone transformations of the data. *Journal of the Royal Statistical Society (Series B), 27*, 251-263.

Lackritz, J. R. (1984). Exact p values for F and t tests. *The American Statistician, 38*, 312-314.

Lewis, C., & Keren, G. (1977). You can't have your cake and eat it too: Some considerations of the error term. *Psychological Bulletin, 84*, 1150-1154.

Loftus, G. R. (1978). On interpretation of interactions. *Memory & Cognition, 6*, 312-319.

Loftus, G. R. (1985a). Evaluating forgetting curves. *Journal of Experimental Psychology: Learning, Memory, & Cognition, 11*, 396-405.

Loftus, G. R. (1985b). Consistency and confoundings: Reply to Slamecka. *Journal of Experimental Psychology: Learning, Memory, & Cognition, 11*, 817-820.

Marcus, R., Peritz, E., & Gabriel, K. R. (1976). On closed testing procedures with special reference to ordered analysis of variance. *Biometrika, 63*, 655-660.

Mathai, A. M., & Rathie, P. N. (1970). The exact distribution for the sphericity test. *Journal of Statistical Research, 4*, 140-159.

Mauchly, J. W. (1940). Significance test for sphericity of a normal n-variate distribution. *Annals of Mathematical Statistics, 11*, 204-209.

Maxwell, C., & Cramer, E. M. (1975). A note on analysis of covariance. *Psychological Bulletin, 82*, 187-190.

Maxwell, S. E., & Bray, J. H. (1986). Robustness of the quasi F statistic to violations of sphericity. *Psychological Bulletin, 99*, 416-421.

Maxwell, S. E., Delaney, H. D., & Dill, C. A. (1984). Another look at ANCOVA versus blocking. *Psychological Bulletin, 95*, 136-147.

Mendoza, J. L., Toothaker, L. E., & Crain, B. R. (1976). Necessary and sufficient conditions for F ratios in the L X J X K factorial design with two repeated factors. *Journal of the American Statistical Association, 71*, 992-993.

Miller, R. G., Jr. (1981). *Simultaneous statistical inference (2nd ed.)*. New York: Springer-Verlag.

Morrison, D. F. (1976). *Multivariate statistical methods*. New York: McGraw-Hill.

Myers, J. (1979). *Fundamentals of experimental design*. Boston: Allyn and Bacon.

Nagarsenker, B. N., & Pillai, K. C. S. (1972). *The distribution of the sphericity test criterion (ARL 72-0154)*. Wright-Patterson Air Force Base, Ohio: Aerospace Research Laboratory, November. NTIS No. AD-754 232.

Newman, D. (1939). The distribution of the range in samples from a normal population, expressed in terms of an independent estimate of standard deviation. *Biometrika, 31*, 20-30.

O'Brien, R. G., & Kaiser, M. K. (1985). MANOVA method for analyzing repeated measures designs: An extensive primer. *Psychological Bulletin, 97,* 316-333.

Overall, J. E., & Spiegel, D. K. (1969). Concerning least squares analysis of experimental data. *Psychological Bulletin, 72,* 311-322.

Overall, J. E., Spiegel, D. K., & Cohen, J. (1975). Equivalence of orthogonal and nonorthogonal analysis of variance. *Psychological Bulletin, 82,* 182-186.

Pearson, E. S., & Hartley, H. O. (1952). *Biometrika tables for statisticians. (Vol. 2).* Cambridge, England: Cambridge University Press.

Pedhazur, E. J. (1977). Coding subjects in repeated measures designs. *Psychological Bulletin, 84,* 298-305.

Peiser, A. M. (1943). Asymptotic formulas for significance levels of certain distributions. *Annals of Mathematical Statistics, 14,* 56-62.

Peritz, E. (1970). *A note on multiple comparisons.* Unpublished manuscript, Hebrew University, Tel Aviv, Israel.

Petrinovich, L. F., & Hardyck, C. D. (1969). Error rates for multiple comparison methods. *Psychological Bulletin, 71,* 43-54.

Pillai, K. C. S., & Nagarsenker, B. N. (1971). On the distribution of the sphericity test criterion in classical and complex normal populations having unknown covariance matrices. *Annals of Mathematical Statistics, 42,* 764-767.

Ramsay, P. H. (1978) Power differences between pairwise multiple comparisons. *Journal of the American Statistical Association, 73,* 479-485.

Rouanet, H., & Lépine, D. (1970). Comparison between treatments in a repeated-measurement design: ANOVA and multivariate methods. *British Journal of Mathematical and Statistical Psychology, 23,* 147-163.

Ryan, T. A. (1959). Multiple comparisons in psychological research. *Psychological Bulletin, 56,* 26-47.

Ryan, T. A. (1960). Significance tests for multiple comparisons of proportions, variances, and other statistics. *Psychological Bulletin, 57,* 318-328.

Saville, D. J., & Wood, G. R. (1986). A method for teaching statistics using N-dimensional geometry. *The American Statistician, 40,* 205-214.

Scheffé, H. (1959). *The analysis of variance.* New York: Wiley.

Shaffer, J. P. (1979). Comparison of means: An F test followed by a modified multiple range procedure. *Journal of Educational Statistics, 4,* 14-23.

Slamecka, N. J. (1985). On comparing rates of forgetting: Comment on Loftus (1985). *Journal of Experimental Psychology: Learning, Memory, & Cognition, 11,* 812-816.

Speed, F. M., & Hocking, R. R. (1976). The use of the R ( )-notation with unbalanced data. *American Statisticain, 30,* 30-33.

Spencer, D. G., Pontecorvo, M. J., & Heise, G. A. (1985). Central cholinergic involvement in working memory. Effects of scopolomine on continuous nonmatching anddiscrimination performance in the rat. *Behavioral Neuroscience, 99*, 1049-1065.

Stoloff, P. H. (1966). *An empirical evaluation of the effects of violating the assumption of homogeneity of covariance for the repeated measures design of the analysis of variance.* University of Maryland, Technical Report TR-66-28, NSG-398.

Timm, N. H. (1975). *Multivariate analysis with applications in education and psychology.* Monterey, Calif.: Brooks/Cole.

Tukey, J. W. (1949) One degree of freedom for nonadditivity. *Biometrics, 5*, 232-242.

Tukey, J. W. (1952). *Allowances for various types of error rates.* Unpublished IMS address, Virginia Polytechnic Institute, Blacksburg, Va.

Tukey, J. W. (1953). *The problem of multiple comparisons.* Unpublished manuscript.

Tukey, J. W. (1991). The philosophy of multiple comparisons. *Statistical Science, 6*, 100-116.

Ury, H. K. (1976). A comparison of four procedures for multiple comparisons among means (pairwise contrasts) for arbitrary sample sizes. *Technometrics, 18*, 89-97.

Weiss, D. J. (1973). FUNPOT: A FORTRAN program for finding a polynomial transformation to reduce any sources of variance in a factorial design. *Behavioral Science, 18*, 150.

Welch, B. L. (1947) The generalization of 'student's' problem when several different population variances are involved. *Biometrika, 34*, 28-35.

Winer, B. J. (1971). *Statistical principles in experimental design (2nd ed.).* New York: McGraw-Hill.

Zwick, R., & Marascuilo, L. A. (1984). Selection of pairwise multiple comparison procedures for parametric and nonparametric analysis of variance models. *Psychological Bulletin, 95*, 148-155.

Index

About the Author

RICHARD S. BOGARTZ is a Professor of Psychology at the University of Massachusetts, Amherst. He has taught at the University of Illinois, the University of Iowa, and received his Ph.D. at UCLA. He is the author of numerous articles in a variety of journals, including *Journal of Experimental Psychology*; *Journal of Mathematical Psychology*; *Journal of Experimental Child Psychology*; *Psychological Bulletin*; *Perception & Psychophysics*; and others.